LexisNexis®

DURGA DAS BASU

Introduction to THE CONSTITUTION of INDIA

First Edition	1960
Second Edition	1962
Third Edition	1964
Fourth Edition	1966
Fifth Edition	1971
Sixth Edition	1976
Seventh Edition	1978
Eighth Edition	1980
Ninth Edition	1982
Tenth Edition	1983
Eleventh Edition	1985
Twelfth Edition	1987
Thirteenth Edition	1990
Fourteenth Edition	1992
Fifteenth Edition	1993
Sixteenth Edition	1994
Seventeenth Edition	1995
Eighteenth Edition	1997
Nineteenth Edition	2001
Twentieth Edition	2008
Twenty-First Edition	2013
Twenty-Second Edition	2015
Twenty-Third Edition	2018
Twenty-Fourth Edition	2020
Twenty-Fifth Edition	2021
Twenty-Sixth Edition	2022
Twenty-Seventh Edition	2024
Twenty-Eighth Edition	**2026**

LexisNexis®

DURGA DAS BASU
Introduction to
THE CONSTITUTION of INDIA

Acharya Dr Durga Das Basu

M A, LL D Calcutta; D Litt (Calcutta, Burdwan; Rabindrabharti; Kalyani); Saraswati, Vacaspati, Vidyavaridhi, Prajnabharati, Nyayaratnakara, Neetibhaskara, Nyayabharati, Manava Ratna.
Honorary Professor, Banaras Hindu University;
Retired Judge, High Court, Calcutta; Formerly Member, Union Law Commission; Tagore Law Professor, Asutosh Memorial; Lecturer, Calcutta University; Recipient National Award, Padmabhushan (1985); National Research Professor of India (1986); National Citizen's Award (1991); Honorary Fellow, Asiatic Society, Calcutta (1994)

28th Edition

2026

LexisNexis®

This book is a publication of **LexisNexis**
(A Division of RELX India Pvt Ltd)
14th floor, Building No 10, Tower–B, DLF Cyber City, Phase-II,
Gurgaon–122002, Haryana, India.
Tel: +91 124 4774444 Fax: +91 124 4774100
Website: www.lexisnexis.co.in / E-mail: help.in@lexisnexis.com

---

RELX India Pvt Ltd – owner of the LexisNexis brand – acquired all the rights in this publication from O.P. Wadhwa, K.K. Wadhwa, V.K. Wadhwa and S.K. Wadhwa in 2008. O.P. Wadhwa, K.K. Wadhwa, V.K. Wadhwa and S.K. Wadhwa built the renowned firm Wadhwa & Co. Nagpur which was founded by their father the late Sri Chetan Das Wadhwa and their mother the late Smt. Ram Pyari Wadhwa.

Dr Durga Das Basu, *Introduction to the Constitution of India*, 28th Edition, 2026.

ISBN: 978-81-19403-79-0

Printed by: Sai Printo Pack Pvt. Ltd., A-102/4, Okhla Industrial Area, Phase-II, New Delhi-110 020

Printed and bound in India.

Certificate of Authenticity

To know if you have purchased a 100% ORIGINAL and AUTHENTIC product, please follow the below verification process:

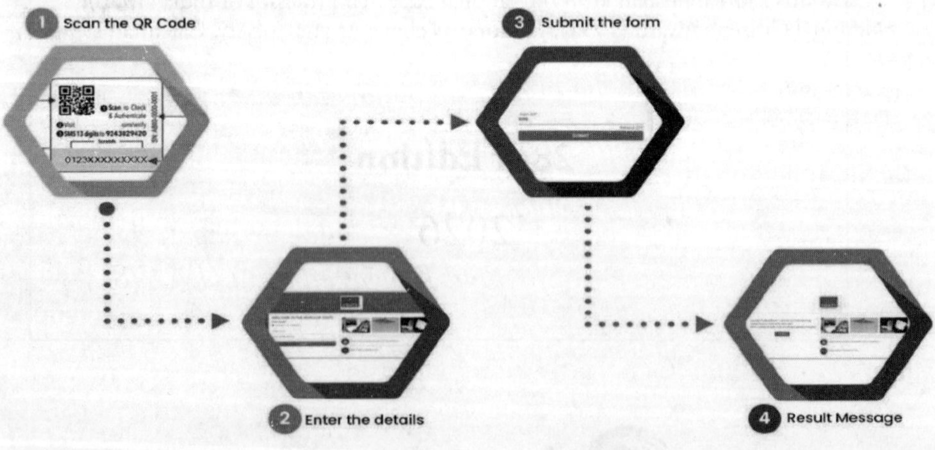

Other modes of verification:
- QR code - user can verify the QR code on VCQRU mobile application.
- Any QR code scanner app – user can also verify the code by scanning QR code via any QR scanner app.

यदा यदा हि धर्मस्य ग्लानिर्भवति भारत।

अभ्युत्थानमधर्मस्य तदात्मानं सृजाम्यहम् ॥

परित्राणाय साधूनां विनाशाय च दुष्कृताम् ।

धर्मसंस्थापनार्थाय सम्भवामि युगे युगे ॥

— *श्रीमद् भगवत् गीता (IV.7/8)*

Whenever there is
Decline of righteousness,
And rise of unrighteousness,
I incarnate myself
To protect the virtuous
And to destroy the wicked,
From Age to Age.

—Shrimad Bhagavad Gita (IV. 7/8)

Pub[illegible]

[illegible] *Introduction to the Constitution of India* is a pioneering [illegible] catering to the needs [illegible] the origin and development of the Constitution [illegible] India [illegible] [illegible] This book [illegible] the Constitution [illegible] constitutional history of India [illegible] 1858 [illegible] the Constitution [illegible] explains the interrelation between [illegible] Contents.

The current edition [illegible] recent amendments to the Constitution [illegible] Supreme Court of India [illegible]

We are confident that this edition [illegible] appreciated and received well.

[illegible]

Publisher's Note

D D Basu Introduction to the Constitution of India is a pioneer work, catering to the needs of anyone who wants to study the origin and development of the Constitution of India. First published in 1960, it has earned a reputation as one of the most incisive publications on the subject. This book offers a systematic exposition of the constitutional document, organised under logical chapters and headings. It traces the constitutional history of India since the Government of India Act, 1858, analyses the provisions of the present Constitution, and explains the interrelation between its diverse contents.

The current edition of the book contains all legislative changes and recent amendments to the Constitution. It also includes notable judgments of the Supreme Court of India such as *Surendra Koli v State of Uttar Pradesh,*[1] *Dr Tanvi Behl v Shrey Goel,*[2] *Sukanya Shantha v UOI,*[3] etc.

We are confident that this edition, like its predecessors, will be appreciated and received well.

* The information provided in this book is updated till 6 February 2026. For any updates subsequent to this date, please refer to the official sources.

1. *Surendra Koli v State of Uttar Pradesh,* AIR 2025 SC 5591.
2. *Dr Tanvi Behl v Shrey Goel,* AIR 2025 SC 1445.
3. *Sukanya Shantha v UOI,* AIR 2024 SC 5201.

PUBLISHER'S NOTE

D.D. Basu's *Introduction to the Constitution of India* is a pioneering work [illegible] development of the Constitution of India, first published in [illegible], it has [illegible] one of the most [illegible] Constitution [illegible] constitutional history of India [illegible] Government of India [illegible] and analyses the provisions of the present Constitution and explains the interrelation between its diverse components.

The current edition of the book contains all the [illegible] amendments to the Constitution. It also includes notes [illegible] of the Supreme Court [illegible] [illegible]

We are confident that this edition, like its predecessors, will be appreciated and received well.

[illegible]

A Tribute to the Great Author

'UNIQUE AND VERSATILE'

Dr Basu was a man of unique and manifold achievements, combined in one :

(i) Born in February, 1910, he actively carried on research till the age of 87, producing creative literature, almost every quarter of the year, comprehending Jurisprudence, Political Science and Religion simultaneously.

(ii) He is remembered as a legend in the world of law and his status as an 'eminent jurist' has been acknowledged by the Government of India by appointing him a full-time member of the Union Law Commission, and a Judge of the Calcutta High Court, on the category of 'eminent jurists'; by conferring upon him the National award Padmabhusan and the National Research Professorship.

(iii) No other member of the Indian Judiciary has been honoured with the aforesaid awards of the Government, together with doctorates from six Universities.

(iv) In the field of Constitutional Law, he introduced the *comparative* method of research, which has been held by Lord Denning, the doyen of world Jurists, as 'a unique contribution to the jurisprudence of the world'.

(v) Dr Basu was the *pioneer* commentator of the Constitution of India (published in September, 1950) when there was no light from any judicial decision in India. His *Commentary on the Constitution of India* has brought the Indian Constitution to the door of every man in the world *who is interested in constitutional government and law.* It has celebrated its Golden Jubilee–rare events in the lifetime of the author of any serious work.

(vi) No other Indian work on Constitutional Law is read from one end of the world to the other, including non-English-speaking countries, such as Japan, Poland, Hungary, West Germany Italy. One of Basu's books has been translated and published in Russia, where the constitutional system has no semblance to that of India.

(vii) No other jurist in India has been compared with 'Blackstone, Coke and Kent', by a Law Journal abroad.

(viii) As an author, he was versatile and *prolific.* His contribution to jurisprudence is not confined to Constitutional Law but comprises authoritative treatises in different branches of law, the total number of pages of the current edition of which exceeds 16,000 in Royal Octavo.

(xi) Dr Basu's talents were not confined to writing. That he was adored by numerous Universities in India and abroad is evidenced by the fact that he held *honoris causa* doctorate from six Universities in India; that he participated at an international seminar at the Chicago Law School; participated in a semi-Government Conference at Ottawa on the future Constitution of Canada; delivered lectures as Guest Lecturer at a score of foreign Universities in the UK, USA and Canada.

In India, he has delivered the prestigious Tagore Law Lectures and the Ashutosh Memorial Lectures of the Calcutta University; and the Honorary Professorship Lectures of the Banaras Hindu University.

(x) He held the rare Doctorate of Law (LL D) of the Calcutta University and D Litt from as many as six Universities.

(xi) He combined in himself all the highest Awards of the Calcutta University– LL D, D Litt, Tagore Law Professorship and Asutosh Memorial Lectureship.

(xii) To crown all, his published research works on Sanskrit scriptures fetched for him a number of Sanskrit titles from various cultural institutions, e.g., *Sarasvati* (Hooghly Sanskrit Parishad); *Vidavaridhi* (Anangamohan Harisabha); *Prajnabharati* (Satyananda Devayratana); *Nyayaratnakara* (Howrah Sanskrit Samaj); *Neetibhaskar* (Nikhil Banga Sanskrit Seva Samity); *Nyaya Bharati* (Sitaramdas Omkarnath Sanskrit Siksha Samsad); *Vacaspati,* Rashtriya Sanskrit Vidyapeetha (Tirupati).

His Bengali Book *Hindu Dharmer Saratatva,* which has run out three editions, has been acknowledged by the Rabindra Bharati University as an original contribution to Comparative Religion, by conferring upon him *honoris causa* D Litt. An English version of this book and Hindi and Oriya translations have been published for the use of non-Indian readers.

(xiii) Apart from thus propagating the message of Indian heritage, breaking through language barriers, Dr Basu donated the copyright with all sale proceeds in these spiritual productions to charitable institutions.

(xiv) All these multifarious activities in the cause of the nation endeared this octogenarian to non-government public bodies such as the Citizen's Club (New Delhi), conferring upon him the National Citizen's Award; the Asiatic Society (Calcutta) by awarding its Honorary Fellowship; the Legal Aid and Advice Society, West Bengal, conferring on him the title *Acharya*; and the Bharat Sevasram Sangha, conferring on him its prestigious award *Manava Ratna.*

Other awarding plaques, medallions or souvenirs include– the Indian Association; the IA Federation Hall Society; the Sankara Institute of Philosophy and Culture, Academy of Comparative Religion, Kal Pratima & St Andrews Memorial Society; Legal Aid Services, West Bengal.

Publishers

CONTENTS

PART I

NATURE OF THE CONSTITUTION

PART II

GOVERNMENT OF THE UNION

PART III

GOVERNMENT OF THE STATES

PART VI

ADMINISTRATION OF SPECIAL AREAS

PART VIII

THE FEDERAL SYSTEM

TABLE OF CASES

A

D

E

F

G

H

I

J

K

N

R

S

T

U

V

PART I

NATURE OF THE CONSTITUTION

CHAPTER 1

THE HISTORICAL BACKGROUND

1. Utility of a Historical Retrospect.

THE very fact that the Constitution of the Indian Republic is the product, not of a political revolution but of the research and deliberations of a body of eminent representatives of the people who sought to improve upon the existing system of administration, makes a retrospect of the constitutional development indispensable for a proper understanding of this Constitution.

Practically, the only respect in which the Constitution of 1949[1] differs from the constitutional documents of the preceding two centuries is that while the latter had been imposed by an imperial power, the Republican Constitution was made by the people themselves through the representatives assembled in a sovereign Constituent Assembly. That explains the majesty and ethical value of this new instrument and also the significance of those of its provisions which have been engrafted upon the pre-existing system.

2. The Government of India Act, 1858.

For our present purposes, we need not go beyond the year 1858 when the British Crown assumed sovereignty over India from the East India Company, and Parliament enacted the first statute for the governance of India under the direct rule of the British Government—the Government of India Act, 1858 (21 & 22 Vict, c 106). This Act serves as the starting point of our survey because it was dominated by the principle of absolute imperial control without any popular participation in the administration of the country, while the subsequent history up to the making of the Constitution is one of the gradual relaxation of imperial control and the evolution of responsible Government. By this Act, the powers of the Crown were to be exercised by the Secretary of State for India, assisted by a Council of 15 members (known as the "Council of India"). The Council was composed exclusively of people from England, some of whom were nominees of the Crown while others were the representatives of the directors of the East India Company. The Secretary of State, who was responsible to the British Parliament, governed India through the Governor-General, assisted by an Executive Council, which consisted of high officials of the Government.

1. The Constitution of India was adopted on 26 November 1949 and some of its provisions [*i.e.*, Articles 5, 6, 7, 8, 9, 60, 324, 366, 367, 379, 380, 388, 391, 392, 393 and 394] were given immediate effect. The remaining provisions of the Constitution, however, became operative on 26 January 1950, which date is referred to in the Constitution as its 'Date of Commencement', and is celebrated in India as the "Republic Day".

2a. Features of the System Introduced by Act of 1858.

The essential features of the system[2] introduced by the Act of 1858 were—

(a) *Centralised administration:* The administration of the country was not only unitary but rigidly centralised. Though the territory was divided into Provinces with a Governor or Lieutenant-Governor aided by his Executive Council at the head of each of them, the Provincial Governments were mere agents of the Government of India and had to function under the superintendence, direction, and control of the Governor-General in all matters relating to the Government of the Province.

(b) *No separation of functions:* There was no separation of functions, and all the authority for the governance of India—civil and military, executive and legislative—was vested in the Governor-General in Council who was responsible to the Secretary of State.

(c) *Absolute control of the Secretary of State:* The control of the Secretary of State over the Indian administration was absolute. The Act vested in him the 'superintendence, direction and control of all acts, operations and concerns which in any way related to the Government or revenues of India'. Subject to his ultimate responsibility to the British Parliament, he wielded the Indian administration through the Governor-General as his agent and his was the last word, whether in matters of policy or of details.[3]

(d) *Bureaucratic administration:* The entire machinery of administration was bureaucratic, totally unconcerned about the public opinion in India.

3. The Indian Councils Act, 1861.

The Indian Councils Act of 1861 introduced a grain of popular element insofar as it provided that the Governor-General's Executive Council, which was so long composed exclusively of officials, should include certain additional *non-official* members, while transacting legislative business as a Legislative Council. But this Legislative Council was neither representative nor deliberative in any sense. The members were nominated and their functions were confined exclusively to a consideration of the legislative proposals placed before it by the Governor-General. It could not, in any manner, criticise the acts of the administration or the conduct of the authorities. Even in legislation, effective powers were reserved to the Governor-General, such as—(a) giving prior sanction to Bills relating to certain matters, without which they could not be introduced in the Legislative Council; (b) vetoing the Bills after they were passed or reserving them for consideration of the Crown; (c) legislating by Ordinances which were to have the same authority as Acts made by the Legislative Council.

Similar provisions were made by the Act of 1861 for Legislative Councils in the Provinces. But even for initiating legislation in these Provincial Councils with respect to many matters, the prior sanction of the Governor-General was necessary.

---

2. Report of the Indian Statutory Commission (*i.e.*, Simon Report), vol I, pp 112 *et seq.*
3. Seton, *India Office,* p 81.

4. The Indian Councils Act, 1892.

Two improvements upon the preceding state of affairs as regards the Indian and Provincial Legislative Councils were introduced by the Indian Councils Act, 1892, namely that: (a) though the majority of official members were retained, the non-official members of the Indian Legislative Council were henceforth to be nominated by the Bengal Chamber of Commerce and the Provincial Legislative Councils, while the non-official members of the Provincial Councils were to be nominated by certain local bodies such as the universities, district boards, and municipalities; (b) the Councils were to have the power of discussing the annual statement of revenue and expenditure, *i.e.*, the Budget, and of addressing questions to the Executive.

This Act is notable for its object, which was explained by the Under-Secretary of State for India thus—

> ...to widen the basis and expand the functions of the Government of India, and to give further opportunities to the *non-official and native elements* in Indian society to take part in the work of the Government.

5. The Morley-Minto Reforms *vide* the Indian Councils Act, 1909.

The first attempt at introducing a representative and popular element was made by the Morley-Minto Reforms, known by the names of the then Secretary of State for India (Lord Morley) and the Viceroy (Lord Minto), which were implemented by the Indian Councils Act, 1909.

The changes relating to the Provincial Legislative Councils were, of course, more advanced. The size of these Councils was enlarged by including elected non-official members so that the official majority was gone. An element of election was also introduced in the Legislative Council at the Centre but the official majority there was maintained.

The deliberative functions of the Legislative Councils were also increased through this Act by giving them the opportunity of influencing the policy of the administration by moving resolutions on the Budget, and on any matter of public interest, save certain specified subjects, such as the Armed Forces, Foreign Affairs and the Indian States.

On the other hand, the positive vice of the system of election introduced by the Act of 1909 was that it provided, for the first time, for separate representation of the Muslim community and, thus, sowed the seeds of separatism[4] that eventually led to the lamentable partition of the country. It can hardly be overlooked that this idea of separate electorates for the Muslims was synchronous with the formation of the Muslim League as a political party (1906).[5]

6. The Government of India Act, 1915.

Subsequent to this, the Government of India Act, 1915 (5 & 6 Geo V, c 61) was passed merely to consolidate all the preceding Government of India Acts so that the existing provisions relating to the Government of India in its executive, legislative and judicial branches could be had from one enactment.

---

4. Panikkar, *Asia and Western Dominance,* 1953, p 155.
5. Nehru, *Discovery of India,* 1956, p 385.

7. The Montagu-Chelmsford Report and the Government of India Act, 1919.

The next landmark in the constitutional development of India is the Montagu-Chelmsford Report which led to the enactment of the Government of India Act, 1919. It was, in fact, an amending Act, but the amendments introduced substantive changes into the existing system.

The Morley-Minto Reforms failed to satisfy the aspirations of the nationalists in India inasmuch as, professedly, the Reforms did not aim at the establishment of a Parliamentary system of Government in the country and provide for the retention of the final decision on all questions in the hands of the irresponsible Executive.

The Indian National Congress, which was established in 1885, was so long under the control of Moderates, became more active during the First World War and started its campaign for self-government (known as the 'Home Rule' Movement). In response to this popular demand, the British Government made a declaration on 20 August 1917, that the policy of His Majesty's Government ("HMG") was that of—

> Increasing association of Indians in every branch of the administration and the gradual development of self-governing institutions with a view to progressive realisation of responsible government in British India as an integral part of the British Empire.

The then Secretary of State for India (Mr ES Montagu) and the Governor-General (Lord Chelmsford), entrusted with the task of formulating proposals for carrying out the above policy and the Government of India Act, 1919, gave a legal shape to their recommendations.

7a. Features of the System Introduced by Act of 1919.

The main features of the system introduced by the Government of India Act, 1919, were as follows—[6]

(a) *Dyarchy in the Provinces:* Responsible Government in the Provinces was sought to be introduced, without impairing the responsibility of the Governor (through the Governor-General), for the administration of the Province, by resorting to device known as 'Dyarchy' or dual government. The subjects of administration were to be divided (by Rules made under the Act) into two categories—Central and Provincial.

The Central subjects were those which were exclusively kept under the control of the Central Government. The Provincial subjects were sub-divided into 'transferred' and 'reserved' subjects. Of the matters assigned to the Provinces, the 'transferred subjects' were to be administered by the Governor with the aid of Ministers responsible to the Legislative Council in which the proportion of elected members was raised to 70 per cent. The foundation of responsible Government was, thus, laid down in the narrow sphere of 'transferred' subjects. The 'reserved subjects', on the other hand, were to be administered by the Governor and his Executive Council without any responsibility to the Legislature.

(b) *Relaxation of Central control over the Provinces:* As stated already, the Rules made under the Government of India Act, 1919, known as the Devolution Rules, made a separation of the subjects of administration into two categories—

---

6. Simon Report, vol I, pp 122-26, 148-56.

Central and Provincial. Broadly speaking, subjects of all-India importance were brought under the category 'Central', while matters primarily relating to the administration of the provinces were classified as 'Provincial'. This meant a relaxation of the previous Central control over the provinces not only in administrative but also in legislative and financial matters. Even the sources of revenue were divided into two categories so that the Provinces could run the administration with the aid of revenue raised by the Provinces themselves and for this purpose, the provincial budgets were separated from the Government of India and the Provincial Legislature was empowered to present its own budget and levy its own taxes relating to the provincial sources of revenue.

At the same time, this devolution of power to the Provinces should not be mistaken for a *federal* distribution of powers. Under the Act of 1919, the Provinces got power by way of delegation from the Centre. The Central Legislature, therefore, retained power to legislate for the whole of India, relating to any subject, and it was subject to such paramount power of the Central Legislature that the Provincial Legislature got the power "to make laws for the peace and good government of the territories for the time being constituting that province".

The control of the Governor-General over Provincial legislation was also retained by a laying down that a Provincial Bill, even though assented to by the Governor, would not become law unless assented to also by the Governor-General, and by empowering the Governor to reserve a Bill for the consideration of the Governor-General if it related to matters specified on this behalf by the Rules made under the Act.

(c) *Indian Legislature made more representative:* No responsibility was, however, introduced at the Centre, and the Governor-General in Council continued to remain responsible only to the British Parliament through the Secretary of State for India. Nevertheless, the Indian Legislature was made more representative and, for the first time, *bi-cameral.* It was to consist of an Upper House, named the Council of State, composed of 60 members of whom 34 were elected, and a Lower House, named the Legislative Assembly, composed of about 144 members of whom 104 were elected. The powers of both the Houses were equal except that the power to vote supply was given exclusively to the Legislative Assembly. The electorates were, however, arranged on a communal and sectional basis, developing the Morley-Minto device further.

The Governor-General's overriding powers in respect of Central legislation were retained in the following forms—(i) his prior sanction was required to introduce Bills relating to certain matters; (ii) he had the power to veto or reserve for consideration of the Crown, any Bill passed by the Indian Legislature; (iii) he had the converse power of certifying any Bill or any grant refused to be passed or made by the Legislature, in which case it would have the same effect as if it was passed or made by the Legislature; (iv) he could make Ordinances, having the force of law for a temporary period, in case of emergency.

7b. Shortcomings under Act of 1919.

The Reforms of 1919, however, failed to fulfil the aspirations of the people in India, and led to an agitation by the Congress (then under the leadership of Mahatma Gandhi) for 'Swaraj' or 'self-government', independent of the British Empire, to be attained through 'Non-cooperation'. The shortcomings of the 1919 system, mainly, were—

(i) *Power remained unitary and centralised:* Notwithstanding a substantial measure of devolution of power to the Provinces, the structure still remained unitary and centralised "with the Governor-General in Council as the keystone of the whole constitutional edifice; and it is through the Governor-General in Council that the Secretary of State and, ultimately, Parliament discharged their responsibilities for the peace, order and good government of India".[7] It was the Governor-General, and not the Courts, who had the authority to decide whether a particular subject was Central or Provincial. The Provincial Legislature could not, without the previous sanction of the Governor-General, take up for consideration any bill relating to a number of subjects.

(ii) *Dyarchy system:* The greatest dissatisfaction came from the working of Dyarchy in the Provincial sphere. In a large measure, the Governor came to dominate ministerial policy by means of his overriding financial powers and control over the official block in the Legislature. In practice, scarcely any question of importance could arise without affecting one or more of the reserved departments. The impracticability of a division of the administration into two water-tight compartments was manifested beyond doubt. The main defect of the system from the Indian standpoint was the control of the purse. Finance, being a reserved subject, was placed in charge of a member of the Executive Council, and not a Minister. It was impossible for any Minister to implement any progressive measure for want of funds and together with this was the further fact that the members of the Indian Civil Service, through whom the Ministers were to implement their policies, were recruited by the Secretary of State and were responsible to him and not to the Ministers. Above all was the overriding power of the Governor who did not act as a constitutional head even with respect to the transferred subjects. There was no provision for collective responsibility of the Ministers to the Provincial Legislature. The Ministers were appointed individually, acted as advisers of the Governor, and differed from members of the Executive Council only in the fact that they were non-officials. The Governor had the discretion to act otherwise than in accordance with the advice of his Ministers; he could certify a grant refused by the Legislature or a Bill rejected by it if it was regarded by him as essential for the due discharge of his responsibilities relating to a reserved subject.

It is no wonder, therefore, that the introduction of ministerial government over a part of the Provincial sphere proved ineffective and failed to satisfy Indian aspirations.

8. The Simon Commission and the Government of India Act, 1935.

The persistent demand for further reforms, attended with the dislocation caused by the Non-cooperation movement, led the British Government, in 1927, to appoint a Statutory Commission, as envisaged by the Government of India Act, 1919 itself (section 84A), to inquire into and report on the working of the Act and, in 1929, to announce that Dominion Status was the goal of Indian political developments. The Commission, headed by Sir John Simon, reported in 1930.

The Report was considered by a Round Table Conference consisting of the delegates of the British Government and of British India as well as of the Rulers of the Indian States (inasmuch as the scheme was to unite the Indian States with

7. Report of the Joint Parliamentary Committee; Simon Report, vol I, pp 232-38.

the rest of India under a federal scheme). A White Paper, prepared on the results of this Conference, was examined by a Joint Select Committee of the British Parliament and the Government of India Bill was drafted in accordance with the recommendations of that Select Committee, and passed, with certain amendments, as the Government of India Act, 1935.

8a. Separate Electorates on the Basis of 'Communal Award'.

Before analysing the main features of the system introduced by this Act, it should be pointed out that this Act went another step forward in perpetuating the communal cleavage between the Muslim and the Non-Muslim communities, by prescribing separate electorates on the basis of the 'Communal Award' which was issued by Mr Ramsay MacDonald, the British Prime Minister, on 4 August 1932, on the ground that the two major communities had failed to come to an agreement. From then onwards, the agreement between the two *religious* communities was continuously hoisted as a condition precedent for any further *political* advance. The Act of 1935, it should be noted, provided separate representation not only for the Muslims, but also for the Sikhs, the Europeans, Indian Christians and Anglo-Indians and, thus, created a serious hurdle in the way of the building up of national unity, which the makers of the future Constitution found it almost insurmountable to overcome even after the Muslims had partitioned for a separate State.

8b. Features of the System Introduced by Act of 1935.

The main features of the governmental system prescribed by the Act of 1935 were as follows—

(a) *Federation and Provincial Autonomy:* While under all the previous Government of India Acts, the Government of India was unitary, the Act of 1935 prescribed a federation, taking the Provinces and the Indian States as units. But it was optional for the Indian States to join the Federation; and since the rulers of the Indian States never gave their consent, the Federation envisaged by the Act of 1935 never came into being.

But though the Part relating to the Federation never took effect, the Part relating to Provincial Autonomy was given effect to since April, 1937. The Act divided legislative powers between the Provincial and Central Legislatures, and within its defined sphere, the Provinces were no longer delegates of the Central Government, but were autonomous units of administration. To this extent, the Government of India assumed the role of a federal government *vis-a-vis* the Provincial Government, though the Indian States did not come into the fold to complete the scheme of federation.

The executive authority of a Province was also exercised by a Governor on behalf of the Crown and not as a subordinate of the Governor-General. The Governor was required to act with the advice of Ministers responsible to the Legislature.

But notwithstanding the introduction of Provincial Autonomy, the Act of 1935 retained control of the Central Government over the Provinces in a certain sphere—by requiring the Governor to act 'in his discretion' or in the exercise of his 'individual judgment' in certain matters. In such matters, the Governor was to act without ministerial advice and under the control and directions of the Governor-General, and, through him, of the Secretary of State.

(b) *Dyarchy at the Centre:* The executive authority of the Centre was vested in the Governor-General (on behalf of the Crown), whose functions were divided into two groups—(i) The administration of defence, external affairs, ecclesiastical affairs, and of tribal areas, was to be made by the Governor-General in his discretion with the help of 'counsellors', appointed by him, who were not responsible to the Legislature; (ii) With regard to matters other than the above reserved subjects, the Governor-General was to act on the advice of a 'Council of Ministers' who were responsible to the Legislature. But even in regard to this latter sphere, the Governor-General might act contrary to the advice so tendered by the ministers if any of his 'special responsibilities' was involved. As regards the special responsibilities, the Governor-General was to act under the control and directions of the Secretary of State.

But, in fact, neither any 'Counsellors' nor any 'Council of Ministers' responsible to the Legislature came to be appointed under the Act of 1935; *the old Executive Council provided by the Act of 1919 continued to advise the Governor-General* until the Indian Independence Act, 1947.

(c) *The Legislature:* The Central Legislature was bi-cameral, consisting of the Federal Assembly and the Council of State. In six of the Provinces, the Legislature was bi-cameral, comprising a Legislative Assembly and a Legislative Council. In the rest of the Provinces, the Legislature was uni-cameral.

The legislative powers of both the Central and Provincial Legislatures were subject to various limitations and neither could be said to have possessed the features of a sovereign Legislature.

The Central Legislature was subject to the following limitations: (i) Apart from the Governor-General's power of veto, a Bill passed by the Central Legislature was also subject to veto by the Crown; (ii) The Governor-General might prevent discussion in the Legislature and suspend the proceedings in regard to any Bill if he was satisfied that it would affect the discharge of his special responsibilities; (iii) Apart from the power to promulgate Ordinances during the recess of the Legislature, the Governor-General had independent powers of legislation, concurrently with those of the Legislature. Thus, he had the power to make temporary Ordinances as well as permanent Acts at any time for the discharge of his special responsibilities; (iv) No bill or amendment could be introduced in the Legislature without the Governor-General's previous sanction, with respect to certain matters, *e.g.*, if the Bill or amendment sought to repeal or amend or was repugnant to any law of the British Parliament extending to India or any Governor-General's or Governor's Act, or if it sought to affect matters as respects which the Governor-General was required to act in his discretion.

There were similar fetters on the Provincial Legislature.

The Instruments of Instructions issued under the Act further required that the Bills relating to a number of subjects, such as those derogating from the powers of a High Court or affecting the Permanent Settlement, when presented to the Governor-General or a Governor for his assent, were to be reserved for the consideration of the Crown or the Governor-General, as the case might be.

(d) *Distribution of legislative powers between the Centre and the Provinces:* Though the Indian States did not join the Federation, the federal provisions of the Government of India Act, 1935, were, in fact, applied as *between the Central Government and the Provinces.*

The division of legislative powers between the Centre and the Provinces is of special interest to the reader in view of the fact that the division made in the Constitution between the Union and the States proceeds largely on the same lines. It was not a mere delegation of power by the Centre to the Provinces as by Rules made under the Government of India Act, 1919. As already pointed out, the Government of India Act of 1935 itself divided the legislative powers between the Central and Provincial Legislatures and, subject to the provisions mentioned below, neither Legislature could transgress the powers assigned to the other.

A three-fold division was made in the Act—(i) There was a *Federal List* over which the Federal Legislature had exclusive powers of legislation. This List included matters such as External Affairs; Currency and Coinage; Naval, Military and Air forces; Census; (ii) There was a *Provincial List* of matters over which the Provincial Legislature had exclusive jurisdiction, *e.g.*, Police, Provincial Public Service, Education; and (iii) There was a *Concurrent List* of matters over which both the Federal and Provincial Legislature had competence, *e.g.*, Criminal law and procedure, Civil procedure, Marriage and Divorce, Arbitration.

The Federal Legislature had the power to legislate with respect to matters enumerated in the Provincial List if a Proclamation of Emergency was made by the Governor-General. The Federal Legislature could also legislate with respect to a Provincial subject if the Legislatures of two or more Provinces desired this in their common interest.

In case of repugnancy in the Concurrent field, a Federal law prevailed over a Provincial law to the extent of the repugnancy, but if the Provincial law having been reserved for the consideration of the Governor-General received his assent, the Provincial law prevailed, notwithstanding such repugnancy.

The allocation of residuary power of legislation in the Act was unique. It was not vested in either the Central or the Provincial Legislature but the Governor-General was empowered to authorise either the Federal or the Provincial Legislature to enact a law with respect to any matter which was not enumerated in the Legislative Lists.

8c. Non-conferment of Dominion Status.

It is to be noted that 'Dominion Status', which was promised by the Simon Commission in 1929, was not conferred by the Government of India Act, 1935.

9. Changes Introduced by the Indian Independence Act, 1947.

The circumstances leading to the enactment of the Indian Independence Act, 1947,[8] is explained in the next Chapter. But the changes introduced by this Act into the structure of Government pending the drawing up of a Constitution for independent India by Constituent Assembly, should be pointed out in the present context, so as to offer a correct and comprehensive picture of the background against which the Constitution was made.

8. For the text of the Government of India Acts, 1800-1935, the Indian Councils Acts, 1861-1909, the Indian Independence Act, 1947 and Orders thereunder, see *M P Jain, Indian Constitutional Law,* Eighth Edition (2023), published by LexisNexis.

In pursuance of the Indian Independence Act, the Government of India Act, 1935, was amended by the Adaptation Orders, both in India and Pakistan, in order to provide an interim Constitution to each of the two Dominions until the Constituent Assembly could draw up the future Constitution. The following were the main results of such adaptations—

(a) *Abolition of the sovereignty and responsibility of the British Parliament:* As has been already explained, by the Government of India Act, 1858, the Government of India was transferred from the East India Company to the Crown. By this Act, the British Parliament became the direct guardian of India, and the office of the Secretary of State for India was created for the administration of Indian affairs—for which the Secretary of State was to be responsible to Parliament. Notwithstanding gradual relaxation of the control, the Governor-General of India and the Provincial Governors remained substantially under the direct control of the Secretary of State until the Indian Independence Act, 1947, so that—

> in constitutional theory, the Government of India is a subordinate official Government under His Majesty's Government.

The Indian Independence Act altered this constitutional position, root and branch. It declared that with effect from the 15 August 1947 (referred to as the 'appointed day'), India ceased to be a Dependency and the suzerainty of the British Crown over the Indian States and the treaty relations with tribal areas also lapsed from the date.

The responsibility of the British Government and Parliament for administration of India having ceased, the office of the Secretary of State for India was abolished.

(b) *The Crown no longer the source of authority:* So long as India remained a Dependency of the British Crown, the Government of India was carried on in the name of His Majesty. Under the Act of 1935, the Crown came into further prominence owing to the scheme of the Act being federal, and all the units of the federation, including the Provinces, drew their authority directly from the Crown. But under the Independence Act, 1947, neither of the two Dominions of India and Pakistan derived its authority from the British Isles.

(c) *The Governor-General and the Provincial Governors to act as Constitutional Heads:* The Governors-General of the two Dominions became the Constitutional Heads of the two new Dominions, as in the case of the other Dominions. This was, in fact, a necessary corollary from 'Dominion Status' which had been denied to India by the Government of India Act, 1935, but conceded by the Indian Independence Act, 1947.

According to the adaptations under the Independence Act, there was no longer any Executive Council as under the Act of 1919 or 'counsellors' as envisaged by the Act of 1935. The Governor-General or the Provincial Governor was to act on the advice of a Council of Ministers having the confidence of the Dominion Legislature or the Provincial Legislature, as the case might be. The words "in his discretion", "acting in his discretion" and "individual judgment" were effaced from the Government of India Act, 1935, wherever they occurred, with the result that there was now no sphere in which these Constitutional Heads could act without or against the wishes of the Ministers. Similarly, the powers of the Governor-General to require Governors to discharge certain functions as his agents were deleted from the Act.

The Governor-General and the Governors lost extraordinary powers of legislation so as to compete with the Legislature, by passing Acts, Proclamations and Ordinances for ordinary legislative purposes, and also the power of certification. The Governor's power to suspend the Provincial Constitution was taken away. The Crown also lost its right of veto and so the Governor-General could not reserve any bill for the signification of His Majesty's pleasure.

(d) *Sovereignty of the Dominion Legislature:* The Central Legislature of India, composed of the Legislative Assembly and the Council of States, ceased to exist on 14 August 1947. From the 'appointed day' and until the Constituent Assemblies of the two Dominions were able to frame their new Constitutions and new Legislatures were constituted thereunder, it was the Constituent Assembly itself, which was to function also as the Central Legislature of the Dominion to which it belonged. In other words, the Constituent Assembly of either Dominion (until it itself desired otherwise), was to have a dual function, *constituent* as well as *legislative*.

The sovereignty of the Dominion Legislature was complete and no sanction of the Governor-General would henceforth be required to legislate on any matter, and there was to be no repugnancy by reason of contravention of any Imperial law.

CHAPTER 4

THE MAKING OF THE CONSTITUTION

1. Demand for a New Constitution to be framed by a Constituent Assembly.

CHAPTER 2

THE MAKING OF THE CONSTITUTION

1. Demand for a New Constitution to be Framed by a Constituent Assembly.

THE demand that India's political destiny should be determined by the Indians themselves had been put forward by Mahatma Gandhi as early as in 1922.

Swaraj, therefore, will not be a free gift of the British Parliament; it will be a declaration of India's full self-expression. That it will be expressed through an Act of Parliament is true but it will be merely a courteous ratification of the *declared wish of the people of India* even as it was in the case of the Union of South Africa [*emphasis added*].

The failure of the Statutory Commission and the Round Table Conference which led to the enactment of the Government of India Act, 1935, to satisfy Indian aspirations accentuated the demand for a Constitution made by the people of India without outside interference, which was officially asserted by the National Congress in 1935. In 1938, Pandit Nehru definitively formulated his demand for a Constituent Assembly thus:

> The National Congress stands for independence and democratic state. It has proposed that the constitution of free India must be framed, without outside interference, by a Constituent Assembly elected on the basis of adult franchise.

This was reiterated by the Working Committee of the Congress in 1939.

2. The Cripps' Mission.

This demand was, however, resisted by the British Government until the outbreak of World War II, when external circumstances forced them to realise the urgency of solving the Indian Constitutional problems. In 1940, the Coalition Government in England recognised the principle that Indians should themselves frame a new Constitution for autonomous India, and in March 1942, when the Japanese were at the doors of India, they sent Sir Stafford Cripps, a member of the Cabinet, with a draft declaration on the proposals of the British Government to be adopted (at the end of the War) for the Constitution of India, provided the two major political parties (Congress and the Muslim League[1]) could come to an agreement to accept them, *viz.*,—

1. As stated earlier, the Muslim League, professedly a communal party, was formed in 1906. While its earlier objective was to secure separate representation of the Muslims in the political system, in its Lahore Resolution of 1940, it asserted its demand for the creation of a separate Muslim State in the Muslim majority areas. This idea was developed into the claim for dividing India into two independent States, when the Cripps offer was announced.

(a) that the Constitution of India was to be framed by an elected Constituent Assembly of the Indian people;

(b) that the Constitution should give India Dominion Status—equal partnership of the British Commonwealth of Nations;

(c) that there should be one Indian Union comprising all the Provinces and Indian States; but that any province (or Indian State) which was not prepared to accept the Constitution would be free to retain its constitutional position existing at that time and with such non-acceding Provinces, the British Government could enter into separate constitutional arrangements.

But the two parties failed to come to an agreement to accept the proposals, and the Muslim League urged—

(a) that India should be divided into two autonomous States on communal lines, and that some of the Provinces, earmarked by Mr Jinnah, should form an independent Muslim State, to be known as "Pakistan";

(b) that instead of one Constituent Assembly, there should be two Constituent Assemblies, *i.e.*, a separate Constituent Assembly for building Pakistan.

3. The Simla Conference.

After the rejection of the Cripps proposals (followed by the dynamic "Quit India" campaign launched by the Congress), various attempts to reconcile the two parties were made including the Simla Conference held at the instance of the Governor-General (Lord Wavell).

4. The Cabinet Delegation.

These having failed, the British Cabinet sent three of its own members,[2] including Cripps himself, to make another serious attempt. But the Cabinet Delegation, too, failed in making the two major parties come to any agreement and were, accordingly, obliged to put forward their own proposals, which were announced simultaneously in India and in England on 16 May 1946.

4a. Features of the Scheme Recommended by the Cabinet Delegation.

The proposals of the Cabinet Delegation sought to effect a compromise between the Union of India and its division. While the Cabinet Delegation definitely rejected the claim for a separate Constituent Assembly and a separate State for Muslims, the scheme which they recommended involved a virtual acceptance of the principle underlying the claim of the Muslim League.

The broad features of the scheme were—

(a) There would be a Union of India, comprising both British India and the States, and having jurisdiction over the subjects of Foreign Affairs, Defence and Communications. All residuary powers would belong to the Provinces and the States.

(b) The Union would have an Executive and a Legislature consisting of representatives of the Provinces and States. But any question raising a

2. The Cabinet Mission consisted of Lord Pethick-Lawrence, Sir Stafford Cripps and Mr AV Alexander.

major communal issue in the Legislature would require for its decision, a majority of the representatives of the two major communities present and voting as well as a majority of all the members present and voting.

(c) The Provinces would be free to form groups with Executives and Legislatures, and each group would be competent to determine the provincial subjects which would be taken up by the group organisation.

The scheme laid down by the Cabinet Mission was, however, recommendatory, and it was contemplated by the Mission that it would be adopted by agreement between the two major parties.

5. Holding of Election for Constituent Assembly and Difference of Opinion on Interpretation of "Grouping Clause".

A curious situation, however, arose after an election for forming the Constituent Assembly was held. The Muslim League joined the election and its candidates were returned. But a difference of opinion had, in the meantime, arisen between the Congress and the League regarding the interpretation of the "grouping clauses" of the proposals of the Cabinet Mission. The British Government intervened at this stage, and explained to the leaders in London that they upheld the contention of the League as correct, and on 6 December 1946, the British Government published the following statement—

> Should a Constitution come to be framed by the Constituent Assembly in which a large section of the Indian population had not been represented, His Majesty's Government would not contemplate forcing such a constitution upon any unwilling part of the country.

5a. Britishers' acknowledgement of Possibility of Two States.

For the first time, thus, the British Government acknowledged the possibility of two Constituent Assemblies and two States.

6. First Meeting of Constituent Assembly.

The result was that on 9 December 1946, when the Constituent Assembly first met, the Muslim League members did not attend, and the Constituent Assembly began to function without Muslim League members.

7. HMG's Statement on Handing Over of Powers of Central Government in British India.

The Muslim League next urged for the dissolution of the Constituent Assembly of India on the ground that it was not representative of all sections of the people of India. On the other hand, the British Government, by their Statement of 20 February 1947, declared—

> (a) that British rule in India would in any case end by June, 1948, after which the British would certainly transfer authority to Indian hands;
>
> (b) that if by that time a fully representative Constituent Assembly failed to work out a Constitution in accordance with the proposals made by the Cabinet Delegation—
>
> > H.M.G. will have to consider to whom the powers of the Central Government in British India should be handed over, on the due date, whether as a whole to some form of Central Government for British India, or in some areas to the existing Provincial Government, or in such other way as seems most reasonable and in the best interests of the Indian people.

7a. Urge for Another Constituent Assembly by Muslim League Members.

The result was inevitable and the League did not consider it necessary to join this Assembly, and went on pressing for another Constituent Assembly for "Muslim India".

8. Arrival of Lord Mountbatten as Governor-General.

The British Government next sent Lord Mountbatten to India as the Governor-General, in place of Lord Wavell, in order to expedite the preparations for the transfer of power, for which they had fixed a rigid time limit.

9. The Mountbatten Plan.

Lord Mountbatten brought the Congress and the League into a definite agreement that the two provinces of the Punjab and Bengal would be partitioned so as to form absolute Hindu and Muslim majority blocks within these Provinces. The League would then get its Pakistan—which the Cabinet Mission had so ruthlessly denied it—*minus* Assam, East Punjab and West Bengal, while the Congress, which was taken as the representative of the people of India other than the Muslims, would get the rest of India where the Muslims were in minority.

The actual decisions as to whether the two Provinces of the Punjab and Bengal were to be partitioned was, however, left to the vote of the members of the Legislative Assemblies of these two Provinces, meeting in two parts, according to a plan known as the "Mountbatten Plan".

9a. Formal Shape Given to the Mountbatten Plan by HMG.

It was given a formal shape by a Statement made by the British Government of 3 June 1947, which provided, *inter alia,* that:

> The Provincial Legislative Assemblies of Bengal and the Punjab (excluding European members) will, therefore, each be asked to meet in two parts, one representing the Muslim majority districts and the other the rest of the Province... The members of the two parts of each Legislative Assembly sitting separately will be empowered to vote whether or not the Province should be partitioned. If a simple majority of *either* Part decides in favour of Partition, division will take place and arrangements will be made accordingly. If partition were decided upon, each part of the Legislative Assembly would decide, on behalf of the areas it represented, whether it would join the existing or a new and separate Constituent Assembly.

It was also proposed that there would be a referendum in the North Western Frontier Province and in the Muslim majority district of Sylhet as to whether they would join India or Pakistan. The Statement further declared HMG's intention "to introduce legislation during the current session for the transfer of power this year on a Dominion Status basis to one or two successor authorities according to decisions taken as a result of the announcement."

The result of the vote according to the above Plan was a foregone conclusion as the representatives of the Muslim majority areas of the two Provinces (*i.e.*, West Punjab and East Bengal) voted for partition and for joining a new Constituent Assembly. The referendum in the North Western Frontier and Sylhet was in favour of Pakistan.

10. Creation of Separate Constituent Assembly for Pakistan.

On 26 July 1947, the Governor-General announced the setting up of a separate Constituent Assembly for Pakistan. The Plan of 3 June 1947, having been carried out, nothing stood in the way of effecting the transfer of power by enacting a statute of the British Parliament in accordance with the declaration.

11. The Indian Independence Act, 1947.

It must be said to the credit of the British Parliament that it lost no time to draft the Indian Independence Bill upon the basis of the above Plan, and this Bill was passed and placed on the Statute Book, with amazing speed, as the Indian Independence Act, 1947 (10 & 11 Geo VI, c 30). The Bill, which was introduced in Parliament on 4 July 1947, received the Royal Assent on 18 July 1947, and came into force from that date.

11a. Outstanding Characteristics of Act of 1947.

The most outstanding characteristics of the Indian Independence Act was that while other Acts of Parliament relating to the Government of India (such as the Government of India Acts from 1858 to 1935) sought to lay down a Constitution for the governance of India by the legislative will of the British Parliament—this Act of 1947 did not lay down any such Constitution. The Act provided that as from 15 August 1947 (which date is referred to in the Act as the "appointed date"), in place of "India" as defined in the Government of India Act, 1935, there would be set up two independent Dominions, to be known as *India* and *Pakistan,* and the Constituent Assembly of each Dominion was to have unlimited power to frame and adopt any Constitution and to repeal any Act of the British Parliament, including the Indian Independence Act.

Under the Act, the Dominion of India got the residuary territory of India excluding the Provinces of Sind, Baluchistan, West Punjab, East Bengal, and the North Western Frontier Province and the district of Sylhet in Assam (which had voted in favour of Pakistan at a referendum, before the Act came into force).

12. Reassembly of the Constituent Assembly of India.

The Constituent Assembly, which had been elected for undivided India and had held its first sitting on 9 December 1946, reassembled on 14 August 1947, as the sovereign Constituent Assembly for the Dominion of India.

13. Composition of the Constituent Assembly of India.

As to its composition, it should be remembered that it had been elected by indirect election by the members of the Provincial Legislative Assemblies (Lower House only), according to the scheme recommended by the Cabinet Delegation [see Table II, *post*]. The essentials of this scheme were as follows—

(1) Each Province and each Indian State or group of States were allotted the total number of seats proportional to their respective populations, roughly in the ratio of one to a million. As a result, the Provinces were to elect 292 members while the Indian States were allotted a minimum of 93 seats.

(2) The seats in each Province were distributed among the three main communities: Muslim, Sikh and General, in proportion to their respective populations.

(3) Members of each community in the Provincial Legislative Assembly elected their own representatives by the method of proportional representation with single transferable vote.

(4) The method of selection in the case of representatives of Indian States was to be determined by consultation.

As a result of the Partition under the Plan of 3 June 1947, a separate Constituent Assembly was set up for Pakistan, as stated earlier. The representatives of Bengal, Punjab, Sind, North Western Frontier Province, Baluchistan and the Sylhet district of Assam (which had joined Pakistan by a referendum) ceased to be members of the Constituent Assembly of India, and there was a fresh election in the new Provinces of West Bengal and East Punjab. In the result, when the Constituent Assembly reassembled on 31 October 1947, the membership of the House was reduced to 299, as in Table II, *post*. Of these, 284 were present on 26 November 1949, and appended their signatures to the Constitution as finally passed.

14. Appointment of the Drafting Committee for Making of Constitution of India.

The salient principles of the proposed Constitution had been outlined by various committees of the Assembly[3] such as the Union Constitution Committee, the Union Powers Committee, Committee on Fundamental Rights, and, after a general discussion of the reports of these Committees, the Assembly appointed a Drafting Committee on 29 August 1947.

15. Draft Constitution of India.

The Drafting Committee, under the Chairmanship of Dr BR Ambedkar, embodied the decision of the Assembly with alternative and additional proposals in the form of a "Draft[4] Constitution of India" which was published in February, 1948. The Constituent Assembly next met in November, 1948, to consider the provisions of the Draft, clause by clause. After several sessions, the consideration of the clauses or second reading was completed by 17 October 1949.

16. Passing of the Constitution of India on 26 November, 1949.

The Constituent Assembly again sat on 14 November 1949, for the third reading and finalized the document on 26 November 1949, on which date the Constitution received the signature of the President of the Assembly and was

3. The important committees of the Constituent Assembly were—
   (a) *Union Powers Committee*: It had 9 members. Shri Jawaharlal Nehru was its Chairman.
   (b) *Committee on Fundamental Rights and Minorities*: It had 54 members. Sardar Vallabhbhai Patel was its Chairman.
   (c) *Steering Committee*: It had 3 members. Dr KM Munshi (Chairman), Shri Gopalswamy Ayyangar and Shri Bishwanath Das.
   (d) *Provincial Constitution Committee*: It had 25 members. Sardar Patel was its Chairman.
   (e) *Committee on Union Constitution*: It had 15 members. Shri Jawaharlal Nehru was its Chairman.
4. The draft was prepared by Sir BN Rau, Adviser to the Constituent Assembly. A 7-member committee chaired by Sir Alladi Krishnaswamy Iyer was set up to examine the draft. Dr BR Ambedkar, who was minister for law from 15 August 1947 to 26 January 1950, piloted the draft Constitution in the Assembly.

declared as passed.

Ours is controlled Constitution not framed by Parliament but by a Constituent Assembly.[5]

17. Dates of Commencement of Provisions of the Constitution.

The provisions relating to short title and commencement [*Articles 393 and 394*], definitions and interpretation [*Articles 366 and 367*], citizenship [*Articles 5 to 9*], elections [*Article 324*], provisional Parliament [now omitted *Articles 379, 380 and 388*], oath or affirmation by the President [*Article 60*], transitional provisions [now omitted *Article 391 and Article 392*], were given immediate effect, *i.e.*, from 26 November 1949. The rest of the provisions of the Constitution came into force on 26 January 1950, and this date is referred to, in the Constitution, as the "date of its commencement".[6]

5. *I.R. Coelho v State of Tamil Nadu*, AIR 2007 SC 861: (2007) 2 SCC 1: (2007) 1 SCALE 197.
6. Since that date, the Constitution has freely been amended, according to the procedure laid down in Article 368, no less than 106 times. [see Table IV, *post*]

CHAPTER 3

THE PHILOSOPHY OF THE CONSTITUTION

1. Constitutional Philosophy.

EVERY Constitution has a philosophy of its own.

1a. The Objectives Resolution of Pandit Nehru.

For the philosophy underlying *our* Constitution, we must look back into the historic Objectives Resolution of Pandit Nehru which was adopted by the Constituent Assembly on 22 January 1947,[1] and which inspired the shaping of the Constitution through all its subsequent stages. It reads thus—

(1) This Constituent Assembly declares its firm and solemn resolve to proclaim India as an Independent Sovereign Republic and to draw up for her future governance a Constitution;

(2) WHEREIN the territories that now comprise British India, the territories that now form the Indian States, and such other parts of India as are outside British India and the States as well as such other territories as are willing to be constituted into the Independent Sovereign India, shall be a Union of them all; and

(3) WHEREIN the said territories, whether with their present boundaries or with such others as may be determined by the Constituent Assembly and thereafter according to the law of the constitution, shall possess and retain the status of autonomous units, together with residuary powers, and exercise all powers and functions of Government and administration, save and except such powers and functions as are vested in or assigned to the Union, or as are inherent or implied in the Union or resulting therefrom; and

(4) WHEREIN all power and authority of the Sovereign Independent India, its constituent parts and organs of Governments are derived from the people; and

(5) WHEREIN shall be guaranteed and secured to all the people of India justice, social, economic and political; equality of status, of opportunity, and before the law; freedom of thought, expression, belief, faith, worship, vocation, association and action, subject to law and public morality; and

(6) WHEREIN adequate safeguards shall be provided for minorities, backward and tribal areas, and depressed and other backward classes; and

(7) WHEREBY shall be maintained the integrity of the territory of the Republic and its sovereign rights on land, sea, and air according to justice and the law of civilised nations; and

(8) This ancient land attain its rightful and honoured place in the world and make its full and willing contribution to the promotion of world peace and the welfare of mankind.

---

1. *Constituent Assembly Debates,* vol 1, (1947) at 304 (moved by Pandit Jawaharlal Nehru on 13 December 1946).

In the words of Pandit Nehru, the aforesaid Resolution was "something more than a resolution. It is a declaration, a firm resolve, a pledge, an undertaking and for all of us a dedication".

The approach of courts must be compatible with constitutional philosophy of which Directive Principles of State Policy constitute an integral part.[2]

1b. Constitution—A Living Instrument.

Constitution is a living instrument. The originalist interpretation rendered to provisions of the Constitution decades back, cannot continue to be valid for all times to come if the Constitution is to continue as a living instrument with continued relevance. Interpretation of law must keep pace with changing needs of society.[3]

1c. Constitution—A Social Document and Modernizing Force.

The Constitution reflects the vision of its founders to give India a collective future based on the values of liberty, equality, and fraternity. Any interpretation of the Constitution must be reflective of the blueprint laid down by its founders.[4] The Constitution is - as Granville Austin[5] put it- a "social document" and a "modernizing force", with its provisions embodying "humanitarian sentiments".

The interpretation of the Constitution is not static. It has evolved with time to give recognition to a broader spectrum of rights to the citizens, as well as to impose additional safeguards against excesses of the State or even private entities, as the case may be. Our interpretation of the Constitution must fill the silences in its text. The framers of the Constitution could not have anticipated every situation that might arise in the future. They also intentionally left certain decisions to the discretion of future generations. However, the choices we make today must align with the broader constitutional framework and values. In filling the gaps, whenever they arise, our interpretation must enhance the foundational values of the Constitution such as equality, dignity, liberty, federalism and institutional accountability. Our interpretation must adhere to the postulate that civil and political rights and socio-economic rights do not exist in a state of antagonism."[6]

2. The Preamble.

It will be seen that the ideal embodied in the above Resolution is faithfully reflected in the Preamble to the Constitution, which, as amended in 1976,[7] summarises the aims and objects of the Constitution:

> WE, THE PEOPLE OF INDIA, having solemnly resolved to constitute India into a SOVEREIGN <u>*SOCIALIST SECULAR*</u> DEMOCRATIC REPUBLIC and to secure to all its citizens:

---

2. *Harjinder Singh v Punjab State Warehousing Corporation,* AIR 2010 SC 1116: 2010 AIR SCW 1357: (2010) 3 SCC 192.
3. *Central Board of Dawoodi Bohra Community v State of Maharashtra,* (2023) 1 SCR 293 : AIR 2023 SC 974.
4. *Sukanya Shantha v UOI,* AIR 2024 SC 5201 : AIR Online 2024 SC 671.
5. Granville Austin, The Indian Constitution: Cornerstone of a Nation, Oxford University Press (1999), at pages 50, xii-xiii.
6. *Sukanya Shantha v UOI,* AIR 2024 SC 5201 : AIR Online 2024 SC 671.
7. The words (in italics and underlined) were inserted by the Constitution (42nd Amendment) Act, 1976.

JUSTICE, social, economic and political;

LIBERTY of thought, expression, belief, faith and worship;

EQUALITY of status and of opportunity;

and to promote among them all

FRATERNITY assuring the dignity of the individual and the unity *and integrity* of the Nation:

IN OUR CONSTITUENT ASSEMBLY this twenty-sixth day of November, 1949, do HEREBY ADOPT, ENACT AND GIVE TO OURSELVES THIS CONSTITUTION.

2a. Importance and Utility of the Preamble.

The importance and utility of the Preamble has been pointed out in several decisions of our Supreme Court.[8] Though, by itself, it is not enforceable in a court of law,[9] the Preamble to a written Constitution states the *objects* which the Constitution seeks to establish and promote and also aids the legal interpretation of the Constitution where the language is found to be *ambiguous*.[10]

The Preamble to our Constitution serves two purposes:

(a) it indicates the *source* from which the Constitution derives its authority;

(b) it also states the *objects* which the Constitution seeks to establish and promote.

The Preamble may be invoked to determine the ambit of the Fundamental Rights and the Directive Principles of State Policy.[11]

For a proper appreciation of the aims and aspirations embodied in our Constitution, therefore, we must turn to the various expressions contained in the Preamble, as reproduced above.

3. Sovereignty.

As has been already explained, the Constitution of India, unlike the preceding Government of India Acts, is not a gift of the British Parliament. It is ordained by the people of India through their representatives assembled in a sovereign Constituent Assembly which was competent to determine the political future of the country in any manner it liked. The words—"We, the people of India...adopt, enact and give to ourselves this Constitution", thus, declare the ultimate sovereignty of the people of India and that the Constitution rests on their authority. These words emphasise the republican and democratic character of the polity and that all power ultimately stems from the people, are indicative of the source of the Constitution.[12]

---

8. *Pradeep Jain (Dr) v UOI,* AIR 1984 SC 1420: (1984) 3 SCC 654; *Steel Authority of India v National Union Water Front Workers,* AIR 2001 SC 3527: (2001) 7 SCC 1; *State of Jharkhand v Harihar Yadav,* (2014) 2 SCC 114.
9. *AK Gopalan v State of Madras,* AIR 1950 SC 27 : (1950) SCR 88, p *198* : 1950 SCJ 174; *UOI v Madan Gopal,* AIR 1954 SC 158 : (1954) SCR 541, p *555*.
10. *Re Berubari Union,* AIR 1960 SC 845, p *846* : (1960) 3 SCR 250.
11. *Kesavananda Bharati Sripadgalvaru v State of Kerala,* AIR 1973 SC 1461: (1973) 4 SCC 225: 1973 Supp SCR 1; *Chandra Bhawan Boarding and Lodging, Bangalore v State of Mysore,* AIR 1970 SC 2042.
12. *SR Chaudhuri v State of Punjab,* AIR 2001 SC 2707: (2001) 7 SCC 126.

Sovereignty means the independent authority of a State. It means that it has the power to legislate on any subject in conformity with constitutional limitations; and that it is not subject to the control of any other State or external power.

4. Republic.

The Preamble declares, therefore, in unequivocal terms that the source of all authority under the Constitution is the people of India and that there is no subordination to any external authority. While Pakistan remained a British Dominion until 1956, India ceased to be a Dominion and declared herself a "Republic" since the making of the Constitution in 1949. It means a Government of the people, by the people and for the people.

We have an elected President as the head of our State, and all office, including that of the President, will be open to all citizens.

5. Sovereignty not Inconsistent with Membership of the Commonwealth.

On and from 26 January 1950, when the Constitution came into force, the Crown of England ceased to have any legal or Constitutional authority over India and no citizen of India was to have any allegiance to the British Crown. But though India declared herself a Republic, she did not sever all ties with the British Commonwealth as did *Eire,* by enacting the Republic of Ireland Act, 1948. In fact, the conception of the Commonwealth itself has undergone a change owing to India's decision to adhere to the Commonwealth, *without acknowledging allegiance to the Crown* which was the symbol of unity of the Old British Empire and also of its successor, the "British Commonwealth of Nations".[13] It is this decision of India which has converted the "British Commonwealth"—a relic of imperialism—into a free association of independent nations under the honourable name of the "Commonwealth of Nations". This historic decision took place at the Prime Ministers' Conference at London on 27 April 1949, where, our Prime Minister, Pandit Nehru, declared that notwithstanding her becoming a sovereign independent Republic, India will continue—

> Her full membership of the Commonwealth of Nations and her acceptance of the King as the symbol of the *free* association of the independent nations and as such the Head of the Commonwealth.

It is to be noted that this declaration is *extra-legal* and there is no mention of it in the Constitution of India. It is a voluntary declaration and indicates a free association and no obligation. It only expresses the desire of India not to sever her friendly relations with the English people even though the tie of political subjugation was severed. The new association was an honourable association between independent states. It accepts the Crown of England only as a *symbolic* head of the Commonwealth (having no functions to discharge in relation to India as belonged to him prior to the Constitution), and having no claim to the allegiance of the citizens of India. Even if the King or Queen of England visits

13. So called since the Imperial Conference 1926. Later it has come to be mentioned simply as "The Commonwealth" [Cf Barker, *Essays on Government,* 1956, pp 16–18].

The concept of Commonwealth as an association has considerably weakened when the United Kingdom virtually segregated itself by refusing to protest against the Racist atrocities committed by the Government of South Africa and later by imposing the visa system upon immigrants from India and some other states.

India, he or she will *not* be entitled to any precedence over the President of India. Again, though as a member of the Commonwealth, India has a right to be represented on Commonwealth conferences, decisions at Commonwealth conferences will not be binding on her and no treaty with a foreign power or declaration of war by any member of the Commonwealth will be binding on her, without her express consent. Hence, this voluntary association of India with the Commonwealth does not affect her sovereignty to any extent and it would be open to India to cut off that association at any time she finds it not to be honourable or useful. As Pandit Nehru explained —

> It is an agreement by free will, to be terminated by free will.[14]

6. Promotion of World Peace.

The great magnanimity with which India took this decision in the face of a powerful opposition at home which was the natural reaction of the manifold grievances under the imperialistic rule, and the great fortitude with which the association has still been maintained, under the pressure of repeated disappointments, the strain of baffling international alignments and the 1976 upsurge of racialism in England, speak volumes about the sincerity of India's pledge to contribute "to the promotion of world peace" which is reiterated in Article 51 of the Constitution:

> The State shall endeavour to —
>
> (a) promote international peace and security;
>
> (b) maintain just and honourable relations between nations;
>
> (c) foster respect for international law and treaty obligations in the dealings of organised peoples with one another; and
>
> (d) encourage settlement of international disputes by arbitration.

6a. One World.

The fraternity which is professed in the Preamble is thus not confined within the bounds of the national territory; it is ready to overflow them to reach the loftier ideal of universal brotherhood, which can hardly be better expressed than in the memorable words of Pandit Nehru:

> The only possible, real object that we, in common with other nations, can have is the object of co-operating in building up some kind of a world structure, call it one world, call it what you like.[15]

Thus, though India declares her sovereignty to manage her own affairs, in no unmistakable terms, the Constitution does not support isolationism or "jingoism". Indian sovereignty is consistent with the concept of "one world", international peace and amity. The International Convention and norms can be read into them in the absence of enacted domestic law occupying the field when there is no inconsistency between them.[16] The rules of Customary International

---

14. *Constituent Assembly Debates*, vol 8, 16 May 1949.
15. *Constituent Assembly Debates*, vol 2, 22 January 1947.
16. *Vishakha v State of Rajasthan,* AIR 1997 SC 3011 : (1997) SCR (Supp 3) 404. In the absence of domestic law occupying the field, to formulate effective measures to check the evil of sexual harassment of working women at all working places, the contents of International Conventions and norms are significant for the purpose of interpretation of the guarantee of gender equality, right to work with human dignity enshrined in Articles 14, 15, 19(1)(g) and 21 of the Constitution and the safeguards against sexual harassment

[Footnote No. 16 Contd.]

Law which are not contrary to municipal law shall be deemed to have been incorporated in the domestic law shall be followed by the courts of law.[17]

7. Democracy.

The picture of a "democratic republic", which the Preamble envisages, is democratic not only from the *political* but also from the *social* standpoint. In other words, it envisages not only a democratic form of government but also a democratic society, infused with the spirit of "justice, liberty, equality and fraternity".

The promise for social, economic and political justice to citizens made by Constitution of India cannot condone policies that turn a blind eye to deliberate infliction of misery on large segments of our population.[18]

7a. Parliamentary/ Representative Democracy.

As a form of government, the democracy which is envisaged, is, of course, a representative democracy and there are in *our* Constitution no agencies of direct control by the people, such as "referendum", or "initiative". The people of India are to exercise their sovereignty through a Parliament at the Centre and a Legislature in each State, which is to be elected on adult franchise[19] and to which the real Executive, namely, the Council of Ministers, shall be responsible. Though there shall be an elected President at the head of the Union and a Governor nominated by the President at the head of each State, neither of them can exercise any political function without the aid and advice of the Council of Ministers[20] which is collectively responsible to the people's representatives in the respective Legislatures (excepting functions which the Governor is authorised by the Constitution itself to discharge in his discretion or on his individual responsibility). The Constitution holds out equality to all the citizens in the matters of choice of their representatives, who are to run the governmental machinery.

Also known as parliamentary democracy, it envisages: (i) representation of the people; (ii) responsible government; and (iii) accountability of the Council of Ministers to the legislature. The essence of this is to draw a direct line of authority from the people through the legislature. The character and content of parliamentary democracy in the ultimate analysis depends upon the quality of

---

[Footnote No. 16 Contd.]

implicit therein. This is implicit from Article 51(c) and enabling power of parliament to enact laws for implementing the International Conventions and norms by virtue of Article 253 read with entry 14 of the Union List in Seventh Schedule of the Constitution. The Parliament has now enacted the Sexual Harassment of Women at Workplace (Prevention, Prohibition and Redressal) Act, 2013 to protect women from sexual harassment at their place of work. The Act penalizes several misconducts of a sexual nature and imposes a mandate on all the public and private organisations to create adequate mechanisms for redressal. See also *UOI v Mudrika Singh*, Civil Appeal No 6859 of 2021 (decided by the Supreme Court on 3 December 2021).

17. *Vellore Citizens' Welfare Forum v UOI*, (1996) 5 SCC 647, p 660.
18. *Nandini Sundar v State of Chhattisgarh*, AIR 2011 SC 2839 (2849) : 2011 AIR SCW 4141 : (2011) 7 SCC 547.
19. The survival of this representative democracy and Parliamentary Government in India for more than seven decades since Independence should silence her critics, since military regime prevailed in her neighbouring countries until recently.
20. This is now expressly ensured by amending Article 74(1) by the Constitution (42nd Amendment) Act, 1976, and the Constitution (44th Amendment) Act, 1978.

persons who man the legislature as representatives of the people. The members of the Legislature, thus, must owe their power directly or indirectly to the people.[21]

7b. Political Justice.

The ideal of a democratic republic enshrined in the Preamble of the Constitution can be best explained with reference to the adoption of universal suffrage and the complete equality between the sexes not only before the law but also in the political sphere. 'Political justice' means the absence of any arbitrary distinction between man and man in the political sphere. In order to ensure the "political" justice held out by the Preamble, it was essential that every person in the territory of India, irrespective of his proprietary or educational qualifications, should be allowed to participate in the political system like any other person. Universal Adult Suffrage was adopted with this object in view. This means that every five years, the members of the Legislatures of the Union and of each State shall be elected by the vote of the entire adult population, according to the principle—"one person, one vote". Various reformative steps have been taken by the Election Commission on the direction of the Supreme Court, *viz.*, the voters have the fundamental right to know about their candidates, and leaving columns blank in the nomination paper amounts to violation of rights.[22] If any sitting member of the Parliament or a State Legislature is convicted of any of the offences mentioned in sub-sections (1), (2) and (3) of section 8 of the Representation of the People Act, 1951 and by virtue of such conviction and/or sentence suffers the disqualifications mentioned therein after the pronouncement of the judgment in *Lily Thomas*,[23] his membership of Parliament or the State Legislature, as the case may be, will not be saved by sub-section (4) of section 8 of the Act which has been held *ultra vires* the Constitution notwithstanding that he files the appeal or revision against the conviction and/or sentence. Further, a person who has no right to vote by virtue of the provisions of sub-section (5) of section 62 of the 1951 Act is not an elector and is, therefore, not qualified to contest the election to the House of the People or the Legislative Assembly of a State.[24] With a view to bring about purity in elections, the Election Commission, upon the direction of the Supreme Court, recognised negative voting on 27 September 2013 and held that a voter could exercise the option of negative voting and reject all candidates as unworthy of being elected. The voter could press the "None of the Above" (NOTA) button in the electronic voting machine and for this, the court also issued necessary direction to the Election Commission for its compliance.[25] The option of NOTA may serve as an elixir in direct elections but in respect of the election to the Council of States which is a different one, it would not only undermine the purity of democracy but also serve the Satan of defection and corruption.[26]

---

21. *SR Chaudhari v State of Punjab,* AIR 2001 SC 2707 : (2001) 7 SCC 126.
22. *UOI v Association for Democratic Reforms,* AIR 2002 SC 2112 : (2002) 5 SCC 294; *People's Union for Civil Liberties v UOI,* AIR 2003 SC 2363 : (2003) 4 SCC 399; *Resurgence India v Election Commission of India,* (2013) 7 Mad LJ 14 : (2013) 4 RCR (Civil) 392 : (2013) 11 Scale 348.
23. *Lily Thomas v UOI,* (2013) 7 SCC 653 : (2013) 2 SCC (LS) 811 : (2013) 8 Scale 469.
24. *Chief Election Commissioner v Jan Chaukidar (Peoples Watch),* (2013) 7 SCC 507 : (2013) 2 SCC (LS) 907 : (2013) 8 Scale 487.
25. *People's Union for Civil Liberties v UOI,* (2013) 10 SCC 1 : (2013) 12 Scale 165 : (2013) 4 RCR (Civil) 669.
26. *Shailesh Manubhai Parmar v Election Commission of India,* AIR 2018 SC 3918: (2018) 9 SCC 100: (2018) 10 SCALE 51.

7c. Economic and Social Democracy.

That this democratic republic stands for the good of *all* the people is embodied in the concept of a "Welfare State" which inspires the Directive Principles of State Policy. The "economic justice" assured by the Preamble can hardly be achieved if the democracy envisaged by the Constitution were confined to a "political democracy". In the words of Pandit Nehru:[27]

> Democracy has been spoken of chiefly in the past, as political democracy, roughly represented by every person having a vote. But a vote by itself does not represent very much to a person who is down and out, to a person, let us say, who is starving or hungry. Political democracy, by itself, is not enough except that it may be used to obtain a gradually increasing measure of economic democracy, equality and the spread of good things of life to others and removal of gross inequalities.

Or, as Dr Radhakrishnan has put it —

> Poor people who wander about, find no work, no wages and starve, whose lives are a continual round of sore affliction and pinching poverty, cannot be proud of the Constitution or its law.[28]

In short, the Indian Constitution promises not only *political* but also *social* democracy, as explained by Dr Ambedkar in his concluding speech in the Constituent Assembly:

> Political democracy cannot last unless there lies at the base of it social democracy. What does social democracy mean? It means a way of life which recognises liberty, equality and fraternity which are not to be treated as separate items in a trinity. They form a union of trinity in the sense that to divorce one from the other is to defeat the very purpose of democracy. *Liberty cannot be divorced from equality, equality cannot be divorced from liberty. Nor can liberty and equality be divorced from fraternity.*

The State in a democratic society derives its strength from the cooperative and dispassionate will of all its free and equal citizens.[29] Social and economic democracy is the foundation on which political democracy would be a way of life in the Indian polity.[30]

The offering of equal opportunity to men and women, irrespective of their caste and creed, in the matter of public employment also implements this democratic ideal. The treatment of the minority, even apart from the constitutional safeguards, clearly brings out that the philosophy underlying the Constitution has not been overlooked by those in power. The fact that members of the Muslim, Christian and other minority communities are as a rule being included in the Council of Ministers of the Union as well as the States, in the Supreme Court, and even in Diplomatic Missions, without any constitutional reservation in that behalf, amply demonstrates that those who are working the Constitution have not missed its true spirit, namely, that every citizen must feel that this country is his own.

---

27. Inaugural address of Pandit Nehru at the Seminar on Parliamentary Democracy on 25 February 1956.
28. Speech of the Vice-President, Inaugural address of Pandit Nehru at the Seminar on Parliamentary Democracy on 25 February 1956.
29. *State of Punjab v GS Gill,* AIR 1997 SC 2324 : (1997) 6 SCC 129.
30. *Samatha v State of Andhra Pradesh,* AIR 1997 SC 3297 : (1997) 8 SCC 191.

7d. Economic Justice.

The banishment of poverty, not by expropriation of those who have, but by the multiplication of the national wealth and resources and an equitable distribution thereof amongst all who contribute towards its production, is the aim of the State envisaged by the Directive Principles. Economic democracy will be installed in our sub-continent to the extent that this goal is reached. In short, economic justice aims at establishing economic democracy and a "Welfare State".

The ideals of economic justice is to make equality of status meaningful and life worth living at its best, removing inequality of opportunity and of status—social, economic and political.[31]

7e. Social Justice.

Social justice is a fundamental right.[32] Social justice is the comprehensive form to remove social imbalance by law harmonising the rival claims or the interests of different groups and/or sections in the social structure or individuals by means of which alone it would be possible to build up a welfare State.[33]

Social justice, read with Article 39A, would include legal justice which means that the system of administration of justice must provide a cheap, expeditious and effective instrument for realization of justice by all sections of the people, irrespective of their social or economic position or their financial resources.[34]

8. Liberty, Equality and Fraternity.

The three have to be secured and protected with social justice and economic empowerment and political justice to all the citizens under the rule of law.[35]

9. Liberty.

Democracy, in any sense, cannot be established unless certain minimal rights, which are essential for a free and civilised existence, are assured to every member of the community. The Preamble mentions these essential individual rights as "freedom of thought, expression, belief, faith and worship" and these are guaranteed against all the authorities of the State by Part III of the Constitution [*vide Articles 19, 25-28*], subject, of course, to the implementation of the Directive Principles for the common good [*Article 31C*] and the Fundamental duties introduced [*Article 51A*], by the 42nd Amendment, 1976.

"Liberty" should be coupled with social restraint and subordinated to the liberty of the greatest number for common happiness.[36]

10. Equality.

Guaranteeing of certain rights to each individual would be meaningless unless all inequality is banished from the social structure and each individual is assured of equality of status and opportunity for the development of the best in him and the means for the enforcement of the rights guaranteed to him. This object is secured in the body of the Constitution, by making illegal all discriminations by the State between citizen and citizen, simply on the

31. *Dalmia Cement (Bharat) Ltd v UOI,* (1996) 10 SCC 104 : (1996) 4 JT SC 555.
32. *Ashok Kumar Gupta v State of UP,* (1997) 5 SCC 201 : 1997 SCC (LS) 1299.
33. *Dalmia Cement (Bharat) v UOI,* (1996) 10 SCC 104 : (1996) 4 JT SC 555.
34. *Babu Ram L v Raghunathji Maharaj,* AIR 1976 SC 1734 : (1976) 3 SCC 492.
35. *SS Bola v BD Sardana,* AIR 1997 SC 3127 : (1997) 8 SCC 522.
36. *SS Bola v BD Sardana,* AIR 1997 SC 3127 : (1997) 8 SCC 522.

ground of religion, race, caste, sex or place of birth [*Article 15(1)*]; by throwing open "public places" to all citizens [*Article 15(2)*]; by abolishing untouchability [*Article 17*]; by abolishing titles of honour [*Article 18*]; by offering equality of opportunity in matters relating to employment under the State [*Article 16*]; by guaranteeing equality before the law and equal protection of the laws, as justiciable rights [*Article 14*].

In addition to the above provisions, to ensure *civic* equality, the Constitution seeks to achieve *political* equality by providing for Universal Adult Franchise [*Article 326*] and by reiterating that no person shall be either excluded from the general electoral roll or allowed to be included in any general or special electoral roll, only on the ground of his religion, race, caste or sex [*Article 325*].

Apart from these general provisions, there are special provisions in the Directive Principles [Part IV] which enjoin the State to place the two sexes on an equal footing in the economic sphere, by securing to men and women equal right to work and equal pay for equal work [*Article 39, clauses (a) and (d)*].

11. From a Socialistic Pattern of Society to Socialism/ Socialist State.

The realisation of so many objectives would certainly mean an expansion of the functions of the State. The goal envisaged by the Constitution, therefore, is that of a "Welfare State"[37] and the establishment of a "socialist state". At the Avadi session in 1955, Congress explained this objective as establishing a "socialistic pattern of society" by a resolution—

> In order to realise the object of Congress...and to *further the objectives stated in the Preamble and Directive Principles of State Policy* of the Constitution of India, planning should take place with a view to the establishment of a *socialistic pattern of society,* where the principal means of production are under social ownership or control, production is progressively speeded up and there is equitable distribution of the national wealth.

How far this end has been already achieved will be explained in Chapter 9, *post*, where it will also be pointed out how, till 1992, the trend had been from a "socialistic pattern" towards a "socialistic state", bringing industries and private enterprises under State ownership and management and carrying on trade and business as a State function.

That the goal of the Indian polity is *socialism* which was ensured by inserting the word "socialist" in the Preamble, by the Constitution (42nd Amendment) Act, 1976. It has been inserted "to spell out expressly the high ideals of socialism". It is to be noted, however, that the "socialism" envisaged by the Indian Constitution is not the usual scheme of State socialism which involves "nationalisation" of all means of production, and the abolition of private property. As the then Prime Minister Indira Gandhi explained—[38]

> We have always said that we have our *own brand* of socialism. We will nationalise the sectors where we feel the necessity. Just nationalisation is not our type of socialism.

Though the word "socialism" is vague, our Supreme Court has observed that its principal aim is to eliminate inequality of income and status and standards of

37. *Cf Crown Aluminum Works v Workmen,* AIR 1958 SC 30 : (1958) 1 SCR 651 : (1958) 1 LLJ 1.
38. *Statesman,* 25 October 1976, p 1; 28 October 1976, p 1.

life, and to provide a decent standard of life to the working people. The Indian Constitution, therefore, does not seek to abolish private property altogether but seeks to put it under restraints so that it may be used in the interests of the nation, which includes the upliftment of the poor. Instead of a total nationalisation of all property and industry, it envisages a "mixed economy", but aims at offering "equal opportunity" to all, and the abolition of "vested interests".[39] From 1992 onwards, the trend is now away from socialism to privatisation. Investment in many public enterprises has been divested in favour of private persons and many industries and services which were reserved for the government sector have been thrown open for private enterprise. This is in keeping with the worldwide trend after the collapse of socialism in the USSR, and East European countries. But the Constitutional obligation to pay compensation to the private owner for State acquisition has been taken away by repealing Article 31, by the Constitution (44th Amendment) Act, 1978, as will be further explained under Chapter 8, *post.*

12. Need for Unity and Integrity of the Nation.

Unity amongst the inhabitants of this vast sub-continent, torn as under by a multitude of problems and fissiparous forces, was the first requisite for maintaining the independence of the country as well as to make the experiment of democracy successful. The ideal of unity has been buttressed by adding the words "and integrity" of the Nation, in the Preamble, by the Constitution (42nd Amendment) Act, 1976. But neither the integration of the people nor a democratic political system could be

39. It must be pointed out, in this context, that both "socialism" and "secularism" are vague words and, in the absence of any explanation of these words in the Constitution, such vagueness is liable to be capitalised by interested political groups and to create confusion in the minds of the masses of the Republic to instruct whom is one of the objects of the Preamble. The Janata Party sought to offer such explanation, by amending Article 366 of the Constitution by the 45th Amendment Bill, 1976, which, however, was thwarted by the Congress opposition in the Rajya Sabha.

In the absence of such explanation, it would remain a matter of controversy whether the object of "socialism" under the Indian Constitution simply means "freedom from exploitation" or State Socialism or even Marxism. Similarly, "secularism" might be used as an instrument of unrestrained communalism or bigotry or even anti-religionism, as distinguished from "equal respect for all religions". Instead of these words serving to elucidate the articles of the Constitution, the meaning of these words shall have to be gathered from the operative provisions, which, in legal interpretation, cannot be controlled by the Preamble. Thus, from Article 43A, which has been introduced by the same 42nd Amendment Act, 1976, it is clear that "socialism", as envisaged by the Preamble, will include "participation of workers" in the management' of an industry, and consequently, profit-sharing. This is, obviously, a step forward from Capitalism to Collectivism.

The Supreme Court is also facilitating the advent of socialism by interpreting other provisions of the Constitution in the light of the word "socialism" in the Preamble [*Excel Wear v UOI,* AIR 1979 SC 25, para 24 : (1978) 4 SCC 224 : (1978) 2 LLJ 527; *Randhir v UOI,* AIR 1982 SC 879, para 8 : (1982) 1 SCC 618; *DS Nakara v UOI,* AIR 1983 SC 130, paras 33–34 : (1983) 1 SCC 305; *Minerva Mills v UOI,* AIR 1980 SC 1789 : (1980) 2 SCC 591].

According to the Supreme Court, the goal of Indian Socialism is "a blend of Marxism and Gandhism, leaning heavily towards Gandhian socialism" [*D S Nakara v UOI,* AIR 1983 SC 130 : (1983) 1 SCC 305].

ensured without infusing a spirit of brotherhood amongst the heterogeneous population, belonging to different races, religions and cultures.[40]

13. Fraternity.

The "Fraternity" cherished by the framers of the Constitution will be achieved not only by abolishing untouchability amongst the different sects of the same community, but by abolishing all communal or sectional or even local or provincial anti-social feelings which stand in the way of the unity of India.

Democracy would indeed be hollow if it fails to generate this spirit of brotherhood amongst all sections of the people—a feeling that they are all children of the same soil, the same Motherland. It becomes all the more essential in a country like India, composed of so many races, religions, languages and cultures.

Article 1 of the Declaration of Human Rights (1948), adopted by the United Nations, says:

> All human beings are born free and equal in *dignity* and rights. They are endowed with reason and conscience and should act towards one another in a spirit of brotherhood.

It is this spirit of brotherhood that the Preamble of *our* Constitution reflects.[41]

14. A Secular State.

The unity and fraternity of the people of India, professing numerous faiths, has been sought to be achieved by enshrining the ideal of a "Secular State", which means that the State protects all religions equally and does not itself uphold any religion as the State religion. The question of Secularism is not one of sentiments, but one of law. The secular objective of the State has been specifically expressed by inserting the word "secular" in the Preamble by the Constitution (42nd Amendment) Act, 1976. The original framers of the Constitution adopted Articles 25, 26 and 27 to further secularism. Secularism was very much embedded in their constitutional philosophy. The 42nd Amendment, which formally inserted secularism into the Preamble, merely made explicit what was already implicit.[42] Secularism is a part of the basic structure of the Constitution. There is no provision in the Constitution making any religion the "established Church" as some other Constitutions do. On the other hand, the liberty of "belief, faith and worship" promised in the Preamble is implemented by incorporating the fundamental rights of all citizens relating to "freedom of religion" in Articles 25-28, which guarantees to each individual, freedom to profess, practise and propagate religion, assure strict impartiality on the part of the State and its institutions towards all religions (see Chapter 8, *post*).

---

40. The Supreme Court has pointed out that in promoting the unity of India, the *common* culture and heritage of India, of which the foundation is the Sanskrit language, must play a leading part [*Santosh Kumar v Secretary, Ministry of HRD,* AIR 1995 SC 293, para 18 : (1994) 6 SCC 579].

41. *S R Bommai v UOI,* AIR 1994 SC 1918 : (1994) 3 SCC 1. See also *Sri Adi Visheshwar of Kashi Vishwanath Temple, Varanasi v State of UP,* (1997) 4 SCC 606, para 26 : (1997) 4 JT SC 124.

42. *Ashok Kumar Thakur v UOI,* (2008) 6 SCC 1 : (2008) 5 Scale 1.

This itself is one of the glowing achievements of Indian democracy when her neighbours, such as Pakistan,[43] Bangladesh, Sri Lanka (Ceylon) and Myanmar (Burma), uphold particular religions as State religions.

15. Dignity of the Individual and Directive Principles.

A fraternity cannot, however, be installed unless the dignity of each of its members is maintained. The Preamble, therefore, says that the State, in India, will assure the dignity of the individual. The Constitution seeks to achieve this object by guaranteeing equal fundamental rights to each individual, so that he can enforce his minimal rights, if invaded by anybody, in a court of law. Seeing that these justiciable rights may not be enough to maintain the dignity of an individual if he is not free from wants and misery, a number of Directives have been included in Part IV of the Constitution, exhorting the State so to shape its social and economic policies that, *inter alia,* "all citizens, men and women equally, have the right to an adequate means of livelihood" [*Article 39(a)*], "just and humane conditions of work" [*Article 42*], and "a decent standard of life and full enjoyment of leisure and social and cultural opportunities" [*Article 43*]. Our Supreme Court has come to hold that the right to dignity is a fundamental right.[44] In a judgment, the Supreme Court has held that the right against sexual harassment is vested in all persons as a part of their right to life and right to dignity under Article 21 of the Constitution.[45]

In order to remove poverty, and to bring about a socio-economic revolution, the list of Directives was widened by the Constitution (42nd Amendment) Act, 1976, and it was provided that—in order that such welfare measures for the benefit of the masses may not be defeated—any measure for the implementation of *any* of the Directives shall be immune from any attack in the Courts on the ground that such measure contravenes any person's fundamental rights under Article 14 or 19.[46]

Swamy Vivekananda had said:

> "Just as a bird cannot fly with its one wing only, a nation will not march forward if the women are left behind."

16. Gender Justice.

Article 39, in Part IV of the Constitution that deals with the Directive Principles of State Policy, provides that the State shall direct its policies towards securing that the citizens, men and women equally, have the right to adequate means of

---

43. Islam is the State religion of Pakistan under the Constitution of 1972. This position had been maintained by the Provisional Constitution Order, 1981, issued by General Zia-ul-Haq, who assumed power in 1977 as the Chief Martial Law Administrator. In Bangladesh, Lieut. General Ershad, the former President and Chief Martial Law Administrator had declared that Islam would be the State religion [*Statesman,* 30 December 1982].

44. *LIC v Consumer Centre,* AIR 1995 SC 1811 : (1995) 5 SCC 482.

45. *UOI v Mudrika Singh,* Civil Appeal No. 6859 of 2021 (decided by the Supreme Court on 3 December 2021).

46. This amendment of Article 31C, by the 42nd Amendment, has not been touched by the 44th Amendment Act, 1978, because the Congress Opposition in the Rajya Sabha thwarted the Janata attempt, through the 45th Amendment Bill, to revert to the pre-1976 position.

livelihood. Clause (*d*) of the said Article provides for equal pay for equal work for both men and women[47] and clause (*e*) stipulates that health and strength of workers, men and women alike, and the tender age of children, are not abused and that citizens are not forced by economic necessity to enter into avocations unsuited to their age or strength.[48] The Fundamental Rights and the Directive Principles are the two quilts of the chariot in establishing the egalitarian social order and, therefore, it is required to interpret the Fundamental Rights in light of the Directive Principles of State Policy.[49] Clause (*e*) of Article 51A makes it clear that all practices derogatory to the dignity of women are to be renounced. A female candidate is not required to furnish information about her menstrual period, last date of menstruation, pregnancy and miscarriage, as calling of such information are indeed embarrassing if not humiliating.[50] The requirement that a married woman should obtain her husband's consent before applying for public employment was held invalid and unconstitutional.[51] Thus, there cannot be any discrimination solely on the ground of gender.

Reservation of seats for women in Panchayats and Municipalities have been provided for under Articles 243D and 243T of the Constitution of India with a view that the women in India are required to participate more in a democratic set-up especially at the grassroots level. Similarly, reservation of seats for women in the board of every co-operative society shall have to be provided for, by law, by the State Legislatures in accordance with Article 243ZJ. Recently, by the Constitution (106th Amendment) Act, 2023,[52] 33% reservation to women has also been provided for, which was lingering from more than 2 decades, in the House of the People (Lok Sabha), the Legislative Assemblies of the States and the Legislative Assembly of the NCT of Delhi by inserting Articles 330A, 332A and by amending Article 239AA(2), respectively. However, such provision shall be implemented after the next census and subsequent delimination exercise and which will continue for a period of 15 years from such commencement.

The sustenance of gender justice is the cultivated achievement of intrinsic human rights. Equality cannot be achieved unless there are equal opportunities for both men and women and if a woman is debarred at the threshold to enter into the sphere of profession for which she is eligible and qualified, it is well-nigh impossible to conceive of equality. It also clips her capacity to earn her livelihood which affects her individual dignity.

47. *Mackinnon Mackenzie v Audrey D'Costa,* (1987) 2 SCC 469 : (1987) 2 SCR 659 : JT (1987) 2 SC 34.
48. *Charu Khurana v UOI,* AIR 2015 SC 839 : 2015 AIR SCW 1 : AIR SC (Civ) 2015 SC 577 : (2015) 1 SCC 192.
49. *Minerva Mills Ltd v UOI,* AIR 1980 SC 1789: (1980) 3 SCC 625; *Society for Unaided Private Schools of Rajasthan v UOI,* AIR 2012 SC 3445 : (2012) 6 SCC 1; *Pramati Educational and Cultural Trust (Registered) v UOI,* AIR 2014 SC 2114 : (2014) 8 SCC 1.
50. Article 51A, Constitution of India; *Neera Mathur v Life Insurance Corporation of India,* AIR 1992 SC 392 : (1992) 1 SCC 286 : JT (1991)4 SC 468.
51. *Maya Devi v State of Maharashtra,* (1986) 1 SCR 743.
52. Whose commencement date is yet to be notified.

The Supreme Court[53] referred to the Convention for Elimination of all forms of Discrimination Against Women, 1979 (for short, "CEDAW") which was ratified by the Government of India in 1993 and framed certain guidelines regard being had to the sexual harassment at work places.

16a. Transgenders as Third Gender.

Self-determination of identity has been held to be an essential facet of Article 21. The Supreme Court while declaring the "Hijra/ Transgender" as "third gender" has held that:[54]

> (1) Hijras, Eunuchs, apart from binary gender, be treated as "third gender" for the purpose of safeguarding their rights under Part III of our Constitution and the laws made by the Parliament and the State Legislature, (2) Transgender persons' right to decide their self-identified gender is also upheld and the Centre and State Governments are directed to grant legal recognition of their gender identity such as male, female or as third gender, (3) We direct the Centre and the State Governments to take steps to treat them as socially and educationally backward classes of citizens and extend all kinds of reservation in cases of admission in educational institutions and for public appointments, (4) Centre and State Governments are directed to operate separate HIV Sero-surveillance Centres since Hijras/Transgenders face several sexual health issues, (5) Centre and State Governments should seriously address the problems being faced by Hijras/Transgenders such as fear, shame, gender dysphoria, social pressure, depression, suicidal tendencies, social stigma, etc. and any insistence for SRS for declaring one's gender is immoral and illegal, (6) Centre and State Governments should take proper measures to provide medical care to TGs in the hospitals and also provide them separate public toilets and other facilities, (7) Centre and State Governments should also take steps for framing various social welfare schemes for their betterment, (8) Centre and State Governments should take steps to create public awareness so that TGs will feel that they are also part and parcel of the social life and be not treated as untouchables, (9) Centre and the State Governments should also take measures to regain their respect and place in the society which once they enjoyed in our cultural and social life.

The Supreme Court has interpreted the law in consonance with the new social needs. This is the recognition of their right of equality as enshrined in Article 14, as well as their human right to life with dignity, which is the mandate of the Article 21 of the Constitution.

17. Fundamental Duties.

The philosophy contained in the Preamble, as explained in the foregoing pages, has been further highlighted by emphasising that each individual shall not only have the fundamental rights in Part III of the Constitution to ensure his liberty of expression, faith and worship, equality of opportunity and the like, but also a corresponding fundamental duty, such as to uphold the sovereignty, unity and integrity of the nation, to maintain secularism and the common brotherhood amongst all the people of India. This has been done by inserting Article 51A, laying down ten [now eleven][55] "Fundamental Duties", by the Constitution (42nd Amendment) Act, 1976 (see, further, under Chapter 8, *post*).

---

53. *Vishaka v State of Rajasthan*, AIR 1997 SC 3011.

54. *National Legal Services Authority v UOI*, AIR 2014 SC 1863 : (2014) 5 SCC 438 : (2014) 3 CTC 46. See also *Justice K S Puttaswamy v UOI*, AIR Online 2018 SC 237 : 2018 SCC OnLine SC 1642 : LNIND 2018 SC 535.

55. *Vide* the Constitution (86th Amendment) Act, 2002, section 4 (w.e.f. 1-4-2010).

A fitting commentary on the foregoing contents of the Preamble to *our* Constitution can be best offered by quoting a few lines from Prof Ernest Barker, one of the modern thinkers on democratic government.[56]

> ... there must be a *capacity* and a *passion* for the enjoyment of liberty—there must be a sense of personality in each, and of respect for personality in all, generally spread through the whole community—before the democratic State can be *truly achieved* . . . Perhaps it can be fairly demanded only in a community which has achieved a *sufficient standard of material existence,* and a *sufficient degree of national homogeneity* to devote itself to an ideal of liberty which has to be *worked out in each by the common effort of all.* If the problems of material existence are still absorbing... the ideal of living a common life of freedom—in other words, of attaining a particular quality of life—will seem an ideal dream. If, again, the problems of national homogeneity are still insistent, and there is *no common feeling of fellowship*—if some sections of the community are regarded by others, whether on the ground of their inferior education, or on the ground of their inferior stock or any other ground, as essentially alien and heterogeneous—the ideal of the common life of freedom will seem equally illusory...

Combining the ideals of political, social and economic democracy with that of equality and fraternity, the Preamble seeks to establish what Mahatma Gandhi described as "the India of My Dreams", namely:

> ... an India, in which the poorest shall feel that it is their country in whose making they have an effective voice;. . .an India in which all communities shall live in perfect harmony. There can be no room in such an India for the curse of untouchability or the curse of intoxicating drinks and drugs. Women will enjoy the same rights as men.[57]

No wonder such a successful combination in the text of our Preamble would receive unstinted approbation from Ernest Barker, who has reproduced this Preamble at the opening of his book on Social and Political Theory, observing that the Preamble to the Constitution of India states:

> In a brief and pithy form the argument of much of the book, and it may accordingly *serve as a key-note.*[58]

---

56. Barker, *Reflections on Government*, Paperback, pp 192–93.
57. MK Gandhi, *India of My Dreams,* pp 9–10.
58. Barker, *Principles of Social and Political Theory,* 1951, Paperback, Preface, pp vi, ix.
    The Supreme Court is relying more and more on the Preamble in interpreting the enacting provisions and implementing the Directive Principles (Part IV) of the Constitution.

CHAPTER 4

OUTSTANDING FEATURES OF OUR CONSTITUTION

1. Drawn from Different Sources.

THE Constitution of India is remarkable for many outstanding features which will distinguish it from other Constitutions even though it has been prepared after "ransacking all the known Constitutions of the world" and most of its provisions are substantially borrowed from others. As Dr Ambedkar observed—[1]

> One likes to ask whether there can be anything new in a Constitution framed at this hour in the history of the world. More than hundred years have rolled when the first written Constitution was drafted. It has been followed by many other countries reducing their Constitutions to writing . . . Given these facts, all Constitutions in their main provisions must look similar. The only new things, if there be any, in a Constitution framed so late in the day are the variations made *to remove the faults and to accommodate it to the needs of the country.*

1a. A Beautiful Patchwork.

So, though our Constitution may be said to be a "borrowed" Constitution, the credit of its framers lies in gathering the best features of each of the existing Constitutions and in modifying them with a view to avoiding the faults that have been disclosed in their working and to adapting them to the existing conditions and needs of this country. So, if it is a "patchwork", it is a "beautiful patchwork".[2]

1b. Criticisms of Constituent Assembly Members.

There were members in the Constituent Assembly who criticised the Constitution which was going to be adopted as a "slavish imitation of the West" or "not suited to the genius" of the people. Many apprehended that it would be unworkable. But the fact that it has survived for about 78 years, while Constitutions have sprung up only to wither away in countries around us, such as Myanmar (earlier, Burma) and Pakistan, belies the apprehension of the critics of the Indian Constitution.

2. The Longest Known Constitution.

The Constitution of India has the distinction of being the most lengthy and detailed constitutional document the world has so far produced.[3] The original Constitution contained as many as 395 Articles and 8 Schedules (to which additions/omissions were made by subsequent amendments). Even after the repeal of several provisions, it still contains 471 Articles and 12 Schedules.

---

1. *Constituent Assembly Debates*, vol 7, pp 35–38.
2. *Constituent Assembly Debates*, vol 7, pp 2, 242; *Constituent Assembly Debates*, vol 11, p 613, 616.
3. The Constitution of the United States, with all its amendments up to date, consists of not more than 7,000 words.

Since its inception, while a number of Articles have been repealed/omitted, 98 Articles and 4 Schedules have been *added* to the Constitution, *viz.*, Articles 21A, 31A to 31C, 39A, 43A, 43B, 48A, 51A, 124A to 124C, 134A, 139A, 224A, 233A, 239A, 239AA, 239AB, 239B, 243A to 243ZT, 244A, 246A, 269A, 279A, 290A, 300A, 312A, 323A, 323B, 330A, 332A, 334A, 338A, 338B, 342A, 350A, 350B, 361A, 361B, 363A, 371A to 371J, 372A and 394A, up to April 2024. The Schedules are Ninth, Tenth, Eleventh and Twelfth.

This extraordinary bulk of the Constitution is due to several reasons:

(i) The framers sought to incorporate the accumulated experience gathered from the working of all the known Constitutions and to avoid all defects and loopholes that might be anticipated in the light of those Constitutions. Thus, while they framed the Chapter on the Fundamental Rights upon the model of the American Constitution, and adopted the Parliamentary system of Government from the United Kingdom, they took the idea of the Directive Principles of State Policy from the Constitution of Eire, and added elaborate provisions relating to Emergencies in the light of the Constitution of the German Reich and the Government of India Act, 1935. On the other hand, our Constitution is more full of words than other Constitutions because it has embodied the modified results of judicial decisions made elsewhere interpreting comparable provisions, in order to minimise uncertainty and litigation.

(ii) Not contented with merely laying down the fundamental principles of governance (as the American Constitution does), the authors of the Indian Constitution followed and reproduced the Government of India Act, 1935, in providing matters of administrative detail—not only because the people were accustomed to the detailed provisions of that Act, but also because the authors had the apprehension that in the present conditions of the country, the Constitution might be perverted unless the form of administration was also included in it. In the words of Dr Ambedkar,—

> .....It is perfectly possible to pervert the Constitution without changing the form of administration.

Any such surreptitious subversion of the Constitution was sought to be prevented by putting detailed provisions in the Constitution itself, so that they might not be encroached upon without amending the Constitution.

The very adoption of the bulk of the provisions from the Government of India Act, 1935, contributed to the volume of the new Constitution inasmuch as the Act of 1935 itself was a lengthy and detailed organic law. So much was borrowed from that Act because the people were familiar with the existing system.

It was also felt that the smooth working of an infant democracy might be jeopardised[4] unless the Constitution mentioned in detail things which were left in other Constitutions to ordinary legislation. This explains why we have in our Constitution detailed provisions about the organisation of the Judiciary, the Services, the Public Service Commissions, Elections and the like. It is the same ideal of "exhaustiveness" which explains why the provisions of the Indian Constitution as to the division of powers between the Union and the States are more numerous than perhaps the aggregate of the provisions relating to that subject in the Constitution of the USA, Australia and Canada.

4. *Constituent Assembly Debates*, vol 11, pp 839–40.

(iii) The vastness of the country (see Table I, *post*), and the peculiar problems to be solved have also contributed towards the bulk of the Constitution. Thus, there is one entire Part [*Part IX*] relating to the Panchayats; one entire Part [*Part IX-A*] relating to the Municipalities; one entire Part [*Part IX-B*] relating to the Co-operative Societies; one entire Part [*Part X*] relating to the Scheduled and Tribal Areas; one entire Part [*Part XVI*] relating to the Scheduled Castes and Scheduled Tribes and other backward classes (including socially and educationally backward classes); one entire Part [*Part XVII*] relating to Official Language; one entire Part [*Part XVIII*] relating to Emergency Provisions; and one entire Part [*Part XXI*] relating to Temporary, Transitional and Special Provisions.

(iv) While the Constitution of the United States deals only with the Federal Government and leaves the states to draw up their own Constitutions, the Indian Constitution provides the Constitutions of both the Union and the Units (*i.e.,* the States), with the same fullness and precision. Since the Units of the federation differed in their historical origins and their political development, special provisions for different classes of the Units[5] had to be made, such as the Part B states (representing the *former Indian States*), the Part C States (representing the Centrally Administered areas) and some smaller Territories in Part D. This also contributed to the bulk of the 1949-Constitution (see Table III, *post*).

Though, as has just been said, the Constitution of the State was provided by the Constitution of India, the erstwhile State of Jammu and Kashmir was accorded a special status and was allowed to make its own State Constitution. Even all the other provisions of the Constitution of India did not directly apply to Jammu and Kashmir but depended upon an Order made for the President in Constitution with the Government of State—for which provision was made in Article 370.

Article 370 now stands substantially modified. On 6 August 2019, in exercise of the powers conferred by clause (3) of Article 370 read with clause (1) of Article 370 of the Constitution of India, the President made a declaration that, as from the 6 August 2019, all clauses of Article 370 shall cease to be operative except the following which shall read as under, namely:

> 370. All provisions of this Constitution, as amended from time to time, without any modifications or exceptions, shall apply to the State of Jammu and Kashmir notwithstanding anything contrary contained in article 152 or article 308 or any other article of this Constitution or any other provision of the Constitution of Jammu and Kashmir or any law, document, judgement, ordinance, order, by-law, rule, regulation, notification, custom or usage having the force of law in the territory of India, or any other instrument, treaty or agreement as envisaged under article 363 or otherwise.

[For details, refer Chapter 15, *post*].

Even after the inauguration of the Constitution, special provisions have been inserted [*e.g., Articles 371 to 371J*], to meet the regional problems and demands in certain States, *i.e.*, States of Maharashtra, Gujarat, Nagaland, Assam, Manipur, Andhra Pradesh, Telangana, Sikkim, Mizoram, Arunachal Pradesh, Goa, Karnataka.

---

5. Of course, some of these provisions have been eliminated by the Constitution (7th Amendment) Act, 1956, which abolished the distinction between different classes of States.

(v) Not only are the provisions relating to the Units elaborately given, the relations between the Federation and the Units and the Units *inter se,* whether legislative or administrative, are also exhaustively codified, so as to eliminate conflicts as far as possible. The lessons drawn from the political history of India which induced the framers of the Constitution to give it a unitary bias, also prompted them to make detailed provisions "regarding the distribution of powers and functions between the Union and the States in all aspects of their administrative and other activities",[6] and also as regards inter-State relations, co-ordination and adjudication of disputes amongst the States.

(vi) There is not only a Bill of Rights containing justiciable fundamental rights of the individual [*Part III*] on the model of the Amendments to the *American* Constitution but also a Part [*Part IV*] containing Directive Principles, which confer no justiciable rights upon the individual but are nevertheless to be regarded as "fundamental in the governance of the country"—being in the nature of "principles of social policy" as contained in the Constitution of *Eire* (*i.e.*, the Republic of Ireland). It was considered by the makers of *our* Constitution that though they could not, owing to their very nature, be made legally enforceable, it was well worth to incorporate in the Constitution some basic non-justiciable rights which would serve as moral restraints upon future governments and thus prevent the policy from being torn away from the idea which inspired the makers of the organic law.

Even the Bill of Rights (*i.e.*, the list of Fundamental Rights) became bulkier than elsewhere because the framers of the Constitution had to include novel matters owing to the peculiar problems of *our* country, eg, untouchability, preventive detention.

To the foregoing list, a notable addition has been made by the 42nd Amendment inserting one new chapter of the Fundamental Duties of Citizens [*Part IVA (Article 51A)*], which though not attended with any legal sanction, have now to be read along with the Fundamental Rights [see, further, under Chapter 8, *post*].

3. More Flexible than Rigid. Another distinctive feature of the Indian Constitution is that it seeks to impart flexibility to a written federal Constitution.

It is only the amendment of a few of the provisions of the Constitution that requires ratification by the State Legislatures and even then ratification by only 1/2 of them would suffice (while the American Constitution requires ratification by 3/4 of the States). The rest of the Constitution may be amended by a special majority of the Union Parliament, *i.e.*, a majority of not less than 2/3 of the members of each House present and voting, which, again, must be majority of the total membership of the House [see Chapter 10, *post*].

On the other hand, Parliament has been given the power to alter or modify many of the provisions of the Constitution by a simple majority as is required for general legislation, by laying down in the Constitution that such changes "*shall not be deemed to be* '*amendments*' *of the Constitution*". Instances to the point are—(a) Changes in the names, boundaries, areas of, and amalgamation and separation of States [*Article 4*]; (b) Abolition or creation of the Second Chamber

6. Dr Rajendra Prasad, *Constituent Assembly Debates*, vol 10, p 891.

of a State Legislature [*Article 169*]; (c) Creation of Legislatures and Council of Ministers for certain Union Territories [*Article 239A(2)*]; (d) Special provisions with respect to Delhi [*Article 239AA(7)*]; (e) Part IX [relating to Panchayats] not to apply to certain areas [*Article 243M(4)*]; (f) Part IX-A [relating to Municipalities] not to apply to certain areas [*Article 243ZC(3)*]; (g) Formation of an autonomous State comprising certain tribal areas in Assam and creation of local Legislature or Council of Ministers or both therefor [*Article 244A*]; (h) All-India Services [*Article 312*]; and (i) Administration of Scheduled Areas and Scheduled Tribes [*Para 7 of the Fifth Schedule* and *Para 21 of the Sixth Schedule*].

Yet another evidence of this flexibility is the power given by the Constitution itself to Parliament to supplement the provisions of the Constitution by legislation. Though the makers of the Constitution aimed at exhaustiveness, they realised that it was not possible to anticipate all exigencies and to lay down detailed provisions in the Constitution to meet all situations and for all times:

(a) In various Articles, therefore, the Constitution lays down certain basic principles and empowers Parliament to supplement these principles by legislation. Thus, (i) as to citizenship, Articles 5–8 only lays down the conditions for acquisition of citizenship at the commencement of the Constitution and Article 11 vests plenary powers in Parliament to legislate on this subject. In pursuance of this power, Parliament has enacted the Citizenship Act, 1955, so that in order to have a full view of the law of citizenship in India, study of the Constitution has to be supplemented by that of the Citizenship Act; (ii) similarly, while laying down certain fundamental safeguards against preventive detention, Article 22(7) empowers Parliament to legislate on some subsidiary matters relating to the subject. The laws made under this power, have, therefore, to be read along with the provisions of Article 22; (iii) again, while banning "untouchability", Article 17 provides that it shall be an offence "punishable in accordance with law", and in exercise of this power, Parliament has enacted the Protection of Civil Rights Act, 1955[7] which must be referred to as supplementing the constitutional prohibition against untouchability; (iv) while the Constitution lays down the basic provisions relating to the election of the President and Vice-President, Article 71(3) empowers Parliament to supplement these constitutional provisions by legislation, and by virtue of this power Parliament has enacted the Presidential and Vice-Presidential Elections Act, 1952.

The obvious advantage of this scheme is that the law made by Parliament may be modified according to the exigencies for the time being, without having to resort to a constitutional amendment.

(b) There are, again, a number of articles in the Constitution which are of a tentative or transitional nature and they are to remain in force only so long as Parliament does not legislate on the subject, eg, exemption of Union property from State taxation [*Article 285*]; suability of the State [*Article 300(1)*].

The Constitution, thus, ensures adaptability by prescribing a variety of modes in which its original text may be changed or supplemented, a fact which has evoked approbation from Prof Wheare—

7. The original title of this Act was the "Untouchability (Offences) Act, 1955". It has been extensively widened and made more rigorous, and renamed as the "Protection of Civil Rights Act, 1955", by Act 106 of 1976.

This variety in the amending process is wise but is *rarely found*.[8]

This wisdom has been manifested in the ease with which Sikkim, a Protectorate since British days, could be brought under the Constitution—first, as an "associate State" (35th Amendment Act), and then as a full-fledged State of the Union (36th Amendment Act, 1975).

4. Substantial Amendments by Various Constitutional Amendment Acts.

It must, however, be pointed out at the outset that many of the original features of the 1949-Constitution have been substantially modified by all the 106 Amendments which have been made up to January 2026.

(i) The 42nd Amendment Act, 1976 (as modified by the 43rd and 44th Amendment Acts, 1977–78), has practically recast the Constitution in vital respects.

(ii) The 73rd Amendment Act, 1992 which was brought into force on 24 April 1993 has added 16 articles which provide for establishment of and elections to Panchayats. They comprise a new part, Part IX. By the same Amendment, a new Schedule 11 has been added which enumerates the functions to be delegated to the Panchayats.

(iii) The 74th Amendment Act, 1992 was passed to establish Municipalities and provides for elections to them. It has inserted Part IX-A consisting of 18 Articles. Schedule 12 inserted by the Amendment mentions the functions to be assigned to the Municipalities. This Amendment came into force on 1 June 1993.

(iv) The 97th Amendment Act, 2011 was passed to promote voluntary formation, autonomous functioning, democratic control and professional management of co-operative societies. It inserted the word "co-operative societies" in Article 19(1)(c). It has further inserted Article 43B in Part IV and Part IXB consisting of 13 Articles (Articles 243ZH to Article 243ZT). This amendment came into force on 15 February 2012.

(v) Interestingly, the Law Commission of India in its various reports, *viz.*, 214th, and 230th Report, and the Department-Related Parliamentary Standing Committee On Home Affairs in its 85th Report on Law's Delays: Arrears in Courts (2001) advocated for reforms in the Judiciary and for removal of "collegium system".

It is in this backdrop that the 99th Constitutional (Amendment) Act, 2014 and the National Judicial Appointment Commission Act, 2014 were enacted in order to bring more transparency in the judicial appointments. As per the amended provisions of the Constitution, the Commission was to consist of: (a) Chief Justice of India (Chairperson, *ex officio*); (b) Two other senior judges of the Supreme Court next to the Chief Justice of India—*ex-officio*; (c) The Union Minister of Law and Justice—*ex-officio*; (d) Two eminent persons (to be nominated by a committee consisting of the Chief Justice of India, Prime Minister of India and the Leader of opposition in the Lok Sabha, or where there is no such Leader of Opposition, then, the Leader of the single largest Opposition Party in Lok Sabha), provided that, of the two eminent persons, one person would be from the Scheduled Castes or Scheduled Tribes or Other Backward Class or minority

8. Wheare, *Modern Constitutions*, p 143.

communities or a woman. The eminent persons shall be nominated for a period of three years and shall not be eligible for re-nomination.

As per the amended Constitution, the functions of the Commission were to (i) recommend persons for appointment as Chief Justice of India, Judges of the Supreme Court, Chief Justices of high courts and other judges of high courts; (b) recommend transfer of Chief Justices and other judges of high courts from one high court to any other high court; and (iii) ensure that the persons recommended are of ability, merit and other criteria mentioned in the regulations related to the act.[9]

However, several writ petitions were later filed in the Supreme Court challenging the above mentioned amendment on the ground that it violated the independence of the judiciary as well as the basic structure of the Constitution. In a five-Judge Bench judgment known as the NJAC Judgment, the majority of the Judges of the Supreme Court declared the 99th Amendment to the Constitution to be unconstitutional on the grounds that clauses (a) and (b) of Article 124A(1) added by the said amendment do not provide an adequate representation to the judicial component in the matter of selection and appointment of judges in the higher judiciary and therefore is violative of the basic structure of the Constitution. It was further held that clause (c) of Article 124A(1) which includes the Union Minister in charge of Law and Justice as an *ex-officio* Member of the NJAC will bring in political influence in the appointment and transfer of Judges which will be in violation of the Independence of Judiciary. It was finally held that clause (d) of the Article 124A which lays down the provision relating to "eminent persons" has not been defined and this vagueness about two member further affects the independence of Judiciary which is the part of the basic structure of our Constitution.[10]

(vi) The Constitution (103rd Amendment) Act, 2019 has amended Articles 15 and 16 to provide for special provisions for the advancement of economically weaker sections of citizens including special provisions relating to their admission to educational institutions including private educational institutions, whether aided or unaided by the State, other than the minority educational institutions referred to in clause (1) of Article 30. A reservation provided under the newly added clause (6) in Article 15 would be in addition to the existing reservations subject to a maximum of 10% of the total seats in each category.

This Amendment Act of 2019 has also added a new clause (6) to Article 16 to provide for reservation of appointments or posts in favour of any economically weaker sections of citizens in addition to the existing reservation and subject to a maximum of 10% of the posts in each category.

9. That constitutional validity of "The Constitutional (99th Amendment) Act, 2014" and "National Judicial Appointment Commission Act, 2014 (No 40 of 2014)" was challenged in *Supreme Court Advocate-on-Record Association v UOI,* AIR 2015 SC (Supp) 2463 : (2016) 5 SCC 1 : (2015) 11 Scale 1 wherein the Supreme Court declared the 99th Amendment to the Constitution to be unconstitutional on the grounds that the clause (a) and (b) of section 124A(1) added by the said amendment do not provide an adequate representation to the judicial component in the matter of selection and appointment of judges in the higher judiciary and, therefore, is violative of the basic structure of the Constitution.

10. *Supreme Court Advocate-on-record Association v UOI,* (2016) 5 SCC 281.

(vii) The most awaited Women Reservation Bill has become an Act (effective date yet to be announced) by way of 106th Constitutional Amedment Act of 2023. This paved the way for the reservation of 1/3rd of seats, on rotational basis, in Parliament, the State Legislatures and the Legislative Assembly of the NCT of Delhi. Within this 33% quota, there would be sub-reservation for Scheduled Castes and Scheduled Tribes. This law, however, is going to be implemented after the next census and the subsequent delimitation exercise—redrawing the Lok Sabha and Assembly constituencies—will determine the particular seats that are to be resertved for women.

5. Reconciliation of a Written Constitution with Parliamentary Sovereignty.

This combination of the theory of "fundamental law", which underlies the written Constitution of the *United States*, with the theory of "Parliamentary sovereignty", which underlies the unwritten Constitution of *England*, is the result of the liberal philosophy of the framers of the Indian Constitution which has been so nicely expressed by Pandit Nehru:

> While we want this Constitution to be as solid and permanent as we can make it, there is no permanence in Constitutions. There should be a certain flexibility. If you make anything rigid and permanent, you stop the nation's growth, the growth of a living, vital, organic people. . . In any event, we could not make this Constitution as rigid that it cannot be *adapted* to changing conditions. When the world is in turmoil and we are passing through a very swift period of transition, what we may do today may not be wholly capable tomorrow.[11]

The flexibility of *our* Constitution is illustrated by the fact that during the first 78 years of its working, it has been amended 106 times. Vital changes have thus been effected by the First, Fourth, Twenty-fourth, Twenty-fifth, Thirty-ninth, Forty-second, Forty-fourth, Seventy-third, Seventy-fourth, Ninety-Seventh, One Hundred Third, and One Hundred Sixth Amendments to the Constitution, including amendments to the fundamental rights, powers of the Supreme Court and the High Courts, reservation to women, etc.

Dr Jennings[12] characterised *our* Constitution as rigid for two reasons: (a) that the process of amendment was complicated and difficult; (b) that matters which should have been left to ordinary legislation having been incorporated into the Constitution, no change in these matters is possible without undergoing the process of amendment. We have seen that the working of the Constitution during seven decades has *not* justified the apprehension that the process of amendment is very difficult [see also Chapter 10, *post*]. But the other part of his reasoning is obviously sound. In fact, his comments on this point have proved to be prophetic. He cited Article 224 as an illustration of a provision which had been unnecessarily embodied in the Constitution:

> An example taken at random is article 224, which empowers a retired judge to sit in a high court. Is that a provision of such constitutional importance that it needs to be constitutionally protected, and be incapable of amendment except with the approval of two-thirds of the members of each House sitting and voting in the Union Parliament?

As Table IV, *post*, will show it has required an amendment of the Constitution, namely, the Seventh Amendment of 1956, to amend this article to provide for

11. *Constituent Assembly Debates,* dated 8 November 1948, pp 322–23.
12. Jennings, "Some Characteristics of the Indian Constitution, 1953", pp 2, 6, 25–26.

the appointment of Additional Judges instead of recalling retired judges. Similar amendments have been required, once to provide that a judge of a high court who is transferred to another high court shall not be entitled to compensation [*Article 222*] and, again, to provide for compensation. It is needless to multiply such instances since they are numerous.

The greatest evidence of flexibility, however, has been offered by the amendments since 1976. The 42nd Amendment Act, 1976, after the Constitution had worked for over quarter of a century, introduced vital changes and upset the balance between the different organs of the State. Of course, behind this flexibility lies the assumption that the Party in power wields more than a two-thirds majority in both Houses of Parliament.

6. A Federal System with Unitary Bias.

Perhaps the most remarkable achievement of the Indian Constitution is to confer upon a federal system the strength of a unitary government. Though normally the system of government is federal, the Constitution enables the federation to transform itself into a unitary State (by the assumption of the powers of States by the Union)—in *emergencies* [*Part XVIII*].

Such a combination of federal and unitary systems in the same constitution is unique in the world. For a correct appreciation of this unique system it is necessary to examine the background upon which federalism has been introduced into India, in the light of the experience in other federal countries. This deserves a separate treatment [see Chapter 5, *post*].

7. Integration of Indian States.

No less an outstanding feature of the new Constitution is the union of some 552 Indian States with the rest of India under the Constitution. Thus, the problem that baffled the framers of the Government of India Act, 1935, and ultimately led to the failure of its federal scheme, was solved by the framers of the Constitution with unique success. The entire sub-continent of India has been unified and consolidated into a compact State in a manner which is unprecedented in the history of this country.

The process by which this formidable task has been formed makes a story in itself.

7a. Status of Indian States under the British Crown.

At the time of the constitutional reforms leading to the Government of India Act, 1935, the geographical entity known as India was divided into two parts—British India and the Indian States. While British India comprised the nine Governors' Provinces and some other areas administered by the Government of India itself, the Indian States comprised some 600 States which were mostly under the personal rule of the Rulers or proprietors. All the Indian States were not of the same order. Some of them were States under the rule of hereditary Chiefs, which had a political status even from before the Mahomedan invasion; others (about 300 in number) were Estates or Jagirs granted by the Rulers as rewards for services or otherwise, to particular individuals or families. But the common feature that distinguished these States from British India was that the Indian States, had *not* been *annexed* by the British Crown. So, while British India was under the direct rule of the Crown through its representatives and according to the statutes of Parliament and enactments of the Indian Legislatures—the Indian States were allowed to remain under the personal rule of their Chiefs and

Princes, under the "suzerainty" of the Crown, which was assumed over the entire territory of India when the Crown took over authority from the East India Company in 1858.

The relationship between the Crown and the Indian States since the assumption of suzerainty by the Crown came to be described by the term "*Paramountcy*". The Crown was bound by engagements of a great variety with the Indian States. A common feature of these engagements was that while the States were responsible for their own internal administration, the Crown accepted responsibility for their external relations and defence. The Indian States had no international life, and for *external* purposes, they were practically in the same position as British India. As regards *internal* affairs, the policy of the British Crown was normally one of non-interference with the monarchical rule of the Rulers, but the Crown interfered in cases of misrule and mal-administration, as well as for giving effect to its international commitments. So, even in the internal sphere, the Indian States had *no legal* right against non-interference.

Nevertheless, the Rulers of the Indian States enjoyed certain personal rights and privileges, and normally carried on their personal administration, unaffected by all political and constitutional vicissitudes within the neighbouring territories of British India.

7b. Place of Indian States in the Federal Scheme Proposed by the Government of India Act, 1935.

The Government of India Act, 1935 envisaged a federal structure for the whole of India, in which the Indian States could figure as units, together with the Governors' Provinces. Nevertheless, the framers of the Act differentiated the Indian States from the Provinces in two material respects, and this differentiation ultimately proved fatal for the scheme itself. The two points of difference were—(a) While in the case of the Provinces accession to the Federation was compulsory or automatic—in the case of an Indian State it was voluntary and depended upon the option of the Ruler of the State; (b) While in the case of the Provinces, the authority of the Federation over the Provinces (executive as well as legislative) extended over the whole of the federal sphere chalked out by the Act—in the case of the Indian States, the authority of the Federation could be limited by the Instrument of Accession and all residuary powers belonged to the State. It is needless to elaborate the details of the plan of 1935, for, as has been stated earlier, the accession of the Indian States to the proposed Federation never came true, and this Part of that Act was finally abandoned in 1939, when World War II broke out.

7c. Cripps' Plan.

When Sir Stafford Cripps came to India with his Plan, it was definitely understood that the Plan proposed by him would be confined to settling the political destinies of British India and that the Indian States would be left free to retain their separate status.

7d. Cabinet Mission's Proposal.

But the Cabinet Mission supposed that the Indian States would be ready to co-operate with the new development in India. So, they recommended that there should be a Union of India, embracing both British India and the States, which would deal only with Foreign Affairs, Defence and Communications, while the State would retain all powers other than these.

7e. Lapse of Paramountcy under the Indian Independence Act, 1947.

When the Indian Independence Act, 1947, was passed, it declared the lapse of suzerainty (paramountcy) of the Crown, in section 7(1)(b) of the Act, which is worth reproduction:

7. (1) As from the appointed day—

(*b*) the suzerainty of His Majesty over the Indian States lapses, and with it, all treaties and agreements in force at the date of the passing of this Act between His Majesty and the rulers of Indian States, all functions exercisable by His Majesty at the date with respect to Indian States, all obligations of His Majesty existing at that date towards Indian States or the rulers thereof, and all powers, rights, authority, or jurisdiction exercisable by His Majesty at that date in or in relation to Indian States by treaty, grant, usage, sufferance or otherwise; and

Provided that notwithstanding anything in paragraph (*b*). . . of this sub-section, effect shall, as nearly as may be, continue to be given to the provision of any such agreement as is therein referred to which relate to customs, transit and communications, posts and telegraphs, or other like matters, until the provisions in question are denounced by the Rulers of the Indian States. . . on the one hand, or by the Dominion or Province or other part thereof concerned on the other hand, or are superseded by subsequent agreements.

7f. Accession to India or Pakistan?

But though paramountcy lapsed and the Indian States regained their position which they had prior to the assumption of suzerainty by the Crown, most of the States soon realised that it was no longer possible for them to maintain their existence independent of and separate from the rest of the country, and that it was in their own interests necessary to accede to either of the two Dominions of India and Pakistan. Of the States situated within the geographical boundaries of the Dominion of India, all (numbering 552) save Hyderabad, Kashmir, Bahawalpur, Junagadh and the NWF States (Chitral, Phulra, Dir, Swat and Amb) had acceded to the Dominion of India by the 15 August 1947, *i.e.*, before the "appointed day" itself.

7g. Problems after Accession and its Solutions.

The problem of the Government of India as regards the States after the accession was two-fold: (a) Shaping the Indian States into sizeable or viable administrative units; and (b) fitting them into the constitutional structure of India.

The first objective was sought to be achieved by a three-fold process of integration (known as the "Patel scheme" after Sardar Vallabhbhai Patel, Minister in-charge of Home Affairs)—

(i) 216 states were merged into the respective Provinces, geographically contiguous to them. These merged states were included in the territories of the states in Part B in the First Schedule of the Constitution. The process of merger started with the merger of Orissa and Chhattisgarh States with the then Province of Orissa on 1 January 1948, and the last instance was the merger of Cooch-Behar with the State of West Bengal in January, 1950.

(ii) 61 states were converted into Centrally administered areas and included in Part C of the First Schedule of the Constitution. This form of integration was resorted to in those cases in which, for administrative, strategic or other special reasons, Central control was considered necessary.

(iii) The third form of integration was the consolidation of groups of States into new viable units, known as Union of States. The first Union formed was the Saurashtra Union consolidating the Kathiawar States and many other States (15 February 1948), and the last one was the Union of Travancore-Cochin, formed on 1 July 1949. As many as 275 states were thus integrated into *five* Unions—Madhya Bharat, Patiala and East Punjab States Union, Rajasthan, Saurashtra and Travancore-Cochin. *These were included in the States in Part B* of the First Schedule. The other three states included in Part B were—Hyderabad, Jammu and Kashmir and Mysore. The cases of Hyderabad and Jammu and Kashmir were peculiar. Jammu and Kashmir acceded to India on 26 October 1947, and so it was included as a state in Part B, but the Government of India agreed to take the accession subject to confirmation by the people of the state, and a Constituent Assembly subsequently confirmed it, in November, 1956. Hyderabad did not formally accede to India, but the Nizam issued a Proclamation recognising the necessity of entering into a constitutional relationship with the Union of India and accepting the Constitution of India subject to ratification by the Constituent Assembly of that State, and the Constituent Assembly of that State ratified this. As a result, Hyderabad was included as a State in Part B of the First Schedule of the Constitution.

We have so far seen how the States in Part B were formed as viable units of administration—being the residue of the bigger Indian States, left after the smaller States had been merged in the Provinces or converted into Centrally Administered Areas. So far as the latter two groups were concerned, there was no problem in fitting them into the body of the Constitution framed for the rest of India. There was an agreement between the Government of India and the Ruler of each of the States so merged, by which the Rulers voluntarily agreed to the merger and ceded all powers for the governance of the States to the Dominion Government, reserving certain personal rights and privileges for themselves.

But the story relating to the States in Part B is not yet complete. At the time of their accession to the Dominion of India in 1947, the States had acceded only on three subjects, *viz.,* Defence, Foreign Affairs and Communications. With the formation of the Unions and under the influence of political events, the Rulers found it beneficial to have a closer connection with the Union of India and all the Rajpramukhs of the Unions as well as the Maharaja of Mysore, signed revised Instruments of Accession by which all these States acceded to the Dominion of India in respect of *all* matters included in the Union and Concurrent Legislative Lists, except only those relating to taxation. Thus, the States in Part B were brought at par with the States in Part A, subject only to the differences embodied in Article 238 and the supervisory powers of the Centre for the transitional period of 10 years [*Article 371*]. Special provisions were made only for Kashmir [*Article 370*] in view of its special position and problems. That Article made special provisions for the partial application of the Constitution of India to that State, with the concurrence of the Government of that State. [See Chapter 15, *post*].

It is to be noted that the Rajpramukhs of the five Unions as well as the Rulers of Hyderabad, Mysore, Jammu and Kashmir all adopted the Constitution of India, by Proclamations.

The process of integration culminated in the Constitution (7th Amendment) Act, 1956, which abolished Part B states as a class and included *all the States in Part A and B in one list.* The special provisions in the Constitution relating to Part B states were, consequently, omitted. The Indian states thus lost their identity and became part of one uniform political organisation embodied in the Constitution of India.[13]

The process of reorganisation is continuing still and the trend is towards conceding the demands of smaller units which were previously Part B States, Union Territories or autonomous parts of states, by conferring upon them the status of a "State", *e.g.*, Nagaland, Meghalaya, Himachal Pradesh, Manipur, Tripura, Mizoram, and Goa. Delhi has been made the National Capital Territory. This process has further been elaborated in Chapter 6 (Territory of India), *post.*

8. Fundamental Rights and Constitutional Remedies.

While the Directive Principles are not enforceable in the courts, the Fundamental Rights, included in Part III, are so enforceable at the instance of any person whose fundamental right has been infringed by any action of the State—executive or legislative—and the remedies for enforcing these rights, namely, the writs of *habeas corpus, mandamus,* prohibition, *quo warranto* and *certiorari,* are also guaranteed by the Constitution. Any law or executive order which offends against a fundamental right is liable to be declared void by the Supreme Court or the High Court.

It is through a misapprehension of these provisions that the Indian Constitution has been described by some critics as a "lawyer's paradise". According to Sir Ivor Jennings, this is due to the fact that the Constituent Assembly was dominated by "the lawyer-politicians". It is they who thought of codifying the individual rights and the prerogative writs though none in *England* would ever cherish such an idea. In the words of Sir Ivor—

> Though no English lawyer would have thought of putting the prerogative writs into a Constitution, the Constituent Assembly did so. . .These various factors have given India a most complicated Constitution. Those of us who claim to be constitutional lawyers can look with equanimity on this exaltation of our profession. But constitutions are intended to enable the process of Government to work smoothly, and not to provide fees for constitutional lawyers. The more numerous the briefs the more difficult the process of government becomes. India has perhaps placed too much faith in us.

With due respect to Sir Ivor Jennings, a great constitutional expert, these observations disclose a failure to appreciate the very foundation of the Indian Constitution. Sir Ivor omits to point out that the fathers of the Indian Constitution preferred the American doctrine of "limited government" to the English doctrine of "Parliamentary sovereignty".

---

13. It should be mentioned, in this context, that the last vestiges of the princely order in India have been done away with by the repeal of Articles 291 and 362, and the insertion of Article 363A, by the Constitution (26th Amendment) Act, 1971 (w.e.f. 28 December 1971), which abolished the Privy Purse granted to the Rulers of the erstwhile Indian States and certain other personal privileges accorded to them under the Constitution — as a result of which the heads of these pre-Independence Indian States have now been brought down to a level of equality with other citizens of India.

In *England,* the birth of modern democracy was due to a protest against the absolutism of an autocratic executive and the English people discovered in Parliamentary sovereignty an adequate solution of the problem that faced them. The English political system is founded on the unlimited faith of the people in the good sense of their elected representatives. Though, of late, detractions from its omnipotent authority have taken place because the ancient institution at Westminster has grown incapable of managing myriads of modern problems with the same ease as in Victorian age, nonetheless, never has anybody in England thought of placing limitations on the authority of Parliament so that it might properly behave.

The Founding Fathers of the *American* Constitution, on the other hand, had the painful experience that even a representative body might be tyrannical, particularly when they were concerned with a colonial Empire. Thus, it is that the Declaration of Independence recounts the attempts of the British "Legislature to extend an unwarrantable jurisdiction over us" and how the British people had been "deaf of the voice of justice". At heavy cost, had the colonists learnt about the frailty and weakness of human nature when the same Parliament which had forced Charles I to sign the Petition of Right (1628) to acknowledge that no tax could be levied without the consent of Parliament, did, in 1765, and the years that followed, insist on taxing the colonies, regardless of their right of representation, and attempt to enforce such undemocratic laws through military rule.

Hence, while the English people, in their fight for freedom against autocracy, stopped with the establishment of the supremacy of the law and Parliament as the sole source of that law, Americans had to go further and to assert that there is to be a law superior to the Legislature itself and that it was the restraints of this paramount written law that could only save them from the fears of absolutism and autocracy which are ingrained in the human nature itself.

As will be more fully explained in the chapter on Fundamental Rights, the Indian experience of the application of the British Rule of Law in India was not altogether happy and there was a strong feeling that it was not administered with even hands by the foreign rulers in India as in their own land. The "Sons of Liberty" in India had known to what use the flowers of the English democratic system, *viz.,* the Sovereignty of Parliament and the Rule of Law, could be put in trampling down the rights of man under an Imperial rule. So, in 1928, long before the dawn of independence in India, the Motilal Nehru Committee asserted that:

> Our first care could be to have our fundamental rights guaranteed in a manner *which will not permit their withdrawal under any circumstances.*

8a. Power of Judicial Review.

Now, judicial review is a necessary concomitant of "fundamental rights", for, it is meaningless to enshrine individual rights in a written Constitution as "fundamental rights" if they are not enforceable, in courts of law, against any organ of the state, legislative or executive. Once this choice is made, one cannot help to be sorry for the litigation that ensues. Whatever apprehensions might have been entertained in some quarters in India at the time of the making of the Indian Constitution, there is hardly anybody in India today who is aggrieved because the Supreme

Court, each year, invalidates a dozen of statutes and a like number of administrative acts on the ground of violation of the fundamental rights.

At the same time, it must be pointed out that since the inauguration of the Constitution, various provisions have been inserted into the Constitution by amendments, which have taken out considerable areas from the pale of judicial review, *e.g.*, by inserting Articles 31A–31C; and by 1995 as many as 284 Acts—Central and State—have been shielded from judicial review on the ground of contravention of the Fundamental Rights, by enumerating them under the Ninth Schedule, which relates to Article 31B.

An independent Judiciary, having the power of "Judicial review", is another prominent feature of *our* Constitution. On the other hand, we have avoided the other-extreme, namely, that of "judicial supremacy", which may be a logical outcome of an over-emphasis on judicial review, as the American experience demonstrates.

Judicial power of the State exercisable by the courts under the Constitution as sentinels of Rule of Law is a basic feature of the Constitution.[14]

Indeed, the harmonization, which our Constitution has effected between Parliamentary Sovereignty and a written Constitution with a provision for judicial review, is a unique achievement of the framers of *our* Constitution. An absolute balance of powers between the different organs of government is an impracticable thing and, in practice, the final say must belong to some one of them. This is why the rigid scheme of Separation of Powers and the checks and balances between the organs in the Constitution of the *United States* has failed in its actual working, and the Judiciary has assumed supremacy under its powers of interpretation of the Constitution to such an extent as to deserve the epithet of the "safety valve" or the "balance-wheel" of the Constitution. As one of her own Judges has said (Chief Justice Hughes), "The Constitution (of the USA) is what the Supreme Court says it is". It has the power to invalidate a law duly passed by the Legislature not only on the ground that it transgresses the legislative powers vested in it by the Constitution or by the prohibitions contained in the Bill of Rights but also on the ground that it is opposed to some general principles said to underlie vague expressions, such as due process, the contents of which not being explicitly laid down in the Constitution, are definable only by the Supreme Court. The American Judiciary thus sits over the *wisdom* of any legislative policy as if it were a third Chamber or super-Chamber of the Legislature.

Under the *English* Constitution, on the other hand, Parliament is supreme and "can do everything that is not naturally impossible" (*Blackstone*) and the courts cannot nullify any Act of Parliament on any ground whatsoever. As May puts it—

> The Constitution has assigned no limits to the authority of Parliament over all matters and persons within its jurisdiction. A law may be *unjust* and contrary to the principles of sound government. But Parliament is not controlled in its discretion and when it errs, its errors can be corrected only by itself.

So, English Judges have denied themselves any power "to sit as a court of appeal against Parliament".

---

14. *GC Kanungo v State of Orissa,* AIR 1995 SC 1655 : (1995) 5 SCC 96, paras 17, 18 ; *L Chandra Kumar v UOI,* AIR 1997 SC 1125 : (1997) 3 SCC 261, paras 62 and 76 and *State of Andhra Pradesh v K Mohanlal,* (1998) 5 SCC 468, para 9.

The *Indian* Constitution wonderfully adopts the *via media* between the American system of Judicial Supremacy and the English principle of Parliamentary Supremacy, by endowing the Judiciary with the power of declaring a law as unconstitutional if it is beyond the competence of the Legislature according to the distribution of powers provided by the Constitution, or if it is in contravention of the fundamental rights guaranteed by the Constitution or of any other mandatory provision of the Constitution, egg, Articles 286, 299, 301, and 304; but, at the same time, depriving the Judiciary of any power of "judicial review" of the wisdom of legislative policy. Thus, it avoided expressions like "due process", and made fundamental rights such as that of liberty and property subject to regulation by the Legislature. But the Supreme Court has discovered "due process" in Article 21 in *Maneka Gandhi's case.*[15] Further, the major portion of the Constitution is liable to be amended by the Union Parliament by a special majority, if in any case, the Judiciary proves too obtrusive. The theory underlying the Indian Constitution in this respect can hardly be better expressed than in the words of Pandit Nehru:

> No Supreme Court, no Judiciary, can stand in judgment over the sovereign will of Parliament, representing the will of the entire community. It can pull up that sovereign will if it goes wrong, but, in the ultimate analysis, where the future of the community is concerned, no Judiciary can come in the way. . . Ultimately, the fact remains that the Legislature must be supreme and must not be interfered with by the Courts of Law in such measures as *social reform.*

Our Constitution thus places the supremacy at the hands of the Legislature as much as that is possible within the bounds of a written Constitution. But, as has been mentioned earlier, the balance between Parliamentary Sovereignty and Judicial Review was seriously disturbed, and a drift towards the former was made, by the Constitution (42nd Amendment) Act, 1976, by inserting some new provisions, *e.g.*, Articles 31D, 32A, 131A, 144A, 226A, 228A, 323A, 323B, and 329A.

The Janata Government, coming to power in 1977, restored the pre-1976 position, to a substantial extent, through the 43rd and 44th Amendments, 1977–78, by repealing the following Articles which had been inserted by the 42nd Amendment—Articles 31D, 32A, 131A, 144A, 226A, 228A, and 329A; and by restoring Article 226 to its original form (substantially).

On the other hand, the Judiciary has gained ground by itself declaring that "judicial review" is a "basic feature" of *our* Constitution, so that so long as the Supreme Court itself does not revise its opinion in this behalf, any amendment of the Constitution to take away judicial review of legislation on the ground of contravention of any provision of the Constitution shall itself be liable to be invalidated by the court. All amendments to the Constitution made on or after 24 April 1973 by which Ninth Schedule is amended by inclusion of various laws therein shall be tested on the touchstone of the basic or essential features of the Constitution as reflected in Article 21 read with Article 14, Article 19 and the principle underlying them. Now no blanket protection available to the laws inserted in the Ninth Schedule by constitutional amendments on or after 24 April 1973 and shall be a matter of constitutional adjudication by examining the

15. *Maneka Gandhi v UOI,* AIR 1978 SC 597 : (1978) 1 SCC 248.

nature and extent of infraction of fundamental right by a statute, sought to be constitutionally protected.[16]

8b. Fundamental Rights Subject to Reasonable Regulation by Legislature. The balancing between supremacy of the Constitution and sovereignty of the Legislature is illustrated by the novel declaration of Fundamental Rights which our Constitution embodies.

The idea of incorporating in the Constitution a "Bill of Rights" has been taken from the Constitution of the United States. But the guarantee of individual rights in *our* Constitution has been very carefully balanced with the need for the *security of the State itself.*

American experience demonstrates that a written guarantee of fundamental rights has a tendency to engender an atomistic view towards society and the State

16. *IR Coelho (dead) by LRs v State of Tamil Nadu,* AIR 2007 SC 861 : (2007) 2 SCC 1. The Hon'ble Supreme Court considered the fundamental question that whether on and after 24 April 1973 when basic structures doctrine was propounded, it is permissible for the Parliament under Article 31B to immunise legislations from fundamental rights by inserting them into the Ninth Schedule and, if so, what is its effect on the power of judicial review of the court. The Hon'ble Supreme Court held that: (i) A law that abrogates or abridges rights guaranteed by Part III of the Constitution may violate the basic structure doctrine or it may not. If former is the consequence of law, whether by amendment of any Article of Part III or by an insertion in the Ninth Schedule, such law will have to be invalidated in exercise of judicial review power of the court. The validity or invalidity would be tested on the principles laid down in this judgment; (ii) The majority judgment in *Kesavananda Bharati's* case read with *Indira Gandhi's* case, requires the validity of each new constitutional amendment to be judged on its own merits. The actual effect and impact of the law on the rights guaranteed under Part III has to be taken into account for determining whether or not it destroys basic structure. The impact test would determine the validity of the challenge; (iii) All amendments to the Constitution made on or after 24 April 1973 by which the Ninth Schedule is amended by inclusion of various laws therein shall have to be tested on the touchstone of the basic or essential features of the Constitution as reflected in Article 21 read with Article 14, Article 19, and the principles underlying them. To put it differently even though an Act is put in the Ninth Schedule by a constitutional amendment, its provisions would be open to attack on the ground that they destroy or damage the basic structure if the fundamental right or rights taken away or abrogated pertains or pertain to the basic structure; (iv) Justification for conferring protection, not blanket protection, on the laws included in the Ninth Schedule by Constitutional Amendments shall be a matter of Constitutional adjudication by examining the nature and extent of infraction of a Fundamental Right by a statute, sought to be Constitutionally protected, and on the touchstone of the basic structure doctrine as reflected in Article 21 read with Article 14 and Article 19 by application of the "rights test" and the "essence of the right" test taking the synoptic view of the Articles in Part III as held in *Indira Gandhi's* case. Applying the above tests to the Ninth Schedule laws, if the infraction affects the basic structure then such a law(s) will not get the protection of the Ninth Schedule. This is our answer to the question referred to us *vide* order dated 14 September 1999 in *IR Coelho v State of Tamil Nadu,* [(1992) 7 SCC 580]; (v) If the validity of any Ninth Schedule law has already been upheld by this Court, it would not be open to challenge such law again on the principles declared by this judgment. However, if a law held to be violative of any rights in Part III is subsequently incorporated in the Ninth Schedule after 24 April 1973, such a violation/infraction shall be open to challenge on the ground that it destroys or damages the basic structure as indicated in Article 21 read with Article 14, Article 19 and the principles underlying thereunder; (vi) Action taken and transactions finalized as a result of the impugned Acts shall not be open to challenge.

which may at times prove to be dangerous to the common welfare. Of course, America has been saved from the dangers of such a situation by reason of her Judiciary propounding the doctrine of "Police Powers" under which the Legislature is supposed to be competent to interfere with individual rights wherever they constitute a "clear danger" to the safety of the State and other collective interests.

Instead of leaving the matter to the off-chance of judicial protection in particular cases, the Indian Constitution makes each of the fundamental rights subject to legislative control under the terms of the Constitution itself, apart from those exceptional cases where the interests of national security, integrity or welfare should exclude the application of fundamental rights altogether [*Articles 31A to 31C*].

8c. Equality—Political, Legal and Social.

Another peculiarity of the chapter on Fundamental Rights in the Indian Constitution is that it aims at securing not merely political or legal equality, but *social* equality as well. Thus, apart from the usual guarantees that the State will not discriminate between one citizen and another merely on the ground of religion, race, caste, sex or place of birth—in the matter of appointment, or other employment, offered by the State—the Constitution includes a prohibition of 'untouchability', in any form and lays down that no citizen may be deprived of access to any public place, of the enjoyment of any public amenity or privilege, only on the ground of religion, race, caste, sex or place of birth.

We can hardly overlook in this context that under the Constitution of the *USA,* racial discrimination persists even today, notwithstanding judicial pronouncements to the contrary. The position in the United Kingdom is no better as demonstrated by current events.

9. Fundamental Rights Checkmated by Fundamental Duties.

Another feature, which was not in the original Constitution has been introduced by the 42nd Amendment, 1976, by introducing Article 51A as Part IVA of the Constitution.

Though the Directives in Part IV of the Constitution were not enforceable in any manner and had to give way before the Fundamental Rights, under the original Constitution, the situation was reversed, through the backdoor, by the 42nd Amendment, 1976, by amending Article 31C—shielding *all* the Directives in Part IV of the Constitution from the Fundamental Rights in Part III. But this object has been frustrated by the majority decision in the case of *Minerva Mills v UOI,*[17] as a result of which Article 31C will shield from unconstitutionality on the ground of violation of Article 13 those laws which implement only the Directives specified in Article 39(b)–(c) and not any other Directive included in Part IV of the Constitution.

In the same direction, the 42nd Amendment Act introduced "Fundamental Duties", to circumscribe the Fundamental Rights, even though the Duties, as such, cannot be judicially enforced (see, further, under Chapter 8, *post*).

17. *Minerva Mills v UOI,* AIR 1980 SC 1789, paras 21–26 : (1980) 2 SCC 591.

10. Universal Franchise without Communal Representation.

The adoption of Universal Adult Suffrage [*Article 326*], *without any qualification* either of sex, property, taxation or the like, is a "bold experiment" in India, having regard to the vast extent of the country and its population, with an overwhelming illiteracy (see Table I, *post*). The suffrage in India, it should be noted, is wider than that in England or the United States. The concept of popular sovereignty, which underlies the declaration in the Preamble that the Constitution is adopted and given by the "people of India" unto themselves, would indeed have been hollow unless the franchise—the only effective medium of popular sovereignty in a modern democracy—were extended to the entire adult population which was capable of exercising the right and an independent electoral machinery (under the control of the Election Commission) was set up to ensure its free exercise. The electorate has further been widened by lowering the voting age from 21 to 18, by the 61st Constitution Amendment Act, 1988.

That, notwithstanding the outstanding difficulties, this bold experiment has been crowned with success will be evident from some of the figures[18] relating to the first General Election held under the Constitution in 1952. Out of a total population of 356 million and an adult population of 180 million, the number of voters enrolled was 173 million and of these no less than 88 million, *i.e.*, over 50% of the enrolled voters, actually exercised their franchise. The orderliness with which 17 General Elections were conducted speaks eloquently of the political attainment of the masses, though illiterate, of this vast sub-continent. In the 18th General Elections held in 2024, the number of persons on the electoral roll had come up to 96.88 crores (having Males—49.7 crores; Females—47.1 crores; Third gender—48,044).

No less creditable for the framers of the Constitution is the abolition of communal representation, which in its trail had brought in the bloody and lamentable partition of India. In the new Constitution, there was no reservation of seats except for the Scheduled Castes and Scheduled Tribes and for the Anglo-Indians—and that only for a temporary period (this period was 10 years in the original Constitution).[19]

11. Parliamentary Form of Government.

It has been stated at the outset, that the form of government introduced by *our* Constitution both at the Union and the States is the Parliamentary Government of the British type.[20] A primary reason for the choice of this system of government was that the people had a long experience of this system under the Government of India Acts,[21] though the British were very slow in importing its features to the fullest length.

The makers of *our* Constitution rejected the Presidential system of government, as it obtains in *America,* on the ground that under that system the Executive and the Legislatures are separate from and independent of each

18. Report of the First General Elections in India (1951–52), vol 1.
19. The Constitution (104th Amendment) Act, 2019 (w.e.f. 25-1-2020) has extended the period to 80 years in respect to reservation of seats for the Scheduled Castes and the Scheduled Tribes in the House of the People and in the Legislative Assemblies of the States, but has not extended the period further for nomination of members of the Anglo-Indian community.
20. Prime Minister Nehru in the Lok Sabha, on 28 March 1957.
21. *Constituent Assembly Debates*, vol 4, 578 (Sardar Patel).

other,[22] which is likely to cause conflicts between them, which *our* infant democracy could ill afford to risk.

But though the British model of Parliamentary or Cabinet form of government was adopted, a hereditary monarch or ruler at the head could not be installed, because India had declared herself a "Republic". Instead of a monarch, therefore, an elected President was to be at the head of the Parliamentary system. In introducing this amalgam, the makers of *our* Constitution followed the *Irish* precedent.

As in the Constitution of *Eire,* the Indian Constitution superimposes an elected President upon the Parliamentary system of responsible government. But though an elected President is the executive head of the Union, he is to act on the advice of his ministers, although whether he so acts according to the advice of his ministers is not questionable in the courts and there is no mode, short of impeachment, to remove the President if he acts contrary to the Constitution.

On the other hand, principle of ministerial responsibility to the Legislature, which under the English system rests on convention, is embodied in the express provisions of *our* Constitution [*Article 75(3)*].

In the words of *our* Supreme Court,[23]

> Our Constitution though federal in its structure, is modelled on the British Parliamentary system where the executive is deemed to have the primary responsibility for the formulation of government policy and its transmission into law, though the condition precedent to the exercise of this responsibility is its retaining the confidence of the legislative branch of the State.....In the Indian Constitution, therefore, we have the same system of parliamentary executive as in England.....

But *our* Constitution is not an exact replica of the Irish model either. The Constitution of *Eire* lays down that the Constitutional powers of the President can only be exercised by him on the advice of Ministers, *except* those which are left to his discretion by the Constitution itself. Thus, the Irish President has an absolute discretion to refuse dissolution of the Legislature to a defeated Prime Minister, contrary to the English practice and convention. But in the Indian Constitution, there is no provision authorising the President to act "in his discretion" on any matter. On the other hand, by amending Article 74(1), the 42nd Amendment Act has explicitly codified the proposition which the Supreme Court had already laid down in several decisions, that the President "*shall,* in the exercise of his functions, act *in accordance with* such advice," *i.e.*, the advice tendered by the Council of Ministers.

The Janata Government has preferred not to disturb this contribution of the 42nd Amendment, except to empower the President by the 44th Amendment, 1978, to refer a matter back to the Council of Ministers, for reconsideration.

12. Role of Conventions under the Constitution.

It is also remarkable that though the framers of the Constitution attempted to make an exhaustive code of organic law, room has been left for the growth of conventions to supplement the Constitution in matters where it is silent. Thus, while the Constitution embodied the doctrine of Cabinet

22. *Constituent Assembly Debates,* vol 7, 984 (Munshi).
23. *Ram Jawaya v State of Punjab,* AIR 1955 SC 549 : (1955) 2 SCR 225; *Shamser Singh v State of Punjab,* AIR 1974 SC 2192 : (1974) 2 SCC 831.

responsibility in Article 75, it was not possible to codify the numerous conventions which answer the problems as they may arise in England, from time to time, in the working of the Cabinet system. Take, *for instance*, the question whether the Ministry should resign whenever there is an adverse vote against it in the House of the People, or whether it is at liberty to regard an accidental defeat on a particular measure as a "snap vote".[24] Again, the Constitution cannot possibly give any indication as to which issue should be regarded as a "vital issue" by a Ministry, so that on a defeat on such an issue the Ministry should be morally bound to resign. Similarly, in what circumstances a Ministry would be justified in advising the President to dissolve Parliament instead of resigning upon an adverse vote, can only be established by convention.

Sir Ivor Jennings in his seminal work "Some Characteristics of the Indian Constitution" is, therefore, justified in observing that—

> The machinery of government is essentially British and the whole collection of British constitutional conventions has apparently been incorporated as conventions.

13. Concluding Remarks.

Before closing this chapter, however, it should be pointed out that since the observations in the case of *Golak Nath,*[25] culminating with *Kesavananda's case,*[26] the Supreme Court had been urging that there are certain "basic" features of the Constitution, which were immune from the power of amendment conferred by Article 368, which, according to the court, was subject to "implied" limitations. On the other hand, the Indira Government had been attempting to thwart this doctrine by successive amendments of Article 368, starting with the 24th Amendment, 1971, and ending with 42nd Amendment Act, 1976, so as to obviate any such conclusion by the Supreme Court.[27] The court has, however, adhered to its view notwithstanding any of these amendments.[28] The present chapter does not enter into that controversy, which will be dealt with in Chapter 10 (Procedure for Amendment), *post.*

The comparative study of any Constitution will reveal that it has certain prominent features which distinguish it from other Constitutions. It is those prominent features which have been summarised in this chapter by way of introducing the reader to the various provisions of the Indian Constitution.

24. *Constituent Aseembly Debates*, vol 7, p 293.
25. *Golak Nath v State of Punjab,* AIR 1967 SC 1643 : (1967) 2 SCR 762.
26. *Kesavananda v State of Kerala,* AIR 1973 SC 1461 : (1973) 4 SCC 225.
27. The Janata Government's efforts to enshrine the "basic features theory" in the Constitution itself, by requiring a *referendum* to amend four "basic features", failed owing to Congress opposition to the relevant amendments of Article 368 of the Constitution, as proposed by the 45th Amendment Bill, 1978. The four basic features mentioned in that Bill were—(i) Secular and democratic character of the Constitution; (ii) Fundamental Rights under Part III; (iii) Free and fair elections to the Legislatures; and (iv) Independence of the Judiciary.
28. *Minerva Mills v UOI,* AIR 1980 SC 1789, paras 21–26, 28, 91, 93–94 : (1980) 2 SCC 591; *Sampat v UOI,* AIR 1987 SC 386; *UOI v Raghubir,* AIR 1989 SC 1933, para 7.

CHAPTER 5

NATURE OF THE FEDERAL SYSTEM

1. India, a Union of States. ARTICLE 1(1) of our Constitution says, "India, that is Bharat, shall be a Union of States".

While submitting the Draft Constitution, Dr. Ambedkar, the Chairman of the Drafting Committee, stated that "although its Constitution may be federal in structure", the Committee had used the term "Union" because of certain advantages. These advantages, as explained by him in the Constituent Assembly, were to indicate two things, viz., (a) that the Indian federation is not the result of an agreement by the units, and (b) that the component units have no freedom to secede from it.

CHAPTER 5

NATURE OF THE FEDERAL SYSTEM

1. India, a Union of States. ARTICLE 1(1) of *our* Constitution says—"India, that is Bharat, shall be a Union of States."

While submitting the Draft Constitution, Dr Ambedkar, the Chairman of the Drafting Committee, stated that "although its Constitution may be federal in structure", the Committee had used the term "Union" because of certain advantages.[1] These advantages, he explained in the Constituent Assembly,[2] were to indicate two things, *viz.*, (a) that the Indian federation is not the result of an agreement by the units, and (b) that the component units have no freedom to secede from it.

The word 'Union', of course, does not indicate any particular type of federation, inasmuch as it is used also in the Preamble of the Constitution of the United States—the model of federation; in the Preamble of the British North America Act (which, according to Lord Haldane, did not create a true federation at all); in the Preamble to the Union of South Africa Act, 1909, which patently set up a unitary Constitution; and even in the Constitution of the USSR (1977), which formally acknowledged a right of secession [*Article 72*] to each Republic, *i.e.*, unit of the Union.

We have, therefore, to examine the provisions of the Constitution itself, apart from the label given to it by its draftsman, to determine whether it provides a federal system as claimed by Dr Ambedkar, particularly in view of the criticisms (as will be presently seen) levelled against its federal claim by some foreign scholars.

2. Federal State. The difficulty of any treatment of federalism is that there is no agreed definition of a federal State. The other difficulty is that it is habitual with scholars on the subject to start with the model of the *United States,* the oldest (1787) of all federal Constitutions in the world, and to exclude any system that does not conform to that model from the nomenclature of 'federation'. But numerous countries in the world have, since 1787, adopted Constitutions having federal features and, if the strict historical standard of the United States be applied to all these later Constitutions, few will stand the test of federalism save perhaps Switzerland and Australia. Nothing is, however, gained by excluding so many recent Constitutions from the federal

---

1. Draft Constitution, 21-2-1948, p iv. [The word 'Union', in fact, had been used both in the Cripps proposals and the Cabinet Mission Plan (see under Chapter 2, *ante*), and in the Objectives Resolution of Pandit Nehru in 1947 (Chapter 3, *ante*), according to which residuary powers were to be reserved to the units].
2. *Constituent Assembly Debates*, vol VII, p 43.

class, for, according to the traditional classification followed by political scientists, Constitutions are either unitary or federal. If, therefore, a Constitution partakes of some features of both types, the only alternative is to analyse those features and to ascertain whether it is *basically* unitary or federal, although it may have subsidiary variations. A liberal attitude towards the question of federalism is, therefore, inevitable particularly in view of the fact that recent experiments in the world of Constitution-making are departing more and more from the 'pure' type of either unitary or a federal system. The Author's views on this subject, expressed in the previous Editions of this book as well as in the *Commentary on the Constitution of India,*[3] now find support from the categorical assertion of a research worker[4] on the subject of federalism (who happens to be an American himself), that the question whether a State is federal or unitary is one of degrees and the answer will depend upon "how many federal features it possesses". Another American scholar[5] has, in the same strain, observed that a federation is more a 'functional' than an 'institutional' concept and that any theory which asserts that there are certain inflexible characteristics without which a political system cannot be federal ignores the fact "that institutions are not the same things in different social and cultural environments".

3. Indian Constitution—Basically Federal, with Unitary Features.

To anticipate the Author's conclusion, the Constitutional system of India is *basically* federal, but, of course, with striking unitary features.[6] In order to come to this conclusion, we have to formulate the essential minimal features of a federal system as to which there is common agreement amongst political scientists.

4. Essential Features of a Federal Polity.

Though there may be difference amongst scholars in matters of detail, the consensus is that a federal system involves the following essential features:

(i) *Dual Government:* While in a Unitary State, there is only one Government, namely the National Government; in a Federal State, there are two Governments—the National or Federal Government and the Government of each component State.

Though a Unitary State may create local sub-divisions, such local authorities enjoy an autonomy of their own but exercise only such powers as are from time to time delegated to them by the national government and it is competent for the National Government to revoke the delegated powers or any of them at its will.

A Federal State, on the other hand, is the fusion of several states into a single State in regard to matters affecting common interests, while each component State enjoys autonomy in regard to other matters. The component States are not mere delegates or agents of the federal Government but both the Federal and State Governments draw their authority from the same source, *viz.,* the Constitution of the land. On the other hand, a component State has no right to

3. Author's *Commentary on the Constitution of India,* 7th (Silver Jubilee) Edn, vol A, pp 33 *et seq.*
4. Prof WT Wagner, *Federal States and their Judiciary,* Moulton and Co, 1969, p 25.
5. Livingstone, *Federation and Constitutional Change,* 1956, pp 6-7.
6. This view of the Author has been affirmed by the 9-Judge Bench Supreme Court decision in *SR Bommai v UOI,* AIR 1994 SC 1918 (para 211) : 1994 (2) SCALE 37 : (1994) 3 SCC 1 : [1994] 2 SCR 644.

secede from the federation at its will. This distinguishes a federation from a confederation.

(ii) *Distribution of Powers:* It follows that the very object for which a Federal State is formed involves a division of authority between the Federal Government and the States, though the method of distribution may not be alike in the Federal Constitutions.

(iii) *Supremacy of the Constitution:* A Federal State derives its existence from the Constitution, just as a corporation derives its existence from the grant of a statute by which it is created. Every power—executive, legislative, or judicial—whether it belongs to the Federation or to the component States, is subordinate to and controlled by the Constitution.

(iv) *Authority of Courts:* In a Federal State, the legal supremacy of the Constitution is essential to the existence of the federal system. It is essential to maintain the division of powers not only between the coordinate branches of the Government, but also between the Federal Government and the States themselves. This is secured by vesting in the Courts a final power to interpret the Constitution and nullify an action on the part of the Federal and State Governments or their different organs which violates the provisions of the Constitution.

The Supreme Court has observed that the Indian Constitution is basically federal in form and is marked by the traditional characteristics of a federal system, namely, supremacy of the Constitution, division of power between the Union and the States and existence of an independent judiciary.[7]

Not much pains need to be taken to demonstrate that the political system introduced by *our* Constitution possesses all the aforesaid essentials of a federal polity. Thus, the Constitution is the supreme organic law of *our* land, and both the Union and the State Governments as well as their respective organs derive their authority from the Constitution, and it is not competent for the States to secede from the Union. There is a division of legislative and administrative powers between the Union and the State Governments and the Supreme Court stands at the head of *our* Judiciary to zealously guard this distribution of powers and to invalidate any action which violates the limitations imposed by the Constitution. This jurisdiction of the Supreme Court may be resorted to not only by a person[8] who has been affected by a Union or State law which, according to him, has violated the constitutional distribution of powers, but also by the Union and the States themselves by bringing a direct action against each other, before the Original Jurisdiction of the Supreme Court under Article 131.[9] It is because of these basic federal features that our Supreme Court has described the Constitution as 'federal'.[10] Moreover, in a Federal Constitution, the distribution of legislative powers between Parliament and the State Legislature involves

7. *Ganga Ram Moolchandani v State of Rajasthan,* AIR 2001 SC 2616 : (2001) 6 SCC 89 : (2001) SCC (LS) 928 : [2001] 3 SCR 992.

8. Cf *Gujarat University v Sri Krishna,* AIR 1963 SC 703 (*715-16*); *Waverly Mills v Rayman & Co,* AIR 1963 SC 90 (*95*).

9. Cf *State of West Bengal v UOI,* AIR 1963 SC 1241.

10. Cf *Atiabari Tea Co v State of Assam,* (1961) 1 SCR 809 (*860*); *Automobile Transport v State of Rajasthan,* AIR 1962 SC 1406 (*1416*) : [1963] 1 SCR 491; *Ref under Article 143,* AIR 1965 SC 745 (para 39).

limitations on legislative powers and, therefore, this requires an authority other than Parliament to ascertain whether such limitations are transgressed.[11]

5. Peculiar Features of Indian Federalism.

But though *our* Constitution provides these essential features of a Federation, it differs from the typical Federal systems of the world in certain fundamental respects:

(A) *Mode of formation:* A Federal Union of the American type is formed by a voluntary agreement between a number of sovereign and independent States, for the administration of certain affairs of general concern.

However, there is an alternative mode of the *Canadian* type (if Canada is admitted into the family of federations), namely, that the provinces of a unitary State may be transformed into a federal union to make themselves autonomous. The provinces of Canada had no separate or independent existence apart from the colonial Government of Canada, and the Union was not formed by any agreement between them, but was imposed by a British statute, which withdrew from the Provinces all their former rights and then re-divided them between the Dominion and the Provinces. Though the Indian Federation resembles the Canadian Federation in its centralising tendency, it even goes further than the Canadian precedent. The federalism in India is not a matter of administrative convenience, but one of principle.[12]

India had a thoroughly centralised Unitary Constitution until the Government of India Act, 1935. The Provincial Governments were virtually the agents of the Central Government, deriving powers by delegation from the latter (see Chapter 1 *ante*).

To appreciate the mode of formation of Federation in India, we must go back to the Government of India Act, 1935, which for the first time introduced the federal concept, and used the expression 'Federation of India' (Section 5) in a Constitutional Act relating to India, since the Constitution has simply continued the federal system so introduced by the Act of 1935, so far as the Provinces of British India are concerned. The foundation for a federal set-up for the nation was laid in the Government of India Act, 1935. Though in every respect the distribution of legislative power between the Union and the States as envisaged in the 1935 Act has not been adopted in the Constitution, but the basic framework is the same.[13] The Supreme Court observed that India has adopted for itself a loose federal structure as it is an "indestructible Union of destructible units".[14]

By the Act of 1935, the British Parliament set up a federal system in the same manner as it had done in the case of *Canada, viz* "by creating autonomous units and combining them into a federation by one and the same Act". All powers hitherto exercised in India were resumed by the Crown and redistributed between the Federation and the Provinces by a direct grant. Under this system, the Provinces derived their authority directly from the Crown and exercised

11. *State of West Bengal v Committee for Protection of Democratic Rights, West Bengal,* 2010 (3) SCC 571; *Madras Bar Association v UOI,* (2014) 10 SCC 1 : (2014) 271 CTR (SC) 257.
12. *SR Bommai v UOI,* AIR 1994 SC 1918; **affirming** by and large, the views of the author at pp 35-55 of C7, vol A.
13. *Prof Yashpal v State of Chhattisgarh,* AIR 2005 SC 2026.
14. *Raja Ram Pal v Hon'ble Speaker, Lok Sabha,* (2007) 3 SCC 184.

legislative and executive powers, broadly free from Central control, within a defined sphere. Nevertheless, the Centre retained control through 'the Governor's special responsibilities' and his obligation to exercise his individual judgment and discretion in certain matters, and the power of the Centre to give direction to the Provinces.[15]

The peculiarity of thus converting a unitary system into a federal one can be best explained in the words of the Joint Parliamentary Committee on Indian Reforms:

> Of course in thus converting a unitary State into a federation we should be taking a step *for which there is no exact historical* precedent. Federations have commonly resulted from an agreement between independent or, at least, autonomous Governments, surrendering a defined part of their sovereignty or autonomy to a new central organism. At the present moment the British Indian Provinces are not even autonomous for they are subject to both administrative and legislative control of the Government and such authority as they exercise has been in the main devolved upon them under a statutory rule-making power by the Governor-General in Council. We are faced with the necessity of *creating autonomous units and combining them* into a federation by one and the same Act.

It is well worth remembering this peculiarity of the origin of the federal system in India. Neither before, nor through the Act of 1935, were the Provinces, in any sense, 'sovereign' States like the States of the American Union. The Constitution, too, has been framed by the 'People of India' assembled in the Constituent Assembly, and the Union of India cannot be said to be the result of any *compact* or agreement between autonomous States. So far as the Provinces are concerned, the progress had been from a unitary to a federal organisation, but even then, this has happened not because the Provinces desired to become autonomous units under a federal union, as in Canada. The Provinces, as just seen, had been artificially made autonomous, within a defined sphere, by the Government of India Act, 1935. What the makers of the Constitution did was to associate the Indian states with these autonomous Provinces into a federal union, which the Indian states had refused to accede to, in 1935.

Some amount of homogeneity of the federating units is a condition for their desire to form a federal union. But in India, the position has been different. From the earliest times, the Indian States had a separate political entity, and there was little that was common between them and the Provinces which constituted the rest of India. Even under the federal scheme of 1935, the Provinces and the Indian States were treated differently; the accession of the Indian States to the system was voluntary while it was compulsory for the Provinces, and the powers exercisable by the Federation over the Indian States were also to be defined by the Instruments of Accession. It is because it was optional with the Rulers of the Indian States that they refused to join the Federal system of 1935. They lacked the 'federal sentiment' (*Dicey*), that is, the desire to form a federal union with the rest of India. But, as already pointed out, the political situation changed with the lapse of paramountcy of the British Crown as

15. Though the federal system as envisaged by the Government of India Act, 1935, could not fully come into being owing to the failure of the Indian States to join it, the provisions relating to the Central Government and the Provinces were given effect to as stated earlier.

a result of which most of the Indian states acceded to the Dominion of India on the eve of the Independence of India.

The credit of the makers of the Constitution, therefore, lies not so much in bringing the Indian states under the federal system but in placing them, as much as possible, on the same footing as the other units of the Federation, under the same Constitution. In short, the survivors of the old Indian states (states in Part B[16] of the First Schedule) were, with minor exceptions, placed under the same political system as the old Provinces (states in Part A). The integration of the units of the two categories has eventually been completed by eliminating the separate entities of states in Part A and States in Part B and replacing them by one category of states, by the Constitution (7th Amendment) Act, 1956.

(B) *Position of the States in the Federation:* In the *United States,* since the States had a sovereign and independent existence prior to the formation of the federation, they were reluctant to give up that sovereignty any further than what was necessary for forming a national government for the purpose of conducting their common purposes. As a result, the Constitution of the federation contains a number of safeguards for the protection of 'State rights', for which there was no need in *India,* as the states were not 'sovereign' entities before. These points of difference deserve particular attention:

(i) *Residuary powers:* While the *residuary* powers are reserved to the States by the American Constitution, these are assigned to the Union by *our* Constitution [*Article* 248].

This alone, of course, is not sufficient to put an end to the federal character of our political system, because it only relates to the *mode* of distribution of powers. *Our* Constitution has simply followed the *Canadian* system in vesting the residuary power in the Union.

(ii) *Own Constitution:* While the Constitution of the *United States of America* merely drew up the constitution of the national government, leaving it "in the main (to the State) to continue to preserve their original Constitution", the Constitution of *India* lays down the constitution for the states as well, and, no state, save the erstwhile State of Jammu and Kashmir, had a right to determine its own (state) constitution.

(iii) *Constitutional amendments:* In the matter of amendment of the Constitution, again, the part assigned to the State is minor, as compared with that of the Union. The doctrine underlying a federation of the *American* type is that the union is the result of an agreement between the component units, so that no part of the Constitution which embodies the compact can be altered without the consent of the covenanting parties. This doctrine is adopted, with variations, by most of the federal systems.

But in *India,* except in a few specified matters affecting the federal structure (see Chapter 10, *post*), the States need not even be consulted in the matter of amendment of the bulk of the Constitution, which may be effected by a Bill in the Union Parliament, passed by a special majority.

(iv) *Division of powers:* Though there is a division of powers between the Union and the States, there is provision in *our* Constitution for the exercise of

16. *Vide* Table III, col (A).

control by the Union both over the administration and legislation of the States. Legislation by a State shall be subject to disallowance by the President, when reserved by the Governor for his consideration [*Article 201*]. Again, the Governor of a State shall be appointed by the President of the Union and shall hold office 'during the pleasure' of the President [*Articles 155-156*]. These ideas are repugnant to the Constitution of the United States or of Australia, but are to be found in the *Canadian* Constitution.

(v) *Union of States:* The *American* federation has been described by its Supreme Court as "an indestructible Union composed of indestructible States".[17]

It comprises two propositions—

(a) The Union cannot be destroyed by any State seceding from the Union at its will.[18]

(b) Conversely, it is not possible for the federal Government to redraw the map of the United States by forming new States or by altering the boundaries of the States as they existed at the time of the compact without the *consent* of the Legislatures of the States concerned. The same principle is adopted in the *Australian* Constitution to make the Commonwealth "indissoluble", with the further safeguard superadded that a popular referendum is required in the affected State to alter its boundaries.

It has been already seen that the first proposition has been accepted by the makers of *our* Constitution, and it is not possible for the States of the Union of India, to exercise any right of secession. It should be noted in this context that by the 16th Amendment of the Constitution in 1963, it has been made clear that even advocacy of secession will not have the protection of the freedom of expression.[19]

But just the contrary of the second proposition has been embodied in *our* Constitution. Under *our* Constitution, it is possible for the Union Parliament to reorganise the States or to alter their boundaries, by a simple majority in the ordinary process of legislation [*Article 4(2)*]. The Constitution does not require that the *consent* of the Legislature of the States is necessary for enabling Parliament to make such laws; only the President has to 'ascertain' the views of the Legislature of the affected States to recommend a Bill for this purpose to Parliament. Even this obligation is not mandatory insofar as the President is competent to fix a time-limit within which a State must express its views, if at all [*proviso to Article 3*]. In the Indian federation, thus, the States are not "indestructible" units as in the *USA*. The ease with which the federal organisation may be reshaped by an ordinary legislation by the Union Parliament has been demonstrated by the enactment of the States Reorganisation Act, 1956, which reduced the number of States from 27 to 14 within a period of six years from the commencement of the Constitution. The same process of disintegration of existing

17. *Texas v White,* (1869) 7 Wall 700.

18. A contrary instance is to be found in the Constitution of the *USSR* which expressly provides that "each Union Republic shall *retain* the right freely to secede from the U.S.S.R." [Article 72 of the Constitution of 1977; see Author's *Select Constitutions of the World,* 1984 Edn, p 188].

19. Author's *Constitutional Law of India,* 6th Edn, 1991, Prentice-Hall of India, p 46.

states, effected by unilateral legislation by Parliament, has led to the formation, subsequently, of several new States—Gujarat, Nagaland, Haryana, Karnataka, Meghalaya, Himachal Pradesh, Manipur, Sikkim, Tripura, Mizoram, Arunachal Pradesh, Goa, Chhattisgarh, Uttarakhand, Jharkhand, and Telangana.

It is natural, therefore, that questions might arise in foreign minds as to the nature of federalism introduced by the Indian Constitution.

(vi) *No theory of equality of State rights:* Not only does the Constitution offer no guarantee to the States against affecting their territorial integrity without their consent—there is no theory of 'equality of State rights' underlying the federal scheme in *our* Constitution, since it is not the result of any agreement between the States.

One of the essential principles of *American* Federalism is the equality of the component States under the Constitution, irrespective of their size or population. This principle is reflected in the equality of representation of the States in the upper House of the Federal Legislature (*i.e.*, in the Senate),[20] which is supposed to safeguard the status and interests of the States in the Federal organisation. To this is superadded the guarantee that no State may, without its consent, be deprived of its equal representation in the Senate [*Article V*].

Under *our* Constitution, there is no equality of representation of the States in the Council of States. As given in the Fourth Schedule, the number of members for the several States varies from 1 to 31. In view of such composition of the Upper Chamber, the federal safeguard against the interests of the lesser States being overridden by the interests of the larger or more populated States is absent under *our* Constitution. Nor can *our* Council of States be correctly described as a federal Chamber insofar as it contains a nominated element of 12 members as against 238 representatives of the States and Union Territories.

(vii) *Special provisions:* Another novel feature introduced into the Indian federalism was the admission of Sikkim as an 'associate State', without being a *member* of the Union of India, as defined in Article 1, which was made possible by the insertion of Article 2A into the Constitution, by the Constitution (35th Amendment) Act, 1974.

This innovation was, however, short lived and its legitimacy has lost all practical interest, since all that was done by the 35th Amendment Act, 1974, has been undone by the 36th Amendment Act, 1975, by which Sikkim has been admitted into the Union of India, *as a full-fledged State* under the First Schedule with effect from 26 April 1975 (see under Chapter 6, *post*). The original federal scheme of the Indian Constitution, comprising States and the Union Territories, has thus been left unimpaired.

Of course, certain special provisions have been laid down in the new Article 371F, as regards Sikkim, to meet the special circumstances of that State. Article 371G makes certain special provisions relating to the State of Mizoram, while Articles 371H, 371I, and 371J insert special provisions for Arunachal Pradesh, Goa and Karnataka, respectively.

(C) *Nature of the Polity:* As a radical solution of the problem of reconciling national unity with 'State rights', the framers of the *American* Constitution made

20. Each of the 50 States of USA has two representatives in the Senate.

a logical division of everything essential to sovereignty and created a dual polity, with a dual citizenship, a double set of officials and a double system of Courts.

(i) *Citizenship:* An *American* is a citizen not only of the State in which he resides but also of the United States, *i.e.,* of the federation, under different conditions; and both the federal and State Governments, each independent of the other, operate *directly* upon the citizen who is thus *subject to two Governments, and owes allegiance to both.* But the *Indian* Constitution, like the Canadian, does not introduce any double citizenship, but single citizenship, *viz*— the citizenship of India [*Article 5*], and birth or residence in a particular state does not confer any separate status as a citizen of that State.

(ii) *Division amongst public officials:* As regards officials similarly, the Federal and State Governments in the *United States,* have their own officials to administer their respective laws and functions. But there is no such division amongst the public officials in India. The majority of the public servants are employed by the States, but they administer both the Union and the State laws as are applicable to their respective States by which they are employed. *Our* Constitution provides for the creation of All-India Services, but they are to be common to the Union and the States [*Article 312*]. Members of the Indian Administrative Service (IAS), appointed by the Union, may be employed either under some Union Department (say, Home or Defence) or under a State Government, and their services are transferable, and even when they are employed under a Union Department, they have to administer both the Union and State laws as are applicable to the matter in question. But even while serving under a State, for the time being, a member of an all-India Service can be dismissed or removed only by the Union Government, even though the State Government is competent to initiate disciplinary proceedings for that purpose.

(iii) *Judiciary:* In the *USA,* there is a bifurcation of the Judiciary as between the Federal and State Governments. Cases arising out of the Federal Constitution and Federal laws are tried by the Federal Courts, while State Courts deal with cases arising out of the State Constitution and State laws. But in *India,* the same system of Courts, headed by the Supreme Court, will administer both the Union and State laws as they are applicable to the cases coming up for adjudication.

(iv) *Election machinery:* The machinery for election, accounts and audit is also similarly integrated.

(v) *Executive functions:* The Constitution of India empowers the Union to entrust its executive functions to a State, by its consent [*Article* 258], and a State to entrust its executive functions to the Union, similarly [*Article* 258A]. No question of 'surrender of sovereignty' by one Government to the other stands in the way of this smooth co-operative arrangement.

(vi) *Emergency provisions:* While the federal system is prescribed for normal times, the Indian Constitution enables the federal government to acquire the strength of a unitary system in *emergencies.* While in normal times, the Union Executive is entitled to give directions to the State Governments in respect of specified matters, when a Proclamation of Emergency is made, the power to give directions extends to *all* matters and the legislative power of the Union extends to State subjects [*Articles 353, 354, and 357*]. The wisdom of these emergency provisions (relating to *external* aggression, as distinguished from 'internal disturbance') has been demonstrated by the fact that during the Chinese aggression of 1962 or the Pakistan aggression of 1965, India could stand as one man, pooling all the resources of the States, notwithstanding the federal organisation.

Even in its normal working, the Federal system is given the strength of a unitary system—

(a) By endowing the Union with exclusive powers of legislation as far as has been found necessary in other countries to meet the ever-growing national exigencies, and, over and above that, by enabling the Union Legislature to take up some subject of State competence, if required in the national interest. Thus, even apart from emergencies, the Union Parliament may assume legislative power (though temporarily) over any subject included in the State List,[21] if the Council of States (Second Chamber of Parliament) resolves, by a two-thirds vote, that such legislation is necessary in the 'national interest' [*Article 249*]. There is, of course, a federal element in this provision inasmuch as such expansion of the power of the Union into the State sphere is possible only with the consent of the Council of States where the States are represented. But, in actual practice, it will mean an additional weapon in the hands of the Union *vis-a-vis* the States so long as the same party has a solid majority in both the Houses of the Union Parliament.

Even though there is a distribution of powers between the Union and the States as under a federal system, the distribution has a strong Central bias and the powers of the States are hedged in with various restrictions which impede their sovereignty even within the sphere limited to them by the distribution of powers basically provided by the Constitution.

(b) By empowering the Union Government to issue directions upon the State Governments to ensure due compliance with the legislative and administrative action of the Union [*Articles 256-257*], and to supersede a State Government which refuses to comply with such directions [*Article 365*].

(c) By empowering the President to withdraw to the Union, the executive and legislative powers of a State under the Constitution if he is, *at any time,* satisfied that the administration of the State cannot be carried on in the normal manner in accordance with the provisions of Constitution, owing to political or other reasons [*Article 356*]. From the federal standpoint, this seems to be anomalous inasmuch as the Constitution-makers did not consider it necessary to provide for any remedy whatever for a similar breakdown of the constitutional machinery at the Centre. Hence, Panikkar is justified in observing—"The Constitution itself has created a kind of paramountcy for the Centre by providing for the suspension of State Governments and the imposition of President's rule under certain conditions such as the breakdown of the administration". *Secondly,* the power to suspend the constitutional machinery may be exercised by the President, not only on the report of the Governor of the State concerned but also *suo motu,* whenever he is satisfied that a situation calling for the exercise of this power has arisen. It is thus a *coercive* power available to the Union against the units of the federation.

---

21. There are three legislative lists in the Seventh Schedule; 98 items in the Union List, 59 items in the State List and 52 items in the Concurrent List [see Table XIX, *post*].

6. A Critique of the Federal System.

But though the above scheme seeks to avoid the demerits of the Federal system, there is perhaps such an emphasis on the strength of the Union government as affects the federal principle as it is commonly understood. Thus, a foreign critic (Prof Wheare)[22] was led to observe that the Indian Constitution provides—

> A system of Government which is quasi-federal.....a *Unitary State* with *subsidiary federal features rather than a Federal State with subsidiary unitary features.*

In his later work in Modern Constitutions[23] he puts it, generically, thus—

> In the class of quasi-federal Constitution it is *probably proper* to include the Indian Constitution of 1950.

Prof Alexandrowicz[24] has taken great pains to combat the view that the Indian federation is a 'quasi-federation'. He seems to agree with this Author,[25] when he says that "India is a case *sui generis*". This is in accord with the Author's observation that—

> The Constitution of India is neither purely federal nor purely unitary but is a combination of both. It is a Union or composite State of a novel type. It enshrines the principle that in spite of federalism, the national interest ought to be paramount.[25]

In fact, anybody who impartially studies the Indian Constitution from close quarters and acknowledges that Political Science today admits of different variations of the federal system cannot but observe that the Indian system is 'extremely federal',[26] or that it is a 'federation with strong centralising tendency'.[27]

Strictly speaking, any deviation from the American model of pure federation would make a system quasi-federal, and, if so, the *Canadian* system, too, can hardly escape being branded as quasi-federal. The difference between the *Canadian* and the *Indian* system lies in the degree and extent of the unitary emphasis. The real test of the federal character of a political structure is, as Prof Wheare has himself observed—[22] That, however, is what appears on paper only. It remains to be seen whether *in actual practice* the federal features entrench or strengthen themselves as they have in Canada, or whether the strong trend towards centralisation which is a feature of most Western Governments in a world of crises, will compel these federal aspects of the Constitution to wither away.

7. Working of Federalism in India.

A survey of the actual working of *our* Constitution for the last 75 years would hardly justify the conclusion that, even though the unitary bonds have in some respects been further tightened, the federal features have altogether 'withered away'.

---

22. KC Wheare, *Federal Government,* 1951, p 28. He relaxes this view in the 4th Edn, 1963, pp 26, 77.
23. Wheare, *Modern Constitutions,* 2nd Edn, 1966, p 21.
24. CH Alexandrowicz, *Constitutional Developments in India,* 1957, pp 157-70.
25. *Vide* Author's *Commentary on the Constitution of India,* 7th Edn, vol A, p 55.
26. Appleby, *Public Administration in India,* 1953, p 51.
27. Jennings, *Some Characteristics of the Indian Constitution,* p 1.

Some scholars in India[28] urged that the unitary bias of *our* Constitution has been accentuated, in its actual working, by two factors so much so that very little is left of federalism. These two factors are—(a) the overwhelming financial power of the Union and the utter dependence of the States upon Union grants for discharging their functions; (b) the comprehensive sweep of the Union Planning Commission (now replaced with NITI Aayog), set up under the concurrent power over planning. The criticism may be justified in point of degree, but not in principle, for two reasons—

(i) Both these controls are aimed at securing a uniform development of the country as a whole. It is true that the bigger States are not allowed to appropriate all their resources and the system of assignment and distribution of tax resources by the Union [*Articles 269, 270, and 272*] means the dependence of the States upon the Union to a large extent. But, left alone, the stronger and bigger States might have left the smaller ones lagging behind, to the detriment of our national strength.

(ii) Even in a country like the United States, such factors have, in practice, strengthened the National Government to a degree which could not have been dreamt of by the fathers of the Constitution. Curiously enough, the same complaint, as in India, has been raised in the United States. Thus, of the centralising power of federal grants, an American writer[29] has observed—

> Here is an attack on federalism, so subtle that it is scarcely realised.....Control of economic life and of these social services (*viz.,* unemployment, old-age, maternity and child welfare) were the two major functions of a State and local governments. The first has largely passed into national hands; the second seems to be passing. If these both go, what we shall have left of State autonomy will be a hollow shell, a symbol.

In fact, the traditional theory of mutual independence of the two governments—federal and States, has given way to "co-operative federalism' in most of the federal countries today.[30]

An American scholar explains the concept of 'co-operative federalism' in these words[30]—

> .....the practice of administrative co-operation between general and regional governments, the partial *dependence* of the regional governments *upon payments* from the general governments, and the fact that the general governments, by the use of *conditional* grants, frequently promote developments in matters which are *constitutionally assigned* to the regions.

Hence, the system of federal co-operation existing under the Indian Constitution, through allocation by the Union of the taxes collected, or direct grants or allocation of plan funds do not necessarily militate against the concept of federalism and that is why Granville Austin[31] prefers to call Indian federalism

28. Eg. Santhanam, *Union-State Relations in India,* 1960, pp vii; 51, 59, 63. At p 70, the learned Author observes—

    "India has practically functioned as a Unitary State though the Union and the States have *tried* to function formally and legally as a Federation."

29. Griffith, *The Impasse of Democracy* 1939, p 196, quoted in Godshall, *Government in the United States,* p 114.
30. Cf Birch, *Federalism,* pp 305-06.
31. Granville Austin, *The Indian Constitution* (1966), pp. 187 *et seq.*

as 'co-operative federalism' which "produces a strong central.....government, yet it does not necessarily result in weak provincial governments that are largely administrative agencies for central policies."

In fact, the federal system in the Indian Constitution is a compromise between two apparently conflicting consideration:

(i) There is a normal division of powers under which the States enjoy autonomy within their own spheres, with the power to raise revenue;

(ii) The need for national integrity and a strong Union government, which the saner section of the people still considers necessary after more than 70 years of working of the Constitution.

8. Indian Federalism as Judicially Interpreted. The interplay of the foregoing two forces has been acknowledged even by the Supreme Court in interpreting various provisions of the Constitution, *e.g.*, in explaining the significance of Article 301[32] thus—

> The evolution of a federal structure or a quasi-federal structure necessarily involved, in the context of the conditions then prevailing, a distribution of powers and a basic part of our Constitution relates to that distribution with the three legislative lists in the Seventh Schedule. The Constitution itself says by Art. 1 that India is a Union of States and in interpreting the Constitution one must keep in the view *the essential structure* of a federal or quasi-federal Constitution, namely, that *the units of the Union have also certain powers as has the Union itself.*
>
> In evolving an integrated policy on this subject our Constitution-makers seem to have kept in mind three main considerations.....first, in the larger interest of India there must be free flow of trade, commerce and intercourse, both inter-State and intra-State; second, *the regional interests must not be ignored altogether,* and third, there must be a power of intervention by the Union in case of crisis to deal with particular problems that may arise in any part of India.....Therefore, in interpreting the relevant articles in Part XIII we must have regard to the *general scheme* of the Constitution of India with special reference to Part III, Part XII.....and their inter-relation to Part XIII *in the context of a federal or quasi-federal Constitution* in which the States have certain powers including the power to raise revenues for their purposes by taxation.

At the same time, there is no denying the fact that the States have occasionally smarted[33] against 'Central dominion' over the States in their exclusive sphere, even in normal times, through the Planning Commission (Planning Commission now replaced by NITI Aayog was not recognised by the Constitution like the Finance Commission, the Public Service Commission or the like). But this is not because the Constitution is not federal in structure[34] or that its provisions envisage unitary control; the defect is *political,* namely, that it is the same party which dominates both the Union and State Governments and that, naturally,

---

32. *Automobile Transport v State of Rajasthan,* AIR 1962 SC 1406 (*1415-16*). In *Kesavananda v UOI,* AIR 1973 SC 1461, some of the judges (paras 302, 599, 1681) considered federalism to be one of the 'basic features' of *our* Constitution. A nine-Judge Supreme Court Bench has in *SR Bommai v UOI,* AIR 1994 SC 1918 laid down that the Constitution is federal and some of the Judges characterised federalism as its basic feature.
33. *Vide* Report of the Centre-State Relations Committee (Rajamannar Committee) (Madras, 1971, pp 7-9).
34. It is interesting to note that even the Rajamannar Committee characterises the system under the Constitution of India as 'federal', but suggests amendment of some of its features which have a unitary trend.

complaints of discrimination or interference with State autonomy are more common in those States which happen to be, for the time being, under the rule of a party different from that of the Union Government. The remedy, however, lies through the ballot box. It is through political forces, again, that the Union Government may be prevented from so exercising its constitutional powers as to assume an 'unhealthy paternalism';[35] but that is beyond the ken of the present work. The remedy for excessive use of the power to impose President's rule in a State, under Article 356, is also political.[36]

The strong Central bias has, however, been a boon to keep India together when we find the separatist forces of communalism, linguism and scramble for power, playing havoc notwithstanding all the devices of Central control, even after five decades of the working of the Constitution. It also shows that the States are not really functioning as agents of the Union Government or under the directions of the latter, for then, events like those in Assam (over the language problem) or territorial dispute between Karnataka and Maharashtra could not have taken place at all.

That the federal system has not withered away owing to the increasing impact of Central bias would be evidenced by a number of circumstances which cannot be overlooked [see, further, Chapter 34, *post*]:

(a) *Co-existence of Central and State Governments:* The most conclusive evidence of the survival of the federal system in India is the co-existence of the Governments of the parties in the States different from that of the Centre. Of course, the reference of the Kerala Education Bill by the President for the advisory opinion of the Supreme Court instead of giving his assent to the Bill in the usual course, has been criticised in Kerala as an undue interference with the constitutional rights of the State, but thanks to the wisdom and impartiality of the Supreme Court, the opinion delivered by the Court[35] was prompted by a purely legalistic outlook free from any political consideration so that the federal system may reasonably be expected to remain unimpaired notwithstanding changes in the party situation so long as the Supreme Court discharges its duties as a guardian of the Constitution.

(b) *Formation of new States:* That Federalism is not dead in India is also evidenced by the fact that new regions are constantly demanding Statehood and that already the Union had to yield to such demand in the cases of Meghalaya, Nagaland, Manipur, Tripura, Mizoram, Arunachal Pradesh, Goa, Chhattisgarh, Uttaranchal and Jharkhand.

(c) *Financial power for States:* Another evidence is the strong agitation for greater financial power for the States. The case for greater autonomy for the States in *all* respects was first launched by Tamil Nadu, as a lone crusader, but in October 1983, it was joined by the States ruled by non-Congress Parties, forming an 'Opposition Conclave', though all the Parties were not prepared to go to the same extent. The enlargement of State powers at the cost of the Union, in the

35. *Re Kerala Education Bill*, AIR 1958 SC 956.

36. It is unfortunate that even the Janata Government formed in 1977 which was determined to undo all mischief alleged to have been caused by the long Congress rule, was not convinced of the need to effectively control the frequent use of the drastic power conferred by Article 356, and that the amendments effected by the 44th Amendment, 1978, in respect of this Article, are not good enough from this standpoint.

political sphere is not, however, shared by other States, on the ground that a weaker Union will be a danger to external security and even internal cohesion, in present-day circumstances. But there is consensus amongst the States, in general, that they should have larger financial powers than those conferred by the existing Constitution, if they are to efficiently discharge their development programmes within the State sphere under List II of the Seventh Schedule. The Morarji Desai Government (1977) sought to pacify the States by conceding substantial grants by way of 'Plan assistance', by what has been called the 'Desai award'.[37]

9. Sarkaria Commission.

It is doubtful, however, whether the agitation for larger constitutional powers in respect of finance will be set at rest by such *ad hoc* palliatives. It is interesting to note that the suggestion, in a previous edition of this book, that the remedy perhaps lay in setting up a Commission for the revision of the Constitution, so that the question of finance may be taken up along with the responsibilities of the Union and the States, on a more comprehensive perspective, has borne fruit in the appointment, in March, 1983, of a one-man Commission, headed by an ex-Supreme Court Judge, J, empowered to recommend changes[38] in the Centre-State relations' in view of the various developments which have taken place since the commencement of the Constitution. The Commission submitted its Report in 1988. The Supreme Court referred to the report in *SR Bommai.*

The proper assessment of the federal scheme introduced by *our* Constitution is that it introduces a system which is to *normally* work as a federal system but there are provisions for converting it into a unitary or quasi-federal system under specified exceptional circumstances.[39] But the exceptions cannot be held to have overshadowed the basic and normal structure.[40] The exceptions are, no doubt,

37. *Statesman,* Calcutta, dated 26 February 1979, p 1.

38. Rao Government, which was in office till 1995, did not implement any of the recommendations made in the Report of the Sarkaria Commission.

39. As Dr Ambedkar explained in the Constituent Assembly (VII *CAD,* 33-34), the political system adopted in the Constitution could be "both unitary as well as federal according to the requirements of time and circumstances".

40. How far the 9-Judge Bench of the Supreme Court in *Bommai's* case (AIR 1994 SC 1918) has adopted the Author's views as expressed in the foregoing discussion will be evident from its following observation:

> The fact that under the scheme of our Constitution, greater power is conferred upon the Centre *vis-a-vis* the States does not mean that states are mere appendages of the Centre. Within the sphere allotted to them, *States are supreme*.....More particularly, the Courts should not adopt an approach, an interpretation, which has the effect of or tends to have the effect of whittling down the powers reserved to the States.....let it be said that federalism in the Indian Constitution is not a *matter of administrative convenience, but one of principle*—the outcome of our own historical process and a recognition of the ground realities (para 276).

This view, expressed by Jeevan Reddy and Agrawal JJ is joined by Pandian J (para 2). The view is supported by Sawant and Kuldip Singh JJ in these words (para 99);

> .....the States have an independent constitutional existence.....they are not satellites nor agents of the Centre. The fact that during emergency and in certain other eventualities their powers are overridden or invaded by the Centre is not *destructive* of the *essential* federal feature of our Constitution.....they are exceptions and have to be resorted to only to meet the exigencies of the *special situations.* The *exceptions are not a rule* (para 99).

unique and numerous; but in cases where the exceptions are not attracted, federal provisions are to be applied without being influenced by the existence of the exceptions. Thus, it will not be possible either for the Union or a State to assume powers which are assigned by the Constitution to the other Government, unless such assumption is sanctioned by some provisions of the Constitution itself. Nor would such usurpation or encroachment be valid by consent of the other party, for the Constitution itself provides the cases in which this is permissible by consent [*e.g., Articles 252, 258(1), and 258A*]; hence, apart from these exceptional cases, the Constitution would not permit any of the units of the federation to subvert the federal structure set up by the Constitution, even by consent. Nor would this be possible by delegation of powers by one Legislature in favour of another.

10. Conclusion.

In fine, it may be reiterated that the Constitution of India is *neither purely federal nor purely unitary but is a combination of both. It is a Union or composite State of a novel type.*[41] It enshrines the principle that "in spite of federalism, the national interest ought to be paramount".[42]

41. Granville Austin, *The Indian Constitution* (1966), p 186, agrees with this view when he describes the Indian federation as 'a *new* kind of federalism to meet India's peculiar needs'.
42. Jennings, *Some Characteristics of the Indian Constitution,* p 55.

CHAPTER 6

TERRITORY OF THE UNION

1. Name of the Union.

AS has been already stated, the political structure prescribed by the Constitution is a Federal Union. The name of the Union is India or *Bharat* [*Article 1(1)*].

2. Territory of India.

The members of this Union at present[1] are 28 States, *i.e.*, Andhra Pradesh, Assam, Bihar, Gujarat, Haryana, Karnataka,[2] Kerala, Madhya Pradesh, Tamil Nadu,[3] Maharashtra, Nagaland, Odisha, Punjab, Rajasthan, Uttar Pradesh, West Bengal, Himachal Pradesh, Manipur, Tripura, Meghalaya,[4] Sikkim, Mizoram, Arunachal Pradesh, Goa, Chhattisgarh,[5] Uttarakhand,[6] Jharkhand[7] and Telangana[8]. Parliament has enacted the Jammu and Kashmir Reorganisation Act, 2019 by which the erstwhile State of Jammu and Kashmir has been reorganised (w.e.f. 31-10-2019) into: (i) the Union Territory of Jammu and Kashmir with a Legislature; and (ii) the Union Territory of Ladakh (comprising Kargil and Leh Districts) without a Legislature [see Chapter 15, *post*].

The expression 'Union of India' should be distinguished from the expression 'territory of India'. While the 'Union' includes only the States which enjoy the status of being members of the federal system and share a distribution of powers with the Union, the "territory of India" includes the entire territory over which the sovereignty of India, for the time being, extends.[9] The phrase "territory of India" cannot mean different territories in different Articles.[10]

---

1. In the original Constitution, there were 27 States placed under three categories,—in Parts A, B and C of the First Schedule, having different status and features (as shown in Table III, Col A, *post*). These States underwent some changes by subsequent legislation until the Constitution (Seventh Amendment) Act of 1956 abolished the three categories and placed all the States on the same footing (being 15 in number)—as a result of the reorganisation made by the States Reorganisation Act, 1956, which was incorporated in the Constitution (Seventh Amendment) Act.
2. The name of Mysore has been changed to 'Karnataka' by the Mysore State (Alteration of Name) Act, 1973.
3. The name of Madras has been changed to 'Tamil Nadu' by the Madras State (Alteration of Name) Act, 1968.
4. The 22nd Amendment Act, 1969, was passed to form an autonomous sub-State within the State of Assam, comprising the tribal areas specified in Part A of the Table to para 20 of the 6th Schedule of the Constitution, to meet the demands of the Hill Tribes for a separate State for themselves, which has since been created and named *Meghalaya*.
5. *Vide* the Madhya Pradesh Reorganisation Act, 2000.
6. *Vide* the Uttar Pradesh Reorganisation Act, 2000.
7. *Vide* the Bihar Reorganisation Act, 2000.
8. *Vide* the Andhra Pradesh Reorganisation Act, 2014 (6 of 2014).
9. *See also* section 3(2) of the Territorial Waters, Continental Shelf, Exclusive Economic Zone and other Maritime Zones Act, 1976.
10. *N Masthan Sahib v Chief Commr*, AIR 1962 SC 797.

Thus, besides the States, there are two other classes of territories, which are included in the 'territory of India', *viz.*: (i) Union Territories; and (ii) Such other territories as may be acquired by India.

2a. Union Territories.

The Union Territories, at present, are 8 in number—Delhi, the Andaman & Nicobar Island, Lakshadweep,[11] Dadra & Nagar Haveli and Daman & Diu,[12] Puducherry,[13] Chandigarh,[14] Jammu and Kashmir, and Ladakh.[15]

For the Union Territory of Puducherry, Parliament has by enacting a law, *viz.*, the Pondicherry (Administration) Act, 1962 under Article 239A, made provisions for a Legislature, etc.

By an amendment to the Constitution, two new Articles, *viz.*, Article 239AA and Article 239AB were inserted in 1992 providing for a Legislature and a Council of Ministers for Delhi. The amendment also renamed the Union Territory of Delhi as the National Capital Territory of Delhi through Article 239AA.[16] The Government of National Capital Territory of Delhi Act, 1991 (1 of 1992) was enacted to supplement the provisions of the Constitution relating to the Legislative Assembly and a Council of Ministers for the National Capital Territory of Delhi and for matters connected therewith or incidental thereto.

Parliament has enacted the Government of National Capital Territory of Delhi (Amendment) Act, 2021, which received the assent of the President on 28 March 2021. It amends certain provisions in the Government of National Capital Territory of Delhi Act, 1991, relating to the powers and responsibilities of the Legislative Assembly and the Lieutenant Governor. The Amendment Act clarifies that the expression "Government", which in the context of legislations to be passed by the Legislative Assembly of Delhi, shall mean the Lieutenant Governor of the National Capital Territory of Delhi.

---

11. The name of the Laccadive, Minicoy and Amindivi Islands has been changed to 'Lakshadweep' by an Act of 1973.
12. The Portuguese enclaves of Dadra and Nagar Haveli, having been integrated with India, after the judgment of the International Court in India's favour, the territory of these two enclaves was constituted a Union Territory, by the Constitution (10th Amendment) Act, 1962. Goa, Daman and Diu was added as a Union Territory, by the Constitution (12th Amendment) Act, 1962. Goa became a State by virtue of Goa, Daman and Diu Reorganisation Act, 1987, separating it from Daman and Diu with effect from 30 May 1987. The Union Territories of Dadra & Nagar Haveli and Daman & Diu have been merged through the enactment of the Dadra and Nagar Haveli and Daman and Diu (Merger of Union Territories) Act, 2019 (wef 26-01-2020).
13. The French Possession of Pondicherry was added by the Constitution (14th Amendment) Act, 1962. The name of Pondicherry has been changed to 'Puducherry' *vide* Act 44 of 2006, section 5 (wef 1-10-2006).
14. Chandigarh was added as a Union Territory by the Constitution (12th Amendment) Act, 1962.
15. Jammu & Kashmir and Ladakh were added as Union Territories by the Jammu and Kashmir Reorganisation Act, 2019 (34 of 2019) (wef 31-10-2019) by demoting the erstwhile State of Jammu & Kashmir.
16. Delhi has now got a special status by the Constitution (69th Amendment) Act, 1991, but has not been promoted to the status of a full-fledged State. See the Author's *Shorter Constitution of India,* 12th Edn, p 756.

The rest of the Union Territories are centrally administered areas, to be governed by the President, acting through an 'Administrator' appointed by him, and issuing regulations for their good government [*Articles 239-240*].

2b. Acquired Territories. Any territory which may, at any time, be acquired[17] by India by purchase, treaty, cession or conquest, will obviously form part of the territory of India. These will be administered by the Government of India subject to legislation by Parliament [*Article 246(4)*].

Thus, the French Settlement of Pondicherry (together with Karaikal, Mahe, and Yanam), which was ceded to India by the French Government in 1954, was being administered as an 'acquired territory' until 1962, inasmuch as the Treaty of Cession had not yet been ratified by the French Parliament. After such ratification, the territory of these French Settlements was constituted a 'Union Territory', in December 1962.

On acquisition of territory, the pre-acquisition laws and the rights acquired therein may continue, only if the new Government chooses to recognise them unequivocally.[18]

3. Historical Account on Integration of Sikkim as an Indian State. The Constitutional developments in Sikkim by way of its integration under the Constitution of India are dramatic.

During British days, Sikkim was an Indian State, under a hereditary monarch called *Chogyal*, subject to British paramountcy. Its external frontier in the Himalayas was demarcated by an agreement with China, in 1890. The Chogyal was a member of the Chamber of Princes.

When India became independent, there was a section of public opinion in Sikkim for merger with India. But the Princely rule of that State and its strategic position stood in the way. Hence, after the lapse of paramountcy, a treaty was entered into between Sikkim and the Government of India, by which the latter undertook the responsibility with regard to the defence, external affairs, and communications of Sikkim. The Government of India was represented in Sikkim by a Political Officer, who was also assigned to Bhutan. Sikkim, thus, became a Protectorate of the Union of India.

3a. The Government of Sikkim Act, 1974. In May 1974, the Sikkimese Congress decided to put an end to monarchical rule, and the Sikkim Assembly passed the Government of Sikkim Act, 1974, for the progressive realisation of a fully responsible government in Sikkim and for furthering its relationship with India. This Act empowered the Government of Sikkim to seek participation and representation of the people of Sikkim in the political institutions of India, for the speedy development of Sikkim in social, economic and political fields.

The Chogyal was made to give his assent to the Government of Sikkim Bill, under which effective power went into the hands of a representative Sikkim

17. 'Acquired' means acquired according to any of the modes recognised by International Law [*N Masthan Sahib v Chief Commr*, AIR 1962 SC 797, 803]. See also *Jose Da Costa v Bascora Sadashiva Sinai Narcornin*, AIR 1975 SC 1843 : (1976) 2 SCC 917.

18. *Vinod Kumar Shantilal Gosalia v Gangadhar Narsingdas Agarwal*, AIR 1981 SC 1946 : (1981) 4 SCC 226 : (1982) 1 SCR 392.

Assembly, and the Chogyal was turned into a normal Constitutional head. The Sikkim Assembly, by virtue of its powers under the Government of Sikkim Act, passed a resolution expressing its desire to be associated with the political and economic institutions of India and for seeking representation for the people of Sikkim in India's Parliamentary system.

3b. The Constitution (35th Amendment) Act, 1974. The Constitution (35th Amendment) Act, 1974, was promptly passed to give effect to this resolution. The main provisions of this Amendment Act were—

(i) Sikkim will not merely be a part of the territory of India, but an 'associate State', which was brought within the framework of the Indian Constitution by inserting Article 2A and Schedule X in the Constitution. These were subsequently omitted by the Constitution (36th Amendment) Act, 1975.

(ii) Sikkim would be entitled to send two representatives to the two Houses, whose rights and privileges would be the same as those of other members of Parliament, except that the representatives of Sikkim would not be entitled to vote at the election of the President or Vice-President of India. They would also be subject to the disqualifications for members of Parliament under the Indian Constitution.

(iii) The defence, communications, external affairs and social welfare of Sikkim would be a responsibility of the Government of India and the people of Sikkim would have the right of admission to institutions for higher education, to the All-India Services and the political institutions in India.

(iv) The Government of Sikkim shall retain residual power on all matters not provided for in Schedule X of the Constitution of India.

There is little doubt that the 35th Amendment Act, 1974, introduced innovations into the original scheme of the Constitution of India. There was no room for any 'associate State' under the Constitution of 1949. India was a federal union of 'States', Union Territories and 'acquired territories' [*Article 1(3)*]. Of course, Article 2 empowered the Parliament of India to admit new 'States' into the 'Union'. But the Constitution (35th Amendment) Act did not seek to admit Sikkim as a new State of the Indian Union. It was to be a territory *associated with India,* and would have representatives in the Indian Parliament without being a part of the territory of India.

The criticism of the introduction of the status of an 'associate State' into the Indian federal system has, however, lost all practical significance, because Sikkim has shortly thereafter been admitted[19] into the Indian Union as the 22nd State in the First Schedule of the Constitution of India.

We shall now advert to this later development. While the Indian Parliament was enacting the Constitution (35th Amendment) Act, the Chogyal resented the development and sought to invoke international intervention. This provoked the

19. The power of Parliament under Article 2 to admit a new State is *not unlimited* but is subject to judicial review, and it is open to the Court to examine whether the terms and conditions for such admission as provided by Parliament are consistent with the Constitutional scheme and the basic features of the Indian Constitution [*RC Poudyal v UOI,* AIR 1993 SC 1804 (para 115)].

progressive sections of the people of Sikkim and led to a resolution being passed by the Sikkim Assembly on 10 April 1975, declaring that the activities of the Chogyal were prejudicial to the democratic aspirations of the people of Sikkim and ran counter to the Agreement of May 1974, executed by the Chogyal. The Assembly further declared and resolved that.

> This institution of the Chogyal is hereby abolished and Sikkim shall henceforth be a *constituent unit of India,* enjoying a democratic and fully responsible government.

3c. The Constitution (36th Amendment) Act, 1975.

This resolution of the Assembly was submitted to the people of Sikkim for their approval. At the referendum so held, there was an overwhelming majority, and the Chief Minister of Sikkim, on behalf of his Council of Ministers, urged the Government of India to implement the result of the referendum. This led to the passing by the Indian Parliament of the Constitution (36th Amendment) Act, 1975, which was later ratified by the requisite number of States under Article 368(2), proviso. By the 36th Constitutional Amendment Act, Sikkim has been admitted into the Union of India as a State, by amending the First and the Fourth Schedules, Articles 80-81, and omitting Article 2A and the 10th Schedule, with retrospective effect from 26 April 1975. Article 371F has, further, been inserted to make some special provisions relating to the administration of Sikkim.

4. 100th Constitutional Amendment on the Land Boundary Agreement with Bangladesh

Both the Houses of the Indian Parliament have unanimously passed the Constitution (119th Amendment) Bill, 2013,[20] for operationalising the Land Boundary Agreement with Bangladesh, 41 years after the accord was signed. India and Bangladesh have a common land boundary of approximately 4096.7 kms. Initially, the India-East Pakistan land boundary was determined as per the Radcliffe Award of 1947. Disputes arose out of some provisions in the Radcliffe Award, which were sought to be resolved through the Bagge Award of 1950. Another effort was made to settle these disputes by the Nehru-Noon Agreement of 1958. However, the issue relating to division of Berubari Union was challenged before the Hon'ble Supreme Court. To comply with the opinion rendered by the Hon'ble Supreme Court of India, the Constitution (Ninth Amendment) Act, 1960 was passed by Parliament. Due to the continuous litigation and other political developments at that time, the Constitution (Ninth Amendment) Act, 1960 could not be notified in respect of territories in former East Pakistan (presently Bangladesh). On 16 May 1974, the Agreement between India and Bangladesh concerning the demarcation of the land boundary and related matters was signed between both the countries to find a solution to the complex nature of the border demarcation involved. In this connection, it was also required to identify the precise area on the ground which would be transferred. Subsequently, the issues relating to demarcation of un-demarcated boundary; the territories in adverse possession; and exchange of enclaves were identified and resolved by signing a Protocol on 6 September 2011, which forms an integral part of the

20. The Constitution (119th Amendment) Bill, 2013 was introduced in Rajya Sabha on 18 December 2013. It was passed by Rajya Sabha on 6 May 2015 and by Lok Sabha on 7 May 2015.

Land Boundary Agreement between India and Bangladesh, 1974. The Protocol was prepared with support and concurrence of the concerned State Governments of Assam, Meghalaya, Tripura, and West Bengal. Accordingly, the Constitution (119th Amendment) Bill, 2013, was passed, which amended the First Schedule of the Constitution, for the purpose of giving effect to the acquisition of territories by India and transfer of territories to Bangladesh through retaining of adverse possession and exchange of enclaves, in pursuance of the aforesaid Agreement of 1974 and its Protocol entered between the Governments of India and Bangladesh. The land swap protocol envisages transferring 111 enclaves with a total area of 17,160.63 acres to Bangladesh, while the neighbouring country is to transfer 51 enclaves with an area of 7,110.02 acres to India. A 6.1-km undefined border stretch will be demarcated with the Bill being passed. The Bill had been moved as the (119th Amendment) Bill and became "the Constitution (100th Amendment) Act, 2015" after the assent of President of India.

5. Formation of New States and Alteration of Boundaries, etc.

It has already been pointed out that the Indian federation differs from the traditional federal system insofar as it empowers Parliament to alter the territory or integrity of its units, namely, the States, without their consent or concurrence. Where the federal system is the result of a compact or agreement between independent States, it is obvious that the agreement cannot be altered without the consent of the parties to it. This is why the American federation has been described as "an indestructible Union of indestructible States". It is not possible for the National Government to redraw the map of the United States by forming new States or by altering boundaries of the States as they existed at the time of the compact *without the consent* of the Legislatures of the States concerned. But since the Federation in India was not the result of any compact between independent States, there was no particular urge to maintain the initial organisation of the States as outlined in the Constitution even though interests of the nation as a whole demanded a change in this respect. The makers of *our* Constitution, therefore, empowered Parliament to reorganise the States by a simple procedure, the essence of which is that the affected State or States may express their views but cannot resist the will of Parliament.[21]

The reason why such liberal power was given to the National Government to reorganise the States is that the grouping of the Provinces under the Government of India Acts was based on historical and political reasons rather than the social, cultural or linguistic divisions of the people themselves. The question of reorganising the units according to natural alignments was indeed raised at the time of the making of the Constitution but then there was not enough time to undertake this huge task, considering the magnitude of the problem.

The provisions relating to the above subjects are contained in Articles 3-4 of the Constitution.

---

21. *Ram Badan Rai v UOI,* AIR 1999 SC 166: JT 1998 (7) SC 478 : (1999) 1 SCC 705 : (1998) 6 SCALE 71.

Article 3 says:

Parliament may by law—

(a) form a new State by separation of territory from any State or by uniting two or more States or parts of States or by uniting any territory to a part of any State,

(b) increase the area of any State,

(c) diminish the area of any State,

(d) alter the boundaries of any State,

(e) alter the name of any State:

Provided that no Bill for the purpose shall be introduced in either House of Parliament except on the recommendation of the President and unless, where the proposal contained in the Bill affects the area, boundaries or name of any of the States, the Bill has been referred by the President to the Legislature of that State for expressing its views thereon within such period as may be specified in the reference or within such further period as the President may allow and the period so specified or allowed has expired.

Explanation I.—In this article, in clauses (*a*) to (*e*), "State" includes a Union territory, but in the proviso, "State" does not include a Union territory.

Explanation II.—The power conferred on Parliament by clause (*a*) includes the power to form a new State or Union territory by uniting a part of any State or Union territory to any other State or Union territory.

One of the basic structures, namely, federal character of the Constitution, is reserved by Article 3 of the Constitution. Thus, it does not violate the basic structure of the Constitution.[22]

Article 4 provides that any such law [including any law made under Article 2] may make supplemental, incidental and consequential provisions for making itself effective and may amend the First and Fourth Schedules of the Constitution, without going through the special formality of a law for the amendment of the Constitution as prescribed by Article 368. These Articles, thus, demonstrate the flexibility of our Constitution. By a simple majority and by the ordinary legislative process, Parliament may form new States or alter the boundaries, etc., of the existing States and thereby change the political map of India.

The law-making power under Articles 3 and 4 is paramount and is neither subject to nor fettered by Article 246 and Lists II and III of the Seventh Schedules. The constitutional validity of law made under Articles 3 and 4 cannot be questioned on the ground of lack of legislative competence with reference to the Lists of the Seventh Schedule.[23]

5a. Procedure for Reorganisation of States.

The only conditions laid down for the making of such a law are—

(a) No Bill for the purpose can be introduced except on the recommendation of the President.

(b) The President shall, before giving his recommendation, refer the Bill to the Legislature of the State which is going to be affected by the changes proposed in the Bill, for expressing its views on the changes *within the period*

22. *PV Krishnaiah v UOI,* AIR 2014 SC 13 (16) (DB).

23. *Mullaperiyar Environmental Protection Forum v UOI,* AIR 2006 SC 1428: (2006) 3 SCC 643.

specified by the President. The President is *not,* however, *bound* by the views of the State Legislature, so ascertained.[24]

Here is, thus, a special feature of the Indian federation, *viz.*, that the territories of the units of the federation may be altered or redistributed if the Union Executive and Legislature so desire.[25] The principles relating to the change of sovereignty in international law are not applicable to a reorganisation of territory of a State under Article 3. When such an adjustment or reorganisation of territories takes place, the existing laws as well as administrative orders in a particular territory continue to be in force and continue to be binding upon the successor State, so long as they are not modified, changed or repudiated by the successor State.[26]

5b. Parliamentary Acts Reorganising States of India. Since the commencement of the Constitution, the foregoing power has been used by Parliament to enact the following Acts:

1. The Assam (Alteration of Boundaries) Act, 1951, altered the boundaries of Assam by ceding a strip of territory from India to Bhutan.
2. The Andhra State Act, 1953, formed a new State named Andhra, by taking out some territory from the State of Madras as it existed at the commencement of the Constitution.
3. The Himachal Pradesh and Bilaspur (New State) Act, 1954, merged the two Part C States of Himachal Pradesh and Bilaspur to form one State, namely, Himachal Pradesh.
4. The Bihar and West Bengal (Transfer of Territories) Act, 1956, transferred certain territories from Bihar to West Bengal.
5. The States Reorganisation Act, 1956, reorganised the boundaries of the different States of India in order to meet local and linguistic demands. Apart from transferring certain territories as between the existing States, it formed the new State of Kerala and merged the former States of Madhya Bharat, Pepsu, Saurashtra, Travancore Cochin, Ajmer, Bhopal, Coorg, Kutch and Vindhya Pradesh in other adjoining States.
6. The Rajasthan and Madhya Pradesh (Transfer of Territories) Act, 1959, transferred certain territories from the State of Rajasthan to that of Madhya Pradesh.
7. The Andhra Pradesh and Madras (Alteration of Boundaries) Act, 1959, made alterations in the boundaries of the States of Andhra Pradesh and Madras.
8. The Bombay Reorganisation Act, 1960, partitioned the State of Bombay to form the new State of Gujarat and to name the residue of Bombay as

24. *Babulal v State of Bombay,* AIR 1960 SC 51 (54): (1960) 1 SCR 605: 62 Bom LR 58; *Pradeep Chaudhary v UOI,* LNIND 2008 SC 3140: (2009) 12 SCC 248: (2009) 7 Scale 12.
25. *State of WB v UOI,* AIR 1963 SC 1241.
26. *Ramkishore Sen v UOI,* AIR 1966 SC 644: (1966) 1 SCR 430; *Director of Industries and Commerce, Government of AP Hyderabad v V Venkata Reddy,* AIR 1973 SC 827: (1973) 1 SCC 99: 1973 (1) SCJ 241; *State of Punjab v Balbir,* AIR 1977 SC 629: (1976) 3 SCC 242.

Maharashtra. Thus, the State of Bombay was split up into two States—Maharashtra and Gujarat.

9. The Acquired Territories (Merger) Act, 1960, provided for the merger into the State of Assam, Punjab, and West Bengal of certain territories acquired by agreements between the Government of India and Pakistan, in 1958 and 1959.

A similar transfer of certain territories from West Bengal and Assam to Pakistan under the aforesaid agreement, was provided for by enacting the Constitution (Ninth Amendment) Act, 1960, because the Supreme Court opined that no territory can be ceded from India to a *foreign country* without amending the Constitution.[27] The lease agreement in perpetuity of some area at Teen Bigha (Indian Territory) to Bangladesh did not amount to lease or surrender of sovereignty, but servitude suffered by India.[28] For later developments, *see* the Constitution (100th Amendment) Act, 2015.

10. The State of Nagaland Act, 1962, formed the new State of Nagaland, with effect form 1 February 1964, comprising the territory of the Naga Hills-Tuensang Area which was previously a Tribal Area in the Sixth Schedule of the Constitution, forming part of the State of Assam.

11. The next change was introduced by the Punjab Reorganisation Act, 1966, by which the State of Punjab was split up into the State of Punjab and Haryana and the Union Territory of Chandigarh with effect from 1 November 1966.

12. The Andhra Pradesh and Mysore (Transfer of Territory) Act, 1968.

13. The Bihar and Uttar Pradesh (Alteration of Boundaries) Act, 1968.

14. The Assam Reorganisation (Meghalaya) Act, 1969, created an autonomous sub-State named Meghalaya, within the State of Assam.

15. Himachal Pradesh was upgraded from the status of a Union Territory to that of a State by the State of Himachal Pradesh Act, 1970.

16. The North Eastern Areas (Reorganisation) Act, 1971, similarly, brought up Manipur, Tripura and Meghalaya into the category of States, and added Mizoram and Arunachal Pradesh to the list of Union territories.

17. The Haryana and Uttar Pradesh (Alteration of Boundaries) Act, 1979.

18. Mizoram, which had been made a Union Territory by the Act of 1971, was elevated to the status of a State, by the State of Mizoram Act, 1986.

19. Arunachal Pradesh, a Union Territory, was made a State by State of Arunachal Pradesh Act, 1986.

20. Goa became a State by virtue of Goa, Daman and Diu Reorganisation Act, 1987, separating it from Daman and Diu with effect from 30 May 1987.

---

27. *Re Berubari Union,* AIR 1960 SC 845. [This cession could not be effected because the constitutionality of the transfer was challenged in the Courts. Though the Supreme Court upheld the transfer, some part of this ceded territory has been retained by West Bengal by agreement with the then Mujibur Rahaman Government of Bangladesh, in 1974].

28. *UOI v Sukumar Sengupta,* AIR 1990 SC 1692 : JT 1990 (2) SC 297.

21. A new State of Chhattisgarh was created by carving out its territory from that of the territories of the Madhya Pradesh by enacting the Madhya Pradesh Reorganisation Act, 2000 (wef 1 November 2000).

22. The State of Uttaranchal came into being on 9 November 2000 by separating its territory out of the territories of the Uttar Pradesh vide the Uttar Pradesh Reorganisation Act, 2000.

23. By enacting the Bihar Reorganisation Act, 2000, the State of Jharkhand was created on 15 November 2000 by carving its territory out of the territories of the Bihar State.

24. By enacting the Andhra Pradesh Reorganisation Act, 2014 the State of Telangana was separated from Andhra Pradesh on 2 June 2014, as a new 29th state of India, with the city of Hyderabad as its capital. Hyderabad will continue to serve as the joint capital city for Andhra Pradesh and Telangana for a period of not more than ten years.

25. The Jammu and Kashmir Reorganisation Act, 2019 provides for the reorganisation of the erstwhile State of Jammu and Kashmir into: (i) the Union Territory of Jammu and Kashmir with a Legislature; and (ii) the Union Territory of Ladakh without a Legislature, with effect from 31 October 2019.

26. The Dadra and Nagar Haveli and Daman and Diu (Merger of Union Territories) Act, 2019 merged the Union Territories of Dadra & Nagar Haveli, and Daman & Diu as the Union Territory of "Dadar and Nagar Haveli and Daman and Diu" with effect from 26-1-2020.

CHAPTER 7

CITIZENSHIP

1. Classification of Population. THE population of a State is divided into two classes—citizens and aliens.

2. Who are Citizens? Citizens are members of the political community to which they belong. They are the people who compose the State. Only a natural person can be a citizen, and not a juristic person like corporations.[1]

3. Citizenship v Nationality. While all citizens are nationals of a State, the reverse is not always true because nationality is a concept of international law while citizenship is a concept of municipal law.[2]

4. Constitutional Rights and Privileges to Citizens Over Aliens. The question of citizenship became particularly important at the time of the making of our Constitution because the Constitution sought to confer certain rights and privileges upon those who were entitled to Indian citizenship while they were to be denied to "aliens". While citizens enjoy full civil and political rights, aliens do not enjoy all of them. In other words, the latter were even placed under certain disabilities.

Thus, citizens of India have the following rights under the Constitution which aliens do not have:

(i) Some of the Fundamental Rights belong to citizens alone, such as Articles 15, 16, and 19.

(ii) Only citizens are eligible for certain offices, such as those of the President [*Article 58(1)(a)*]; Vice-President [*Article 66(3)(a)*]; Judge of the Supreme Court [*Article 124(3)*] or of a High Court [*Article 217(2)*]; Attorney-General [*Article 76(1)*]; Governor of a State [*Article 157*]; Advocate-General [*Article 165*].

(iii) The right of suffrage for election to the House of the People (of the Union) and the Legislative Assembly of every State [*Article 326*] and the right to become a member of Parliament [*Article 84*] and of the Legislature of a State [*Article 191(d)*] are also confined to citizens.

All the above rights are denied to aliens, whether they are "friendly" or "enemy" aliens. But "enemy aliens" suffer from a special disability; they are not entitled to the benefit of the procedural provisions in clauses (1)-(2) of Article 22 relating to arrest and detention. An alien enemy includes not only subjects of a

---

1. *State Trading Corporation of India Ltd. v CTO,* AIR 1963 SC 1811.
2. *State Trading Corporation of India Ltd. v CTO,* AIR 1963 SC 1811.

State at war with India but also Indian citizens who voluntarily reside in or trade with such a State.

5. Constitutional and Statutory Basis of Citizenship in India.

The Constitution, however, did not intend to lay down a permanent or comprehensive law relating to citizenship in India. It simply described the classes of persons who would be deemed to be the citizens of India *at the date of the commencement* of the Constitution and left the entire law of citizenship to be regulated by some future law made by Parliament [*Article 11*]. In exercise of this power, Parliament has enacted the Citizenship Act (57 of 1955), making elaborate provisions for the acquisition and termination of citizenship *subsequent to the commencement* of the Constitution; the provisions of this Act are to be read with the provisions of Part II of the Constitution, in order to get a complete picture of the law of Indian citizenship.

In view of the fact that the Act of Parliament only deals with the modes of acquisition of citizenship *subsequent* to the commencement of the Constitution, it would be convenient to deal with them separately.

6. Constitutional Provisions Relating to Citizenship.

Under Articles 5-8 of the Constitution, the following persons became citizens of India at the commencement of the Constitution (*i.e.*, 26 January 1950)—

I. Every person who is born as well as domiciled in the "territory of India"—irrespective of the nationality of his parents [*Article 5(a)*].

II. Every person who is domiciled in the "territory of India", either of whose parents was born in the territory of India—irrespective of the nationality of his parents or the place of birth of such person [*Article 5(b)*].

III. Every person who or whose father or mother was not born in India, but who (a) had his domicile in the "territory of India"; and (b) had been ordinarily residing in the territory of India for not less than five years[3] immediately preceding the commencement of the Constitution. In this case also, the nationality of the person's parents is immaterial [*Article 5(c)*]. Thus, a subject of a Portuguese Settlement, residing in India for not less than five years immediately preceding the commencement of the Constitution, with the intention of permanently residing in India, would become a citizen of India at the commencement of the Constitution.

The expression "every person", under Article 5, includes: (i) a prisoner; (ii) a member of the armed forces (but subject to Article 33).[4] Mere domicile is not sufficient to confer the citizenship of India on a person.[5]

IV. A person who had migrated from Pakistan, provided [*Article 6*]—

(a) he or either of his parents or grand-parents was born in "India" as defined in the Government of India Act, 1935 (as originally enacted); and

3. It is not necessary that the person should have resided in India for every day of this period; what is required is residence during the period without any serious break [*Evelyn Attaullah v Justin Attaullah,* AIR 1953 Cal 530].

4. *State of Maharashtra v Prabhakar Pandurang Sangzgiri,* AIR 1966 SC 424 : (1966) 1 SCR 702; *Sunil Batra v Delhi Administration,* AIR 1978 SC 1675 : (1978) 4 SCC 494; *Lt Col Prithi Pal Singh Bedi v UOI,* AIR 1982 SC 1413 : (1982) 3 SCC 140.

5. *DP Joshi v State of Bombay,* AIR 1955 SC 334 : (1955) 1 SCR 1215.

(b) (i) if he had migrated before 19 July 1948—he has ordinarily resided within the "territory of India" since the date of such migration (in this case, no registration of the immigrant is necessary for citizenship); or

(b) (ii) if he had migrated on or after 19 July 1948—he further makes an application before the commencement of this Constitution for registering himself as a citizen of India to an officer appointed by the Government of India, and is registered by that officer, being satisfied that the applicant has resided in the territory of India for at least six months before such application.

V. A person who migrated from India to Pakistan after 1 March 1947, but had subsequently *returned* to India under a permit[6] issued under the authority of the Government of India for resettlement or permanent return or under the authority of any law provided he gets himself registered in the same manner as under Article 6(b)(ii), as stated above [*Article 7*].

By 'migration' is meant voluntarily moving to India but not for a specific purpose and for a limited period of time.[7] Migration, referred to in Article 7, refers to migration between 1-3-1947 and 26-1-1950; and does not extend to migrations after that date, which will be governed by the Citizenship Act, 1955.[8]

VI. A person who, or any of whose parents or grand-parents, was born in "India" as defined in the Government of India Act, 1935 (as originally enacted) but who is ordinarily residing in any country outside India (whether *before or after* the commencement of this Constitution) on an application to the diplomatic or consular representative of India in the country of his residence [*Article 8*]. Provision was, thus, made for Indians living in foreign countries at the date of commencement of the Constitution.

Every person who is, or is deemed to be, a citizen of India under Articles 5 to 8 shall, subject to the provisions of the Citizenship Act, 1955, continue to be such citizen [*Article 10*]. This means that the law enacted by Parliament can make changes even in Articles 5 to 8.

6a. One Citizenship in India.

It should be noted in this context, that *our* Constitution, though federal, provides for one citizenship only, namely, the citizenship of India. In federal States like the *USA* and *Switzerland*, there is a dual citizenship, namely, federal or national citizenship and citizenship of the State where a person is born or permanently resides, and there are distinct rights and obligations flowing from the two kinds of citizenship. In India, a person born or resident in any State can acquire only one citizenship, namely, that of India and the civic and political rights which are *conferred by the Constitution* upon the citizens of India can be equally claimed by any citizens of India, irrespective of his birth and residence in any part of India.

Permanent residence within a State may, however, confer advantages in certain other matters, which should be noted in this context:

6. Permit should be a valid one [*Naziranbai v State*, AIR 1957 MB 1].
7. *Kulathil Mammu v State of Kerala*, AIR 1966 SC 1614; *Delhi Administration v Iqbal Mohammad*, AIR 1971 SC 472.
8. *State of Andhra Pradesh v Khader Abdul*, AIR 1961 SC 1467; *State of Madhya Pradesh v Peer Md*, AIR 1963 SC 645.

(a) So far as employments under the Union are concerned, there shall be no qualification for residence within any particular territory, but by Article 16(3) of the Constitution, Parliament is empowered to lay down that as regards any particular class or classes of employment *under a State* or a Union Territory residence within that State or Territory shall be a necessary qualification. This exception in the case of State employments has been engrafted for the sake of efficiency, insofar as it depends on familiarity with local conditions.

It is to be noted that it is Parliament which would be the sole authority to legislate in this matter and that State Legislatures shall have no voice. To this extent, invidious discrimination in different States is sought to be avoided. Parliament, in the exercise of this power, enacted the Public Employment (Requirement as to Residence) Act, 1957, for a temporary duration. By this Act, Parliament empowered the Central Government to make rules, having force for a specified period, prescribing a residential requirement only for appointment to non-Gazetted posts in Andhra Pradesh, Himachal Pradesh, Manipur and Tripura. Since the expiry of this Act in 1974, nobody can be denied employment in any State on the ground of his being a non-resident in that State.[9]

(b) As will be seen in the chapter on Fundamental Rights, Article 15(1), which prohibits discrimination on grounds only of race, religion, caste, sex or place of birth, does not mention *residence*. It is, therefore, constitutionally permissible for a State to confer special benefits upon its residents in matters other than those in respect of which rights are conferred by the Constitution upon all citizens of India. One of these, for instance, is the matter of levying fees for admission to State educational institutions. The Supreme Court has held that because discrimination on the ground of residence is not prohibited by Article 15, it is permissible for a State to offer a concession to its residents in the matter of fees for admission to its State Medical College.[10]

6b. Domicile.

"Domicile" has been defined to be the country which is taken to be a man's permanent home. In other words, "domicile" means the place where a person's habitation is fixed without any present intention of moving therefrom.[11]

Domicile is basically a legal concept for the purpose of determining what is the personal law applicable to an individual and even if an individual has no permanent home, he is invested with a domicile by law. There are two main classes of domicile: domicile of origin that is communicated by operation of law to each person at birth, that is the domicile of his father or his mother according as he is legitimate or illegitimate and domicile of choice which every person of full age is free to acquire in substitution for that which he presently possesses. The domicile of origin attaches to an individual by birth while the domicile of choice is acquired by residence in a territory subject to a distinctive legal system, with the intention to reside there permanently or indefinitely. Now the area of domicile, whether it be domicile of origin or domicile of choice, is the country

9. *Pandurangrao v APPSC,* AIR 1963 SC 268, p 272 : (1963) 1 SCR 707.
10. *DP Joshi v State of Bombay,* AIR 1955 SC 334 : (1955) 1 SCR 1215.
11. *Central Bank of India v Ram Narain,* AIR 1955 SC 36.

which has the distinctive legal system and not merely the particular place in the country where the individual resides.[12]

The Constitution recognises only one domicile, namely, the domicile in India. Article 5 of the Constitution is clear and explicit on this point and it refers only to one domicile, namely, "domicile in the territory of India". The legal system which prevails throughout the territory of India is one single indivisible system. Though different domicile rules in different States actually defeat the advantages of single-citizenship. It engenders provincialism. The concept of "domicile" has no relevance to the applicability of municipal laws, whether made by the Union of India or by the States. It would not, therefore, be right to say that a citizen of India is domiciled in one State or another, forming part of the Union of India. The domicile which he has, is only one domicile, namely, domicile in the territory of India. When a person who is permanently resident in one State goes to another State with the intention to reside there permanently or indefinitely, his domicile does not undergo any change: he does not acquire a new domicile of choice. His domicile remains the same, namely, Indian domicile. Moreover, to think in terms of state domicile will be highly detrimental to the concept of unity and integrity of India.[13]

7. The Citizenship Act, 1955. The various modes of acquisition of citizenship prescribed by the Citizenship Act, 1955, are discussed in the ensuing paragraphs.

7a. Citizenship by Birth. Every person born in India—(i) on or after 26 January 1950, but before the 1 July 1987; (ii) on or after 1 July 1987 but before the commencement of the Citizenship (Amendment) Act, 2003 (*i.e.*, up to 2-12-2004) and either of whose parents is a citizen of India at the time of his birth; (iii) on or after the commencement of the Citizenship (Amendment) Act, 2003 (*i.e.*, 3-12-2004) where—(I) both of his parents are citizen of India; or (II) one of whose parents is a citizen of India and the other is not an illegal migrant[14] at the time of his birth, shall be a citizen of India by birth. However, a

---

12. *Halsbury's Laws of England,* 4th Edn, vol 8, paras 421 & 422; *Wicker v Homes,* [1858] 7 HL Cases 124; *UOI v Rashid,* (1969) 2 SCWR 52; *Kedar Pandey v Narain Bikram Sah,* AIR 1966 SC 160; *Raza Dabshani v State of Bombay,* AIR 1966 SC 1436; *State of Bihar v Amar Singh Kumar,* AIR 1955 SC 282; *Dr Tanvi Behl v Shrey Goel,* AIR 2025 SC 1445 : AIROnline 2025 SC 99.
13. *Dr Pradeep Jain v UOI,* AIR 1984 SC 1420 : (1984) 3 SCC 654; *Madhu Arya v State of Uttarakhand,* AIR 2011 Uttar 50; *Animesh Sil v State of Bihar,* (2011) 1 Pat LJR 1164 (Pat—DB); *Smriti Sinha v State of Jharkhand,* AIR 2003 Jhar (NOC) 431.
14. The expression "illegal migrant", as per section 2(1)(*b*), means a foreigner who has entered into India—
    (i) without a valid passport or other travel documents and such other document or authority as may be prescribed by or under any law in that behalf; or
    (ii) with a valid passport or other travel documents and such other document or authority as may be prescribed by or under any law in that behalf but remains therein beyond the permitted period of time.

    Provided that any person belonging to Hindu, Sikh, Buddhist, Jain, Parsi or Christian community from Afghanistan, Bangladesh or Pakistan, who entered into India on or before 31-12-2014 and who has been exempted by the Central Government by or under section 3(2)(*c*) of the Passport (Entry into India) Act, 1920 or from the application of the provisions of the Foreigners Act, 1946 or any rule or order made thereunder, shall not be treated as illegal migrant for the purposes of this Act.

person shall not be a citizen of India by virtue of mere birth if at the time of his birth—(a) either his father or mother possesses such immunity from suits and legal process as is accorded to an envoy of a foreign sovereign power accredited to the President of India and he or she, as the case may be, is not a citizen of India; or (b) his father or mother is an enemy alien and the birth occurs in a place then under occupation by the enemy [*section 3 of the 1955 Act*].

7b. Citizenship by Descent.

Broadly speaking, a person born outside India (i) on or after 26 January 1950, but before the 10 December 1992, if his father is a citizen of India at the time of his birth; or (ii) on or after the 10 December 1992, if either of his parents is a citizen of India at the time of his birth, shall be a citizen of India by descent. However, a minor[15] who is a citizen of India by virtue of descent and is also a citizen of any other country shall cease to be a citizen of India if he does not renounce the citizenship or nationality of another country within six months of attaining full age[16] [*section 4 of the 1955 Act*].

7c. Citizenship by Registration.

Several classes of persons (who have not otherwise acquired Indian citizenship) can acquire Indian citizenship by registering themselves to that effect before the prescribed authority, *e.g.*, persons of Indian origin who are ordinarily resident in India and have been so resident for seven years immediately before making the application for registration; persons who are married to citizens of India; a person of full age and capacity who has been registered as an Overseas Citizen of India for five years and who has been residing in India for one year before making an application for registration [*section 5 of the 1955 Act*].

7d. Citizenship by Naturalisation.

A foreigner, not being an illegal migrant, can acquire Indian citizenship, on application for naturalisation to the Government of India [*section 6 of the 1955 Act*].

7e. Citizenship by Incorporation of Territory.

If any new territory becomes a part of India, the Government of India shall specify the persons of that territory who shall be the citizens of India [*section 7 of the 1955 Act*].

7f. Citizenship by Assam Accord.

In 1985, a special provision was also added as to citizenship of persons of Indian Origin covered by the Assam Accord. Under sub-section 2 of section 6A, two conditions are required to be satisfied—(i) persons who are of Indian Origin (undivided India) came before 1 January 1966 to Assam from the specified territory; and (ii) have been "ordinarily resident" in Assam as it existed in 1985 since the date of entry in Assam [*section 6A of the 1955 Act*].[17]

7g. Overseas Citizenship.

The Government of India in 2003 and 2005, by amending the Citizenship Act, 1955, introduced the concept of Overseas Citizenship of India, which most people mistakenly referred to as "dual citizenship" provision. Persons of Indian Origin of certain categories who migrated from India and acquired citizenship of a foreign country,

---

15. A person who has not attained the age of 18 years.
16. A person shall be deemed to be of full age if he is not a minor, and of full capacity if he is not of unsound mind.
17. *State of Arunachal Pradesh v Khudiram Chakma*, AIR 1994 SC 1461.

other than Pakistan and Bangladesh, are eligible to be granted an Overseas Citizenship of India on an application made in this behalf to the Central Government as long as their home country allow dual citizenship in some form or the other under their local laws.

Citizenship (Amendment) Act, 2015: In 2015, the Citizenship (Amendment) Act, 2015 was passed by Parliament substituting the words "overseas citizen of India" with the words "Overseas Citizen of India (OCI) Cardholder" and making enabling provisions for registration of OCI Cardholder, conferment of certain rights on such citizens, renunciation of overseas citizenship and cancellation of registration as Overseas Citizen of India Cardholder [*sections 7A-7D of the 1955 Act*]:

(i) *Registration and conferment of rights on OCI Cardholder:* The Act outlines certain qualifications for registering a person as an Overseas Citizen of India. The Act provides certain additional grounds for registering for an Overseas Citizen of India Card. These are: (i) a minor child whose parent(s) are Indian citizens; or (ii) spouse of foreign origin of an Indian citizen or spouse of foreign origin of an Overseas Citizen of India cardholder subject to certain conditions; or (iii) great grandchild of a person who is a citizen of another country, but who meets one of several conditions (*for example,* the great grandparent must be a citizen of India at the time of commencement of the Constitution or any time afterwards).

An Overseas Citizen of India is entitled to some benefits[18] such as a multiple-entry, multi-purpose lifelong visa to visit India. However, he is not entitled to certain rights conferred on an Indian citizen, such as equality of opportunity in matters of public employment; election as President and Vice-President; appointment as a Judge of the Supreme Court and High Courts; registration as a voter.[19]

---

18. What is meant to be granted to OCIs is a limited right, which is a statutory right and not a fundamental or constitutional right. The grant of the limited right is by the Central Government by notification. Therefore, what right is granted depends on the policy of the Central Government. It is not automatic on the attaining of the status of an OCI. There cannot be a presumption that a right that is not taken away by a notification is deemed to have been granted. See *Sorab Singh Gill v UOI,* WP No. 18093 of 2009, dated 18-3-2010 (Punj); *Karm Kumar v UOI,* (2010) SCC OnLine Del 2579; *Pranav Bajpe v State of Karnataka,* WA 1177 of 2019, dated 9-12-2020 (Karn).

Refer, Ministry of Home Affairs, Notification No. SO 1050(E), dated 4-3-2021. Though the impugned notification dated 4-3-2021 is based on a policy and in the exercise of the statutory power of a Sovereign State, the provisions as contained therein shall apply prospectively only to persons who are born in a foreign country subsequent to 4-3-2021, *i.e.,* the date of the notification and who seek for a registration as OCI cardholder from that date since at that juncture the parents would have a choice to either seek for citizenship by descent or to continue as a foreigner in the background of the subsisting policy of the Sovereign State. Hence, the notification being sustainable prospectively, the impugned portion of the notification which provides for supersession of the notifications dated 11-4-2005, 5-1-2007 and 5-1-2009 and the clause 4(*ii*), its proviso and *Explanation* (1) thereto shall operate prospectively in respect of OCI cardholders who have secured the same subsequent to 4-3-2021 [*Anushka Rengunthwar v UOI,* (2023) 2 MLJ 35 (SC) : LNIND 2023 SC 77].

19. Refer, Ministry of Home Affairs (Foreigners Division), Order, F. No. 26011/52/2016-OCI, dated 11-12-2017 and Ministry of Home Affairs (Foreigners Division), Order, F. No. 26011/52/2016-OCI, dated 2-8-2018.

The Citizenship Act provides that any person who is/has been a citizen of Pakistan or Bangladesh or any other country which is notified by the Central Government will be ineligible to apply for Overseas Citizenship of India. The Amending Act 2015 extends this provision to cover persons whose parents/grandparents/great grandparents were citizens of any of the above countries.

The Act also introduces a new provision which allows the Central Government to register a person as an Overseas Citizen of India cardholder even if she/he does not satisfy any of the listed qualifications. This is permissible if special circumstances exist.[20]

(ii) *Renunciation and cancellation of overseas citizenship*: The Act provides that where a person renounces their overseas citizenship, their minor child shall also cease to be an Overseas Citizen of India. The Amending Act extends this provision to cover spouses of Overseas Citizen of India cardholders. The Amending Act also allows the Central Government to cancel the Overseas Citizenship of India card where it is obtained by the spouse of an Indian citizen or Overseas Citizen of India cardholder, if: (i) the marriage is dissolved by a court; or (ii) the spouse enters into another marriage even while the first marriage has not been dissolved.

(iii) *Merger of Overseas Citizen of India and Persons of Indian Origin schemes*: Currently, the Central Government provides for schemes for Indian origin persons, and their families, the Persons of Indian Origin card and the Overseas Citizen of India card. Persons of Indian Origin enjoy fewer benefits than Overseas Citizens of India. For example, they are entitled to visa free entry into India for 15 years, while Overseas Citizens of India are provided a lifelong visa. The Amending Act provides that the Central Government may notify that Persons of Indian Origin cardholders shall be considered to be Overseas Citizen of India cardholders from a specified date, *i.e.*, 9 January 2015 *vide Ministry of Home Affairs, Notification, F. No. 26011/01/2014-IC, dated 9-1-2015.*

Thus, the concept of OCI Cardholder is distinct from Indian citizenship not only with regard to the procedure for grant of citizenship and the privileges consequent upon registration but also with regard to the cancellation of the citizenship.[21]

7h. Accelerated Citizenship to Persecuted Religious Minorities from Afghanistan, Pakistan or Bangladesh.

The migrants from Hindu, Sikh, Buddhist, Jain, Parsi or Christian communities from Afghanistan, Pakistan or Bangladesh, who had entered into India without valid travel documents or if the validity of their documents had expired, were regarded as "illegal migrants" and were ineligible to apply for Indian citizenship under section 5 or section 6 of the Citizenship Act, 1955.

Before the enactment of the Citizenship Amendment Act, 2019, the said migrants had been exempted from the adverse penal consequences of the Passport (Entry into India) Act, 1920 and the Foreigners Act, 1946. Subsequently in 2016, the Central Government made them eligible for long term visa to stay in India.

20. Ministry of Home Affairs (Foreigners Division), Order, F. No. 26011/158/2016-OCI, dated 11-1-2019.
21. *Satish Nambiar v UOI,* AIR 2008 Bom 158.

The Citizenship Amendment Act, 2019 (47 of 2019) has amended the Citizenship Act, 1955, with effect from 10 January 2020, to provide for Indian Citizenship to migrants from persecuted religious minority communities [*i.e.*, Hindu, Sikh, Buddhist, Jain, Parsi or Christian] from Afghanistan, Pakistan or Bangladesh, who have entered into India up to the cut of date of 31 December 2014 [*section 2(1)(b), proviso*].[22] The Central Government or an authority specified by it shall grant the certificate of registration or certificate of naturalization, subject to such conditions, restrictions and manner as may be prescribed [*section 6B(1)*]. However, the provisions of section 6B shall not apply to tribal area of Assam, Meghalaya, Mizoram or Tripura as included in the Sixth Schedule to the Constitution and the area covered under "The Inner Line"[23] notified under the Bengal Eastern Frontier Regulation, 1873.

On 11 March 2024, the Ministry of Home Affairs officially announced the rules for the Citizenship Amendment Act, 2019 *vide Ministry of Home Affairs, Notification No. GSR 172(E), dated 11-3-2024.* The Citizenship (Amendment) Rules, 2024 amended the Citizenship Rules, 2009, *inter alia*, by inserting rules 10A, 11A and 13A, and amending rules 14, 15, 17 and 38.

8. Loss of Indian Citizenship.

The Citizenship Act, 1955, also lays down how the citizenship of India may be *lost*—whether it was acquired under the Citizenship Act, 1955, or prior to it under the provisions of the Constitution (*i.e.*, under *Articles* 5–8). It may happen in any of the three ways—renunciation, termination and deprivation:

(a) Renunciation is a voluntary act by which a person holding the citizenship of India as well as that of another country may abjure one of them [*section 8*].

(b) Termination shall take place by operation of law as soon as a citizen of India voluntarily acquires the citizenship of another country. However, this provision shall not apply to a citizen of India who, during any war in which India may be engaged, voluntarily acquires the citizenship of another country, until the Central Government otherwise directs. [*section 9*].

(c) Deprivation is a compulsory termination of the citizenship of India, by an order of the Government of India, if it is satisfied as to the happening of certain contingencies, *e.g.*, that Indian citizenship had been acquired by a person by fraud,[24] or that he has shown himself to be disloyal or disaffected towards the Constitution of India [*section 10*].

If a person has acquired citizenship of India and a question arises whether or not he has lost the citizenship by acquisition of the citizenship of another country, that question has to be resolved by the authority prescribed under the Citizenship Act, 1955.[25] The Central Government is vested with exclusive

22. According to Intelligence Bureau records, the immediate beneficiaries of the Amended Act will be 31,313 people, which include 25,447 Hindus, 5,807 Sikhs, 55 Christians, 2 Buddhists and 2 Parsis.

23. The Inner Line Permit, which include Arunachal Pradesh, Mizoram and Nagaland. The inclusion of Manipur in Inner Line Permit was also announced on 9 December 2019.

24. *Ghaurul Hasan v State of Rajasthan,* AIR 1967 SC 107.

25. *Lal Babu Hussein v Electoral Registration Officer,* (1995) 3 SCC 100 (SC).

jurisdiction to determine the foregoing question, and that question cannot be determined by any Court, either by suit or in a proceeding under Article 226 or under Article 32.[26]

If a person voluntarily migrates to a foreign State after 26-1-1950, he will lose his Indian citizenship under the provisions of the 1955 Act.[27]

9. National Register of Citizens (NRC).

As per section 14A of the Citizenship Act, 1955, the Central Government may compulsorily register every citizen of India and issue national identity card to him. The Central Government may maintain a National Register of India Citizens and for that purpose establish a National Registration Authority. Procedure to be followed for compulsory registration of citizens shall be such as may be prescribed.[28]

As of now, it has only been implemented for the State of Assam. However, it continues to be litigated in the Supreme Court. The experience with Assam NRC shows that many people were declared "foreigners" because their documents were deemed insufficient. In December 2022, audit by the Comptroller and Auditor General of India revealed several irregularities in the Assam NRC.

26. *State of Andhra Pradesh v Khader Abdul,* AIR 1961 SC 1467; *Akbar Khan v UOI,* AIR 1962 SC 70; *State of Madhya Pradesh v Peer Md,* AIR 1963 SC 645. See also *Ayub Khan Mohd v Commissioner of Police,* AIR 1965 SC 1623; *Moinuddin Syed Khawaja v Government of India,* AIR 1967 SC 1143.
27. *Abdul Sattar Haji Ibrahim Patel v State of Gujarat,* AIR 1965 SC 810.
28. See *Abdul Kuddus v UOI,* AIR 2019 SC 2834 : (2019) 6 SCC 604 (SC); *Sirajul Hoque v State of Assam,* (2019) 5 SCC 534 (SC); *Assam Public Works v UOI,* (2020) 11 SCC 778 (SC); *Assam Sanmilita Mahasangha v UOI,* (2019) 5 SCC 534 (SC).

CHAPTER 8

FUNDAMENTAL RIGHTS AND FUNDAMENTAL DUTIES

1. Individual and Fundamental Rights in England.

THE Constitution of England is *unwritten*. Hence, there is, in England, no code of Fundamental Rights as exists in the Constitution of the United States or in other written Constitutions of the world. This does not mean, however, that in England there is no recognition of those basic rights of the individual without which democracy becomes meaningless. The object, in fact, is secured here in a different way. The foundation of individual rights in England may be said to be negative, in the sense that an individual has the right and freedom to take whatever action he likes, so long as he does not violate any rule of the ordinary law of the land. Individual liberty is secured by judicial decisions determining the rights of individuals in particular cases brought before the courts.

The Judiciary is the guardian of individual rights in England as elsewhere; but there is a fundamental difference. While in England, the courts have the fullest power to protect the individual against executive tyranny, the courts are powerless as against legislative aggression upon individual rights. In short, there are no fundamental rights binding upon the Legislature in England. The English *Parliament* being theoretically "omnipotent", there is no law which it cannot change. As has been already said, the individual has rights, but they are founded on the ordinary law of the land which can be changed by Parliament like other laws. So, there is no right which may be said to be "fundamental" in the strict sense of the term. Another vital consequence of the supremacy of Parliament is that the English Court has no power of judicial review over legislation at all. It cannot declare any law as unconstitutional on the ground of contravention of any supposed fundamental or natural right.

2. Individual Rights between England and USA, Compared.

The fundamental difference in approach to the question of individual rights between England and the United States is that while the English were anxious to protect individual rights from the abuses of executive power, the framers of the American Constitution were apprehensive of tyranny not only from the Executive but also from the Legislature—*i.e.,* a body of men who for the time being form the majority in the Legislature.

3. American Bill of Rights.

So, the American Bill of Rights (contained in the first 10 Amendments of the Constitution of the USA) is equally binding upon the Legislature as upon the Executive. The result has been the establishment in the United States of a "judicial supremacy", as opposed to the "Parliamentary supremacy" in England. The courts in the

United States are competent to declare an Act of Congress as unconstitutional on the ground of contravention of any provision of the Bill of Rights. Further, it is beyond the competence of the Legislature to modify or adjust any of the fundamental rights in view of any emergency or danger to the State. That power has been assumed by the Judiciary in the United States.

4. History of Demand for Fundamental Rights in India.

In *India,* the Simon Commission and the Joint Parliamentary Committee which were responsible for the Government of India Act, 1935, had rejected the idea of enacting declarations of fundamental rights on the ground that "abstract declarations are useless, unless there exist the will and the means to make them effective". But nationalist opinion, since the time of the Nehru Report,[1] was definitely in favour of a Bill of Rights, because the experience gathered from the British regime was that a subservient Legislature might serve as a handmaid to the Executive in committing inroads upon individual liberty.

Regardless of the British opinion, therefore, the makers of our Constitution adopted Fundamental Rights to safeguard individual liberty and also for ensuring (together with the Directive Principles) social, economic and political justice for every member of the community.[2] That they have succeeded in this venture is the testimony of an ardent observer of the Indian Constitution.[3]

> In India it appears that the Fundamental Rights have both created a new equality. . . and have helped to preserve individual liberty. . . The number of rights cases brought before high courts and the Supreme Court attest to the value of the Rights, and the frequent use of prerogative writs testifies to their popular acceptance as well. *The classic arguments against the inclusion of written rights in a Constitution have not been borne out in India.* In fact, the reverse may have been the case.

4a. Judiciary Competent to Declare a Law as Unconstitutional and Void.

So, the Constitution of India has embodied a number of Fundamental Rights in Part III of the Constitution, which are (subject to exceptions, to be mentioned hereafter) to act as limitations not only upon the powers of the Executive but also upon the powers of the Legislature. Though the model has been taken from the Constitution of the United States, the Indian Constitution does not go so far, and rather effects a compromise between the doctrines of Parliamentary sovereignty and judicial supremacy. On the other hand, the Parliament of India cannot be said to be sovereign in the English sense of legal omnipotence—for, the very fact that Parliament is created and limited by a written Constitution enables *our* Parliament to legislate only subject to the limitations and prohibitions imposed by the Constitution, such as, the Fundamental Rights, the distribution of legislative powers, etc. In case any of these limitations are transgressed, the Supreme Court and the high courts are competent to declare a law as unconstitutional and void. Now there is no blanket protection available to the laws inserted in the Ninth Schedule by constitutional amendments on or after 24 April 1973 (the date of the judgment of *Kesavananda*

1. Report published in 1928 by a Committee headed by Pandit Motilal Nehru which was appointed by the All Parties Conference to outline the principles for a Constitution of India.
2. Author's *Human Rights in Constitutional Law,* Prentice-Hall of India, 1994, pp 1, 41, and 46.
3. Granville Austin, *The Indian Constitution,* 1966, p 114.

Bharati v State of Kerala)[4] and it shall be a matter of constitutional adjudication by examining the nature and extent of infraction of fundamental rights by a statute, sought to be constitutionally protected.[5] So far as the contravention of Fundamental Rights is concerned, this duty is specially enjoined upon the courts by the Constitution [*Article* 13], by way of abundant caution. Clause (2) of Article 13 says—

> The State shall not make any law which takes away or abridges the rights conferred by this Part and any law made in contravention of this clause shall, to the extent of the contravention, be void.

To this extent, *our* Constitution follows the *American* model rather than the English.

4b. Judiciary's Powers Weaker than Legislature. But the powers of the Judiciary *vis-a-vis* the Legislature are weaker in India than in the United States in the following respects:

Firstly, while the declarations in the American Bill of Rights are absolute and the power of the State to impose restrictions upon the fundamental rights of the individual in the collective interests had to be evolved by the Judiciary—in India, this power has been expressly conferred upon the Legislatures by the Constitution itself in the case of the major fundamental rights, of course, leaving a power of judicial review in the hands of the Judiciary to determine the reasonableness of the restrictions imposed by the Legislature.

Secondly, by a somewhat hasty step, the Janata Government, headed by Morarji Desai, has taken out an important fundamental right, namely, the right of Property, by omitting Articles 19(1)(*f*) and 31, by the 44th Amendment Act, 1978. Of course, the provision in Article 31(1) has, by the same amendment, been transposed to a new article— Article 300A, which is *outside* Part III of the Constitution and has been labelled as "Chapter IV" of Part XII (which deals with "Finance, Property, Contracts and Suits")—but that is not a "fundamental right".

While under the Congress rule for 30 years, the ambit of the Fundamental Rights embodied in Part III of the original Constitution had been circumscribed by multiple amendments, bit by bit, the death blow to one of the Fundamental Rights came from the Janata Government.

The net result of the foregoing amendments inflicted upon the right to property are—

(i) The right not to be deprived of one's property save by authority of law is no longer a "fundamental right". Hence, if anybody's property is taken away by executive fiat without the authority of law or in contravention of a law, the aggrieved individual shall have no right to move the Supreme Court under Article 32.

(ii) If a Legislature makes a law depriving a person of his property, he cannot challenge the reasonableness of the restrictions imposed by such law, invoking Article 19(1)(*f*), because that provision has *ceased to exist.*[6]

---

4. *Kesavananda Bharati v State of Kerala,* AIR 1973 SC 1461 : (1973) 4 SCC 225.
5. *IR Coelho (dead) by LRs v State of Tamil Nadu,* AIR 2007 SC 861 : (2007) 2 SCC 1..
6. This amendment, thus, silences that voice of the Judiciary which had been articulated, prior to 1978, through cases such as *Kochunni v State of Madras,* AIR 1960 SC 1080, p *1092* : (1960) 3 SCR 887; *Panipat Sugar Mills v UOI,* AIR 1973 SC 537 : (1973) 1 SCC 129; *Saraswati Syndicate v UOI,* AIR 1975 SC 460 : (1974) 2 SCC 630.

(iii) Since clause (2) of Article 31 has vanished, the individual's right to property is no longer a guarantee against the Legislature in respect of any compensation for loss of such property. Article 31(2) [in the original Constitution] embodied the principle that if the State makes a compulsory acquisition or requisitioning of private property, it must (a) make a law; (b) such law must be for a public purpose; and (c) some compensation must be paid to the expropriated owner.

Of course, by the 25th Amendment of 1971, during the regime of Mrs Gandhi, the requirement of "compensation" was replaced by "an amount", the adequacy of which could no longer be challenged before the Courts. Nevertheless, the Supreme Court held, the aggrieved individual might complain if the "amount" so offered was *illusory* or amounted to "confiscation".[7] But even such an innocuous possibility has been foreclosed by the 44th Amendment.

The short argument advanced in the Statement of Objects and Reasons of the 45th Amendment Bill for deleting the fundamental right to property is that it was only being converted into a *legal* right. What is meant is that while Article 19(1)(*f*) and 31(2) of the *original* Constitution operated as limitations on the Legislature itself, the 45th Amendment Bill installs the Legislature as the guardian of the individual's right to property, without any fetter on its goodwill and wisdom. But if the Legislature could be presumed to be so infallible and innocent, this would be a good argument for omitting *all* the fundamental rights from Part III. As it has been pointed out earlier, the very justification of putting limitations on the Legislature by adopting a guarantee of Fundamental Rights is that history has proved that the group of human beings constituting, for the time being, the majority in a Legislative body, are not always infallible and that is why constitutional safeguards are necessary to permanently protect the individual from legislative tyranny.

Thirdly, by subsequent amendments, the arena of Fundamental Rights has been narrowed down by introducing certain exceptions to the operation of fundamental rights, namely, Articles 31A, 31B, 31C, and 31D.[8]

(a) Of these, Articles 31A, and 31C are exceptions to the fundamental rights enumerated in Articles 14 and 19; this means that any law falling under the ambit of Article 31A (eg, a law for agrarian reform), or Article 31C (a law for the implementation of any of the Directive Principles contained in Part IV of the Constitution), cannot be invalidated by any Court on the ground that it contravenes any of the fundamental rights guaranteed by Article 14 (equality before law); Article 19 (freedom of expression, assembly, etc.).

(b) Article 31B, however, offers almost complete exception to all the fundamental rights enumerated in Part III. If any enactment is included in the Ninth Schedule, which is to be read along with Article 31B, then such enactment shall be immune from constitutional invalidity on the ground of contravention of any of the fundamental rights. But shall be open to challenge on the ground of

7. *Cf Kesavananda Bharati v State of Kerala,* AIR 1973 SC 1461, pp *1554, 1606, 1637, 1776, 2051*; *State of Karnataka v Ranganatha,* AIR 1978 SC 215, p *228* : (1977) 4 SCC 471.

8. Article 31D, which had been inserted by the Constitution (42nd Amendment) Act, 1976, has since been repealed by the 43rd Amendment Act, 1977.

damage to the basic structure of the Constitution subsequent to 24 April 1973 (ie, the date of decision in *Kesavananda's* case).[9]

(c) The right to property is now considered to be not only a constitutional or statutory right but also a human right. Human rights have been historically considered in the realm of individual rights such as, right to health, right to livelihood, right to shelter and employment etc. but now human rights are gaining a multifaceted dimension. Right to property is also considered very much a part of the new dimension. Therefore, even claim of adverse possession has to be read in that context. With the expanding jurisprudence of the European Court of Human Rights, the court has taken an unkind view to the concept of adverse possession. Therefore, it will have to be kept in mind that the courts around the world are taking an unkind view toward statutes of limitation overriding property rights.[10]

Fourthly, by the 42nd Amendment Act, 1976, a countervailing factor has been introduced, namely, the Fundamental Duties mentioned in Article 51A. Though these Duties are not themselves enforceable in the courts nor their violation, as such, punishable, nevertheless, if a court, before which a fundamental right is sought to be enforced, has to read all parts of the Constitution, it may refuse to enforce a fundamental right at the instance of an individual who has patently violated any of the Duties specified in Article 51A.[11] If so, the emphasis of the original Constitution on fundamental rights has been minimised.

Fifthly, the category of "fundamental rights" under our Constitution is exhaustively enumerated in Part III of the Constitution. The *American* Constitution (Ninth Amendment) expressly says that *the enumeration of certain rights* in the Bill of Rights "shall not be construed to deny or disparage others *retained* by the people". This rests on the theory of inalienable natural rights which can by no means be lost to the individual in a free society; the guarantee of some of them in the written Constitution cannot, therefore, render obsolete any right which inhered in the individual even before the Constitution, eg, the right to engage in political activity. But there is no such unenumerated right under *our* Constitution.

As was observed in the early case of *A K Gopalan v State of Madras,*[12] the Legislatures under *our* Constitution being sovereign except insofar as their sovereignty has been limited by the Constitution either expressly or by necessary implication, the courts cannot impose any limitation upon that sovereignty either on the theory of the "spirit of the Constitution" or of that of "natural rights", ie, rights other than those which are enumerated in Part III of the Constitution.[13]

9. See Author's *Constitutional Law of India,* Prentice-Hall of India, 1991, pp 109, *et seq.*
10. *P T Munichikkanna Reddy v Revamma,* AIR 2007 SC 1753 : (2007) 6 SCC 59; Universal Declaration of Human Rights, 1948 under section 17(i) and 17(ii) also recognises right to property: "17 (i) Everyone has the right to own property alone as well as in association with others. (ii) No-one shall be arbitrarily deprived of his property".
11. This is the result specifically provided for in Article 59 of the 1977—Soviet Constitution: "Citizens' exercise of their rights and freedoms is inseparable from the performance of their duties and obligations".
12. *A K Gopalan v State of Madras,* AIR 1950 SC 27 : (1950) 1 SCR 88.
13. This proposition has been buttressed by the decision in *ADM Jabalpur v Shivkant Shukla,* AIR 1976 SC 1207 : (1976) 2 SCC 521, that the embodiment of certain rights as

[Footnote No. 13 Contd.]

Any expansion of the Fundamental Rights under the Indian Constitution must, therefore, rest on judicial interpretation and the Supreme Court has gone ahead in this direction by enlarging the scope of Article 21.[14]

It should not be supposed, however, that there is no other justiciable right provided by *our* Constitution outside Part III. Limitations upon the State are imposed by other provisions of the Constitution and these limitations give rise to corresponding rights to the individual to enforce them in a court of law if the Executive or the Legislature violates any of them. Thus, Article 265 says that "no tax shall be levied or collected except by authority of law". This provision confers a right upon an individual not to be subjected to arbitrary taxation by the Executive, and if the Executive seeks to levy a tax without legislative sanction, the aggrieved individual may have his remedy from the courts.[15] Tax illegally levied must be refunded since its retention may offend Article 265 of the Constitution.[16] The new provision in Article 300A belongs to this category.[17] Similarly, Article 301 says that "subject to the provisions of this Part, trade, commerce and intercourse throughout the territory of India shall be free". If the Legislature or the Executive imposes any restriction upon the freedom of trade or intercourse which is not justified by the other provisions of Part XIII of the Constitution, the individual who is affected by such restriction may challenge the action by appropriate legal proceedings.[18]

What, then, is the distinction between the "fundamental rights" included in Part III of the Constitution and those rights arising out of the limitations contained in the other Parts[19] which are equally justiciable? Though the rights of both these classes are equally justiciable, the constitutional remedy by way of an application direct to the Supreme Court under Article 32, which is itself included in Part III, as a "fundamental right", is available only in the case of *fundamental*

[Footnote No. 13 Contd.]

"fundamental rights" in Part III of the Constitution has completely replaced the pre-Constitution rights founded on common law or otherwise; for instance, the right to personal liberty is exclusively contained in Article 21 and the validity of any law depriving personal liberty, today, cannot be challenged on the ground of violation of any common law rule in that behalf (paras 61, 77, 83, 247, 264, 280). But the situation has been muddled because some Judges have asserted "Rule of Law" to be a "basic feature" of our Constitution, — apart from its specific and express provisions [*Indira Nehru Gandhi v Raj Narain,* AIR 1975 SC 2299 (Ray CJ, Khanna J, Chandrachud J)].

14. Eg, right to travel abroad deduced from "personal liberty" in Article 21 [*Maneka v UOI,* AIR 1978 SC 597, para 54 : (1978) 1 SCC 248, **affirming** *Satwant Singh Sawhney v D Ramarathnam Assistant Passport Officer,* AIR 1967 SC 1836, p *1844–45*]; so also right to privacy deduced from Article 19 and 21 [*Justice K S Puttaswamy v UOI,* AIR 2017 SC 4161 (a nine judge Bench). Similarly, the rights to speedy trial and free legal aid have been deduced from Article 21 [*Sheela v UOI,* AIR 1986 SC 1773 : 1986 SCC (Cr) 337: (1986) 3 SCC 596 : (1986) 3 SCR 443; *Suk Das v Arunachal Pradesh,* AIR 1986 SC 991 : (1986) 2 SCC 401].
15. *State of Kerala v Joseph,* AIR 1958 SC 296 : 1958 Ker LT 362; *Firm Gulam Hussain Haji Yakub v State of Rajasthan,* AIR 1963 SC 379 : (1963) 2 SCR 255.
16. *Mafatlal Industries Ltd v UOI,* (1997) 5 SCC 536 : (1996) Supp 10 SCR 585; *CIT, Bhopal v Shelly Products,* (2003) 5 SCC 461; *State of Uttar Pradesh v Vam Organic Chemicals Ltd,* AIR 2003 SC 4650 : (2004) 1 SCC 225.
17. *Bishambhar v State of Uttar Pradesh,* AIR 1982 SC 33.
18. *Atiabari Tea Co v State of Assam,* AIR 1961 SC 232 : (1961) 1 SCR 809.
19. Excepting, of course, the non-justiciable rights, e.g., the "Directive Principles of State Policy", in Part IV.

rights. If the right follows from some *other* provision of the Constitution, say, Article 265 or Article 301, the aggrieved person may have his relief by an ordinary suit or, by an application under Article 226 to the high court, but an application under Article 32 shall not lie, unless the invasion of the non-fundamental right involves the violation of some fundamental right as well.[20]

5. Amendability of Fundamental Rights—a Basic Feature.

As the word "fundamental" suggests, under some Constitutions, fundamental rights are immune from constitutional amendment; in other words, they are conferred a special sanctity as compared with other provisions of the Constitution. But this principle has been rejected by the Indian Constitution, as it stands interpreted by amendments of the Constitution themselves and judicial decisions.

Of course, no part of the Constitution of India can be changed by ordinary legislation unless so authorised by the Constitution itself (*e.g.*, Article 4); but *all* parts of the Constitution except the basic features can be amended by an Amendment Act passed under Article 368, including the fundamental rights. This proposition has been established after a history of its own:

A. Until the case of *Golak Nath,*[21] the Supreme Court had been holding that no part of our Constitution was unamendable and that Parliament might, by passing a Constitution Amendment Act, in compliance with the requirements of Article 368, amend any provision of the Constitution, including the Fundamental Rights and Article 368 itself.[22]

According to this earlier view,[23] thus, the courts could act as the guardian of fundamental rights only so long as they were not amended by the Parliament of India by the required majority of votes. In fact, some of the amendments of the Constitution so far made were effected with a view to superseding judicial pronouncements which had invalidated social or economic legislation on the ground of contravention of fundamental rights. Thus, the narrow interpretation of clause (2) of Article 19 by the Supreme Court in the cases of *Ramesh Thappar v State of Madras*[24] and *Brij Bhushan v State of Delhi*[25] was superseded by the Constitution (First Amendment) Act, 1951, while the interpretation given to Article 31 in the cases of *State of West Bengal v Gopal,*[26] *Dwarkadas v Sholapur Spinning Co,*[27] and *State of West Bengal v Bela Banerjee,*[28] was superseded by the Constitution (Fourth Amendment) Act, 1955.

---

20. *Syed Ahmed v State of Mysore,* AIR 1975 SC 1443, para 6 : (1975) 2 SCC 131; *Dt. Collector v Ibrahim,* AIR 1970 SC 1275 : (1970) 1 SCC 386.
21. *Golak Nath v State of Punjab,* AIR 1967 SC 1643 : (1967) 2 SCR 762. According to the majority in *Kesavananda Bharati v State of Kerala,* AIR 1973 SC 1461, the "basic features" are not amendable at all, though, curiously, Fundamental Rights are not included in the list of basic features as formulated by the majority.
22. *Shankari Prasad v UOI,* (1952) SCR 89; *Sajjan Singh v State of Rajasthan,* AIR 1965 SC 845.
23. *Shankari Prasad v UOI,* (1952) SCR 89; *Sajjan Singh v State of Rajasthan,* AIR 1965 SC 845.
24. *Ramesh Thappar v State of Madras,* (1950) SCR 594.
25. *Brij Bhushan v State of Delhi,* (1950) SCR 605.
26. *State of West Bengal v Subodh Gopal,* (1954) SCR 587.
27. *Dwarkadas v Sholapur Spinning Co,* (1954) SCR 674; *State of West Bengal v Bela Banerjee,* (1954) SCR 558.
28. *State of West Bengal v Bela Banerjee,* (1954) SCR 558; *Ram Narain v State of Delhi,* AIR 1953 SC 277 : (1953) Cr LJ 1113.

B. But the Supreme Court cried halt to the process of amending the Fundamental Rights through the amending procedure laid down in Article 368 of the Constitution, by its much-debated decision in *Golak Nath v State of Punjab.* In *Golak Nath's case*, overruling its two earlier decisions in *Shankari Prasad* and *Sajjan Singh's* cases, the Supreme Court held that Fundamental Rights, embodied in Part III, had been given a "transcendental position" by the Constitution, so that no authority functioning under the Constitution, including Parliament exercising the amending power under Article 368, was competent to amend the Fundamental Rights.

C. But by the 24th Amendment Act, 1971, Articles 13 and 368 were amended to make it clear that Fundamental Rights were amendable under the procedure laid down in Article 368, thus *overriding* the majority decision of the Supreme Court in *Golak Nath v State of Punjab.*

The majority decision in *Kesavananda Bharati's* case upheld the validity of these amendments and also *overruled Golak Nath's case,* holding that *it is competent for Parliament* to amend Fundamental Rights under Article 368, which does not make any exception in favour of fundamental rights; nor does Article 13 comprehend Acts amending the Constitution itself. At the same time *Kesavananda's* case also laid down that there were implied limitations on the power to "amend" and that power cannot be used to alter the "basic features" of the Constitution.

A big limitation that stands in the way of Parliament, acting by a special majority, to introduce drastic changes in the Constitution, is the judicially innovated doctrine of "*basic features*" which can be eliminated only if a Bench larger than the "13-Judge Bench" in *Kesavananda's* case be prepared to overturn the decision in that case. In the meantime, applying *Kesavananda,* the majority of the Constitution Bench has invalidated clauses (4) and (5) of Article 368 as violative of the basic features of the Constitution.[29]

The Fundamental Rights form the basic structure of the Constitution. Any law that abrogates or abridges such rights would be violative of the doctrine of basic structure. Article 32 being a fundamental right, it is the duty of the court to ensure that no fundamental right is contravened or abridged by any statutory or constitutional provision.[30]

A violation of separation of powers need not rise to such a level that the Apex Court considers it an abrogation of the basic structure.[31] It is important to note that separation of powers between three organs–*the Legislature, the Executive* and *the Judiciary*–is also nothing but a consequence of principles of equality enshrined in Article 14 of the Constitution of India. Accordingly, breach of the separation of judicial powers, may amount to negation of equality under Article 14. Stated thus, a legislation can be invalidated on the basis of breach of the separation of powers, since such breach is negation of equality under Article 14 of the Constitution.[32]

---

29. *Minerva Mills v UOI,* AIR 1980 SC 1789, paras 21, 28.
30. *State of West Bengal v Committee for Protection of Democratic Rights,* (2010) 3 SCC 571.
31. *Mohmadhusen A K Shaikh v UOI,* AIR 2008 SC (Supp) 734 : (2009) 2 SCC 1, p 41 : (2009) 1 SCC (Crl) 620.
32. *State of Tamil Nadu v State of Kerala,* AIR 2014 SC 2407 : (2014) 12 SCC 696.

6. Classification of Fundamental Rights.

The provisions of Part III of *our* Constitution which enumerate the Fundamental Rights are more elaborate than those of any other existing written constitution relating to fundamental rights, and cover a wide range of topics.

I. The Constitution itself classifies the Fundamental Rights under seven groups as follows:

(a) Right to equality.

(b) Right to particular freedoms.

(c) Right against exploitation.

(d) Right to freedom of religion.

(e) Cultural and educational rights.

(f) Right to property.

(g) Right to constitutional remedies.

Of these, the right to property has been *eliminated* by the 44th Amendment Act, so that only *six* freedoms now remain, in Article 19(1). The rights falling under each of the six categories are shown in Table V, *post*.

II. Another classification which is obvious is from the point of view of persons to whom they are available. Thus—

(a) Some of the fundamental rights are granted only to *citizens*—(i) Protection from discrimination on grounds only of religion, race, caste, sex or place of birth [*Article 15*]; (ii) Equality of opportunity in matters of public employment [*Article 16*]; (iii) Freedoms of speech, assembly, association, movement, residence and profession [*Article 19*]; (iv) Cultural and educational rights of minorities [*Article 30*].

(b) Some of the fundamental rights, on the other hand, are available to *any person* on the soil of India—citizen or foreigner—(i) Equality before the law and equal protection of the Laws [*Article 14*]; (ii) Protection in respect of conviction against *ex post facto* laws, double punishment and self-incrimination [*Article 20*]; (iii) Protection of life and personal liberty against action without authority of law [*Article 21*]; (iv) Right against exploitation [*Article 23*]; (v) Freedom of religion [*Article 25*]; (vi) Freedom as to payment of taxes for the promotion of any particular religion [*Article 27*]; (vii) Freedom as to attendance at religious instruction or worship in State educational institutions [*Article 28*].

III. Some of the Fundamental Rights are *negatively* worded, as prohibitions to the State, *e.g.*, Article 14 says—"The State *shall not* deny to any person equality before the law . . ." Similar are the provisions of Articles 15(1); 16(2); 18(1); 20; 22(1); and 28(1). There are others, which *positively* confer some benefits upon the individual [*e.g.*, the right to religious freedom, under Article 25, and the cultural and educational rights, under Articles 29(1), and 30(1)].

IV. Still another classification may be made from the standpoint of the extent of limitation imposed by the different fundamental rights upon legislative power.

(i) On the one hand, we have some fundamental rights, such as under Article 21, which are addressed against the Executive but impose no limitation upon the Legislature at all. Thus, Article 21 simply says that—

> No person shall be deprived of his life or personal liberty except according to procedure established by law.

It was early held by our Supreme Court that a competent Legislature is entitled to lay down any procedure for the deprivation of personal liberty, and that the courts cannot interfere with such law on the ground that it is unjust, unfair or unreasonable. In this view, the object of Article 21 is not to impose any limitation upon the legislative power but only to ensure that the Executive does not take away a man's liberty except under the authority of a valid law, and in strict conformity with the procedure laid down by such law. In later cases, however, the Supreme Court has found it difficult to immunise laws made under Article 21 from attack on the ground of "unreasonableness" under a relevant clause of Article 19(1), or Article 14, and Supreme Court decisions show an increasing inclination in that direction.[33]

(ii) To the other extreme are Fundamental Rights which are intended as absolute limitations upon the legislative power so that it is not open to the Legislature to regulate the exercise of such rights, *e.g.*, the rights guaranteed by Articles 15, 17, 18, 20, and 24.

(iii) In between the two classes stand the rights guaranteed by Article 19 which itself empowers the Legislature to impose reasonable restrictions upon the exercise of these rights, in the public interest. Though the individual rights guaranteed by Article 19 are, in general, binding upon both the Executive and the Legislature, these "authorities" are permitted by the Constitution to make valid exceptions to the rights within limits imposed by the Constitution. Such grounds, in brief, are security of the state, public order, public morality and the like.

7. Fundamental Rights Available Against the State and Private Individuals.

All the above rights are available against the *State*. It is now settled that the rights which are guaranteed by Articles 19[34] and 21[35] are guaranteed against State action as distinguished from violation of such rights by *private individuals*. In case of violation of such rights by individuals, the ordinary legal remedies may be available but not the constitutional remedies.

"State action", in this context, must, however, be understood in a wider sense. For interpreting the words "State" wherever it occurs in the Part on Fundamental Rights, a definition has been given in Article 12 which says that, unless the context otherwise requires, "the State" will include not only the Executive and Legislative organs of the Union and the States, but also local bodies (such as municipal authorities) as well as "other authorities".[36] This latter expression refers to any authority or body of persons exercising the power to issue orders, rules, bye-laws or regulations having the force of law, *e.g.*, a Board having the power to issue statutory rules, or exercising governmental powers. Even the act

33. *Cf Maneka v UOI,* AIR 1978 SC 597, paras 54–56, 63 — a seven Judge Bench; *Sunil v Delhi Administration,* AIR 1978 SC 1675, para 228 : (1978) 4 SCC 494; *Hussainara Khatoon v State of Bihar,* AIR 1979 SC 1360, p *1365*; *State of Maharashtra v VG Champalal,* AIR 1981 SC 1675 (*1677*); *Sher Singh v State of Punjab,* AIR 1983 SC 465.
34. *Bishan Das v State of Punjab,* AIR 1961 SC 1570.
35. *Samdasani v Central Bank,* (1952) SCR 391.
36. *Ramana v IAAI,* AIR 1979 SC 1628.

of a private individual may become an act of the state if it is *enforced* or *aided* by any of the authorities just referred to.[37]

Unaided private minority schools over which the Government has no administrative control because of their autonomy under Article 30(1) of the Constitution is not State within the meaning of Article 12 of the Constitution.[38]

The Constitution (93rd Amendment) Act, 2005, inserting clause (5) of Article 15 and the Constitution (86th Amendment) Act, 2002, inserting Article 21A, do not alter the basic structure or framework of the Constitution and are declared constitutionally valid. The Right of Children to Free and Compulsory Education Act (or Right to Education Act), 2009 is not *ultra vires* Article 19(1)(*g*) of the Constitution. However, the Right of Children to Free and Compulsory Education Act, 2009 insofar as it applies to minority schools, aided or unaided, covered under clause (1) of Article 30 of the Constitution, is *ultra vires* the Constitution.[39]

Article 21-A was added by the Constitution (86th Amendment) Act, 2002 thus making free and compulsory education to children of the age of 6 to 14 years, a fundamental right, within the meaning of Part III of the Constitution.[40]

It should be noted, however, that there are certain rights included in Part III which are available not only against the State but also against private individuals, *e.g.*, Article 15(2) [equality in regard to access to and use of places of public resort]; Article 17 [prohibition of untouchability]; Article 18(3)-(4) [prohibition of acceptance of foreign title]; Article 23 [prohibition of traffic in human beings]; Article 24 [prohibition of employment of children in hazardous employment]. But these provisions in Part III are not *self-executory,* that is to say, these articles are not directly enforceable; they would be indirectly enforceable; only if some law is made to give effect to them, and such law is violated. It follows that the classification of fundamental rights into *executory* and *self-executory* is another possible mode of classification.

We may now proceed to a survey of the various fundamental rights, in particular.

8. Article 14—Equality before the Law and Equal Protection of the Laws.

Article 14 of the Constitution provides—

> The State shall not deny to any person equality before the law or the equal protection of the laws within the territory of India.

Prima facie, the expression "equality before the law" and "equal protection of the laws" may seem to be identical, but, in fact, they mean different things. While equality before the law is a somewhat *negative* concept implying the absence of any special *privilege* by reason of birth, creed or the like, in favour of any individual and the equal subjection of all classes to the ordinary

37. *Kochunni v State of Madras (I)*, AIR 1959 SC 725 (*730*).

38. *Mrs Satimbla Sharma v St Paul's Senior Secondary School,* AIR 2011 SC 2926 : (2011) 8 JT SC 611: (2011) 6 SLT 250 : LNIND 2011 SC 2635 .

39. *Pramati Educational and Cultural Trust v UOI,* AIR 2014 SC 2114 : (2014) 8 SCC 1.

40. The Legislature has enacted the Right of Children to Free and Compulsory Education Act, 2009 to provide for free and compulsory education to all children of the age of 6 to 14 years. The said Act was amended in 2019 to substitute section 16 of the Act so as to empower the appropriate Government to take a decision as to whether to hold back a child in the fifth class or in the eighth class or in both classes, or not to hold back a child in any class, till the completion of elementary education.

law—equal protection of the laws is a more *positive* concept, implying the *right* to equality of treatment in equal circumstances. It is well settled that guarantee of equality before law is a positive concept and cannot be enforced in a negative manner. If an illegality or an irregularity has been committed in favour of any individual or group of individuals, others cannot invoke the jurisdiction of courts and tribunals to require the state to commit the same irregularity or illegality in their favour.[41] If the method of allocation (of Coal Blocks by the Government) violates Article 14, the consequence of such illegal allocation must follow. The Supreme Court declared allotment of coal blocks by the Government since 1993 to 2011 as invalid, as the allotments were made i) without any objective criteria; ii) without application of mind; iii) without following guidelines or desired recommendations of Ministries or State Government concerned; iv) without assessment of comparative merit; and v) without assessment of applicant's requirements *vis-a-vis* capacity of block to be allotted.[42] Natural resources constitute public property/national asset, and while distributing them, the state is bound to act in consonance with the principles of equality and public trust, and ensure that no action is taken which may be detrimental to public interest. The grant of licences bundled with spectrum, is *ex-facie* arbitrarily illegal and violative of Article 14 of the Constitution.[43]

The concept of equality and equal protection of laws in its proper spectrum encompasses social and economic justice in a political democracy.[44] The principle of "equality" is the essence of democracy and accordingly a basic feature of Constitution.[45]

8a. Equality before the Law.

Equality before the law, as a student of English Constitutional law knows, is the second corollary from *Dicey's*[46] concept of the Rule of Law. Equality before law is correlative to the concept of Rule of Law for all round evaluation of healthy social order.[47] The doctrine of equality before law is a necessary corollary to the concept of the rule of law.[48] It is a declaration of equality of all persons within the territory of India, implying thereby the absence of any privilege in favour of any individual.[49] It means that no man is above the law of the land and that every person, whatever be his rank or status, is subject to the ordinary law and amenable to the jurisdiction of the ordinary tribunals. Against, every citizen from the Prime Minister down to the humblest peasant, is under the same responsibility for every act done by him without lawful justification and in this respect, there is no distinction between officials and private citizens. It follows that the position will be the same in India. But even in England, certain exceptions are recognised to the above rule of equality in the public interests.

41. *State of West Bengal v Debasish Mukherjee,* AIR 2011 SC 3667 (*3677*), see also *Fuljit Kaur v State of Punjab,* AIR 2010 SC 1937 : (2010) 11 SCC 455 (equality cannot be claimed in illegality).
42. *Manohar Lal Sharma v The Principal Secretary,* (2014) 9 SCC 614 : (2014) 9 SCC 516-A.
43. *Centre for Public Interest Litigation v UOI,* (2012) 3 SCC 1 : (2012) 2 Mad LJ 111 (SC).
44. *Dalmia Cement (Bharat) Ltd v UOI,* (1996) 10 SCC 104.
45. *M Nagraj v UOI,* AIR 2007 SC 71 : (2006) 8 SCC 212.
46. *Law of the Constitution,* 9th Edn, p 202.
47. *Dalmia Cement (Bharat) Ltd v UOI,* (1996) 10 SCC 104.
48. *Ashutosh Gupta v State of Rajasthan,* (2002) 4 SCC 34.
49. *Amita v UOI,* (2005) 13 SCC 721 : (2005) 7 JT SC 288 : (2005) 6 Scale 397.

The concept of equality before law does not involve the idea of absolute equality amongst all, which may be a physical impossibility. Article 14 guarantees the similarity of treatment and not identical treatment. Article 14 does not require that the legislative classification should be scientifically or logically perfect.[50] A person would be treated unequally only if that person was treated worse than others, and those others must be those who are "similarly situated" to the complainant.[51] Classification for the purpose of legislation cannot be done with mathematical precision. The legislature enjoys considerable latitude while exercising its wisdom taking into consideration myriad circumstances, enriched by its experience and strengthened by people's will. So long as the classification can withstand the test of Article 14, it cannot be questioned why one subject was included and the other left out and why one was given more benefit than the other.[52] The concept of equality permits rational or discriminating discrimination. Conferment of special benefits or protection or rights to a particular group of citizens for rational reasons is envisaged under Article 14 and is implicit in the concept of equality.[53] The right to equality under Article 14 of the Constitution is available against the State, it cannot be claimed against unaided private minority school.[54]

The exceptions allowed by the *Indian* Constitution are—

(1) The President or the Governor of a state shall not be answerable to any court for the exercise and performance of the powers and duties of his office or for any act done or purporting to be done by him in the exercise and performance of those powers and duties.

(2) No criminal proceeding whatsoever shall be instituted or continued against the President or a Governor in any court during his term of office.

(3) No civil proceeding in which relief is claimed against the President or the Governor of a state shall be instituted during his term of office in any court in respect of any act done or purporting to be done by him in his personal capacity, whether before or after he entered upon his office as President or Governor of such state, until the expiration of two months next after notice in writing has been delivered to the President or the Governor, as the case may be, or left at his office stating the nature of the proceedings, the cause of action therefor, the name, description any place of residence of the party by whom such proceedings are to be instituted and the relief which he claims [*Article* 361].

The above immunities, however, shall not bar—(i) Impeachment proceedings against the President. (ii) Suits or other appropriate proceedings against the Government of India or the Government of a state.

Besides the above constitutional exceptions, there will, of course, remain the exceptions acknowledged by the comity of nations in every civilized country, *e.g.*, in favour of foreign Sovereigns and ambassadors.

---

50. *Ashutosh Gupta v State of Rajasthan,* (2002) 4 SCC 34. See also *Dharam Dutt v UOI,* AIR 2004 SC 1295.
51. *Glanrock Estate (P) Ltd v State of Tamil Nadu,* (2010) 10 SCC 96, p *111* : (2010) 9 JT SC 568: (2010) 9 Scale 270.
52. *Ombalika Das v Hulisa Shaw,* (2002) 4 SCC 539.
53. *TMA Pai Foundation v State of Karnataka,* (2002) 8 SCC 481 : (2002) 9 JT SC 25.
54. *Satimbla Sharma v St Paul's Senior Secondary School,* AIR 2011 SC 2926.

8b. Equal Protection of the Laws.

Equal protection of the laws, on the other hand, would mean "that among equals, the law should be equal and equally administered, that likes should be treated alike. . ." Equal protection requires affirmative action by the State towards unequals by providing facilities and opportunities.[55] The "substantive equality" and "distributive justice" are at the heart of understanding of guarantee of "equal protection before the law". The State can treat unequals differently with the objective of creating a level playing field in the social economic and political spheres.[56]

In other words, it means the right to equal treatment in *similar circumstances* both in the privileges conferred and in the liabilities imposed by the laws.[57] Article 14 proceeds on the premise that equality of treatment is required to be given to persons who are equally circumstanced. Implicit in the concept of equality is the concept that the persons who are in fact unequally circumstanced, cannot be treated on a par.[58] However, unequals cannot be clubbed.[59] None should be favoured and none should be placed under any disadvantage, in circumstances that do not admit of any reasonable justification for a different treatment. Thus, it does not mean that every person shall be taxed equally, but that persons under the same character should be taxed by the same standard. What Article 14 prohibits is "class legislation" and not "classification for purpose of legislation". The legislature can classify persons for legislative purposes so as to bring them under a well-defined class. A classification would be justified unless it is patently arbitrary. If there is equality and uniformity in each group, the law would not become discriminatory though due to some fortuitous circumstances some included in a class get an advantage over others, but they should not be singled out for special treatment.[60] The classification should not be arbitrary; it should be reasonable and be based on qualities and characteristics that have relation to the object of legislation.[61]

But if there is any *reasonable* basis for classification, the Legislature would be entitled to make a different treatment. The legislature is competent to exercise its discretion and make classification.[62] The reasonable classification must be found on an intelligible differentia which distinguishes persons or things that are grouped together from those that are left out of the group and the differentia has a rational nexus to the object sought to be achieved by the legislation in question.[63] It is for the legislature to identify the class of the people to be given protection and on what basis such protection was to be given. The court cannot

---

55. *Panchayat Varga Shramajivi Samudaik Sahakari Khedut Co-op Society v Haribhai Mevabhai,* AIR 1996 SC 2578.
56. *UOI v Rakesh Kumar,* AIR 2010 SC 3244 : (2010) 4 SCC 50, p 73 : (2010) 2 SCR 483.
57. *State of West Bengal v Anwar Ali,* (1952) SCR 289; *Ramana v IAAI,* AIR 1979 SC 1628; *John Vallamation v UOI,* AIR 2003 SC 2902.
58. *TMA Pai Foundation v State of Karnataka,* (2002) 8 SCC 481.
59. *Onkar Lal Bajaj v UOI,* AIR 2003 SC 2562.
60. *State of Andhra Pradesh v Nallamilli Rami Reddi,* (2001) 7 SCC 708. See also *Dharam Dutt v UOI,* AIR 2004 SC 1295.
61. *John Vallamatom v UOI,* AIR 2003 SC 2902.
62. *Anukul Chandra Pradhan v UOI,* (1997) 6 SCC 1.
63. *National Council for Teacher Education v Shri Shyam Shikha Prakashan Sansthan,* (2011) 3 SCC 238 (*255*).

interfere.[64] State has wide discretion in respect of classification of objects, persons and things for the purposes of taxation.[65] The Legislature can devise classes for the purpose of taxing or not taxing, exempting or not exempting, granting incentives and prescribing rate of tax, benefits or concessions.[66] Thus, it may: (i) exempt certain classes of property from taxation at all, such as charities, libraries and the like; (ii) impose different specific taxes upon different trades and professions; (iii) tax real and personal property in different manner and so on.

The guarantee of "equal protection", thus, is a guarantee of equal treatment of persons in "equal circumstances", permitting differentiation in different circumstances. In other words—

> The principle of equality does not mean that every law must have universal application for all persons who are not by nature, attainment or circumstance in the same position as the varying needs of different classes of persons often require separate treatment.[67]
>
> The principle does not take away from the State the power of classifying persons for legitimate purposes.[68]
>
> A Legislature which has to deal with diverse problems arising out of an infinite variety of human relations must, of necessity, have the power of making special laws to attain particular objects; and for that purpose it must have large powers of selection or classification of persons and things upon which such laws are to operate.[69]

In order to be "reasonable", a classification must not be arbitrary, but must be rational, that is to say, it must not only be based on some qualities or characteristics which are to be found in all the persons grouped together and not in others who are left out but those qualities or characteristics must have a reasonable relation to the *object* of the legislation.[70] The reasonableness of a provision depends upon the circumstances obtaining at a particular time and the urgency of the evil sought to be controlled. The possibility of the power being abused is no ground for declaring a provision violative of Article 14.[71] In order to pass the test, two conditions must be fulfilled, namely, that: (1) the classification must be founded on an intelligible differentia which distinguishes those that are grouped together from others; and (2) that differentia must have a rational relation to the object sought to be achieved by the Act.[72]

In *Sukanya Shantha v UOI,*[73] the Supreme Court has summarised the constitutional standards laid down under Article 14 can be as follows: First, the Constitution permits classification if there is intelligible differentia and

---

64. *D C Bhatia v UOI,* (1995) 1 SCC 104.
65. *State of Kerala v Aravind Ramakant Modawdakar,* (1999) 7 SCC 400, para 6.
66. *State of Uttar Pradesh v Kamla Palace,* AIR 2000 SC 617 : (2000) 1 SCC 557, para 12.
67. *Dhirendra v Legal Remembrancer,* (1955) 1 SCR 224; *Sarbananda Sonowal v UOI,* AIR 2005 SC 2920.
68. *Chiranjit Lal v UOI,* (1950) 1 SCR 869.
69. *Onkar Lal Bajaj v UOI,* AIR 2003 SC 2562.
70. *Ameeroonissa v Mehboob,* (1953) SCR 404 (*414*); *Pathumma v State of Kerala,* AIR 1978 SC 771.
71. *J K Industries Ltd v Chief Inspector of Factories & Boilers,* (1996) 6 SCC 665, para 39.
72. *Amita v UOI,* (2005) 13 SCC 721 : (2005) 7 JT SC 288 : (2005) 6 Scale 397.
73. *Sukanya Shantha v UOI,* AIR 2024 SC 5201 : AIR Online 2024 SC 671.

reasonable nexus with the object sought. Second, the classification test cannot be merely applied as a mathematical formula to reach a conclusion. A challenge under Article 14 has to take into account the substantive content of equality which mandates fair treatment of an individual. Third, in undertaking classification, a legislation or subordinate legislation cannot be manifestly arbitrary, i.e. courts must adjudicate whether the legislature or executive acted capriciously, irrationally and/or without adequate determining principle, or did something which is excessive and disproportionate. In applying this constitutional standard, courts must identify the "real purpose" of the statute rather than the "ostensible purpose" presented by the State, as summarized in ADR. Fourth, a provision can be found manifestly arbitrary even if it does not make a classification. Fifth, different constitutional standards have to be applied when testing the validity of legislation as compared to subordinate legislation.

It is not possible to exhaust the circumstances or criteria which may accord a reasonable basis for classification in all cases. It depends on the object of the legislation in view and whatever has a reasonable relation to the *object or purpose* of the legislation is a reasonable basis for classification of the persons or things coming under the purview of the enactment. Thus—

(i) The basis of classification may be *geographical*.[74]

(ii) The classification may be according to difference in time.[75]

(iii) The classification may be based on the difference in the *nature* of the trade, calling or occupation, which is sought to be regulated by the legislation.[76]

Similarly, higher educational qualification is a permissible basis of classification for promotion[77] as it has nexus with higher efficiency on the promotional post.[78] A case of over classification shall be discriminatory and invalid as it would violate the provisions of Article 14 of the Constitution.[79]

Thus, it has been held that—

(a) In offences relating to women, *e.g.*, adultery (now declared unconstitutional by the Supreme Court, see discussion *infra*), women in India may be placed in a more favourable position, having regard to their social status and need for protection[80] (see under Article 15, *post*).

(b) In a law of prohibition, it would not be unconstitutional to differentiate between civil and military personnel, or between foreign visitors and Indian citizens—for they are not similarly circumstanced from the standpoint of need for prohibition of consumption of liquor.[81]

74. *TMA Pai Foundation v State of Karnataka,* (2002) 8 SCC 481.
75. *TMA Pai Foundation v State of Karnataka,* (2002) 8 SCC 481.
76. *Hathi Singh v UOI,* AIR 1960 SC 923; *State of Haryana v Jai Singh,* AIR 2003 SC 1696.
77. *T R Kothandraman v Tamil Nadu Water Supply & Drainage Board,* (1994) 6 SCC 282, para 16; *Assam State Electricity Board v Gajendra Nath Pathak,* (1997) 11 SCC 3, paras 6 and 7.
78. *Food Corp of India v Om Prakash Sharma,* AIR 1998 SC 2682 : (1998) 7 SCC 676, paras 19 and 32.
79. *P Venugopal v UOI,* (2008) 5 SCC 1.
80. *Yusuf v State of Bombay,* AIR 1954 SC 321.
81. *State of Bombay v Balsara,* (1951) 2 SCR 682.

(c) Exemption to the candidate who stood first in the Forest Rangers College from selection as Assistant Conservator by the Public Service Commission, it being based on reasonable classification, is not *ultra vires* Article 14.[82]

The guarantee of equal protection applies against substantive as well as procedural laws.[83] The decision-making process should be transparent, fair and open.[84] The procedure for distribution of State largesses must be transparent, just, fair and non-arbitrary. Non-transparency promotes nepotism and arbitrariness.[85] The role model for governance and decision taken thereof should manifest equity, fair play and justice. The cardinal principle of governance in a civilized society based on rule of law not only has to base on transparency but must create an impression that the decision-making was motivated on the consideration of probity. The Government has to rise above the nexus of vested interests and nepotism and eschew window-dressing. The act of governance has to withstand the test of judiciousness and impartiality and avoid arbitrary or capricious actions.[86] Hence the discretion vested by a statute is to be exercised fairly and judicially and not arbitrarily[87] but subject to the requirements of law.[88] In the absence of rules, the action of the government is required to be fair and reasonable.[89] From the standpoint of the latter, it means that all litigants, who are similarly situated, are able to avail themselves of the same procedural rights for relief and for defence, without discrimination. The discrimination presupposes, classification of similarly situated persons into different groups without any reasonable basis, for extending dissimilar benefits or treatment.[90]

Of course, if the differences are of a *minor* or *unsubstantial* character, which have not prejudiced the interests of the person or persons affected, there would not be a denial of equal protection.[91] Again, a procedure different from that laid down by the ordinary law can be prescribed for a particular class of persons if the discrimination is based upon a reasonable classification having regard to the object which the legislation has in view and the policy underlying it. Thus, in a law which provides for the externment of undesirable persons who are likely to jeopardize the peace of the locality, it is not an unreasonable discrimination to provide that a suspected person shall have no right to cross-examine the witnesses who depose against him, for the very object of the legislation which is an extraordinary one would be defeated if such a right were given to the suspected person.[92] In the Reference on the Special Courts Bill, 1978,[93] the Supreme Court has held that the setting up of a Special Court for the expeditious

82. *S Ramesha v State of Karnataka,* AIR 1996 SC 718.
83. *Lachmandas v State of Bombay,* (1952) SCR 710 (*726*).
84. *Dutta Associates Pvt Ltd v Indo Merchantiles Pvt Ltd,* (1997) 1 SCC 53, para 7.
85. *Common Cause, A Registered Society v UOI,* AIR 1996 SC 3538 : (1996) 6 SCC 530, paras 24 and 25 : *ABL International Ltd v Export Credit Guarantee Corporation of India Ltd,* (2004) 3 SCC 553.
86. *Onkar Lal Bajaj v UOI,* AIR 2003 SC 2562, para 36.
87. *Rakesh Kumar v Sunil Kumar,* AIR 1999 SC 935 : (1999) 2 SCC 489, para 21 :.
88. *Dharambir Singh v UOI,* (1996) 6 SCC 702, para 4.
89. *Style (Dress Land) v Union Territory, Chandigarh,* (1999) 7 SCC 89, para 10.
90. *State of Himanchal Pradesh v Anjana Devi,* (2009) 5 SCC 108.
91. *Amita v UOI,* (2005) 13 SCC 721 : (2005) 7 JT SC 288 : (2005) 6 Scale 397.
92. *Gurbachan v State of Bombay,* (1952) SCR 737, p *744*.
93. *Re The Special Courts Bill, 1978,* AIR 1979 SC 478, paras 74, 78, 80–89 — seven-Judge Bench).

trial of offences committed during the Emergency period [from 25 June 1975 to 27 March 1977] by high public officials, in view of the congestion of work in the ordinary criminal courts and in view of the need for a speedy termination of such prosecutions in the interests of the functioning of democracy under the Constitution of India, is a reasonable classification. But to include in the Bill any offence committed during any period prior to the Proclamation of Emergency in June, 1975, was unconstitutional inasmuch as such classification has no reasonable nexus with the object of the Bill. The provision under Article 14 of the constitution would be violated if there is arbitrary discrimination among the educational institutions similarly situated.[94]

Any procedure which comes in the way of a party in getting a fair trial would be violative of Article 14.[95] Article 14 of the Constitution should not be stretched too far, otherwise it will make the functioning of the administration impossible.[96]

The guarantee of equal protection includes absence of any *arbitrary* discrimination by the laws themselves or in the matter of their *administration.* Thus, even where a statute itself is not discriminatory, but the public official entrusted with the duty of carrying it into operation applies it against an individual, not for the purpose of the Act but *intentionally for the purpose of injuring him,* the latter may have that executive act annulled by the court on the ground of contravention of the guarantee of equal protection. Of course, it is for the aggrieved individual to establish beyond doubt that the law was applied against him by the public authority "*with an evil eye and an unequal hand*".[97] Wide discretionary power conferred by a statute on any authority must be exercised reasonably in furtherance of public policy and for the public good and the public cause. The authority must record reasons for the said exercise of power even if the statute does not expressly enjoin upon the authority to do so.[98] The action of "State" must satisfy the principal requirements of Article 14 *viz.*, treating persons similarly situated equally and grant of equal protection to them. Reasonableness and fairness is the heart and soul of Article 14.[99] In short, Article 14 hits "*arbitrariness*" of State action in any form.[100]

An act which is discriminatory is liable to be labelled as arbitrary.[101] Arbitrariness in the making of an order by an authority can manifest itself in different forms. Non-application of mind by the authority making the order is one of them. Application of mind is best demonstrated by disclosure of mind by

94. *State of Uttar Pradesh v Committee of MMTDSV Mandir*, (2010) 1 SCC 639.
95. *Dwarka Prasad Agarwal v B D Agarwal,* AIR 2003 SC 2686.
96. *Dilip Kumar Garg v State of Uttar Pradesh,* (2009) 4 SCC 753 (*757*).
97. *Amita v UOI,* (2005) 13 SCC 721 : (2005) 7 JT SC 288 : (2005) 6 Scale 397.
98. *Consumer Action Group v State of Tamil Nadu,* AIR 2000 SC 3060.
99. *Delhi Development Authority v Joint Action Committee, Allottee of SFS Flats,* (2008) 2 SCC 672, para 43.
100. *State of West Bengal v Committee for Protection of Democratic Rights,* (2010) 3 SCC 571; *Royappa v State of Tamil Nadu,* AIR 1974 SC 555; *Ajay v Khalid,* AIR 1981 SC 487; *D S Nakara v UOI,* AIR 1983 SC 130, para 14. *Budhan Choudhry v State of Bihar*, AIR 1955 SC 191 : (1955) 1 SCR 1045.
101. *State of Andhra Pradesh v Mc Dowell & Co,* AIR 1996 SC 1627 : (1996) 3 SCC 709, para 44.

the authority making the order and disclosure is best done by recording the reasons that led the authority to pass the order.[102]

The court will not interfere in the policy decisions of the Government unless the government-action is arbitrary or invidiously discriminatory.[103] The Government policy is not subject to judicial review unless it is demonstrably arbitrary, capricious, irrational, discriminatory or violative of constitutional or statutory provisions.[104]

Two wrongs do not make a right. A party cannot claim that, since something wrong has been done; direction should be given to do another wrong. It would not be setting a wrong right but would be perpetuating another wrong. In such matters there is no discrimination involved. The concept of equal treatment presupposes the existence of similar legal foothold and does not countenance repetition of a wrong action to bring forth wrongs on a par.[105]

It is the duty of state to allay fears of citizens regarding discrimination and arbitrariness.[106] However, protective discrimination in favour of SCs and STs is a part of Constitutional scheme of social and economic justice[107] to integrate them into the national mainstream so as to establish an integrated social order with equal dignity of person.[108] There are two dimensions of Article 14 in its application to a legislation and rendering the legislation invalid, now well-recognised, which are: (i) discrimination, based on an impermissible or invalid classification; and (ii) excessive delegation of powers; conferment of uncanalised and unguided powers on the Executive, whether in the form of delegated legislation or by way of conferment of authority to pass administrative orders—if such conferment is without any guidance, control or checks, it is violative of Article 14 of the Constitution.[109]

In *Board of Control for Cricket in India v Netaji Cricket Club*, the Supreme Court while considering the role and the nature of functions being discharged by the BCCI, held that the Board's control over the sport of cricket was deep and pervasive and that it exercised enormous public functions, which made it obligatory for the Board to follow the doctrine of "fairness and good faith".[110] The BCCI is not "State" within the meaning of Article 12, as the Board was not created by any statute, nor a part of the share capital held by the Government.[111] The "nature of duties and functions" which the BCCI performs *viz.* it regulates and controls the game to the exclusion of all others, it formulates rules,

102. *East Coast Railway v Mahadeo Appa Rao*, (2010) 7 SCC 678 (*686*).
103. *Shiba Kumar Dutta v UOI*, 1998 AIR (SC) 2911 : (1997) 3 SCC 545, para 2 : (1999) 1 LLJ 1123.
104. *Krishnan Kakkanth v Government of Kerala*, AIR 1997 SC 128 : (1997) 9 SCC 495, paras 35–38.
105. *UOI v International Trading Co*, (2003) 5 SCC 437. See also *Sanjay Kumar Manjul v Chairman, UPSC*, (2006) 8 SCC 42; *Ekta Shakti Foundation v Government of NCT of Delhi*, AIR 2006 SC 2609; *State of Uttar Pradesh v Neeraj Awasthi*, (2006) 1 SCC 667; *Vishal Properties (P) Ltd v State of Uttar Pradesh*, (2007) 11 SCC 172
106. *Style (Dress Land) v Union Territory, Chandigarh*, (1999) 7 SCC 89, para 9.
107. *Ashok Kumar Gupta v State of Uttar Pradesh*, (1997) 5 SCC 201, para 46.
108. *PGI of Medical Education & Research v K L Narasimhan*, (1997) 6 SCC 283, para 24.
109. *Subramanian Swamy v CBI*, AIR 2014 SC 2140 : (2014) 8 SCC 682.
110. *Board of Control for Cricket in India v Netaji Cricket Club*, (2005) 4 SCC 741.
111. *Zee Telefilms Ltd v UOI*, (2005) 4 SCC 649.

regulations norms and standards covering all aspect of the game, it enjoys the power of choosing the members of the national team and the umpires, it exercises the power of disqualifying players which may at times put an end to the sporting career of a person, it spends crores of rupees on building and maintaining infrastructure like stadia, running of cricket academies and Supporting State Associations, it frames pension schemes and incurs expenditure on coaches, trainers etc., it sells broadcast and telecast rights and collects admission fee to venues where the matches are played etc. all these activities are undertaken with the tacit concurrence of the State Government and the Government of India who are not only fully aware but supportive of the activities of the Board. The State has not chosen to bring any law or taken any other step that would either deprive or dilute the Board's monopoly in the field of cricket. On the contrary, the Government of India have allowed the Board to select the national team which is then recognized by all concerned and applauded by the entire nation including at times by the highest of the dignitaries when they win tournaments and bring laurels home. Those distinguishing themselves in the international arena are conferred highest civilian awards like the Bharat Ratna, Padma Vibhushan, Padma Bhushan and Padma Shri apart from sporting awards instituted by the Government. Any organisation or entity that has such pervasive control over the game and its affairs and such powers as can make dreams end up in smoke or come true cannot be said to be undertaking any private activity. The functions of the Board are clearly public functions, and the entity discharging the same is answerable on the standards generally applicable to judicial review of State action. Therefore, BCCI may not be State under Article 12 of the Constitution but is certainly amenable to writ jurisdiction under Article 226 of the Constitution of India.[112]

9. Article 15—Prohibition of Discrimination on Grounds of Religion, Race, Caste, Sex or Place of Birth.

As just stated, a particular aspect of the equality guaranteed by Article 14 is the prohibition against discrimination contained in Article 15 of the Constitution which runs thus:

(1) The State shall not discriminate against any citizen on grounds only of religion, race, caste, sex, place of birth or any of them.

(2) No citizen shall on grounds only of religion, race, caste, sex, place of birth or any of them be subject to any disability, liability, restriction or condition with regard to—

(a) access to shops, public restaurants, hotels and places of public entertainment; or

(b) the use of wells, tanks, bathing ghats, roads and places of public resort maintained wholly or partly out of State funds or dedicated to the use of general public.

(3) Nothing in this article shall prevent the State from making any special provision for women and children.

(4) Nothing in this article or in clause (2) of article 29 shall prevent the State from making any special provision for the advancement of any socially and educationally backward classes of citizens or for the Scheduled Castes and the Scheduled Tribes.

112. *Board of Control for Cricket in India v Cricket Association of Bihar*, LNIND 2015 SC 49 : (2015) 3 SCC 251, AIR 2015 SC 3194.

(5) Nothing in this article or in sub-clause (g) of clause (1) of article 19 shall prevent the State from making any special provision, by law, for the advancement of any socially and educationally backward classes of citizens or for the Scheduled Castes or the Scheduled Tribes in so far as such special provisions relate to their admission to educational institutions including private educational institutions, whether aided or unaided by the State, other than the minority educational institutions referred to in clause (1) of article 30.

The scope of this Article is very wide. While the prohibition in clause (1) is levelled against state action, the prohibition in clause (2) is levelled against individuals as well.

Clause (1) says that any act of the state, whether political, civil or otherwise, shall not discriminate as between citizens on grounds only of religion, race, caste, sex, place of birth or any of them. The plain meaning of this prohibition is that no person of a particular religion, caste, etc., shall be treated unfavourably by the state when compared with persons of any other religion or caste *merely* on the ground that he belongs to the particular religion or caste, etc. The significance of the word "only" is that if there is any other ground or consideration for the differential treatment besides those prohibited by this Article, the discrimination will not be unconstitutional.[113] Thus, discrimination in favour of a particular sex will be permissible if the classification is the result of other considerations besides the fact that the person belongs to that sex, eg physical or intellectual fitness for some work. For instance, women may be considered to be better fitted for the job of a nurse while they may not be considered eligible for employment in heavy industries like a steel factory. Such discrimination, being based on a ground *other than* sex, would not be considered to be unconstitutional. Discrimination in favour of men on the ground of sex alone is not permissible under Article 15(1) of the Constitution but the discrimination in favour of women is permissible in view of clause (3) of Article 15 of the Constitution.[114]

But if a person is sought to be discriminated against simply because he belongs to a particular community, race or sex, he can get the state action annulled through a court. While racial discrimination still persists as a malignant growth upon Western society, it speaks volumes for Indian achievement that a possible victim of racial discrimination, in India, can obtain relief direct from the highest court of the land, by means of a petition for an appropriate writ, and, yet, no such complaint has so far come before the courts.

As already stated, in regard to the public places specified in clause (2), the protection is available even against discriminatory acts by private individuals. Clause (2) provides that so far as places of public entertainment are concerned, no person shall be subjected to discrimination on the grounds only of religion, race, caste, sex, place of birth or any of them, whether such discrimination is the result of an act of the state or of any other individual. Even wells, tanks, bathing ghats, roads, and places of public resort which are owned by private individuals are subject to this prohibition provided they are maintained wholly or partly out of state funds or they have been dedicated to the use of the general public.

113. *State of Kerala v Aravind Ramakant Modawdakar,* (1999) 7 SCC 400, para 6.
114. *Ashok Kumar Malpani v State of Madhya Pradesh,* AIR 2010 MP 64 (*105*) (DB).

The above prohibitions against discrimination, however, would not preclude the state from—

(a) making special provision for women and children;

(b) making special provision for the advancement of any socially and educationally backward classes of citizens or for the Scheduled Castes and the Scheduled Tribes.

These exceptional classes of people require special protection and hence any legislation which is necessary for the making of special provisions for persons of these classes, would not be held to be unconstitutional.

The Constitution recognises caste as a proscribed ground of discrimination under Article 15(1), and envisions a society free from caste-prejudices. Furthermore, the Constitution provides for the enumeration of certain castes and tribes as Scheduled Castes and Scheduled Tribes in order to facilitate protective discrimination and overall promote equitable distribution of resources. Article 15(4) allows the state to make special provisions for the advancement of socially and educationally backward classes of citizens, which includes Scheduled Castes and Scheduled Tribes. In that sense, caste can be ground for classification, as long as it is used to grant benefits to the victims of caste-discrimination. However, as evident from the language of Article 15(1), caste cannot be a ground to discriminate against members of marginalized castes. Any use of caste as a basis for classification must withstand judicial scrutiny to ensure it does not perpetuate discrimination against the oppressed castes. While caste-based classifications are permissible under certain constitutional provisions, they are strictly regulated to ensure they serve the purpose of promoting equality and social justice.[115]

Similarly, though discrimination on the ground of caste only is prohibited by clause (1) of the Article, it would be permissible under clause (4) for the State to reserve seats for the members of the backward classes or of the Scheduled Castes or Tribes or to grant them fee concessions, in public educational institutions.[116] Article 15(4) of the Constitution does not make any mandatory provision for reservation and the power to make reservation under this article is discretionary and no writ can be issued to effect reservation.[117] Article 15(4) envisages the policy of compensatory or protective discrimination but it should be reasonable and consistent with the ultimate public interest i.e., national interest and the interest of community or society as a whole[118] but the provision cannot be justifiably invoked in granting remission to the convicted persons belonging to the scheduled castes and scheduled tribes as it would not be a measure for their "advancement". However, the benefit obtained was permitted to be retained.[119] It was held that an SC/ST candidate selected for admission to a course on the basis of merit as a general candidate should not be treated as a reserved candidate[120] and reservation for admission to the

115. *Sukanya Shantha v UOI,* AIR 2024 SC 5201 : AIR Online 2024 SC 671.

116. *Chitralekha v State of Mysore,* AIR 1964 SC 1823 (*1827*).

117. *Gulshan Prakash v State of Haryana,* AIR 2010 SC 288 : (2010) 1 SCC 477 (*484*).

118. *Preeti Srivastava (Dr) v State of Madhya Pradesh,* AIR 1999 SC 2894 : (1999) 7 SCC 120, paras 13, 15 and 62.

119. *State of Madhya Pradesh v Mohan Singh,* AIR 1996 SC 2106 : (1995) 6 SCC 32, para 5.

120. *PGI of Medical Education & Research v K L Narasimhan,* (1997) 6 SCC 283, para 5.

specialities/ super-specialities in post-graduate and doctoral course in medicine is permissible.[121]

Clause (5) was inserted by the Constitution (93rd Amendment) Act, 2005 with effect from 20 January 2006. It empowers the State to make special provision, by law, for the advancement of any socially and educationally backward classes of citizens or for the Scheduled Castes or the Scheduled Tribes regarding their admission to educational institutions including private ones whether aided or unaided by the State, excepting the minority institutions. The placement of clause (5) of Article 15 of the Constitution in the equality code is of great significance. What it does is that it enlarges as opposed to truncating, an essential and indeed a primordial feature of the equality code.[122] Article 15(5) inserted by the Constitution (93rd Amendment) Act, 2005 is valid to the extent that it permits reservation for socially and educationally backward classes ('SEBCs') in state or state aided educational institutions subject to the exclusion of the "creamy layer" from OBCs. Exclusion of minority educational institutions from the purview of Article 15(5) held to be valid. However there is difference of opinion with regard to question of validity of inclusion of private unaided institutions within the purview of Article 15(5).[123]

Article 15 of the Constitution has been amended *vide* the Constitution (103rd Amendment) Act, 2019. The 2019 Amendment Act has added a new clause (6) to provide for special provisions for the advancement of economically weaker sections of citizens including special provisions relating to their admission to educational institutions including private educational institutions, whether aided or unaided by the State, other than the minority educational institutions referred to in clause (1) of Article 30. A reservation provided under the newly added clause (6) would be in addition to the existing reservations subject to a maximum of ten per cent of the total seats in each category. Clause (6) of Article 15 provides as follows:

> (6) Nothing in this article or sub-clause (g) of clause (1) of article 19 or clause (2) of article 29 shall prevent the State from making,—
>
> (a) any special provision for the advancement of any economically weaker sections of citizens other than the classes mentioned in clauses (4) and (5); and
>
> (b) any special provision for the advancement of any economically weaker sections of citizens other than the classes mentioned in clauses(4) and (5) in so far as such special provisions relate to their admission to educational institutions including private educational institutions, whether aided or unaided by the State, other than the minority educational institutions referred to in clause (1) of article 30, which in the case of reservation would be in addition to the existing reservations and subject to a maximum of ten per cent. of the total seats in each category.
>
> *Explanation.*—For the purposes of this article and article 16, "economically weaker sections" shall be such as may be notified by the State

121. *PGI of Medical Education & Research v K L Narasimhan,* (1997) 6 SCC 283, paras 21 and 23.
122. *Indian Medical Association v UOI,* AIR 2011 SC 2365, p 2417 : (2011) 7 SCC 179.
123. *Ashok Kumar Thakur v UOI,* (2008) 6 SCC 1.

from time to time on the basis of family income and other indicators of economic disadvantage.

10. Article 16—Equality of Opportunity in Matters of Public Employment. As a corollary from the general assurance of absence of discrimination by the state on grounds only of religion, race, caste, sex, or place of birth [*Article 15*], the Constitution guarantees equality of opportunity in matters of public employment. Article 16 says that—

(1) There shall be equality of opportunity for all citizens in matters relating to *employment* or appointment to any *office* under the State.

(2) No citizen shall, on grounds only of religion, race, caste, sex, descent, place of birth, residence or any of them, be ineligible for, or discriminated against in respect of, any employment or office under the State.

(3) Nothing in this article shall prevent Parliament from making any law prescribing, in regard to a class or classes of employment or appointment to an office under the Government of, or any local or other authority within, a State or Union territory, any requirement as to residence within that State or Union territory prior to such employment or appointment.

(4) Nothing in this article shall prevent the State from making any provision for the reservation of appointments or posts in favour of any backward class of citizens which, in the opinion of the State, is not adequately represented in the services under the State.

(4A) Nothing in this article shall prevent the State from making any provision for reservation in matters of promotion, with consequential seniority, to any class or classes of posts in the services under the State in favour of the Scheduled Castes and the Scheduled Tribes which, in the opinion of the State, are not adequately represented in the services under the State.

(4B) Nothing in this article shall prevent the State from considering any unfilled vacancies of a year which are reserved for being filled up in that year in accordance with any provision for reservation made under clause (4) or clause (4A) as a separate class of vacancies to be filled up in any succeeding year or years and such class of vacancies shall not be considered together with the vacancies of the year in which they are being filled up for determining the ceiling of fifty per cent. reservation on total number of vacancies of that year.

(5) Nothing in this article shall affect the operation of any law which provides that the incumbent of an office in connection with the affairs of any religious or denominational institution or any member of the governing body thereof shall be a person professing a particular religion or belonging to a particular denomination.

The expression "matters relating to employment or appointment" contained in Article 16(1) includes all matters in relation to employment both prior and subsequent to the employments which are incidental to the employment and form part of the terms and conditions of such employment.[124] The principle of merit-cum-seniority puts greater emphasis on merit and ability and where the promotion is governed by this principle seniority plays a less significant role. However, seniority is to be given weightage when merit and ability, more or less are equal among the candidates who are to be promoted.[125] The final seniority list once published cannot be disturbed at the behest of person who chose not to

124. *Amita v UOI,* (2005) 13 SCC 721, para 12.
125. *HSED Corp Ltd v Seema Sharma,* AIR 2009 SC 2592.

challenge it for years. Its sanctity must be maintained unless there are very compelling reasons to do so in order to do substantial justice.[126] Determination of seniority is a vital aspect in the service career of an employee. It must be based on some principles which are just and fair. This is the mandate of Article 16 of the Constitution.[127]

The true import of equality of opportunity is not simply a matter of legal equality. Its existence depends not merely on the absence of disabilities but on the presence of abilities and opportunity of excellence in each cadre/grade[128] as equality of opportunity means equality as between the members of the same class of employees and not between that of separate independent classes.[129] All persons similarly situated should be treated similarly. Only because one person has approached the court that would not mean the persons similarly situated should be treated differently.[130] When regular vacancies in posts are to be filled up, a regular process of recruitment or appointment has to be resorted to as per the constitutional scheme, and cannot be done in a haphazard manner based on patronage or other considerations. Hence, appointment/recruitment of temporary, contractual, casual, daily-wage or *ad hoc* employment *dehors* the constitutional scheme cannot be regularised. Such appointees cannot claim to be made permanent.[131] An *ad hoc* appointment is always to a post but not to the cadre/service and is also not made in accordance with provisions contained in the recruitment rules for regular appointment.[132] An *ad hoc* appointment is not entitled to family pension only because services of *ad hoc* employee continued. The continuation of *ad hoc* employee would not mean that thereby this status has been changed. An *ad hoc* employee does not hold status of Government servants.[133] Like other employers, the government is also entitled to pick and choose from amongst a large number of candidates offering themselves for employment. But this can be done on one condition that all the applicants must be given an equal opportunity along with others who qualify for the same post. The selection test must not be arbitrary and technical qualifications and standards should be prescribed where necessary.[134]

A person cannot be excluded from a state service merely because he is a Brahmin,[135] even though this result is reached by reason of a distribution of posts amongst communities according to a ratio or quota. Government jobs or service cannot be denied to the persons suffering from AIDS.[136] This equality is to be observed by the state not only in the matter of appointments to the public services, but also in the matter of any other public employment, where the

126. *Rajendra Pratap Singh Yadav v State of Uttar Pradesh,* AIR 2011 SC 2737.
127. *D P Das v UOI,* AIR 2011 SC 294, p *2950*; see also *Amarjeet Singh v Devi Ratan,* AIR 2010 SC 3676; *M P Palanisamy v A Krishna,* AIR 2009 SC 2809.
128. *Jagdish Lal v State of Haryana,* AIR 1997 SC 2366 : (1997) 6 SCC 538, para 14 :.
129. *UOI v No. 664950 IM Havildar/Clerk,* AIR 1999 SC 1412 : (1999) 3 SCC 709, para 15.
130. *State of Karnataka v C Lalitha,* (2006) 2 SCC 747, para 29.
131. *Secretary, State of Karnataka v Umadevi (3),* AIR 2006 SC 1806. See also *Punjab State Warehousing Corp v Manmohan Singh,* (2007) 9 SCC 337.
132. *State of Rajasthan v Jagdish Narain Chaturvedi,* AIR 2010 SC 157 (*162*).
133. *State of Haryana v Shakuntala Devi,* AIR 2009 SC 869.
134. *Amita v UOI,* (2005) 13 SCC 721, para 12.
135. *Venkataramana v State of Madras,* AIR 1951 SC 229.
136. *'X' v Hospital 'Z',* (1998) 8 SCC 296, para 45.

relationship of master and servant exists between the state and the employee.[137] It bars discrimination not only in the matter of initial appointment but also of promotion and termination of the service itself[138] as "employment" includes promotion.[139]

This right is a safeguard not only against communal discrimination, but also against local discrimination or even against discrimination against the weaker sex.

The right to be considered for promotion by the Departmental Promotion Committee is a fundamental right guaranteed under Article 16, provided a person is eligible and is in the zone of consideration;[140] but the "consideration" must be "fair" according to established principles governing service jurisprudence.[141]

The only exceptions to the above rule of equality are—

(a) Residence within the state may be laid down by Parliament as a condition for particular classes of employment of appointment under any state or other local authority [*Article 16(3)*].

By virtue of this power, Parliament enacted the Public Employment (Requirement as to Residence) Act, 1957, empowering the Government of India to prescribe residence as condition for employment in certain posts and services in the State of Andhra Pradesh and in the Union Territories of Himachal Pradesh, Manipur and Tripura (Now States). This Act having expired in 1974, there is no provision to prescribe residence as a condition for public employment, except that for Andhra Pradesh special provisions have been made by inserting a new Article 371D (*post*) in the Constitution itself.

(b) The state may reserve any post or appointment in favour of any backward class of citizens who, in the opinion of the state, are not adequately represented in the services under that state [*Article 16(4)*]. This is to provide socio-economic equality to the disadvantaged.[142] The expression "backward class of citizens" contained in Article 16(4) would take Scheduled Castes and Scheduled Tribes within its purview.[143]

(c) Offices connected with a religious or denominated institution may be reserved for members professing the particular religion or belonging to the particular denomination to which the institution relates [*Article 16(5)*].

(d) The claims of the members of the Scheduled Castes and Scheduled Tribes shall be taken into consideration in the matter of appointment to services and posts under the Union and the states, as far as may be consistent with the

137. *Achutan v State of Kerala,* AIR 1959 SC 490.

138. *General Manager v Rangachari,* AIR 1962 SC 36; *Kunj Behari v UOI,* AIR 1963 SC 518, p *527.*

139. *Ajit Singh (II) v State of Punjab,* (1999) 7 SCC 209, para 22.

140. *Delhi Jal Board v Mahinder Singh,* (2007) 7 SCC 210, para 5.

141. *Badrinath v Government of Tamil Nadu,* (2000) 8 SCC 395, para 58(1).

142. *State of Uttar Pradesh v Dr Dina Nath Shukla,* AIR 1997 SC 1095 : (1997) 9 SCC 662, para 7.

143. *E V Chinnaiah v State of Andhra Pradesh,* (2005) 1 SCC 394, para 58.

maintenance of efficiency of the administration [*Article 335*] but the *proviso*[144] to Article 335 providing for giving relaxation in qualifying marks in any examination or lowering the standard of evaluation in favour of the members of the SC & ST hits the consideration of maintenance of efficiency in administration and has done away with the emphasis on it laid down by the Apex Court in some cases.[145] The Supreme Court has held[146] that while Article 16(4) is apparently without any limitation upon the power of reservation conferred by it, it has to be read together with Article 335 which enjoins that in taking into consideration the claims of the members of the Scheduled Castes and Scheduled Tribes in the making of appointments in connection with the affairs of the Union or a State, the policy of the State should be consistent with "the maintenance of efficiency of administration".[147] The result is that—

> There can be no doubt that the Constitution-makers assumed. . .that while making adequate reservation under article 16(4) care would be taken not to provide for unreasonable, excessive or extravagant reservation. . .Therefore, like the special provision improperly made under article 15(4), reservation made under article 16(4) beyond the permissible and legitimate limits would be liable to be challenged as a *fraud on the Constitution.*[148]

However, the Constitution (82nd Amendment) Act, 2000 inserted a proviso to Article 335 almost closing the door for consideration of maintenance of efficiency of administration in the making of appointments to services and posts in connection with the affairs of the Union or of a State inasmuch as the proviso empowered the State to relax the qualifying marks in any examination or lower the standards of evaluation, for reservation in matters of promotions of the members of the SC/ST to any classes of services or posts in connection with the affairs of the Union or a State.

The concession relating to reservation would be applicable only when a Scheduled Caste or Scheduled Tribe candidate came within the number of available vacancies.[149]

It is to be noted carefully that the prohibition against discrimination in the matter of public employment is attracted where the discrimination is based *only* on any of the grounds enumerated, namely, religion, race, caste, sex, descent, place of birth or residence. It does not prevent the State, like other employers, to pick and choose from a number of candidates, either for appointment or for promotion, on grounds of efficiency, discipline and the like.[150] It is also to be noted that though reservation in favour of backward classes is permissible under

144. *Vide* the Constitution (82nd Amendment) Act, 2000.
145. *Indra Sawhney v UOI,* (1992) Supp 3 SCC 217 and *S Vinod Kumar v UOI,* (1996) 6 SCC 580. *Faculty Association of AIIMS v UOI,* (2013) 11 SCC 246 : (2013) 5 Mad LJ 833; *Jagdish Saran v UOI,* AIR 1980 SC 820 : (1980) 2 SCC 768; *Pradeep Jain v UOI,* AIR 1984 SC 1420 : (1984) 3 SCC 654; *Preeti Srivastava v State of Madhya Pradesh,* (1999) 7 SCC 120 : (1999) 4 AWC 2853 (SC); The Constitution (102nd) Amendment does not violate any basic feature of the Constitution. *Dr Jaishri Laxmanrao Patil v The Chief Minister,* LNIND 2021 SC 170 : (2021) SCC Online 170
146. *General Manager v Rangachari,* AIR 1962 SC 36, p *42–44.*
147. *Amita v UOI,* (2005) 13 SCC 721, para 12.
148. *Balaji v State of Mysore,* AIR 1963 SC 647, p *664.*
149. *Pragjyotish Gaonlia Bank v Brij Lal Das,* (2009) 3 SCC 323, p *329.*
150. *Banarsidas v State of Uttar Pradesh,* (1956) SCR 358, p *361–62.*

clause (4) of Article 16, no such reservation is possible in favour of women; nor is any other discrimination in favour of women possible, eg relaxation of rules of recruitment or standard of qualification or the like. The courts and tribunals can neither prescribe the qualification nor upon the power of the concerned authority so long as the qualification prescribed by the employer is reasonably relevant and has a rational nexus with the functions and duties attached to the post and are not violative of any provision of Constitution Statute and Rules.[151] The court cannot interfere with the methods of reservation unless there is some clear illegality.[152]

For the furtherance of *social* equality, the Constitution provides for the abolition of the evil of "untouchability" (see Article 17, *post*) and the prohibition of conferring titles by the state.

A nine-Judge Bench of the Supreme Court has in *Indra Sawhney's* case[153] (popularly known as the Mandal Commission case) laid down the following important points which summarise the law on the issue of reservations in Government employment:

1. Article 16(4) is exhaustive of the provisions that can be made in favour of the backward classes in the matter of employment.

2. Backward classes of citizens is not defined in the Constitution. There is an integral connection between caste, occupation, poverty and social backwardness. In the Indian context, lower castes are treated as backwards. A caste may by itself constitute a class.

3. The backward classes can be identified in Hindu society with reference to castes along with other criteria such as traditional occupation, poverty, place of residence, lack of education etc, and in communities where caste is not recognised the rest of the criteria would apply.

4. The backwardness contemplated by Article 16(4) is mainly social. It need not be both social and educational.

5. "Means-test" signifies imposition of an income limit for the purpose of excluding persons from the backward classes. Those whose income is above that limit are referred to as the "creamy layer". Income or the extent of property can be taken as a measure of social advancement and on that basis the "creamy layer" of a given caste can be excluded.[154]

---

151. *Chandigarh Administration v Usha K Wale*, AIR 2011 SC 2956, p *2961*.

152. *Nair Service Society v T Beermasthan*, (2009) 55 SCC 545, p*563*.

153. *Indra Sawhney v UOI*, (1992) Supp (3) SCC 217. Parliament has enacted the National Commission for Backward Classes Act, 1993, to set up a National Commission for backward classes. See also *Ashoka Kumar Thakur (8) v UOI*, (2007) 4 SCC 361; The Constitution (102nd) Amendment does not violate any basic feature of the Constitution. *Dr Jaishri Laxmanrao Patil v The Chief Minister*, LNIND 2021 SC 170 : (2021) SCC Online 170.

154. *Indra Sawhney v UOI*, (1992) Supp (3) SCC 217. Parliament has enacted the National Commission for Backward Classes Act, 1993, to set up a National Commission for backward classes. See also *Ashoka Kumar Thakur (8) v UOI*, (2007) 4 SCC 361; The Constitution (102nd) Amendment does not violate any basic feature of the Constitution. *Dr Jaishri Laxmanrao Patil v The Chief Minister*, LNIND 2021 SC 170 : (2021) SCC Online 170.

6. For getting reservations a class must be backward and should not be adequately represented in the services under the State.

7. The reservations contemplated in Article 16(4) should not exceed 50%.

8. The rule of 50% should be applied to each year. It cannot be related to the total strength of the class, service or cadre etc.

9. Reservation of posts under Article 16(4) is confined to initial appointment only and cannot extend to providing reservation in the matter of *promotion.* If a reservation in promotion exists it shall continue for five years (16 November 1997). By the Constitution (77th Amendment) Act, 1995, this limitation of time has been removed by inserting clause (4A) to enable it to continue reservation in promotion for the SC and ST.[155]

10. Identification of backward classes is subject to judicial review.

Sub-division of Other Backward Classes contemplated in the Mandal Commission case is not applicable to Scheduled Castes and Scheduled Tribes. Hence sub-classification or subgrouping of SC & ST is not permitted.[156]

Article 16(4) is an enabling provision and confers a discretionary power on the State to make reservation, if required, but it confers no constitutional right upon the members of the backward classes to claim reservation.[157]

The vacancies reserved could be "carried forward" for a maximum period of three years if candidates from backward classes were not available after which they were to lapse. By inserting clause (4B) in Article 16 by the Constitution (81st Amendment) Act, 2000, the state has been empowered to consider such unfilled vacancies as a separate class to be filled up in any succeeding year or years, however the Hon'ble Supreme Court put certain limitations on powers available to the state under Article 16(4-A) and (4-B) and the same are: (i) the ceiling limit of a maximum of 50% reservation (quantitative limitation); (ii) the principle of creamy layer (qualitative exclusion); (iii) the compelling reasons for exercise of power under, namely backwardness and inadequacy of representation; and (iv) the overall administrative efficiency as required by Article 335.[158]

The Constitution (103rd Amendment) Act, 2019 has amended Article 16 of the Constitution of India. It has added a new clause (6) to provide for reservation of appointments or posts in favour of any economically weaker sections of citizens in addition to the existing reservation and subject to a maximum of 10% of the posts in each category. Clause (6) of Article 16 provides as follows:

> (6) Nothing in this article shall prevent the State from making any provision for the reservation of appointments or posts in favour of any economically weaker sections of citizens other than the classes mentioned in clause (4), in addition to

155. The Constitution (85th) Amendment Act, 2001 has amended clause (4A) of Article 16 and substituted the words "in matters of promotion, with consequential seniority to any class", for the words "in matters of promotion to any class".

156. *E V Chinnaiah v State of Andhra Pradesh,* (2005) 1 SCC 394, para 38.

157. *S Pushpa v Sivachanmugavelu,* AIR 2005 SC 1038.

158. *M Nagaraj* v *UOI,* (2006) 8 SCC 212. The judgment in M Nagaraj has been overruled in part in *Jarnail Singh v Lachhmi Narain Gupta,* (2018) 7 Mad LJ 573 : LNIND 2018 SC 488.

the existing reservation and subject to a maximum of ten per cent of the posts in each category.

11. Relation between Articles 14, 15 and 16. As the Supreme Court has observed,[159] Articles 14–16, taken together, enshrine the principle of equality and absence of discrimination.

While the principle is generally stated in Article 14, which extends to all persons—citizens or aliens, Articles 15 and 16 deal with particular aspects of that equality. Thus,

(a) Article 15 is available to *citizens* only and it prohibits discrimination against any citizen in any matter at the disposal of the State on any of the specified grounds, namely, religion, race, caste, sex or place of birth.

(b) Article 16 is also confined to citizens, but it is restricted to one aspect of public discrimination, namely, employment under the State.

In matters not coming under Articles 15 and 16, if there is any discrimination, the validity of that can be challenged under the general provision in Article 14.

In other words, Article 14 lays down the rule of equality in the widest term, while Article 15 prohibits discrimination on the grounds specified therein but covering the entire range of State activities. Article 16 embodies the same rule but is narrower in scope since it is confined to State activities relating to office or employment under the State. Both Articles 15 and 16 operate subject to exceptions therein.[160]

As compared to Article 16, Article 15 is a general provision having a wider application, and it does not contain 'residence' as one of the prohibitory grounds, and apparently one can say that Article 15 does not bar the State from making 'residence' as a requirement, for admission in colleges or like matters. However, both Article 15 and Article 16 are different facets of the concept of equality, embodied in Article 14 and therefore, a legislation can still be struck down if it creates an unjustifiable classification, such as between residents of a State and all others.[161]

12. Article 17—Abolition of Untouchability. Article 17 of the Constitution says—

> Untouchability' is abolished and its practice in any form is forbidden. The enforcement of any disability arising out of 'untouchability' shall be an offence punishable in accordance with law.

The vision of the founding fathers of the Constitution to liberate the society from blind and ritualistic adherence to mere traditional superstitious beliefs *sans* reason or rational basis has found expression in the form of Article 17.[162] Article 17 enunciates that everyone is born equal. There cannot be any stigma attached to the existence, touch or presence of any person. By way of Article 17, our Constitution strengthens the equality of status of every citizen.[163] It is absolutely

159. *Dasaratha v State of Andhra Pradesh,* AIR 1961 SC 564 (*569*); *Devadasan v UOI,* AIR 1964 SC 179; *General Manager v Rangachari,* AIR 1962 SC 36 (*40–41*).
160. *Ewanlangki-E-Rymbai v Jaintia Hills District Council,* AIR 2006 SC 1589.
161. *Dr Tanvi Behl v Shrey Goel,* AIR 2025 SC 1445 : AIROnline 2025 SC 99.
162. *N Adithayan v Travancore Devaswom Board,* (2002) 8 SCC 106, para 16.
163. *Sukanya Shantha v UOI,* AIR 2024 SC 5201 : AIR Online 2024 SC 671.

imperative to abolish the caste system as expeditiously as possible for the smooth functioning of rule of law and democracy in our country.[164] To implement the mandate of Article 17, Parliament, in exercise of this power, has enacted the several legislations such as the Untouchability (Offenses) Act, 1955, Scheduled Castes and the Scheduled Tribes (Prevention of Atrocities) Act, 1989, Employment of Manual Scavengers and Construction of Dry Latrines (Prohibition) Act, 1993, and Prohibition of Employment as Manual Scavengers and their Rehabilitation Act, 2013. The laws enacted under Article 17 aim to provide dignity to the affected individuals.[165]

The Untouchability (Offences) Act, 1955 has been amended and renamed (in 1976) as the Protection of Civil Rights Act, 1955.

The word "untouchability" has not, however, been defined either in the Constitution or in the above Act. It has been assumed that the word has a well-known connotation—primarily referring to any social practice which looks down upon certain depressed classes solely on account of their *birth* and disables them from having any kind of intercourse with people belonging to the so-called higher classes or castes. The Act declares certain acts as offences, when done on the ground of "untouchability", and prescribes the punishments therefor, eg.:

(a) refusing admission to any person to public institutions, such as hospital, dispensary, educational institution;

(b) preventing any person from worshipping or offering prayers in any place of public worship;

(c) subjecting any person to any disability with regard to access to any shop, public restaurant, hotel or public entertainment or with regard to the use of any reservoir, tap or other source of water, road, cremation ground or any other place where "services are rendered to the public".

The sweep of the Act has been enlarged in 1976, by including within the offence of practising untouchability, the following—

(i) *insulting* a member of a Scheduled Caste on the ground of untouchability;

(ii) *preaching* untouchability, directly or indirectly;

(iii) *justifying* untouchability on historical, philosophical or religious grounds or on the ground of tradition of the caste system.

The penal sanction has been enhanced by providing that: (a) in the case of subsequent convictions, the punishment may range from one to two years' imprisonment; (b) a person convicted of the offence of "untouchability" shall be disqualified for *election* to the Union or a State Legislature.

If a member of a Scheduled Caste is subjected to any such disability or discrimination, the court shall presume, unless the contrary is proved, that such act was committed on the ground of "untouchability". In other words, in such cases, there will be a statutory presumption of an offence having been committed under this Act.

164. *State of Uttar Pradesh v Ram Sanjeevan*, (2010) 1 SCC 529 (*531*).

165. *Sukanya Shantha v UOI*, AIR 2024 SC 5201 : AIR Online 2024 SC 671.

The prohibition of untouchability in the Constitution has thus been given a realistic and effective shape by this Act.

13. Article 18—Abolition of Titles. "Title" is something that hangs to one's name, as an appendage. During the British rule, there was a complaint from the nationalists that the power to confer titles was being abused by the Government for imperialistic purposes and for corrupting public life. The Constitution seeks to prevent such abuse by prohibiting the state from conferring any title at all.

It is to be noted that—

(a) The ban operates only against the state. It does not prevent other public institutions, such as Universities, to confer titles or honours by way of honouring their leaders or men of merit.

(b) The state is not debarred from awarding military or academic distinctions, even though they may be used as titles.[166]

(c) The state is not prevented from conferring any distinction or award, say, for social service, *which cannot be used as a title, that is, as an appendage to one's name.* Thus, the award of *Bharat Ratna or Padma Vibhushan* cannot be used by the recipient *as a title* and does not, accordingly, come within the constitutional prohibition.

In 1954, the Government of India introduced decorations (in the form of medals) of four categories, namely, *Bharat Ratna, Padma Vibhushan, Padma Bhushan* and *Padma Shri.* While the Bharat Ratna was to be awarded for "exceptional services towards the advancement of Art, Literature and Science, and in recognition of *public service* of the higher order", the others would be awarded for "distinguished public service in any field, including service rendered by government servants", in order of the degree of the merit of their service.

Though the foregoing awards were mere *decorations* and not intended to be used as appendage to the names of the persons to whom they are awarded, there was a vehement criticism from some quarters that the introduction of these awards violated Article 18. The critics pointed out that even though they may not be used as titles, the decorations tend to make distinctions according to rank, contrary to the Preamble which promises "equality of status". The critics gained strength on this point from the fact that the decorations are divided into several classes, superior and inferior, and that holders of the *Bharat Ratna* have been assigned a place in the "Warrant of Precedence" (Ninth place, ie, just below the Cabinet Ministers of the Union), which is usually meant for indicating the rank of the different dignitaries and high officials of the State, in the interests of discipline in the administration. The result was the creation of a rank of persons on the basis of Government recognition, in the same way as the conferment of nobility would have done.

Another criticism, which seems to be legitimate, is that there is no sanction, either in the Constitution or in any existing law, against a recipient of any such decoration appending it to his name and, thus, using it as a title. Any such use is obviously inconsistent with the prohibition contained in Article 18(1) but it is not

166. At present the Government of India awards *decorations* for acts of gallantry, such as *Param Vir Chakra, Maha Vir Chakra, Vir Chakra.*

made an offence either by the Constitution or by any law. The apprehensions of the critics on this point were unfortunately justified by the fact that in describing the author on the Title of an issue of the Hamlyn Lectures, the decoration "*Padma Vibhushan*" was, in fact, appended as a title.

The protest raised by Acharya Kripalani against the award of such decorations, which went unheeded earlier was honoured by the Janata regime (1977)—by putting a stop to the practice of awarding *Bharat Ratna,* etc. by the *Government.* But it was *restored* by Mrs Gandhi after her come-back.

In this context, it is to be noted that Article 18(1) itself makes an exception in favour of granting by the State of any *military* or *academic* distinction.

The matter was taken to court, and the Supreme Court has now held[167] that non-military awards by way of recognition of *merit* of *extraordinary work* (eg, the Padma awards) are not titles of nobility and hence, do not violate Article 14 or 18, provided they are not used as titles or prefixes or suffixes to the name of the awardee.

14. Article 19—The Six Freedoms.

Apart from the rights flowing from the above prohibition, certain positive rights are conferred by the Constitution in order to promote the ideal of liberty held out by the Preamble. The foremost amongst these are the *six* fundamental rights in the nature of "freedom" which are guaranteed to the citizens by the Constitution of India [*Article 19*]. These were popularly known as the "seven freedoms" under our Constitution. It has already been pointed out that in the original Constitution, there were seven freedoms in Article 19(1) but that one of them, namely, "the right to acquire, hold and dispose of property" has been *omitted* by the Constitution (44th Amendment) Act, 1978, leaving only six freedoms in this Article. They are—1. Freedom of speech and expression; 2. Freedom of assembly; 3. Freedom of association; 4. Freedom of movement; 5. Freedom of residence and settlement; 6. Freedom of profession, occupation, trade or business.

Since Article 19 forms the core of *our* chapter on Fundamental Rights, it is essential for the reader to be familiar with the text of this Article, as it stands amended:

> 19. (1) All citizens shall have the right—
>
> (a) to freedom of speech and expression;
>
> (b) to assemble peaceably and without arms;
>
> (c) to form associations or unions [168][or co-operative societies];
>
> (d) to move freely throughout the territory of India;
>
> (e) to reside and settle in any part of the territory of India; and
>
> (f) .....[169]
>
> (*g*) to practise any profession, or to carry on any occupation, trade or business.
>
> (2) Nothing in sub-clause (a) of clause (1) shall affect the operation of any existing law, or prevent the State from making any law, insofar as such law imposes reasonable restrictions on the exercise of the right conferred by the said sub-clause

167. *Bala v UOI,* (1996) 1 SCC 361, paras 18–30, 32, CB.

168. Inserted by the Constitution (97th Amendment) Act, 2011, section 2.

169. Sub-clause (f) of Article 19(1) has been omitted by the Constitution (44th Amendment), 1978, wef 20-6-1979.

in the interests of the sovereignty and integrity of India, the security of the State, friendly relations with foreign States, public order, decency or morality, or in relation contempt of court, defamation or incitement to an offence.

(3) Nothing in sub-clause (b) of the said clause shall affect the operation of any existing law insofar as it imposes, or prevent the State from making any law imposing, in the interests of the sovereignty and integrity of India or public order, reasonable restrictions on the exercise of the right conferred by the said sub-clause.

(4) Nothing in sub-clause (c) of the said clause shall affect the operation of any existing law insofar as it imposes, or prevent the State from making any law imposing, in the interests of the sovereignty and integrity of India or public order or morality, reasonable restrictions on the exercise of the right conferred by the said sub-clause.

(5) Nothing in sub-clauses (d) and (e) of the said clause shall affect the operation of any existing law insofar as it imposes, or prevent the State from making any law imposing, reasonable restrictions on the exercise of any of the rights conferred by the said sub-clauses either in the interests of the general public or for the protection of the interests of any Scheduled Tribe.

(6) Nothing in sub-clause (g) of the said clause shall affect the operation of any existing law insofar as it imposes, or prevent the State from making any law imposing, in the interests of the general public, reasonable restrictions on the exercise of the right conferred by the said sub-clause, and, in particular, *nothing in the said sub-clause, shall affect the operation* of any existing law insofar as it relates to, or prevent the State from making any law relating to—

(i) the professional or technical qualifications necessary for practising any profession or carrying on any occupation, trade or business, or

(ii) the carrying on by the State, or by a corporation owned or controlled by the State, of any trade, business, industry or service, whether to the exclusion, complete or partial, of citizens or otherwise.

The freedom of speech is the matrix, the indispensable condition of nearly every other form of freedom. It is the well spring of civilisation and without it liberty of thought would shrivel. Public decency and morality is outside the purview of the protection of free speech and expression and thus a balance should be maintained between freedom of speech and expression and public decency and morality.[170] The state is duty bound to ensure the prevalence of conditions in which of these freedoms can be exercised.[171]

Even though the constitutional freedom of speech and expression is not absolute and can be subjected to reasonable restrictions on grounds such as decency and morality.[172]

Flying of National Flag is a symbol of expression coming within the preview of Article 19(1)(a).[173] A voter's speech or expression in case of election would include casting of votes, that is to say, a voter speaks out or expresses by casting vote.[174] Right to information is an integral part of freedom of expression,

170. *Maqbool Fida Hussain v Raj Kr Pandey,* 2008 Cr LJ 4107.

171. *Indibility Creative Pvt Ltd v Govt of West Bengal,* AIR Online 2019 SC 242 : 2019 SCC OnLine SC 520 : LNIND 2019 SC 341 (It is the duty of the state to ensure that the right to freedom of speech and expression is not silenced by the fear of the mob).

172. *S Khushboo v Kanniammal,* AIR 2010 SC 3196, p *3208.*

173. *UOI v Naveen Jindal,* (2004) 2 SCC 510, para 37.

174. *UOI v Association for Democratic Reforms,* AIR 2002 SC 2112; *People's Union for Civil Liberties (PUCL) v UOI,* AIR 2003 SC 2363.

particularly a voter's right to know the antecedents/assets of a candidate contesting election.[175] The right to information of a voter is a facet of Article 19(1)(a) which guarantees to the voter the right to information concerning the affairs of the public and the government. The right to information under Article 19(1)(a) can only be restricted based on the grounds stipulated in Article 19(2). Therefore, the statutory amendments and the Electoral Bond Scheme which mandates non-disclosure of information on political funding are violative of the right to information under Article 19(1)(a) of the Constitution.[176] Right to speech implies the right to silence. It implies freedom, not to listen, and not to be forced to listen.[177]

The dignity of the courts and the people's faith in administration must not be tarnished because of biased and unverified reporting. In order to avoid such biased reporting, one must be careful to verify the facts and do some research on the subject being reported before a publication is brought out.[178] Giving of a call for bandh and its enforcement by any association, organisation or political party would be illegal and unconstitutional.[179]

No citizen has a fundamental right under Article 19(1)(c) to become a member of a voluntary association or a cooperative society. His right is governed by the provisions of the statute. So, the right to become or to continue being a member of the society is a statutory right.[180] Mere membership of a banned organisation will not make a person a criminal unless he resorts to violence or incites people to violence or creates public disorder by violence or incitement to violence.[181]

No citizen can claim to have trade in noxious or dangerous goods. Hence, intoxicating liquor being a noxious material, no citizen can claim any inherent right or privilege to sell intoxicating liquor by retail.[182] Education used to be charity or philanthropy in the good old times. Gradually, it became an occupation.[183] The establishment and running of an educational institution where a large number of persons are employed as teachers or administrative staff, and an activity is carried on that results in imparting of knowledge to the students, must necessarily be regarded as an occupation, even if there is no element of profit generation. All citizens have a right to establish and administer educational institutions under Article 19(1)(g) and the minorities have a special right under Article 30.[184]

---

175. *People's Union for Civil Liberties (PUCL) v UOI,* AIR 2003 SC 2363; *People's Union for Civil Liberties v UOI,* AIR 2004 SC 1442.
176. *Association For Democratic Reforms v UOI,* AIR 2024 SC 1441 : AIROnline 2024 SC 117 : 2024 INSC 113.
177. *Re Noise Pollution (V),* AIR 2005 SC 3136.
178. *Sanjoy Narayan, Hindustan Times v High Court of Allahabad,* (2011) 13 SCC 155, p *157.*
179. *All India Dravida Munnetra Kazhagam v Government of Tamil Nadu¸* (2009) 5 SCC 452, p *457.*
180. *Zoroastrian Cooperation Housing Society Ltd v District Registrar, Co-op Societies (Urban),* AIR 2005 SC 2306.
181. *Arup Bhuyan v State of Assam,* (2011) 3 SCC 377 (*379*).
182. *Secretary to Government Tamil Nadu v K Vinayagamurthy,* (2002) 7 SCC 104, para 7.
183. *P A Inamdar v State of Maharashtra,* AIR 2005 SC 3226.
184. *TMA Pai Foundation v State of Karnataka,* (2002) 8 SCC 481.

14a. Limitations upon the Freedoms.

Absolute individual rights cannot be guaranteed by any modern state. The guarantee of each of the above rights is, therefore limited by *our* Constitution itself by conferring upon the "State" a power to impose by its laws reasonable restrictions as may be necessary in the larger interests of the community. This is what is meant by saying that the Indian Constitution attempts "to strike a balance between individual liberty and social control".[185] Since the goal of our constitutional system is to establish a "welfare State", the makers of the Constitution did not rest with the enumeration of uncontrolled individual rights, in accordance with the philosophy of *laissez faire,* but sought to ensure that where collective interests were concerned, individual liberty must yield to the common good; but, instead of leaving it to the courts to determine the grounds and extent of permissible state regulation of individual rights as the American Constitution does, the makers of our Constitution specified the permissible limitations in clauses (2) to (6) of Article 19 itself.

The "State", in this context, includes not only the legislative authorities of the Union and the states but also other local or statutory[186] authorities, eg, municipalities, local boards, etc, within the territory of India or under the control of the Government of India. So, all of these authorities may impose restrictions upon the above freedoms, provided such restrictions are reasonable and are relatable to any of the grounds of public interest as specified in clauses (2)–(6) of Article 19.

Thus—

(i) The Constitution guarantees freedom of speech and expression. But this freedom is subject to reasonable restrictions imposed by the State relating to: (a) defamation; (b) contempt of court; (c) decency or morality; (d) security of the State; (e) friendly relations with foreign State; (f) incitement to an offence; (g) public order; (h) maintenance of the sovereignty and integrity of India.[187]

"Decency or morality" is not confined to sexual morality alone. It indicates that the action must be in conformity with the current standards of behaviour or propriety.[188] Hence, seeking votes at an election on the ground of the candidate's religion in a secular state, is against the norms of decency and propriety of the society.[189]

It is evident that freedom of speech and expression cannot confer upon an individual a licence to commit illegal or immoral acts or to incite others to

---

185. *Gopalan v State of Madras,* (1950) SCR 88 (*253–54*).
186. *Rajasthan State Electricity Board v Mohan,* AIR 1967 SC 1856.
187. Sovereignty and Integrity of India were added as new grounds for the restriction of the freedoms of speech, assembly and association, by the Constitution (16th Amendment) Act, 1963. After this amendment, it would be competent for the Legislatures to combat movements like the DMK movement in the South and the Plebiscite movement in *Kashmir* or parties advocating anarchism, by enacting appropriate laws. In pursuance of this amendment Parliament has enacted the Unlawful Activities (Prevention) Act, 1967 [see Author's *Law of the Press* (Prentice-Hall of India), 2nd Edn, pp 455 *et seq*].
188. *Ramesh Yeshwant Prabhoo (Dr) v Prabhakar Kashinath Kunte,* AIR 1996 SC 1113 : (1996) 1 SCC 130, paras 28 and 29.
189. *Ramesh Yeshwant Prabhoo (Dr) v Prabhakar Kashinath Kunte,* AIR 1996 SC 1113 : (1996) 1 SCC 130, paras 28 and 29.

overthrow the established government by force or unlawful means. No one can exercise his right of speech in such a manner as to violate another man's such right.[190]

Analysis of the offences involving speech and expression under IPC as well as in other special enactments shows that the eight heads of restrictions in Article 19(2) are so exhaustive that the laws made for protection of the individual, sections of society, classes of citizens, the court, the country and the State, have been saved.[191]

(ii) Similarly, the freedom of *assembly* is subject to the qualification that the assembly must be peaceable and without arms and subject to such reasonable restrictions as may be imposed by the "State" in the interests of public order. In other words, the right of meeting or assembly shall not be liable to be abused so as to create public disorder or a breach of the peace, or to prejudice the sovereignty or integrity of India.[192]

(iii) Again, all citizens have the right to *form associations* or *unions,* but subject to reasonable restrictions imposed by the state in the interests of public order or morality or the sovereignty or integrity of India. Thus, this freedom will not entitle any group of individuals to enter into a criminal conspiracy or to form any association dangerous to the public peace or to make illegal strikes or to commit a public disorder, or to undermine the sovereignty or integrity of India.[193]

(iv) Similarly, though every citizen shall have the right to *move* freely throughout the territory of India or to *reside* and *settle* in any part of the country—this right shall be subject to restrictions imposed by the state in the interests of the general public or for the protection of any Scheduled Tribe.

This Fundamental right can also be exercised in relation to the Scheduled Area.[194]

---

190. *Secretary, Ministry of Information & Broadcasting v Cricket Association of Bengal,* AIR 1995 SC 1236 : (1995) 2 SCC 161, para 152.

191. *Kaushal Kishor v State of UP,* (2023) 4 SCC 1 (SC) : 2023 SCC OnLine SC 6.

192. *Indra Sawhney v UOI,* (1992) Supp 3 SCC 217 and *S Vinod Kumar v UOI,* (1996) 6 SCC 580. *Faculty Association of AIIMS v UOI,* (2013) 11 SCC 246 : (2013) 5 Mad LJ 833; *Jagdish Saran v UOI,* AIR 1980 SC 820 : (1980) 2 SCC 768; *Pradeep Jain v UOI,* AIR 1984 SC 1420 : (1984) 3 SCC 654; *Preeti Srivastava v State of Madhya Pradesh,* (1999) 7 SCC 120 : (1999) 4 AWC 2853 (SC); The Constitution (102nd) Amendment does not violate any basic feature of the Constitution. *Dr Jaishri Laxmanrao Patil v The Chief Minister,* LNIND 2021 SC 170 : (2021) SCC Online 170

193. Under the Unlawful Activities (Prevention) Act, 1967 an association may be declared unlawful leading to banning of its activities. This can be done only after a tribunal presided over by a High Court judge upholds the validity of the declaration after hearing the association. Earlier National Socialist Council of Nagaland, Liberation Tigers of Tamil Eelam (LTTE), National Council of Khalistan and United Liberation Front of Assam (ULFA) were declared unlawful. On 10 December 1992 the RSS, VHP, Bajrang Dal, Islamic Sevak Sangh and Jamait-e-Islami Hindi were declared unlawful. Justice Bahri tribunal has held that the ban on RSS and Bajrang Dal is unjustified. Hence the notification pertaining to them has no effect.

194. *Adivasis for Social and Human Rights Action v UOI,* 2023 SCC OnLine SC 601 : AIR 2023 SC 2658.

(v) Again, every citizen has the right to practise any profession or to carry on any *occupation, trade or business,* but subject to reasonable restrictions imposed by the state in the interests of the general public and subject to any law laying down qualifications for carrying on any profession or technical occupation, or enabling the state itself to carry on any trade or business to the exclusion of the citizens.

14b. Scope for Judicial Review.

As pointed out earlier, one of the striking features of the provisions relating to Fundamental Rights in *our* Constitution is that the very declaration of the major Fundamental Rights is attended with certain limitations specified by the Constitution itself. In the *United States*, the Bill of Rights itself does not contain any such limitations to the rights of the individuals guaranteed thereby, but in the enforcement of those rights the courts had to invent doctrines like that of "Police Power of the State" to impose limitations on the rights of the individual in the interests of the community at large. However, as explained above in Article 19 of *our* Constitution, there is a distinct clause attached to each of the rights declared, containing the limitations or restrictions which may be imposed by the State on the exercise of each of the rights so guaranteed. For example, while the freedom of speech and expression is guaranteed, an individual cannot use this freedom to defame another which constitutes an offence under the law. A law which may be made by the State under any of the specified grounds, such as public order, defamation, contempt of court, cannot be challenged as unconstitutional or inconsistent with the guarantee of freedom of expression except where the restrictions imposed by the law can be held to be "unreasonable" by a court of law.

That is how the competing interests of individual liberty and of public welfare have been sought to be reconciled by the framers of *our* Constitution. As Mukherjee, J explained in the leading case of *A K Gopalan v State of Madras*[195]—

> There cannot be any such thing as absolute or uncontrolled liberty wholly freed from restraint for that would lead to anarchy and disorder. The possession and enjoyment of all rights . . . are subject to such reasonable conditions as may be deemed to the governing authority of the country to be essential to the safety, health, peace, general order and morals of the community. The question, therefore, arises in each case of *adjusting the conflicting interests* of the individual and of the society. . . Ordinarily every man has the liberty to order his life as he pleases, to say what he will, to go where he will, to follow any trade, occupation or calling at his pleasure and to do any other thing which he can lawfully do without let or hindrance by any other person. On the other hand, for the very protection of these liberties the society must arm itself with certain powers. ... What the Constitution, therefore, attempts to do in declaring the rights of the people is to strike a balance between individual liberty and social security. ... Article 19 of the Constitution gives a list of individual liberties and prescribes in the various clauses the restraints that may be placed upon them by law so that they may not conflict with public welfare or general morality.

It is by way of interpretation of the word "reasonable" that the court comes into the field, and in each case when an individual complains to the court that his Fundamental Right has been infringed by the operation of a law, or an executive order issued under a law, the court has got to determine whether the restriction

195. *A K Gopalan v State of Madras,* AIR 1950 SC 27 : (1950) 1 SCR 88.

imposed by the law is reasonable and if it is held to be unreasonable in the opinion of the court, the court will declare the law (and the order, if any) to be unconstitutional and void.[196]

14c. Tests of Reasonableness of a Restriction.

The expression "reasonable restriction" seeks to strike a balance between the freedoms guaranteed by any of the sub-clauses of Article 19(1) and the social control permitted by any of the exceptions in clauses (2) to (6). It is to be seen, therefore, what criteria or tests have been laid down by the Supreme Court for determining whether the restriction is reasonable or not. The Supreme Court has said[197–198] that a restriction is reasonable only when there is a proper balance between the rights of the individual and those of the society. Where the lands were given to landless persons as a social welfare measure to improve the conditions of poor landless persons, the conditions imposed against the transfer for the particular period of such granted land cannot be said to constitute any unreasonable restriction.[199]

The test of reasonableness should, therefore, be applied to each individual statute impugned and not abstract or general pattern of reasonableness can be laid down as applicable to all cases. The *nature of the right* alleged to have been infringed, the underlying *purpose of the restrictions* imposed, the *extent* and *urgency of the evil* sought to be remedied thereby, the *disproportion* of the imposition, the *prevailing conditions* at the time, should all enter into the judicial verdict.[200] Thus, the formula of subjective satisfaction of the Government and its officers with an advisory Board to review the materials on which the Government seeks to override a basic freedom guaranteed to the citizen, may be viewed as reasonable only in very exceptional circumstances (eg, in providing internment or externment for the security of the state), and within the narrowest limits, and not to curtail a right such as the freedom of association, in the absence of any emergent or extraordinary circumstances.[201] All the attendant circumstances must be taken into consideration and one cannot dissociate the actual *contents* of the restrictions from the *manner of their imposition* or the *mode of putting them into practice.*[202]

The Supreme Court has held that in examining the reasonableness of a statutory provision, whether it violated the fundamental right guaranteed under Article 19, one has to keep in mind:

(1) The Directive Principles of the State Policy.

(2) The restrictions must not be arbitrary or of an excessive nature, going beyond the requirement of the interest of the general public.

---

196. *Mohd Hanif Qureshi v State of Bihar,* (1959) SCR 629.

197. *Dwarka Prasad v State of Uttar Pradesh,* (1954) SCR 803.

198. *Chintamanrao v State of Madhya Pradesh,* (1952) SCR 759; *State of Maharashtra v Himmatbhai,* AIR 1970 SC 1157.

199. *Bhadrappa v Tolacha Naik,* (2008) 2 SCC 104 (*107*).

200. *State of Madras v Row,* (1952) SCR 597 (*607*); *Laxmi Khandsari v State of Uttar Pradesh,* AIR 1981 SC 873. (This proposition is now to be read subject to the exceptions under Articles 31B, 31C.)

201. *Bhadrappa v Tolacha Naik,* (2008) 2 SCC 104 (*107*).

202. *N B Khare v State of Delhi* (1950) SCR 519; *Gurbachan v State of Bombay,* (1952) SCR 737 (*742*).

(3) No abstract or general pattern or a mixed principle to judge the reasonableness of the restrictions can be laid down so as to be of universal application and the same will vary from case to case as also with regard to the changing conditions, values of human life, social philosophy of the constitution, prevailing conditions and surrounding circumstances.

(4) A just balance has to be struck between the restrictions imposed and social control envisaged by Article 19(6).

(5) Prevailing social values as also social needs which are intended to be satisfied by the restrictions.

(6) There must be a direct and proximate nexus or reasonable connection between the restrictions imposed and the object sought to be achieved by the Act, that being so a strong presumption in favour of the constitutionality of the Act will naturally arise.[203]

The role of the Courts is to be a gatekeeper (and a conscience keeper) to strictly check the entry of restrictions into the temple of fundamental rights and to protect such rights limited by lawful restrictions, and not to protect the restrictions and make the rights residual privileges.[204]

14d. Substantive and Procedural Reasonableness. It follows, therefore, that the question of reasonableness should be determined from both the *substantive* and *procedural* standpoints. Hence—

(a) In order to be reasonable, the restriction imposed must have a reasonable relation to the collective object which the legislation seeks to achieve and must not go in excess of that object, or, in other words, the restriction must not be greater than the mischief to be prevented. Legislation which arbitrarily or excessively invades the right cannot be said to contain the quality of reasonableness.[205] Thus—

> The object of an Act was "to provide measures for the supply of adequate labour for agricultural proposes in *bidi* manufacturing areas". But the order of the Deputy Commissioner made thereunder forbade *all* persons residing in certain villages from engaging in the manufacture of *bidis* during the agricultural season. The Supreme Court invalidated the order on the ground that it imposed an unreasonable restriction upon the freedom of business [*Article 19(1)(g)*] of those engaged in the manufacture of *bidis* because—
>
> The object of the Act could be achieved by legislation restraining the employment of *agricultural* labour in the manufacture of bidis *during the agricultural season* or by regulating hours of work on the business of making *bidis*. A *total* prohibition of the manufacture imposes an *unreasonable* and *excessive* restriction on the lawful occupation of manufacturing *bidis*.[206]

(b) While the foregoing aspect may be said to be the *substantive* aspect of reasonableness, there is another aspect, *viz*, the *procedural aspect*, relating to the manner in which the restrictions have been imposed. That is to say, in order to be reasonable, not only the restriction must not be *excessive*, the procedure or

---

203. *MRF Ltd v Inspector Kerala Govt*, (1998) 8 SCC 227, para 13.
204. *Kaushal Kishor v State of UP*, (2023) 4 SCC 1 (SC) : 2023 SCC OnLine SC 6.
205. *Dwarka Prasad v State of Uttar Pradesh*, (1954) SCR 803.
206. *Dwarka Prasad v State of Uttar Pradesh*, (1954) SCR 803.

manner of imposition of the restriction must also be *fair and just.* In order to determine whether the restrictions imposed by a law are procedurally reasonable, the court must take into consideration all the attendant circumstances such as the *manner* of its imposition, the mode of putting it into practice. Broadly speaking, a restriction is unreasonable if it is imposed in a manner which violates the principles of natural justice, for example, if it seeks to curtail the right of association or the freedom of business of a citizen without giving him *an opportunity to be heard.*[207] It has also been laid down that in the absence of extraordinary circumstances it would be unreasonable to make the exercise of a fundamental right depend on the subjective satisfaction of the Executive.[208]

The rights of hawking for carrying a business on streets cannot be denied if they are properly regulated under Article 19(6) of the Constitution[209] but hawkers carrying on trade or business on pavements of roads cannot claim right under Article 21 as right to carry on trade or business is not covered by Article 21.[210]

14e. Freedom of the Press.

There is no specific provision in our Constitution guaranteeing the freedom of the press because freedom of the press is included[211] in the wider freedom of "expression" which is guaranteed by Article 19(1)(a). Freedom of expression means the freedom to express not only one's *own* views but also the views of *others* and, by *any* means, including printing. Since however, the freedom of expression is not an absolute freedom and is subject to the limitations contained in clause (2) of Article 19, laws may be passed by the State imposing reasonable restrictions on the freedom of the press in the interests of the security of the State, the sovereignty and integrity of India, friendly relations with foreign States, public order, decency or morality, or for the prevention of contempt of court, defamation or incitement to an offence. Absolute, unlimited and unfettered freedom of press at all times and in all the circumstances would lead to disorder and anarchy.[212]

The newspapers serve as a medium of exercise of freedom of speech.[213] Any expression of opinion would not be immune from the liability for exceeding the limits. If a citizen, in the garb of exercising the right of free expression guaranteed under Article 19(1) tries to scandalise the court or undermines the dignity of the court, then the court would be entitled to exercise the power under contempt provisions.[214]

The Press, as such, has no special privileges in India. From the fact that the measure of the freedom of the Press is the same as that of an ordinary citizen under Article 19(1)(a), several propositions emerge[215]—

207. *Dwarka Prasad v State of Uttar Pradesh,* (1954) SCR 803; *AP Merchants' Association v UOI,* AIR 1971 SC 2346.
208. *Bhadrappa v Tolacha Naik,* (2008) 2 SCC 104 (*107*).
209. *Gainda Ram v MCD,* (2010) 10 SCC 715, p *716.*
210. *Sodan Singh v New Delhi Municipal Committee,* (1989) 4 SCC 155.
211. *Express Newspapers v UOI,* AIR 1958 SC 578.
212. *Re Harijai Singh,* AIR 1997 SC 73 : (1996) 6 SCC 466, para 10.
213. *Hindustan Times v State of Uttar Pradesh,* (2003) 1 SCC 591.
214. *Re, Arundhati Roy,* AIR 2002 SC 1375.
215. *N Adithayan v Travancore Devaswom Board,* (2002) 8 SCC 106, para 16.

I. The Press is not immune from—

(a) the ordinary forms of taxation;

(b) the application of the general laws relating to industrial relations;

(c) the regulation of the conditions of service of the employees.

II. But in view of the guarantee of freedom of expression, it would not be legitimate for the State—

(a) to subject the Press to laws which take away or abridge the freedom of expression or which would curtail circulation[216] and thereby narrow the scope of dissemination of information or fetter its freedom to choose its means of exercising the right *or* would undermine its independence by driving it to seek Government aid;[217]

(b) to single out the Press for laying upon it excessive and prohibitive burdens which would restrict the circulation, impose a penalty on its right to choose the instruments for its exercise or to seek an alternative media;[218]

(c) to impose a specific tax upon the Press deliberately calculated to limit the circulation of information.[219]

When the constitutionality of an enactment specially directed against the Press is challenged, the court has to test it by the standard of substantive and procedural reasonableness, as explained earlier. An enactment of this nature, the Punjab Special Powers (Press) Act, 1956, came up before the Supreme Court in *Virendra v State of Punjab,*[220] and the court annulled one of its provisions, while upholding another, on the following grounds:

> A law which empowers the Government to prohibit, for a *temporary* period, the entry of literature of a *specified class,* likely to cause communal disharmony would not be held to be unreasonable, if it complies with the procedural requirements of natural justice. But it would be unreasonable if it empowered the State Government to prohibit the bringing into the State of *any* newspaper, on its being satisfied that such action was necessary for the maintenance of communal harmony or public order, inasmuch as it placed the whole matter at the subjective satisfaction of the State Government without even providing for a right of representation to the party affected.

Since the expiry of the Press (Objectionable Matter) Act, 1951, in 1956, there was no all-India Act for the control of the Press in India. But in 1976, the Parliament enacted the Prevention of Publication of Objectionable Matter Act, 1976, with more rigorous provisions, and in a *permanent* form. In April, 1977, the Janata Government *repealed* this Act. Subsequently, however, this position was

---

216. *Bennett Coleman v UOI,* AIR 1973 SC 106 [see Author's *Casebook on Indian Constitutional Law,* vol 1, pp 207–49].
217. *Bennett Coleman v UOI,* AIR 1973 SC 106 [see Author's *Casebook on Indian Constitutional Law,* vol 1, pp 207–49].
218. *Bennett Coleman v UOI,* AIR 1973 SC 106 [see Author's *Casebook on Indian Constitutional Law,* vol 1, pp 207–49].
219. *Gainda Ram v MCD,* (2010) 10 SCC 715, p *716.*
220. *Virendra v State of Punjab,* AIR 1958 SC 986.

further buttressed by inserting a new Article in the Constitution itself—Article 361A[221]—by the Constitution (44th Amendment) Act, 1978.

14f. Censorship.

Censorship of the press, again, is not specially prohibited by any provision of the Constitution. Like other restrictions, therefore, its constitutionality has to be judged by the test of "reasonableness" within the meaning of clause (2).[222]

Soon after the commencement of the Constitution and prior to the insertion of the word "reasonable" in clause (2), the question of validity of censorship came up before *our* Supreme Court, in the case of *Brij Bhushan v State of Delhi.*[223]

The facts of this case were as follows:

> Section 7(1)(c) of the East Punjab Safety Act, 1949, provided that "the Provincial Government . . . if satisfied that such action is necessary for preventing or combating any activity prejudicial to the *public safety* or the maintenance of *public order may,* by order in writing addressed to a printer, publisher, editor require that any matter relating to a particular subject or class of subjects shall before publication be submitted for *scrutiny*".
>
> Similar provisions of the Madras Maintenance of Public Order Act, 1949, were challenged in the allied case of *Ramesh Thappar v State of Madras.*[224]
>
> The majority of the Supreme Court had no difficulty in holding that the imposition of pre-censorship on a journal was an obvious restriction upon the freedom of speech and expression guaranteed by clause (1)(a) of article 19, that 'public safety' or 'public order' was not covered by the expression 'security of the State', and the impugned law was not, therefore, saved by clause (2) as it then stood.

Shortly after these decisions,[225] clause (2) was amended by the Constitution (First Amendment) Act, 1951, inserting "public order" in clause (2). Hence, the ground relied upon by the majority in the cases of *Ramesh Thappar*[226] and *Brij Bhushan* is no longer available. The word "reasonable" was also inserted in clause (2) by the same amendment. The result of this twofold amendment is that if censorship is imposed in the interests of public order, it cannot at once be held to be unconstitutional as fetter upon the freedom of circulation but its "reasonableness" has to be determined with reference to the circumstances of its imposition. In this sense, the introduction of the word "reasonable" has not been an unmixed blessing. For, censorship of the press, in *times of peace,* is something unimaginable either in England or in the United States in modern times. But under *our* Constitution, as the Supreme Court decision in *Virendra v State of Punjab,*[227] suggests, even at a time of peace, censorship may be valid if it is subjected to reasonable safeguards, both from the substantive and procedural

221. See Author's *Shorter Constitution of India,* 14th Edn, 2008.
222. *Virendra v State of Punjab,* AIR 1958 SC 986.
223. *Brij Bhushan v State of Delhi,* (1950) SCR 605; *Ramesh Thappar v State of Madras,* (1950) SCR 594 (*597*).
224. *Brij Bhushan v State of Delhi,* (1950) SCR 605; *Ramesh Thappar v State of Madras,* (1950) SCR 594 (*597*).
225. *S Khushboo v Kanniammal,* AIR 2010 SC 3196, p *3208.*
226. *Brij Bhushan v State of Delhi,* (1950) SCR 605; *Ramesh Thappar v State of Madras,* (1950) SCR 594 (*597*).
227. *Bennett Coleman v UOI,* AIR 1973 SC 106 [see Author's *Casebook on Indian Constitutional Law,* vol 1, pp 207–49].

standpoints, but not otherwise. The provisions before the Court[228] were sections 2 and 3 of the Punjab Special Powers (Press) Act, 1956, which were similar to that in section 7(1)(c) of the East Punjab Public Safety Act, 1949 (which had been impugned in *Brij Bhushan's* case),[229] except that in the Act of the 1956 what was authorised was even more drastic than pre-censorship, *viz*—a total *prohibition.* The court held that section 2, which provided for a right of representation against the order of the authority and limited the power to a specified period and as to publications of a specified class, was valid; but that section 3, which had no such safeguards, constituted an unreasonable restriction.

It would, therefore, follow that a provision for pre-censorship for a limited period in emergent circumstances and subject to procedural safeguards, eg, as in section 144 of the Criminal Procedure Code, 1973, is valid.[230] If, however, it is left to the absolute discretion[231] of the executive authority, it must be held to be unreasonable. The Supreme Court has, similarly, upheld the validity of a law sanctioning pre-censorship of motion pictures to protect the interests safeguarded by Article 19(2), eg, public order and morality.[232] The Constitutionality of section 66A of the Information Technology Act, 2000, was challenged on the ground that it infringes the fundamental right to free speech and expression and is not saved by any of the eight subjects covered in Article 19(2). Further it casts the net very wide—"all information" that is disseminated over the internet is included within its reach. The Supreme Court held that section 66A creates an offence which is vague and overbroad, and therefore, unconstitutional under Article 19(1)(a) and not saved by Article 19(2).[233]

It should be noted that when a Proclamation of Emergency is made under Article 352, Article 19 itself, remains suspended [*Article* 358], so that pre-censorship may be imposed, without any restraint (see chapter 28, *post*). Thus, immediately after the Proclamation of Emergency on the ground of internal disturbance[234] in June, 1975, a Censorship Order was issued (26 June 1975), under rule 48(1) of the Rules made under the Defence and Internal Security of India Act, 1971. It should be noted that on the defeat of Mrs Gandhi at the election of 1977, the Proclamation of Internal Emergency[235] was revoked on the 21st, and the Press Censorship Order was revoked on the 22 March 1977.

228. *Bennett Coleman v UOI,* AIR 1973 SC 106 [see Author's *Casebook on Indian Constitutional Law,* vol 1, pp 207–49].
229. *Brij Bhushan v State of Delhi,* (1950) SCR 605; *Ramesh Thappar v State of Madras,* (1950) SCR 594 (*597*).
230. *Babulal v State of Maharashtra,* AIR 1961 SC 884.
231. *Bennett Coleman v UOI,* AIR 1973 SC 106 [see Author's *Casebook on Indian Constitutional Law,* vol 1, pp 207–49].
232. *Abbas v UOI,* AIR 1971 SC 481; see Author's *Casebook on Indian Constitutional Law,* vol 1, p 276.
233. *Shreya Singhal v UOI,* WP (C) No. 167 of 2012, decided on 24 March 2015 (Supreme Court of India) (Bench: J Chelameswar, RF Nariman, JJ).
234. As will be more fully explained in chapter 28, *post,* the 44th Amendment Act, 1978, has amended Article 352(1), omitting "internal disturbance" therefrom, so that it will no longer be possible to make any Proclamation of Emergency on the ground of *internal disturbance.* A Proclamation of Emergency can hereafter be valid under Article 352(1) only on the ground of (a) war; or (b) external aggression; or (c) *armed rebellion.*
235. *Abbas v UOI,* AIR 1971 SC 481; see Author's *Casebook on Indian Constitutional Law,* vol 1, p 276.

The denial of security clearance to operate a news channel is a restriction on the freedom of press, and such restriction is constitutionally permissible only on the grounds stipulated in Article 19(2).[236]

Article 19 would also be inapplicable in cases where Articles 31A to 31C are attracted. These exceptions to Fundamental Rights, which have been introduced by subsequent amendments, will be discussed at the end of this chapter.

14g. Freedom of Press Relating to Court Proceedings.

In an important case which arose from an order of a Division Bench of the high court of Judicature at Madras wherein the high court while hearing a writ petition under Article 226 of the Constitution alleged to have made certain oral remarks, attributing responsibility to the Election Commission for surge in the number of cases of COVID-19, due to its failure to implement appropriate COVID-19 safety measures and protocol during the elections,[237] the Supreme Court observed:

> This Court stands as a staunch proponent of the freedom of the media to report court proceedings. This we believe is integral to the freedom of speech and expression of those who speak, of those who wish to hear and to be heard and above all, in holding the judiciary accountable to the values which justify its existence as a constitutional institution.

The Supreme Court further observed that:

> the duty to preserve the independence of the judiciary and to allow freedom of expression of the judges in court is one end of the spectrum. The other end of the spectrum, which is equally important, is that the power of judges must not be unbridled and judicial restraint must be exercised, before using strong and scathing language to criticize any individual or institution.

14h. Access to Internet.

In *Anuradha Bhasin v UOI*,[238] the Supreme Court held that the right to freedom of speech and expression and the freedom to practice any profession or carry on any trade, business or occupation over the medium of internet enjoys Constitutional protection under Articles 19(1)(a) and 19(1)(*g*) of the Constitution of India. Any restriction upon such fundamental rights should be in consonance with the mandate under Articles 19(2) and 19(6), inclusive of the test of proportionality.

15. Article 20—Protection in Respect of Conviction for Offences.

Article 20 guarantees protection in certain respects against conviction for offences, by prohibiting—

(a) Retrospective criminal legislation, commonly known as *ex post facto* legislation.

(b) Double jeopardy or punishment for the same offence more than once.

(c) Compulsion to give self-incriminating evidence.

236. *Madhyamam Broadcasting Limited v UOI*, 2023 SCC OnLine SC 366 : (2023) 3 MLJ 97.

237. *Chief Election Commissioner of India v MR Vijayabhaskar*, LNIND 2021 SC 171 : Civil Appeal No 1767 of 2021 (SC), decided on 6 May 2021.

238. *Anuradha Bhasin v UOI*, LNIND 2020 SC 18 : (2020) SCC Online SC 25.

15a. Prohibition Against *ex post facto* Legislation.

The provision against *ex post facto* legislation is contained in clause (1) of Article 20 of our Constitution which runs as follows—

> No person shall be convicted of any offence except for violation of a law in force at the time of the commission of the act charged as an offence, nor be subjected to a penalty greater than that which might have been inflicted under the law in force at the time of the commission of the offence.

This is a limitation upon the law-making power of the Legislatures in India. A law is said to be prospective when it affects acts done or omission made after the law comes into effect. The majority of laws are prospective in their operation. But sometimes the Legislature may give retrospective effect to a law, that is to say, to bring within the operation of the law, not only future acts and omissions but also acts or omissions committed even prior to the enactment of the law in question. Though ordinarily a Legislature can enact prospective as well as *retrospective* laws, according to the present clause a Legislature shall not be competent to make a *criminal law* retrospective so as to provide that a person may be convicted for an act which was not an offence under the law in force at the time of commission of that act or to subject an accused to a penalty greater than that which might have been inflicted under the law in force at the time of the commission of the offence. In other words, when the Legislature declares an act to be an offence or provides a penalty for an offence, it cannot make the law retrospective so as to prejudicially affect the persons who have committed such acts prior to the enactment of that law.[239] Enlarging a penal provision for prosecution would be violative of Article 20(1).[240]

15b. Immunity from Double Prosecution and Punishment.

The prohibition against double jeopardy is contained in clause (2) of Article 20 which runs thus—

> No person shall be prosecuted and punished for the same offence more than once.

The expression "double jeopardy" is used in the American law but not in *our* Constitution. Nevertheless, clause (2) of Article 20, in effect, lays down a similar principle. As has been laid down by the Supreme Court in *Venkataraman v UOI,*[241] Article 20(2) refers to *judicial* punishment and gives immunity to a person from being prosecuted and punished for the same offence more than once. In other words, if a person has been prosecuted and punished in a previous proceeding of an offence, he cannot be prosecuted and punished for the same offence again in a subsequent proceeding. A person cannot be punished for the same offence twice and cannot be compelled to be a witness against himself.[242] If any law provides for such double punishment, such law would be void. The Article, however, does not give immunity from proceedings other than proceedings before a court of law or a judicial tribunal. Hence, a Government servant who has been punished for an offence in a court of law may

---

239. *Kedar Nath v State of West Bengal,* (1954) SCR 30. See also *Star India (P) Ltd v Commissioner of Central Excise, Mumbai & Goa,* (2005) 7 SCC 203, para 7; *C Gupta v Glaxo-Smithkline Pharmaceuticals Ltd,* (2007) 7 SCC 171, para 23.
240. *Sakshi v UOI,* (2004) 5 SCC 518, para 20.
241. *Venkataraman v UOI,* (1954) SCR 1150. See also *UOI v Sunil Kumar Sarkar,* AIR 2001 SC 1092; *State of Punjab v Dalbir Singh,* (2001) 9 SCC 212.
242. *Manu Sharma v State (NCT of Delhi),* (2010) 6 SCC 1, p 80.

yet be subjected to *departmental proceedings* for the same offence, or conversely.[243] If the accused was neither convicted nor acquitted of the charges against him in the first trial, his retrial would not amount to double jeopardy.[244] Prosecution and punishment under two sections of an Act, the offences under the two sections being distinct from each other, does not amount to double jeopardy.[245]

15c. Accused's Immunity from being Compelled to give Evidence Against Himself. The immunity from self-incrimination is conferred by clause (3) of Article 20 which says—

> No person accused of any offence shall be compelled to be a witness against himself.

The scope of this immunity has, *prima facie*, been widened by *our* Supreme Court by interpreting the word "witness" to comprise both oral and documentary evidence, so that no person can be compelled to furnish *any kind of evidence* which is reasonably likely to support a prosecution against him. Such evidence must, however, be in the nature of a communication. The prohibition is not attracted where any object or document is searched and seized from the possession of the accused.[246] For the same reason, the clause does not bar the medical examination of the accused or the obtaining of thumb-impression or specimen signature from him.[247]

Secondly, the immunity does not extend to civil proceedings or other than criminal proceedings.[248] It has also been explained by the Supreme Court[249] that in order to claim the immunity from being compelled to make a self-incriminating statement, it must appear that a *formal accusation* has been made against the person at the time when he is asked to make the incriminating statement. He cannot claim the immunity at some general inquiry or investigation on the ground that his statement may at some later stage lead to an accusation.[250] In administrative and quasi criminal proceedings the protection of Article 20(3) becomes available only after a person has been formally accused of committing an offence. The compulsory administration of the narco analysis technique amounts to "testimonial compulsion" and thereby triggers the protection of Article 20(3) of the Constitution.[251]

After the introduction of section 54A in the CrPC, an accused is under an obligation to stand for identification parade. An accused cannot resist subjecting

243. *Sakshi v UOI,* (2004) 5 SCC 518, para 20.
244. *O P Dahiya v UOI,* (2003) 1 SCC 122. See also *Shiv Parshad Pandey v CBI,* AIR 2003 SC 1974.
245. *State of Rajasthan v Hat Singh,* AIR 2003 SC 791; *State (NCT of Delhi) v Navjot Sandhu,* (2005) 11 SCC 600.
246. *M P Sharma v Satish,* (1954) SCR 1077.
247. *State of Bombay v Kathi Kalu,* AIR 1961 SC 1808. See also *State (NCT of Delhi) v Navjot Sandhu,* (2005) 11 SCC 600.
248. *Maqbool v State of Bombay,* (1953) SCR 730.
249. *State of Rajasthan v Hat Singh,* AIR 2003 SC 791; *State (NCT of Delhi) v Navjot Sandhu,* (2005) 11 SCC 600.
250. *Raja Narayanlal v Maneck,* AIR 1961 SC 29, p *38*; *Veera v State of Maharashtra,* AIR 1976 SC 1167.
251. *Selvi v State of Karnataka,* AIR 2010 SC 1974 : (2010) 7 SCC 263; see also *Balasahib v State of Maharashtra,* (2011) 1 SCC 364.

himself to the TIP on the ground that he cannot be forced or coerced for the same. If the coercion is sought to be imposed in getting from an accused evidence which cannot be procured save through positive volitional act on his part, the constitutional guarantee as enshrined under Article 20(3) of the Constitution will step in to protect him. However, if that evidence can be procured without any positive volitional evidentiary act on the part of the accused, Article 20(3) of the Constitution will have no application. The accused while subjecting himself to the TIP does not produce any evidence or perform any evidentiary act. As explained very succinctly by the learned Judges of the Calcutta High Court as above, it may be a positive act and even a volitional act, but only to a limited extent, when the accused is brought to the place where the TIP is to be held. It is certainly not his evidentiary act. The accused concerned may have a legitimate ground to resist facing the TIP saying that the witnesses had a chance to see him either at the police station or in the Court, as the case may be, however, on such ground alone he cannot refuse to face the TIP. It is always open for the accused to raise any legal ground available to him relating to the legitimacy of the TIP or the evidentiary value of the same in the course of the trial. However, the accused cannot decline or refuse to join the TIP.[252]

16. Freedom of Person or Personal Liberty. Freedom of person or personal liberty is sought to be ensured by *our* Constitution by means of a two-fold guarantee, namely—

(a) By providing that no person can be deprived of his liberty except according to law [*Article 21*];

(b) By laying down certain specific safeguards against arbitrary arrest or detention [*Article 22*].

17. Article 21—Protection of life and Personal Liberty. Article 21 of *our* Constitution provides that—

> No person shall be deprived of his life or personal liberty except according to the procedure established by law.

This Article reminds us of one of the famous clauses of the Magna Carta:

> No man shall be taken or imprisoned, disseized or outlawed, or exiled, or in any way destroyed save . . by the law of the land.

It means that no member of the Executive shall be entitled to interfere with the liberty of a citizen unless he can support his action by some provision of law. In short, no man can be subjected to any physical coercion that does not admit of legal justification. When, therefore, the State or any of its agents deprives an individual of his personal liberty, such action can be justified only if there is a law to support such action and the procedures prescribed by such law have been "strictly and scrupulously"[253] observed. The word "law" which figures in Article 21 of the Constitution would mean a validity enacted law and in order to be a valid law it must be just, fair and reasonable.[254]

---

252. *Mukesh Singh v State (NCT of Delhi)*, 2023 SCC OnLine SC 1061.

253. *Ram Narain v State of Bombay*, 1959 AIR 459 : (1952) SCR 652.

254. *Delhi Airtech Services Pvt Ltd v State of Uttar Pradesh*, AIR 2012 SC 573, *593* : (2011) 9 SCC 354.

Again, as under the English Constitution, personal freedom is secured by the Indian Constitution by the judicial writ of *habeas corpus* (see under "*Habeas Corpus*", *post*) [*Articles 32 and 226*] by means of which an arrested person may have himself brought before the court and have the ground of his imprisonment examined, and regain his freedom if the court finds that there is no legal justification for his imprisonment. The court will also set the prisoner free where there is a law authorising the deprivation of liberty of a person but there has been no strict compliance with the conditions imposed by the law. The Supreme Court has more than once observed that "those who feel called upon to deprive other persons of their personal liberty in the discharge of what they conceive to be their duty, must strictly and scrupulously observe the forms and rules of the law".[255]

But in no country can there be any absolute freedom of the individual. The principle underlying the *English* Constitution is that it is the people's representatives, assembled in Parliament, who shall determine how far the rights of the individuals should go and how far they should be curtailed in the collective interests or for the security of the State itself, according to exigencies of the time. This was the theory adopted by the Constitution of India in saying that life and personal liberty are subject to "the procedure established by law".

17a. Judicial Review.

The Supreme Court has, however infused judicial review by holding that "procedure" inherently meant a fair procedure, so that Article 21 has been turned into a safeguard against arbitrary legislation. The history of this change in view is as follows:

I. Until the 1978-decision in *Maneka's* case,[256] the view which prevailed in *our* Supreme Court was that there was no guarantee in *our* Constitution against arbitrary *legislation* encroaching upon personal liberty. Hence, if a competent Legislature makes a law providing that a person may be deprived of his liberty in certain circumstances and in a certain manner, the validity of the law could not be challenged in a court of law on the ground that the law is unreasonable, unfair or unjust.[257] Under the "Due Process", clause of the *American* Constitution (5th and 14th Amendments), the court has assumed the power of declaring unconstitutional any law which deprives a person of his liberty otherwise than in accordance with the court's notions of "due process", ie, reasonableness and fairness. In *England,* this is not possible inasmuch as courts have no power to invalidate a law made by Parliament. In the result, personal liberty is, in England, "a liberty confined and controlled by law". It exists only so far as it is not taken away or limited by laws made by the representatives of the people. In *AK Gopalan v State of Madras,*[258] the majority of *our* Supreme Court propounded the view that by adopting the expression "procedure established by law", Article 21 of our Constitution had embodied the English concept of

255. *Selvi v State of Karnataka,* AIR 2010 SC 1974 : (2010) 7 SCC 263; see also *Balasahib v State of Maharashtra,* (2011) 1 SCC 364.

256. *Cf Maneka v UOI,* AIR 1978 SC 597, paras 54–56, 63 — a seven Judge Bench; *Sunil v Delhi Administration,* AIR 1978 SC 1675, para 228 : (1978) 4 SCC 494; *Hussainara Khatoon v State of Bihar,* AIR 1979 SC 1360, p *1365*; *State of Maharashtra v VG Champalal,* AIR 1981 SC 1675 (*1677*); *Sher Singh v State of Punjab,* AIR 1983 SC 465.

257. *AK Gopalan v State of Madras,* (1950) SCR 88; *Jayanarayana Sukul v State of West Bengal,* AIR 1970 SC 675.

258. *AK Gopalan v State of Madras,* (1950) SCR 88; *Jayanarayana Sukul v State of West Bengal,* AIR 1970 SC 675.

personal liberty in preference to that of American "Due Process", even though, according to the minority,[259] the result of such interpretation was to throw "the most important fundamental right to life and personal liberty" "at the mercy of legislative majorities." The result, according to the majority, is due to the difference in the basic approach, namely, that—

> Although our Constitution has imposed some limitations on the legislative authorities yet subject to and outside such limitations our Constitution has left our Parliament and the State legislatures supreme in their respective fields. In the main ... our Constitution has *preferred the supremacy of the legislature to that of the judiciary.*[260]

It was also held[261–262] that there is no safeguard for personal liberty under our Constitution besides Article 21, such as natural law or common law. In the result, when personal liberty is taken away by a competent legislation, the person affected can have no remedy.[263]

II. It is a striking feature of the development of constitutional law of India that after a long struggle, which may be said to have started tangibly since 1971, the *minority* view in *Gopalan's* case[264] has come to triumph in the seven-Judge decision in *Maneka's* case,[265] which we have already noted. This case[266] has categorically laid down the following propositions, overturning the majority in *Gopalan*.[267]

(a) Articles 19 and 21 are not water-tight compartments. On the other hand, the expression of "personal liberty" in Article 21 is of the widest amplitude, covering a variety of rights of which some have been included in Article 19 and given *additional* protection. Hence, there may be some overlapping between Articles 19 and 21.

(b) In the result, a law coming under Article 21 must *also* satisfy the requirements of Article 19. In other words, a law made by the State which seeks to deprive a person of his personal liberty must prescribe a *procedure* for such deprivation which *must not be arbitrary, unfair or unreasonable.*

---

259. *AK Gopalan v State of Madras,* (1950) SCR 88; *Jayanarayana Sukul v State of West Bengal,* AIR 1970 SC 675.
260. *AK Gopalan v State of Madras,* (1950) SCR 88; *Jayanarayana Sukul v State of West Bengal,* AIR 1970 SC 675.
261. *Delhi Airtech Services Pvt Ltd v State of Uttar Pradesh,* AIR 2012 SC 573, *593* : (2011) 9 SCC 354.
262. *ADM Jabalpur v Shivkant Shukla,* AIR 1976 SC 1207.
263. *AK Gopalan v State of Madras,* (1950) SCR 88; *Jayanarayana Sukul v State of West Bengal,* AIR 1970 SC 675.
264. *AK Gopalan v State of Madras,* (1950) SCR 88; *Jayanarayana Sukul v State of West Bengal,* AIR 1970 SC 675.
265. *Cf Maneka v UOI,* AIR 1978 SC 597, paras 54–56, 63 — a seven Judge Bench; *Sunil v Delhi Administration,* AIR 1978 SC 1675, para 228 : (1978) 4 SCC 494; *Hussainara Khatoon v State of Bihar,* AIR 1979 SC 1360, p *1365*; *State of Maharashtra v Champalal,* AIR 1981 SC 1675 (*1677*); *Sher Singh v State of Punjab,* AIR 1983 SC 465.
266. *Cf Maneka v UOI,* AIR 1978 SC 597, paras 54–56, 63 — a seven Judge Bench; *Sunil v Delhi Administration,* AIR 1978 SC 1675, para 228 : (1978) 4 SCC 494; *Hussainara Hussainara v State of Bihar,* AIR 1979 SC 1360, p *1365*; *State of Maharashtra v CVG hampalal,* AIR 1981 SC 1675 (*1677*); *Sher Singh v State of Punjab,* AIR 1983 SC 465.
267. *AK Gopalan v State of Madras,* (1950) SCR 88; *Jayanarayana Sukul v State of West Bengal,* AIR 1970 SC 675.

(c) Once the test of reasonableness is imported to determine the validity of a law depriving a person of his liberty, it follows that such law shall be invalid if it violates the principles of natural justice, eg, if it provides for the impounding of a passport without giving the person affected an opportunity to be heard or to make a representation against the order proposed.[268]

From *Gopalan*[269] to *Maneka,*[270] thus, the judicial exploration has completed its trek from the North to the South Pole. The decision in *Maneka's* case[271] is being followed by the Supreme Court in subsequent cases.

The Supreme Court has held that the right to life as enshrined in Article 21 means something more than survival or animal existence and would include the right to live with human dignity. It would include right to minimum subsistence allowance during suspension and all those aspects which go to make a man's life meaningful, complete and worth living. It would, thus, include—

(1) The right to life under Article 21 of the Constitution does not include the right to die. An assisted suicide and active euthanasia are not legal. Euthanasia can be made lawful only by legislation.[272] The Constitution Bench of the Supreme Court in *Gian Kaur's* case held that both, euthanasia and assisted suicide are not lawful in India. However, the Supreme Court in *Aruna Ramchandran Shanbaug's* case noted, that there is no statutory provision in our country as to the legal procedure for withdrawing life-support given to a person in PVS (Permanent Vegetative State) or who is otherwise incompetent to take a decision in this connection. The Supreme Court held that passive euthanasia should be permitted in our country and further laid down the law/procedure in this connection which will continue to be the law until the Parliament makes a law on the subject.[273] In March 2018, a five-judge Constitution Bench of the Supreme Court gave legal sanction to passive euthanasia, permitting "living will" by patients on withdrawing medical support if they slip into irreversible coma. The Supreme Court held that the right to die with dignity is a fundamental right.

(2) Fair trial means a trial in which bias or prejudice for or against the accused, the witnesses, or the cause which is being tried is eliminated. If the witnesses are threatened or are forced to give false evidence that also

268. *Cf Maneka v UOI,* AIR 1978 SC 597, paras 54–56, 63 — a seven Judge Bench; *Sunil v Delhi Administration,* AIR 1978 SC 1675, para 228 : (1978) 4 SCC 494; *Hussainara Khatoon v State of Bihar,* AIR 1979 SC 1360, p *1365*; *State of Maharashtra v VG Champalal,* AIR 1981 SC 1675 (*1677*); *Sher Singh v State of Punjab,* AIR 1983 SC 465.

269. *AK Gopalan v State of Madras,* (1950) SCR 88; *Jayanarayana Sukul v State of West Bengal,* AIR 1970 SC 675.

270. *Cf Maneka v UOI,* AIR 1978 SC 597, paras 54–56, 63 — a seven Judge Bench; *Sunil v Delhi Administration,* AIR 1978 SC 1675, para 228 : (1978) 4 SCC 494; *Hussainara Khatoon v State of Bihar,* AIR 1979 SC 1360, p *1365*; *State of Maharashtra v Champalal,* AIR 1981 SC 1675 (*1677*); *Sher Singh v State of Punjab,* AIR 1983 SC 465.

271. *Cf Maneka v UOI,* AIR 1978 SC 597, paras 54–56, 63 — a seven Judge Bench; *Sunil v Delhi Administration,* AIR 1978 SC 1675, para 228 : (1978) 4 SCC 494; *Hussainara Khatoon v State of Bihar,* AIR 1979 SC 1360, p *1365*; *State of Maharashtra v Champalal,* AIR 1981 SC 1675 (*1677*); *Sher Singh v State of Punjab,* AIR 1983 SC 465.

272. *Gian Kaur v State of Punjab,* (1996) 2 SCC 648.

273. *Aruna Ramachandra Shanbagu v UOI,* (2011) 4 SCC 454, p *512* : (2011) 4 SCC 524.

would not result in a fair trial.[274] In the absence of fair trial, the Supreme Court can give order for re-trial even after acquittal, if the acquittal is unmerited and based on tainted evidence etc.[275]

(3) Subjecting a person to the narco analysis lie detector and BEAP tests in an interlocutory manner violates prescribed boundaries of privacy. No victim of an offence can be compelled to undergo any of such tests. Such a forcible administration would be an unjustified intrusion into mental privacy.[276]

(4) Involving ill equipped, barely literate youngsters in counter insurgency activities wherein their lives are placed in danger could not be conceived under the rubric of livelihood. The act of using such youngsters in counter insurgency activities is necessarily revelatory of disrespect for the life of the tribal youth, and defiling of their human dignity.[277]

(5) "*Khap Panchayats*" often decree or encourage honour killings or other atrocities in an institutionalised way on boys and girls of different castes and religion who wish to get married or have been married, or interfere with personal lives of people. This is wholly illegal and has to be ruthlessly stamped out.[278]

(6) Custodial death is perhaps one of the worst crimes in a civilized society governed by the rule of law. The rights inherent in Articles 21 and 22(1) of the Constitution require to be jealously and scrupulously protected. We cannot wish away the problem. Any form of torture or cruel, inhuman or degrading treatment would fall within the inhibition of Article 21 of the Constitution, whether it occurs during investigation interrogation or otherwise.[279]

(7) The principle of Rule of law and due process are closely linked with human rights protection. Such rights can be protected effectively when a citizen has recourse to the court of law. Failure to accord fair hearing either to the accused or the prosecution violates even minimum standards of due process of law. Since a fair hearing requires an opportunity to preserve the process, it may be vitiated and violated by an overhasty, stage-managed, tailored and partisan trial.[280]

(8) The recent jurisprudential development with regard to delay in execution of death sentence, the Supreme Court commuted the death sentence into life imprisonment, while holding that the execution of sentence of death of the accused, notwithstanding the existence of supervening circumstances, is in violation of Article 21 of the Constitution. One of the supervening circumstances sanctioned by the Supreme Court of India for commutation of death sentence into life imprisonment is the undue, inordinate and unreasonable delay in execution of death sentence, as it attributes to torture. The nature of delay i.e., whether it is undue or unreasonable, must

274. *Himanshu Singh Sabharwal v State of Madhya Pradesh*, AIR 2008 SC 1943, p *1947*.
275. *Zahira Habibulla H Sheikh v State of Gujarat*, (2004) 4 SCC 158.
276. *Selvi v State of Karnataka*,: AIR 2010 SC 1974 : (2010) 7 SCC 263, p *379*.
277. *Nandini sundar v State of Chhattisgarh*, AIR 2011 SC 2839, p *2865*.
278. *Arumugam Servai v State of Tamil Nadu*, AIR 2011 SC 1859, p *1863*.
279. *Rajjammal v State of Tamil Nadu*, 2008 Cr LJ 2280 : (2008) 3 Mad LJ 167.
280. *Zahira Habibulla H Sheikh v State of Gujarat*, (2004) 4 SCC 158.

be appreciated based on the facts of individual cases and no exhaustive guidelines can be framed in this regard. In *Shatrughan Chauhan's*[281] case, the Supreme Court of India observed that:

> .....it is well established that Article 21 of the Constitution does not end with the pronouncement of sentence but extends to the stage of execution of that sentence, as already asserted, prolonged delay in execution of sentence of death has a dehumanizing effect on the accused. Delay caused by circumstances beyond the prisoners' control mandates commutation of death sentence.

A nation must prioritize human dignity-ensuring that every person, regardless of their background or identity, is able to live with respect, equality, and freedom. Thus, human dignity forms the bedrock of social justice and a just, compassionate society. The right to live with dignity extends even to the incarcerated, and they have inherent dignity. They are to be treated in a humanely and without cruelty.[282]

Caste prejudices and discrimination hinder the growth of one's personality. Therefore, Article 21 provides for the right to overcome caste barriers as a part of the right to life of individuals from marginalized communities. The protection provided by Article 21 can be seen as a constitutional guarantee that individuals from marginalized communities should have the freedom to break free from these traditional social restrictions. It extends beyond mere survival to ensure that they can flourish in an environment of equality, respect, and dignity, without being subjected to caste-based discrimination which stifles their personal growth.[283].

Adopting a liberal interpretation, the Supreme Court has read several rights in Article 21 to make "life" more meaningful and worth living. They may be enumerated as under:

1. Right not be subjected to bonded labour and to be rehabilitated after release.
2. Right to livelihood.
3. Right to decent environment.
4. Right to appropriate life insurance policy.
5. Right to good health.
6. Right to food, water, education (not professional or special), medical care and shelter.
7. Prisoner's right to have necessities of life.
8. Right to speedy, fair and open trial.
9. Right of women to be treated with decency and dignity.
10. Right of privacy.
11. Right to go abroad.

---

281. *Noel Riley v Attorney General,* (PC) (1982) Cr LR 679; *Shatrughan Chauhan v UOI,* (2014) 3 SCC 1 : (2014) 2 SCC (Cri) 1; *V Sriharan @ Murugan v UOI,* AIR 2014 SC 1368 : (2014) 4 SCC 242; *Devender Pal Singh Bhullar v State (NCT of Delhi),* AIR 2013 SC 1975 : (2013) 6 SCC 195.
282. *Sukanya Shantha v UOI,* AIR 2024 SC 5201 : AIR Online 2024 SC 671.
283. *Sukanya Shantha v UOI,* AIR 2024 SC 5201 : AIR Online 2024 SC 671.

12. Right against solitary confinement.
13. Right against bar fetters and handcuffing.
14. Right to legal aid.
15. Right against delayed execution.
16. Right against custodial violence.
17. Right against public hanging.
18. Right to health and medical aid of workers.
19. Right to doctor's assistance.
20. Right to social justice and economic empowerment.
21. Right to freedom from noise pollution.
22. Right to reputation.
23. Right to family pension (release).
24. Right of decent burial or cremation.
25. Right to information.
26. Right to hearing.
27. Right of appeal from judgment of conviction.
28. Right to be free from adverse effects of climate change.[284]
29. Right to safe, well-maintained, and motorable roads.[285]

17b. Unnatural Offences.

The Constitutionality of "unnatural offences" such as homosexuality as a crime (section 377 IPC) was challenged before the Delhi High Court in 2001 and in 2009, the Delhi High Court, after considering various constitutional provisions and new developments declared that section 377 IPC, insofar as it criminalises consensual sexual acts of adults in private, is violative of Articles 21, 14 and 15 of the Constitution. It was provided that the clarification in the judgment will hold, till the Parliament chooses to amend the law to effectuate the recommendation of the Law Commission of India in its 172nd Report. However, the Supreme Court of India in *Suresh Kumar Kaushal v Naz Foundation*[286] reversed the Delhi High Court's 2009 verdict, and held that the 150-year-old section 377, criminalising gay sex, "does not suffer from the vice of unconstitutionality". However, in the light of its judgment in "*National Legal Services Authority v UOI*" recognising the transgender community as a third gender, along with male and female, the Supreme Court of India agreed to reconsider its verdict in "*Suresh Kumar Kaushal v Naz Foundation*".

A Constitution Bench of the Supreme Court in *Navtej Singh Johar*[287] overruled *Suresh Kumar Koushal* and held that consensual carnal intercourse among adults in private space, does not in any way harm public decency or morality. The court held that so far as section 377 penalises any consensual

284. *M K Ranjitsinh v UOI,* 2024 SCC OnLine SC 570.
285. *Umri Pooph Pratappur (UPP) Tollways Pvt. Ltd. v M.P. Road Development Corporation,* 2025 INSC 907.
286. *Suresh Kumar Koushal v NAZ Foundation,* AIR 2014 SC 563 : 2014 Cr LJ 784.
287. *Navtej Singh Johar v UOI,* AIR 2018 SC 4321.

sexual relationship between two adults, be it homosexuals (man and man), heterosexuals (man and woman) or lesbians (woman and woman), cannot be regarded as constitutional. However, if anyone engages in any kind of sexual activity with animal, said aspect of section 377 is constitutional and it shall remain a penal offence.

Previous judgments have established that queer and LGBTQ+ couples too have the right to union or relationship under Article 21, "be it mental, emotional or sexual" flowing from the right to privacy, right to choice, and autonomy. This, however, does not extend to a right to claim entitlement to any legal status for the said union or relationship.[288]

17c. Adultery.

In *Joseph Shine v UOI,*[289] another Constitution Bench of the Supreme Court decriminalised adultery and held section 497 of the Indian Penal Code unconstitutional as violative of Articles 14 and 21 of the Constitution. Before, it was struck down, the cognizance of the offence was limited to adultery committed with a married woman, and the male offender alone was made liable to punishment.

In *Joseph Shine*, the Supreme Court observed that treating adultery an offence would tantamount to the State entering into a real private realm. The act, ie, adultery does not fit into the concept of a crime. If it is treated as a crime, there would be immense intrusion into the extreme privacy of the matrimonial sphere. It is better to be left as a ground for divorce, the Supreme Court observed.

17d. Right to Privacy.

The right to privacy as a fundamental right stands established, with conclusive determination of the nine judge Bench judgment of the Supreme Court in *KS Puttaswamy v UOI.*[290] The majority judgment and five concurring judgments of other five judges have declared, in no uncertain terms and most authoritatively, right to privacy to be a fundamental right. This judgment also discusses in detail the scope and ambit of right to privacy. The right to privacy though not expressly guaranteed in the Constitution of India is now recognised as a basic fundamental right.

18. Article 21A—Right to Education.

The Constitution (86th Amendment) Act, 2002 has inserted Article 21A (wef 1-4-2010) which provides that—

> The State shall provide free and compulsory education to all children of the age of six to fourteen years in such manner as the State may, by law, determine.

The right of a child should not be restricted only to free and compulsory education, but it should be extended to have quality education without discrimination on the ground of child's economic, social and cultural background.[291] The right of child to free and compulsory education has now become a part of the Fundamental Rights under Article 21A of the Constitution. The total indifference of the Governmental authorities is leading to violation of

288. *Supriyo alias Supriya Chakraborty v UOI,* 2023 SCC OnLine SC 1348.

289. *Joseph Shine v UOI,* AIR 2018 SC 4898.

290. *KS Puttaswamy v UOI,* AIR 2017 SC 4161 : (2017) 10 SCC 1 : 2017 SCC OnLine SC 996. See also *Central Public Information Officer, Supreme Court v Subhash Chandra Agarwal,* AIR Online 2019 SC 1449 : 2019 SCC OnLine SC 1459 : LNIND 2019 SC 899.

291. *State of Tamil Nadu v K Shyam Sunder,* (2011) 8 SCC 737, p *756.*

the Fundamental Rights of the children.[292] It is the Constitutional obligation of the State to provide for free and compulsory education of children till they complete the age of 14 years.[293]

In a democratic society, a right to education is indispensable in the interpretation of right to development as a human right. Thus, right to development is also considered to be a basic human right.[294] However in a 2012 ruling the Hon'ble Supreme Court held that Rights of children to free and compulsory education guaranteed under Article 21A and Right to Education Act, 2009 can be enforced against the schools defined under section 2(n) of the Act, except unaided minority and non-minority schools not receiving any kind of aid or grants to meet their expenses from the appropriate governments or local authorities.[295]

19. Article 22—Protection Against Arbitrary Arrest and Detention. Apart from the foregoing judicial salvage, let us now advert to the safeguards which the Constitution itself has provided in Article 22 against arbitrary arrest and detention. Hence, in a case coming under Article 22, the requirements of both Articles 21 and 22 must be complied with.

The procedural safeguards against arbitrary arrest and detention, provided for in clauses (1) and (2) of Article 22, are—

(a) No person who is arrested shall be detained in custody without being informed, as soon as may be, of the grounds for such arrest.

(b) No such person shall be denied the right to consult, and to be defended by, a legal practitioner of his choice.

(c) Every person who is arrested and detained in custody shall be produced before the nearest magistrate within a period of 24 hours of arrest excluding the time necessary for the journey from the place of arrest to the court of the magistrate and no such person shall be detained in custody beyond the said period without the authority of a magistrate.

The above safeguards are not, however, available to—(a) an enemy alien; (b) a person arrested or detained under a law providing for preventive detention.

Article 22(1) provides that the arrested person shall not be detained in custody without being informed, as soon as may be, of the grounds for such arrest. Thus where arrested person being indisputably informed about the grounds of arrest and the endorsement on the said document, his arrest is not violative of the Article 22(1).[296] The grounds of arrest informed in writing must convey to the arrested person all basic facts on which he was being arrested so as to provide him an opportunity of defending himself against custodial remand and to seek bail.[297]

---

292. *Environmental & Consumer Protection Foundation v Delhi Administration,* (2011) 13 SCC 16.
293. *State of Uttar Pradesh v Pawan Kumar Dwivedi,* (2014) 9 SCC 692.
294. *Election Commission of India v St. Mary's School,* (2008) 2 SCC 390, p *402.*
295. *Society for Un-aided Private Schools of Rajasthan v UOI,* (2012) 6 SCC 1.
296. *Ram Kishor Arora v Directorate of Enforcement,* AIR 2024 SC 220 : AIR Online 2023 SC 1127.
297. *Prabir Purkayastha v State (NCT of Delhi),* AIR 2024 SC 2967 : AIROnline 2024 SC 372.

Right under Article 22(2) of the Constitution is available only against illegal detention by the police and it is not available against custody in jail of a person pursuant to a judicial order.[298]

19a. Preventive Detention.

The Constitution itself authorises the Legislature to make laws providing for "*Preventive detention*" for reasons connected with the security of a State, the maintenance of public order, or the maintenance of supplies and services essential to the community, or for reasons connected with Defence, Foreign Affairs or the Security of India [Seventh Schedule, List I, Entry 9; List III, Entry 3].

So, it would be competent to the Legislature to enact that a person should be detained or imprisoned *without trial* for any of the above reasons and against such laws, the individual shall have no right of personal liberty. The Constitution, however, imposes certain safeguards against abuse of the above power [*Articles 22(4)–(7)*]. It is these safeguards which constitute fundamental rights against arbitrary detention and it is because of these safeguards that "preventive detention" has found a place in the Part of "Fundamental Rights" in *our* Constitution. The relevant provisions of Article 22 explain as follows:

When a person has been arrested under a law of *preventive detention*—

(i) The Government is entitled to detain such person in custody only for *three months*. If it seeks to detain the arrested person for more than 3 months, it must obtain a report from an Advisory Board—who will examine the papers submitted by the Government and by the accused—as to whether the detention is justified.

(ii) The person so detained shall, as soon as may be, be informed of the grounds of his detention excepting facts which the detaining authority considers to be against the public interest to disclose. The detenu has the right to be supplied with copies of all documents, statements and other materials relied upon on the ground of detention without delay.[299]

(iii) The person detained must have the earliest opportunity of making a representation against the order of detention.[300]

A law which violates any of the conditions imposed by Article 22, as stated above, is liable to be declared invalid and an order of detention which violates any of these conditions will, similarly, be invalidated by the Court, and the detenu shall forthwith be set free.[301]

Parliament has the power to prescribe, by law, the maximum period for which a person may be detained under a law of preventive detention.

Preventive detention means detention of a person without trial. It is so called in order to distinguish it from *punitive* detention. The object of punitive detention is to *punish* a person *for what he has done* and after he is tried in the courts for the illegal act committed by him. The object of preventive detention, on the other hand, is to *prevent him from doing* something and the detention in

298. *Pragyna Singh Thakur v State of Maharashtra*, (2011) 10 SCC 445, p *464*.

299. *Thahira Haris v Government of Karnataka*, (2009) 11 SCC 438, p *446*.

300. *Delhi Airtech Services Pvt Ltd v State of Uttar Pradesh*, AIR 2012 SC 573, *593* : (2011) 9 SCC 354.

301. *Tarapada v State of West Bengal*, (1951) SCR 212, for the grounds on which the courts can interfere with an order of detention, see Author's *Shorter Constitution of India*, 14th Edn, 2008 under Article 22; *Constitutional Law of India*, 1991, pp 84 *et seq*.

this case takes place on the apprehension that he is going to do something wrong which comes within any of the grounds specified by the Constitution, *viz.,* acts prejudicial to the security of the State, public order, maintenance of supplies and services essential to the community; defence; foreign affairs or security of India. In fact, preventive detention is resorted to in such circumstances that the evidence in possession of the authority is not sufficient to make a charge or to secure the conviction of the detenu by legal *proofs* but may still be sufficient to justify his detention on the *suspicion* that he would commit a wrongful act unless he is detained.

Preventive detention is something unknown in the United States of America or the United Kingdom, in times of peace. The adoption (in India) on a permanent footing, of the power of the Executive to arrest persons on suspicion, which is tolerated in other countries only in emergencies, cannot, on principle, be justified by any lover of liberty. But no proper assessment of this provision of *our* Constitution is possible without taking note of the following circumstances:

Firstly, detention without trial was not a new idea introduced by the makers of *our* Constitution, for the first time. It was in existence since the early days of British India, under the notorious Bengal Regulation III of 1818 (the Bengal State Prisoners Regulation) and similar enactments in Madras and Bombay which laid no fetters upon the powers of the Government to detain a person on suspicion. Then came rule 26 of the Rules framed under the Defence of India Act, 1939, which authorised the Government to detain a person whenever it was "satisfied with respect to that particular person that such detention was necessary to prevent him from acting in any manner prejudicial" to the defence and safety of the country and the like.[302] This was, of course, a wartime measure modelled on similar legislation in England, during World War II, the validity of which had been upheld by the House of Lords.[303] But even after the cessation of the War, preventive detention was continued in India as an instrument to suppress apprehended breach of public order, public safety and the like by the Provincial Maintenance of Public Order Acts, under which there was a spate of litigation. The framers of *our* Constitution simply made it possible for such legislation to be continued under the Constitution, subject to certain safeguards laid down therein, because they painfully visualised that the circumstances which had necessitated such abnormal legislation in the past had not disappeared at the birth of India's Independence. It is common knowledge that the Republic had its birth amidst anti-social and subversive forces and the ravages of communal madness involving colossal loss of lives and property. In order to save the infant Republic from the inroads of any such subversive elements, therefore, this power had to be conferred upon the State. But the framers of the Constitution improved upon the existing law by subjecting the power of preventive detention to certain Constitutional safeguards upon the violation of which the individual could have a right to approach the Supreme Court or the high courts because the safeguards are fundamental rights, for the enforcement of which the constitutional remedies would lie. There have been a number of cases in which the courts have nullified orders of preventive detention, in proceedings for *habeas corpus.*

302. *Emperor v Sibnath,* AIR 1945 PC 156.
303. *Liversidge v Anderson,* (1942) AC 206.

Secondly, the above provisions of the Constitution are not self-executory but require a law to be made by the Legislature, conforming to the conditions laid down in the Article, and preventive detention can subsist only so long as the Legislature permits. The Preventive Detention Act, 1950 was, thus, passed by the Indian Parliament which constituted the law of preventive detention in India. It was a temporary Act, originally passed for one year only. Several times since then, the term of the Act was extended until it expired at the end of 1969. The revival of anarchist forces obliged Parliament to enact a new Act, named the Maintenance of Internal Security Act (popularly known as MISA) in 1971, having provisions broadly similar to those of the Preventive Detention Act of 1950. In 1974, Parliament passed the Conservation of Foreign Exchange and Prevention of Smuggling Activities Act, 1974 (commonly referred to as the 'COFEPOSA'), as an economic adjunct of the MISA. While the MISA was, in general, aimed at subversive activities, the COFEPOSA is aimed at anti-social activities like smuggling, racketing in foreign exchange and the like. MISA was repealed in 1978, but COFEPOSA still remains. Further, power of preventive detention has been conferred on the Central and State Governments to safeguard defence and security of the country and to maintain public order and essential supplies and services by enacting the National Security Act, 1980,[304] and the Prevention of Black Marketing and Maintenance of Supplies of Essential Commodities Act, 1980.[305] With the increase in terrorist activities, the government had to pass in 1985 the Terrorist and Disruptive Activities (Prevention) Act, 1985 (commonly called TADA). This has widely been used to curb terrorism. However, TADA was repealed in 1995. For the same purposes, the Prevention of Terrorism Act, 2002 (commonly called POTA) was enacted on 28 March 2002 but that too was repealed on 21 September 2004.

It may be mentioned that the number of detenus, during the Emergency of 1975–76, had soared up to 1,75,000. On the eve of coming to power, the Janata Party promised to abolish detention without trial. After coming to power, the Janata Government came to realise the reality of the problem. Eventually, in April, 1978, the MISA was *repealed* by the Parliament. But the Government refused to repeal the COFEPOSA because while the former related to political detention, the latter was aimed at *social* offences which required extra power to check when inflation, black marketing, smuggling and the like were rampant.

The provisions in clauses (2)–(7) of Article 22 could not be altogether omitted, so long as preventive detention was authorised by COFEPOSA. The Janata Government, therefore, sought to alleviate the rigours of the procedure for preventive detention, by effecting changes in clauses (4) and (7), by enacting the Constitution (44th Amendment) Act, 1978. But the relevant provision of this Amendment Act could not be brought into effect immediately since some changes in the machinery of the Advisory Boards had to be made. Hence, the Amendment Act of 1978 empowered the Central Government to bring into force these provisions by issuing notifications. Paradoxically, however, before any such notification could be issued, the Janata Government had its fall and Mrs Gandhi

304. *AK Roy v UOI,* AIR 1982 SC 710, paras 52, 113.

305. In order to cope with the increase in terrorist activities, Government was obliged to enact a temporary Act, *viz* the Terrorist and Disruptive Activities (Prevention) Act, 1987 (called *TADA*). This Act has not been renewed after it lapsed, without affecting previous cases under the Act.

returned to power in January, 1980. The Government has not issued any such notification notwithstanding adverse comments by the Supreme Court in view of the inordinate delay.[306] In the result, the original clauses relating to preventive detention in Article 22 subsist till today and the relevant provisions of the Amendment Act of 1978, solemnly passed by Parliament, remain a *dead-letter.*

Some states have enacted State laws, authorising preventive detention[307] which recall the *old* Preventive Detention Act of 1950. It should be pointed out in this context that the legislative power to enact law of preventive detention is divided by the Constitution between the Union and the states. The Union has exclusive power [Entry 9 of *List* I, Seventh *Schedule*] only when such law is required for reasons connected with Defence, Foreign Affairs or the Security of *India.* A state has power, concurrently with the Union, to provide for preventive detention for reasons connected with security of the *State,* maintenance of public order, or the maintenance of supplies and services essential to the community [Entry 3 of List III]. A state has therefore a say in the matter of abolishing preventive detention on these grounds because it is a responsibility of the state to maintain public order [Entry 1 of List II], production, supply and distribution of goods [Entry 27 of List II].

So long as the concurrent power of the states to legislate for preventive detention with respect to the aforesaid grounds remains and any of them feels the need for retaining or making state laws for preventive detention, it is practically difficult for the Union Government to impose its will on such states. Till then, the existence of Article 22 on the Constitution will be beneficial, rather than prejudicial, to the cause of liberty, because the validity of such state laws can be challenged on the ground of contravention of the safeguards laid down in Article 22.[308]

In these circumstances, Article 22 continues to be on the Constitution as a necessary evil.

20. Article 23—Right Against Exploitation. As an adjunct to the guarantee of personal liberty and the prohibition against discrimination, *our* Constitution lays down certain provisions to prevent exploitation of the weaker sections of the society by unscrupulous individuals or even by the state.

Article 23 says:

(1) Traffic in human beings and *begar* and other similar forms of forced labour are prohibited and any contravention of this provision shall be an offence punishable in accordance with law.

(2) Nothing in this article shall prevent the State from imposing compulsory service for public purposes, and in imposing such service the State shall not make any discrimination on grounds only of religion, race, caste or class or any of them.

---

306. *Dwarka Prasad v State of Uttar Pradesh,* (1954) SCR 803.

307. Some States have made laws authorising preventive detention relating to subject within their jurisdiction; *eg,* J & K Public Safety Act, 1977; AP Detention Act, 1970; Rajasthan PD Act, 1970; UP Rashtra Virodhi Tatwa Nivaran Adhiniyam, 1970; West Bengal Prevention of Violent Activities Act, 1970; MP Security & Public Order Maintenance Act, 1980. Preventive detention is provided for by the following Central Acts; COFEPOSA, 1974; NASA, 1980. Prevention of Blackmarketing and Maintenance of Supplies of Essential Commodities Act, 1980.

308. *Delhi Airtech Services Pvt Ltd v State of Uttar Pradesh,* AIR 2012 SC 573, *593* : (2011) 9 SCC 354.

Article 23(1) provides an enforceable fundamental right against social and economic exploitation. It aims to prohibit human trafficking, "begar", and "other similar forms of forced labour". Like Articles 15(2) and 17, it is enforceable both against the State and non-state actors. At the same time, the scope of the provision is wide, as it has left the term "begar" undefined, and supplemented by the phrase "other similar forms of forced labour". The "other similar forms" can be many. The framers of the Constitution consciously left the terms undefined so that future interpretation is not restrictive.[309]

Slavery in its ancient form may not so much be a problem in every state today but its newer forms which are labelled in the Indian Constitution under the general term "exploitation" are no less a serious challenge to human freedom and civilisation. It is in this view that *our* Constitution, instead of using the word "slavery" uses the more comprehensive expression "traffic in human beings" which includes a prohibition not only of slavery but also of traffic in women or children or the crippled, for immoral or other purposes.[310] Our Constitution also prohibits forced labour of any form which is similar to *begar,* an indigenous system under which landlords sometimes used to compel their tenants to render free service.[311] What is prohibited by the clause is therefore the act of compelling a person to render gratuitous service where he was lawfully entitled either not to work or to receive remuneration for it. The clause therefore does not prohibit forced labour as punishment for a criminal offence. Nor would it prevent the State from imposing compulsory recruitment or conscription for public purposes, such as military or even social service.

Article 23 has an element of force.[312]

21. Article 24—Prohibition of Employment of Children in Factories, etc.

Special provision for the protection of children is made in Article 24 which says:

> No child below the age of fourteen years, shall be employed to work in any factory or mine or engaged in any other hazardous employment.

It is to be noted that the prohibition imposed by this Article is absolute and does not admit of any exception for the employment of a child in a factory or mine or in any other "hazardous employment", eg, in a railway or a port. The Supreme Court directed that children should not be employed in hazardous jobs in factories and positive steps should be taken for the welfare of such children as well as improving the quality of their life[313] and the employers of children below 14 years must comply with the provisions of the Child Labour (Prohibition and

---

309. *Sukanya Shantha v UOI,* AIR 2024 SC 5201 : AIR Online 2024 SC 671.

310. *Sanjit v State of Rajasthan,* AIR 1953 SC 328, para 4; *People's Union for Democratic Rights v UOI,* AIR 1982 SC 1473, paras 14–15.

311. A bold step towards the abolition of forced labour and of economic and physical exploitation of the weaker sections of the people has been taken by the enactment, by Parliament, of the Bonded Labour System (Abolition) Act, 1976.

312. *State of Gujarat v Hon'ble High Court of Gujarat,* AIR 1998 SC 3164 : (1998) 7 SCC 392, paras 20 and 21 .

313. *MC Mehta v State of Tamil Nadu,* (1991) 1 SCC 283, paras 5, 7, 8, 9 and 11.

Regulation) Act providing for compensation, employment of their parents/guardians and their education.[314]

22. Articles 25 to 28—Freedom of Conscience and Free Profession, Practice and Propagation of Religion.

India, under the Constitution, is a "Secular State", ie, a state which observes an attitude of *neutrality and impartiality towards all religions.* A secular state is founded on the idea that the state is concerned with the relation between man and man and not with the relation between man and God which is a matter for individual conscience. The state shall treat all religions and religious groups equally and with equal respect without in any manner interfering with their individual right of religion, faith and worship. There is no justification for interfering in someone's religious belief by any means.[315] The attitude of impartiality towards all religions is secured by the Constitution by several provisions [*Articles 25–28*]:

Firstly, there shall be no "State religion" in India. The state will neither establish a religion of its own nor confer any special patronage upon any particular religion. It follows from this that—

(a) the state will not compel any citizen to pay any taxes for the promotion or maintenance of any particular religion or religious institution [*Article 27*];

(b) no religious instruction shall be provided in any educational institution *wholly provided* by state funds;

(c) even though religious instruction be imparted in educational institutions *recognised* by or *receiving aid* from the state, no person attending such institution shall be compelled to receive that religious instruction without the consent of himself or of his guardian (in case the pupil be a minor). In short, while religious instruction is totally banned in state-owned educational institutions, in other denominational institutions it is not totally prohibited but it must not be imposed upon people of other religions without their consent [*Article 28*].

Secondly, every person is guaranteed the freedom of conscience and the freedom to profess, practise and propagate his own religion, subject only—

(a) to restrictions imposed by the state in the interests of public order, morality and health (so that the freedom of religion may not be abused to commit crimes or anti-social acts, eg, to commit the practice of infanticide, and the like);

(b) to regulations or restrictions made by the state relating to any economic, financial, political or other *secular* activity which may be *associated* with religious practice, but do not really appertain to the freedom of conscience;

(c) to measures for social reform and for throwing open of Hindu religious institutions of a *public* character to all classes and sections of Hindus.

Subject to the above limitations, a person in India shall have the right not only to entertain any religious belief but also to practise the observances dictated by such belief, and to preach his views to others [*Article 25*].

---

314. *MC Mehta v State of Tamil Nadu,* AIR 1997 SC 699 : (1996) 6 SCC 756, paras 27–29 and *Bandhua Mukti Morcha v UOI,* AIR 1997 SC 2218 : (1997) 10 SCC 549, para 12.

315. *Dara Singh v Republic of India,* (2011) 2 SCC 490, p *531.*

Thirdly, not only is there the freedom of the individual to profess, practise and propagate his religion, there is also the right guaranteed to every religious group or denomination—

(a) to establish and maintain institutions for religious and charitable purposes;

(b) to manage its own affairs in matters of religion;

(c) to own and acquire movable and immovable property; and

(d) to administer such property in accordance with law [*Article 26*].

To those who have any idea as to what part religion plays in the entire being of the common man in India, the bold pronouncements in the above Articles must appear to be astoundingly progressive, and more so, if we consider that while the other half of the truncated territory, consisting of a large mass of Hindu minority, has adopted Islam as the state religion in her Constitution, India stands firm, regardless of her environments. It is to be noted that this guarantee is available not only to the citizens of India but to all persons, including aliens.[316]

The ambit of the freedom of religion guaranteed by Articles 25–26 has been widened by the judicial interpretation that what is guaranteed by Articles 25 and 26 is the right of the *individual* to practise and propagate not only matters of faith or belief but also all those rituals and observances which are regarded as integral parts of a religion by the followers of its doctrines.[317] Of course, religion is a matter of faith but it is not necessarily theistic and there are well-known religions in India like Buddhism and Jainism which do not believe in God. On the other hand, though a religion undoubtedly has its basis in a system of beliefs or doctrines which are regarded by those who profess that religion as conducive to their spiritual well-being, it would not be correct to say that religion is nothing else but a doctrine of belief.[318] Similarly, each religious denomination or organisation enjoys complete autonomy in the matter of deciding as to what rites and ceremonies are *essential* according to the tenets of the religion they hold.[319] Regulation by the state, again, cannot interfere with things which are essentially religious.[320] But the court has the right to determine whether a particular rite or observance is regarded as essential by the tenets of a particular religion,[321] and to interfere if a particular practice offends against public health or morality, or, not being an essentially religious practice, contravenes any law of social, economic or political regulation.

It should be pointed out in this context that the word "secular" is a dubious word, capable of diverse meanings and one of its dictionary meanings is "concerned with the affairs of the *world*" as opposed to religious affairs. This has not only caused confusion amongst teachers of Political Science and Law in India but has also been taken advantage of by interested parties. This state of

316. *Commissioner, Hindu Religious Endowments v Lakshmindra,* (1954) SCR 1005.

317. *Hanif Quareshi v State of Bihar,* AIR 1958 SC 731.

318. *Hanif Quareshi v State of Bihar,* AIR 1958 SC 731.

319. *Hanif Quareshi v State of Bihar,* AIR 1958 SC 731.

320. *Ratilal v State of Bombay,* (1954) SCR 1055.

321. *Sardar Sarup Singh v State of Punjab,* AIR 1959 SC 860, p *866*; *Moti Das v Sahi,* AIR 1959 SC 942, p *950*; *Jagadiswaranand v Police Commissioner,* AIR 1984 SC 51, para 10.

confusion has been set at rest by authoritative pronouncements made by the Supreme Court, in a nine-judge decision, as follows:[322]

(a) Secularism, in India, does not mean that the state should be hostile to religion but that it should be *neutral* as between the different religions.

(b) Every individual has the freedom to profess and practise his own religion, and it cannot be contended that "if a person is a devout Hindu or a devout Muslim, he ceases to be secular".

(c) The use of the vague word "secular" in the Preamble would *not* override the enacted provisions in Articles 25–30 or Article 351, so that the preference of Sanskrit in the academic syllabus as an *elective*[323–324] subject, while not conceding this status to Arabic or Persian or the like, would *not* militate against the basic tenets of secularism.

(d) The neutrality of the state would be violated if religion is used for *political* purposes and advocated by the political parties for their political ends. An appeal to the electorate on grounds of religion offends secular democracy (para 128). Politics and religion cannot be mixed (para 131). If a State Government does this, it will be a fit case for application of Article 356 of the Constitution against it.

(e) It is in this sense that secularism is to be regarded as a *basic feature* of the Constitution.

22a. Right to Religion and Gender Equality.

In 2018, a Constitution Bench of the Supreme Court (with 4:1 majority) on a petition filed by Indian Young Lawyers Association[325] under Article 32 of the Constitution allowed the entry of women between the ages of 10 and 50 in the Sabarimala temple. The Supreme Court held that Article 25(1), by employing the expression all persons, demonstrates that the freedom of conscience and the right to freely profess, practise and propagate religion is available to every person including women. The right guaranteed under Article 25(1) has nothing to do with gender or, for that matter, certain physiological factors specifically attributable to women.

The Supreme Court held that the exclusionary practice being followed at the Sabarimala temple violates the right of Hindu women to freely practise their religion and this denial denudes them of their right to worship. The right to practise religion under Article 25(1) is equally available to both men and women of all age groups professing the same religion. The exclusion of entry of women of the age group of 10–50 years, is a clear violation of the right of Hindu women to practise their religious beliefs which, in consequence, makes their fundamental right of religion under Article 25(1) a dead letter.

---

322. *SR Bommai v UOI,* AIR 1994 SC 1918.
323. *Santosh Kumar v Ministry of HRD,* (1994) 6 SCC 579.
324. *SR Bommai v UOI,* AIR 1994 SC 1918. A nine-judge Bench decision.
325. *Indian Young Lawyers Association v State of Kerala,* AIR Online 2018 SC 243 : (2018) 6 Andh LD 102 : LNIND 2018 SC 492.

Hearing the review petitions and several fresh petitions on the issue, the Supreme Court observed that the court should evolve a judicial policy befitting to its plenary powers to do substantial and complete justice and for an authoritative enunciation of the constitutional principles by a larger bench. The Constitution Bench of the Supreme Court[326] (with 3:2 majority) referred the matter to a larger bench of not less than seven judges. The Supreme Court held that the debate about the constitutional validity of practices restricting the entry of women generally in the place of worship is not limited to this case, but also arises in respect of entry of Muslim women in a Durgah/Mosque as also in relation to Parsi women married to a non-Parsi into the holy fire place of an Agyari. There is yet another seminal issue relating to the practice of female genital mutilation followed in Dawoodi Bohra community pending consideration before the Supreme Court.

22b. Propagation and Conversion.

It is amazing that some Christian leaders assert that the word 'propagate' in Article 25(1) gives them a fundamental right to convert people of other Faiths into Christianity, *by any means.* This assertion, followed by agitation, is particularly amazing because it seeks to undermine the decision of the Supreme Court in *Stainislaus's* case[327] in January, 1977, which had been brought by a Christian Father, who sought to invalidate a Madhya Pradesh Act, because it made it a penal offence to convert or to attempt to convert a person by means of "force, fraud or allurement". Orissa had earlier passed a similar Act (which used the word "inducement" in place of 'allurement') and the constitutionality of that Act had been challenged by several members of the Christian community, including a Christian Society, a Professor of Geology and several priests. Both the Acts were taken up together by the Supreme Court[328] and the contentions of the Christian community were rejected *in toto,* by the Supreme Court, laying down the following propositions of law which are, under the Constitution, binding upon all courts in India:

(i) The right to "propagate", in Article 25(1), gives to each member of every religion the right to spread or disseminate the tenets of his religion (say, by advocacy or preaching), but it would *not* include the *right to convert* another, because each man has the same freedom of "conscience" guaranteed by that very provision [*Article 25(1)*], on which the Christians relied.

(ii) The equal freedom of conscience, belonging to each man, under Article 25(1), means that he has the freedom to choose and hold any faith of his choice and *not to be converted* into another religion by means of force, fraud, inducement or allurement. He can, of course, voluntarily adopt another religion, but "force, fraud, inducement or allurement" takes away the free consent from the would-be convert.

(iii) Even assuming that a particular religion had the right to propagate its tenets by any means, including conversion—the State has the right and duty to intervene if such activity of conversion offended against "public order, morality

326. *Kantaru Rajeevaru v Indian Young Lawyers Association,* AIR Online 2019 SC 1450 : (2020) 2 SCC 1 : LNIND 2019 SC 901.
327. *Stainislaus v State of MP,* AIR 1977 SC 908.
328. *Stainislaus v State of MP,* AIR 1977 SC 908.

or health", because the guarantee of freedom of religion in Article 25(1) is subject to the limitations of "public order, morality, or health" as follows:

> 25. (1) Subject to public order, morality and health and to the other provisions of this Part, all persons are equally entitled to freedom of conscience and the right freely to profess, practise and propagate religion.

(iv) If any such right to convert be conceded, such right would belong to *every* religion, so that there would inevitably be a breach of the public peace if *every* religious community carried on a campaign to convert people belonging to other faiths, by the use of force, fraud, inducement or allurement. The state was, therefore, constitutionally authorised, nay, enjoined—to maintain public order by prohibiting and penalising conversion (including attempt to convert) if force, fraud, inducement or allurement was used by the person or persons advocating conversion in any particular case. This is exactly what had been done by the MP and Orissa Acts.

The Supreme Court, therefore, upheld[329] the Constitutional validity of both the MP and Orissa Acts, after rejecting every plea raised on behalf of the Christian parties. After this pronouncement of the Supreme Court, the Arunachal Pradesh Legislature passed a Bill, modelled exactly on the MP and Orissa Acts, which had been held to be valid by the Supreme Court and submitted it to the President for his assent; a private member of Parliament (Shri OP Tyagi) presented before the *Lok Sabha* a similar Bill, which, if passed by Parliament, would be applicable to all the States of India. The Christian community at once started agitations and demonstrations against these two Bills, with threats against severer resistance if these measures were passed. They politicised the issue, with the slogan that it was a campaign against the Christian religion in particular.[330] This contention involves *suppressio veri* (suppression of truth) on the following points:

(i) Neither of the disputed Bills was levelled against the Christian religion as such but would have operated against *any* religious community (including the Hindu, Muslim, Sikh, etc) which resorted to any of these unlawful means—force, fraud, inducement or allurement, in order to convert a member of another Faith to its own fold.

(ii) That *all* the legal points now raised against these two pending Bills were taken by the Christian parties to the Madhya Pradesh and Orissa Acts case but were definitely rejected by the Supreme Court.

(iii) Those who rely on the International Charters in support of their freedom to convert have not mentioned Article 18(2) of the International Covenant on Civil and Political Rights, 1966, which says:

> No one shall be subject to *coercion* which would impair his freedom to have or to adopt a religion or belief of his choice.

---

329. *Stainislaus v State of MP,* AIR 1977 SC 908.

330. Owing to the dissolution of Parliament on the resignation of Sri Desai, Tyagi's Bill has lapsed. The Arunachal Bill has become law with President's assent, but no challenge against it in the courts appears to have yet been made. [A registered letter addressed to the Pope John Paul enquiring of the scriptural authority to justify conversion against a person's free will, remains unanswered.]

This freedom of every man to adopt a religion of his choice is guaranteed by clause (1) of Article 18. The two clauses, read together, mean that every individual shall have the freedom to choose his own religion or belief in worship and this freedom shall not be impaired by the use of *coercion* by any individual attempting to induce him to adopt another religion. So far as the disputed Indian Bills ban the use of *force* as a means of conversion, it is perfectly in line with this International Charter. When *fraud* is used, the freedom of choice of the individual sought to be converted is similarly impaired. The only dispute which may possibly be raised by the Indian Christians is as to the use of *inducement or allurement.* But such means, too, impair the freedom of choice of an individual and his resultant choice or volition cannot be said to be *free,* within the meaning of Article 18(1) of the International Covenant, referred to. The validity of use of these two words in an Indian Bill would rest not on the wording of the International Covenant which is the resultant of various international factors, but on the interpretation of the words "public order and morality" in Article 25(1) of our Constitution, which constitutes the supreme law of this land.

(iv) If the agitators were dissatisfied with the Supreme Court's interpretation of Article 25(1), they were free to challenge the constitutionality of the provisions of the disputed Bills after they were passed[331] and to persuade the judges of the Supreme Court to revise their views as expressed in the *Stainislaus'* case;[332] but there was not the least justification to denounce the Bills as a crusade against the Christians in particular, when they were nothing but a codification of the principles laid down by the highest tribunal of the land and on the model of the State statutes which had been approved by that tribunal in the *Stainislaus'* case.[333]

23. Articles 29 and 30.

Apart from the foregoing guarantee of freedom of conscience and religion, there are certain general provisions which are aimed at ensuring the effectiveness of the above guarantee by prohibiting any discrimination by the State on the ground of religion alone:

(i) The state shall not discriminate against a citizen, in any matter [*Article 15(1)*], and, in particular, in the matter of employment [*Article 16(2)*], only upon the ground of religion.

(ii) Similar discrimination is banned as regards access to or use of public places [*Article 15(2)*]; admission into any educational institution maintained or aided by the state [*Article 29(2)*], the right to vote [*Article 325*].

(iii) Where a religious community is in the minority, the Constitution goes further to enable it to preserve its culture and religious interests by providing that—

(a) The state shall not impose upon it any culture other than the community's own culture [*Article 29(1)*];

---

331. *TMA Pai Foundation v State of Karnataka,* (2002) 8 SCC 481. See also *SK Md Rafique v Managing Committee, Contai Rehmania High Madrasah,* LNIND 2020 SC 2 : 2020 SCC Online SC 4 (The Supreme Court while upholding the West Bengal Madrasah Service Commission Act held that there is no Absolute Right of Appointment for Minority Educational Institutions).

332. *Stainislaus v State of MP,* AIR 1977 SC 908.

333. *Stainislaus v State of MP,* AIR 1977 SC 908.

(b) Such community shall have the right to establish and administer educational institutions of its choice and the state shall not, in granting aid to educational institutions, discriminate against such an educational institution maintained by a minority community on the ground that it is under the management of a religious community [*Article 30*]. Full compensation has to be paid if the state seeks to acquire the property of a minority educational institution [*Article 30(1A)*].

The expression "minority" has been used in two senses—one based on religion and the other on the basis of language. Since reorganisation of the states in India has been on linguistic lines, therefore, for the purpose of determining the minority, the unit will be the State and not the whole of India. Hence, minorities have to be considered state-wise. It is a relative term and is referred to, to represent the linguistic or religious sections or groups forming less than 50% of the total population of the state.[334]

The sum-total of the above provisions make *our* State more secular than even the USA. The *secular* nature of our Constitution has been further highlighted by inserting this word in the Preamble, by the Constitution (42nd Amendment) Act, 1976.[335] A word of caution should, however, be uttered in this context. What is meant by "secularism" or the safeguards of the minority, are exhaustively enumerated in Articles 25–30 and allied provisions (as to minority rights, see, further, under chapter 32, *post*). If a minority community presses for any *extra* favours outside these specific provisions in the name of "secularism" or the party in power yields them for political reasons, it might be re-introducing those vices of communalism from which India suffered so much during the later British regime and which the fathers of the Constitution eliminated from the Constitution of free India, eg, communal representation in the Legislatures[336] or communal reservation in public employment. For instance, if Government seeks to justify an appointment to a public office, high or low, not on the ground of merit, but on the ground that the appointee belongs to a religious minority, such discrimination would violate the Fundamental Right of any other community under Article 16(2), not to be "discriminated against" on the ground of "religion" or the like. Instead of safeguarding the rights of a minority community, it would deny the rights of the *majority* and other minority communities which are guaranteed by the Constitution itself. Neither secularism nor minority rights can, therefore, be allowed to be an argument for *preference* of the minority or to undermine the national unity and strength, for which the confidence of the majority is no less necessary. But a minority educational institution has the power to reserve only upto 50% seats for students belonging to its own community.[337]

---

334. *TMA Pai Foundation v State of Karnataka,* (2002) 8 SCC 481. See also *SK Md Rafique v Managing Committee, Contai Rehmania High Madrasah,* LNIND 2020 SC 2 : 2020 SCC Online SC 4 (The Supreme Court while upholding the West Bengal Madrasah Service Commission Act held that there is no Absolute Right of Appointment for Minority Educational Institutions).
335. See Author's *Constitutional Law of India,* Prentice-Hall of India, 6th Edn, 1991, pp 1, 3.
336. Nobody who has read Indian Constitutional History can afford to forget that it was the "Communal Award" of 1932, providing for separate representation for the Muslims and non-Muslims, which ultimately led to the lamentable partition of India.
337. *St Stephens College v University of Delhi,* (1992) 1 SCC 558.

An institution retains its minority character as long as it continues to achieve two objectives, *viz,* (i) to enable such minority to conserve its religion and language; and (ii) to give a thorough, good, general education to children belonging to such minority.[338]

The right to establish and administer would include the right to have choice of medium of instruction.[339] The Supreme Court[340] has summarised general principles relating to establishment and administration of educational institutions by minorities thus:

(*i*) The right of minorities to establish and administer educational institutions of their choice comprises the following rights:

(*a*) to choose its governing body in whom the founders of the institution have faith and confidence to conduct and manage the affairs of the institution;

(*b*) to appoint teaching staff (teachers/lecturers and Headmasters/ Principals) as also non-teaching staff, and to take action if there is dereliction of duty on the part of any of its employees;

(*c*) to admit eligible students of their choice and to set up a reasonable fee structure;

(*d*) to use its properties and assets for the benefit of the institution.

(*ii*) The right conferred on minorities under Article 30 is only to ensure equality with the majority and not intended to place the minorities in a more advantageous position *vis-a-vis* the majority. There is no reverse discrimination in favour of minorities. The general laws of the land relating to national interest, national security, social welfare, public order, morality, health, sanitation, taxation, etc. applicable to all, will equally apply to minority institutions also.

(*iii*) The right to establish and administer educational institutions is not absolute. Nor does it include the right to mal-administer. There can be regulatory measures for ensuring educational character and standards and maintaining academic excellence. There can be checks on administration as are necessary to ensure that the administration is efficient and sound, so as to serve the academic needs of the institution. Regulations made by the State concerning generally the welfare of students and teachers, regulations laying down eligibility criteria and qualifications for appointment, as also conditions of service of employees (both teaching and non-teaching), regulations to prevent exploitation or oppression of employees, and regulations prescribing syllabus and curriculum of study fall under this category. Such regulations do not in any manner interfere with the right under Article 30(1).

(*iv*) Subject to the eligibility conditions/qualifications prescribed by the state being met, the unaided minority educational institutions will have the

338. *P A Inamdar v State of Maharashtra,* AIR 2005 SC 3226.

339. *Usha Mehta v State of Maharashtra,* (2004) 6 SCC 264.

340. *Secretary, Malankara Syrian Catholic College v T Jose,* (2007) 1 SCC 386, para 19. See also *P A Inamdar v State of Maharashtra,* AIR 2005 SC 3226.

freedom to appoint teachers/lecturers by adopting any rational procedure of selection.

However, the right of the minorities is not absolute and is subject to regulations.[341] Reasonable regulations can be imposed for protecting the larger interest of the state and the nation. While imposing the regulations, the state shall be cautious not to destroy the minority character of the institution.[342]

The Preamble to *our* Constitution aims at securing the "unity and integrity of the nation". Religious and cultural safeguards have been guaranteed by the Constitution to minority communities in order to ensure them "justice, freedom of thought, expression, belief, faith and worship". But if any minority community goes on clamouring for *more* than what the framers of the Constitution offered to them, it would simply *perpetuate* the insular objectives of these communities and India would never grow up into a Nation, inspired with the ideal of "unity and integrity of the Nation". To revert to the ante-independence vortex of communalism and separatism would imperil the very foundation of Independence. On the other hand, secularism which means *neutrality* of the state towards *all* religions will itself be violated if the Government suppresses the religious or other legal rights of the majority community to appease the demands of an aggressive minority.

24. A History of the Right to Property under the Constitution of India.

The Constitution of 1949 had a three-fold provision for safeguarding the right of private property. It not only guaranteed the right of *private ownership* but also the right to *enjoy* and *dispose* of property free from restrictions other than reasonable restrictions.

24a. The Constitution of 1949.

Firstly, it guaranteed to every citizen the right to acquire any property by any lawful means such as inheritance, personal earning or otherwise, to hold it as his own and to dispose it freely, limited only by: (a) reasonable restrictions to serve the exigencies of public welfare; and (b) any other reasonable restrictions that may be imposed by the State to protect the interests of any Scheduled Tribe [*Article 19(1)(f)*].[343]

The restrictions must, of course, be "reasonable", from the substantive as well as the procedural standpoints. Thus—

(a) The restriction must not be in excess of the requirement of the interest of the general public for which the restriction is sought to be imposed.[344]

(b) A restriction would be procedurally unreasonable if, in the absence of extraordinary circumstances, it is imposed without notice or without hearing or without assigning any reason, on the subjective satisfaction of an administrative authority.[345]

Secondly, the Constitution guaranteed that no person shall be deprived of his property save by the authority of law [*Article 31(1)*]. This implied that, short of

341. *Islamic Academy of Education v State of Karnataka,* (2003) 6 SCC 697.
342. *Usha Mehta v State of Maharashtra,* (2004) 6 SCC 264, para 10.
343. Article 19(1)(f) was omitted by 44th Amendment Act.
344. *State of Bombay v Balsara,* (1951) SCR 682.
345. *Raghubir Singh v Court of Wards,* (1953) SCR 1049.

the consent of the owner, a man's property can be taken only by the consent of the nation as embodied in the laws passed according to the Constitution. Any property which is seized by the Police or the Government[346] without proper legal authority will be released at the intervention of the courts. As against its own subjects, a sovereign cannot exercise an "Act of State", and the private property of a subject cannot be taken away by an *executive* order,[347] as distinguished from an order made in exercise of power conferred by a statute.

This clause was intended to be a protection against executive, but not against legislative, appropriation of property. The Supreme Court, however, held that the law which seeks to deprive a person of his property must be a valid law, which means a law enacted by a competent Legislature and not inconsistent with any of the Fundamental Rights guaranteed by Part III of the Constitution.[348]

Thirdly, the Constitution enjoined that if the state wants to *acquire* the private property of an individual or to *requisition* (ie, to take over its possession for a temporary period) it, it could do so only on two conditions—

(a) that the acquisition or requisitioning is for a *public purpose;*

(b) that when such a law is passed, it must provide for payment of an *amount* to the owner—either by fixing the amount or by specifying the *principle* upon which it is to be determined and given [*Article 31(2)*].[349]

24b. Amendments up to Constitutional 42nd Amendment Act, 1976.

The provisions of the Constitution as to the obligation to pay compensation for acquisition of property for public purposes, however, underwent serious changes as a result of amendments of the Constitution by the 1st, the 4th, the 17th, the 25th and the 42nd Amendment Acts.[350] The net result of these amendments is as follows—

A. Though the Legislature was under a constitutional obligation to pay compensation, the *adequacy* of the compensation shall not be liable to be questioned in a court of law. In other words, when a law provided for the acquisition of person's property for a public purpose, he would not be entitled to challenge the validity of that law in a court of law on the ground that the Legislature had not provided for payment of the full value of his property. This (Fourth) Amendment (1955) in Article 31(2) was necessitated by the fact that even the word "compensation" *simpliciter* was interpreted by the Supreme Court[351] as implying "full compensation", ie, the market value of the property at the date of the acquisition. The Government thought that it was not practicable to implement its programme of national planning and development if the full market value was to be paid from the inadequate

346. *Wazir Chand v State of Himachal Pradesh,* AIR 1954 SC 415; *Virendra v State of Punjab,* AIR 1957 SC 896.

347. *Dwarka Nath Tewari v State of Bihar,* AIR 1959 SC 249; *Virendra Singh v State of Uttar Pradesh,* (1955) 1 SCR 415.

348. *Kochunni v State of Madras,* AIR 1960 SC 1080 : 1960 Ker LJ 1077; *Kunnathat Thathunni v State of Kerala,* AIR 1961 SC 552 : (1961) 3 SCR 77.

349. Article 31 was repealed by the 44th Amendment Act.

350. For the text of Articles 31A–31D, as amended up-to-date, see Author's *Constitution Law of India,* Prentice-Hall of India, 1991, pp 97ff. Of these, Article 31D has been *omitted* by the Constitution (43rd Amendment) Act, 1977.

351. *State of West Bengal v Bela Banerjee,* (1954) SCR 558, p *563* : (1954) SCA 41.

resources of the infant Republic for every inch of the property which was to be nationalised. But even after the foregoing amendment, the Supreme Court continued to hold that the very word "compensation" implied full monetary equivalent of the property taken away from the owner, i.e., its market value at the date of the acquisition.[352]

By the 25th Amendment of 1971, therefore, the word "compensation" in clause (2) of Article 31 was substituted by the word "*amount*". But, again, the majority of the Supreme Court reserved an area *for* judicial intervention, in the Full Bench case of *Kesavananda v State of Kerala,*[353] by holding that the amount which was fixed by the Legislature could not be arbitrary or *illusory,* but must be determined by a principle which is relevant to the acquisition of property. [The Indira Government reacted by putting specified laws of acquisition beyond the pale of Article 31 altogether, by engrafting the exceptions in Articles 31A–31D,[354] which will be mentioned presently.]

B. By a number of successive amendments, certain exceptions to Article 31(2) were introduced, in Articles 31A–31D,[355] to exclude the obligation to pay any amount as compensation in the case of laws providing for acquisition by the State or nationalisation, if such laws relate to matters specified in these exceptional provisions. These exceptions to the obligations under Article 31 may now be examined in particular:

(a) Article 31A relates to a law for the acquisition by the State of any "estate" or other intermediate interest in *land.* The object of taking out the acquisition of intermediate interests in land from the obligation to pay compensation was to make it possible for the Government to effect agrarian reform which was so urgently needed to protect the interests of the tenants as well as to improve the agricultural wealth of the country.

In order to facilitate agrarian reform as well as social control of the means of production, it has been provided in Article 31A that not only a law providing for the acquisition by the State of any estate or of any rights therein or the extinguishment or modification of any such rights, but also certain other laws, such as a law providing for the taking over of the management of any property by the State for a limited period either in the public interest or in order to secure the proper management of the property, shall be constitutionally valid even though it takes away or abridges any of the rights conferred by Articles 14 and 19.

(b) While Article 31A excepts certain *classes* of laws, Article 31B, read with the Ninth Schedule, gives a blanket cover to *particular enactments* which are, for the time being specified in the Ninth Schedule. Their number, in 2000 is 284. They have been altogether immunised from attack, on the ground of contravention of any of the Fundamental Rights.

(c) Article 31C, as inserted by the 25th Amendment Act, 1971, provided that any law which seeks to implement the Directive in Article 39(b) or 39(c), ie, the plan of socialistic distribution of wealth, and the means of production shall not be void for inconsistency with Articles 14 or 19.

---

352. *R C Cooper v UOI,* AIR 1970 SC 564, pp *608, 614.*
353. *Kesavananda Bharati v State of Kerala,* AIR 1973 SC 1461.
354. *Cooper v UOI,* AIR 1970 SC 564, pp *608, 614.*
355. *Cooper v UOI,* AIR 1970 SC 564, pp *608, 614.*

But the effectiveness of Article 31C was crippled by the decision of the majority of the Supreme Court in the case of *Kesavananda*[356] that judicial review is one of the essential features of the Indian Constitution which cannot be taken away by the process of amendment under Article 368, and that, accordingly, that part of Article 31C, which stated that any legislative declaration that a particular law was made to implement the Directives in Article 39(b)–(c) shall not be open to question in a court, is itself unconstitutional.

24c. The 42nd and 43rd Amendments.

Undaunted by *Kesavananda,*[357] Parliament enlarged the scope of Article 31C, by the *42nd Amendment* Act, 1976, by including within its protection any law to implement *any* of the Directive Principles enumerated in Part IV of the Constitution—not merely in Article 39(b)–(c). As a result of this, if any law of acquisition was made with the object of giving effect to *any of the Directives,* the reasonableness of such a law cannot be questioned under Article 14 or 19. *Minerva Mills*[358] has, however, nullified this extension.

(d) The last faggot of exceptions Article 31D, has been repealed by the 43rd (Constitution Amendment) Act, 1977, and need not bother the reader.[359]

24d. The 44th Amendment Act, 1978.

While the Congress Government for over a quarter of a century had eaten into the vitals of Article 31(2) by successive amendments, as outlined above, it was left to the Janata Government to *eliminate* the right of property altogether from the list of Fundamental Rights in Part III. This has been effected by the 44th Amendment Act, 1978, which we have already discussed in connection with Judicial Review. Nevertheless, its incidents may be recapitulated in order to give a definite idea as to how much of the right to property remains under the Indian Constitution after April, 1979, and in what shape.

(a) Article 19(1)(f) has been repealed.

(b) Article 31(1) has been taken out of Part III, and made a separate Article, *viz,* 300A, which reads as follows:

> No person shall be deprived of his property save by authority of law.

The word "law" which figures in Article 300A of the Constitution would mean a validity enacted law and in order to be a valid law it must be just, fair and reasonable.[360]

The compensation has to be understood in relation to the right to property. The right of the ousters is protected only to a limited extent as enumerated in Article 300A of the Constitution.[361]

356. *Kesavananda Bharati v State of Kerala,* AIR 1973 SC 1461.
357. *Kesavananda Bharati v State of Kerala,* AIR 1973 SC 1461.
358. *SR Bommai v UOI,* AIR 1994 SC 1918. A nine-judge Bench decision.
359. For the text of Articles 31A–31D, as amended up-to-date, see Author's *Constitution Law of India,* Prentice-Hall of India, 1991, pp 97ff. Of these, Article 31D has been *omitted* by the Constitution (43rd Amendment) Act, 1977.
360. *Delhi Airtech Services Pvt Ltd v State of Uttar Pradesh,* AIR 2012 SC 573, p *593* : (2011) 9 SCC 354.
361. *State of Madhya Pradesh v Narmada Bachao Andolan,* (2011) 7 SCC 639, p *686*; see also *KT Plantation Pvt Ltd v State of Karnataka,* (2011) 9 SCC 1, *Delhi Airtech Services Pvt. Ltd v State of Uttar Pradesh,* (2011) 9 SCC 354.

The result, in short, is that if an individual's property is taken away by a public official without legal authority or in excess of the power conferred by law in this behalf, he can no longer have speedy remedy direct from the Supreme Court under Article 32 (because the right under Article 300A is *not* a fundamental right). He shall have to find his remedy from the high court under Article 226 or by an ordinary suit.

(c) Clauses (2A)–(6) of Article 31 have been omitted.

(d) Clause (2) of Article 31 has been omitted,[362] but its proviso has been *transferred* to Article 30, as clause (1A) to that Article.

(e) Though Article 31 itself has been deleted, Article 31A which was originally inserted as an exception to Article 31 has been retained, with the omission of any reference to Article 31. Article 31A, therefore, remains to operate as an exception to Articles 14 and 19, to shield the five classes of laws specified in Article 31A(1). Curiously, however, the second proviso to Article 31A(1) has been retained, giving a right to full compensation to the actual tiller, even though Article 31 has been omitted and a reference to Article 31 has been omitted from clause (1) to Article 31A, to which the second proviso operates as an exception.

The above patchwork is bound to create confusion in the mind of a lay reader. It would, accordingly, be profitable to outline the vestiges of the right to compensation which survive the onslaught of the 44th Amendment. These are twofold:

Though the mass of citizens shall no longer have any guaranteed right to compensation if his property is acquired or requisitioned and the Legislature shall have no constitutional obligation to provide for payment of any solatium to the expropriated owner, two exceptions to this general position are allowed by the 44th Amendment in two cases of *acquisition:*

(a) If the property acquired belongs to an educational institution established and administered by a *minority,* the law of acquisition must provide for such compensation as would not abrogate the right of a minority "to establish and administer educational institution", which is guaranteed by Article 30(1). Shorn of innuendo, this means that if the State chooses to acquire a minority educational institution, it must offer full market value or adequate compensation so that the minority community may set up that institution at a suitable alternative site.

(b) If the State seeks to acquire the land which is *personally cultivated* by the owner and such land does not exceed the statutory *ceiling,* the State must pay to such owner full market value of his land as well as any building or structure standing thereon or appurtenant thereto. Though both the foregoing exceptions may be beneficial so far as they go, there is much to comment from the standpoint of constitutional law as from the national standpoint.

(i) As regards the concession in favour of a minority educational institution—it is somewhat inexplicable why no such guarantee should be made in favour of

---

362. A serious controversy has been raised as to whether, notwithstanding such repeal, a law can be struck down on the ground that it provides for *no* compensation or *illusory* compensation.

In 1995, a Division Bench of the Supreme Court [*Jilubhai v State of Gujarat,* AIR 1995 SC 142] has answered this question in the affirmative.

educational institutions managed by members of a *majority* community. Is not education as pure and adorable whether it comes through the Ganges or the Jordan? In their over-zealousness for the addition of a special guarantee in favour of the minority which the fathers of the original Constitution did not envisage,[363] the fathers of the 44th Amendment took no time to ponder that by eliminating Article 31(2), they were taking away a right which had been guaranteed to all persons in India. Legally speaking, the new provision in Article 30(1A) is a tail which has lost its head by the repeal of Article 31(2).[364]

(ii) As to the right of a small tiller of land to full compensation for his land and building or other structures, one fails to understand why similar right should not be guaranteed to a poorer man who has not an inch of agricultural land but has a humble hut to lay his head at night. He may be a day labourer, a petty pensioner or a landless peasant who tills another man's land. Are they less deserving?

Would it not be pertinent to point out in this context that even in the 1977-Constitution of the USSR, there was Article 13 which stated:[365]

> .....The personal property of citizens of the USSR may include articles of everyday use, personal consumption and convenience, the implements and other objects of a small holding.....or for building an *individual dwelling*. The personal property of citizens and the right to inherit it are *protected by the State.....*

In short, in the USSR, every individual had the guaranteed right to hold and inherit a dwelling, irrespective of his being an agriculturist, and the duty of the state to protect this right would obviously mean that the state cannot acquire or deprive the owner of his dwelling house unless otherwise provided by the Constitution.

The over-zealous political leaders of India should know that the provision in the 1982-Constitution of the *Chinese* Republic, too, is in the same strain. Though Article 6 provides for social ownership of the "means of production", Article 13, at the same time guarantees to the individual to own personal property, acquired by his personal income:

> The *State protects* the right of citizens to own lawfully earned income, savings, *houses* and other *lawful property*.

Article 39, further, declares, as a fundamental right, that:

> The citizens'. . . *homes* are inviolable.

The net result of the foregoing provisions seems to be that the state cannot take away an individual's dwelling house and similar personal property, even by legislation, so that no question of compensation for compulsory acquisition may arise.

---

363. The Janata Government, which undertook to unwind the changes introduced by the Indira Government into the Constitution, forgot, in the present context, that there was no proviso to clause (2) of Article 31 in the original Constitution of 1949. In 1971, when the word "compensation" was substituted by the word "amount", by the same 25th Amendment Act, the proviso was introduced by Mrs Gandhi to safeguard the right of a minority educational institution to full compensation while all the world outside had no such right under the Constitution of India as amended by her Government. It is that proviso which was nurtured by the Janata Government, by the 44th Amendment Act, while repealing Article 31(2) itself.

364. *R Gandhi v UOI,* (1999) 8 SCC 106, para 13.

365. Author's *Shorter Constitution of India,* 9th Edn, pp 668ff; *Comparative Constitutional Law,* pp 184 *et seq.*

In view of the drastic effects of the abolition of Articles 19(1)(f) and 31(2), some jurists in *India* have put forth their belief that the Supreme Court would come to the rescue of the expropriated owners by holding that notwithstanding the omission of such constitutionally guaranteed right to compensation, the court would derive such right from the legislative power contained in Entry 42 of List III—"Acquisition and requisitioning of property", read with the common law doctrine of "Eminent Domain". Unfortunately, it has not been possible for the Author to persuade himself to this anachronistic assumption for reasons which have been elaborately given in the Author's bigger works.

In the circumstances, there is a case for restoration of *some* relief for the poorer sections of property-owners (as distinguished from capitalists or owners of the means of production). But such relief can be more easily brought about by a further amendment of the Constitution than leaving it to the off-chances of "judicial amendment".

25. Article 32—Constitutional Remedies for Enforcement of Fundamental Rights.

Abstract declarations of fundamental rights in the Constitution are useless, unless there is the *means* to make them effective. Constitutional experience in all countries shows that the reality of the existence of such rights is tested only in the courts.

The power of the courts to enforce obedience to the Fundamental Rights, again, depends not only upon the impartiality and independence of the Judiciary, but also upon the effectiveness of the instruments available to it to compel such obedience against the Executive or any other authority. Under the Anglo-American system, such means have been found in the writs or judicial processes such as *habeas corpus, mandamus,* prohibition, *certiorari* and *quo warranto.*

The Indian Constitution lays down the following provisions for the enforcement of the Fundamental Rights guaranteed by the Constitution, in the light of the above experience:

(a) The Fundamental Rights are guaranteed by the Constitution not only against the action of the Executive but also against that of the Legislature. Any act of the Executive or of the Legislature which takes away or abridges any of these rights shall be void and the courts are empowered to declare it as void [*Article 13*]. The Supreme Court strikes at the arbitrary action of the State.[366] It has jurisdiction to enforce the fundamental rights against private bodies and individuals and award compensation for violation of the fundamental rights. It can exercise its jurisdiction *suo motu* or on the basis of PIL.[367] Where fundamental rights, particularly the right to life and personal liberty under Article 21 are violated by State machinery, appropriate monetary compensation may be an effective remedy.[368]

(b) Apart from the power to treat a law as void for being in contravention of the provisions of the Constitution guaranteeing the Fundamental Rights, the Judiciary

366. *R Gandhi v UOI,* (1999) 8 SCC 106, para 13.

367. *Bodhisattawa Gautam v Subhra Chakraborty,* AIR 1996 SC 922 : (1996) 1 SCC 490 paras 6 and 7.

368. *Khursheed Ahmad Chohan v Union of Territory of Jammu and Kashmir,* AIR 2025 SC 3393 : 2025 INSC 876.

has been armed with the power to issue the writs mentioned above (*habeas corpus, etc*), in order that it may enforce such rights against any authority in the State, at the instance of an individual whose right has been violated.

The power to issue these writs for the enforcement of the Fundamental Rights is given by the Constitution to the Supreme Court and high courts [*Articles 32 and 226*].

(c) The rights so guaranteed shall not be suspended except during a Proclamation of Emergency—in the manner laid down by the Constitution [*Article 359*].

Though a Fundamental Right may be enforced by other proceedings, such as a declaratory suit under the ordinary law or an application under Article 226 or by way of defence to legal proceedings brought against an individual, a proceeding under Article 32 is described by the Constitution as a "constitutional remedy" for the enforcement of the Fundamental Rights included in Part III and the right to bring such proceeding before the Supreme Court is itself a Fundamental Right in Part III.

Article 32 is thus the cornerstone of the entire edifice set up by the Constitution. Commenting on this Article, in the Constituent Assembly,[369] Dr Ambedkar said:

> If I was asked to name any particular article of the Constitution as *the most important*—an article *without which this* Constitution *would be a nullity*—I would not refer to any other article except this one. It is the very soul of the Constitution and the very heart of it.

The relevant provisions in clauses (1) and (2) of Article 32 should be noticed:

> (1) The right to move the Supreme Court by appropriate proceedings for the enforcement of the rights conferred by this Part is guaranteed.
>
> (2) The Supreme Court shall have power to issue directions or orders or writs, including writs in the nature of *habeas corpus, mandamus,* prohibition, *quo warranto* and *certiorari,* whichever may be appropriate for the enforcement of any of the rights conferred by this Part.

(a) Article 32, thus, provides a guaranteed remedy for the enforcement of those rights, and this remedial right is itself made a Fundamental Right, being included in Part III.[370] The Supreme Court is thus constituted the protector and guarantor of Fundamental Rights, and it cannot, consistently with the responsibility so laid upon it, refuse to entertain applications seeking protection against infringement of such right, on technical grounds.[371] Thus, though a writ may ordinarily be refused on the ground that the petitioner has another adequate legal remedy open to him, an application under Article 32 cannot be refused merely on this ground where a Fundamental Right appears to have been infringed.[372]

369. *Constituent Assembly Debates*, 1948, vol 7, 953.

370. *Kochunni v State of Madras,* AIR 1959 SC 725; *Kharak Singh v State of Uttar Pradesh,* AIR 1963 SC 1295 : (1964) 1 SCR 332; *Rashid Ahmed v Municipal Board,* (1950) 1 SCR 566.

371. *Rural Litigation v State of Uttar Pradesh,* (1989) Supp 1 SCC 504, para 16.

372. *Basappa v Nagappa,* (1955) 1 SCR 250; *Kharak Singh v State of Uttar Pradesh,* AIR 1963 SC 1295 : (1964) 1 SCR 332 (overruled in part by a nine judge Bench judgment in *Justice KS Puttaswamy v UOI,* AIR 2017 SC 4161).

25a. Prerogative Writs. (b) The Supreme Court can make any order appropriate to the circumstances, unfettered by the technicalities of the English "Prerogative writs".[373]

On the other hand, the sole object of Article 32 is the enforcement of the fundamental rights guaranteed by the Constitution. Whatever other remedies may be open to a person aggrieved, he has no right to complain under Article 32, where no "fundamental" right has been infringed. For the same reason, no question other than relating to a Fundamental Right will be determined in a proceeding under Article 32.[374]

The expression "prerogative writ" is one of *English* common law which refers to the extraordinary writs granted by the Sovereign, as fountain of justice, on the ground of inadequacy of ordinary legal remedies. In course of time these writs came to be issued by the high court of Justice as the agency through which the Sovereign exercised his judicial powers and these prerogative writs were issued as extraordinary remedies in cases where there was either no remedy available under the ordinary law or the remedy available was inadequate. These writs are—*habeas corpus, mandamus,* prohibition, *certiorari* and *quo warranto.*

25b. Difference between the Jurisdiction of the Supreme Court and the High Courts to Issue Writs.

In a sense, the power of the high courts to issue these writs is wider than that of the Supreme Court inasmuch as under Article 32 of the Constitution the Supreme Court has the power to issue these writs only for the purpose of enforcement of the Fundamental Rights whereas under Article 226, a high court can issue these writs not only for the purpose of enforcement of Fundamental Rights but also for the redress of any other injury or illegality, owing to contravention of the *ordinary law,* provided certain conditions are satisfied, for which, see chapter 22 and 23, *post.*[373]

Thus,—(a) an application to a high court under Article 226 will lie not only where a Fundamental Right has been infringed but also where some other limitation imposed by the Constitution, outside Part III, has been violated, eg, where a State Legislature has imposed a sales tax in contravention of the

373. It should be pointed out in the present context that by the 42nd Amendment Act, 1976, various conditions and limitations had been imposed on the writ jurisdiction of both the Supreme Court and the high courts, by introducing provisions such as Articles 32A, 131A, 144A, 226A, 228A, and substituting Article 226 itself [see Author's *Constitution Amendment Acts,* pp 100–07; 126–28]. All these fetters have since been removed by the 43rd and 44th Amendment Acts, 1977–78, brought by the Janata Government, so that the provisions in Articles 32 and 226 have been *restored to their original condition.*

But Articles 323A and 323B, inserted in 1976, have been kept intact. In pursuance of Article 323A, the Administrative Tribunals Act has been enacted in 1985, by which service matters have been taken away from the jurisdiction of the high courts under Article 226, and vested in Administrative Tribunals, so far as Union Government servants are concerned [see, further, under chapter 29, *post*] but subsequently in *L Chandra Kumar v UOI,* (1997) 3 SCC 261, paras 62 and 76, the Supreme Court has declared the sections of the Articles 323A and 323B and the legislations enacted in pursuance thereof infringing the powers of judicial review of the Supreme Court and the high courts under Articles 32 and 222/227 as unconstitutional.

374. *Amar Singhji v State of Rajasthan,* AIR 1955 SC 504.

limitations imposed by Article 286.[375] But an application under Article 32 shall not lie in any case unless the right infringed is a "Fundamental Right" enumerated in Part III of the Constitution.[376]

(b) Another point of distinction between the two jurisdictions is that while the Supreme Court can issue a writ against any person or Government within the territory of India, a high court can, under Article 226, issue a writ against any person, Government or other authority only if such person, Government or authority is physically resident or located within the territorial jurisdiction of the high court, ie, within the State to which the territorial jurisdiction of the particular high court extends or if the cause of action arises within such jurisdiction.[377]

As stated earlier, the Supreme Court has been assigned by the Constitution a special role as "the protector and guarantor of fundamental rights,"[378] by Article 32(1). In an appropriate case, when the court feels that the investigation by the police authorities is not in proper direction and in order to do complete justice in the case and where the high police officials are involved in the crime, it is always open to the court to hand over the investigation to the independent agency like CBI.[379]

In order to invoke the jurisdiction under Article 32 to approach the Supreme Court directly, it has to be shown as to why the high court had not been approached, could not be approached or it was futile to approach the high court.[380] The availability of an alternative remedy does not in any manner affect the maintainability of the writ petition under Article 32 of the Constitution. Wherever the facts of the case are not in dispute, and the issue involves the interpretation of rules which are of significant importance having a far-reaching effect, it would be a fit case for this Court to exercise its discretion and entertain the writ petition under Article 32 even if there is an alternative remedy available.[381] Invocation of jurisdiction of the Supreme Court under Article 32 of the Constitution cannot be said to be inappropriate where the direction was given for the production of a minor child who was illegally removed to India by his mother from a foreign country and the child was traced through CBI, on the writ petition filed by the father who was foreign citizen.[382]

---

375. *State of Bombay v United Motors,* (1953) SCR 1069.

376. *Tarapada v State of West Bengal,* (1951) SCR 212, for the grounds on which the courts can interfere with an order of detention, see Author's *Shorter Constitution of India,* 14th Edn, 2008 under Article 22; *Constitutional Law of India,* 1991, pp 84 *et seq.*

377. See clause (1A), introduced in Article 226, by the Constitution (15th Amendment) Act, which has been made clause (2), by the 42nd Amendment.

378. *Environmental & Consumer Protection Foundation v Delhi Administration,* (2011) 13 SCC 16.

379. *Rubabbuddin Sheikh v State of Gujarat,* AIR 2010 SC 3175 : (2010) 2 SCC 200, p *216*; see also *Rubabbuddin Sheikh (2) v State of Gujarat,* AIR 2007 SC 1914, p *1917*; *Subrat Chattoraj v UOI,* (2014) 8 SCC 768.

380. *UOI v Paul Nanickan,* (2003) 8 SCC 342, para 22.

381. *Ravikumar Dhansukhlal Maheta v High Court of Gujarat,* AIR 2024 SC 3256 : AIROnline 2024 SC 405.

382. *V Ravichandran v UOI,* (2010) 1 SCC 174, p *198*.

25c. The Supreme Court as the Guardian of Fundamental Rights.

Where, therefore, the infringement of a Fundamental Right has been established, the Supreme Court cannot refuse relief under Article 32 on the ground—

(a) That the aggrieved person may have his remedy from some other court or under the ordinary law;[383] or

(b) That disputed facts have to be investigated or evidence has to be taken before relief may be given to the petitioner;[384] or

(c) That the petitioner has not asked for the proper writ applicable to his case. In such a case, the Supreme Court must grant him the proper writ and, if necessary, modify it to suit the exigencies of the case.[385]

(d) Generally only the person effected may move the court but the Supreme Court has held that in social or public interest actions, any person may move the court. This is called expansion of the "right to be heard". It favours Public Interest Litigation.[386] Following English and American decisions, the Supreme Court has admitted exceptions from the strict rules relating to affidavit *locus standi* and the like in the case of a class of litigations classified as "public interest litigation" (PIL) i.e., where the public in general are interested in the vindication of some right or the enforcement of some public duty.[387]

Another consequence which results from the guarantee of the constitutional remedy under Article 32 is this:

Not only is this remedy immune from being overridden by legislation but any law which renders *nugatory* or *illusory* the Supreme Court's power to grant this remedy shall be void. This was illustrated in the leading case of *A K Gopalan v State of Madras,*[388, 389] where the Supreme Court invalidated section 14 of the Preventive Detention Act, 1950, as it originally stood. The section was as follows:

> (1) No Court shall, except for the purpose of a prosecution for an offence punishable under sub-section (2), allow any statement to be made or any evidence to be given before it or the substance of any communication made under section 7 of the grounds on which a detention order has been made against any person or of any representation made by him against such order; and notwithstanding anything contained in any other law, no Court shall be entitled to require any public officer to produce before it, or to disclose the substance of, any such communication or representation made, or the proceedings of an advisory board or that part of the report of an advisory board which is confidential.
>
> (2) It shall be an offence punishable with imprisonment for a term which may extend to one year, or with fine, or with both for any person to disclose or publish without the previous authorisation of the Central Government or the State

383. *Himmatlal v State of MP,* (1954) SCR 1122.
384. *Rural Litigation v State of Uttar Pradesh,* (1989) Supp 1 SCC 504, para 16.
385. *Rural Litigation v State of Uttar Pradesh,* (1989) Supp 1 SCC 504, para 16.
386. *Basappa v Nagappa,* (1955) 1 SCR 250; *Kharak Singh v State of Uttar Pradesh,* AIR 1963 SC 1295 : (1964) 1 SCR 332 (overruled in part by a nine judges Bench judgment in *Justice KS Puttaswamy v UOI,* AIR 2017 SC 4161).
387. *People's Union for Democratic Rights v UOI,* AIR 1982 SC 1473, para 1.
388. *Gopalan v State of Madras,* (1950) SCR 88 (*253–54*).
389. For the facts and principles of this decision of the Supreme Court and other leading cases, read Author's *Casebook on Indian Constitutional Law,* vol 1, pp 447 *et seq.*

> Government, as the case may be, any contents or matter purporting to be contents of any such communication or representation as is referred to in sub-section (1) . . . .

The Supreme Court struck down the above provision on the ground that it contravened Article 32 by way of preventing the Supreme Court from *effectively exercising* its powers under Article 32. The following observations of Mahajan J are illuminating:

> This section is in the nature of an iron curtain around the acts of the authority making the order of preventive detention. The Constitution has guaranteed to the detained person the right to be told the grounds of detention. He has been given a right to make a representation [*Vide* article 22(5)], yet section 14 *prohibits the disclosure of the grounds furnished to him or the contents of the representation made by him in a Court of law* and makes a breach of this injunction punishable with imprisonment.
>
> Now it is quite clear that if an authority passes an order of preventive detention for reasons not connected with any of the six subjects mentioned in the 7th Schedule, this court can always declare the detention illegal and release the detenu, but it is not possible for this court to function if there is a prohibition against disclosing the grounds which have been served upon him. It is only by an examination of the grounds that it is possible to say whether the grounds fall within the ambit of the legislative power contained in the Constitution or are outside its scope. Again something may be served on the detenu as being grounds which are not grounds at all. In this contingency it is the right of the detained person under article 32 to move this court for enforcing the right under Article 22(5) that he be given the real grounds on which the detention order is based. This Court would be disabled from exercising its functions under article 32 and adjudicating on the point that the grounds given satisfy the requirements of the sub-clause if it is not open to it to see the grounds that have been furnished. It is a guaranteed right of the person detained to have the very grounds which are the basis of the order of detention. This court would be entitled to examine the matter and to see whether the grounds furnished are the grounds on the basis of which he has been detained or they contain some other vague or irrelevant material. The whole purpose of furnishing a detained person with the grounds is to enable him to make a representation refuting these grounds and of proving his innocence. In order that this Court may be able to safeguard this fundamental right and to grant him relief *it is absolutely essential that the detenu is not prohibited under penalty of punishment to disclose the grounds to the Court and no injunction by law can be issued to this Court disabling it from having a look at the grounds.* Section 14 creates a substantive offence if the grounds are disclosed and it also lays a duty on the court not to permit the disclosure of such grounds. *It virtually amounts to a suspension of a guaranteed right* provided by the Constitution inasmuch as it indirectly by a stringent provision makes administration of the law by this court impossible and at the same time it deprives a detained person from obtaining justice from this court. In my opinion, therefore, this section when it prohibits the disclosure of the grounds contravenes or abridges the rights given by Part III to a citizen and is *ultra vires* the powers of Parliament to that extent."[390]

There is provision in the Constitution for empowering courts other than the Supreme Court or the high courts to issue the writs, by making a law of Parliament. But no such law has yet been passed,— with the result that no courts

390. *Makhan Singh v State of Punjab,* (1952) SCR 368; *Keshav Nilkanth v Commissioner of Police,* (1956) SCR 653.

other than the Supreme Court or the high courts have got the power to issue these writs. The incidents of the several kinds of writs which *our* Supreme Court and the high courts are authorised by the Constitution to issue may now be noted.

26. *Habeas corpus*, Writ of.

A writ of *habeas corpus* is in the nature of an order calling upon the person who has detained another to produce the latter before the court, in order to let the court know on what ground he has been confined and to set him free if there is no legal justification for the imprisonment. The words "*habeas corpus*" literally mean "to have a body". By this writ, therefore, the court secures the body of a person who has been imprisoned to be brought before itself to obtain knowledge of the reason why he has been imprisoned and to set him free if there is no lawful justification for the imprisonment. The writ may be addressed to any person whatever, an official or a private person, who has another person in his custody and disobedience to the writ is met with punishment for contempt of court. The writ of *habeas corpus* is thus a very powerful safeguard to the subject against arbitrary acts not only of private individuals but also of the executive. *Habeas corpus* petition becomes infructuous if the detenu is produced before the Magistrate.[391]

Habeas corpus writ is a prerogative writ which is an extraordinary remedy, and recourse to such a remedy should not be permitted unless the ordinary remedy provided by the law is either not available or is ineffective.[392]

The different purposes for which the writ of *habeas corpus* is available may, accordingly, be stated as follows:

(a) For the enforcement of Fundamental Rights. It has already been explained that under *our* Constitution the right of personal liberty is guaranteed against the State by Article 21 which says that "no person shall be deprived of his life or personal liberty except according to procedure established by law". Hence, if the Executive has arrested and detained any person without the authority of any law or in contravention of the procedure established by the law which authorises the detention, or the law which authorises the imprisonment is itself invalid or unconstitutional, the high court or the Supreme Court may issue a writ of *habeas corpus* against the authority which has kept the person in custody and order the release of the person under detention.

(b) It will also issue where the order of imprisonment or detention is *ultra vires* the statute which authorises the imprisonment or detention.[393]

The writ of *habeas corpus* is, however, *not* issued in the following cases:

(i) Where the person against whom the writ is issued or the person who is detained is not within the jurisdiction of the court.

(ii) To secure the release of a person who has been imprisoned by a court of law on a criminal charge.[394]

---

391. *Harbans Kaur v UOI,* (1995) 1 SCC 623, para 16.
392. *Nirmala v Kulwant Singh,* AIR 2024 SC 2344 : AIROnline 2024 SC 299.
393. *Makhan Singh v State of Punjab,* (1952) SCR 368; *Keshav Nilkanth v Commissioner of Police,* (1956) SCR 653.
394. *Janardhan Reddy v State of Hyderabad,* (1951) 2 SCR 344.

(iii) To interfere with a proceeding for contempt by a court of record or by Parliament.

(iv) where a person is committed to jail custody by a competent court, by an order which *prima facie* does not appear to be without jurisdiction or wholly illegal.[395]

27. *Mandamus*, Writ of.

Mandamus literally means a command. It demands some activity on the part of the body or person to whom it is addressed. In short, it commands the person to whom it is addressed to perform some public or quasi-public legal duty which he has refused to perform and the performance of which cannot be enforced by any other adequate legal remedy. It is, therefore, clear that *mandamus* will not issue unless the applicant has a legal right to the performance of legal duty of a *public* nature and the party against whom the writ is sought is bound to perform that duty. It is a discretionary remedy and the high court may refuse to grant *mandamus* where there is an alternative remedy for redress of the injury complained of. In the matter of enforcement of Fundamental Rights, however, the question of alternative remedy does not weigh so much with the court since it is the *duty* of the Supreme Court or the high court to enforce the Fundamental Rights. In India, *mandamus* will lie not only against officers and other persons who are bound to do a public duty but also against the Government itself for, Articles 226 and 361 provided that appropriate proceedings may be brought against the Government concerned. The writ is also available against inferior courts or other judicial bodies when they have refused to *exercise their jurisdiction* and thus to perform their duty. The purposes for which a writ may be issued may now be analysed as follows:

(a) For the enforcement of Fundamental Rights, whenever a public officer or a Government has done some act which violates the Fundamental Right of a person, the court would issue a writ of *mandamus* restraining the public officer or the Government from enforcing that order or doing that act against the person whose Fundamental Right has been infringed. Thus, where the petitioner, who was otherwise eligible for appointment to the Subordinate Civil Judicial Service, was not selected owing to the operation of a "Communal Rotation Order" which infringed the Fundamental Right guaranteed to the petitioner by Article 16(1), the court issued an order directing the State of Madras "to consider and dispose of the petitioner's application for the post after taking it on the file on its merits and without applying the rule of communal rotation".[396]

(b) Apart from the enforcement of Fundamental Rights, *mandamus* is available from a high court for various other purposes, eg,—

(i) To enforce the performance of a statutory duty where a public officer has got a power conferred by the Constitution or a statute. The court may issue a *mandamus* directing him to exercise the power in case he refuses to do it.

---

395. *Col Dr B Ramachandra Rao v State of Orissa*, (1972) 3 SCC 256; *Subrata Roy Sahara v UOI*, (2014) 8 SCC 470.

396. *B Venkataramana v State of Madras*, AIR 1951 SC 229.

(ii) The writ will also lie to compel any person to perform his public duty where the duty is imposed by the Constitution or a statute or statutory instrument.

(iii) To compel a court or judicial tribunal to exercise its jurisdiction when it has refused to exercise it.

(iv) To direct a public official or the Government *not* to enforce a law which is unconstitutional.

The courts are normally reluctant to issue any direction to government for making a law.[397]

Mandamus will not be granted against the following persons:

(i) The President, or the Governor of a state, for the exercise and performance of the powers and duties of his office or for any act done or purporting to be done by him in the exercise and performance of those powers and duties [*Article* 361, *post*].

(ii) *Mandamus* does not lie against a private individual or body whether incorporated or not except where the state is in collusion with such private party,[398] in the matter of contravention of any provision of the Constitution, or a statute or a statutory instrument.[399]

28. Prohibition, Writ of.

The writ of prohibition is a writ issued by the Supreme Court or a high court to an inferior court forbidding the latter to continue proceedings therein in excess of its jurisdiction or to usurp a jurisdiction with which it is not legally vested. In other words, the object of the writ is to compel inferior courts to keep themselves within the limits of their jurisdiction. The writ of prohibition differs from the writ of *mandamus* in that while *mandamus* commands activity, prohibition commands inactivity. Further, while *mandamus* is available not only against judicial authorities but also against administrative authorities, prohibition as well as *certiorari* is issued only against judicial or *quasi-judicial* authorities. Hence, prohibition is not available against a public officer who is not vested with judicial functions. Where excess of jurisdiction is apparent on the face of the proceedings, a writ of prohibition is not a matter of discretion but may be had *of right.* In India, a writ of prohibition may be issued not only in cases of absence or excess of jurisdiction but also in cases where the court or tribunal assumes jurisdiction under a law which itself contravenes some Fundamental Right guaranteed by the Constitution. The Supreme Court can issue the writ only where a Fundamental Right is affected by reason of the jurisdictional defect in the proceedings.

Though prohibition and *certiorari* are both issued against courts or tribunals exercising judicial or *quasi-judicial* powers, *certiorari* is issued to *quash* the order or decision of the tribunal while prohibition is issued to *prohibit* the tribunal from making the *ultra vires* order or decision. It follows, therefore, that while

397. *Saurabh Chaudri v UOI,* AIR 2004 SC 361 : (2003) 11 SCC 146, para 77; *Re, Networking of Rivers,* (2004) 11 SCC 360, para 8.

398. *Saurabh Chaudri v UOI,* AIR 2004 SC 361 : (2003) 11 SCC 146, para 77; *Re, Networking of Rivers,* (2004) 11 SCC 360, para 8.

399. *Sohan Lal v UOI,* AIR 1957 SC 529.

prohibition is available during the pendency of the proceedings and before the order is made, *certiorari* can be issued only after the order has been made.

Briefly speaking, therefore, while prohibition is available at an earlier stage, *certiorari* is available at a later stage, on similar grounds. The object of both is to secure that the jurisdiction of an inferior court or tribunal is properly exercised and that it does not usurp the jurisdiction which it does not possess.

29. *Certiorari*, Writ of.

The conditions necessary for the issue of the writ of *certiorari* are—

I. There should be a tribunal or officer having legal authority to determine questions affecting rights of subjects and having a duty to act judicially.

II. Such tribunal or officer must have acted without jurisdiction or in excess of the legal authority vested in such *quasi-judicial* authority, or in contravention of the rules of natural justice or there is an "error apparent on the face of its record".

III. The Supreme Court, early, took the view that the writ of *certiorari* would not issue against purely administrative action. It would issue only if the authority has a *duty* to proceed judicially, that is to say, to come to a decision after hearing the parties interested in the matter and without reference to any extraneous consideration.[400]

But later decisions have obliterated the distinction between administrative and quasi-judicial bodies. The *current view* is that even if the governing statute does not require that before making an order affecting an individual, he must be heard, such a requirement would be implied by the court where the right of property or some other civil right of the individual is affected. To omit to do this is to deny natural justice, and in such cases, the court may quash the so-called administrative decision, by means of a writ of *certiorari,* under Article 226.[401]

IV. A tribunal may be said to act without jurisdiction in any of the following circumstances—

(a) Where the court is not properly constituted, that is to say, where persons who are not qualified to sit on the tribunal have sat on it and pronounced the decision complained against.

(b) Where the subject-matter of enquiry is beyond the scope of the tribunal according to the law which created it.

(c) Where the court has assumed a jurisdiction on the basis of a wrong decision of facts upon the existence of which the jurisdiction of the tribunal depends.

(d) Where there has been a failure of justice either because the tribunal has violated the principles of natural justice or because its decision has been obtained by fraud, collusion or corruption.

V. When the decision of an inferior tribunal is vitiated by an error "apparent on the face of the record", it is liable to be quashed by *certiorari,* even though

---

400. *Province of Bombay v Khusaldas,* (1950) SCR 621.

401. *AK Kraipak v UOI,* AIR 1970 SC 150, p *156*; *Kesava Mills v UOI,* AIR 1973 SC 389 (paras 7–8) : (1973) 1 SCC 380; *DFO v Ram Sanehi Singh,* AIR 1973 SC 205 : (1971) 3 SCC 864; *Erusian Equipment v State of West Bengal,* AIR 1975 SC 266; *Joseph v Executive Engineer,* AIR 1978 SC 930.

the court may have acted within its jurisdiction. "Error", in this context, means "error of *law*". Where the tribunal states on the face of the order the grounds on which they made it and it appears that in law these grounds were not such as to warrant the decision to which they had come, *certiorari* would issue to quash the decision.[402] The writ of *certiorari* would not be maintainable where the high court has nowhere stated that the lower courts had committed an error of jurisdiction or they had acted illegally and improperly.[403]

In all such cases, a high court can issue a writ of *certiorari* to quash the decision of the inferior tribunal; and the Supreme Court can also issue the writ in such cases, provided some Fundamental Right has also been infringed by the order complained against.

30. *Quo Warranto*, Writ of. *Quo warranto* is a proceeding whereby the court enquires into the legality of the claim which a party asserts to a public office, and to oust him from its enjoyment if the claim be not well founded.

The conditions necessary for the issue of a writ of *quo warranto* are as follows:

(i) The office must be public and it must be created by a statute or by the constitution itself.

(ii) The office must be a substantive one and not merely the function or employment of a servant at the will and during the pleasure of another.

(iii) There has been a contravention of the Constitution or a statute or statutory instrument, in appointing such person to that office.[404]

The fundamental basis of the proceeding of *quo warranto* is that the public has an interest to see that an unlawful claimant does not usurp a public office. It is, however, a discretionary remedy which the court may grant or refuse according to the facts and circumstances of each case. A writ of *quo warranto* may, thus, be refused where it is vexatious or where it would be futile in its result or where the petitioner is guilty of laches or where there is an alternative remedy for ousting the usurper. Where the application challenges the validity of an appointment to a public office, it is maintainable at the instance of *any* person, whether any fundamental or other legal right of such person has been infringed or not.

A writ of *quo warranto* lies against the person who is not entitled to hold an office of public nature and is only an usurper of the office. Such a person is required to show, by what authority he is entitled to hold that office. The challenge can be made on the grounds such as he does not fulfil the required qualifications or suffers from any disqualification debarring him to hold such office.[405] A writ of *quo warranto* lies only when the appointment is contrary to a statutory provision.[406]

---

402. *Hari Vishnu v Ahmad,* (1955) 1 SCR 1104, p *1123*; *Nagendra v Commissioner,* AIR 1958 SC 398, p *412*.

403. *Mohd Shahnawaj Akhtar v District Judge, Varanasi,* (2010) 5 SCC 510, p *512*.

404. The Supreme Court can issue this writ in a proceeding under Article 32 only if a Fundamental Right has been violated by an appointment.

405. *BR Kapur v State of TN,* (2001) 7 SCC 231; *Centre for PIL v UOI,* AIR 2011 SC 1267 : (2011) 4 SCC 1.

406. *Hari Bansh Lal v Sahodar Prasad Mahto,* AIR 2010 SC 3515 : (2010) 9 SCC 655.

Quo warranto is thus a very powerful instrument for safeguarding against the usurpation of public offices.

31. Parliament's Power to Modify or Restrict Fundamental Rights. The limitations upon the enforcement of the Fundamental Rights are as follows:

(i) Parliament shall have the power to modify the application of the Fundamental Rights[407] to the members of the Armed Forces, Police Forces or intelligence organisations so as to ensure proper discharge of their duties and maintenance of discipline amongst them [*Article 33*].[408]

In exercise of this power, Parliament has enacted the Army and Air Force Acts of 1950 and the Navy Act, 1957, which empower the Central Government to make Rules restricting the Fundamental Rights of the defence personnel, for the sake of discipline—which is absolutely essential to maintain the security of India. By a circular issued under such Rules, Government of India has ordered that no concession can be offered in favour of any member of the Defence Forces for the purpose of offering prayers during *office hours.* It is a pity that a fundamentalist Muslim Organisation, named All India Muslim Forum, has raised objection against the circular articulated by Muslim members in Parliament, on various grounds. None of these grounds are, however, tenable in view of the express provision in Article 33 of the Constitution of India, which silences the argument that no such restriction was imposed in respect of Muslims during the British regime and also that it would hurt the "sentiments" of the Muslims. Nor does the argument that the withdrawal of such concession would be contrary to the guarantee of secularism hold water because, *firstly,* Article 25(1) makes it "expressly" subject to the *other* provisions of this Part, in which Article 33 is included. *Secondly,* what Article 25 guarantees is equality of treatment as amongst different religions. If no such concession exists in favour of the members of any other religion, no question of discrimination against Muslims can possibly arise. Above all, the defence of the nation is a *secular* duty of each citizen of India, regardless of his religious beliefs or rites. Nothing can be allowed by the independent Republic which can possibly jeopardise the defence of the Nation.

A similar instance was the claim of a section of Muslims to postpone the elections fixed for February, 1995, on the ground of Ramzan. This has, of course, been turned down by the Election Commission on the ground that no

407. Article 33 was amended by the Constitution (50th Amendment) Act, 1984. For the amended text of Article 33 see Author's *Shorter Constitution of India,* 14th Edn, 2008.

408. Article 33 of the Constitution entrusts to Parliament to determine, by law, the extent to which any of the rights conferred by Part III of the Constitution can be restricted or abrogated in their application to the members of the Armed Forces. Besides the requirement that a restriction must be determined by law, Article 33 postulates a nexus between the restriction or abrogation and the need for the proper discharge of duties and the maintenance of discipline among members of the Armed Forces. The restrictions imposed upon Fundamental Rights in exercise of the power conferred by Article 33 must be "absolutely necessary for ensuring proper discharge of duties and the maintenance of discipline". *UOI v Lt Cdr Annie Nagaraja,* (2020) SCC OnLine SC 326 : (2020) 3 Mad LJ 388 : LNIND 2020 SC 207; *Secretary, Ministry of Defence v Babita Puniya,* LNIND 2020 SC 134; *Lt Col Prithi Pal Singh Bedi v UOI,* AIR 1982 SC 1413 : (1982) 3 SCC 140 : (1982) 1 Scale 676; *R Viswan v UOI,* AIR 1983 SC 658 : (1983) 3 SCC 401 : (1983) 3 SCR 60 : (1983) 1 Scale 497.

such religious plea can stop the electoral process. It is also doubtful if there is any religious scripture which requires Muslims to suspend their normal duties on the days of fasting, which is spread over one month.

(ii) When martial law has been in force in any area, Parliament may, by law, indemnify any person in the service of the Union or a State for any act done by him in connection with the maintenance or restoration of order in such area or validate any sentence passed or act done while martial law was in force [*Article* 34].

(iii) The Fundamental Rights guaranteed by the Constitution will remain suspended, while a Proclamation of Emergency is made by the President under Article 352 [see *post*]. The effect of such Proclamation in this behalf is twofold—

(a) As soon as a Proclamation of Emergency is made, the State shall be freed from the limitations imposed by Article 19. This means that the Legislature shall be competent to make any law and the Executive shall be at liberty to take any action, even though it contravenes or restricts the right of freedom of speech and expression, assembly, association, movement, residence, profession or occupation. So far as these rights are concerned, the citizen shall thus have no protection against the executive or legislative authorities during the operation of the Proclamation of Emergency. The enlargement of the power of the State under Article 358 will continue only so long as the Proclamation itself remains in operation; Article 19 will revive as soon as the Proclamation expires. But the citizen shall have no remedy for acts done against him during the period of the Proclamation, in violation of the above rights [*Article* 358].

(b) The other consequence depends upon the issue of a further Order by the President. Where a Proclamation of Emergency is in operation, the President may by Order declare that the right *to move a court* for the enforcement of any of the Fundamental Rights shall remain *suspended* for the period during which the Proclamation remains in force [*Article* 359]. In such a case, however, the right to move the courts would be revived after the Proclamation ceases to be in force, or earlier, if so specified in the President's Order. In other words, if such an Order is issued, the Supreme Court and the high courts shall be powerless to issue the prerogative writs or to make any other order for the enforcement of any Fundamental Right, including those which are conferred by Articles other than Article 19 with the exception of those conferred by Articles 20 and 21.

This Order of the President, however, shall not be final. Such Order shall, as soon as may be after it is made, be laid before each House of Parliament, and it will be within the competence of Parliament to disapprove of it.[409]

The 44th Amendment Act, 1978, has further provided that a law or executive order will be shielded under Article 358 or 359 only, if the law in question contains a recital to the effect that it has been made in relation to the Proclamation of Emergency; and the executive order has been issued under such law. *Secondly,* Articles 20–21 *cannot* be suspended by any Order under Article 359.

---

409. As to Proclamation of Emergency and Orders made under Article 359, see, further, under Emergency Provisions, chapter 28, *post.*

As the Constitution stands today, two other matters must be mentioned which limit the operation of the Fundamental Rights, as they were devised in the 1949-Constitution, and are not confined to times of "Emergency" but operate *even in normal times.* These are:

I. The exceptions to Fundamental Rights; and

II. The Fundamental Duties.

31a. Exceptions to Fundamental Rights. I. Articles 31A–31D, introduced by successive amendments, constitute exceptions to the application of Fundamental Rights, wholly, or partially.[410] Of these, Article 31D has subsequently been repealed (by the 43rd Amendment Act, 1977).

31b. Fundamental Duties. II. The Fundamental Duties[411] are 11 in number, incorporated in Article 51A [Part IVA], which has been inserted by the *42nd Amendment* Act, 1976. Under this Article, it shall be the duty of every citizen of India—

(i) to abide by the Constitution and respect its ideals and institutions, the National Flag and the National Anthem;

(ii) to cherish and follow the noble ideals which inspired our national struggle for freedom;

(iii) to protect the sovereignty, unity and integrity of India;

(iv) to defend the country;

(v) to promote the spirit of common brotherhood amongst all the people of India;

(vi) to preserve the rich heritage of our composite culture;

(vii) to protect and improve the natural environment;

(viii) to develop the scientific temper and spirit of inquiry;

(ix) to safeguard public property;

(x) to strive towards excellence in all spheres of individual and collective activity.

[412](xi) who is a parent or guardian to provide opportunities for education to his child or, as the case may be, ward between the age of six and fourteen years.

In this context, it would be better to remove a misnomer involved in the expression "composite culture" in clause (f) of Article 51A. The Supreme Court has now pointed out that the foundation of this composite culture is the Sanskrit language and literature which is the great binding force "for the different peoples of this great country and it should be preferred in the educational

---

410. Article 31D, which had been inserted by the Constitution (42nd Amendment) Act, 1976, has since been repealed by the 43rd Amendment Act, 1977.

411. It is interesting to note that the Author suggested at p 289 of vol A of the 6th Edn of the Commentary, that a separate part should be engrafted to incorporate fundamental duties.

412. Inserted by the Constitution (86th Amendment) Act, 2002, section 4.

system for the preservation of that heritage,—apart from the duty of the Government under Article 351".[413]

To quote the Supreme Court:

> Though the people of this country differed in a number of ways, they all were proud to regard themselves as participants in a *common* heritage, and that heritage, *emphatically,* is the heritage of Sanskrit.[413]

The reason is that the original population of India was Hindu. Thereafter this country was subjected to Muslim and British rule. Because of its wonderful tolerance, the Hindu culture imbibed these alien cultures and thus grew up a "composite culture" in India [*Para* 118]:[414]

> Hindu religion developed resilience to accommodate and imbibe with tolerance the cultural richness with religious assimilation and became a land of religious tolerance [*Para* 118][414] ... each religion made its contribution to enrich the *composite* Indian culture as a happy blend or synthesis. *Our* religious tolerance (thus) received reflections in *our Constitutional* creed [*Para* 126].[414]

Of course, there is no provision in the Constitution for direct enforcement of any of these Duties[415] nor for any sanction to prevent their violation. But it may be expected that in determining the constitutionality of any law, if a court finds that it seeks to give effect to any of these Duties, it may consider such law to be "reasonable" in relation to Article 14 or 19, and thus save such law from unconstitutionality. It would also serve as a warning to reckless citizens against anti-social activities such as burning the Constitution, destroying public property and the like.[416]

The Supreme Court has held that since the Duties are obligatory for a citizen, it would follow that the state should also strive to achieve the same goal. The court may, therefore, issue suitable *directions* in these matters, in appropriate cases.[417] The Supreme Court in order to give effect to Fundamental Duties as enshrined under Article 51A(g) read with Articles 21, 47, 48B, adopted principle of "sustainable development" as a balancing concept and further held that "Precautionary Principle" and "Polluter Pays Principle" are acceptable as part of the law of the country and should be implemented by court of law. The Hon'ble Supreme Court further held that the rules of the customary international law which are not contrary to the municipal law shall be deemed to have been incorporated in the domestic law and shall be followed by the courts of law.[418] A common thread runs through Parts III, IV and IVA of the Constitution of India. One Part enumerates the Fundamental Rights, the second declares the fundamental principles of governance and the third lays down the Fundamental Duties of the citizens. While interpreting any of these provisions, it shall always be advisable to examine the scope and impact of such interpretation on all the three constitutional aspects emerging from these Parts. Fundamental Duties, as defined in Article 51A, are not made enforceable by a writ of court just as the

---

413. *Santosh Kumar v Ministry of HRD,* (1994) 6 SCC 579.
414. *Stainislaus v State of MP,* AIR 1977 SC 908.
415. *Ramsharan v UOI,* AIR 1989 SC 549, para 14.
416. See, further, Author's *Constitutional Law of India,* 6th Edn, 1991, pp 134–35.
417. *Rural Litigation v State of Uttar Pradesh,* AIR 1987 SC 359, para 20.
418. *Vellore Citizen's Welfare Forum v UOI,* AIR 1996 SC 2715 : (1996) 5 SCC 647.

Fundamental Rights are, but it cannot be lost sight of that "duties" in Part IVA Article 51A are prefixed by the same word "fundamental" which was prefixed by the founding fathers of the Constitution to "rights" in Part III. Every citizen of India is fundamentally obligated to develop a scientific temper and humanism. He is fundamentally duty-bound to strive towards excellence in all spheres of individual and collective activity so that the nation constantly rises to higher levels of endeavour and achievements. State is, all the citizens placed together and hence though Article 51A does not expressly cast any fundamental duty on the State, the fact remains that the duty of every citizen of India is the collective duty of the State.[419]

419. *Re Ramlila Maidan Incident*, (2012) 5 SCC 1; *AIIMS Students' Union v AIIMS*, (2002) 1 SCC 428.

[illegible] which was preceded by [illegible] consequences of the [illegible] scientific temper and humanism [illegible] the Government and [illegible] the subject [illegible] of the State.

[illegible]

CHAPTER 9

DIRECTIVE PRINCIPLES OF STATE POLICY

PART IV of the Constitution [*Articles 36–51*] contains the Directive Principles of State Policy.

1. Classification of the Directives.

As shown in Table VI, *post*, these principles may be classified under several groups:

(i) Certain ideals, particularly economic, which, according to the framers of the Constitution, the State[1] should strive for.

(ii) Certain directions to the Legislature and the Executive intended to show in what manner the State should exercise their legislative and executive powers.

(iii) Certain rights of the citizens, which shall not be enforceable by the courts like the "Fundamental Rights", are, but which the State shall nevertheless aim at securing, by regulation of its legislative and administrative policy.

2. Scope of the Directives.

It shall be the duty of the State[1] to follow these principles, both in the matter of administration as well as in the making of laws. They embody the object of the State under the republican Constitution, namely, that it is to be a "Welfare State" and not a mere "Police State". Most of these Directives, it will be seen, aim at the establishment of the economic and social democracy, which is pledged for in the Preamble.

3. Nature of the Economic Democracy.

According to Sir Ivor Jennings,[2] the philosophy underlying most of these provisions is "Fabian socialism without the socialism, for, only 'the nationalisation'[3] of the means of 'production, distribution and exchange' is missing". This much is clear, however, that *our* Constitution (as framed in 1949) did not adhere to any particular "ism" but sought to effect a compromise between individualism and

---

1. "State", in this context, has the same meaning as in the Chapter on Fundamental Rights. This means that not only the Union and State authorities, but also local authorities shall have a moral obligation to follow the Directives, *e.g.*, the promotion of cottage industries, prohibition of consumption of intoxicants or of the slaughter of cows, calves and other milch cattle, improvement of public health and of the level of nutrition of the people.
2. Sir Ivor Jennings, *Some Characteristics of the Indian Constitution,* p 13.
3. The power to nationalise is implicit in Article 39(b), if that is necessary to ensure a better "distribution" of the ownership of material resources to subserve the common good [*State of Karnataka v Ranganathan,* AIR 1978 SC 215, paras 82–83 : (1977) 4 SCC 471].

socialism by eliminating the vices of unbridled private enterprise and interest by social control and welfare measures as far as possible.

3a. Socialistic Pattern of Society.

This is why a "*Socialistic pattern of society*", not "*socialism*", was declared to be the objective of our planning by Pandit Nehru:[4]

> Socialism to some people means two things: Distribution, which means cutting off the pockets of the people who have too much money, and nationalisation. Both these are desirable objectives, but neither is by itself Socialism.
>
> Any attempt to distribute by affecting the productive machinery is utterly wrong; to do so would be to weaken ourselves. The basis of Socialism is greater wealth; there cannot be any Socialism of poverty. Therefore, the process of equalisation has to be phased.
>
> Secondly, there is the question of nationalisation. I think it is dangerous merely to nationalise something without being prepared to work it properly. To nationalise we have to select things. My idea of Socialism is that *every individual in the State should have equal opportunity for progress.*

3b. Trends Towards Collectivism.

It must be mentioned, in this context, that the governmental policy, at the Union level, had demonstrated a greater bias towards collectivism during the regime of his daughter, Mrs Indira Gandhi, and quite a number of industries, trades and other means of production were nationalised during the three decades since independence, either directly or through the agency of State-owned or State-controlled corporations, *e.g.*, banking, insurance, aviation, coal mines.

3c. 'Socialist' Objective of State.

It should, however, be mentioned that though the objective of the State has been described to be "Socialist", by the amendment of the Preamble by the Constitution (42nd Amendment) Act, Mrs Gandhi had said that this socialism did not indicate collectivism, but the offering of equal opportunities to all through socio-economic reform.

4. Various Constitutional Amendments in Part IV.

I. By the Constitution (42nd Amendment) Act, 1976, certain other changes have been introduced in Part IV, adding 2 new Directives, to accentuate the socialistic bias of the Constitution:

(i) *Equal justice and free legal aid:* Article 39A has been inserted to enjoin the State to provide free legal aid to the poor and to take other suitable steps to ensure equal justice to all, which is offered by the Preamble.[5]

(ii) *Workers' participation in management of industries:* Article 43A has been inserted in order to direct the State to ensure the participation of workers in the management of industry and other undertakings (this is what is known as "profit-sharing"). This is a positive step in advancement of socialism in the sense of economic justice.[6]

---

4. *Hindustan Standard,* Delhi, 17 May 1958, p 7. See also, Second Five Year Plan, p 22.
5. The Central Government notified the Legal Services Authority Act, 1987 to bring into force a piece of legislation that would provide free legal aid to the poor and arming the *Lok Adalat* with the status of a civil court.
6. Mere insertion of the word "Socialist" in the Preamble does not introduce Socialism in the collectivist sense, for, according to the canons of interpretation, a Preamble merely serves

[Footnote No. 6 Contd.]

Further, Article 39 has been amended to include that the State shall, in particular, direct its policy towards securing that children are given opportunities and facilities to develop in a healthy manner and in conditions of freedom and dignity and that childhood and youth are protected against exploitation and against moral and material abandonment [*Article 39(f)*].

II. The Janata Government sought to implement the promise of *economic justice and equality of opportunity* assured by the Preamble, by inserting clause (2) in Article 38[7] (by the 44th Amendment Act, 1978), as follows:

> (2) The State shall, in particular, strive to minimise the inequalities in income, and endeavour to eliminate inequalities in status, facilities and opportunities, not only amongst individuals but also amongst groups of people residing in different areas or engaged in different vocations.

This innocently-looking amendment is to be read along with the elimination of the Fundamental Right to Property. These together have paved the way for confiscatory taxation and for equalising salaries and wages for different vocations and different categories of work, which would usher in a socialistic society, even without resorting to nationalisation of the means of production.

III. The Constitution (86th Amendment) Act, 2002 altered Article 45, making provisions for early childhood care and education for children below the age of 6 years, in place of the erstwhile provision for free and compulsory education until the age of 14 years.

IV. The Constitution (97th Amendment) Act, 2011, has inserted Article 43B to promote voluntary formation of co-operative societies. Article 43B provides that:

> The State shall endeavour to promote voluntary formation, autonomous functioning, democratic control and professional management of co-operative societies.

The Constitution (97th Amendment) Act was passed in the year 2011, received the Presidential assent on 12 January 2012 and came into force with effect from 15 February 2012. The Supreme Court[8] has struck down most parts

[Footnote No. 6 Contd.]

as a key to the enacting provisions but cannot add to or modify *the law* as laid down in the enacting provisions of the Constitution.

The Supreme Court has, however, observed that the insertion of the word "socialist" in the Preamble would enable the Courts "to lean more and more in favour of nationalisation and State ownership of industry" [*Excel Wear v UOI,* AIR 1979 SC 25 (para 24) : (1978) 4 SCC 224 : 1978 (2) LLJ 527]. This means that in upholding laws of nationalisation, the Court would liberally interpret the Directives in the light of omission of Articles 19(1)(f) and 31(2), by the Constitution (44th Amendment) Act, 1978.

7. Article 38 enjoins the State to strive to promote the welfare of the people by securing and protecting, as effectively as it may, the social order in which justice—social, economic and political—shall inform all the institutions of national life. It directs the State to strive to minimise inequalities in income and endeavour to eliminate inequalities in status, facilities, opportunities among individuals and groups of people residing in different areas or engaged in different avocations [*Dalmia Cement (Bharat) Ltd v UOI,* (1996) 10 SCC 104, para 21 : (1996) 4 JT 555].

8. Constitutionality of the Constitution (97th Amendment) Act, 2011 was challenged in *Rajendra N Shah v UOI,* (2013) 2 GLR 1698 : LNIND 2013 GUJ 16 wherein the Gujarat High Court declared the Constitution (97th Amendment) Act, 2011, inserting Part IX-B,

[Footnote No. 8 Contd.]

of the Constitution (97th Amendment) Act on the ground that it required ratification by at least one-half of the State Legislatures as per Article 368(2).

5. Comparison of Directives with Fundamental Rights.

The Directives, however, differ from the Fundamental Rights contained in Part III of the Constitution or the ordinary laws of the land in the following respects:

(i) *Limitations on State v instructions to State:* While the Fundamental Rights constitute limitations upon State action, the Directive Principles are in the nature of instruments of instruction to the Government of the day to do certain things and to achieve certain ends by their actions.

(ii) *Implementation:* The Directives, however, require to be implemented by legislation, and so long as there is no law carrying out the policy laid down in a Directive, neither the State nor an individual can violate any existing law or legal right under colour of following a Directive.

(iii) *Justiciability v non-justiciability:* The Directives are not enforceable in the Courts and do not create any justiciable rights in favour of the individuals. From the standpoint of the individual, the difference between the Fundamental Rights and the Directives is that between justiciable and non-justiciable rights—a classification which has been adopted by the framers of *our* Constitution from the Constitution of *Eire.* Thus, though the Directive under Article 43 enjoins the State to secure a living wage to all workers, no worker can secure a living wage by means of an action in a Court, so long as it is not implemented by appropriate legislation. In other words, the Courts are not competent to compel the Government to carry out any Directive, *e.g.,* to provide for free compulsory education within the time limited by pre-substituted Article 45, or to undertake legislation to implement any of the Directive Principles.

6. Conflict between Directives and Fundamental Rights.

It may be observed that the declarations made in Part IV under the head "Directive Principles of State Policy" are in many cases of a wider import than the declarations made in Part III as "Fundamental Rights". Hence, the question of priority in case of conflict between the two classes of provisions may easily arise.

(i) *Fundamental rights to prevail (earliest view):* But while the Fundamental Rights are enforceable by the Courts [*Articles 32 and 226*] and the Courts are bound to declare as void any law that is inconsistent with any of the Fundamental Rights, the Directives are not so enforceable by the Courts [*Article 37*] and the

[Footnote No. 8 Contd.]

containing Articles 243ZH to 243ZT as *ultra vires* the Constitution of India for not taking recourse to Article 368(2) providing for ratification by the majority of the State Legislatures. Against this order, the Union of India preferred an appeal before the Supreme Court. The Supreme Court in *UOI v Rajendra N Shah,* 2021 SCC OnLine SC 474, decided on 20-7-2021, by a majority of 2:1 upheld the judgment of the High Court except to the extent that it had struck down Part IX-B of the Constitution in its entirety. The Supreme Court held that since the Constitutional (97th Amendment) Act dealt with an entry which was an exclusive State subject, it required a ratification by at least one-half of the State Legislatures as per Article 368(2) of the Constitution. The Supreme Court held that that Part IX-B is operative only insofar as it concerns Multi-State Cooperative Societies both within various States and in Union Territories of India.

Courts cannot declare as void any law which is otherwise valid on the ground that it contravenes any of the "Directives". Hence, in case of any conflict between Parts III and IV of the Constitution, the former shall prevail in the Courts.[9]

(ii) *Total immunity by Article 31C:* The foregoing general proposition, laid down, above in (i), by the Supreme Court in 1951, must, however, be read subject to a major exception. Article 31C, introduced in 1971 and expanded by the Constitution (42nd Amendment) Act, says that though the Directives themselves are not directly enforceable in the Courts, if any law is made to implement *any* of the *Directives* contained in Part IV, it would be totally immune from unconstitutionality on the ground of contravention of the Fundamental Rights conferred by Articles 14 and 19.[10]

(iii) *Principle of harmonious construction to be adopted:* This attempt to confer a primacy upon the Directives as against the Fundamental Rights has, however, been foiled by the majority of the Supreme Court Bench in the *Minerva Mills* case[11] in two respects:

(a) It has struck down the widening of Article 31C to include *any or all* of the Directives in Part IV, on the ground that such total exclusion of judicial review would offend the "basic structure" of the Constitution. As a result, Article 31C is restored to its pre-1976 position, so that a law would be protected by Article 31C only if it has been made to implement the Directive in Article 39(b)-(c) and not any of the other Directives included in Part IV.

(b) It has also been held that there is a fine balance in the original Constitution as between the Directives and the Fundamental Rights, which should be adhered to by the courts, by a harmonious reading of the two categories of provisions, *instead of giving any general preference to the Directive Principles.*

It is also to be noted that outside these two Fundamental Rights [in Articles 14 and 19], the general proposition laid down in 1951[12] shall subsist. Thus, by way of implementing the Directive in Article 45,—to provide free and compulsory education to children,—the State cannot override the Fundamental Right, under Article 30(1), of minority communities to establish educational institutions of their own choice. The Supreme Court observed that:

> The directive principles of State policy have to conform to and run as subsidiary to the Chapter on Fundamental Rights. Nevertheless, in determining the scope and ambit of the fundamental rights relied on by or on behalf of any person or body the court may not entirely ignore these directive principles of State policy laid down in Part IV of the Constitution but should adopt the principle of harmonious construction and should attempt to give effect to both as much as possible.[13]

The integrative approach towards Fundamental Rights and Directive Principles, which says that the both should be interpreted and read together, has now come to hold the field. It has now become a judicial strategy to read Fundamental Rights along with Directive Principles with a view to define the

9. *State of Madras v Champakam,* AIR 1951 SC 226 : (1951) 2 SCR 525 (531).
10. Article 31 having been repealed, reference thereto has been omitted from Article 31C by the 44th Amendment Act, 1978.
11. *Minerva Mills v UOI,* AIR 1980 SC 1789 : (1980) 2 SCC 591.
12. *State of Madras v Champakam,* AIR 1951 SC 226 : (1951) 2 SCR 525 (531).
13. *Re The Kerala Education Bill, 1957, Reference Under Article 143(1) of The Constitution of India,* AIR 1958 SC 956 : [1959] 1 SCR 995.

scope and ambit of the former. For the most part, Directive Principles have been used to broaden and to give depth to some Fundamental Rights and to imply some more rights therein for the people over and above those that are expressly stated in the Fundamental Rights.

The fundamental rights and the directive principles are the two wheels of the chariot as an aid to make social and economic democracy true.[14]

The Supreme Court of India in *National Legal Services Authority v UOI,*[15] observed:

> Speaking for the vision of our founding fathers, in *Rangnatha Reddy,*[16] the Supreme Court speaking through Justice Krishna Iyer observed:
>
> The social philosophy of the Constitution shapes creative judicial vision and orientation. Our nation has, as its dynamic doctrine, economic democracy sans which political democracy is chimerical. We say so because our Constitution, in Parts III and IV and elsewhere, ensouls such a value system, and the debate in this case puts precisely this soul in peril....Our thesis is that the dialectics of social justice should not be missed if the synthesis of Parts III and Part IV is to influence State action and court pronouncements. Constitutional problems cannot be studied in a socio-economic vacuum, since socio-cultural changes are the source of the new values, and sloughing off old legal thought is part of the process the new equity-loaded legality. A judge is a social scientist in his role as constitutional invigilator and fails functionally if he forgets this dimension in his complex duties.
>
> While interpreting Article 21, the Supreme Court has comprehended such diverse aspects as children in jail entitled to special treatment (*Sheela Barse v UOI,* [1986] 3 SCC 596), health hazards due to pollution (*Mehta MC v UOI,*[1987] 4 SCC 463), beggars' interest in housing (*Kalidas v State of J&K,* [1987] 3 SCC 430), health hazards from harmful drugs (*Vincent Panikurlangara v UOI,* AIR 1987 SC 990), right of speedy trial (*Reghubir Singh v State of Bihar,* AIR 1987 SC 149), handcuffing of prisoners (*Aeltemesh Rein v UOI,* AIR 1988 SC 1768), delay in execution of death sentence, immediate medical aid to injured persons (*Parmanand Katara v UOI,* AIR 1989 SC 2039), starvation deaths (*Kishen v State of Orissa,* AIR 1989 SC 677), the right to know (*Reliance Petrochemicals Ltd v Indian Express Newspapers Bombay Pvt Ltd,* AIR 1989 SC 190), right to open trial (*Kehar Singh v State (Delhi Admn.),* AIR 1988 SC 1883), inhuman conditions an*(sic)* after-care home(*Vikram Deo Singh Tomar v State of Bihar,* AIR 1988 SC 1782).
>
> A most remarkable feature of this expansion of Article 21 is that many of the non-justiciable Directive Principles embodied in Part IV of the Constitution have now been resurrected as enforceable fundamental rights by the magic wand of judicial activism, playing on Article 21 eg (a) Right to pollution-free water and air (*Subhash Kumar v State of Bihar,* AIR 1991 SC 420), (b) Right to a reasonable residence (*Shantistar Builders v Narayan Khimalal Totame,* AIR 1990 SC 630), (c) Right to food, clothing, decent environment and even protection of cultural heritage (*Ram Sharan Autyanuprasi v UOI,* AIR 1989 SC 549), (d) Right of every child to a full development (*Shantistar Builders v Narayan Khimalal Totame,* AIR 1990 SC 630), (e) Right of residents of hilly-areas to access to roads (*State of HP v Umed Ram Sharma,* AIR 1986 SC 847), (f) Right to education (*Mohini Jain v State of Karnataka,* AIR 1992 SC 1858), but not for a professional degree (*Unni Krishnan JP v State of AP,* AIR 1993 SC 2178).

---

14. *Jilubhai Nanbhai Khachar v State of Gujarat,* AIR 1995 SC 142 : 1995 Supp (1) SCC 596 (para 47).
15. *National Legal Services Authority v UOI,* AIR 2014 SC 1863 : (2014) 5 SCC 438.
16. *State of Karnataka v Ranganatha Reddy,* AIR 1978 SC 215 : (1977) 4 SCC 471.

A corollary of this development is that while so long the negative language of Art. 21 and use of the word 'deprived' was supposed to impose upon the State the negative duty not to interfere with the life or liberty of an individual without the sanction of law, the width and amplitude of this provision has now imposed a positive obligation (*Vincent Panikurlangara v UOI*, AIR 1987 SC 990) upon the State to take steps for ensuring to the individual a better enjoyment of his life and dignity, eg (i) Maintenance and improvement of public health (*Vincent Panikurlangara v UOI*, AIR 1987 SC 990), (ii) Elimination of water and air pollution (*Mehta MC v UOI*, [1987] 4 SCC 463), (iii) Improvement of means of communication (*State of HP v Umed Ram Sharma*, AIR 1986 SC 847). (iv) Rehabilitation of bonded labourers (*Bandhuva Mukti Morcha v UOI*, AIR 1984 SC 802), (v) Providing human conditions if prisons (*Sher Singh v State of Punjab*, AIR 1983 SC 465) and protective homes (*Sheela Barse v UOI*, [1986] 3 SCC 596), (vi) Providing hygienic condition in a slaughter-house (*Buffalo Traders Welfare Association v Maneka Gandhi*, [1994] Suppl (3) SCC 448)

The common golden thread which passes through all these pronouncements is that Article 21 guarantees enjoyment of life by all citizens of this country with dignity, viewing this human rights in terms of human development.

7. Special Importance to Right to Education.

It is significant to note that among several Articles enshrined under Part IV of the Indian Constitution, Article 45 had been given much importance, as education is the basic necessity of the democracy and if the people are denied their right to education, then democracy will be paralyzed; and it was, therefore, emphasised that the objectives enshrined under Article 45 in Part IV should be achieved within ten years of the adoption of the Constitution. By establishing the obligations of the State, the Founding Fathers made it the responsibility of future Governments to formulate a programme in order to achieve the given goals, but the unresponsive and sluggish attitude of the Government to achieve the objectives enshrined under Article 45, belied the hopes and aspirations of the people. Although several States have enacted legislations to provide free and compulsory primary education such as the Kerala Education Act, 1958; the Punjab Primary Education Act 1960; the Gujarat Compulsory Primary Education Act 1961; the UP Basic Education Act 1972; the Rajasthan Primary Education Act 1964.[17]

However, the Judiciary showed keen interest in providing free and compulsory education to all the children below the age of 14 years. In the case of *Mohini Jain v State of Karnataka*,[18] the Hon'ble Supreme court held that right to education is a Fundamental Right enshrined under Article 21 of the Constitution. The right to education springs from right to life. The right to life under Article 21 and the dignity of the individual cannot fully be appreciated without the enjoyment of right to education. The Supreme Court observed:

"Right to life" is the compendious expression for all those rights which the courts must enforce because they are basic to the dignified enjoyment of life. It extends to the full range of conduct which the individual is free to pursue. The right to education flows directly from right to life. The right to life under Article 21 and the dignity of an individual cannot be assured unless it is accompanied by

17. *Maharshi Mahesh Yogi Vedic Vishwavidyalaya v State of MP*, (2013) 15 SCC 677 : LNIND 2013 SC 587; *Mohini Jain v State of Karnataka*, AIR 1992 SC 1858 : (1992) 3 SCC 666; *Unni Krishnan P v State of Andhra Pradesh*, AIR 1993 SC 2178 : (1993) 1 SCC 645; *Bandhua Mukti Morcha v UOI*, AIR 1997 SC 2218 : (1997) 10 SCC 549 : JT (1997) 5 SC 285.
18. *Mohini Jain v State of Karnataka*, (1992) 3 SCC 666.

the right to education. The State Government is under an obligation to make endeavour to provide educational facilities at all levels to its citizens.

In the case of *Unni Krishnan JP v State of Andhra Pradesh*,[19] the Supreme Court while examining the decision of Mohini Jain's case, partly overruled that decision and held that the right to education is implicit in the right to life and personal liberty guaranteed by Article 21 and must be interpreted in the light of the Directive Principles of State Policy contained in Articles 41, 45 and 46, however, limited the State obligation to provide educational facilities as follows: (i) Every citizen of this country has a right to free education until he completes the age of 14 years; (ii) Beyond that stage, his right to education is subject to the limits of the economic capacity of the State.

Again, in *Bandhua Mukti Morcha v UOI*,[20] K Ramaswamy J and Saghir Ahmad J, while observing that illiteracy has many adverse effects in a democracy governed by a rule of law, held that educated citizens could meaningfully exercise their political rights, discharge social responsibilities satisfactorily and develop spirit of tolerance and reform. Therefore, compulsory education is one of the essentials for the stability of democracy, social integration and to eliminate social evils. The Supreme Court, by rightly and harmoniously construing the provisions of Parts III and IV of the Constitution, has made right to education, a basic fundamental right.

Under the backdrop of the aforementioned declarations by the Supreme Court of India, the Government of India by the Constitutional (86th Amendment) Act, 2002, had added a new Article, Article 21A, which provides that "the State shall provide free and compulsory education to all children of the age of 6 to 14 years in such manner as the State may, by law determine". In this regard, the Central Government has made the Right of Children to Free and Compulsory Education Act, 2009 (35 of 2009), which has been effective from 1-4-2010. Further, they strengthened Article 21A by adding clause (*k*) to Article 51A, which provides for those who are a parent or guardian to provide opportunities for education to his/her child or ward between the age of 6 and 14 years.

On the basis of the Constitutional mandate provided under Articles 21A, 41, 45, 46 and 51A(*k*) and various judgments of the Supreme Court of India, both the Government of India as well as the Supreme Court of India, have taken several steps to eradicate illiteracy, improve the quality of education and simultaneously ensure that school dropouts are brought to *nil.* Some of these programmes are the National Technology Mission, District Primary Education Programme, Nutrition Support for Primary Education, National Open School, Mid-Day Meal Scheme, Sarva Siksha Abhiyan and other State specific initiatives.

8. Sanction behind the Directives.

Though these Directives are not enforceable by the courts and, if the Government of the day fails to carry out these objects, *no Court* can make the Government ensure them, yet these principles have been declared to be "fundamental in the governance of the country", such that "it shall be the duty of the State to apply these principles in making laws" [*Article 37*].

---

19. *Unni Krishnan JP v State of Andhra Pradesh,* (1993) 1 SCC 645.
20. *Bandhua Mukti Morcha v UOI,* (1997) 10 SCC 549.

The sanction behind them is, in fact, *political.* As Dr Ambedkar observed in the Constituent Assembly,—

> "if any Government ignores them, they will certainly have to answer for them before the *electorate* at the election time".[21]

It would also be a patent weapon at the hands of the Opposition—to discredit the Government on the ground that any of its executive or legislative acts is opposed to the Directive Principles.

8a. Author's View. The Author discerns a more effective sanction for enforcement of the Directives, which does not appear to have been properly appreciated in any quarters so far. Article 355 says—

> It shall be the *duty* of the *Union* . . . to ensure that the government of every State is carried on in accordance with the provisions of this Constitution.

Indisputably, Part IV (containing the Directive Principles) is a part of the Constitution. On the other hand, even though the Directives are not enforceable in the courts of law, Article 37 unequivocally enjoins that "it shall be the *duty* of the *State* to apply these principles in making laws". If so, it should be the *duty* of the Union to see that every State takes steps for implementing the Directives, as far as possible. Hence, it should be competent for the Union to issue directions against particular States to introduce "free and compulsory education for children" [*Article 45*], or to prevent "slaughter of cows, calves and other milch and draught cattle" [*Article 48*], or to introduce "prohibition of consumption of alcoholic drinks" [*Article 47*], and so on. In case of refusal to comply with such directions issued by the Union, it may apply Article 365 against such recalcitrant State. Otherwise, the Directives in Part IV shall ever remain a dead-letter.

9. Utility of the Directives—Criticisms. Owing to the legal deficiencies of the Directives, the utility of their incorporation in the Constitution, which is a *legal* instrument, has been questioned from different quarters:

(i) Sir Ivor Jennings,[22] thus, characterised them as "pious aspiration" and also questioned the utility of importing into India of the 19th century English philosophy of "Fabian socialism without the socialism".

(ii) Prof Wheare has criticised them in stronger terms—

> When one peruses the terms of these Articles one cannot deny that it would be *foolish* to allow Courts to concern themselves with these matters . . . It may be doubted whether there is any gain, on balance, in introducing these *paragraphs of generalities* into a Constitution anywhere at all, if it is intended that the Constitution should command the respect as well as affection of the people. If the Constitution is to be taken *seriously,* the interpretation and fulfilment of these general objects of policy will raise *great difficulties* for legislatures, and these difficulties will bring the Constitution, the Courts and the legislature into *conflict* and disrepute. If these declarations are, however, to be treated as 'words', they will bring discredit upon the Constitution also.[23]

---

21. *Constituent Assembly Debates,* vol 7, 41, 476 (Dr Ambedkar).
22. Ivor Jennings, *Some Characteristics of the Indian Constitution,* 1953, pp 31–33.
23. Wheare, *Modern Constitutions,* p 47.

10. Utility of the Directives—Praises. Nevertheless, their incorporation in the Constitution has been justified by a consensus of opinion as well as the working of the Constitution since 1950:

(i) Sir BN Rau, who advised the division of individual rights into two categories—those which were enforceable in the courts and those which were not—stated that the latter class which are known in the Constitution as "Directives" were intended as "*moral precepts* for the authorities of the State . . . they have at least an educative value". That educative value is to remind those in power for the time being that the goal of the Indian polity is to introduce "socialism in the economic sphere" (as per Panikkar), or "*economic* democracy" as distinguished from "*political* democracy" (as per Ambedkar), which simply means "one person one vote". It reminds the authorities that they must ensure "social security and better standards of sanitation" and emphasise "the duty towards women and children and the obligations towards backward and tribal classes" (Panikkar).

(ii) Granville Austin considers these Directives to be "aimed at furthering the goals of the social revolution or . . . to foster this revolution by establishing the conditions necessary for its achievement". He explains:

> By establishing these positive obligations of the State, the members of the Constituent Assembly made it the responsibility of future Indian governments to find a middle way between individual liberty and the public good, between preserving the property and the privilege of the few and bestowing benefits on the many in order to liberate the powers of all men equally for contributions to the common good.[24]

In short, the Directives emphasise, in amplification of the Preamble, that the goal of the Indian polity is not *laissez faire,* but a welfare State, where the State has a positive duty to ensure to its citizens social and economic justice and the dignity of the individual. It would serve as an "Instrument of Instructions" upon all future Governments, irrespective of their party creeds. The socialistic approach has been further emphasised by the Constitutional 42nd and 44th Amendment Acts, as discussed earlier.

(iii) Though these Directives are not enforceable by the Courts and if the Government of the day fails to carry out these objects, no Court can make the Government ensure them, yet these principles have been declared to be *fundamental* in the governance of the country, and a Government which rests on popular vote can hardly ignore them, while shaping its polity.[25]

(iv) Again, while at the time of the drafting of the Constitution, the Directives were considered by many as a surplusage because they were not justiciable, the working of the Constitution during the last few years has demonstrated the utility of the Directives even in the courts thusly:

(a) *Constitutional validity of laws:* Though the courts cannot declare a law to be *invalid* on the ground that it contravenes a Directive Principle, nevertheless the constitutional validity of many laws has been *maintained* with reference to the Directives so that they do not serve as mere "*moral homily*" as Prof Wheare had anticipated in 1950. For instance, it has been held that when a law is challenged as

24. Granville Austin, *The Indian Constitution,* pp 50–52.
25. *Constituent Assembly Debates,* vol 7, 41, 476 (Dr Ambedkar).

constituting an invasion of the Fundamental Right specified in Article 14 or 19, the court would uphold the validity of such law if it had been made to implement a Directive, holding that it constituted a "reasonable classification" for the purpose of Article 14[26]; a "reasonable restriction" under Article 19[27]; or a "public purpose" within the meaning of (now omitted) Article 31(2).[28]

The Constitution has since been amended to dispense with the need for judicial interpretation to reach the above conclusion. In 1971, Article 31C was inserted in the Constitution to provide that a law to implement Article 39(b)-(c) would be immune from the limitation imposed by Articles 14, 19 or (now omitted) 31. In 1976, this protection was extended to any law to give effect to *any* of the Directives included in Part IV, by the Constitution (42nd Amendment) Act. The Supreme Court has, however, resisted that extension.[29]

(b) *Principle of harmonious construction:* Even as regards Fundamental Rights other than those under Articles 14, 19 and (now omitted) 31[30], though the Directives cannot directly override them, in determining the scope and ambit of the Fundamental Rights themselves, the court may not entirely ignore the Directive Principles and should adopt the principle of harmonious construction so as to give effect to both as much as possible.[31]

Again, the Supreme Court has relied upon Article 39A in determining the duty of the State in making a law under Article 21, depriving a person of his personal liberty, and held that where a prisoner has a right of appeal, the State should provide him a free copy of the judgment and also engage a counsel for him at the cost of the State.[32-33]

(c) *Interpretation of a legislation:* Not only in the matter of determining the constitutional validity of a legislation, but also in its interpretation, the court should bear in mind that the Directive Principles are not in conflict with but complementary to the Fundamental Rights, and enable the State to impose certain *duties* upon the citizens, insofar as the Directives are implemented, *e.g.*, in making a law to ensure minimum wages to workers, in accordance with the Directive in Article 43.[34]

(d) *Directives by Supreme Court:* Though the Directive Principles, as such, are not enforceable by the courts, the Supreme Court has issued directives, in proper

---

26. *Orient Weaving Mills v UOI,* AIR 1963 SC 98 : (1962) Supp 3 SCR 481.
27. *State of Bombay v Balsara,* AIR 1951 SC 318 : (1951) SCR 682; *Hanif Quareshi v State of Bihar,* AIR 1958 SC 731 : (1959) SCR 629.
28. *State of Bihar v Kameshwar,* AIR 1952 SC 252 : (1952) 1 SCR 889 (Mahajan and Aiyyar JJ).
29. *Minerva Mills v UOI,* AIR 1980 SC 1789 : (1980) 2 SCC 591.
30. Article 31 having been repealed, reference thereto has been omitted from Article 31C by the 44th Amendment Act, 1978.
31. *Ref on the Kerala Education Bill,* AIR 1958 SC 956 : (1959) 1 SCR 995; *State of TN v Abu,* AIR 1984 SC 326, paras 10–11 : (1984) 1 SCC 515; *Bandhua Mukti Morcha,* AIR 1984 SC 802, para 10 : (1984) 3 SCC 161 : (1984) Lab IC 560 .
32. *MH Hoskot v State of Maharashtra,* AIR 1978 SC 1548, para 24 : (1978) 3 SCC 544 : 1978 CrLJ 1678.
33. *Kishore Chand v State of HP,* AIR 1990 SC 2140 : (1991) 1 SCC 286, paras 12–13 : (1991) SCC (Cr) 172.
34. *CB Boarding & Lodging v State of Mysore,* AIR 1970 SC 2042, para 13 : (1970) 1 SCC 43.

cases, enjoining the Government to perform their positive duties to achieve the goals envisaged by the Directives.[35]

(v) On the other hand, the Constitution itself has been amended, successively (*e.g.*, 1st, 4th, 17th, 25th, 42nd and 44th), to modify those "Fundamental Rights" by reason of whose existence the State was experiencing difficulty in effecting agrarian, economic and social reforms which are envisaged by the Directive Principles.[36]

11. Implementation of the Directives.

It would not be an easy task to survey the progress made by the Governments of the Union and the States in implementing such a large number of Directives over a period of over seven decades since the promulgation of the Constitution. Nevertheless, a brief reference to some of the outstanding achievements may be made in order to illustrate that the Directives have not been taken by the Government in power as "pious homilies", as was supposed by many when they were engrafted in the Constitution.

(a) *Even distribution of material resources [Article 39(b)]:* The greatest progress in carrying out the Directives has taken place as regards Article 39(b), which directs that the State should ensure that the ownership and control of the material resources of the community are so distributed as best to serve the common good. The distribution of largesse of the State is to serve the common good of as many persons as possible.[37] In an agrarian country like India, the main item of material resources is no doubt agricultural. Since the time of the permanent settlement, this important source of wealth had been being largely appropriated by a group of hereditary proprietors and other intermediaries known variously in different parts of the country, such as, *zamindars, jagirdars, inamdars,* etc., while the actual tillers of the soil were being impoverished by the operation of various economic forces, apart from high rents and exploitation by the intermediaries. The Planning Commission, in its First Plan, therefore, recommended an abolition of these intermediaries so as to bring the tillers of the soil in direct relationship with the State. This reform has, by this time, been carried out almost completely throughout India. Simultaneously, legislation has been undertaken in many of the States for the improvement of the condition of the cultivators as regards security of tenure, fair rents, and the like. In order to prevent the concentration of land holdings even among the actual cultivators, legislation has been enacted in many of the States, fixing a ceiling, that is to say, a maximum area of land which may be held by an individual owner.

It has already been stated how these reforms have been facilitated by amending the Constitution, to shield these laws from challenge in the courts.

(b) *Self-governance power to Panchayats [Article 40]:* A large number of laws have been enacted to implement the directive in Article 40 to organise village panchayats and endow them with powers of self-government. It is stated that there are about 2,68,837 Gram Panchayats, 6751 Intermediate Tiers and 679

35. *D S Nakara v UOI,* AIR 1983 SC 130, paras 33–34 : (1983) 1 SCC 305; *Sheela Barse v State of Maharashtra,* AIR 1983 SC 378, paras 1, 3 : (1983) 2 SCC 96 : 1983 Cr LJ 642; *People's Union v UOI,* AIR 1982 SC 1473, para 7 : (1982) 2 SCC 494; *Lingappa v State of Maharashtra,* AIR 1985 SC 389, paras 14, 16 : (1985) 1 SCC 479.
36. Inserting Articles 31A–31C and the Ninth Schedule in the Constitution.
37. *Mahinder Kumar Gupta v UOI,* (1995) 1 SCC 85, para 5 : (1995) 1 Mad LJ (SC) 64.

Zila Panchayats in the country.[38] Though the Constitution and functions of the panchayats vary according to the terms of the different State Acts, generally speaking, the panchayats, elected by the entire adult population in the villages, have been endowed with powers of civic administration such as medical relief, maintenance of village roads, streets, tanks and wells, provision of primary education, sanitation and the like.

Besides civic functions, the panchayats also exercise judicial powers. Legal practitioners are excluded from these village tribunals. Though owing to lack of proper education, narrow-mindedness and sectional interests in the rural areas, the system of panchayat administration is still under controversy. After the Constitution (73rd and 74th Amendment) Acts, almost all the States have enacted laws vesting various degrees of powers of self-government in the hands of panchayats.

(c) *Promotion of cottage industries [Article 43]:* For the promotion of cottage industries, which is a State subject, the Central Government has established several Boards to help the State Governments, in the matters of finance, marketing, and the like. These are—All-India Khadi and Village Industries Board; All-India Handicrafts Board; All-India Handloom Board; Small-scale Industries Board; Silk Board; Coir Board. Besides, the National Small Industries Corporation has been set with certain statutory functions, and the Khadi and Village Industries Commission has been set up for the development of the Khadi and village industries.

(d) *Compulsory pre-primary child care and education [Article 45]:* The Government has formulated the Central Right of Children to Free and Compulsory Education (RTE) Rules, 2010 for Union Territory without State Legislature. It has also formulated Model RTE Rules which were to be adopted by the concerned States based on the ground realities prevailing in that particular State.

(e) *Raising the level of nutrition and standard of living, and improving public health [Article 47]:* For raising the standard of living, particularly of the rural population, the Government of India launched its Community Development Project in 1952. Later on, Integrated Rural Development Programme (IRDP) (1978–79), National Rural Employment Programme (NREP), Rural Landless Employment Guarantee Programme (RLEGP), Drought Prone Areas Programme (DPAP), Desert Development Programme (DDP) and some other schemes were launched.

Though legislation relating to prohibition of intoxicating drinks and drugs had taken place in some of the Provinces long before the Constitution came into being, not much of effective work had been done until, in pursuance of the Directive in the Constitution, the Planning Commission took up the matter and drew up a comprehensive scheme through its Prohibition Enquiry Committee. Since then, prohibition has been introduced in several States/Union Territories, in whole or in part.[39]

38. Source: *https://egramswaraj.gov.in/* (last accessed on 26 April 2024).

39. Such States include Gujarat, Bihar, Mizoram and Nagaland. Other States/Union Territories which had previously enforced but later repealed the prohibition were Andhra Pradesh, Haryana, Kerala, Manipur, Tamil Nadu and Lakshadweep.

Though the States' paucity of financial resources is the primary reason for the failure to fully implement this Directive so far, it would be only candid to record that ultimately, failure of the people to imbibe the Gandhian ideal of life is at the back of this failure. The spread of the malady of intoxication amongst the younger generation since independence is, in fact, alarming. It should be pointed out that a fresh impetus was given to the programme of prohibition by the Janata Prime Minister, Mr Desai, a staunch advocate of the Gandhian philosophy in this matter.

Dry days are specific days when the sale of alcohol is prohibited in the States, by the respective State Government, which otherwise allow sale and consumption of alcohol. These days generally include Republic Day, Independence Day, Gandhi Jayanti and Election voting days.

(g) *Separation of Judiciary from Executive [Article 50]:* As to the separation of the Executive from the Judiciary, the slow progress and diverse methods in the various States has been replaced by a uniform system by Union legislation, in the shape of the Criminal Procedure Code, 1973, which has placed the function of judicial trials in the hands of "Judicial Magistrates", who are members of the judiciary and are under the complete control of the High Courts.

12. Directives Contained in other Parts of the Constitution.

Besides the Directives contained in Part IV, there are certain other Directives addressed to the State in other Parts of the Constitution. Those Directives are also non-justiciable. These are—

(a) Article 335 enjoins that the claims of the members of the Scheduled Castes and the Scheduled Tribes shall be taken into consideration, consistently with the maintenance of efficiency of administration, in the making of appointments to services and posts in connection with the affairs of the Union or of a State.[40]

(b) Article 350A enjoins every State and every local authority within the State to provide adequate facilities for instruction in the mother-tongue at the primary stage of education to children belonging to linguistic minority groups.

(c) Article 351 enjoins the Union to promote the spread of the Hindi language and to develop it so that it may serve as a medium of expression of all the elements of the composite culture of India.

Though the Directives contained in above Articles are not included in Part IV, Courts have given similar attention to them on the application of the principle that all parts of the Constitution should be read together.[41]

40. *Balaji v State of Mysore,* AIR 1963 SC 649, p *664* : (1963) Supp (1) SCR 439; *Devadasan v UOI,* AIR 1964 SC 179, *188* : (1964) 4 SCR 680.
41. See, *R R Dalavai v State of TN,* AIR 1976 SC 1559 : (1976) 3 SCC 748.

CHAPTER 10

PROCEDURE FOR AMENDMENT

1. Nature of the Amending Process.

THE nature of the amending process envisaged by the makers of *our* Constitution can be best explained by referring to Pandit Nehru's observation that the Constitution should not be so rigid that it cannot be adapted to the changing needs of national development and strength.

There was also a *political* significance in adopting a "facile procedure" for amendment, namely, that any popular demand for changing the political system should be capable of realisation, if it assumed a considerable volume. In the words of Dr Ambedkar, explaining the proposals for amendment introduced by him in the Constituent Assembly:

> Those who are dissatisfied with the Constitution have only to obtain in two-thirds majority, and if they cannot obtain even a two-thirds majority in the Parliament elected on adult franchise in their favour, their dissatisfaction with the Constitution cannot be deemed to be shared by the general public.[1]

Elements of flexibility were therefore imported into a Federal Constitution, which is inherently rigid in its nature. According to the traditional theory of federalism, either the process of amendment of the Constitution is entrusted to a body other than the ordinary Legislature, or a special procedure is prescribed for such amendment in order to ensure that the federal compact may not be disturbed at the will of one of the parties of the federation, *viz.,* the federal Legislature.

2. Modes for Effecting any Constitutional Amendment.

But, as has been explained at the outset, the framers of *our* Constitution were also inspired by the need for the sovereignty of Parliament elected by universal suffrage to enable it to achieve a dynamic national progress. They, therefore, prescribed an easier mode for changing those provisions of the Constitution which did not primarily affect the federal system. This was done in two ways—

(a) *Amendment by simple majority:* By providing that the alteration of certain provisions of the Constitution were "*not to be deemed to be amendment of the Constitution*". The result is that such provisions can be altered by the Union Parliament in the ordinary process of legislation, that is, by a simple majority.

(b) *Amendment by following mandatory and special constitutional procedure:* Other provisions of the Constitution can be changed only by

1. *CAD,* dated 25 November 1949, pp. 225-26.

the process of "amendment" which is prescribed in Article 368. But a differentiation has been again made in the procedure for amendment, according to the nature of the provisions sought to be amended.

While in all cases of amendment of the Constitution, a Bill has to be passed by the Union Parliament by a special majority, in the case of certain provisions which affect the *federal structure,* a further step is required, *viz.,* a ratification by the Legislature of at least half of the States, before the Bill is presented to the President for his assent [*Article 368*]. But even in this latter group of cases, the law which eventually effects the amendment is a law made by Parliament, which is the ordinary legislative organ of the Union. There is thus no separate *constituent body* provided for by *our* Constitution for the amending process. The procedure for amendment is—

I. An amendment of the Constitution may be initiated only by the introduction of a Bill for the purpose in either House of Parliament, and when the Bill is passed in each House by a majority (*i.e.*, more than 50%) of the total membership of that House *and* by a majority of not less than two-thirds of the members of that House *present and voting,* it shall be presented to the President for his assent and upon such assent being given to the Bill, the Constitution shall stand amended in accordance with the terms of the Bill.

II. If, however, such amendment seeks to make any change[2] in the following provisions, namely,—(a) The manner of election of the President [*Articles 54 and 55*]; (b) Extent of the executive power of the Union and the States [*Articles 73 and 162*]; (c) Goods and Services Tax Council [*Article 279A*]; (d) The Supreme Court and the High Courts [*Chapter IV of Part V, Chapter V of Part VI, and Article 241*]; (e) Distribution of legislative power between the Union and the States [*Chapter I of Part XI*]; (f) Any of the Lists in the Seventh Schedule; (g) Representation of the States in Parliament [*Articles 80, 81 and the Fourth Schedule*]; and (h) Provisions of Article 368 itself,—the amendment shall also require to be ratified by the Legislatures of not less than one-half of the States by resolutions to that effect passed by those Legislatures before the Bill making provision for such amendment is presented to the President for assent[3] [*Article 368(2)*].

3. General and Distinctive Features for Amending Indian Constitution.

It is clear from the above that the amending process prescribed by *our* Constitution has certain distinctive features as compared with the corresponding provisions in the leading Constitutions of the world. The procedure for amendment must be classed as "rigid" insofar as it requires a special majority and, in some cases, a special procedure for amendment as compared with the procedure prescribed for ordinary legislation. But the procedure is not as complicated or difficult as in the *USA* or in any other rigid Constitution. Thus, the general and distinctive features for amending the Indian Constitution are as follows:

---

2. The word 'change' means a change in the remedy while the right remains intact. But such change may not be a direct change in the language of any of the provisions specified in clauses (a) to (h), but may be a change 'in effect'. See also, *Shri Kihota Hollohon v Zachilhu,* AIR 1993 SC 412: 1992 (1) SCR 686: (1992) Supp 2 SCC 651 (CB).
3. See *Table IV,* post, for instances where such ratification has been obtained for amending the Constitution.

(a) *Constituent power:* Subject to the special procedure laid down in Article 368, *our* Constitution vests constituent power upon the ordinary Legislature of the Union, *i.e.*, Parliament (of course, acting by a special majority), and there is no separate body for amending the Constitution, as exists in some other Constitutions (*e.g.*, a Constitutional Convention).

(b) *Introduction of Bill in Union Parliament:* The State Legislatures cannot initiate any Bill or proposal for amendment of the Constitution. The only mode of initiating a proposal for amendment is to introduce a Bill in either House of the Union Parliament.

(c) *Passing of Constitutional Amendment Bills:* Subject to the provisions of Article 368, Constitution Amendment Bills are to be passed by Parliament in the same way as ordinary Bills.[4] In other words, they may be initiated in *either* House, and may be amended like other Bills, subject to the majority required by Article 368. But for the special majority prescribed, they must be passed by both the Houses, like any other Bill.

It would be pointed out, in this context, that there is another important point on which the passage of a Constitution Amendment Bill differs from the procedure relating to the passage of a Bill for ordinary legislation. Article 108 provides that if there is a disagreement between the two Houses of Parliament regarding the passage of a Bill, the deadlock may be solved by a *joint session* of the two Houses. But it is clear from Article 108(1), that the procedure for joint session is applicable only to Bills for ordinary legislation which come under Chapter 2 of Part V of the Constitution, and *not* to Bills for amendment of the Constitution, which are governed by the self-contained procedure contained in Article 368(2). The requirement of a special majority in both Houses, in Article 368(2) would have been nugatory had the provision as to joint session been available in this sphere.

(d) *Previous sanction of the President:* The previous sanction of the President is not required for introducing in Parliament any Bill for amendment of the Constitution.

(e) *Ratification by State Legislatures:* The requirement relating to ratification by the State Legislatures is more liberal than the corresponding provisions in the American Constitution. While the latter requires ratification by not less than three-fourths of the States, under *our* Constitution ratification by not less than half of them suffices.

(f) *President obligated to give assent:* In the case of an ordinary Bill, governed by Article 111, when the Bill, after being passed by both Houses of Parliament, is presented to the President, he may, instead of assenting to it, declare that he "withholds assent therefrom". In the latter case, the Bill cannot become an "Act". But the amendment of Article 368 in 1971 has made it *obligatory* for the President to give his assent to a Bill for amendment of the Constitution, when it is presented to him after its passage by the Legislature.

In short, though the formality of the President's assent has been retained in the case of an amendment of the Constitution, in order to signify the date when the amendment Bill becomes operative as a part of the Constitution, the President's power to veto a Bill for amendment of the Constitution has been taken away, by

4. *Shankari Prasad v UOI,* AIR 1951 SC 458; *Sajjan v State of Rajasthan,* AIR 1965 SC 845.

substituting the words "*shall* give his assent" in clause (2) of the Article 368, as it stands after the Constitution (24th Amendment) Act, 1971.

4. Constitution Amendment Act—Whether a "Law" under Article 13?

There has been a historical controversy as to whether an amendment of the Constitution, made in the manner provided for under Article 368, must have to conform to the requirements of Article 13(2), as a "law" as defined in Clause (3) of Article 13; or, in other words, whether a Constitution Amendment Act would be void if it seeks to take away or is inconsistent with a fundamental right enumerated in Part III of the Constitution.

A. *Pre-Golak Nath judgment:* Until the case of *Golak Nath,*[5] the Supreme Court had been holding that no part of our Constitution was "unamendable" and that Parliament may, by passing a Constitution Amendment Act, in compliance with the requirements of Article 368, amend any provision of the Constitution, including the Fundamental Rights and Article 368 itself. It was held that "law" in Article 13(2) referred to ordinary legislation made by Parliament as a *legislative* body and would not include an amendment of the Constitution, which was passed by Parliament in its *constituent* capacity.

B. *Golak Nath judgment:* But, in *Golak Nath's* case, a majority of six judges in a special bench of 11 overruled the previous decisions[6] and took the view that, though there is no express exception from the ambit of Article 368, the Fundamental Rights included in Part III of the Constitution cannot, by their very nature, be subject to the process of amendment provided for in Article 368 and that if any of such Rights is to be amended, a new Constituent Assembly must be convened for making a new Constitution or radically changing it.

The majority in *Golak Nath's* case rested its conclusion on the view that the power to amend the Constitution was also a legislative power conferred by Article 245 by the Constitution, so that Constitution amendments would also be "law" within the purview of Article 13(2).

C. *Post-Golak Nath judgment:* After the *Golak Nath* decision, Parliament sought to supersede it by amending Article 368 itself, by the Constitution (24th Amendment) Act, 1971, as a result of which an amendment of the Constitution passed in accordance with Article 368, would not be "law" within the meaning of Article 13 and the validity of a Constitution Amendment Act would not be open to judicial review on the ground that it takes away or affects a Fundamental Right [*Article* 368(3)]. Even after this specific amendment of the Constitution, the controversy before the Supreme Court did not cease because the validity of the 24th Constitution Amendment Act itself was challenged in a case from Kerala (*Kesavananda v State of Kerala*)[7], which was heard by a full bench of 13 Judges. The majority of the Full Court upheld the validity of the 24th Amendment and overruled the case of *Golak Nath.*

The question has thus been *settled* in favour of the view that a Constitution Amendment Act, passed by Parliament, is not "law" within the meaning of Article 13. The majority in *Kesavananda's* case upheld the validity of clause (4) of Article 13 [and a corresponding provision in Article 368(3)], which had

5. *Golak Nath v State of Punjab,* AIR 1967 SC 1643.
6. *Shankari Prasad v UOI,* AIR 1951 SC 458; *Sajjan v State of Rajasthan,* AIR 1965 SC 845.
7. *Kesavananda Bharati v State of Kerala,* AIR 1973 SC 1461 (FB).

been inserted by the Constitution (24th Amendment) Act, 1971, and reads as follows:

> *Nothing in this article (ie, Article 13), shall apply to any amendment made under Article 368.*

As a result, Fundamental Rights in India can be amended by an Act passed under Article 368, and the validity of a Constitution Amending Act cannot be questioned on the ground that that Act invaded or encroached upon any Fundamental Right.

5. "Basic Features" of the Constitution not Amendable.

Another question which has been mooted since the case of *Golak Nath* is, whether, outside Part III (Fundamental Rights), there is any other provision of the Constitution of India which is immune from the process of amendment in Article 368. Though the majority in *Kesavananda's* case has overturned the majority view in *Golak Nath* that Fundamental Rights cannot be amended under Article 368, it affirmed another proposition asserted by the majority in *Golak Nath's* case, namely, that—

(i) There are certain *basic features* of the Constitution of India, which cannot be altered in exercise of the power to amend it, under Article 368. If, therefore, a Constitution Amendment Act seeks to alter the basic structure or framework of the Constitution, the court would be entitled to annul it on the ground of *ultra vires,* because the word "amend", in Article 368, means only changes other than altering the very structure of the Constitution, which would be tantamount to making a new Constitution.[8]

(ii) These basic features, without being exhaustive, are—the sovereignty and territorial integrity of India, the federal system, judicial review, and the Parliamentary system of government.

(iii) Applying this doctrine that judicial review is a basic feature of the Constitution of India, the majority in *Kesavananda's* case held the second part of section 3 of the Constitution (25th Amendment) Act, 1971, relating to Article 31C, as invalid. The portion so invalidated read —

> ...and no law containing a declaration that it is for giving effect to such policy shall be called in question in any Court on the ground that it does not give effect to such policy.

Article 31C, which was introduced by section 3 of the 25th Amendment Act, provided—(a) that if any law seeks to implement the Directive Principle contained in Article 39(b)–(c), *i.e.,* regarding socialistic control and distribution of the material resources of the country, such law shall not be void on the ground of contravention of Article 14 or 19; (b) it further provided that if anybody challenges the constitutionality of any such law, the court would be precluded from entering even into the preliminary question, namely, whether such law is, in fact, a law, "giving effect to" Article 39(b) or (c), if on the face of the Act, there was a declaration by the Legislature that it is for giving effect to such Directive policy. In other words, by adding a declaration to an Act, the Legislature was empowered by the Constitution (25th Amendment) Act, to deprive the courts of their power to determine the validity of the Act on the ground that it contravened some provision

8. The observations to the contrary in *Sanjeev Coke Co v Bharat Coking Coal Ltd,* AIR 1983 SC 239, para 13, do not suffice to overturn either *Kesavananda* or *Minerva Mills.*

of the Constitution. The majority in *Kesavananda* held that Article 368 did not confer any such power to take away judicial review, in the name of "amending" the Constitution.

5a. Author's Views on Unamendability of "Basic Features".

The foregoing view of the majority in *Kesavananda's* case as to "basic features" is debatable inasmuch as there is no express limitation upon the amending power conferred by Article 368(1). If it is supposed that there are some implied limitations, it is difficult to appreciate how the court, after holding that the Fundamental Rights did *not* constitute such inviolable part of the Constitution, could come to the conclusion that judicial review, which is an adjunct of Fundamental Rights, could be so considered. It would, therefore, be no wonder if another full bench of the Supreme Court comes to overturn this view in *Kesavananda's* case, on the grounds —

(i) that Article 368(1), as it stands amended in 1971, makes it clear that not only the procedure, but also the 'power' to amend the Constitution is conferred by Article 368 itself and cannot be derived from somewhere else, such as Article 245. Hence, the limitations, if any, upon the amending power must be found from Article 368 itself and not from any theory of implied limitation;

(ii) that the word 'repeal' in Article 368(1) also makes it clear that 'amendment', under Article 368, includes a repeal of any of its provisions, including any supposed 'basic' or 'essential' provision;

(iii) that the Constitution of India makes no distinction between 'amendment' and 'total revision', as do some other Constitutions, such as the Swiss Constitution. Hence, there is no bar to change the whole Constitution, in exercise of the amending power, which is described as the '*constituent power*' [*Article* 368(1)] and that, accordingly, it would not be necessary to convene a Constituent Assembly to revise the Constitution *in toto*.

5b. Validity of Constitutional Amendment, Whether can be Challenged?

The Indira Gandhi Government sought to arrest these implications of *Kesavananda,* and cut the fetters sought to be imposed on the sovereignty of Parliament (as a constituent body), by inserting two clauses (4)–(5) in Article 368, by the 42nd Amendment Act, 1976.[9] Clause (5) declares that "there shall be no limitation" "on the constituent power of Parliament to amend" the provisions of this Constitution and that at any rate, the validity of no Constitution Amendment Act "shall be called in question in any court on *any* ground" [Clause (4)].

The foregoing attempt to preclude judicial review of Constitution Amending Acts has, however, been nullified by the Supreme Court, by striking down clauses (4)–(5) as inserted in Article 368 by the 42nd Amendment Act, by its decision in the *Minerva Mills* case,[10] on the ground that judicial review is a "basic feature" of

9. The observations to the contrary in *Sanjeev Coke Co v Bharat Coking Coal Ltd,* AIR 1983 SC 239, para 13, do not suffice to overturn either *Kesavananda* or *Minerva Mills.*

10. *Minerva Mills v UOI,* AIR 1980 SC 1789. Clauses (4) and (5), inserted in Article 368 by the Constitution (42nd Amendment) Act, 1976, have been declared invalid by the Supreme Court Constitution Bench, on the ground that these clauses which removed all limitations upon the power of Parliament to amend the Constitution and precluded judicial review of a Constitution Amendment Act, on *any* ground, sought to destroy an "essential feature" or "basic structure" of the Constitution. *Madras Bar Association v UOI,* (2014) 10 SCC 1.

the Indian Constitutional system which cannot be taken away even by amending the Constitution.

6. Article 368 as Interpreted by the Supreme Court. So far, the decision in *Kesavananda* has been followed in subsequent cases by the Supreme Court. As a result, Article 368, as so interpreted by the highest court, leads to the following propositions:

(i) Any part of the Constitution may be amended after complying with the procedure laid down in Article 368.

(ii) No referendum or reference to a Constituent Assembly would be required to amend any provision of the Constitution.

(iii) But no provision of the Constitution or any part thereof can be amended if it takes away or destroys any of the "basic features" of the Constitution. Thus, apart from the procedural limitation expressly laid down in Article 368, the substantive limitation founded on the doctrine of "basic features", has been introduced into *our* Constitution, by judicial innovation. The constitutional values/overarching principles would fall outside the amending power under Article 368 of the Constitution. The Parliament cannot amend the Constitution to abrogate these principles so as to rewrite the Constitution.[11]

7. List of Basic Features. The Supreme Court has refused to foreclose its list of "basic features". From the various decisions so far, the following list may be drawn up:[12]

(a) Supremacy of the Constitution.
(b) Rule of law.
(c) Principle of separation of powers between the Legislature, the Executive and the Judiciary.
(d) Objectives specified in the Preamble to the Constitution.
(e) Judicial review [Articles 32 and 226/227].
(f) Federalism.
(g) Secularism.
(h) Sovereign, Democratic, Republican structure.
(i) Freedom and dignity of the individual.
(j) Unity and integrity of the Nation.
(k) Principle of equality [not every feature of equality, but the quintessence of equal justice].
(l) Essence of other Fundamental Rights in Part III.
(m) Concept of social and economic justice—to build a welfare State; Part IV *in toto*.
(n) Balance between Fundamental Rights and Directive Principles.
(o) Parliamentary system of Government.
(p) Free and fair elections.

11. *Glanrock Estate (P) Ltd v State of Tamil Nadu,* (2010) 10 SCC 96, p 100.
12. See Article 368 of *Durga Das Basu, Shorter Constitution of India,* published by LexisNexis.

(q) Limitations upon the amending power conferred by Article 368.

(r) Independence of the Judiciary but within the four corners of the Constitution and not beyond that.

(s) Effective access to justice.

(t) Powers of the Supreme Court under Articles 32, 136, 141 and 142.

(u) Legislation seeking to nullify the awards made in exercise of the judicial power of the State by Arbitration Tribunals constituted under an Act.[13]

(v) Reasonableness.[14]

(w) Social justice.[15]

(x) Article 21 r/w Articles 14 and 19; Articles 15 and 14 r/w Article 16(4), (4-A) & (4-B); Articles 20 and 32, etc., including the principles or essence underlying them.[16]

8. Brief Account on Constitutional Amendments since 1950. Since its commencement on 26 January 1950, Constitution of India has been amended *106 times till February 2026* by passing Acts of Parliament in the manner prescribed by Article 368.[17] Since all these Amendment Acts

13. *G C Kanungo v State of Orissa,* AIR 1995 SC 1655 : (1995) 5 SCC 96, para 28.
14. *M Nagaraj v UOI,* (2006) 8 SCC 212.
15. *M Nagaraj v UOI,* (2006) 8 SCC 212.
16. *I R Coelho v State of Tamil Nadu,* AIR 2007 SC 861.
17. The question of rigidity or flexibility of the procedure for amendment prescribed by Article 368 was so long clouded by the fact that the Congress Party had a monolithic control over the Legislatures both at the Union and in the States. It was this extraordinary fact that enabled the Union Government to overcome the *double* majority safeguard in Article 368(2), and to bring 106 amendments in 78 years. The rigidity of the double majority requirement has, on the other hand, been demonstrated by the difficulties which the Janata Government (1977–78) had to face to obtain the passage of an amendment bill to do away with the undemocratic features of the 42nd Amendment, on which they had the support of the consensus of enlightened public opinion. It is to be noted that—

    (a) Article 368(2) requires that a Constitution Amendment Bill must be passed by the double majority in *each* House of Parliament, so that if the Janata Government failed to obtain that majority in the *Rajya Sabha,* it could not resort to a 'joint sitting' of both Houses, as prescribed by Article 108 in the case of *ordinary* legislation.

    (b) The requirement of double majority may be illustrated with the strength of the Janata Party in the *Rajya Sabha* in September, 1977. The Rajya Sabha having a total membership of 250 members (roughly),—under the first part of Article 368(2), a Constitution Amendment Bill could be passed only if at least 126 members voted for it. But since the Janata Party had a following of 41 only (roughly) in the *Rajya Sabha,* they could not rely on their own strength, in obtaining a passage of such Bill.

    The second part of Article 368(2) is no less, perhaps more, rigorous. It requires that two-third of the members who are present on the date of voting on the Constitution Amendment Bill and actually tender their vote, must vote in favour of the Bill. If so, the Bill could be passed only if 168 members voted in its favour; and that was too much for the Janata Party commanding only 41 members of their own.

    That is why the fate of the amendment Bill proposed by the Janata depended on the pleasure of the Congress Party. In order to avoid opposition from the Congress (O), the Janata Government, therefore, divided their proposals into two Bills. In the first

[Footnote No. 17 Contd.]

have been mentioned, with full particulars, in Table IV, *post,* it is needless to reproduce them hereunder.

8a. The 42nd, 43rd and 44th Amendments. Nevertheless, the 42nd, 43rd and the 44th Amendments must be given a fuller treatment in view of its serious repercussions in the political as well as the legal world. All previous amendments paled into insignificance after the passing of the 42nd Amendment Act, 1976, which alone would illustrate how momentous the amending power under the Indian Constitution is, and how easy it is to change extensive and vital provisions of the Constitution, without any elaborate formalities, *when the ruling party has a comfortable majority in both the Houses of Parliament.*

The 42nd Amendment Act was practically a "revision" of the Constitution, for the following reasons:

(i) In extent, it introduced changes in the Preamble, as many as 53 Articles, as well as the 7th Schedule.

(ii) As to substantive changes, it sought to change the vital principles underlying the 1949-Constitution:

I. *Judicial Review of ordinary laws:* It made, for the first time, a distinction between Union and State laws, for the purpose of challenging their constitutionality on the ground of contravention of any provision of the Constitution and provided, broadly, (a) that a High Court could not pronounce invalid any Central law, including subordinate legislation under such law, on the ground of unconstitutionality; (b) that the Supreme Court could not, in its jurisdiction under Article 32, pronounce a State law as unconstitutional, unless a Central law had also been challenged in such proceeding. If any law was made to implement any of the directives included in Part IV [*Article 31C*] or in exercise of the new power under Article 31D to ban anti-national activities or associations, the validity of such law could not be challenged on the ground of contravention of

---

[Footnote No. 17 Contd.]

instance, the less controversial proposals were included in the Bill which was passed in 1977 as the 43rd Amendment Act. The next Bill (45th Bill, which became the 44th Amendment Act, 1978), met with stiffer resistance because Congress(O) now joined hands with Congress(I) to sabotage the more vital parts of this latter Bill—thus defeating, for instance, the clause which sought to amend Article 368 itself—to introduce referendum.

The same difficulty faced Mrs. Gandhi after her return to power in January, 1980. She failed to make any substantial amendment to the Constitution before 1984 as she could not command the required majority in the Rajya Sabha [*Statesman,* 4 November 1982, p 1].

The Congress(I) Governments' two Bills (64th and 65th Amendment Bills, 1989) to amend the Constitution to insert provisions regarding Nagarpalika and Panchayats fell through in the Rajya Sabha on 13 October 1989, being just two votes short of the required majority. The Lok Sabha had passed them on 10 August 1989.

The Constitution (64th Amendment) Bill, 1990, relating to amendment of Article 356 in relation to Punjab, was passed by Rajya Sabha on 28 March 1990.

In Lok Sabha (30 March 1990) on the motion for consideration of the Bill only 236 votes were in favour (five against). The motion was declared as not carried for want of required majority (majority of the total membership of the House). A fresh Bill had to be brought for passing the amendment.

The procedure prescribed by Article 368(2), *per se,* cannot therefore be described as flexible.

Articles 14, 19, and 31. Above all, an artificial majority of judges was required both in the Supreme Court and the high courts, in order to pronounce a law as unconstitutional and invalid.

II. *Judicial Review of Constitution Amendment Acts:* By amending Article 368, it was provided that a law, which is described as a Constitution Amendment Act, would be completely immune from challenge in a court of law, whether on a procedural or substantive ground. Thus, even if such a Bill had not been passed in conformity with the *procedure* laid down in Article 368 itself, nobody would be entitled to challenge it in any court on that ground,—a position which is juristically absurd.

III. *Fundamental Duties:* For the first time, a chapter on Fundamental *Duties* [*Article* 51A] was introduced in order to counteract the sweep of Fundamental Rights. Even though no sanction has been appended to these Duties, it is obvious that if a court takes these Duties into consideration along with Fundamental Rights, the scope of the free play of the rights would, to that extent, be narrowed down.

IV. *Fundamental Rights devalued:* By expanding the scope of Article 31C, it was provided that if any law seeks to implement *any* of the Directive Principles included in Part IV, such law would be altogether immune from judicial review on the ground of contravention of Fundamental Rights. This is exactly the reverse of what was provided in the 1949-Constitution. The load on Fundamental Rights, in short, became ruthlessly heavy after the cumulative burden of Articles 31A, 31B, 31C, 31D, and 51A.

When the Janata Party came to power towards the end of March, 1977, they sought to take early steps to fulfil their election pledge to undo the extensive mischief which had been done to the Constitution by the 42nd Amendment Act, as outlined above. But owing to the fact that the Janata Party had no majority—not to speak of a 2/3 majority—in the *Rajya Sabha,* which was required to pass a Constitution Amending Bill under Article 368, their attempts in this behalf were chequered and only partially successful. The first step was abortive, namely, that the 43rd Amendment Bill which was introduced in the *Lok Sabha* in April, 1977, had to be left over till the next Session, hoping to gain some more seats in the *Rajya Sabha* at the periodical election to be held to that House in the meantime. Eventually, the 43rd Amendment Act, 1977, was passed with the aid of the votes of Congress(O). The attitude of that Party, however, changed, when the next Bill (*viz.,* the 45th) was taken to the *Rajya Sabha* in 1978, as a result of which this Bill was enacted, only *in a truncated shape,* as the 44th Amendment Act, 1978.

The changes made by the 43rd and the 44th Amendment Acts are summarised in Table IV, *post.* Briefly speaking,—

(i) The 43rd Amendment Act, 1977, simply repealed those provisions which had been added by the 42nd Amendment Act to curb judicial review, *e.g.,* Articles 31D, 32A, 144A, 226A, and 228A.

(ii) The changes made by the 44th Amendment Act are more extensive:

(a) It not only omitted some more of the Articles which had been inserted by the 42nd, *e.g.,* Articles 257A, and 329A; but also made amendments in other Articles in order to restore those provisions to their pre-1976 text, *e.g.,* Article 226.

(b) Apart from combating the mischiefs introduced by the 42nd Amendment, the 44th Amendment Act introduced additional changes, *e.g.*, by omitting the Fundamental Right to Property in Article 19(1)(f) and Article 31(2).

(c) Since the Janata Government failed to secure the passage of a number of clauses of the 45th Amending Bill, the stamp of the 42nd Amendment on various provisions, such as Article 368, still remains. Besides, the Janata Government have themselves retained some of the provisions as amended by the 42nd Amendment, which they considered to beneficial, *e.g.*, Articles 74(1) and 311.

8b. The 73rd and 74th Amendments.

Of the subsequent amendments, the 73rd and 74th Amendment Acts of 1992 deserve special mention inasmuch as they have introduced the electoral system for the composition of the units of local government below the States, *viz.,* the Panchayats in the rural areas, and the Municipalities in the urban areas.

8c. The 97th Amendment.

The constitutionality of the Constitution (97th Amendment) Act, 2011 was challenged in *Rajendra N Shah v UOI* wherein, the Gujarat High Court delivered its judgment dated 22 May 2013, WP(PIL) No 166 of 2012, and declared the Constitution (97th Amendment) Act 2011, which inserted Part IXB containing Articles 243ZH to 243ZT, as *ultra vires* the Constitution of India for not taking recourse to Article 368(2) of the Constitution, *i.e.*, providing for ratification by the majority of the State Legislatures. The Supreme Court by a majority of 2:1 upheld the judgment of the High Court, except to the extent that it struck down Part IX-B of the Constitution in its entirety. The Supreme Court held that, since the Constitutional (97th Amendment) Act dealt with an entry which was an exclusive state subject, it required a ratification by at least one-half of the State Legislatures as per Article 368(2) of the Constitution.[18]

9. Dangers of Frequent Amendments.

It is evident that, instead of being rigid,[19] as some critics supposed during the early days of the Constitution,[20] the procedure for amendment has rather proved to be too flexible in view of the ease with which as many as 106 amendments have been made during the 78 years of the working of the Constitution. So long as the party in power at the Centre has a solid majority in Parliament and in more than half of the State Legislatures, the apprehension of impartial observers should be not upon the difficulty of amendment but as to the possibility of its being used too often either to achieve political purposes or to get rid of judicial decisions[21]

18. Against the Order/Judgment dated 22 April 2013 of the Gujarat High Court in WP (PIL) No 166 of 2012, the Union of India preferred an appeal bearing CA No 9108–9109/ 2014 titled, "*UOI v Rajendra N Shah*" to the Supreme Court. The Supreme Court in *UOI v Rajendra N Shah,* 2021 SCC OnLine SC 474 : Civil Appeal Nos 9108–9109 of 2014, held that the Constitutional (97th Amendment) Act required a ratification by at least one-half of the state legislatures as per Article 368(2) of the Constitution. The Supreme Court held that that Part IX-B is operative only insofar as it concerns Multi-State Cooperative Societies both within various States and in Union Territories of India.

19. *M Nagaraj v UOI,* (2006) 8 SCC 212.

20. *Cf* Jennings, *Some Characteristics of the Indian Constitution,* pp 9–10.

21. *Cf* Ramaswami Aiyar's Foreword to Krishnaswami Aiyar's *Constitution and Fundamental Rights,* p 9.

which may appear to be unwholesome to the party in power. Judges may, of course, err but, as has already been demonstrated, even the highest tribunal is likely to change its views in the light of further experience.[22] In the absence of serious repercussions or emergent circumstances or a special contingency (*e.g.*, to admit Sikkim—by the 35th and 36th Amendments), the process of constitutional amendment should not be resorted to for the purpose of overriding unwelcome judicial verdicts so often as would generate in the minds of the lay public an irreverence for the Judiciary—thus shaking the very foundation of constitutional government.

The Hon'ble Supreme Court finally settled the law that all amendments to the Constitution made on or after 24 April 1973 by which Ninth Schedule is amended, by inclusion of various laws therein, shall be tested on the touchstone of the basic or essential features of the Constitution, as reflected in Article 21 read with Articles 14, 19 and the principles underlying them. Now, there is no blanket protection available to the laws inserted in the Ninth Schedule by Constitutional amendments on or after 24 April 1973, and it shall be a matter of constitutional adjudication by examining the nature and extent of infraction of Fundamental Right by a statute, sought to be constitutionally protected.[23]

22. Thus, in *Bengal Immunity Co v State of Bihar,* (1955) 2 SCR 603, the Supreme Court overruled its previous majority decision in *State of Bombay v United Motors,* (1953) SCR 1069, as regards the power of a State in which goods are delivered for consumption to tax the sale or purchase of such goods though it is in the course of inter-State trade or commerce. It was observed in this case that there was no provision in the Constitution to bind the Supreme Court by its own decisions.

23. *I R Coelho (dead) by LRs v State of Tamil Nadu,* (2007) 2 SCC 1. (please see also Chapter 4, *ante*).

PART II

GOVERNMENT OF THE UNION

PART II

GOVERNMENT OF THE UNION

CHAPTER 11

THE UNION EXECUTIVE

1. President and Vice-President. At the head of the Union Executive stands the President of India; and the second being the Vice-President of India.

2. Election of President and Vice-President. *A. President:* The President of India is elected[1] by indirect election, that is, by an electoral college, in accordance with the system of proportional representation by means of the single transferable vote.[2]

The electoral college[3] shall consist of—

(a) The elected members of both Houses of Parliament;

(b) The elected members of the Legislative Assemblies of the States; and the elected members of the Legislative Assemblies of Union Territories of Delhi and Puducherry [*Article 54*].

As far as practicable, there shall be uniformity of representation of the different states at the election, according to the population and the total number of elected members of the Legislative Assembly of each state, and parity shall also be maintained between the States as a whole and the Union [*Article 55*]. This second condition seeks to ensure that the votes of the states, in the aggregate, in the electoral college for the election of the President, shall be equal to that of the people of the country as a whole. In this way, the President shall be a representative of the nation as well as a representative of the people in the different states. It also gives recognition to the status of the states in the federal system.

The system of indirect election was criticised by some as falling short of the democratic ideal underlying universal franchise, but indirect election was supported by the framers of the Constitution, on the following grounds—

(i) Direct election by an electorate of some 510 million people would mean a tremendous loss of time, energy and money;

(ii) Under the system of responsible Government introduced by the Constitution, real power would vest in the ministry; so, it would be anomalous to elect the President directly by the people without giving him real powers.[4]

---

1. For the results of the elections so far held, see Table X, Part B.
2. As to how the system of Proportional Representation would work, see Author's *Commentary on the Constitution of India*, 7th Edn, vol E/1, pp 84–90.
3. At the Presidential election held in 2007, 2012 and 2017, the electoral college consisted of 4896 members of which the break-up was 543 Lok Sabha + 233 Rajya Sabha + 4120 State Assembly members. At the Presidential election held in 2022, the electoral college consisted of 776 MPs and 4,033 MLAs [excluding 90 MLAs of the dissolved J&K Legislative Assembly].
4. *Constituent Assembly Debates*, vol 4, pp 734, 846.

B. Vice-President: The election of the Vice-President, like that of the President, shall be indirect and in accordance with the system of proportional representation by means of the single transferable vote. But his election shall be different from that of the President inasmuch as the State Legislatures shall have no part in it. The Vice-President shall be elected by an electoral college consisting of the members of both Houses of Parliament[5] [*Article 66(1)*].

A sitting MP undergoing imprisonment allowed to cast his vote in the election of Vice-President by issuing suitable directions to the police and Election Commission. The MP was allowed to travel by air at his own cost.[6]

3. Qualifications for Election as President and Vice-President. In order to be qualified for election as President, a person must—

(a) be a citizen of India;
(b) has completed the age of 35 years;
(c) be qualified for election as a member of the House of the People; and
(d) must *not* hold any office of profit under the Government of India or the Government of any State or under any local or other authority subject to the control of any of the said Government [*Articles 58(1) and 58(2)*].

Similarly, in order to be qualified to be elected as Vice-President, a person must be:

(a) a citizen of India;
(b) has completed 35 years of age;
(c) be qualified for election as a member of the Council of States[7]; and
(d) must *not* hold an office of profit save that of President, Vice-President, Governor or Minister for the Union or State [*Articles 66(3) and 66(4)*].

But a sitting President or Vice-President of the Union or the Governor of any State or a Minister, either for the Union or for any State, is not disqualified for election as President [*Explanation to Article 58(2); and Explanation to 66(4)*].

3a. Office of Profit. In order to be an office of profit, the office must carry various pecuniary benefits such as providing official accommodation or a chauffeur driven car.[8] It must be shown that (i) there was a permanent office, (ii) income or profit accrued from that office, and (iii) the candidate held that office.[9]

5. The original Constitution provided that the Vice-President would be elected by the two Houses of Parliament, assembled at *a joint meeting*. This cumbrous procedure of a joint meeting of the two Houses for this purpose has been done away with, by amending Article 66(1) by the Constitution (11th Amendment) Act, 1961. As amended, the members of both Houses remain the voters, but they may vote by secret ballot, without assembling at a joint meeting.
6. *Mohd. Shahabuddin v State of Bihar*, (2007) 10 SCC 28.
7. The reason for this difference between the qualifications for election as President and Vice-President is obvious, namely, that the Vice-President is normally to act as the Chairman of the Council of States.
8. *Purno Agitok Sangma v Pranab Mukherjee*, AIR 2013 SC 372.
9. *Rabindra Kumar Nayak v Collector, Mayurbhanj, Orissa*, AIR 1999 SC 1120.

4. Doubts and Disputes Relating to or Connected with the Election of a President or Vice-President.

Determination of doubts and disputes relating to the election of a President or Vice-President is dealt with in Article 71, as follows—

(a) Such disputes shall be decided by the Supreme Court whose jurisdiction shall be *exclusive* and *final*.

(b) No such dispute can be raised on the ground of any vacancy in the electoral college which elected the President or Vice-President.

(c) If the election of a President or Vice-President is declared void by the Supreme Court, acts done by him prior to the date of such decision of the Supreme Court shall not be invalidated.

(d) Barring the decision of such disputes, other matters relating to the election of President or Vice-President may be regulated by law made by Parliament.

5. Term of Office of President and Vice-President.

A. President: The President's term of office is five years from the date on which he enters upon his office; but he is eligible for re-election[10] [*Articles 56-57*].

The President's office may terminate within the term of five years in either of two ways—

(i) By resignation in writing under his hand addressed to the Vice-President of India,

(ii) By removal for violation of the Constitution, by the process of impeachment [*Article 56*]. The only ground for impeachment specified in Article 61(1) is "violation of the Constitution".

B. Vice-President: The term of office of the Vice-President is five years. His office may terminate earlier than the fixed term either by resignation or by removal or due to death. A formal impeachment is *not* required for his removal. He may be removed by a resolution of the Council of States passed by a majority of its members and agreed to by the House of People [*Article 67, proviso (b)*].

Though there is no specific provision (corresponding to Article 57) making a Vice-President eligible for re-election, the *Explanation* to Article 66 suggests that a sitting Vice-President is eligible for re-election and Dr S Radhakrishnan was, in fact, elected for a second term in 1957.

5a. Procedure for Impeachment of President.

An impeachment is a quasi-judicial procedure in Parliament. *Either House* may prefer the charge of violation of the Constitution before the other House which shall then either investigate the charge itself or cause the charge to be investigated.

But the charge cannot be preferred by a House unless—

(a) a resolution containing the proposal is moved after a 14 days' notice in writing signed by not less than one-fourth of the total number of members of that House; and

(b) the resolution is then passed by a majority of not less than two-third of the total membership of the House.

---

10. In his speech in Parliament in 1961, Prime Minister Nehru observed that we should adopt a *convention* that no person shall be a President for more than two terms, and that no amendment of the Constitution was necessary to enjoin this.

The President shall have a right to appear and to be represented at such investigation. If, as a result of the investigation, a resolution is passed by not less than two-third of the total membership of the House before which the charge has been preferred declaring that the charge has been sustained, such resolution shall have the effect of removing the President from his office with effect from the date on which such resolution is passed [*Article 61*].

Since the Constitution provides the mode and ground for removing the President, he cannot be *removed* otherwise than by impeachment, in accordance with the terms of Articles 56 and 61.

6. Conditions of Office of President and Vice-President.

A. President: The President shall not be a member of either House of Parliament or of a House of the Legislature of any State, and if a member of either House of Parliament or of a House of the Legislature of any State be elected President, he shall be deemed to have vacated his seat in that House on the date on which he enters upon his office as President. The President shall not hold any other office of profit [*Articles 59(1) and (2)*].

The President shall be entitled without payment of rent to the use of his official residence and shall be also entitled to such emoluments, allowances and privileges as may be determined by Parliament by law (and until provision in that behalf is so made, such emoluments, allowances and privileges as are specified in the Second Schedule of the Constitution) [*Article 59(3)*].[11] By passing the Finance Act, 2018, Parliament has amended the President's Emoluments and Pension Act, 1951 (30 of 1951) and raised the emoluments to Rs 5,00,000/- *per mensem* with effect from 1 January 2016. It is noteworthy that Parliament inserted the term "Emolument and" in the title of "the President's Pension Act, 1951" and "section 1A" *vide* the President's Pension (Amendment) Act, 1985 (77 of 1985), wef 26-12-1985. The emoluments and allowances of the President shall not be diminished during his term of office [*Article 59(4)*].

B. Vice-President: The Vice-President shall not be a member of either House of Parliament or of a House of the Legislature of any State, and if a member of either House of Parliament or of a House of the Legislature of any State be elected Vice-President, he shall be deemed to have vacated his seat in that House on the date on which he enters upon his office as Vice-President. He shall not hold any other office of profit [*Articles 66(2) and 64*].

When the Vice-President thus acts as, or discharges the functions of the President, under Article 65, he shall cease to perform the duties of the Chairman of the Council of States and then the Deputy Chairman of the Council of States shall acts as it Chairman [*Article 91*]. In such a case, he gets the emolument of the President; otherwise, he gets the salary of the Chairman of the Council of States under Article 97 [*proviso to Article 64; and 65(3)*].[12]

---

11. Rs 10,000 originally, raised to Rs 20,000 in 1990 and to Rs 50,000 in 1998 (wef 1-1-1996), and to Rs 1,50,000/- *vide* the President's Emoluments and Pension (Amendment) Act, 2008 (wef 1-1-2006) and further increased to Rs 500000/- *vide* the Finance Act, 2018 (w.r.e.f. 1-1-2016.

12. Article 65(3) is to be read with para 4 of Part A of the Second Schedule,—the result of which is that until Parliament legislates on this subject (no such law has so far been passed by Parliament till 1987), a Vice-President, while acting as or discharging the

[Footnote No. 12 Contd.]

There is no bar to a member of the Union or State Legislature being elected President or Vice-President, but the two offices cannot be combined in one person. In case a member of the Legislature is elected President or Vice-President, he shall be deemed to have vacated his seat in that House of the Legislature to which he belongs on the date on which he enters upon his office as President or Vice-President [*Articles 59(1) and 66(2)*].

7. Whether a Member of Legislature may become President or Vice-President?

8. Vacancy in the Office of President.

A vacancy in the office of the President may be caused in any of the following ways—

(i) On the expiry of his term of five years;

(ii) By his death;

(iii) By his resignation;

(iv) On his removal by impeachment;

(v) Otherwise, *e.g.*, on the setting aside of his election as President [*Article 65(1)*].

(a) When the vacancy is going to be caused by the *expiration of the term* of the sitting President, an election to fill the vacancy must be *completed* before the expiration of the term [*Article 62(1)*]. But in order to prevent an "interregnum", owing to any possible delay in such completion, it is provided that the outgoing President must continue to hold office, notwithstanding that his term has expired, until his successor enters upon his office [*Article 56(1), proviso (c)*]. There is no scope for the Vice-President getting a chance to act as President in this case.

(b) In case of a vacancy arising by reason of any cause *other than* the expiry of the term of the incumbent in office, an election to fill the vacancy must be held as soon as possible after, and in no case later than six months from the date of occurrence of the vacancy [*Article 62(2)*]. Immediately after such vacancy arises, say, by the death of the President, and until a new President is elected, as above, it is the Vice-President who shall act as President [*Article 65(1)*]. It is needless to point out that the new President who is elected shall be entitled to the full term of five years from the date he enters upon his office.

[Footnote No. 12 Contd.]

functions of the President, shall receive the same emoluments and privileges and allowances as the President gets under Article 59(3). Since 1996, that emolument is a sum of Rs 50,000/- per mensem which has been further revised to Rs 1,25,000/- *vide* the Salaries and Allowances of Officers of Parliament (Amendment) Act, 2008 wref from 1-1-2006.

When the Vice-President does not act as President, his only function is that of the Chairman, Council of States, under Article 97. By passing the Salaries and Allowances of Officers of Parliament (Amendment) Act, 1998, the salary of the Chairman of the Council of States has been raised to Rs 40,000/- *per mensem, vide* Act 26 of 1998 (wef 1-1-1996). The salary of the Chairman of the Council of States has been raised to "one lakh twenty-five thousand rupees *per mensem vide* the Salaries and Allowances of Officers of Parliament (Amendment) Act, 2008 w.e.f. 1-1-2006 and has been further raised to four lakh rupees per mensem (wref 1-1-2016 *vide* the Finance Act, 2018 (13 of 2018). He is entitled to daily allowance as admissible to Members of Parliament.

(c) Apart from a permanent *vacancy,* the President may be temporarily *unable* to discharge his functions, owing to his absence from India, illness or any other cause, in which case the Vice-President shall *discharge his functions* until the date on which the President resumes his duties [*Article 65(2)*].

8a. Vacancy in the Office of Both President and Vice-President.

Parliament has enacted the President (Discharge of Functions) Act, 1969 to provide that in the event of occurrence of vacancy in the office of both the President and the Vice-President, by reason of death, resignation, removal or otherwise, the Chief Justice of India, or in his absence, the senior-most judge of the Supreme Court of India available shall discharge the functions until a new President is elected. The disqualification under Article 58(2) will not be attracted to such person because he is only to discharge the functions of the President and not seeking election as President.[13]

9. Functions of the Vice-President.

The Vice-President is the highest dignitary of India, coming next after the President [see Table IX]. No functions are, however, attached to the office of the Vice-President as such. The normal function of the Vice-President is to act as the *ex-officio* Chairman of the Council of States. But if there occurs any vacancy in the office of the President by reason of his death, resignation, removal or otherwise, the Vice-President shall *act* as *President* until a new President is elected and enters upon his office [*Article 65(1)*].

The Vice-President shall *discharge the functions* of the President during the temporary absence of the President, illness *or any other cause* by reason of which he is unable to discharge his functions [*Article 65(2)*]. No machinery having been prescribed by the Constitution to determine when the President is unable to discharge his duties owing to absence from India or a like cause, it becomes a somewhat delicate matter as to who should move in the matter on any particular occasion.

It is to be noted that the above provision of the Constitution has not been put into use prior to 20 June 1960, though President, Dr Rajendra Prasad had been absent from India for a considerable period during his foreign tour in the year 1958. It was during the 15 day visit of Dr Rajendra Prasad to the Soviet Union in June 1960, that for the first time, the Vice-President, Dr Radhakrishnan was given the opportunity of acting as the President owing to the "inability" of the President to discharge his duties.

The second occasion took place in May, 1961, when President Rajendra Prasad became seriously ill and was incapable of discharging his functions. After a few days of crisis, the President himself suggested that the Vice-President should discharge the functions of the President until he resumed his duties. It appears that the power to determine when the President is unable to discharge his duties or when he should resume his duties has been understood to belong to the President himself. In the event of occurrence of vacancy in the office of both the President and the Vice-President by reason of death, resignation, removal etc. the Chief Justice of India or in his absence the senior most Judge of the Supreme Court available shall discharge the functions until a new President is elected. In 1969 when on the death of Dr Zakir Hussain, the Vice-President Shri V V Giri

13. *Arun Kumar v UOI,* AIR 1982 Raj 67.

resigned, Shri Hidyatullah, CJ, discharged the functions from 20 July 1969 to 24 August 1969.

10. Nature of the Powers of the President. The Constitution says that the "executive power of the Union shall be vested in the President" [*Article 53*]. The President of India shall thus be the head of the "executive power" of the Union.

The "executive power" primarily means the execution of the laws enacted by the Legislature, but the business of the Executive in a modern State is not as simple as it was in the days of Aristotle. Owing to the manifold expansion of the functions of the State, all residuary functions have practically passed into the hands of the Executive. The executive power may, therefore, be shortly defined as "the power of carrying on the business of government" or "the administration of the affairs of the State", excepting functions which are vested by the Constitution in any other authority. The ambit of the executive power has been thus explained by *our* Supreme Court[14]—

> It may not be possible to frame an exhaustive definition of what executive function means and implies. Ordinarily the executive power connotes the residue of governmental functions that remain after legislative and judicial functions are taken away, subject, of course, to the provisions of the Constitutions or of any law...
>
> The executive function comprises both the determination of the policy as well as carrying it into execution, the maintenance of order, the promotion of social and economic welfare, the direction of foreign policy, in fact, the carrying on or supervision of the general administration of the State.[15]

11. Constitutional limitations on President's Powers. Before we take up an analysis of the different powers of the Indian President, we should note the *constitutional limitations* under which he is to exercise his executive powers.

Firstly, he must exercise these powers according to the Constitution [*Article 53(1)*]. Thus, Article 75(1) explicitly requires that Ministers (other than the Prime Minister) can be appointed by the President only on the advice of the Prime Minister. There will be a violation of this provision if the President appoints a person as Minister from outside the list submitted by the Prime Minister. If the President violates any of the mandatory provisions of the Constitution, he will be liable to be removed by the process of impeachment.

Secondly, the executive powers shall be exercised by the President of India *in accordance with the* advice of his Council of Ministers [*Article 74(1)*].

Prior to 1976, there was no express provision in the Constitution that the President was bound to act in accordance with the advice tendered by the Council of Ministers, though it was *judicially established*[16] that the President of India was not a real executive, but a constitutional head, who was bound to act according to the advice of Ministers, so long as they commanded the confidence

---

14. *Ram Jawaya v State of Punjab,* AIR 1955 SC 549 : (1955) 2 SCR 225, pp *238–39.*
15. *Ram Jawaya v State of Punjab,* AIR 1955 SC 549 : (1955) 2 SCR 225, pp *238–39.*
16. *Shamser Singh v State of Punjab,* AIR 1974 SC 2192; *Rao v Indira,* AIR 1971 SC 1002, p 1005; *A Sanjeevi Naidu v State of Madras,* AIR 1970 SC 1102, p 1106.

of the majority in the House of the People [*Article 75(3)*].[17] The 42nd Amendment Act, 1976 amended Article 74(1) to clarify this position.

Article 74(1), as so amended, reads:

> There shall be a Council of Ministers with the Prime Minister at the head to aid and advise the President who shall, in the exercise of his functions, act in accordance with such advice.

The word "shall" makes it obligatory for the President to act in accordance with ministerial advice.

The Janata Government *retained* the foregoing text of Article 74(1), as amended by the 42nd Amendment Act. But by the 44th Amendment Act, a proviso was added to Article 74(1) as follows:

> Provided that the President may require the Council of Ministers to reconsider such advice, either generally or otherwise, and the President shall act in accordance with the advice tendered after such reconsideration.

The net result after the 44th Amendment, therefore, is that except in certain marginal cases referred to by the Supreme Court,[18] the President shall have no power to act in his discretion in any case. He *must* act according to the advice given to him by the Council of Ministers, headed by the Prime Minister, so that refusal to act according to such advice will render him liable to impeachment for violation of the Constitution. This is subject to the President's power to send the advice received from the Council of Ministers, in a particular case, back to them for their reconsideration; and if the Council of Ministers adhere to their previous advice, the President shall have no option but to act in accordance with such advice. The power to return for reconsideration can be exercised only once, on the same matter.

It may be said, accordingly, that the powers of the President will be the powers of his Ministers, in the same manner as the prerogatives of the English Crown have become the "privileges of the people" (*Dicey*).[19] An inquiry into the powers of the Union Government, therefore, presupposes an inquiry into the provisions of the Constitution which vest powers and functions in the President.

12. Executive Powers of the President. The various powers that are included within the comprehensive expression "executive power" in a modern State have been classified by political scientists under the following heads:

(a) *Administrative power, i.e.,* the execution of the laws and the administration of the departments of government.

(b) *Military power, i.e.,* the command of the armed forces and the conduct of war.

(c) *Legislative power, i.e.,* the summoning, prorogation, etc., of the legislature, initiation of and assent to legislation and the like.

17. *Shamser Singh v State of Punjab*, AIR 1974 SC 2192; *Rao v Indira*, AIR 1971 SC 1002, p 1005; *A Sanjeevi Naidu v State of Madras*, AIR 1970 SC 1102, p 1106.
18. *Shamser Singh v State of Punjab*, AIR 1974 SC 2192; *Rao v Indira*, AIR 1971 SC 1002, p 1005; *A Sanjeevi Naidu v State of Madras*, AIR 1970 SC 1102, p 1106.
19. Dicey's, *Law of the Constitution*, 10th Edn, p 468.

(d) *Judicial power, i.e.,* granting of pardons, reprieves, etc. to persons convicted of crime.

The Indian Constitution, by its various provisions, vests power in the hands of the President under each of these heads, subject to the limitations just mentioned.

12a. Administrative Powers.

In the matter of administration, not being a real head of the Executive like the American President, the Indian President shall *not* have any administrative function to discharge nor shall he have that power of control and supervision over the Departments of the Government as the American President possesses. But though the various Departments of Government of the Union will be carried on under the control and responsibility of the respective Ministers in charge, the President will remain the *formal* head of the administration, and as such, all executive action of the Union must be expressed to be taken in the *name* of the President. The only mode of ascertaining whether an order or instrument is made by the Government of India will be to see whether it is expressed in the name of the President and authenticated in such manner as may be prescribed by rules to be made by the President [*Article 77*]. For the same reason, all contracts and assurances of property made on behalf of the Government of India must be expressed to be made by the President and executed in such manner as the President may direct or authorise [*Article 299*].

Again, though he may not be the "real" head of the administration, all officers of the Union shall be his "subordinates" [*Article 53(1)*] and he shall have a right to be informed of the affairs of the Union [*Article 78(b)*].

The administrative power also includes the power to *appoint and remove* the high dignitaries of the State. Under *our* Constitution, the President shall have the power to appoint—(i) The Prime Minister of India; (ii) Other Ministers of the Union; (iii) The Attorney-General for India; (iv) The Comptroller and Auditor-General of India; (v) The Judges of the Supreme Court; (vi) The Judges of the high courts of the States; (vii) The Governor of a State; (viii) A Commission to investigate interference with water-supplies; (ix) The Finance Commission; (x) The Union Public Service Commission and Joint Commissions for a group of States; (xi) The Chief Election Commissioner and other members of the Election Commission; (xii) A Special Officer for the Scheduled Castes and Tribes; (xiii) A Commission to report on the administration of Scheduled Areas; (xiv) A Commission to investigate into the condition of backward classes; (xv) A Commission on Official Language; (xvi) Special Officer for linguistic minorities.

In making some of the appointments, the President is required by the Constitution to consult persons other than his ministers as well. Thus, in appointing the judges of the Supreme Court the President shall consult the Chief Justice of India and such other judges of the Supreme Court and of the high courts as he may deem necessary [*Article 124(2)*]. These conditions will be referred to in the proper places, in connection with the different offices.

The President shall also have the power to remove: (i) his Ministers, individually; (ii) the Attorney-General for India; (iii) the Governor of a State; (iv) the Chairman or a member of the Public Service Commission of the Union or of a State, on the report of the Supreme Court; (v) a judge of the Supreme Court or of a High Court or the Election Commissioner, on an address of Parliament.

It is to be noted that besides the power of appointing the above specified functionaries, the Indian Constitutions does not vest in the President any absolute power to appoint *inferior officers* of the Union as is to be found in the *American* Constitution. The Indian Constitution thus seeks to avoid the undesirable "spoils system" of America, under which about 20% of the federal civil offices are filled in by the President, without consulting the Civil Service Commission, and as a reward for party allegiance. The Indian Constitution avoids the vice of the above system by making the "Union Public Services and the Union Public Service Commission"—a legislative subject for the Union Parliament, and by making it obligatory on the part of the President to consult the Public Service Commission in matters relating to appointment [*Article 320(3)*], except in certain specified cases. If in any case the President is unable to accept the advice of the Union Public Service Commission, the Government has to explain the reasons therefore, in Parliament. In the matter of removal of the civil servants, on the other hand, while those serving under the Union hold office during the President's pleasure, the Constitution has hedged in the President's pleasure by laying down certain conditions and procedure subject to which only the pleasure may be exercised [*Article 311(2)*].

12b. Military Power. The military powers of the Indian President shall be lesser than those of either the American President or of the English Crown.

The Supreme command of the Defence Forces is, of course, vested in the President of India, but the Constitution expressly lays down that the exercise of this power shall be regulated by law [*Article 53(2)*]. This means that though the President may have the power to take action as to declaration of war or peace or the employment of the Defence Forces, it is competent for Parliament to regulate or control the exercise of such powers. The President's powers as Commander-in-Chief cannot be construed, as in the USA, as a power independent of legislative control.

Secondly, since the Constitution enjoins that certain acts cannot be done without the authority of law, it must be held that such acts cannot be done by the President without approaching Parliament for sanction, *e.g.*, acts which involve the expenditure of money [*Article 114(3)*], such as the raising, training and maintenance of the Defence Forces.

12c. Diplomatic Power. The diplomatic power is a very wide subject and is sometimes spoken of as identical with the power over foreign or external affairs, which comprise "all matters which bring the Union into relation with any foreign country". The legislative power as regards these matters as well as the power of making treaties and implementing them, of course, belongs to Parliament. But though the *final* power as regards these things is vested in Parliament, the Legislature cannot take the initiative in such matters. The task of *negotiating* treaties and agreements with other countries, subject to ratification by Parliament, will thus belong to the President, acting on the advice of his Ministers.

Again, though diplomatic representation as a subject of legislation belongs to Parliament, like the heads of other States, the President of India will represent India in international affairs and will have the power of appointing Indian representatives to other countries and of receiving diplomatic representatives of other States, as shall be recognised by Parliament.

12d. Legislative Powers.

Like the Crown of England, the President of India is a component part of the Union Parliament and here is one of the instances where the Indian Constitution departs from the principle of Separation of Powers underlying the Constitution of the United States. The legislative powers of the Indian President, of course according to ministerial advice, [*Article 74(1)*] are various and may be discussed under the following heads:

(a) *Summoning, Prorogation, Dissolution:* Like the English Crown *our* President shall have the power to summon or prorogue the Houses of Parliament and to dissolve the lower House.[20] He shall also have the power to summon a joint sitting of both Houses of Parliament in case of a deadlock between them [*Articles 85 and 108*].

(b) *The Opening Address:* The President shall address both Houses of Parliament assembled together, at the first session after each general election to the House of the People and at the commencement of the first session of each year, and "inform Parliament of the causes of its summons" [*Article 87*].

The practice during the last five decades shows that the President's Opening Address is being used for purposes similar to those for which the "Speech from the Throne" is used in England, *viz.,* to announce the programme of the Cabinet for the session and to raise a debate as to the political outlook and matters of general policy or administration. Each House is empowered by the Constitution to make rules for allotting time "for *discussion* of the matters referred to in such address and for the precedence of such discussion over other business of the House".

(c) *The Right to Address and to send Messages:* Besides the right to address a joint sitting of both Houses at the commencement of the first session, the President shall also have the right to address either House or their joint sitting, at any time, and to require the attendance of members for this purpose [*Article 86(1)*]. This right is no doubt borrowed from the English Constitution, but there it is not exercised by the Crown except on ceremonial occasions.

Apart from the right to address, the Indian President shall have the right to send messages to either House of Parliament either in regard to any pending Bill or to other matter, and the House must then consider the message "with all convenient despatch" [*Article 86(2)*]. Since the time of George III, the English Crown has ceased to take any part in legislative or to influence it and messages are now sent only on formal matters. The American President, on the other hand, possesses the right to recommend legislative measures to Congress by messages though Congress is not bound to accept them.

The Indian President shall have the power to send messages not only on legislative matters but also "otherwise". Since the head of the Indian Executive is represented in Parliament by his Ministers, the power given to the President to send messages regarding legislation may appear to be superfluous, unless the

20. The Council of States, also called the upper House, is *not* subject to dissolution, but is a permanent body. One-third of its members retire every two years [*Article* 83(1)].

President has the freedom to send message differing from the Ministerial policy, in which case again it will open a door for friction between the President and the Cabinet.

It is to be noted that during the 78 years of the working of *our* Constitution, the President has not sent any message to Parliament nor addressed it on any occasion other than after each general election and at the opening of the first session each year.

(d) *Nominating Members to the Houses:* Though the main composition of the two Houses of Parliament is elective, either direct or indirect, the President has been given the power to nominate certain members to both the Houses upon the supposition that adequate representation of certain interests will not be possible through the competitive system of election. Thus, (i) In the Council of States, 12 members are to be nominated by the President from persons having special knowledge or practical experience of literature, science, art and social service [*Article 80(1)*]; (ii) The President is also empowered to nominate not more than two members to the House of the People from the Anglo-Indian community, if he is of opinion that the Anglo-Indian community is not adequately represented in that House [*Article 331*][21].

(e) *Laying Reports, etc., before Parliament:* The President is brought into contact with Parliament also through his power and duty to cause certain reports and statements to be laid before Parliament, so that Parliament may have the opportunity of taking action upon them. Thus, it is the duty of the President to cause to be laid before Parliament—(a) the Annual Financial Statement (Budget) and the Supplementary Statement, if any; (b) the report of the Auditor-General relating to the accounts of the Government of India; (c) the recommendations made by the Finance Commission, together with an explanatory memorandum of the action taken thereon; (d) the report of the Union Public Service Commission, explaining the reasons where any advice of the Commission has not been accepted; (e) the report of the Special Officer for Scheduled Castes and Tribes; (f) the report of the Commission on backward classes; (g) the report of the Special Officer for linguistic minorities.

(f) *Previous sanction to legislation:* The Constitution requires the previous sanction or recommendation of the President for introducing legislation on some matters, though, of course, the Courts are debarred from invalidating any legislation on the ground that the previous sanction was not obtained, where the President has eventually *assented* to the legislation [*Article 255*]. These matters are:

(i) *A Bill for the formation of new States or the alteration of boundaries,* etc., of existing States [*Article 3*]. The exclusive power of *recommending* such legislation is given to the President in order to enable him to obtain the views of the affected States before initiating such legislation.

(ii) A Bill providing for any of the matters specified in Article 31A(1) [*1st proviso to Article 31A(1)*].

(iii) A Money Bill [*Article 117(1)*].

21. Please refer Chapter 32 for changes made by the Constitution (104th Amendment) Act, 2019.

(iv) A Bill which would involve expenditure from the Consolidated Fund of India even though it may not, strictly speaking, be a Money Bill *[Article 117(3)]*.

(v) A Bill affecting taxation in which States are interested, or affecting the principles laid down for distributing moneys to the States, or varying the meaning of the expression of "agricultural income" for the purpose of taxation of income, or imposing a surcharge for the purposes of the Union under Chapter I of Part XII [*Article 274(1)*].

(vi) State Bills imposing restrictions upon the freedom of trade [*Article 304, proviso*].

(g) *Assent to legislation and Veto:*

(A) *Veto over Union Legislation:* A Bill will not be an Act of the Indian Parliament unless and until it receives the assent of the President. When a Bill is presented to the President, after its passage in both Houses of Parliament, the President shall be entitled to take any of the following three steps:

(i) He may declare his assent to the Bill; or

(ii) He may declare that he withholds his assent to the Bill; or

(iii) He may, *in the case of Bills other than Money Bills,* return the Bill for reconsideration of the Houses, with or without a message suggesting amendments. A Money Bill cannot be returned for reconsideration.

In case of (iii), if the Bill is passed again by both House of Parliament with or without amendment and again presented to the President, it would be obligatory upon him to declare his assent to it [*Article 111*].

Generally speaking, the object of arming the Executive with this power is to prevent hasty and ill-considered action by the Legislature. But the necessity for such power is removed or at least lessened when the Executive itself initiates and conducts legislation or is responsible for legislation, as under the Parliamentary or Cabinet system of Government. As a matter of fact, though a theoretical power of veto is possessed by the Crown in *England,* it has never been used since the time of Queen Anne.

Where, however, the Executive and the Legislature are separate and independent from each other, the Executive, not being itself responsible for the legislation, should properly have some control to prevent undesirable legislation. Thus, in the *United States,* the President's power of veto has been supported on various grounds, such as: (a) to enable the President to protect his own office from aggressive legislation; (b) to prevent a particular legislation from being placed on the statute book which the President considers to be unconstitutional (for though the Supreme Court possesses the power to nullify a statute on the ground of unconstitutionality, it can exercise that power only in the case of clear violation of the Constitution, regardless of any question of policy, and only if a proper proceeding is brought before it *after* the statute comes into effect); (c) to check legislation which he deems to be practically inexpedient or, which he thinks does not represent the will of the American people.

From the standpoint of effect on the legislation, executive vetos have been classified as absolute, qualified, suspensive and pocket vetos.

(B) *Absolute Veto:* The *English* Crown possesses the prerogative of absolute veto, and if it refuses assent to any bill, it cannot become law, notwithstanding any vote of Parliament. But this veto power of the Crown has become *obsolete* since 1700, owing to the development of the Cabinet system, under which all public legislation is initiated and conducted in the Legislature by the Cabinet. Judged by practice and usage, thus there is at present no executive power of veto in England.

(C) *Qualified Veto:* A veto is "qualified" when it can be overridden by an extraordinary majority of the Legislature and the Bill can be enacted as law with such majority vote, overriding the executive veto. The veto of the *American* President is of this class. When a Bill is presented to the President, he may, if he does not assent to it, return the Bill within 10 days, with a statement of his objections, to that branch of Congress in which it originated. Each House of Congress then reconsiders the Bill and if it is adopted again in each House, by a two-thirds vote of the members present—the Bill becomes a law, notwithstanding the absence of the President's signature. The qualified veto is then overridden. But if it fails to obtain that two-thirds majority, the veto stands and the Bill fails to become law. In the result, the qualified veto serves as a means to the Executive to point out the defects of the legislation and to obtain a reconsideration by the Legislature, but ultimately the extraordinary majority of the Legislature prevails. The qualified veto is thus a useful device in the United States where the Executive has no power of control over the Legislature, by prorogation, dissolution or otherwise.

(D) *Suspensive Veto:* A veto is suspensive when the executive veto can be overridden by the Legislature by an *ordinary* majority. To this type belongs the veto power of the *French* President. If, upon a reconsideration, Parliament passes the Bill again by a simple majority, the President has no option but to promulgate it.

(E) *Pocket Veto:* There is a fourth type of veto called the "pocket veto" which is possessed by the *American* President. When a Bill is presented to him, he may neither sign the Bill nor return the Bill for reconsideration within ten days. He may simply let the Bill lie on his desk until the 10 days limit has expired. But, if in the meantime, Congress has adjourned (ie, before expiry of the period of ten-days from presentation of the Bill to the President), the Bill fails to become a law. This method is known as the "pocket veto", for, by simply withholding a Bill presented to the President during the last few days of the session of Congress the President can prevent the Bill to become law.

The veto power of the Indian President is a combination of the absolute, suspensive and pocket vetos. Thus,—

(i) As in *England,* there would be an end to a Bill if the President declares that he withholds his assent from it. Though such refusal has become obsolete in England since the growth of the Cabinet system under which it is the Cabinet itself which is to initiate the legislation as well as to advise a veto, such a provision was made in the Government of India Act, 1935. Even with the introduction of full Ministerial responsibility, the same provision has been incorporated in the Constitution of India. Normally, this power will be exercised only in the case of "private" members' Bills. In the case of a Government Bill, a situation may, however, be imagined, where after the passage of a Bill and before it is assented to by the President, the Ministry resigns and the next Council of Ministers, commanding a majority in Parliament, advises the President to use his veto power against the Bill. In such a contingency, it would be constitutional on the part of the President to use his veto power even though the Bill had been duly passed by Parliament.[22]

(ii) If, however, instead of refusing his assent outright, the President remits the Bill or any portion of it for reconsideration, a re-passage of the Bill by an *ordinary* majority would compel the President to give his assent. This power of the Indian President, thus, differs from the qualified veto in the United States insofar as no extraordinary majority is required to effect the enactment of a returned Bill. The effect of a return by the Indian President its thus merely "suspensive". [As has been stated earlier, this power is not available in the case of Money Bills.]

(iii) Another point to be noted is that the Constitution does not prescribe any time-limit within which the President is to declare his assent or refusal, or to return the Bill. Article 111 simply says that if the President wants to return the Bill, he shall do it "as soon as possible" after the Bill is presented to him. By reason of this absence of a time-limit, it seems that the Indian President would be able to exercise something like a "pocket veto", by simply keeping the Bill on his desk for an indefinite time,[23] particularly, if he finds that the Ministry is shaky and is likely to collapse shortly.

(F) *Disallowance of State legislation:* Besides the power to veto Union legislation, the President of India shall also have the power of disallowance or return for reconsideration of a Bill of the State Legislature, which may have been reserved for his consideration by the Governor of the State [*Article 201*].

---

22. The only instance of the exercise of the President's veto power over a Bill passed by Parliament, so far, has been in regard to the PEPSU Appropriation Bill. It was passed by Parliament under Article 357, by virtue of the Proclamation under Article 356. The Proclamation was, however revoked on 7 March 1954, and the Bill was presented for assent of the President on 8 March 1954. The President withheld his assent to the Bill on the ground that on 8 March 1954, Parliament had no power to exercise the legislative powers of the Pepsu State and that, accordingly, the President could not give his assent to the Bill to enact a law which was beyond the competence of Parliament to enact on that date.

    The Salary, Allowances and Pension of Members of Parliament (Amendment) Bill, 1991 was passed by the Houses of Parliament on the last day of its sitting, without obtaining the President's recommendation as required by Article 117(1). It was presented to the President for his assent on 18 March 1991. The President withheld his assent to it. (*Rajya Sabha, Parliamentary Bulletin Part I,* dated 9 March 1992).

    This shows that the veto power is necessary to prevent the enactment of Bills which appear to be *ultra vires* or unconstitutional at the time when the Bill is ready for the President's assent. It also shows that there may be occasions when Government may have to advise the President to veto a Bill which had been introduced by the Government itself.

23. In 1986, both the Houses passed the Indian Post Office (Amendment) Bill, 1986. It was widely criticised as curtailing the Freedom of the Press. President Zail Singh did not declare his assent or that he withheld his assent. It was all the time in the "pocket" of the President.

    After the formation of the National Front Government in December, 1989, the President R Venkataraman referred it back for reconsideration and the Prime Minister declared that it would be brought again before the Houses of Parliament, with suitable changes. It appears certain that it has been given up.

Reservation of a State Bill for the assent of the President is a discretionary power[24] of the Governor of a State. In the case of any Bill presented to the Governor for his assent after it has been passed by both Houses of the Legislature of the State, the Governor may, instead of giving his assent or withholding his assent, reserve the Bill for the consideration of the President.

In one case reservation is compulsory, *viz.,* where the law in question would derogate from the powers of the high court under the Constitution [*Article 200, second proviso*].

In the case of a Money Bill so reserved, the President may either declare his assent or withhold his assent. But in the case of a Bill, other than a Money Bill, the President may, instead of declaring his assent or refusing it, direct the Governor to *return* the Bill to the Legislature for reconsideration. In this latter case, the Legislature must reconsider the Bill within six months and if it is passed again, the Bill shall be presented to the President again. But it shall not be obligatory upon the President to give his assent in this case too [*Article 201*].

It is clear that a Bill which is reserved for the consideration of the President shall have no legal effect until the President declares his assent to it. But no time limit is imposed by the Constitution upon the President either to declare his assent or that he withholds his assent. As a result, it would be open to the President to keep a Bill of the State Legislature pending at his hands for an indefinite period of time, without expressing his mind.

In a strictly Federal Constitution like that of the *United States,* the States are autonomous within their sphere and so there is no scope for the Federal Executive to veto measures passed by the State Legislatures. Thus, in the Constitution of *Australia,* too, there is no provision for reservation of a State Bill for the assent of the Governor-General and the latter has no power to disallow State Legislation.

But *India* has adopted a federation of the Canadian type. Under the *Canadian* Constitution, the Governor-General has the power not only of refusing his assent to a Provincial legislation, which has been reserved by the Governor for the signification of the Governor-General's assent, but also of directly disallowing a Provincial Act, even where it has not been reserved by the Governor for his assent. These powers thus give the Canadian Governor-General a control over Provincial legislation, which is unknown in the United States of America or Australia. This power has, in fact, been exercised by the Canadian Governor-General not only on the ground of encroachment upon Dominion powers, but also on grounds of policy, such as injustice, interference with the freedom of criticism and the like. The Provincial Legislature is to this extent subordinate to the Dominion Executive.

There is no provision in the Constitution of India for a direct disallowance of State legislation by the Union President, but there is provision for disallowance of such bills as are *reserved* by the State Governor for assent of the President. The President may also direct the Governor to return the Bill to the State Legislature for reconsideration; if the Legislature again passes the Bill by an ordinary majority, the Bill shall be presented again to the President for his reconsideration. But if he refuses his assent again, the Bill fails. In short, there is no means of overriding the President's veto, in the case of State legislation. So,

24. *Hoechst Pharmaceuticals v State of Bihar*, AIR 1983 SC 1019, para 89.

the Union's control over State legislation shall be absolute, and no grounds are limited by the Constitution upon which the President shall be entitled to refuse his assent. As to reservation by the Governor, it is to be remembered that the Governor is a nominee of the President. So, the power of direct disallowance will be virtually available to the President through the Governor.

These powers of the President in relation to State legislation will thus serve as one of the bonds of Central control, in a federation tending towards the unitary type.

(h) *The Ordinance-making Power:* The President shall have the power to legislate by Ordinances at a time when it is not possible to have a Parliamentary enactment on the subject, immediately [*Article 123*].

The ambit of this Ordinance-making power of the President is co-extensive with the legislative powers of Parliament, that is to say, it may relate to any subject in respect of which Parliament has the right to legislate and is subject to the same constitutional limitations as legislation by Parliament. Thus, an Ordinance cannot contravene the Fundamental Rights any more than an Act of Parliament. In fact, Article 13(3)(a) doubly ensures this position by laying down that "'law' includes any 'Ordinance'". Subject to this limitation, the Ordinance may be of any nature as Parliamentary legislation may take, eg it may be retrospective or may amend or repeal any law or Act of Parliament itself. Of course, an Ordinance shall be of temporary duration. This independent power of the Executive to legislate by Ordinance is a relic of the Government of India Act, 1935, but the provisions of the Constitution differ from that of the Act of 1935 in several material respects as follows:

Firstly, this power is to be exercised by the President on the advice of his Council of Ministers (and not in the exercise of his "individual judgment" as the Governor-General was empowered to act, under the Government of India Act, 1935).

Secondly, the Ordinance must be laid before Parliament when it reassembles, and shall automatically cease to have effect at the expiration of six weeks from the date of re-assembly unless disapproved earlier by Parliament. In other words an Ordinance can exist at the most only for six weeks from the date of re-assembly. If the Houses are summoned to re-assemble on different dates the period of six weeks is to be counted from the later of those dates. The Supreme Court in *Krishna Kumar Singh v State of Bihar,*[25] held that the requirement of laying an ordinance before the parliament is a mandatory constitutional obligation cast upon the government and the failure to comply with this is a serious constitutional infraction and the abuse of the constitutional process.[26]

Thirdly, the Ordinance-making power will be available to the President only when *either* of the two Houses of Parliament has been prorogued or is otherwise not in session, so that it is not possible to have a law enacted by Parliament. He shall have no such power while both Houses of Parliament are in session. The President's Ordinance-making power under the Constitution is, thus, *not* a co-ordinate or parallel power of legislation available while the Legislature is capable of legislating.

25. *Krishna Kumar Singh v State of Bihar,* (2017) 3 SCC 1.
26. *Krishna Kumar Singh v State of Bihar,* (2017) 3 SCC 1.

Any legislative power of the executive (independent of the legislature) is unimaginable in the *USA,* owing to the doctrine of Separation of Powers underlying the American Constitution and even in *England,* since the *Case of Proclamations,* (1610) 2 St Tr 723. But the power to make Ordinances during recesses of Parliament has been justified in *India,* on the ground that the President should have the power to meet with a pressing need for legislation when either House is not in session.

> It is not difficult to imagine cases where the powers conferred by the ordinary law existing at any particular moment may be difficult to deal with a situation which may suddenly and immediately arise. The Executive must have the power to issue an Ordinance as the Executive cannot deal with the situation by resorting to the ordinary process of law because the Legislature is not in session.

Even though the legislature is not in session, the President cannot promulgate an Ordinance unless he is satisfied that there are circumstances which render it necessary for him to take "immediate action". Clause (1) of Article 123 says—

> If at any time, except when both Houses of Parliament are in session, the President is satisfied that circumstances exist which render it necessary for him to take immediate action, he may promulgate such Ordinances as the circumstances appear to him to require.

But "immediate action" has no necessary connection with an "emergency" such as is referred to in Article 352. Hence, the promulgation of an Ordinance is not dependent upon the existence of an armed rebellion or external aggression. The only test is whether the circumstances which call for the legislation are so serious and imminent that the delay involved in summoning the Legislature and getting the measure passed in the ordinary course of legislation cannot be tolerated. But the sole judge of the question whether such a situation has arisen is the President himself and it was held in some earlier cases a court cannot enquire into the propriety of his satisfaction even where it is alleged that the power was not exercised in good faith.[27]

---

27. *Lakhi Narayan v Province of Bihar,* AIR 1950 FC 59; *State of Punjab v Satya Pal,* AIR 1969 SC 903, p *912.* The proposition arrived at in these cases now stand modified in a case from Bihar, decided by the Supreme Court in December, 1986—*D C Wadhawa v State of Bihar,* AIR 1987 SC 579. In this case, it was established that the Government of Bihar, instead of laying before the State Legislature an Ordinance as required by Article 213(2)(a) of the Constitution [corresponding to Article 123(2)(a)] or having an Ordinance replaced by an Act of the Legislature, before the expiry of the Ordinance on the lapse of the time specified in the Constitution, would prolong its duration by re-promulgating it, ie, by issuing another new Ordinance to replace the Ordinance which would have otherwise expired. In this manner, some 256 Ordinances were kept alive (up to a length of 14 years in some cases) without getting an Act passed by the State Legislature in place of the expiring Ordinance. The Supreme Court held that the power of the Governor to promulgate an Ordinance was in the nature of an emergency power. Hence, though in some rare cases when an Act to replace an Ordinance could not be passed by the Legislature in time as it was loaded with other business; but if it was made a usual practice so as to establish legislation by the Executive (or an "Ordinance Raj") instead of by the Legislature, as envisaged by the Constitution, that would amount to a *fraud* on the Constitution, on which ground, the court would strike down the repromulgated Ordinance. The substance of this decision is, therefore, that in extreme cases, a court may invalidate an Ordinance on the ground of *fraud* and it affirms the trend since *Cooper's* case.

But if on the expiry of an Ordinance it is repromulgated and this is done repeatedly, then it is an abuse of the power and a fraud on the Constitution.[28]

In *Cooper's* case,[29] however, the Supreme Court expressed the view that the genuineness of the President's satisfaction could possibly be challenged in a court of law on the ground that it was *mala fide, e.g.,* where the President has prorogued a House of Parliament in order to make an Ordinance relating to a controversial matter, so as to by-pass the verdict of the Legislature.

The Indira Government wanted to silence any such judicial interference in the matter of making an Ordinance by inserting Clauses (4) in Article 123, laying down that the President's satisfaction shall be *final* and could not be questioned in *any* court on *any* ground.

The Janata Government overturned the foregoing change. The net result is that the observation in *Cooper's* case re-enters the field and the door for judicial interference in a case of *mala fides* is reopened. To establish *mala fides* may not be an easy affair; but the revival of *Cooper's* observation may serve as a potential check on any arbitrary power to prorogue the House of Parliament in order to legislate by Ordinance.

It is true that when the Ordinance-making power is to be exercised on the advice of a Ministry which commands a majority in Parliament, it makes little difference that the Government seeks to legislate by an Ordinance instead of by an Act of Parliament, because the majority would have ensured a safe passage of the measure through Parliament even if a Bill had been brought instead of promulgating the Ordinance. But the argument would not hold good where the Government of the day did *not* carry an overwhelming majority. Article 123 would, in such a situation, enable the Government to enact a measure for a temporary period by an Ordinance, not being sure of support in Parliament if a Bill had been brought. Even where the Government has a clear majority in Parliament, a debate in Parliament which takes place where a Bill is introduced not only gives a nation-wide publicity to the "pros and cons" of the measure but also gives to the two Houses a chance of making amendments to rectify unwelcome features or defects as may be revealed by the debate. All this would be absent where the Government elects to legislate by Ordinance. It is evident, therefore, that there is a likelihood of the power being abused even though it is exercisable on the advice of the Council of Ministers,[30] because the Ministers themselves might be tempted to resort to an Ordinance simply to avoid a debate in Parliament and may advise the President to prorogue Parliament at any time, having this specific object in mind.

It is clear that there should be some safeguard against such abuse. So far as the merits of the Ordinance are concerned, Parliament, of course, gets a chance to review the measure when Government seeks to introduce a Bill to replace it. It may also pass resolutions disapproving of the Ordinance, if and when the Government is obliged to summon the Parliament for other purposes [*Article* 123(2)(a)]. But the real question is how to enable Parliament to tell the Government, short of passing a vote of censure or of no-confidence, that it does not approve of the conduct of the Government in making the Ordinance instead

28. *D C Wadhawa v State of Bihar*, AIR 1987 SC 579.
29. *R C Cooper v UOI*, AIR 1970 SC 564, p *588, 644*; *A K Roy v UOI*, AIR 1982 SC 710.
30. *Samsher v State of Punjab*, AIR 1974 SC 2192, para 30.

of bringing a Bill for the purpose? The House of the people has made a Rule requiring that whenever the Government seeks to replace an Ordinance by a Bill, a statement "explaining the circumstances which necessitated immediate legislation by Ordinance" must accompany such Bill. The statement merely informs the House of the grounds advanced by the Government. A general discussion takes place on the resolution approving the Ordinance and generally a resolution is moved by the opposition disapproving the Ordinance.

12e. Pardoning Power.

Almost all Constitutions confer upon the head of the Executive the power of granting pardons to persons who have been tried and convicted of some offence. The object of conferring this "judicial" power upon the Executive is to correct possible judicial errors, for, no human system of judicial administration can be free from imperfections.

In *Kehar Singh's* case,[31] the following principles were laid down: (a) The convict seeking relief has no right to insist on oral hearing; (b) No guideline needs be laid down by the Supreme Court for the exercise of the power; (c) The power is to be exercised by the President on the advice of the Central Government; (d) The President can go into the merits of the case and take a different view; (e) Exercise of the power by the President is not open to judicial review, except to the limited extent as indicated in *Maru Ram's* case.[32] The court can interfere only where the Presidential decision is wholly irrelevant to the object of Article 72 or is irrational, arbitrary, discriminatory or *mala fide*. The power exercised under Article 72/161 of the Constitution can be subjected to limited judicial review. This power of clemency is to be exercised cautiously and in appropriate cases, which in effect, mitigate the sentence of punishment awarded and which do not, in any way wipe out the conviction.[33] However, the delay in deciding the mercy petitions under the Articles 72 and 161 has come under heavy criticism by the Supreme Court. The Supreme Court, while taking note of the contemporary jurisprudential development with regard to delay in execution of death sentence, commuted the death sentence into life imprisonment. The fact that no time limit is prescribed to the President/Governor for disposal of the mercy petition, should compel the government to work in a more systematised manner to repose the confidence of the people in the institution of democracy and as such the Supreme Court implored upon the government to render its advice to the President within a reasonable time, so that the President is in a position to arrive at a decision at the earliest.[34] It is the duty of the Executive to promptly process the mercy petitions invoking Articles 72 or 161 of the Constitution and forward the petitions along with requisite documents to the concerned constitutional functionary without undue delay.[35]

31. *Kehar Singh v UOI,* AIR 1989 SC 653.
32. *Maru Ram v UOI,* AIR 1980 SC 2147, paras 62, 72(a) [Const Bench] **followed** in *S R Bommai v UOI,* (1994) 3 SCC 1, para 73—9-Judges Bench. See also *Vinay Sharma v UOI,* AIR 2020 SC 1451.
33. *State of Haryana v Jagdish,* AIR 2010 SC 1690, p 1699 : (2010) 4 SCC 216.
34. *Noel Noel Riley v Attorney General,* (PC), (1982) Crl Law Review 679; *Shatrughan Chauhan v UOI,* (2014) 3 SCC 1; *V Sriharan @ Murugan v UOI,* AIR 2014 SC 1368 : (2014) 4 SCC 242; *Devender Pal Singh Bhullar v State (NCT of Delhi),* AIR 2013 SC 1975 : (2013) 6 SCC 195.
35. *State of Maharashtra v Pradeep Yashwant Kokade,* AIR 2025 SC 1 : AIROnline 2024 SC 818.

It should be noted that what has been referred to above as the "pardoning power" comprises a group of analogous powers each of which has a distinct significance and distinct legal consequences, *viz.,* pardon, reprieve, respite, remission, suspension, commutation. Thus, while a *pardon rescinds* both the sentence and the conviction and absolves the offender from all punishment and disqualifications, *commutation* merely substitutes one form of punishment for another of a lighter character, eg, each of the following sentences may be commuted for the sentence next following it: death; rigorous imprisonment; simple imprisonment; fine. *Remission,* on the other hand, reduces the amount of sentence without changing its character, eg, a sentence of imprisonment for one year may be remitted to six months. *Respite* means awarding a lesser sentence instead of the penalty prescribed, in view of some special fact, eg, the pregnancy of a woman offender. *Reprieve* means a stay of execution of a sentence, eg, pending a proceeding for *pardon* or *commutation.*

Under the Indian Constitution, the pardoning power shall be possessed by the President as well as the State Governors, under Articles 72 and 161, respectively as follows—

	President		*Governor*
1.	Has the power to grant pardon, reprieve, respite, suspension, remission or commutation in respect of punishment or sentence by *court-martial.*	1.	No such power.
2.	Do, where the punishment or sentence is for an offence against a law relating to a matter to which the *executive power of the union extends.*	2.	Powers similar to those of President in respect of an offence against a law relating to a matter to which the *executive power of the State* extends (except as to death sentence for which see *below*).
3.	Do, in *all cases* where the sentence is one of *death.*	3.	No power to pardon in case of sentence of death. But the power to suspend, remit or commute a sentence of death, if conferred by law, remains, unaffected.

In the result, the President shall have the pardoning power in respect of—

(i) All cases of punishment by a court martial. (The Governor shall have no such power)

(ii) Offences against laws made under the Union and Concurrent Lists. (As regards laws in the Concurrent sphere, the jurisdiction of the President shall be concurrent with that of the Governor) Separate provision has been made as regards sentences of death.

(iii) The *only* authority for pardoning a sentence of death is the President. But though the Governor has no power to pardon a sentence of death, he has, under section 54 of the Indian Penal Code, 1860 and sections 432–433 of the Criminal Procedure Code, 1973, the power to suspend, remit or commute a sentence of death in certain circumstances. This power is left intact by the Constitution, so that as regards suspension, remission or commutation, the Governor shall have a concurrent jurisdiction with the President. These powers of the President and the Governor under Articles 72 and 161 of the Constitution to grant remission to a convict have to be exercised on the advice of the Council of Ministers of the Union and the State respectively.[36]

12f. Miscellaneous Powers.

As the head of the executive power, the President has been vested by the Constitution with certain powers which may be said to be residuary in nature, and are to be found scattered amongst numerous provisions of the Constitution. Thus,—

(a) *Rule-making power:* The President has the constitutional authority to make *rules* and regulations relating to various matters, such as, how his orders and instruments shall be authenticated; the paying into custody of and withdrawal of money from, the public accounts of India; the number of members of the Union Public Service Commission, their tenure and conditions of service; recruitment and conditions of service of persons serving the Union and the secretarial staff of Parliament; the prohibition of simultaneous membership of Parliament and of the Legislature of a State; the procedure relating to the joint sittings of the Houses of Parliament in consultation with the Chairman and the Speaker of the two Houses; the manner of enforcing the orders of the Supreme Court; the allocation among States of emoluments payable to a Governor appointed for two or more States; the discharge of the functions of a Governor in any contingency not provided for in the Constitution; specifying Scheduled Castes and Tribes; specifying matters on which it shall not be necessary for the Government of India to consult the Union Public Service Commission.

(b) *Power to give instructions to Governor:* He has the power to give instructions to a Governor to promulgate an Ordinance if a Bill containing the same provisions requires the previous sanction of the President under the Constitution [*Article 213(1), proviso*].

(c) *Presidential reference to Supreme Court:* He has the power to refer any question of public importance for the opinion of the Supreme Court. Presidential reference was made in the backdrop of the decision rendered by the Supreme Court in *Centre for Public Interest Litigation v UOI*,[37] [popularly known as "2G Spectrum's case"], wherein eight questions were referred to the Hon'ble Supreme Court for its opinion/advice, however the Hon'ble Supreme Court only considered five questions and declined to give its opinion on remaining three questions.[38] [*Article 143*; see Chapter 22 under "Advisory Jurisdiction"].

(d) *Power to appoint Commissions:* He has the power to appoint certain Commissions for the purpose of reporting on specific matters, such as,

36. *UOI v Sriharan*, (2016) 7 SCC 1.
37. *Centre for Public Interest Litigation v UOI*, (2012) 3 SCC 1.
38. *Re Special Reference No 1 of 2012*, (2012) 10 SCC 1.

Commissions to report on the administration of Schedules Areas and welfare of Scheduled Tribes and Backward Classes; the Finance Commission; Commission on Official Language; an Inter-State Council.

(e) *Special powers relating to Union Territories:* He has some special powers relating to "Union Territories", or territories which are directly administered by the Union. Not only is the administration of such Territories to be carried on by the President through an Administrator, responsible to the President alone, but the President has the final legislative power (to make regulations) relating to the Andaman and Nicobar Islands; the Lakshadweep; Dadra and Nagar Haveli and Daman and Diu, and Puducherry;[39] and may even repeal or amend any law made by Parliament as may be applicable to such Territories [*Article 240*].

(f) *Special powers to administer Scheduled Areas, etc.:* The President shall have certain special powers in respect of the administration of Scheduled Area and Tribes, and Tribal Area in Assam:

(i) Subject to amendment by Parliament, the president shall have the power, by order, to declare an area to be a Scheduled Area or declare that an area shall cease to be a Scheduled Area, alter the boundaries of Scheduled Areas, and the like [*Fifth Schedule, para 6*].

(ii) A Tribes Council may be established by the direction of the President in any State having Scheduled Areas and also in States having Scheduled Tribes therein *but* not Scheduled Areas [*Fifth Schedule, para 4*].

(iii) All regulations made by the Governor of a State for the peace and good government of the Scheduled Areas of the State must be submitted forthwith to the President and until assented to by him, such regulations shall have no effect [*Fifth Schedule, para 5(4)*].

(iv) The President may, at any time, require the Governor of a State to make a report regarding the administration of the Scheduled Areas in that State and give directions as to the administration of such Areas [*Fifth Schedule, para 3*].

(g) *Special powers and responsibilities towards SCs and STs:* The President has certain special powers and responsibilities as regards Scheduled Castes and Tribes:

(i) Subject to modification by Parliament, the President has the power to draw up and notify the lists of Scheduled Castes and Tribes in each State and Union Territory. Consultation with the Governor is required in the case of the list relating to a State [*Articles 341-342*].

(ii) The President shall appoint a Special Officer to investigate and report on the working of the safeguards provided in the Constitution for the Scheduled Castes and Tribes [*Article 338*].

---

39. As regards the Union Territories of: (a) Goa, Daman & Diu; (b) Pondicherry; (c) Mizoram; and (d) Arunachal Pradesh, the President's power to make regulations has ceased, since the setting up of a Legislature in each of these Territories, after the amendments of Article 240(1), in 1962, 1971 and 1975. So far as Mizoram, Arunachal Pradesh and Goa are concerned, they have been promoted to the category of States, in 1986–87.

(iii) The President may at any time and shall at the expiration of 10 years from the commencement of the Constitution, appoint a Commission for the welfare of the Scheduled Tribes in the States [*Article 339*].

The foregoing may be said to be an account of the President's normal powers.

12g. Emergency Powers.

Besides these, he shall have certain extraordinary powers to deal with emergencies, which deserve a separate treatment [see Chapter 28, *post*]. For the present, it may be mentioned that the situations that would give rise to these extraordinary powers of the President are of three kinds:

(a) *Firstly,* the President is given the power to make a "Proclamation of Emergency" on the ground of threat to the security of India or any part thereof, by war, external aggression or *armed rebellion.*[40] The object of this Proclamation is to maintain the security of India and its effect is, *inter alia,* assumption of wider control by the Union over the affairs of the States or any of them as may be affected by armed rebellion or external aggression.

(b) *Secondly,* the President is empowered to make a Proclamation that the Government of a State cannot be carried on in accordance with the provisions of the Constitution. The break-down of the constitutional machinery may take place either as a result of a political deadlock or the failure by a State to carry out the directions of the Union [*Articles 356 and 365*]. By means of a Proclamation of this kind, the President may assume to himself any of the governmental powers of the State and to Parliament the powers of the Legislature of the State.

(c) *Thirdly,* the President is empowered to declare that a situation has arisen whereby "the financial stability or credit of India or of any part thereof is threatened" [*Article 360*]. The object of such Proclamation is to maintain the financial stability of India by controlling the expenditure of the States and by reducing the salaries of the public servants, and by giving directions to the States to observe canons of financial propriety, as may be necessary.

13. Cabinet System of Government.

The framers of *our* Constitution intended that though formally all executive powers were vested in the President, he should act as the constitutional head of the Executive like the English Crown, acting on the advice of Ministers responsible to the popular House of the Legislature.

But while the *English* Constitution leaves the entire system of Cabinet Government to convention, the Crown being legally vested with absolute powers and the Ministers being in theory nothing more than the servants of the Crown, the framers of *our* Constitution enshrined the foundation of the Cabinet system in the body of the written Constitution itself, though, of course, the details of its working had necessarily to be left to be filled up by convention and usage.[41]

---

40. The words "armed rebellion" have been substituted for "internal disturbance", by the 44th Amendment Act, 1978.
41. For further study of the Cabinet system in India, see Author's *Commentary on the Constitution of India,* 7th Edn, vol E/1, pp 195–293.

While the Prime Minister is selected by the President, the other Ministers are appointed by the President on the advice of the Prime Minister [*Article 75(1)*] and the allocation of portfolios amongst them is also made by him. PM/CMs cannot be constitutionally prohibited to give advice under Article 75(1) or Article 164(1) to President/Governor in respect of a person for becoming a Minister, who is charged for serious or heinous offences, or offences relating to corruption. However, it can always be legitimately expected, regard being had to the role of a Minister in the Council of Ministers, and keeping in view the sanctity of the oath he takes, the Prime Minister, while living up to the trust reposed in him, would consider not choosing a person with criminal antecedents against whom charges have been framed for heinous or serious criminal offences or charges of corruption to become a Minister of the Council of Ministers.[42] Further, the President's power of dismissing an individual Minister is virtually a power in the hands of the Prime Minister. In selecting the Prime Minister, the President must obviously be restricted to the leader of the party in majority in the House of the People, or, a person who is in a position to win the confidence of the majority in that House.

14. Council of Ministers.

Under *our* Constitution, there is no bar to the *appointment* of a person from outside the Legislature as Minister. But he cannot continue as Minister for more than six months unless he secures a seat in either House of Parliament (by election or nomination, as the case may be), in the meantime. Article 75(5) says—

> A Minister who for any period of six consecutive months is not a member of either House of Parliament shall at the expiration of that period cease to be a Minister.

The number of members of the Council of Ministers was not specified in the Constitution. It is determined according to the exigencies of the time. At the end of 1961, the strength of the Council of Ministers of the Union was 47, at the end of 1975, it was raised to 60, and in 1977, it was reduced to 24, while in July 1989, it was again raised to 58. The National Front Government (headed by Sri VP Singh) started with only 22 Ministers. All the Ministers, however, do not belong to the same rank.[43] The National Democratic Alliance Government

14a. Number of Ministers in the Council.

42. *Manoj Narula v UOI,* (2014) 9 SCC 1. The Supreme Court quoted the memorable words of Dr. Rajendra Prasad dated on 26 November 1949:
Whatever the Constitution may or may not provide, the welfare of the country will depend upon the way in which the country is administered. That will depend upon the men who administer it. It is a trite saying that a country can have only the Government it deserves. Our Constitution has provision in it which appear to some to be objectionable from one point or another. We must admit that the defects are inherent in the situation in the country and the people at large. If the people who are elected are capable and men of character and integrity, they would be able to make the best even of a defective Constitution. If they are lacking in these, the Constitution cannot help the country. After all, a Constitution like a machine is a lifeless thing. It acquires life because of the men who control it and operate it, and India needs today nothing more than a set of honest men who will have the interest of the country before them..."

43. In July, 1989, their number was (a) Members of the Cabinet—18; (b) Ministers of State—40 (total 58). In July 1990, (a) the Members of the Cabinet—18; (b) Ministers of State—18; and (c) Deputy Ministers—5. In March 1992, the total was 57. In September, 1995—(a) Members of the Cabinet—20, and (b) Ministers of State—50. In December 1996,

[Footnote No. 43 Contd.]

(headed by Mr. A B Bajpai) had 29 Cabinet Ministers and 44 State Ministers (no Deputy Ministers). However, sub-clause (1A) has been inserted to Article 75 by the Constitution (91st Amendment) Act, 2003 which provides that the total number of Ministers, including the Prime Minister, shall not exceed 15% of the total number of the members of the House of People (wef 1-1-2004). The Constitution does not classify the members of the Council of Ministers into different ranks. All this has been done informally, following the English practice. It has now got legislative sanction, so far as the Union is concerned, in section 2 of the Salaries and Allowances of Ministers Act, 1952, which defines "Minister" as a "Member of the Council of Ministers, by whatever name called, and includes a Deputy Minister".

Describing a person as Deputy Prime Minister is descriptive only, and such description does not confer on him any powers of Prime Minister, Hence, oath as Deputy Prime Minister is not invalid.[44]

14b. Salaries, etc., of Ministers.

The Council of Ministers is thus a composite body, consisting of different categories. At the Centre, these categories are three, as stated above. The salaries and allowances of Ministers shall be such as Parliament may from time to time by law determine. Each Minister gets a sumptuary allowance at a varying scale, according to his rank, and a residence, free of rent.

The rank of the different Ministers is determined by the Prime Minister according to whose advice the President appoints the Ministers [*Article 75(1)*], and also allocates business amongst them [*Article 77*]. While the Council of Ministers is collectively responsible to the House of the People [*Article 75(3)*], Article 78(c) enjoins the Prime Minister, when required by the President, to submit for the consideration of the Council of Ministers any matter on which a decision has been taken by a Minister but which has not been considered by the Council,—in practice, the Council of Ministers seldom meets as a body. It is the Cabinet, an inner body *within the Council,* which shapes the policy of the Government.

Ministers may be chosen from members of either House and a Minister who is a member of one House has a right to speak in and to take part in the proceedings of the other House though he has no right to vote in the House of which he is not a member [*Article 88*].

14c. Cabinet Meetings.

While Cabinet Ministers attend meetings of the Cabinet of their own right, Ministers of State are not members of the Cabinet and they can attend only if invited to attend any particular meeting. A Deputy Minister assists the Minister in charge of a Department of Ministry and takes no part in Cabinet deliberations.

[Footnote No. 43 Contd.]

there were 20 cabinet ministers and 19 ministers of State. In November 2000, there were 29 Cabinet Ministers, 44 State Ministers and no Deputy Ministers. On 22 May 2008, there were 32 Cabinet Ministers, 8 Ministers of State (independent charge) and 40 other Ministers of State. On 15 June 2018, there were 27 Cabinet Ministers, 11 Ministers of State (independent charge) and 37 Ministers of State. On 31 December, 2023, there were 28 Cabinet Ministers, 3 Ministers of State (independent charge) and 42 Ministers of State.

44. *KM Sharma v Devi Lal,* AIR 1990 SC 528: (1990) 1 SCC 438: JT 1990 (1) SC 5.

15. Ministerial Responsibility to Parliament. As to Ministerial responsibility, it may be stated that the Constitution follows in the main the English principle except as to the *legal* responsibility of individual Ministers for acts done by or on behalf of the President.

15a. Collective Responsibility. The principle of collective responsibility is codified in Article 75(3) of the Constitution—

> The Council of Ministers shall be collectively responsible to the House of the People.

So, the Ministry, as a body, shall be under a constitutional obligation to resign as soon as it loses the confidence of the popular House of the Legislature. The collective responsibility is to the House of the People even though some of the Ministers may be members of the Council of States.

The "collective responsibility" has two meanings: the first, that all the members of a government are unanimous in support of its policies and exhibit that unanimity on public occasions although while formulating the policies, they might have differed in the cabinet meeting; the second, that the Ministers, who had an opportunity to speak for or against the policies in the Cabinet are thereby personally and morally responsible for their success and failure.[45]

Of course, instead of resigning, the Ministry shall be competent to advise the President or the Governor to exercise his power of dissolving the Legislature, on the ground that the House does not represent the views of the electorate faithfully.

A statement made by a Minister, if traceable to any affairs of the State or for protecting the Government, can be attributed vicariously to the Government by invoking the principle of collective responsibility, so long as such statement represents the view of the Government also. If such a statement is not consistent with the view of the Government, then it is attributable to the Minister personally.[46]

15b. Individual Responsibility to the President. The principle of individual responsibility to the head of the State is embodied in Article 75(2)—

> The Ministers shall hold office during the pleasure of the President.

The result, is that though the Ministers are collectively responsible to the Legislature, they shall be individually responsible to the Executive head and shall be liable to dismissal even when they may have the confidence of the Legislature. But since the Prime Minister's advice will be available in the matter of dismissing other Ministers individually, it may be expected that this power of the President will virtually be, as in England, a power of the Prime Minister against his colleagues—to get rid of an undesirable colleague even where that Minister may still possess the confidence of the majority in the House of the People. Usually, the Prime Minister exercises this power by asking an undesirable colleague to resign, which the latter readily complies with, in order to avoid the odium of a dismissal.

---

45. *Common Cause, A Registered Society v UOI,* AIR 1999 SC 2979 : (1999) 6 SCC 667, para 3.
46. *Kaushal Kishor v State of UP,* (2023) 4 SCC 1 (SC) : 2023 SCC OnLine SC 6.

15c. Legal Responsibility.

But, as stated earlier, the English principle of legal responsibility has not been adopted in *our* Constitution. In *England,* the Crown cannot do any public act without the counter-signature of a Minister who is liable in a court of law if the act done violates the law of the land and gives rise to a cause of action in favour of an individual. But *our* Constitution does not expressly say that the President can act only *through* Ministers and leaves it to the President to make rules as to how his orders, etc., are to be authenticated; and on the other hand, provides that the courts will not be entitled to enquire what advice was tendered by the Ministers to the executive head. Hence, if an act of the President is, according to the rules made by him, authenticated by a Secretary to the Government of India, there is no scope for a Minister being legally responsible for the act even though it may have been done on the advice of the Minister.

16. Special Position of the Prime Minister.

As in England, the Prime Minister is the "keystone of the Cabinet arch". Article 74(1) of *our* Constitution expressly states that the Prime Minister shall be "at the head" of the Council of Ministers. Hence, the other Ministers cannot function when the Prime Minister dies or resigns.

In *England,* the position of the Prime Minister has been described by Lord Morley as "*primus inter pares*", *i.e.,* "first among equals". In theory, all Ministers or members of the Cabinet have an equal position, all being advisers of the Crown, and all being responsible to Parliament in the same manner. Nevertheless, the Prime Minister has a pre-eminence, by convention and usage. Thus,—

(a) The Prime Minister is the leader of the party in majority in the popular House of the Legislature.

(b) He has the power of selecting the other Ministers and also advising the Crown to dismiss any of them individually, or require any of them to resign. Virtually, thus, the other Ministers hold office at the pleasure of the Prime Minister.

(c) The allocation of business amongst the Ministers is a function of the Prime Minister. He can also transfer a Minister from one Department to another.

(d) He is the chairman of the Cabinet, summons its meetings and presides over them.

(e) While the resignation of other Ministers merely creates a vacancy, the resignation or death of the Prime Minister dissolves the Cabinet.

(f) The Prime Minister stands between the Crown and the Cabinet. Though individual Ministers have the right of access to the Crown on matters concerning their own departments, any important communication, particularly relating to policy, can be made only through the Prime Minister.

(g) He is in charge of coordinating the policy of the Government and has, accordingly, a right of supervision over all the departments.

In *India,* all these special powers will belong to the Prime Minister inasmuch as the conventions relating to Cabinet Government are, in general, applicable. But some of these have been codified in the Constitution itself. The power of advising the President as regards the appointment of other Ministers is, thus, embodied in Article 75(1). As to the function of acting as the channel of communication between the President and the Council of Ministers, Article 78 provides—

> It shall be the duty of the Prime Minister—
>
> (a) to communicate to the President all decisions of the Council of Ministers relating to the administration of the affairs of the Union and proposals for legislation;
>
> (b) to furnish such information relating to the administration of the affairs of the Union and proposals for legislation as the President may call for; and
>
> (c) if the President so requires to submit for the consideration of the Council of Ministers any matter on which a decision has been taken by a Minister but which has not been considered by the Council.

Thus, even though any particular Minister has tendered any advice to the President without placing it before the Council of Ministers, the President has (through the Prime Minister) the power to refer the matter to be considered by the Council of Ministers. The unity of the Cabinet system will thus be enforced in India through the provisions of the written Constitution.

17. Position of President.

It is no wonder that the position of the President under *our* Constitution has evoked much interest amongst political scientists in view of the plentitude of powers vested in an elected President holding for a fixed term, saddled with limitations of Cabinet responsibility.

In a Parliamentary form of Government, the tenure of office of the virtual executive is *dependent* on the will of the Legislature; in a Presidential Government, the tenure of office of the Executive is *independent* of the will of the Legislature (*Leacock*). Thus, in the Presidential form of which the model is the *United States*—the President is the *real* head of the Executive who is elected by the people for a fixed term. He is independent of the Legislature as regards his tenure and is not responsible to the Legislature for his acts. He may, of course, act with the advice of ministers, but they are appointed by him as his *counsellors* and are responsible to him and not to the Legislature. Under the Parliamentary system represented by *England,* on the other hand, the head of the Executive (the Crown) is a mere titular head, and the virtual executive power is wielded by the Cabinet, a body formed of the members of the Legislature and responsible to the popular House of the Legislature for their office and actions.

Being a Republic, *India* could not have a hereditary monarch. So, an elected President is at the head of the executive power in India. The tenure of his office is for a fixed term of years as of the American President. He also resembles the American President inasmuch as he is removable by the Legislature under the special quasi-judicial procedure of impeachment. But, on the other hand, he is more akin to the English King than the American President insofar as he has no "functions" to discharge, on his own authority. *All* the powers and "functions" [*Article 74(1)*] that are vested by the Constitution in the President are to be exercised on the advice of the Ministers responsible to the Legislature as in England. While the so-called Cabinet of the American President is responsible to himself and not to Congress, the Council of Ministers of *our* President shall be responsible to Parliament.

The reason why the framers of the Constitution discarded the *American* model after providing for the election of the President of the Republic by an electoral college formed of members of the Legislatures not only of the Union but also of the States, has thus been explained:[47]

> In combining stability with responsibility, they gave more importance to the latter and preferred the system of "daily assessment of responsibility" to the theory of "periodic assessment" upon which the American system is founded. Under the American system, conflicts are bound to occur between the Executive, Legislature and Judiciary; and on the other hand, according to many modern American writers the absence of co-ordination between the Legislature and the Executive is a source of weakness of the American political system. What is wanted in India on her attaining freedom from one and a half century of bondage is a *smooth* form of Government which would be conducive to the manifold development of the country without the least friction—and to this end, the Cabinet or Parliamentary system of Government of which India has already had some experience, is better suited than the Presidential.

18. President, whether to Act on Advice of Council of Ministers?

A more debatable question that has been raised is whether the Constitution *obliges* the President to act only on the advice of the Council of Ministers, on every matter. The controversy, on this question, was highlighted by a speech delivered by the President Dr. Rajendra Prasad at a ceremony of the Indian Law Institute (28 November 1960)[48] where he urged for a study of the relationship between the President and the Council of Ministers, observing that—

> There is no provision in the Constitution which in so many words lays down that the President shall be bound to act in accordance with the advice of his Council of Ministers.

The above observation came in contrast with the words of Dr. Rajendra Prasad himself with which he, as the President of the Constituent Assembly, summed up the relevant provisions of the Draft Constitution:

> Although there is no specific provision in the Constitution itself making it binding on the President to accept the advice of his ministers, it is hoped that the convention under which in England the King always acted on the advice of his ministers would be established in this country also and the President would become a constitutional President in all matters.

Politicians and scholars, naturally, took sides on this issue, advancing different provisions of the Constitution to demonstrate that the "President under *our* Constitution is not a figure-head" (*Munshi*)[49] or that he was a mere Constitutional head similar to the English Crown.

---

47. *Constituent Assembly Debates*, vol 4, pp 580, 734; vol 7, pp 32, 974, 984.
48. The suggestion of President Dr. Rajendra Prasad, in his speech at the Indian Law Institute, that the position of the Indian President was not identical with that of the British Crown, must be read with his quoted observation in the Constituent Assembly [*Constituent Assembly Debates*, vol 10, p 988] which, as a contemporaneous statement, has a great value in assessing the intent of the makers of the Constitution, and the meaning behind Article 74(1), as it stood up to 1976.
49. K M Munshi, *The President under the Indian Constitution*, 1963, p 8.

When the question went up to the Supreme Court, the court took the latter view, relying on the interpretation of the words "aid and advise" in the Dominion Constitution Acts, in these words, in *Ram Jawaya's* case:

> Under article 53(1) of our Constitution the executive power of the Union is vested in the President. But under article 74 there is to be a Council of Ministers with the Prime Minister at the head to aid and advise the President in the exercise of his functions. *The President has thus been made a formal or constitutional head of the executive and the real executive powers are vested in the Ministers or the Cabinet.* The same provisions obtain in regard to the Government of States; the Governor, occupies the position of the head of the executive in the State but it is virtually the Council of Ministers in each State that carries on the executive Government. In the Indian Constitution, therefore, we have the same system of parliamentary executive as in England and the Council of Ministers consisting, as it does, of the members of the legislature is like the British Cabinet, 'a hyphen which joins, a buckle which fastens', the legislative part of the State to the executive part.

The foregoing interpretation was reiterated by the Supreme Court in several later decisions,[50] so that, so far as judicial interpretation was concerned, it was settled that the Indian President is a constitutional head of the Executive like the British Crown. In *Rao v Indira's* case, a unanimous court observed—

> The Constituent Assembly did not choose the Presidential system of Government.

The Indira Government sought to put the question beyond political controversy, by amending the Constitution itself. Article 74(1) was thus substituted, by the Constitution (42nd Amendment) Act, 1976:

> (1) There shall be a Council of Ministers with the Prime Minister at the head to aid and advise the President who *shall, in the exercise of his functions, act in accordance with such advice.*

Though the Janata Government sought to wipe off the radical changes infused into the Constitution by Mrs. Gandhi's Government, it has *not* disturbed the foregoing amendment made in Article 74(1). The only change made by the 44th Amendment Act over the 1976—provision is to add a proviso which gives the President one chance to refer the advice given to the Council of Ministers back for a reconsideration; but if the Council of Ministers reaffirm their previous advice, the President shall be *bound* to act according to that advice. Article 74(1), as it stands after the 44th Amendment, 1978, stands thus:

> (1) There shall be a Council of Ministers with the Prime Minister at the head to aid and advise the President who shall, in the exercise of his functions, act in accordance with such advice.
>
> *Provided* that the President may require the Council of Ministers to reconsider such advice, either generally or otherwise, and the President shall act in accordance with the advice tendered after such reconsideration.

The position to-day, therefore, is that the debate whether the President of India has any power to act contrary to the advice given by the Council of Ministers has become *meaningless.* By amending the Constitution in 1976 and

50. *Sanjeevi v State of Madras,* AIR 1970 SC 1102, p 1106; *U N Rao v Indira Gandhi,* AIR 1971 SC 1002, p 1005; *Shamser Singh v State of Punjab,* AIR 1974 SC 2192.

1978, a seal has been put to the controversy which had been mooted by President Dr Rajendra Prasad at the Indian Law Institute that there was no provision in the Indian Constitution to make it obligatory upon the President to act only in accordance with the advice tendered by the Council of Ministers, on each occasion and under all circumstances.

But, at the same time, the amendment so made has erred on the other side, by making it an *absolute* proposition, without keeping any reserve for situations when the advice of a Prime Minister is not available (*e.g.*, in the case of death);[51] or the advice tendered by the Prime Minister is improper, according to British conventions, *e.g.*, when Prime Minister defeated in Parliament successively asks for its dissolution.[52]

So far as the contingency arising from the death of the Prime Minster is concerned, it instantly operates to dissolve the existing Council of Ministers. Hence, it would appear that notwithstanding the 1976-78 amendments of Article 74(1), the President shall have the power of acting without ministerial advice, during the time taken in the matter of choosing a new Prime Minister, who, of course, must command majority in the House of the People. In this contingency, no Council of Ministers exists, on the death of the erstwhile Prime Minister.

But, as regards the contingency arising out of a demand for dissolution by a Prime Minister who is defeated in the House of the People, it cannot be said that no Council of Ministers is in existence. On the amended Article 74(1), the President of India, must act upon the request of the defeated Council of Ministers even if such request is improper, *e.g.*, on a second occasion of defeat. If so, the position in India would differ from the principles of Cabinet Government as they prevail in the UK.

19. Attorney-General of India.

The office of the Attorney-General is one of the offices placed on a special footing by the Constitution. He is the first Law Officer of the Government of India, and as such, his duty shall be—(i) to give advice on such legal matters and to perform such other duties of a legal character as may, from time to time, be referred or assigned to him by the President; and (ii) to discharge the functions conferred on him by the Constitution or any other law for the time being in force [*Article 76*].

Though the Attorney-General of India is not (as in England) a member of the Cabinet, he shall also have the right to speak in the Houses of Parliament or in any Committee thereof, but shall have no right to vote [*Article 88*]. By virtue of his office, he is entitled to privileges of a member of Parliament [*Article 105(4)*]. In the performance of his official duties, the Attorney-General shall have a right of audience in all courts in the territory of India.

The Attorney-General for India shall be appointed by the President and shall hold office during the pleasure of the President. He must have the same qualifications as are required to be a judge of the Supreme Court. He shall

51. *Samsher v State of Punjab*, AIR 1974 SC 2192, para 30.
52. D D Basu, *Commentary on the Constitution of India*, 5th Edn, vol 2, LexisNexis, 2014, p 593, where it is stated—

"Constitutional writers agree that a dismissal of the Cabinet by the Crown, would now be an unconstitutional act, except in the abnormal case of a Cabinet refusing to resign or to appeal to the electorate upon a vote of no confidence in the Commons." See the instances given in *Shamser Singh's* case [AIR 1974 SC 2192, para 153].

receive such remuneration as the President may determine. He is not a whole-time counsel for the Government nor a Government servant.

20. Comptroller and Auditor-General of India. Another pivotal office in the Government of India is that of Comptroller and Auditor-General (CAG) who controls the entire financial system of the country [*Article 148*]—at the Union as well as State levels.

As observed by Dr Ambedkar, the CAG of India shall be the most important officer under the Constitution of India. For, he is to be the guardian of the public purse and it is his duty to see that not a farthing is spent out of the Consolidated Fund of India or of a State without the authority of the appropriate Legislature. In short, he shall be the impartial head of the audit and accounts system of India. In order to discharge this duty properly, it is highly essential that this office should be independent of any control of the Executive.

The foundation of parliamentary system of Government, as has been already seen, is the responsibility of the Executive to the Legislature and the essence of such control lies in the system of financial control by the Legislature. In order to enable the Legislature to discharge this function properly, it is essential that this Legislature should be aided by an agency, fully independent of the Executive, who would scrutinise the financial transactions of the Government and bring the results of such scrutiny before the Legislature. There was an Auditor-General of India even under the Government of India Act, 1935, and that Act secured the independence of the Auditor-General by making him irremovable except "in like manner and on the like grounds as a Judge of the Federal Court". The office of the CAG, in the Constitution, is substantially modelled upon that of the Auditor-General under the Government of India Act, 1935.

20a. Conditions of Service. The *independence* of the Comptroller and Auditor-General has been sought to be secured by the following provisions of the Constitution—

(a) Though appointed by the President, the Comptroller and Auditor-General may be *removed* only on an address from both Houses of Parliament, on the grounds of: (i) "proved misbehaviour"; or (ii) "incapacity".

He is thus excepted from the general rule that all civil servants of the Union hold their office at the pleasure of the President [*Article 310(1)*].

(b) His salary and conditions of service shall be statutory (ie, as laid down by Parliament by law) and shall not be liable to variation to his disadvantages during his term of office. Under this power, Parliament has enacted the Comptroller and Auditor-General's (Conditions of Service) Act, 1971 which, as amended, provides as follows:

(i) The term of office of the Comptroller and Auditor-General shall be six years from the date on which he assumes office. But—

- (a) He shall vacate office on attaining the age of 65 years, if earlier than the expiry of the six year term;
- (b) He may, at any time, resign his office, by writing under his hand, addressed to the President of India;

(c) He may be removed by impeachment [*Articles 148(1); and 124(4)*].

(ii) His salary shall be equal to that of a Judge of the Supreme Court (which is now Rs 2,50,000, wef 1-1-2016).

(iii) On retirement, he shall be eligible to an annual pension as per the high court and Supreme Court Judges (Salaries and Conditions of Service) Amendment Act, 2018 (10 of 2018).

(iv) In other matters his conditions of service shall be determined by the Rules applicable to a member of the IAS, holding the rank of a Secretary to the Government of India.

(v) He shall be disqualified for any further Government "office" after retirement[53] so that he shall have no inducement to please the Executive of the Union or of any State.

(vi) The salaries, etc., of the Comptroller and Auditor-General and his staff and the administrative expenses of his office shall be charged upon the Consolidated Fund of India and shall thus be non-votable [*Article 148*].

On the above points, thus, the position of the Comptroller and Auditor-General shall be similar to that of a Judge of the Supreme Court.[54]

20b. Duties and Powers.

The Comptroller and Auditor-General shall perform such *duties* and exercise such *powers* in relation to the accounts of the Union and of the States as may be prescribed by Parliament. In exercise of this power, Parliament has enacted the Comptroller and Auditor-General's (Duties, Powers and Conditions of Service) Act, 1971, which, as amended in 1976, relieves him of his pre-Constitution duty to *compile* the accounts of the Union; and the States may enact similar legislation with the prior approval of the President,—to separate accounts from audit also at the State level, and to relieve the Comptroller and Auditor-General of his responsibility in the matter of preparation of accounts, either of the States or of the Union.

The material provisions of this Act relating to the duties of the Comptroller and Auditor-General are—

53. There was a vehement public criticism that this prohibition in Article 148(4) was violated by the appointment of a retired Comptroller and Auditor-General as the Chairman of the Finance Commission. According to judicial decisions, an "office" is an employment, which embraces the ideas of tenure, duration, emolument and duties. Now, the Finance Commission is an office created by Article 280 of the Constitution itself, with a definite tenure, emoluments and duties as defined by the Finance Commission (Miscellaneous Provisions) Act, 1951, read with Article 280 of the Constitution. Apparently, therefore, the membership of the Finance Commission is an office under the Government of India, which comes within the purview of Article 148(4).

54. But, as Dr Ambedkar pointed out in the Constituent Assembly (*Constituent Assembly Debate*, vol 8, p 407), in one respect the independence of the Comptroller and Auditor-General falls short of that of the Chief Justice of India. While the power of appointment of the staff of the Supreme Court has been given to the Chief Justice of India [*Article* 146(1)], the Comptroller and Auditor-General has no power of appointment, and, consequently, no power of disciplinary control with respect to his subordinates. In the case of the Comptroller and Auditor-General, these powers have been retained by the Government of India though it is obviously derogatory to the administrative efficiency of this highly responsible functionary.

(a) to audit and report on all expenditure from the Consolidated Fund of India and of each State and each Union Territory having a Legislative Assembly as to whether such expenditure has been in accordance with the law;

(b) similarly, to audit and report on all expenditure from the Contingency Funds and Public Accounts of the Union and of the States;

(c) to audit and report on all trading, manufacturing, profit and loss accounts, etc., kept by any Department of the Union or a State;

(d) to audit the receipts and expenditure of the Union and of each State to satisfy himself that the rules and procedures in that behalf are designed to secure an effective check on the assessment, collection and proper allocation of revenue;

(e) to audit and report on the receipts and expenditure of: (i) all bodies and authorities "substantially financed" from the Union or State revenues; (ii) Government companies; (iii) other corporations or bodies, when so required by the laws relating to such corporations or bodies.

20c. Compared with his British Counterpart.

As has been just stated, the duty of preparing the accounts was a relic of the Government of India Act, 1935, which has no precedent in the British system, under which the accounts are prepared, not by the Comptroller and Auditor-General, but by the respective Departments. The legislation to separate the function of preparation of accounts from the Comptroller and Auditor-General of India, thus, brings this office at par with that of his British counterpart in one respect.

But there still remains another fundamental point of difference. Though the designation of his office indicates that he is to function both as Comptroller and Auditor, *our* Comptroller and Auditor-General is so far exercising the functions only of an Auditor. In the exercise of his functions as Comptroller, the English Comptroller and Auditor-General controls the receipt and issue of public money and his duty is to see that the whole of the public revenue is lodged in the account of Exchequer at the Bank of England and that nothing is paid out of that account without legal authority. The Treasury cannot, accordingly, obtain any money from the public Exchequer without a specific authority from the Comptroller, and, this he issues on being satisfied that there is proper legal authority for the expenditure. This system of control over issues of the public money not only prevents withdrawal for an unauthorised purpose but also prevents expenditure in excess of the grants made by Parliament.

In India, the Comptroller and Auditor-General has no such control over the *issue* of money from the Consolidated Fund and many Departments are authorised to draw money by issuing cheques without specific authority from the Comptroller and Auditor-General, who is concerned only *at the audit stage* when the expenditure has already taken place. This system is a relic of the past, for, under the Government of India Acts, even the designation "Comptroller" was not there and the functions of the Auditor-General were ostensibly confined to audit. After the commencement of the Constitution, it was thought desirable that *our* Comptroller and Auditor-General should also have the control over issues as in England, particularly for ensuring that "the grants voted and appropriations made by Parliament are not exceeded". But no action has as yet been taken to introduce the system of Exchequer Control over issues as it has been found that the entire system of accounts and financial control shall have to be overhauled before the control can be centralised at the hands of the Comptroller and Auditor-General.

The functions of the Comptroller and Auditor-General have been the subject of controversy, in regard to two questions:

(a) The first is, whether in exercising his function of audit, the Comptroller and Auditor-General has the jurisdiction to comment on extravagance and suggest economy, apart from the legal authority for a particular expenditure. The orthodox view is that when a statute confers power or discretion upon an authority to sanction expenditure, the function of audit comprehends a scrutiny of the *propriety* of the exercise of such power in particular cases, having regard to the interests of economy, besides its legality. But the Government Departments resent on the ground that such interference is incompatible with their responsibility for the administration. In this view, the Departments are supported by academicians such as Appleby,[55] according to whom the question of economy is inseparably connected with the efficiency of the administration and that, having no responsibility for the administration, the Comptroller and Auditor-General or his staff has no competence on the question of economy:

> Auditors do not know and cannot be expected to know very much about good administration; their prestige is highest with others who do not know much about administration... Auditing is a necessary but highly pedestrian function with a *narrow perspective and very limited usefulness.*[56]

(b) Another question is, whether the audit of the Comptroller and Auditor-General should be extended to industrial and commercial undertakings carried on by the Government through private limited companies, who are governed by the Articles of their Association, or to statutory public corporations or undertakings which are governed by statute. It was rightly contended by a former Comptroller and Auditor-General[57] that inasmuch as money is issued out of the Consolidated Fund of India to invest in these companies and corporations on behalf of the Government, the audit of such companies must necessarily be a right and responsibility of the Comptroller and Auditor-General, while, at present, the Comptroller and Auditor-General can have no such power unless the Articles of Association of such companies or the governing statutes provide for audit by the Comptroller and Auditor-General. The result is that the report of the Comptroller and Auditor-General does not include the results of the scrutiny of the accounts of these corporations and the Public-Accounts Committee or Parliament have little material for controlling these important bodies, spending

55. Appleby A's, *Re-examination of India's Administrative System,* p 28.
56. Appleby A's, *Re-examination of India's Administrative System,* p 28.
57. Narhari Rao's statement before the Public Accounts Committee, 1952.

> public money. On behalf of the Government, however, this extension of the function of the Comptroller and Auditor-General has been resisted on the ground that the Comptroller and Auditor-General lacks the business or industrial experience which is essential for examining the accounts of these enterprises and that the application of the conventional machinery of the Comptroller and Auditor-General is likely to paralyse these enterprises which are indispensable for national development.

As has just been stated, this defect has been partially remedied by the Act of 1971 which enjoins the Comptroller and Auditor-General to audit and report on the receipts and expenditure of "Government companies" and other bodies which are "substantially financed" from the Union or State revenues, irrespective of any specific legislation in this behalf.

enterprises. On behalf of the Government, however, the extension of the function of the Comptroller and Auditor-General has been resisted on the ground that the Comptroller and Auditor-General lacks the business or commercial experience which is essential for examining the accounts of these enterprises, and that the application of the conventional machinery of the Comptroller and Auditor-General is likely to paralyse the [illegible] development.

As has just been stated, the position has been affected by the Act of 1971 which enjoins the Comptroller and Auditor-General to audit and report on the receipts and expenditure of Government companies and other bodies which are substantially financed from the Union or State revenues, irrespective of any specific legislation in this behalf.

CHAPTER [illegible]

THE UNION LEGISLATURE

CHAPTER 12

THE UNION LEGISLATURE

1. Parliamentary System of Government.

AS has been explained at the outset, *our* Constitution has adopted the Parliamentary system of Government which effects a harmonious blending of the legislative and executive organs of the State inasmuch as the executive power is wielded by a group of members of the Legislature who command a majority in the popular Chamber of the Legislature and remain in power so long as they retain that majority.

2. Functions of Parliament.

The functions of Parliament as the legislative organ follow from the above feature of the Parliamentary system:

I. *Providing the Cabinet:* It follows from the above that the first function of Parliament is that of providing the Cabinet and holding them responsible. Though the responsibility of the Cabinet is to the popular Chamber, the membership of the Cabinet is not necessarily restricted to that Chamber and some of the members are usually taken from the upper Chamber.

II. *Control of the Cabinet:* It is a necessary corollary from the theory of ministerial responsibility that it is a business of the popular Chamber to see that the Cabinet remains in power so long as it retains the confidence of the majority in that House. This is expressly secured by Article 75(3) of *our* Constitution.

III. *Criticism of the Cabinet and of individual Ministers:* In modern times, both the executive and the legislative policies are initiated by the Cabinet, and the importance of the legislative function of Parliament has, to that extent, diminished from the historical point of view. But the critical function of Parliament has increased in importance and is bound to increase if Cabinet Government is to remain a "responsible" form of Government instead of being an autocratic one. In this function, both the Houses participate and are capable of participating, though the power of bringing about a downfall of the Ministry belongs only to the popular Chamber (*i.e.*, the House of the People) [*Article 75(3)*].

While the Cabinet is left to formulate the policy, the function of Parliament is to bring about a discussion and criticism of that policy on the floor of the House, so that not only the Cabinet can get the advice of the deliberative body and learn about its own errors and deficiencies, but the nation as a whole can be appraised of an alternative point of view, on the evaluation of which representative democracy rests in theory.

IV. *An organ of information:* As an organ of information, Parliament is more powerful than the Press or any other private agency, for Parliament secures the information *authoritatively*, from those in the know of things. The information is collected and disseminated not only through the debates but through the specific medium of "Questions" to Ministers.

V. *Power to make legislations:* The next function of the Legislature is that of making laws [*Articles 107-108; and 245*] which belongs to the Legislature equally under the Presidential and Parliamentary forms of Government. In India, since the inauguration of the Constitution, the volume of legislation is steadily rising in order to carry out the manifold development and other measures necessary to establish a welfare State.

VI. *Financial control:* Parliament has the sole power not only to authorise expenditure for the public services and to specify the purposes to which that money shall be appropriated, but also to provide the ways and means to raise the revenue required, by means of taxes and other impositions and also to ensure that the money that was granted has been spent for the authorised purposes. As under the English system, the lower House possesses the dominant power in this respect, under *our* Constitution [*Article 109*].

3. Constitution of Parliament. *The Parliament* of India consists of the President and two Houses. The lower House is called the House of the People[1]

1. The first general election under the Constitution took place in the winter of 1951–52. The first Lok Sabha, which held its first sitting on 13 May 1952 was dissolved by the President on 4 April 1957.

The second general election was held in the winter of 1956–57, and the second Lok Sabha held its first sitting on 10 May 1957.

The third general election was held in February, 1962, and the third Lok Sabha had its first sitting on 16 April 1962.

The fourth general election was held in February, 1967, and the fourth Lok Sabha had its first sitting on 16 March 1967 and was prematurely dissolved on 27 December 1970.

The fifth general election, which was thus a mid-term election, was held in March, 1971, and the fifth Lok Sabha had its first sitting on 19 March 1971.

The sixth general election was held in March 1977, after the dissolution of the Lok Sabha on 18 January 1977, during its second extended term. Excepting in Kerala, there was no simultaneous election to the Legislative Assemblies of the States. The sixth Lok Sabha had its first sitting on 25 March 1977.

The seventh general election was held in January, 1980 and the first sitting was on 21 January 1980.

The eighth general election was held in December, 1984 and the first sitting was on 15 January 1985.

The ninth general election was held in November, 1989 and the ninth Lok Sabha had its first sitting on 18 December 1989.

The tenth general election was held on 20 May, 12 and 15 June 1991 and the 10th Lok Sabha had its first sitting on 20 June 1991.

The 11th general election was held in May 1996 and the 11th Lok Sabha had its first sitting on 22 May 1996.

The 12th general election was held in February, 1998 and the 12th Lok Sabha had its first sitting on 23 March 1998.

The 13th general election was held in September and October, 1999 and the 13th Lok Sabha had its first sitting on 20 October 1999.

The 14th general election was held in April and May, 2004 and the 14th Lok Sabha had its first sitting on 2 June 2004.

The 15th general election was held in 16 April 2009 and 13 May 2009 and the 15th Lok Sabha had its first sitting on 1 June 2009.

The 16th general election was held running in nine phases from 7 April to 12 May 2014 and the 16th Lok Sabha had its first sitting on 4 June 2014.

[Footnote No. 1 Contd.]

while the upper House is known as the Council of States[2] [*Article 79*].

(The *Hindi* names "*Lok Sabha*" and "*Rajya Sabha*" have been adopted by the House of the People and the Council of States, respectively.)

The President is a part of the Legislature, like the English Crown, for, even though he does not sit in Parliament, except for the purpose of delivering his opening address [*Article 87*], a *Bill passed by the Houses* of Parliament cannot become law without the President's assent. The other legislative functions of the President, such as the making of Ordinances while both Houses are not in sitting, have already been explained.

4. Composition of the Council of States. The Council of States shall be composed of not more than 250 members, of whom: (a) 12 shall be nominated by the President; and (b) the remainder (*i.e.*, 238) shall be representatives of the States and the Union Territories [*Article 80*].

(i) *Nominated members:* The 12 nominated members shall be chosen by the President from amongst persons having "special knowledge or practical experience in literature, science, art, and social service" [*Article 80(3)*]. The Constitution thus adopts the principle of nomination for giving distinguished persons a place in the upper Chamber.

(ii) *Representation of States:* The representatives of each State shall be elected by the elected members of the Legislative Assembly of the State in accordance with the system of proportional representation by means of the single transferable vote [*Article 80(4)*]. The words "representative of the State" does not in any manner connote that the representative must also be an elector or a voter registered in the State itself. It is no part of federal principle that the representatives of the State must belong to that State. If the Indian Parliament, in its wisdom has chosen not to require a residential qualification, it would definitely not violate the basic feature of federalism.[3]

(iii) *Representation of Union Territories:* The representatives of the Union Territories shall be chosen in such manner as Parliament may prescribe [*Article 80(5)*]. Under this power, Parliament has prescribed[4] that the representatives of Union Territories to the Council of States shall be indirectly elected by members of an electoral college for that Territory, in accordance with the system of proportional representation by means of the single transferable vote.

The Council of States thus reflects a federal character by representing the Units of the federation. But it does not follow the American principle of equality of State representation in the Second Chamber. In India, the number of

---

[Footnote No. 1 Contd.]

The 17th general election was held running in seven phases from 11 April to 19 May 2019 and the 17th Lok Sabha had its first sitting on 17 June 2019.

The 18th general election was held from 19 April to 1 June 2024 in seven phases, whose result were declared on 4 June 2024.

2. The Rajya Sabha was first constituted on 3 April 1952 and it held its first sitting on 13 May 1952, and the retirement of the 1st batch of the members of the Rajya Sabha took place on 2 April 1954.
3. *Kuldip Nayar v UOI*, AIR 2006 SC 3127: (2006) 7 SCC 1.
4. Sections 27A, 27H of Representation of the People Act, 1950.

representatives of the States to the Council of States varies from 1 (Nagaland) to 31 (Uttar Pradesh). See, Table XI, *post*.

There is no difference in the status between elected and nominated members of the Rajya Sabha except that the elected members can participate in the election of the President of India whereas the nominated cannot do so.[5]

5. Composition of the House of the People. The House of the People has a variegated composition. The Constitution prescribes a maximum number as follows:

(a) Not more than 530 representatives of the States [*Article 81(1)(a)*];

(b) Not more than 20 representatives of Union Territories [*Article 81(1)(b)*].

(c) Not more than two members of the Anglo-Indian community, nominated by the President, if he is of the opinion that the Anglo-Indian community is not adequately represented in the House of the People [*Article 331*].[6]

(i) The representatives of the States shall be directly elected by the people of the State on the basis of adult suffrage. Every citizen who is not less than 18[7] years of age and is not otherwise disqualified, *e.g.*, by reason of non-residence, unsoundness of mind, crime or corrupt or illegal practice, shall be entitled to vote at such election [*Article 326*]. The bulk of the members of the House are thus directly elected by the people.

(ii) The members from the Union Territories are to be chosen in such manner as Parliament may by law provide. Under this power, Parliament has enacted[8] that representatives of all the Union Territories shall be chosen by direct election.

5a. Territorial Constituencies for Election to the House of the People. The election to the House of the People being direct, requires that the territory of India should be divided into suitable territorial constituencies, for the purpose of holding such elections. Article 81(2), as it stands after the Constitution (Seventh Amendment) Act, 1956, has provided for uniformity of representation in two respects—(a) as between the different States; and (b) as between the different constituencies in the same State, thus:

> (a) there shall be allotted to each State a number of seats in the House of the People in such manner that the ratio between that number and the population of the State is, so far as practicable, the same for all States; and
>
> (b) each State shall be divided into territorial constituencies in such manner that the ratio between the population of each constituency and the number of seats allotted to it is, so far as practicable, the same throughout the State.

The Election Commission is empowered to make changes only in the description of a constituency under the updating of Delimitation of Parliamentary and Assembly Constituencies Order, 1976, but not in the boundaries or area or extent of any constituency shown in the Order.[9]

---

5. *Kuldip Nayar v UOI*, AIR 2006 SC 3127: (2006) 7 SCC 1.
6. Please refer to Chapter 32 for changes made by the Constitution (104th Amendment) Act, 2019.
7. As amended by the Constitution (61st Amendment) Act, 1988.
8. The Union Territories (Direct Election to the House of the People) Act, 1965.
9. *Election Commission of India v Mohd Abdul Ghani*, (1995) 6 SCC 721.

6. System of Proportional Representation. While the system of separate electorates was abandoned by the Constitution, the system of proportional representation was partially adopted for the second Chamber in the Union and State Legislatures.

(a) *Council of States:* As regards the Council of States, proportional representation by single transferable vote has been adopted for the indirect election by the elected members of the Legislative Assembly of each State, in order to give some representation to minority communities and parties [*Article 80(4)*].

(b) *Legislative Council of a State:* Similarly, proportional representation is prescribed for election to the Legislative Council of a State by electorates consisting of municipalities, district boards and other local authorities and of graduates and teachers of three years standing resident in the State [*Article 171(3)*].

(c) *House of the People and Legislative Assembly of a State:* As regards the House of the People [*Article* 81] and the Legislative Assembly of a State, however, the system of proportional representation has been abandoned and, instead, the Constitution has adopted the single member constituency with reservation of seats (at the general election) for some backward communities, namely, the Scheduled Castes and Tribes [*Articles* 330, and 332].

The reasons for not adopting proportional representation for the House of the People were thus explained in the Constituent Assembly—

(i) Proportional representation presupposes literacy on a large scale. It presupposes that every voter should be a literate, at least to the extent of being in a position to know the numerals and mark them on the ballot paper. Having regard to the position of literacy in this country at present, such a presumption would be extravagant.

(ii) Proportional representation is ill-suited to the Parliamentary system of government laid down by the Constitution. One of the disadvantages of the system of proportional representation is the fragmentation of the Legislature into a number of small groups. Although the British Parliament appointed a Royal Commission in 1910 to consider the advisability of introducing proportional representation and the Commission recommended it, Parliament did not eventually accept the recommendations of the Commission on the ground that the proportional representation would not permit a stable Government. Parliament would be so divided into small groups that every time anything happened which displeased certain groups in Parliament, they would on those occasions withdraw support to the Government with the result that the Government, losing the support of certain groups, would fall to pieces.

What India needed, at least in view of the existing circumstances, was a stable Government, and, therefore, proportional representation in the lower House to which the Government would be responsible could not be accepted. In this connection, Dr Ambedkar said in the Constituent Assembly—

> I have not the least doubt in my mind, whether the future Government provides relief to the people or not, our future Government must do one thing—they must maintain a stable Government and maintain law and order.[10]

10. *Constituent Assembly Debates,* vol 7, 1262.

7. Duration of Houses of Parliament.

(a) *Council of States:* The Council of States is not subject to dissolution. It is a permanent body, but (as nearly as possible) one-third of its members retire on the expiration of every second year, in accordance with provisions made by Parliament in this behalf. It follows that there will be an election of one-third of the membership of the Council of States at the beginning of every third year [*Article 83(1)*]. The order of retirement of the members is governed by the Council of States (Term of Office of Members) Order, 1952, made by the President in exercise of powers conferred upon him by the Representation of the People Act, 1951.

(b) *House of the People:* The normal life of the House of the People is five years,[11] but it may be dissolved earlier by the President. On the other hand, the normal term may be extended by an Act passed by Parliament itself[12] during the period when a "Proclamation of Emergency" (made by the President under Article 352) remains in operation. The Constitution, however, sets a limit to the power of Parliament thus to extend its own life during a period of Emergency: the extension cannot be made for a period exceeding one year at a time (*i.e.*, by the same Act of Parliament), and, in any case, such extension cannot continue beyond a period of six months after the Proclamation of Emergency ceases to operate [*proviso to Article 83*].

8. Sessions of Parliament, Prorogation and Dissolution.

The President's power—(a) to summon either House; (b) to prorogue either House; and (c) to dissolve the House of the People has already been noted (in the chapter—"The Union Executive", *ante*).

As regards summoning, the Constitution imposes a duty upon the President, namely, that he must summon each House at such intervals that six months shall not intervene between its last sitting in one session and the date appointed for its first sitting in the next session [*Article 85(1)*]. The net result of this provision is that Parliament must meet at least twice a year and not more than six months shall elapse between the date on which a House is prorogued and the commencement of its next session. Articles 85 and 87 of the Constitution were amended so as to do away with the summoning of the Parliament twice a year and the constitutional requirement of the President's special address at the commencement of each session. The House is now prorogued only once a year and the President addresses both the Houses of Parliament only at the commencement of the first session of each year.[13]

It would, in this context, be useful to distinguish prorogation and dissolution from adjournment. A "session" is the period of time between the first meeting of a Parliament, and its prorogation or dissolution. The period between the prorogation of Parliament and its re-assembly in a new session is termed "recess". Within a session, there are a number of daily "sittings" separated by adjournments, which postpone the further consideration of business for a specified time—hours, days or weeks.

---

11. By the 42nd Amendment Act, 1976, the Indira Government, extended this term to six years but it has been restored to five years, by the 44th Amendment Act, 1978.
12. This power was used during the Emergency on the ground of internal disturbance (1975–77).
13. *Ramdas Athawale v UOI*, AIR 2010 SC 1310 : (2010) 4 SCC 1, p 8.

The sitting of a House may be terminated by: (a) dissolution; (b) prorogation; or (c) adjournment.

(i) As stated already, only the House of the People is subject to dissolution. *Dissolution* may take place in either of two ways—(a) By efflux of time, ie, on the expiry of its term of five years, or the terms as extended during a Proclamation of Emergency; (b) By an exercise of the President's power under Article 85(2).

(ii) While the powers of dissolution and prorogation are exercised by the President on the advice of his Council of Ministers, the power to adjourn the daily sittings of the House of the People and the Council of States belongs to the Speaker and the Chairman, respectively.

A *dissolution* brings the House of the People to an end (so that there must be a fresh election), while *prorogation* merely terminates a session. *Adjournment* does not put an end to the existence of a session of Parliament but merely postpones the further transaction of business for a specified time, hours, days or weeks.

(iii) A *dissolution* ends the very life of the existing House of the People so that *all matters* pending before the House lapse with the dissolution. If these matters have to be pursued, they must be re-introduced in the next House after fresh election. Such pending business includes not only notices, motions, etc., but Bills, including Bills which originated in the Council and were sent to the House, as well as Bills originating in the House and transmitted to the Council which were pending in the Council on the date of dissolution. But a Bill pending in the Council which has not yet been passed by the House shall not lapse on dissolution. A dissolution would not, however, affect a joint sitting of the two Houses summoned by the President to resolve a disagreement between the Houses if the President has notified his intention to hold a joint sitting before the dissolution [*Article 108(5)*].

Though in *England* prorogation also wipes all business pending at the date of prorogation, in *India*, all Bills pending in Parliament are expressly saved by Article 107(3). In the result, the only effect of a *prorogation* is that pending notices, motions and resolutions lapse, but Bills remain unaffected. *Adjournment* has no such effect on pending business.

9. Qualifications for Membership of Parliament.

In order to be chosen as a member of the Parliament, a person: (a) must be a citizen of India; (b) must be not less than 30 years of age in the case of the Council of States and not less than 25 years of age in the case of the House of the People. Additional qualifications may be prescribed by Parliament by law [*Article 84*].

The age of a person, in an election petition has to be determined not only on the basis of the materials placed on record but also upon taking into consideration the circumstances attending thereto. The Electoral Roll and Election Commission identity card are not conclusive proof of the age of a candidate.[14]

10. Disqualifications for Membership.

A person shall be disqualified for being chosen as, and for being, a member of either House of Parliament—

14. *Sushil Kumar v Rakesh Kumar*, AIR 2004 SC 230: (2003) 8 SCC 673.

(a) if he holds any office of profit under the Government of India or the Government of any State (other than an office exempted by Parliament by law) but not a Minister for the Union or for a State; or

(b) if he is of unsound mind and stands so declared by a competent Court;

(c) if he is an undischarged insolvent;

(d) if he is not a citizen of India or has voluntarily acquired citizenship of a foreign State or is under acknowledgment of allegiance or adherence to a foreign power;

(e) if he is so disqualified by or under any law made by Parliament [*Article 102(1)*].

Further, he shall be disqualified for being a member of either House of Parliament if he is so disqualified under the Tenth Schedule [*Article 102(2)*]. Such proceeding gets started before the Speaker only on a complaint being made that certain persons belonging to a political party has incurred disqualification on the ground of defection.[15]

It may be noted that sex is no disqualification for membership of Parliament and that in the 13th General Election, as many as 32 women secured election to the House of the People.

A time has come the Parliament must make law to ensure that persons facing serious criminal cases do not enter into the political stream. It is one thing to take cover under the presumption of innocence of the accused but it is equally imperative that persons who enter public life and participate in law making should be above any kind of serious criminal allegation. Substantial efforts have to be undertaken to cleanse the polluted stream of politics by prohibiting people with criminal antecedents so that they do not even conceive of the idea of entering into politics. They should be kept at bay.[16]

10a. Question whether Member is Disqualified or not?

If any question arises as to whether a member of either House of Parliament has become subject to any of the above disqualifications, the President's decision, in accordance with the opinion of the Election Commission, shall be final [*Article 103*].

10b. Penalty for Disqualified Members.

A penalty of Rs 500 per day may be imposed upon a person who sits or votes in either House of Parliament knowing that he is not qualified or that he is disqualified for membership thereof [*Article 104*].

11. Vacation of Seats by Members.

A member of Parliament shall *vacate* his seat in the following cases [*Article 101*]:

(i) *Dual membership:* (a) If a person be chosen to membership of both Houses of Parliament he must vacate his seat in one of the two Houses, as may be prescribed by Parliament by law; (b) Similarly, if a person is elected to the Union Parliament and a State Legislature then he must resign his seat in the

15. *Pema Khandu v Speaker, Arunachal Pradesh,* 2016 (3) Gau LR 676: 2016 (2) Gau LT 1050.

16. *Public Interest Foundation v UOI,* (2019) 3 SCC 224. See further, *Rambabu Singh Thakur v Sunil Arora,* (2020) 3 SCC 733: 2020 SCC OnLine SC 178; *Brajesh Singh v Sunil Arora,* LNIND 2021 SC 227: (2021) 10 SCC 241.

State Legislature; otherwise his seat in Parliament shall fall vacant at the expiration of the period specified in the rules made by the President.

(ii) *Disqualification:* If a person incurs any of the disqualifications mentioned in Article 102, as discussed above, his seat will thereupon become vacant immediately.

(iii) *Resignation:* A member may resign his seat by writing addressed to the Chairman of the Council of States or the Speaker of the House of the People, as the case may be, and thereupon his seat shall be vacant, unless such resignation is not voluntary or genuine. The word 'genuine' relates to the authenticity of the letter of resignation. The word 'voluntary' implies free will of the member concerned.[17]

(iv) *Absence without permission:* The House may declare a seat vacant if the member in question absents himself from all meetings of the House for a period of 60 days without permission of the House. In computing the period of said 60 days, any period during which the House is prorogued or is adjourned for more than four consecutive days shall not be taken in account.

12. Salaries and Allowances of Members of Parliament. Under the Salaries, Allowances and Pension of Members of Parliament Act, 1954, as amended by the Finance Act, 2018, a member of Parliament is entitled to a salary at the rate of Rs 1,00,000 (One Lakh) per mensem during the whole term of his office *plus* an allowance at the rate of Rs 2,000 for each day during any period of residence on duty at the place where Parliament or any Committee thereof is sitting or where any other business connected with his duties as Member of Parliament is transacted. Together with this, he is entitled to travelling allowance, free transit by railways, steamer and other facilities as prescribed by rules framed under the Act. He shall also be entitled to a pension, since a 1976 Amendment, on a graduated scale for each five year term as member of either House.

13. Officers of Parliament. Each House of Parliament has its own presiding officer and secretarial staff.

The Speaker can appoint the Secretary General in Lok Sabha on contract basis who may be an in-service officer or an outsider or even a retired person.[18]

14. Speaker and Deputy Speaker of the House of the People. There shall be a *Speaker* to preside over the House of the People. In general, his position is similar to that of the Speaker of the English House of Commons.

The House of the People will, as soon as may be after its first sitting, choose two members of the House to be, respectively, Speaker and Deputy Speaker [*Article 93*]. The Speaker or the Deputy Speaker will normally hold office during the life of the House, but his office may terminate earlier in any of the following ways: (i) By his ceasing to be a member of the House; (ii) By resignation in writing, addressed to the Deputy Speaker, and *vice versa*; (iii) By *removal* from office by a resolution, passed by a majority of all the then members of the House [*Article 94*]. Such a resolution shall not be moved unless at least 14

17. *Shrimanth Balasaheb Patil v The Karnataka Legislative Assembly*, LNIND 2019 SC 904: (2020) 2 SCC 595.

18. *PK Sandhu v Shiv Raj V Patil*, AIR 1997 SC 2357: (1997) 4 SCC 348.

days' notice has been given of the intention to move the resolution. While a resolution for his removal is under consideration, the Speaker shall not preside but he shall have the right to speak in, and to take part in the proceedings of, the House, and shall have a right of vote except in the case of equality of votes [*Article 96*].

At other meetings of the House, the Speaker shall preside. The Speaker will not vote in the first instance, but shall have and exercise a casting vote in the case of equality of votes. The absence of vote in the first instance will make the position of the Speaker as impartial as in England, and the casting vote is given to him only to resolve a deadlock.

The Speaker will have the final power to maintain order within the House of the People and to interpret its Rules of Procedure. In the absence of a quorum, it will be the duty of the Speaker to adjourn the House or to suspend the meeting until there is a quorum.

The Speaker's conduct in regulating the procedure or maintaining order in the House will not be subject to the jurisdiction of any court [*Article 122*]. But the Speaker/Chairman, while acting as an adjudicating authority of questions as to disqualification on ground of defection does not enjoy the constitutional immunity under Article 122 or 212 of the Constitution.[19]

Besides presiding over his own House, the Speaker possesses certain powers not belonging to the Chairman of the Council of States—

(a) The Speaker shall preside over a joint sitting of the two Houses of Parliament [*Article 118(4)*].

(b) When a Money Bill is transmitted from the Lower House to the Upper House, the Speaker shall endorse on the Bill his certificate that it is a Money Bill [*Article 110(4)*]. The decision of the Speaker as to whether a Bill is Money Bill is final and once the certificate is endorsed by the Speaker on a Bill, the subsequent procedure in the passage of the Bill must be governed by the provisions relating to Money Bills.

The scope of judicial review in matters under Article 110(3) is extremely restricted. There is a presumption of legality in favour of the Speaker's decision and onus is on the person challenging its validity to show that such certification was grossly unconstitutional or tainted with blatant substantial illegality. Courts ought not to replace the Speaker's assessment or take a second plausible interpretation. Instead, judicial review is restricted to instances where there is a complete disregard to the Constitutional scheme itself. It is not the function of Constitutional Courts to act as appellate forums, especially on the opinion of the Speaker, for doing so would invite the risk of paralysing the functioning of the Parliament.[20]

While the office of Speaker is vacant or the Speaker is absent from a sitting of the House, the Deputy Speaker presides, except when a resolution for his *own* removal is under consideration.

---

19. *Padi Kaushik Reddy v State of Telangana*, AIR 2025 SC 3618 : AIROnline 2025 SC 687.
20. *Rojer Mathew v South Indian Bank Ltd*, AIR Online 2019 SC 1514 : (2019) SCC OnLine SC 1456 : LNIND 2019 SC 902.

While the House of the People has a Speaker elected by its members from among themselves, the Chairman of the Council of States (who presides over that House) performs that function *ex-officio.* It is the Vice-President of India who shall *ex-officio* be the Chairman of the Council of States and shall preside over that House and shall function as the Presiding Officer of that House so long as he does not officiate as the President of India during a casual vacancy in that office. When the Chairman acts as the President of India, the Office of the Chairman of the Council of States falls vacant and the duties of the office of the Chairman shall be performed by the Deputy Chairman. The Chairman may be removed from his office only if he is removed from the office of the Vice-President, the procedure for which has already been stated. Under the Salaries and Allowances of Officers of Parliament Act, 1953, as amended by the Finance Act, 2018, the salary of the Chairman is the same as that of the Speaker, *viz.*, Rs 4,00,000 (Four Lakh) plus a sumptuary allowance of Rs 2,000 per mensem, but when the Vice-President acts as the President he shall be entitled to the emoluments and allowances of the President [*Article 65(3)*] and during that period he shall cease to earn the salary of the Chairman of the Council of States. The functions of the Chairman in the Council of States are similar to those of the Speaker in the House of the People except that the Speaker has certain special powers according to the Constitution, for instance, of certifying a Money Bill, or presiding over a joint sitting of the two Houses, which have been already mentioned.

15. Chairman of the Council of States.

Privileges are certain rights belonging to each House of Parliament collectively and some others belonging to the members individually, without which it would be impossible for either House to maintain its independence of action or the dignity of its position.

16. Powers, Privileges and Immunities of Parliament and its Members.

Both the Houses of Parliament as well as of a State Legislature have similar *privileges* under *our* Constitution.

Clauses (1)-(2) of Articles 105 and 194 of *our* Constitution deal only with two matters, *viz.*, freedom of speech and right of publication.

As regard privileges relating to *other* matters, the position, as it stands after the 44th Amendment, 1978, is as follows—The privileges of members of *our* Parliament were to be the same as those of members of the House of Commons (as they existed at the commencement of the Constitution), until *our* Parliament itself takes up legislation relating to privileges in whole or in part. In other words, if Parliament enacts any provision relating to any particular privilege at any time, the English precedents will to that extent be superseded in its application to *our* Parliament. No such legislation having been made by *our* Parliament, the privileges were the same as in the House of the Commons, subject to such exceptions as necessarily follow from the difference in the constitutional set-up in India. Reference to House of Commons was omitted in 1978.

In an earlier case,[21] the Supreme Court held that if there was any conflict between the existing privileges of Parliament and the Fundamental Rights of a citizen, the former shall prevail, for, the provisions in Articles 105(3) and 194(3)

21. *Pandit M S M Sharma v Shri Krishna,* AIR 1959 SC 395 : (1959) SCR Supl 1 806.

of the Constitution, which confer upon the Houses of *our* Legislatures the same British privileges as those of the House of Commons, are independent provisions and are not to be construed as subject to Part III of the Constitution, guaranteeing the Fundamental Rights. For instance, if the House of a Legislature expunges a portion of its debates from its proceedings, or otherwise prohibits its publication, anybody who publishes such prohibited debate will be guilty of contempt of Parliament and punishable by the House and the Fundamental Right of freedom of expression [*Article 19(1)(a)*] will be no defence. But in a later case,[22] the Supreme Court has held that though the existing privileges would not be fettered by Article 19(1)(*a*), they must be read subject to Articles 20–22 and 32. Further, the Supreme Court held that:

> the provisions of Article 105(2) of the Constitution confer immunity on a Member of Parliament from criminal prosecution only in respect of the "freedom of speech" and the "right to give vote" by him in Parliament or any committee thereof. The immunity or protection is available only in regard to these parliamentary or official activities. Such immunity is not available for any acts done in his private or personal capacity. The conduct of a Member of Parliament involving the commission of offences of bribery and criminal conspiracy having been done in personal capacity cannot, on any reasoning, be held to be acts done in the discharge or purported discharge of his parliamentary or official duty in Parliament. Taking of bribe is obviously a criminal act. Therefore, the court proceedings that fall within the ambit of clause (2) of Article 105 can be only those which "arise out of" and are subsequent to "anything said" or "any vote given" in Parliament or any committee thereof and not those which arose from outside antecedent conduct of the Members of Parliament.[23]

It has been held that the interpretation placed in the judgment of the majority in *PV Narasimha Rao's* case resulted in a paradoxical outcome. Such an interpretation is contrary to the text and purpose of Articles 105 and 194. Members of the House or indeed the House itself cannot claim privileges which are not essentially related to their functioning. Constitution envisions probity in public life. Corruption and bribery of members of the Legislature erode the foundation of the Parliamentary democracy. Bribery is not protected by parliamentary privilege. Delivery of result is irrelevant to the offence of bribery.[24] Voting for elections to the Rajya Sabha falls within the ambit of Article 194(2). Thus, the said case cannot be concurred with and, hence, overruled.[25]

Bribery is not protected by parliamentary privilege. Bribery is not in respect of anything said or any vote given. Bribery is not immune under clause (2) of Article 105 and Article 194 because a member engaging in bribery commits a crime which is unrelated to their ability to vote or to make a decision on their vote. Same principle applies to bribery in connection with a speech in the House or a Committee. Individual member of the Legislature cannot assert a claim of privilege to seek immunity under Articles 105 and 194 from prosecution on a

---

22. *Ref under Article 143*, AIR 1965 SC 745, pp *764, 767*.
23. *PV Narasimha Rao v State*, AIR 1998 SC 2120 : (1998) 4 SCC 626.
24. Offence of bribery is agnostic to the performance of the agreed action and crystallizes on the exchange of illegal gratification. It does not matter whether the vote is cast in the agreed direction or if the vote is cast at all. Offence of bribery is complete at the point in time when the legislator accepts the bribe.
25. *Sita Soren v UOI*, (2024) 3 SCR 462 (SC) : 2024 INSC 161.

charge of bribery in connection with a vote or speech in the Legislature. Such a claim to immunity fails to fulfil the twofold test that the claim is tethered to the collective functioning of the House and that it is necessary to the discharge of the essential duties of a legislator.[26]

Extent of this immunity must be tested on the anvil of the test of intrinsic relation to the functioning of the House and the necessity test. The phrase "in respect of" is significant to delineate the ambit of the immunity granted under clause (2) of Article 105. Words "in respect of" apply to the phrase "anything said or any vote given," and in the latter part to a publication by or with the authority of the House. Expressions "anything" and "any" must be read in the context of the accompanying expressions in Articles 105(2) and 194(2). Words "anything" or "any" may not be interpreted without reading the operative word on which it applies, *i.e.*, "said" and "vote given" respectively. Words "anything" and "any" when read with their respective operative words mean that a member may claim immunity to say as they feel and vote in a direction that they desire on any matter before the House. These are absolutely outside the scope of interference by the courts. Words "in respect of" means 'arising out of' or 'bearing a clear relation to' and cannot be interpreted to mean anything which may have even a remote connection with the speech or vote given.[27]

Protection under Articles 105 and 194 has been colloquially called "parliamentary privilege" and not "legislative privilege". It cannot be restricted to only law-making on the floor of the House but extends to other powers and responsibilities of elected members, taking place in the Legislature or Parliament, even when the House is not sitting.[28]

The manner of enforcement of privilege by the Legislature can result in judicial scrutiny, though subject to the restrictions contained in the other Constitutional provisions, for example, Article 122 or 212.[29]

16a. Privileges Classified. The privileges of each House may be divided into two groups—(a) those which are enjoyed by the members individually; and (b) those which belong to each House of Parliament, as a collective body.

Two constituent elements of privileges are: First is the sum of rights enjoyed by the House of Parliament collectively and the second is the rights enjoyed by members of the House individually. Rights and immunities such as the power to regulate its own procedure, the power to punish for contempt of the House or to expel a member, belong to the first element of privileges held by the House as a collective body for its proper functioning, protection of members, and vindication of its own authority and dignity. Second element of rights exercised individually by members of the House includes freedom of speech and freedom from arrest, among others. Privilege exercised by members individually is in turn qualified by its necessity, in that the privilege must be such that "without which they could not discharge their functions". These privileges enjoyed by members of the House individually are a means to ensure and facilitate the effective

26. *Sita Soren v UOI*, (2024) 3 SCR 462 (SC) : 2024 INSC 161.
27. *Sita Soren v UOI*, (2024) 3 SCR 462 (SC) : 2024 INSC 161.
28. *Sita Soren v UOI*, (2024) 3 SCR 462 (SC) : 2024 INSC 161.
29. *Raja Ram Pal v Hon'ble Speaker, Lok Sabha*, (2007) 3 SCC 184.

discharge of the collective functions of the House. Privileges enjoyed by members of the House which exceed those possessed by other bodies or individuals, are not absolute or unqualified. Thus, the privileges and immunities enshrined in Articles 105 and 194 belong to the House collectively. Exercise of the privileges individually by members must be tested on the anvil of whether it is tethered to the healthy and essential functioning of the House.[30]

(A) The privileges enjoyed by the members individually are: (i) Freedom from arrest; (ii) Exemption from attendance as jurors and witnesses; (iii) Freedom of speech.

(i) *Freedom from Arrest:* Section 135A of the Code of Civil Procedure, 1908, *as amended* by Act 104 of 1976, exempts a member from arrest during the continuance of a meeting of the Chamber or Committee thereof of which he is a member or of a joint sitting of the Chambers or Committees, and during a period of 40 days before and after such meeting or sitting. This immunity is, however, confined to arrest in civil cases and does not extend to arrest in criminal case or under the law of Preventive Detention.

(ii) *Freedom of Attendance as Witness:* According to the English practice, a member cannot be summoned, without the leave of the House, to give evidence as a witness while Parliament is in session.

(iii) *Freedom of Speech:* As in England, there will be freedom of speech within the walls of each House in the sense of immunity of action for anything said therein. While an ordinary citizen's right of speech is subject to the restrictions specified in Article 19(2), such as the law relating to defamation, a Member of Parliament cannot be made liable in any court of law in respect of anything said in Parliament or any Committee thereof. But this does not mean unrestricted licence to speak anything that a member may like, regardless of the dignity of the House. The freedom of speech is therefore "subject to the rules" framed by the House under its powers to regulate its internal procedure.

The Constitution itself imposes another limitation upon the freedom of speech in Parliament, namely, that no discussion shall take place in Parliament with respect to the conduct of any judge of the Supreme Court or of a high court in the discharge of his duties except upon a motion for presenting an address to the President praying for the removal of the Judge [*Article 121*].

(B) The privileges of the House *collectively* are—(i) The right to publish debates and proceedings and the right to restrain publication by others; (ii) The right to exclude others; (iii) The right to regulate the internal affairs of the House, and to decide matters arising within its walls; (iv) The right to publish Parliamentary misbehaviour; (v) The right to punish members and outsiders for breach of its privileges.

Thus, each House of Parliament shall have the power—

(i) To exclude strangers from the galleries at any time. Under the Rules of Procedure, the Speaker and the Chairman have the right to order the "withdrawal of strangers from any part of the House".

30. *Sita Soren v UOI,* (2024) 3 SCR 462 (SC) : 2024 INSC 161.

(ii) To regulate its internal affairs. Each House of Parliament has the right to control and regulate its proceedings and also to decide any matter arising within its walls, without interference from the courts. What is said or done within the walls of Parliament cannot be inquired into in a court of law.

(iii) To punish members and outsiders for breach of its privileges. Each House can punish for contempt or breach of its privileges, and the punishment may take the form of admonition, reprimand or imprisonment. Thus, in the famous *Blitz case*, the editor of the newspaper was called to the Bar of the House of the People and reprimanded for having published an article derogatory to the dignity of a member in his capacity as member of the House. In 1990, Sri KK Tewari, a former Minister was reprimanded by the Rajya Sabha. In 2005, both Rajya Sabha and Lok Sabha took stern action of expulsion against certain Members of Parliament in famous "cash for query case" on the ground that the conduct of the members was unethical and unbecoming of the Members of Parliament and their continuance as MPs is untenable.[31] What constitutes breach of privileges or contempt of Parliament has been fairly settled by a number of precedents in England and India. Broadly speaking:

> Any act or omission which obstructs or impedes either House of Parliament in the performance of its functions or which obstructs or impedes any member or officer of such House in the discharge of his duty or which has a tendency, directly or indirectly, to produce such results as may be treated as a contempt, even though there is no precedent of the offence.[32]

17. Ordinary Bills. The different stages in the legislative procedure in Parliament relating to Bills *other than Money Bills* are as follows:

1. *Introduction:* A Bill other than Money or financial Bills may be introduced in either House of Parliament [*Article 107(1)*] and requires passage in both Houses before it can be presented for the President's assent. A Bill may be introduced either by a Minister or by a private Member. The difference in the two cases is that any Member other than a Minister desiring to introduce a Bill has to give notice of his intention and to ask for leave of the House to introduce which is, however, rarely opposed. If a Bill has been published in the official gazette before its introduction, no motion for leave to introduce the Bill is necessary. Unless published earlier, the Bill is published in the official gazette as soon as may be after it has been introduced.

2. *Motions after introduction:* After a Bill has been introduced or on some subsequent occasion, the Member in charge of the Bill may make one of the following motions in regards to the Bill, *viz.*—

(a) That it be taken into consideration;

(b) That it be referred to a Select Committee;

(c) That it be referred to a Joint Committee of the House with the concurrence of the other House;

(d) That it be circulated for the purpose of eliciting public opinion thereon.

---

31. *Raja Ram Pal v Hon'ble Speaker, Lok Sabha*, (2007) 3 SCC 184.
32. May, *Parliamentary Practice*, 15th Edn, p 109.

On the day on which any of the aforesaid motions is made or on any subsequent date to which the discussion is postponed, the principles of the Bill and its general provisions may be discussed. Amendments to the Bill and clause by clause consideration of the provisions of the Bill take place when the motion that the Bill be taken into consideration is carried.

3. *Report by Select Committee:* It has already been stated that after introduction of the Bill the Member in charge or any other Member by way of an amendment may move that the Bill be referred to a Select Committee. When such a motion is carried, a Select Committee of the House considers the provisions of the Bill (but not the principles underlying the Bill which had, in fact, been accepted by the House when the Bill was referred to the Select Committee). After the Select Committee has considered the Bill, it submits its report to the House and after the report is received, a motion that the Bill as returned by the Select Committee be taken into consideration lies. When such a motion is carried, the clauses of the Bill are open to consideration and amendments are admissible.

4. *Passing of the Bill in the House where it was introduced:* When a motion that the Bill be taken into consideration has been carried and no amendment of the Bill has been made or after the amendments are over, the Member in charge may move that the Bill be passed. This stage may be compared to the third reading of a Bill in the House of Commons. After the motion that the Bill may be passed is carried,[33] the Bill is taken as passed so far as that House is concerned.

5. *Passage in the other House:* When a Bill is passed in one House, it is transmitted to the other House. When the Bill is received in the other House it undergoes all the stages as in the originating House subsequent to its introduction. The House which receives the Bill from another House can, therefore, take either of the following courses:

(i) It may reject the Bill altogether. In such a case the provisions of Article 108(1)(*a*) as to joint sitting may be applied by the President.

(ii) It may pass the Bill with amendments. In this case, the Bill will be returned to the originating House. If the House which originated the Bill accepts the Bill as amended by the other House, it will be presented to the President for his assent [*Article 111*]. If however the originating House does not agree to the amendments made by the other House and there is final disagreement as to the amendments between the two Houses, the President may summon a joint sitting to resolve the deadlock [*Article 108(1)(b)*].

(iii) It may take no action on the Bill, ie, keep it lying on its Table. In such a case, if more than six months elapse from the date of the reception of the Bill, the President may summon a joint sitting [*Article 108(1)(c)*].

6. *President's Assent:* When a Bill has been passed by both Houses of Parliament either singly or at a joint sitting as provided in Article 108, the Bill is presented to the President for his assent. If the President withholds his assent, there is an end to the Bill. If the President gives his assent, the Bill becomes an Act from the date of his assent. Instead of either refusing assent or giving assent,

33. Except in the case of Bills for the amendment of the Constitution (*Article* 368), all Bills and other questions before each House are passed or carried by a simple majority [*Article* 100(1)].

the President may return the Bill for reconsideration of the Houses with a message requesting them to reconsider it. If, however, the Houses pass the Bill again with or without amendments and the Bill is presented to the President for his assent after such reconsideration, the President shall have no power to withhold his assent from the Bill.

18. Money Bills. A Bill is deemed to be a "Money Bill" if it contains only provisions dealing with all or any of the following matters:

(a) the imposition, abolition, remission, alteration or regulation of any tax; (b) the regulation of the borrowing of money by the Government; (c) the custody of the Consolidated Fund or the Contingency Fund of India, the payment of moneys into or the withdrawal of moneys from any such fund; (d) the appropriation of moneys out of the Consolidated Fund of India; (e) the declaring of any expenditure to be expenditure charged on the Consolidated Fund of India or the increasing of the amount of any such expenditure; (f) the receipt of money on account of the Consolidated Fund of India or the public account of India or the custody or issue of such money or the audit of the accounts of the Union or of a State; or (g) any matter incidental to any of the matters specified in sub-clauses (a)-(f) [*Article 110*].

But a Bill shall not be deemed to be a Money Bill by reason only that it provides for imposition of fines or other pecuniary penalties, or for the demand or payment of fees for licences or fees for services rendered, or by reason that it provides for the imposition, abolition, remission, alteration or regulation of any tax by any local authority or body for local purposes.

If any question arises, whether a Bill is a Money Bill or not, the decision of the Speaker of the House of the People thereon shall be final. This means that the nature of a Bill which is certified by the Speaker as a Money Bill shall not be open to question either in a court of law or in the either House or even by the President.

When a Bill is transmitted to the Council of States or is presented for the assent of the President, it shall bear the endorsement of the Speaker that it is a Money Bill. As pointed out earlier, this is one of the special powers of the Speaker.

The following is the procedure for the passing of Money Bills in Parliament:

(1) A Money Bill shall not be introduced in the Council of States.

(2) After a Money Bill has been passed by the House of the People, it shall be transmitted (with the Speaker's certificate that it is a Money Bill) to the Council of States for its recommendations. The Council of States cannot reject a Money Bill nor amend it by virtue of its own powers. It must, within a period of 14 days from the date of receipt of the Bill, return the Bill to the House of the People which may thereupon either accept or reject all or any of the recommendations of the Council of States.

(3) If the House of the People accepts any of the recommendations of the Council of States, the Money Bill shall be deemed to have been passed by both Houses with the amendments recommended by the Council of States and accepted by the House of the People.

(4) If the House of the People does not accept any of the recommendations of the Council of States, the Money Bill shall be deemed to have been passed by both Houses in the form in which it is passed by the House of the People without any of the amendments recommended by the Council of States.

(5) If a Money Bill passed by the House of the People and transmitted to the Council of States for its recommendations is not returned to the House of the People within the said period of 14 days, it shall be deemed to have been passed by both Houses at the expiration of the said period in the form in which it was passed by the House of the People [*Article 109*].

Thus, Money bills as defined under Article 110(1) include bills which contain only provisions covered by sub-clauses (a)-(g). These Money Bills can be introduced only in the Lok Sabha and the role of the Rajya Sabha is merely consultative. Unlike in the case of ordinary Bills, where the Upper House can block the proposed legislation and act as a check on the power of the directly elected Lower House, in case of Money Bills, the Rajya Sabha merely has the ability to recommend amendments, that too only within 14 days. In case the Lok Sabha refuses to accept those recommendations or in case no recommendations are made by the Rajya Sabha within the period of 14 days, the Money Bill can be directly sent for Presidential ratification and thereafter it becomes valid law.

The Constitution of India by, Article 110(4), requires that every Money Bill be certified to be so by the Speaker before it is transmitted to the Rajya Sabha for their non-binding consideration. The Speaker of the Lok Sabha hence is the only appropriate authority to decide the nature of a Bill under Article 110(3).[34]

The introduction of Aadhaar (Targeted Delivery of Financial and Other Subsidies, Benefits and Services) Act, 2016, is justified as a Money Bill on the ground that the main provision is a part of Money Bill and other are only incidental and, therefore, covered by clause (g) of Article 110. However, Chandrachud J while dissenting was of the view that introducing one provision in the Act which is covered within the parameters of Article 110 does not render the entirety of the Act a money bill where its other provisions travel beyond the parameters set out in Article 110. In his opinion, passing of a bill as a money bill, when it does not qualify for it, damages the delicate balance of bicameralism.[35]

18a. Money Bills and Financial Bills. Generally speaking, a Financial Bill may be said to be any Bill which relates to revenue or expenditure. But it is in a technical sense that the expression is used in the Constitution.

The definition of a "Money Bill" is given in Article 110 and no Bill is a Money Bill unless it satisfies the requirements of this Article. It lays down that a Bill is a Money Bill if it contains *only* provisions dealing with all or any of the six matters

---

34. The issue and question of Money Bill, as defined under Article 110(1) of the Constitution, and certification accorded by the Speaker of the Lok Sabha in respect of Part-XIV of the Finance Act, 2017 was referred to a larger Bench by a five judge Constitution Bench in *Rojer Mathew v South Indian Bank Ltd,* AIR Online 2019 SC 1514 : (2019) SCC OnLine SC 1456 : LNIND 2019 SC 902.

35. *KS Puttaswamy (Aadhaar-5J) v UOI,* (2019) 1 SCC 1.

specified in that Article or matters incidental thereto. These six specified matters have already been stated. On the question whether any Bill comes under any of the sub-clauses of Article 110, the decision of the Speaker of the House of the People is final and his certificate that a particular Bill is a Money Bill is not liable to be questioned. Shortly speaking, thus, only those Financial Bills are Money Bills which bear the certificate of the Speaker as such.

Financial Bills which do not receive the Speaker's certificate are of two classes. These are dealt with in Article 117 of the Constitution—

(i) To the first class belongs a Bill which contains any of the matters specified in Article 110 but does not consist *solely* of those matters, for example, a Bill which contains a taxation clause, but does not deal solely with taxation [*Article 117(1)*].

(ii) Any ordinary Bill which contains provisions involving expenditure from the Consolidated Fund is a Financial Bill of the second class [*Article 117(3)*].

The incidents of these three different classes of Bills are as follows—

(i) A Money Bill cannot be introduced in the Council of States nor can it be introduced except on the recommendation of the President. Again, the Council of States has no power to amend or reject such a Bill. It can only recommend amendments to the House of the People.

(ii) A Financial Bill of the first class, *i.e.*, to say, a Bill which contains any of the matters specified in Article 110 but does not exclusively deal with such matters, has two features in common with a Money Bill, *viz.*, that it cannot be introduced in the Council of States and also cannot be introduced except on the recommendation of the President. But not being a Money Bill, the Council of States has the same power to reject or amend such a Financial Bill as it has in the case of non-Financial Bills subject to the limitation that an amendment other than for reduction or abolition of a tax cannot be moved in either House without the President's recommendation. Such a Bill has to be passed in the Council of States through three readings like ordinary Bills and in case of a final disagreement between the two Houses over such a Bill, the provision for joint sitting in Article 108 is attracted. Only Money Bills are excepted out of the provisions relating to a joint sitting [*Article 108(1)*].

(iii) A Bill which merely involves expenditure and does not include any of the matters specified in Article 110, is an ordinary Bill and may be initiated in either House and the Council of States has full power to reject or amend it. But it has only *one special incident* in view of the financial provision (*i.e.*, provision involving expenditure contained in it) *viz.*, that it must not be *passed* in either House unless the President has recommended the consideration of the Bill. In other words, the President's recommendation is not a condition precedent to its introduction as in the case of Money Bills and other Financial Bills of the first class but in this case it will be sufficient if the President's recommendation is received before the Bill is *considered.* Without such recommendation, however, the consideration of such Bill cannot take place [*Article 117(3)*].

But for this special incident, a Bill which merely involves expenditure is governed by the same procedure as an ordinary Bill, including the provision of a joint sitting in case of disagreement between the two Houses.

19. Provisions for Removing Deadlock between Two Houses of Parliament.

It has already been made clear that any Bill, *other than a Money Bill,* can become a law only if it is agreed to by both the Houses, with or without amendments. A machinery should then exist, for resolving a deadlock between the two Houses if they fail to agree either as to the provisions of the Bill as introduced or as to the amendments that may have been proposed by either House.

(A) As regards Money Bills, the question does *not* arise, since the House of the People has the final power of passing it, the other House having the power only to make recommendation for the acceptance of the House of the People. In case of disagreement over a Money Bill, thus, the lower House has the plenary power to override the wishes of the upper Houses, *i.e.*, the Council of States.

(B) As regards all other Bills (including "Financial Bills"), the machinery provided by the Constitution for resolving a disagreement between the two Houses of Parliament is a joint sitting of the two Houses [*Article 108*].

The President may notify to the Houses his intention to summon them for a joint sitting in case of disagreement arising between the two Houses in any of the following ways:—

If, after a Bill has been passed by one House and transmitted to the other Houses—

(a) the Bill is rejected by the other House; or

(b) the Houses have finally disagreed as to the amendments to be made in the Bill; or

(c) more than six months have elapsed from the date of the reception of the Bill by the other House without the Bill being passed by it.

No such notification can be made by the President if the Bill has already lapsed by the dissolution of the House of the People; but once the President has notified his intention to hold a joint sitting, the subsequent dissolution of the House of the People cannot stand in the way of the joint sitting being held.

As stated earlier, the Speaker will preside at the joint sitting; in the absence of the Speaker, such person as is determined by the Rules of Procedure made by the President (in consultation with the Chairman of Council of States and the Speaker of the House of People) shall preside [*Article 118(4)*]. The Rules, so made, provide that

> During the absence of the Speaker from any joint sitting, the Deputy Speaker of the House or, if he is also absent, the Deputy Chairman of the Council or, if he is also absent, such other person as may be determined by the Members present at the sitting, shall preside.

There are restrictions on the amendments to the Bill which may be proposed at the joint sitting:

(a) If, after its passage in one House, the Bill has been rejected or has not been returned by the other House, only such amendments may be proposed at the joint sitting as are made necessary by the delay in the passage of the Bill.

(b) If the deadlock has been caused because the other House has proposed amendments to which the originating House cannot agree, then: (i) amendments necessary owing to the delay in the passage of the Bill, as well as, (ii) other amendments as are relevant to the matters with respect to which the House have disagreed, may be proposed at the joint sitting.

If at the joint sitting of the two Houses the Bill, with such amendments, if any, as are agreed to in joint sitting, is passed by a majority of the *total number* of members of both Houses *present and voting,* it shall be deemed for the purposes of this Constitution to have been passed by both the Houses.

It is to be carefully noted that the procedure for joint sitting, as prescribed by Article 108, is confined to Bills for ordinary legislation and does *not* extend to a Bill for amendment of the Constitution, which is governed by Article 368(2), and must, therefore, be passed by each House, separately, by the special majority laid down. That is why the 43rd Amendment Bill, introduced in the *Lok Sabha* in April 1977, could not overcome the apprehended resistance in the *Rajya Sabha,* by resorting to a joint sitting, as carelessly suggested in some newspaper articles. The 45th Amendment Bill suffered mutilation in the *Rajya Sabha,* for the same reason.

20. Financial Legislation in Parliament.

At the beginning of every financial year, the President shall, in respect of the financial year, cause to be laid before both the Houses of Parliament a statement of the estimated receipts and expenditure of the Government of India for that year. This is known as the "annual financial statement" (*i.e.*, the "Budget") [*Article 112*]. It also states the ways and means of meeting the estimated expenditure.

20a. Policy Statement in the Budget.

In conformity with the usual Parliamentary practice in the United Kingdom, the Budget not only gives the estimates for the ensuing year but offers an opportunity to the Government to review and explain its financial and economic policy and programme to the Legislature to discuss and criticise it. The Annual Financial Statement in *our* Parliament thus contains, apart from the estimates of expenditure, the ways and means to raise the revenue,—

(a) An analysis of the actual receipts and expenditures of the closing year, and the causes of any surplus or deficit in relation to such year;

(b) An explanation of the economic policy and spending programme of the Government in the coming year and the prospects of revenue.

20b. Votable and Non-votable Expenditure.

The estimates of expenditure embodied in the annual financial statement shall show separately—(a) the sums required to meet expenditure described by this Constitution as expenditure *charged upon* the Consolidated Fund of India; and (b) the sums required to meet other expenditure proposed to be made from the Consolidated Fund of India.

(a) So much of the estimates as relates to expenditure charged upon the Consolidated Fund of India shall *not* be submitted to the vote of Parliament but each House is competent to discuss any of these estimates.

(b) So much of the estimates as relates to other expenditure shall be submitted in the form of demands for grants to the House of the People, and that House shall have power to assent, or to refuse to assent, to any demand, or to assent to any demand subject to a reduction of the amount specified therein. No demand for a grant shall however be made except on the recommendation of the President [*Article 113*].

In practice, the presentation of the Annual Financial Statement is followed by a general discussion in both the Houses of Parliament. The estimates of expenditure, *other than those which are charged,* are then placed before the House of the People in the form of "demands for grants".

No money can be withdrawn from the Consolidated Fund except under an Appropriation Act, passed as follows:

As soon as may be after the demands for grants have been voted by the House of the People, there shall be introduced a Bill to provide for the appropriation out of the Consolidated Fund of India of all moneys required to meet—(a) the grants so made by the House of the People; and (b) the expenditure charged on the Consolidated Fund of India.

This Bill will then be passed as a Money Bill, subject to this condition that no amendment shall be proposed to any such Bill in either House of Parliament which will have the effect of varying the amount or altering the destination of any grant so made or of varying the amount of any expenditure charged on the Consolidated Fund [*Article 114*].

20c. Expenditure Charged on the Consolidated Fund of India.

The following expenditure shall be expenditure charged on the Consolidated Fund of India [*Article 112(3)*]—

(a) the emoluments and allowances of the President and other expenditure relating to his office; (b) the salaries and allowances of the Chairman and the Deputy Chairman of the Council of States and the Speaker and the Deputy Speaker of the House of the People; (c) debt charges for which the Government of India is liable; (d) (i) the salaries, allowances and pensions payable to or in respect of judges of the Supreme Court; (ii) the pensions payable to or in respect of judges of the Federal Court; (iii) the pensions payable to or in respect of judges of any high court; (e) the salary, allowances and pension payable to or in respect of the Comptroller and Auditor-General of India; (f) any sums required to satisfy any judgment, decree or award of any court or arbitral tribunal; (g) any other expenditure declared by this Constitution or by Parliament by law to be so charged.

20d. Relative Parts Played by the two Houses in Financial Legislation.

As has been already explained, financial business in Parliament starts with the presenting of the Annual Financial Statement. This Statement is caused to be laid by the President before *both* Houses of Parliament [*Article 112*]. After the Annual Financial Statement is presented, there is a general discussion of the Statement as a whole in *either* House. This discussion is to be a general discussion relating to a policy involving a review and criticism of the administration and a valuation of the grievances of the people. No motion is moved at this stage nor is the Budget submitted to vote.

The Council of States shall have *no further business* with the Annual Financial Statement beyond the above general discussion. The voting of the grants, *i.e.,* of the demands for expenditure made by Government, is an exclusive business of the House of the People. In the House of the People, after the general discussion is over, estimates are submitted in the form of demands for grants on the particular heads and it is followed by a vote of the House on each of the heads [*Article 113(2)*].

After the grants are voted by the House of the People, the grants so made by the House of the People as well as the expenditure charged on the Consolidated Fund of India are incorporated in an Appropriation Bill. It provides the legal authority for the withdrawal of these sums from the Consolidated Fund of India.

Similarly, the taxing proposals of the budget are embodied in another Bill known as the Annual Finance Bill.

Both these Bills being Money Bills, the special procedure relating to Money Bills shall have to be followed. It means that they can be introduced *only in the House of the People* and after each Bill is passed by the House of the People, it shall be transmitted to the Council of States which shall have the power only to make *recommendations* to the House of the People within a period of 14 days but no power of amending or rejecting the Bill. It shall lie at the hands of the House of the People to accept or reject the recommendations of the Council of States. In either case, the Bill will be deemed to be passed as soon as the House of the People decides whether it would accept or reject any of the recommendations of the Council of States and thereafter the Bill becomes law on receiving the assent of the President.

20e. Parliament's Control over the Financial System.

The financial system consists of two branches—revenue and expenditure.

(i) As regards revenue, it is expressly laid down by our Constitution [*Article 265*] that no tax shall be levied or collected except by authority of law. The result is that the Executive cannot impose any tax without legislative sanction. If any tax is imposed without legislative authority, the aggrieved person can obtain his relief from the courts of law.

(ii) As regards expenditure, the pivot of parliamentary control is the Consolidated Fund of India. This is the reservoir into which all the revenues received by the Government of India as well as all loans raised by it are paid and the Constitution provides that no moneys shall be appropriated out of the Consolidated Fund of India except in accordance with law [*Article 266(3)*]. This law means an Act of Appropriation passed in conformity with Article 114. Whether the expenditure is charged on the Consolidated Fund of India or it is an amount voted by the House of the People, no money can be issued out of the Consolidated Fund of India unless the expenditure is authorised by an Appropriation Act [*Article 114(3)*]. It follows, accordingly, that the executive cannot spend the public revenue without parliamentary sanction.

While an Act of Appropriation ensures that there cannot be any expenditure of the public revenues without the sanction of Parliament, Parliament's control over the expenditure cannot be complete unless it is able to ensure economy in the volume of expenditure. On this point, however, a reconciliation has to be made between two conflicting principles, namely, the need for parliamentary control and the responsibility of the Government in power for the administration and its policies.

20f. Committee on Estimates. The Government has the sole initiative in formulating its policies and in presenting its demands for carrying out those policies. Parliament can hardly refuse such demands or make drastic cuts in such demands without reflecting on the policy and responsibility of the Government in power. Nor is it expedient to suggest economies in different items of the expenditure proposed by the Government when the demands are presented to the House for its vote, in view of the shortage of time at its disposal. The scrutiny of the expenditure proposed by the Government is, therefore, made by the House in the informal atmosphere of a Committee, known as the Committee on Estimates. After the Annual Financial Statement is presented before the House of the People, this Committee of the House, annually constituted, examines the estimates, in order to:

(a) report to the House what economies, improvements, in organisation, efficiency or administrative reform, consistent with the policy underlying the estimates, may be effected;

(b) suggest alternative policies in order to bring efficiency and economy in administration;

(c) examine whether the money is well laid out within the limits of the policy implied in the estimates;

(d) suggest the form in which estimates are to be presented to Parliament.

Though the report of the Estimates Committee is not debated in the House, the fact that it carries on its examination throughout the year and places its views before the members of the House as a whole exerts a salutary influence in checking Governmental extravagance in making demands in the coming year, and in moulding its policies without friction in the House.

The third factor to be considered is the system of parliamentary control to ensure that the expenditure sanctioned by Parliament has actually been spent in terms of the law of Parliament, ie, the Appropriation Act or Acts. The office of the Comptroller and Auditor-General is the fundamental agency which helps Parliament in this work. The Comptroller and Auditor-General is the guardian of the public purse and it is his function to see that not a paisa is spent without the authority of Parliament. It is the business of the Comptroller and Auditor-General to audit the accounts of the Union and to satisfy himself that the expenditure incurred has been sanctioned by Parliament and that it has taken place in conformity with the rules sanctioned by Parliament. The Comptroller and Auditor-General then submits his report of audit relating to the accounts of the Union to the President who has to lay it before each House of Parliament.

20g. Committee on Public Accounts. After the report of the Comptroller and Auditor-General is laid before the Parliament, it is examined by the Public Accounts Committee. Though this is a Committee of the House of the People (having 15 members from that House), by an agreement between the two Houses, seven members of the Council of States are also associated with this Committee, in order to strengthen it. The Chairman of the Committee is generally a member of the Lok Sabha who is not a member of the ruling party.

In scrutinising the Appropriation Accounts of the Government of India and the report of the Comptroller and Auditor-General thereon it shall be the duty of the Committee on Public Accounts to satisfy itself—

(a) that the moneys shown in the accounts as having been disbursed were legally available for and applicable to the service or purpose to which they have applied or charged;

(b) that the expenditure conforms to the authority which governs it; and

(c) that every re-appropriation has been made in accordance with the provisions made in this behalf under rules framed by competent authority.

This Committee, in short, scrutinises the report of the Comptroller and Auditor-General in details and then submits its report to the House of the People so that the irregularities noticed by it may be discussed by Parliament and effective steps taken.

20h. Credit of Government Money.

All moneys received by or on behalf of the Government of India will be credited to either of two funds—the Consolidated Fund of India, or the "public account" of India. Thus,

(a) Subject to the assignment of certain taxes to the States, all *revenues* received by the Government of India, all *loans* raised by the Government and all moneys received by that Government in *repayment of loans* shall form one consolidated fund to be called "the Consolidated Fund of India" [*Article 266(1)*].

(b) All other public moneys received by or on behalf of the Government of India shall be credited to the Public Account of India [*Article 266(2)*], *e.g.*, moneys received by an officer or court in connection with affairs of the Union [*Article 284*].

No money out of the Consolidated Fund of India (or of a State) shall be appropriated except in accordance with a law of Appropriation. The procedure for the passing of an Appropriation Act has been already noted.

21. Contingency Fund of India.

Article 267 of the Constitution empowers Parliament and the Legislature of a State to create a "Contingency Fund" for India or for a State, as the case may be. The "Contingency Fund" for India has been constituted by the Contingency Fund of India Act, 1950. The Fund will be at the disposal of the executive to enable advances to be made, from time to time, for the purpose of meeting *unforeseen expenditure,* pending authorisation of such expenditure by the Legislature by supplementary, additional or excess grants. The amount of the Fund is subject to be regulated by the appropriate Legislature.

The custody of the Consolidated Fund of India and the Contingency Fund of India, the payment of moneys into such Funds, withdrawal of moneys therefrom, custody of public moneys other than those credited to such Funds, their payment into the public accounts of India and the withdrawal of moneys from such account and all other matters connected with or ancillary to matters aforesaid shall be regulated by law by Parliament, and, until provision in that behalf is so made shall be regulated by rules made by the President [*Article 283*].

22. Constitutional Position of the Council of States as Compared with that of the House of the People.

Though *our* Council of States does not occupy as important a place in the constitutional system as the American Senate, its position is not so inferior as that of the House of Lords as it stands today. *Barring the specific provisions with respect to which the lower House has special functions,* eg with respect to money Bills (see *below),* the Constitution proceeds on a theory of equality of status of the two Houses.

This equality of status was explained by the Prime Minister Pandit Nehru himself,[36] in these words—

> Under our Constitution Parliament consists of two Houses, each functioning in the allotted sphere laid down in the Constitution. We derive authority from that Constitution. Sometimes we refer back to the practice and conventions prevailing in the Houses of Parliament of the United Kingdom and even refer erroneously to an Upper House and a Lower House. I do not think that is correct. Nor is it helpful always to refer back to the procedure of the British Parliament which has grown up in the course of several hundred years and as a result of conflicts originally with the authority of the King and later between the Commons and the Lords. We have no such history behind us, though in making our Constitution we have profited by the experience of others.
>
> Our guide must, therefore, be our own Constitution which has clearly specified the functions of the Council of States and the House of the People. To call either of these Houses an Upper House or a Lower House is not correct. Each House has full authority to regulate its own procedure within the limits of the Constitution. Neither House by itself, constitutes Parliament. It is the two Houses together that are the Parliament of India ...That Constitution treats the two Houses equally, except in certain financial matters which are to be the sole purview of the House of the People. In regard to what these are, the Speaker is the final authority.

The Constitution also makes no distinction between the two Houses in the matter of selection of Ministers. In fact, during all these years, there have been several Cabinet Ministers from amongst the members of the Council of States, such as the Ministers for Home Affairs, Law, Railway and Transport, Production, Works, Housing and Supply, etc. But the responsibility of such member, as Minister, is to the House of the People [*Article* 75(3)].

The exceptional provisions which impose limitations upon the powers of the Council of States, as compared with the House of the People are:

(1) A Money Bill shall not be introduced in the Council. Even a Bill having financial provisions cannot be introduced in the Council.

(2) The Council has no power to reject or amend a Money Bill. The only power it has with respect to Money Bills is to suggest "recommendations" which may or may not be accepted by the House of the People, and the Bill shall be deemed to have been passed by both Houses of Parliament, without the concurrence of the Council, if the Council does not return the Bill within 14 days of its receipt or makes recommendations which are not accepted by the House.

(3) The Speaker of the House has got the sole and final power deciding whether a Bill is a Money Bill.

36. Statement in the Rajya Sabha, dated 6 May 1953. Similar views were reiterated in the other House (HP Deb, 12 May 1953).

(4) Though the Council has the power to discuss, it has no power to vote money for the public expenditure and demands for grants are not submitted for the vote of the Council.

(5) The Council of Ministers is responsible to the House of the People and not to the Council [*Article 75(3)*].

(6) Apart from this, the Council suffers, by reason of its numerical minority, in case a joint session is summoned by the President to resolve a deadlock between the two Houses [*Article 108(4)*].

On the other hand, the Council of States has certain special powers which the other House does not possess and this certainly adds to the prestige of the Council:

(a) Article 249 provides for temporary Union legislation with respect to a matter in the State List, if it is necessary in the national interest, but in this matter a special role has been assigned by the Constitution to the Council. Parliament can assume such legislative power with respect to a State subject only if the Council of States declares, by a resolution supported by not less than two-thirds of its members present and voting, that it is necessary or expedient in the national interest that Parliament should make laws for the whole or any part of the territory of India with respect to that matter while the resolution remains in force.

(b) Similarly, under Article 312 of the Constitution, Parliament is empowered to make laws providing for the creation of one or more All-India Services common to the Union and the States, if the Council of States has declared by a resolution supported by not less than two-thirds of the members present and voting that it is necessary or expedient in the national interest so to do.

In both the above matters, the Constitution assigns a special position to the Council because of its federal character and of the fact that a resolution passed by two-thirds of its members would virtually signify the consent of the States.

Notwithstanding these special functions, and the theory of equality propounded by Pandit Nehru, it is not possible for the Council of States, by reason of its very composition, to attain a status of equality with the House of the People. Even though there is no provision in the Constitution, corresponding to Article 169 relating to the upper Chamber in the States, for the abolition of the upper Chamber in Parliament, there has been, since the inauguration of the Constitution, a feeling in the House of the People that the Council serves no useful purpose and is nothing but a "device to flout the voice of the People", which led even to the motion of a Private Member's Resolution for the abolition of the Council. It was stayed for the time being only at the intervention of the then Prime Minister Pandit Nehru on the ground that the working of the Council was yet too short to adjudge its usefulness.

(c) The most extreme instance of its importance, during its career, has been shown by the Council of States in the matter of constitutional amendment. Under Article 368(2), a Bill for the amendment of the Constitution, in order to be law, must be passed in *each* House of Parliament by the specified special majority, and the device of joint sitting under Article 108 is *not* available to remove the opposition by the *Rajya Sabha* in respect of a Bill for amendment of the

Constitution. While the Janata party had an overwhelming majority in the *Lok Sabha,* the Congress [(O) and (I) together] had an imposing majority in the *Rajya Sabha* so that there was no chance of the 43rd Amendment Bill, 1977, being passed by a two-thirds majority in the *Rajya Sabha,* as its composition existed in April, 1977. The progress of the 43rd Amendment Bill had, therefore, to be halted after its introduction in the *Lok Sabha,* since the Congress party declared its intention to oppose the consideration of this Bill. The opposition of the two Congress Parties also truncated the 45th Constitution Amendment Bill, while in the *Rajya Sabha.*

The Constitution (64th Amendment) Bill, 1989 and the Constitution (65th Amendment) Bill, 1989 could not secure the requisite majority in the *Rajya Sabha* and hence could not be passed (13 October 1989), even though they had earlier been duly passed by the *Lok Sabha.*

23. Doctrine of Occupied Field.

The consistent view of the Supreme Court is that wherever the field is covered by the Parliamentary law in terms of List I and List III, the law made by the State Legislature would, to the extent of repugnancy, be void. Of course, there has to be a direct conflict between the laws. The direct conflict is not necessarily to be restricted to the obedience of one resulting in disobedience of other but even where the result of one would be in conflict with the other. It is difficult to state any one principle that would uniformly be applicable to all cases of repugnancy. It will have to be seen in the facts of each case while keeping in mind the laws which are in conflict with each other. Where the field is occupied by the Centre, subject to the exceptions stated in Article 254, the State law would be void.[37]

37. *Maa Vaishno Devi Mahila Mahavidyalaya v State of UP,* (2013) 2 SCC 617.

PART III

GOVERNMENT OF THE STATES

CHAPTER 13

THE STATE EXECUTIVE

1. State Executive.

As stated at the outset, *our* Constitution provides for a federal Government, having separate systems of administration for the Union and its Units, namely, the States. The Constitution contains provisions for the governance of both. It lays down a uniform structure for the State Government, in Part VI of the Constitution, which is applicable to all the States including the erstwhile State of Jammu & Kashmir. [Refer to Chapter 15 for details]

Broadly speaking, the pattern of Government in the States is the same as that for the Union, namely, a parliamentary system—the executive head being a constitutional ruler who is to act according to the advice of Ministers responsible to the State Legislature (or its popular House, where there are two Houses)—except in matters in respect of which the Governor of a State is empowered by the Constitution to act 'in his discretion' [*Article 163(1)*].

2. Governor.

At the head of the executive power of a State is the Governor just as the President stands at the head of the executive power of the Union. The executive power of the State is vested in the Governor and all executive action of the State has to be taken in the name of the Governor. Normally, there shall be a Governor for each State, but an amendment of 1956 makes it possible to appoint the same person as the Governor for the two or more States [*Article 153*].

3. Appointment and Term of Office of Governor.

The Governor of a State is not elected but is appointed by the President [*Article 155*] and holds his office at the pleasure of the President [*Article 156(1)*]. Any citizen of India who has completed 35 years of age is eligible for the office [*Article 157*], but he must not hold any other office of profit, nor be a member of the Legislature of the Union or of any State. There is no bar to the selection of a Governor from amongst members of a Legislature but if a Member of a Legislature is appointed Governor, he ceases to be a Member immediately upon such appointment [*Article 158*]. There is no bar to a person being appointed Governor more than once.[1]

The normal term of a Governor's office shall be five years, but it may be terminated earlier, by—(i) dismissal by the President, at whose 'pleasure' he

---

1. Thus, Sri VV Giri, who was appointed Governor of UP in 1958, was appointed Governor of Kerala in 1960 for the unexpired portion of his term and in June 1962 he was reappointed Governor of Kerala for a second term, limited up to June 1964 (*Statesman,* 10 June 1962), Srimati Padmaja Naidu, Governor of West Bengal, also got a second term.

holds the office [*Article 156(1)*]; (ii) resignation [*Article 156(2)*]. The grounds upon which a Governor may be removed by the President are not laid down in the Constitution, but it is obvious that this power will be sparingly used to meet with cases of gross delinquency, such as bribery, corruption, treason, and the like or violation of the Constitution.[2]

3a. Why an Appointed Governor?

The original plan in the Draft Constitution was to have elected Governors. But in the Constituent Assembly, it was replaced by the method of appointment by the President, upon the following arguments:[3]

(a) It would save the country from the evil consequences of still another election, run on personal issues. To sink every province into the vortex of an election with millions of primary voters but with no possible issue other than personal, would be highly detrimental to the country's progress.

(b) If the Governor were to be elected by direct vote, then he might consider himself to be superior to the Chief Minister, who merely returned from a single constituency, and this might lead to frequent *friction* between the Governor and the Chief Minister.

But under the Parliamentary system of Government prescribed by the Constitution, the Governor was to be the constitutional head of the State—the real executive power being vested in the Ministry responsible to the Legislature.

> When the whole of the executive power is vested in the Council of Ministers, if there is another person who believes that he has got the backing of the province behind him, and, therefore, at his discretion he can come forward and intervene in the governance of the province, it would really amount to a surrender of democracy.[3]

(c) The expenses involved and the elaborate machinery of election would be out of proportion to the powers vested in this Governor who was to act as a mere constitutional head.

(d) A Governor elected by adult franchise to be at the top of the political life in the State would soon prefer to be the Chief Minister or a Minister with effective powers. The party in power during the election would naturally put up for Governorship a person who was not as outstanding as the future Chief Minister with the result that the State would not be able to get the best man of the party. All the process of election would have to be gone through only to get a second rate man of the party elected as Governor. Being subsidiary in importance to the Chief Minister, he would be the nominee of the Chief Minister of the State, which was not a desirable thing.

(e) Through the procedure of appointment by the President, the Union Government would be able to maintain intact its control over the States.

(f) The method of election would encourage separatist tendencies. The Governor would then be the nominee of the Government of that particular

2. A glaring exception to this sound principle took place when the President, on the advice of the National Front Prime Minister Sri VP Singh, in December 1989, asked all the Governors to resign, simply because another Party had come to power at the Union. Of course, eventually, some of them were not required to resign.
3. Constituent Assembly Debates, vol. VII, p 455.

province to stand for the Governorship. The stability and unity of the Governmental machinery of the country as a whole could be achieved only by adopting the system of nomination.

> He should be a more detached figure acceptable to the province, otherwise he could not function, and yet may not be a part of the party machine of the province. On the whole it would probably be desirable to have people from outside, eminent in something, education or other fields of life who would naturally co-operate fully with the Government in carrying out the policy of the Government and yet represent before the public something above politics.[3]

The arguments which were advanced, in the Constituent Assembly, *against* nomination are also worthy of consideration:

(i) A nominated Governor would not be able to work for the welfare of a State because he would be a foreigner to that State and would not be able to understand its special needs.

(ii) There was a chance of friction between the Governor and the Chief Minister of the State no less under the system of nomination, if the Premier of the State did not belong to the same party as the nominated Governor.[4]

(iii) The argument that the system of election would not be compatible with the Parliamentary or Cabinet system of Government is not strong enough in view of the fact that even at the Centre there is an elected President to be advised by a Council of Ministers. Of course, the election of the President is not direct but indirect.

(iv) An appointed Governor under the instruction of the Centre might like to run the administration in a certain way contrary to the wishes of the Cabinet. In this tussle, the Cabinet would prevail and the President-appointed Governor would have to be recalled. The system of election, therefore, was far more compatible with good, better and efficient Government plus the right of self-Government.

(v) The method of appointment of the head of the State executive by the federal executive is repugnant to the strict federal system as it obtains in the *USA* and *Australia*.

3b. Status of Appointed Governors so Far.

In actual working, it may be said that in States where one party has a clear majority, the part played by the Governor has been that of a constitutional and impartial head, but in those states where there are multiple parties with an uncertain command over the Legislature, the Governor has acted as a mere agent of the Centre in various matters, such as inviting a person to form a Ministry, because he belonged to the ruling party at the Centre, even though he had no clear following (as in the case of Sri Rajagopalachari in Madras, after the General election in 1952) or bringing about the removal of a Ministry having the confidence of the Legislature, by means of a report under Article 356 (as happened in Kerala in 1959, in the case of the Communist Ministry headed by

4. Indeed there did occur some friction between the Governor and the Chief Minister during 1987-89 in Andhra Pradesh and Kerala where they belonged to different political parties. But, strikingly, there was disagreement between the Governor Govind Narain Singh and the Chief Minister of Bihar (1985); and Governor Smt. Sarla Grewal and the Chief Minister of Madhya Pradesh (1989) even though hailing from the same party.

Sri Namboodiripad). Nevertheless, there is one aspect in which the system of appointing an outsider by the Centre has proved to be beneficial, and that is the prevention of disruptive and separatist forces from impairing the national unity and strength as might otherwise have been possible without the knowledge of the Centre, under a locally elected Governor.

It is from this standpoint alone that one can tolerate the patently undemocratic instances of appointing a retiring or a retired member of the Indian Civil Service or the Indian Administrative Service (who is obviously a veteran bureaucrat) or of the Armed Forces as a Governor.

4. Conditions of Governor's Office.

A Governor gets a monthly emolument of Rs 3,50,000,[5] together with the use of an official residence free of rent and also such allowances and privileges as are specified in the Governor's (Emoluments, Allowances and Privileges) Act, 1982 as amended in 2009 (wef 1 January 2006). The emolument and allowances of a Governor shall not be diminished during his term of office [*Articles 158(3)-(4)*].

5. Powers of the Governor.

The Governor has no diplomatic or military powers like the President, but he possesses executive, legislative and judicial powers analogous to those of the President.

5a. Executive Powers.

Apart from the power to appoint his Council of Ministers, the Governor has the power to appoint the Advocate-General and the Members of the State Public Service Commission. The Ministers as well as Advocate-General hold office during the pleasure of the Governor, but the Members of the State Public Service Commission cannot be removed by him, they can be removed only by the President on the report of the Supreme Court on reference made by the President and, in some cases, on the happening of certain disqualifications [*Article 317*].

The Governor has no power to appoint judges of the state high court but he is entitled to be consulted by the President in the matter [*Article 217(1)*].

Like the President, the Governor has the power to nominate members of the Anglo-Indian community to the Legislative Assembly of his State, if he is satisfied that they are not adequately represented in the Assembly; but while the President's corresponding power with regard to the House of the People is limited to a maximum of two members, in the case of the Governor the limit is one member only, since the Constitution (23rd Amendment) Act, 1969 [*Article 333*].

As regards, the upper Chamber of the State Legislature (in States where the Legislature is bi-cameral), namely, the Legislative Council, the Governor has a power of nomination of members corresponding to the power of the President in relation to the Council of States, and the power is similarly exercisable in respect of "persons having special knowledge or practical experience in

5. The Governors (Emoluments, Allowances and Privileges) Act, 1982 (43 of 1982); Emoluments of Governor as enhanced *vide* Act No 27 of 1998, section 2 (wef 1 January 1996). Section 3 was again substituted by Act 1 of 2009 and made effective from 1 January 2006. The salary of the Governor of a State has been further enhanced to Rs. 350000/- per mensem by the Finance Act, 2018 and made effective from 1 January 2016.

respect of matters such as literature, science, art, co-operative movement and social service" [*Article 171(5)*]. It is to be noted that 'co-operative movement' is not included in the corresponding list relating to the Council of States. The Governor can so nominate 1/6th part of the total members of the Legislative Council.

5b. Legislative Powers.

As regards *legislative* powers, the Governor is a part of the State Legislature [*Article 164*] just as the President is a part of Parliament. Again, he has a right of addressing and sending messages, and summoning, proroguing and dissolving, in relation to the State Legislature, just as the President has in relation to Parliament.[6] He also possesses a similar power of causing to be laid before the State Legislature the annual financial statement [*Article 202*] and of making demands for grants and recommending 'Money Bills' [*Article 207*].

His powers of 'veto' over State legislation and of making Ordinances are dealt with separately. (See, Chapter 14, *post.*)

5c. Judicial Powers.

The Governor has the power to grant pardons, reprieves, respites, or remission of punishments or to suspend, remit or commute the sentence of any person convicted of any offence against any law relating to a matter to which executive power of the State extends [*Article 161*]. He is also consulted by the President in the appointment of the Chief Justice and the Judges of the High Court of the State.

5d. Emergency Power.

The Governor has no emergency powers[7] to meet the situation arising from external aggression or *armed rebellion* as the President has [*Article 352(1)*], but he has the power to make a report to the President whenever he is satisfied that a situation has arisen in which Government of the State cannot be carried on in accordance with the provisions of the Constitution [*Article 356*], thereby inviting the President to assume to himself the functions of the Government of the State or any of them. [This is popularly known as 'President's Rule'.]

6. Council of Ministers.

As has already been stated, the Governor is a constitutional head of the State executive, and has, therefore (subject to his discretionary functions noted below), to act on the advice of a Council of Ministers [*Article* 163]. The provisions relating to the Council of Ministers of the Governor are, therefore, subject to exceptions to be stated presently, similar to those relating to the Council of Ministers of the President.

---

6. Of course, as has been pointed out in other contexts, the Upper House of the Union Legislature, *ie,* the Council of States or of the State Legislature, *ie,* the Legislative Council, is not subject to dissolution but is subject to a system of periodical retirement. Hence, the President or the Governor's power of dissolution must be understood to refer to the dissolution of the House of the People and the Legislative Assembly, respectively.

   In those States where the State Legislature consists of one House only [*Article* 168(1)(b)], a dissolution of the Legislative Assembly results in the dissolution of the State Legislature (because there is no Legislative Council to survive).

7. Only the Governor of erstwhile State of Jammu & Kashmir was vested with the power to impose Governor's Rule under section 92 of the Constitution of J&K.

7. Appointment of Council of Ministers.

At the head of a State Council of Ministers is the *Chief Minister* (corresponding to the *Prime Minister* of the Union). The Chief Minister is appointed by the Governor,[8] while the other Ministers are appointed by the Governor on the advice of the Chief Minister. The Chief Minister cannot be constitutionally prohibited to give advice under Article 164(1) to the Governor in respect of a person, for becoming a Minister, who is charged for serious or heinous offences or offences relating to corruption.[9] The Council of Ministers shall be collectively responsible to the Legislative Assembly of the State and individually responsible to the Governor. The Ministers are jointly and severally responsible to the Legislature. He or they, is or are, publicly accountable for the acts or conducts in the performance of duties.[10] Any person[11] may be appointed a Minister (provided he has the confidence of the Legislative Assembly), but he ceases to be a Minister if he is not or does not remain, for a period of six consecutive months, a member of the State Legislature. No right is conferred on the non-member Minister concerned even during the period of six months when he is permitted to continue in office, to vote in the House. None of the powers or privileges of an MLA extend to that non-legislator Minister.[12] The salaries and allowances of Ministers are governed by laws made by the State Legislature [*Article 164*].

The Legislature of Assam lacks competence to enact the Assam Parliamentary Secretaries (Appointment, Salaries, Allowances and Miscellaneous Provisions) Act creating the post of Parliament Secretaries who are of the rank and status of a Minister of State in violation of Article 164(1A). This is wholly irrational way of construing the scope of Article 194(3) and Entry 39 of List I.[13]

8. Relationship between the Governor and his Ministers.

It may be said that, in general, the relation between the Governor and his ministers is similar to that between the President and his ministers, with this important difference that while the Constitution does not empower the President to exercise any function 'in his discretion', it authorises the Governor to exercise some functions 'on his discretion'. In this respect, the principle of Cabinet responsibility in the States differs from that in the Union.

Article 163(1) says—

> There shall be a Council of Ministers ... to aid and advise the Governor in the exercise of his functions, *except* in so far as he is by or under this Constitution required to exercise his functions or any of them in his discretion.

---

8. The Governor may appoint a person to be the Chief Minister on his own estimation that such person is likely to command a majority in the State Assembly and he can exercise this power even before the Assembly is fully constituted. Such act, itself, would not establish *mala fides* on the part of the Governor [*Rajnarain v Bhajanlal,* (1982) P&H, dated 20 October 1982; *Statesman* (D)/21 October 1982].
9. *Manoj Narula v UOI,* (2014) 9 SCC 1.
10. *Secretary, Jaipur Development Authority, Jaipur v Daulat Mal Jain,* (1997) 1 SCC 35 (para 10).
11. It is striking that no member of the 1975 Abdullah Ministry of Jammu & Kashmir was initially a member of the State Legislature.
12. *SR Chaudhuri v State of Punjab,* AIR 2001 SC 2707: (2001) 7 SCC 126.
13. *Bimolangshu Roy v State of Assam,* AIR 2017 SC 3552: (2018) 14 SCC 408.

It is because of this discretionary jurisdiction of the Governor that no amendment was made by the 42nd Amendment Act in Article 163(1) as in Article 74(1), which we have noticed in Chapter 11.

In the exercise of the functions which the Governor is empowered to exercise in his discretion, he will *not* be required to act according to the advice of his ministers or even to seek such advice. Again, if any question arises whether any matter is or is not a matter as regards which the Governor is required by the Constitution to act in his discretion, the decision of the Governor shall be final, and the validity of anything done by the Governor shall not be called into question on the ground that he ought or ought not to have acted in his discretion [*Article 163(2)*].

8a. Discretionary Functions of Governor.

The functions which are specially required by the Constitution to be exercised by the Governor in his discretion are—

(a) Para 9(2) of the 6th Schedule which provides that the Governor of Assam shall, in his discretion, determine the amount payable by the State of Assam to the District Council, as royalty accruing from licences for minerals.[14]

(b) Article 239(2) [added by the Constitution (7th Amendment) Act, 1956] which authorises the President to appoint the Governor of a State as the administrator of an adjoining Union Territory and provides that where a Governor is so appointed, he shall exercise his functions as such administrator 'independently of his Council of Ministers'.

8b. Other Discretionary Functions of Governor.

In view of the responsibility of the Governor to the President and of the fact that the Governor's decision as to whether he should act in his discretion in any particular matter is final [*Article 163(2)*], it would be possible for a Governor to act without ministerial advice in certain *other* matters, according to the circumstances, even though they are not specifically mentioned in the Constitution as discretionary functions.[15]

(i) As an instance to the point may be mentioned the making of a report to the President under Article 356, that a situation has arisen in which the Government of State cannot be carried on in accordance with the provisions of the Constitution. Such a report may possibly be made against a Ministry in power— for instance, if it attempts to misuse its powers to subvert the Constitution. It is obvious that in such a case the report cannot be made according to ministerial advice. No such advice again, will be available where one Ministry has resigned and another alternative Ministry cannot be formed. The making of a report under Article 356, thus, must be regarded as a function to be exercised by the Governor in the exercise of his discretion.

Obviously, the Governor is also the medium through whom the Union keeps itself informed as to whether the State is complying with the Directives issued by the Union from time to time.

---

14. The Naga Hills-Tuensang Area has been taken out of this discretionary sphere, by making it a separate State, named Nagaland. Hence, para 18 of the 6th Schedule has been omitted in 1971.
15. *Samsher v State of Punjab*, AIR 1974 SC 2192 (paras 47, 88, 153).

(ii) Further, after such a Proclamation as to failure of the Constitution machinery in the State is made by the President, the Governor acts as the agent of the President as regards those functions of the State Government which have been assumed by the President under the Proclamation [*Article 356(1)(a)*]. However, the validity of the Proclamation issued by the President under Article 356(1) is judicially reviewable to the extent of examining whether it was issued on the basis of any material at all or whether the material was relevant or whether the Proclamation was issued in the malafide exercise of the power. The Supreme Court or the High court can strike down the proclamation if it is found to be malafide or based on wholly irrelevant or extraneous grounds.[16] The power conferred by Article 356 upon the President is a conditioned power. It is not an absolute power.[17]

(iii) In some other matters, such as the reservation of a Bill for consideration of the President [*Article 200*], the Governor may not always be in agreement with his Council of Ministers, particularly when the Governor happens to belong to a party other than that of the Ministry. In such cases, the Governor may, in particular situations, be justified in acting without ministerial advice, if he considers that the Bill in question would affect the powers of the Union or contravene any of the provisions of the Constitution even though his Ministry may be of a different opinion.[18-19]

Article 200 of the Constitution relating to the passage of Bills except money Bills, requires Bills passed by the Legislative Assembly of a State, or in case of a State having a Legislative Council, a bill passed by both the houses of the Legislature of the State, to be presented to the Governor for assent. Such Bills become law on receipt of assent of the Governor.

The second proviso to Article 200 of the Constitution mandates the Governor to reserve for the consideration of the President, any Bill, which in the opinion of the Governor would, if it became law, so derogate from the powers of the high court, as to endanger the position which that court is, by the Constitution, designed to fill.[20]

9. Special Responsibilities of Governor.

Besides the above functions to be exercised by the Governor 'in his discretion', there are certain functions under the amended Constitution which are to be exercised by the Governor 'on his special responsibility'—which practically means the same thing as 'in his discretion', because though in cases of special responsibility, he is to

16. *SR Bommai v UOI,* (1994) 3 SCC 1 : [1994] 2 SCR 644 : AIR 1994 SC 1918.
17. *Rameshwar Prasad v UOI,* (2006) 2 SCC 1 : AIR 2006 SC 980; *KK Abu v UOI,* AIR 1965 Ker 229; *Special Reference No 1 of 2002* (popularly known as Gujarat Assembly Election matter), [(2002) 8 SCC 237].
18. This happened in the case of the Kerala Education Bill [*vide Re Kerala Education Bill* AIR 1958 SC 956]. In *Hoechst Pharmaceuticals v State of Bihar,* AIR 1953 SC 1019 : 1983 SCR (3) 130 (para 89), the function under Article 200 has been held to be discretionary.
19. In some cases, the Supreme Court has observed that unless a particular provision of the Constitution expressly *requires* the Governor to act in his discretion, his power to act without the advice of Ministers cannot be drawn by implication [*Sanjeevi v State of Madras,* (1970) 2 SCC 672 (*677*)]. But this observation is now to be read subject to the exceptional contingencies mentioned in the seven-Judge decision in *Samsher v State of Punjab,* AIR 1974 SC 2192 : 1975 SCR (1) 814, *above.*
20. See *Rajendra Diwan v Pradeep Kumar Ranibala,* LNIND 2019 SC 991.

consult his Council of Ministers, the final decision shall be 'in his individual judgment', which no court can question. Such functions are—

(i) Under Article 371(2), as amended,[21] the President may direct that the Governor of Maharashtra or Gujarat shall have a special responsibility for taking steps for the development of certain areas in the State, such as Vidarbha, Saurashtra.

(ii) The Governor of Nagaland shall, under Article 371A(1)(b) (introduced in 1962), have similar responsibility with respect to law and order in that State so long as internal disturbances caused by the hostile Nagas in that State continue.

(iii) Similarly, Article 371C(1), as inserted in 1971, empowers the President to direct that the Governor of Manipur shall have special responsibility to secure the proper functioning of the Committee of the Legislative Assembly of the State consisting of the members elected from the Hill Areas of that State.

(iv) Article 371F(g), inserted by the Constitution (36th Amendment) Act, 1975, similarly, imposes a special responsibility upon the Governor of Sikkim "for peace and for an equitable arrangement for ensuring the social and economic advancement of different sections of the population of Sikkim".

(v) Article 371H(a), inserted by the Constitution (55th Amendment) Act, 1986, similarly, imposes a special responsibility upon the Governor of Arunachal Pradesh "with respect to law and order in the State of Arunachal Pradesh and in the discharge of his functions in relation thereto, the Governor shall, after consulting the Council of Ministers, exercise his individual judgment as to the action to be taken".

> "Provided that if any question arises whether any matter is or is not a matter as respects which the Governor is under this sub-clause required to act in the exercise of his individual judgment, the decision of the Governor in his discretion shall be final, and the validity of anything done by the Governor shall not be called in question on the ground that he ought or ought not to have acted in the exercise of his individual judgment:
>
> Provided further that if the President on receipt of a report from the Governor or otherwise is satisfied that it is no longer necessary for the Governor to have special responsibility with respect to law and order in the State of Arunachal Pradesh, he may by order direct that the Governor shall cease to have such responsibility with effect from such date as may be specified in the order;"

(vi) Article 371J, inserted by the Constitution (98th Amendment) Act, 2012, similarly, imposes a special responsibility upon the Governor of Karnataka for:

> 1. (a) establishment of a separate development board for Hyderabad-Karnataka region, (b) equitable allocation of funds for developmental expenditure over the said region, (c) equitable opportunities and facilities for the people belonging to the said region in matters of public employment, education and vocational training, and may provide for;
>
> 2. (a) reservation of proportion of seats in educational and vocational training institutions in Hyderabad-Karnataka Region for students of the Region and (b) identification of posts or classes of posts under the State Government and in any

21. That is, as amended by the Constitution (7th Amendment) Act, 1956, and the Bombay Reorganisation Act, 1960. By the Constitution (32nd Amendment) Act, 1973, Andhra Pradesh has been taken out of Article 371 and provided for separately, in the *new* Article 371D.

body or organisation under the control of the State Government in the Hyderabad-Karnataka region and reservation of a proportion of such posts for persons of the Hyderabad-Karnataka Region.

In the discharge of such special responsibility, the Governor has to act according to the directions issued by the President from time to time, and subject thereto, he is to act 'in his discretion'. It has been held by the Supreme Court that the measure of discretionary power of the Governor, is limited to the scope postulated under Article 163(1). The discretionary power of the Governor extends to situations, wherein a constitutional provision expressly requires the Governor to act in his own discretion and the same cannot be construed otherwise.[22]

10. President's Control over the Governor.

It is obvious that as regards matters on which the Governor is empowered to act in his discretion or on his 'special responsibility', the Governor will be under the complete control of the President.

As regards other matters, however, though the President will have a personal control over the Governor through his power of appointment and removal,[23] it does not seem that the President will be entitled to exercise any effective control over the State Government against the wishes of a Chief Minister who enjoys the confidence of the State Legislature, though, of course, the President may keep himself informed of the affairs in the State through the reports of the Governor, which may even lead to the removal of the Ministry, under Article 356, as stated above.

11. Whether Governor is Competent to Dismiss a Chief Minister?

A sharp controversy has of late arisen upon the question whether a Governor has the power to dismiss a Council of Ministers, headed by the Chief Minister, on the *assumption* that the Chief Minister and his Cabinet have lost their majority in the popular House of the Legislature. The controversy has been particularly intriguing inasmuch as two Governors acted in contrary directions under similar circumstances. In West Bengal, in 1967, Governor Dharma Vira, being of the view that the United Front Ministry, led by Ajoy Mukherjee, had lost majority in the Legislative Assembly, owing to defections from that Party, asked the Chief Minister to call a meeting of Assembly at a short notice, and, on the latter's refusal to do so, dismissed the Chief Minister with his Ministry. On the other hand, in Uttar Pradesh in 1970, Governor Gopala Reddy dismissed Chief Minister Charan Singh, on a similar assumption, without even waiting for the verdict of the Assembly which was scheduled to meet only a few days later. Quite a novel thing happened in Uttar Pradesh in 1998 when Governor Romesh Bhandari, being of the view that the Chief Minister Kalyan Singh Ministry had lost majority in the Assembly, dismissed him without affording him opportunity to prove his majority on the floor of the House and appointed Shri Jagdambika Pal as the Chief Minister which was challenged by Shri Kalyan Singh before the High Court which by an

22. *Nabam Rebia v Deputy Speaker*, 2016 (2) SCALE 58 : (2016) 8 SCC 1.

23. The dismissal of the Tamil Nadu Governor, Prabhudas Patwari in October, 1980 [*Statesman*, 31 October 1980] demonstrates that the President's 'pleasure' under Article 156(1) can be used by the Prime Minister to dismiss any Governor for political reasons, and without assigning any cause.

interim order put Shri Kalyan Singh again in position as the Chief Minister. This order was challenged by Shri Jagdambika Pal before the Supreme Court which directed a "composite floor test" to be held between the contending parties which resulted in Shri Kalyan Singh securing majority. Accordingly, the impugned interim order of the High Court was made absolute.[24]

Before answering the question with reference to the preceding instances, it should be noted that the Cabinet system of Government has been adopted in *our* Constitution from the United Kingdom and some of the salient conventions underlying the British system have been codified in our Constitution. In the absence of anything to the contrary in the context, therefore, it must be concluded that the position under our Constitution is the same as in the United Kingdom.

In *England,* Ministers being legally the servants of the Crown, at law, the Crown has the power to dismiss each Minister individually or collectively. But upon the growth of the Parliamentary system, it has been established that the Ministers, *collectively*, hold their office so long as they command a majority in the House of Commons. This is known as the 'collective responsibility' of Ministers. The legal responsibility of the Ministers, as a collective body, to the Crown has thus been replaced by the *political* responsibility of the Ministry to Parliament, and the Crown's power to dismiss a Prime Minister of his Cabinet has become obsolete,—the last instance being 1783.[25] The Crown retains, however, his power to dismiss a Minister individually and, in practice, this power is exercised by the Crown on the advice of the Prime Minister himself, when he seeks to weed out an undesirable colleague.

Be that as it may, the above two propositions as they exist today in England have been codified in Clauses (1) and (2) of Article 164 of our Constitution as follows :

> (1) ... and the Ministers shall hold office at the pleasure of the Governor;
>
> (2) The Council of Ministers shall be collectively responsible to the Legislative Assembly of the State.

In the above context, the legitimate conclusion that can be drawn is that—

(a) The Governor has the power to dismiss an individual Minister at any time.

(b) He can dismiss a Council of Ministers or the Chief Minister (whose dismissal means a fall of the Council of Ministers), *only* when the Legislative Assembly has *expressed* its want of confidence in the Council of Ministers, either by a direct vote of no-confidence or censure or by defeating an important measure or the like, and the Governor does not think fit to dissolve the Assembly. The Governor cannot do so at his pleasure on his *subjective estimate* of the strength of the Chief Minister in the Assembly at any point of time, because it is for the Legislative Assembly to enforce the collective responsibility of the Council of Ministers to itself, under Article 164(2).

The above view of the Author has been upheld by the Supreme Court in *SR Bommai v UOI,*[26] (a nine-Judge Bench) by observing that wherever a doubt arises

24. *Jagdambika Pal v UOI,* (1999) 9 SCC 95 : AIR 1998 SC 998 : 1998 (2) SCALE 82.
25. *Vide Halsbury's Law of England,* 4th Edn, 1974, vol 8, pp 696-97.
26. *SR Bommai v UOI,* (1994) 3 SCC 1 : 1994 AIR 1918.

whether a Ministry has lost the confidence of the House, the only way of testing is on the floor of the House. The assessment of the strength of the Ministry is not a matter of private opinion of any individual, be he the Governor or the President.

12. Advocate-General for the State.

Each State shall have an Advocate-General for the State, an official corresponding to the Attorney-General of India, and having similar functions for the State. He shall be appointed by the Governor of the State and shall hold office during the pleasure of the Governor. Only a person who is qualified to be a Judge of a High Court can be appointed as Advocate-General. He receives such remuneration as the Governor may determine [*Article 165*]. The person beyond age of 62 years can also be appointed as Advocate-General.[27]

He shall have the right to speak and to take part in the proceedings of, but no right to vote in the Houses of the Legislature of the State [*Article 177*].

12a. Additional Advocate-General.

The Governor may appoint an Additional Advocate-General. His appointment is not in the constitutional scheme and does not hold constitutional office. However, such appointments must be held to have been made by the State in exercise of its executive power.[28]

27. *State of Uttaranchal v Balwant Singh Chaufal,* AIR 2010 SC 2550: 2010 AIR SCW 1029: (2010) 3 SCC 402.

28. *MT Khan v Government of Andhra Pradesh,* AIR 2004 SC 2934: (2004) 2 SCC 267.

CHAPTER 14

THE STATE LEGISLATURE

THOUGH a uniform pattern of Government is prescribed for the States, in the matter of the composition of the Legislature, the Constitution makes a distinction between the bigger and the smaller states. While the Legislature of every state shall include the Governor and, in some of the states, it shall consist of two Houses, namely, the Legislative Assembly and the Legislative Council, while in the rest, there shall be only one House, *i.e.*, the Legislative Assembly [*Article 168*].

1. The Bi-cameral and Uni-cameral Legislatures.

Owing to changes introduced since the inauguration of the Constitution, in accordance with the procedure laid down in Article 169, the States having two Houses[1] are Andhra Pradesh,[2] Bihar, Karnataka, Maharashtra, Tamil Nadu,[3] Telangana[4] and Uttar Pradesh[5] [*Article 168(1)(a)*]. It follows that in the remaining states, the Legislature is uni-cameral, that is, consisting of the Legislative Assembly only [*Article 168(1)(b)*].

A Legislative Assembly shall have its Speaker and Deputy Speaker, and a Legislative Council shall have its Chairman and Deputy Chairman, and the provisions relating to them are analogous to those relating to the corresponding officers of the Union Parliament.

2. Creation and Abolition of Legislative Councils in States.

But the above list is not permanent in the sense that the Constitution provides for the *abolition* of the Second Chamber (that is, the Legislative Council) in a State where it exists as well as for the *creation* of such a Chamber in a State where there is none at present, by a simple procedure

1. (a) The Legislative Council in Andhra Pradesh has been abolished by the Andhra Pradesh Legislative Council (Abolition) Act, 1985. (b) By reason of section 8(2) of the Constitution (Seventh Amendment) Act, 1956, Madhya Pradesh shall have a second House (Legislative Council) only after a notification to this effect has been made by President. No such notification having been made so far, Madhya Pradesh is still having one Chamber. (c) The Legislative Council of Tamil Nadu has been abolished in August, 1986, by passing the Tamil Nadu Legislative Council (Abolition) Act, 1986.
2. Revived by the Andhra Pradesh Legislative Council Act, 2005 (1 of 2006).
3. Inserted by the Tamil Nadu Legislative Council Act, 2010 (16 of 2010), section 3 (w. e. f. date of commencement of this Act has not notified so far).
4. State of Telangana has been created as the 29th State *vide* the Andhra Pradesh Reorganisation Act, 2014 (wef 2-6-2014).
5. West Bengal has abolished its Legislative Council wef 1-8-1969 by a notification under the West Bengal Legislative Council (Abolition) Act, 1969, and Punjab has abolished its Legislative Council, under the Punjab Legislative Council (Abolition) Act, 1969.

which does not involve an amendment of the Constitution. The procedure prescribed is a resolution of the Legislative Assembly of the State concerned passed by a special majority (*i.e.*, a majority of the total membership of the Assembly not being less than two-thirds of the members actually present and voting), followed by an Act of Parliament [*Article 169*].

This apparently extraordinary provision was made for the States (while there was none corresponding to it for the Union Legislature) in order to meet the criticism, at the time of the making of the Constitution, that some of *our* states being of poorer resources, could ill afford to have the extravagance of two Chambers. This device was, accordingly, prescribed to enable each state to have a Second Chamber or not according to its own wishes. It is interesting to note that, taking advantage of this provision, the State of Andhra Pradesh, in 1957, *created* a Legislative Council, leading to the enactment of the Legislative Council Act, 1957, by Parliament. Through the same process, it has been abolished in 1985. On the other hand, West Bengal and Punjab have abolished their Second Chambers, pursuing the same procedure.

3. Composition of the Legislative Council.

The size[6] of the Legislative Council shall vary with that of the Legislative Assembly,—the membership of the Council being not more than one-third of the membership of the Legislative Assembly but not less than 40. This provision has been adopted so that the Upper House (the Council) may not get a predominance in the Legislature [*Article 171(1)*].

The system of composition of the Council as laid down in the Constitution is not final. The final power of providing the composition of this Chamber of the State Legislature is given to the Union Parliament [*Article 171(2)*]. But until Parliament legislates on the matter, the composition shall be as given in the Constitution, which is as follows: It will be a partly nominated and partly elected body—the election being an indirect one and in accordance with the principle of proportional representation by the single transferable vote. The members being drawn from various sources, the Council shall have a variegated composition.

Broadly speaking, fifth-sixth of the total number of members of the Council shall be indirectly elected and one-sixth will be nominated by the Governor. Thus —

(a) One-third of the total number of members of the Council shall be elected by electorates consisting of members of *local bodies,* such as municipalities, district boards.

(b) One-twelfth shall be elected by electorates consisting of *graduates* of three years' standing residing in that state.

(c) One-twelfth shall be elected by electorates consisting of persons engaged for at least three years in *teaching* in educational institutions within the state, not lower in standard than secondary schools.

(d) One-third shall be elected by members of the Legislative Assembly from amongst persons who are *not members* of the Assembly.

(e) The remainder shall be nominated by the Governor from persons having knowledge or practical experience in respect of such matters as literature, science, art, co-operative movement and social service (The

6. See Table XIV for membership of the State Legislatures.

courts cannot question the *bona fides* or propriety of the Governor's nomination in any case).

4. Composition of the Legislative Assembly.

The Legislative Assembly of each State shall be composed of members chosen by *direct* election on the basis of adult suffrage from territorial constituencies. The number of members of the Assembly shall be not more than 500 nor less than 60. However, the Assembly in Nagaland shall not be less than 46 members; Sikkim, Arunachal Pradesh and Goa shall not be less than 30 members; and Mizoram shall not be less than 40 members.

There shall be a proportionately equal representation according to population in respect of each territorial constituency within a state. There will be a readjustment by Parliament by law, upon the completion of each census.

As stated already, the Governor has the power to nominate *one* member of the Anglo-Indian community as he deems fit, if he is of the opinion that they are not adequately represented in the Assembly [*Article 333*]. Such reservation will cease on the expiration of 70[7] years from the commencement of the Constitution [*Article 334*].

5. Duration of the Legislative Council.

The Legislative Council shall not be subject to dissolution. But one-third of its members shall retire on the expiry of every second year [*Article 172(2)*]. It will thus be a permanent body like the Council of States, only a fraction of its membership being changed every third year.

6. Duration of the Legislative Assembly.

The duration of the Legislative Assembly is five years, but—

(i) It may be dissolved sooner than five years, by the Governor.[8]

---

7. The original period of 10 years has been extended to 70 years, gradually by the Constitution (8th Amendment) Act, 1959, the 23rd Amendment Act, 1969, the 45th Amendment Act, 1980, the 62nd Amendment Act, 1989, the 79th Amendment Act, 1999, and the Constitution (95th Amendment) Act, 2009 (wef 25-1-2010). This period has been further extended to *eighty* years by the Constitution (104th) Act, 2019 (wef 25-1-2020) in respect to reservation of seats for the Scheduled Castes and the Scheduled Tribes in the House of the People and in the Legislative Assemblies of the States. The Constitution (104th) Act, 2019 (wef 25-1-2020) has not extended the period further for nomination of members of the Anglo-Indian community.

8. In this context, we should refer to the much-debated question as to whether the Governor has any discretion to dissolve the Assembly without or against the advice of the Chief Minister, or through the device of suspending the State Legislature under Article 356. In the general election to the *Lok Sabha*, held in March, 1977, the Congress Party was routed by the Janata Party. It was urged by the Janata Government at the Centre that in view of this verdict, the Congress Party had no moral right to continue in power in nine States, *viz.*, Bihar, Haryana, Himachal Pradesh, Madhya Pradesh, Orissa, Punjab, Rajasthan, Uttar Pradesh, West Bengal. In pursuance of this view, the Union Home Minister (Mr Charan Singh) issued on, 18 April 1977, an "appeal" to the Chief Ministers of these nine States to advise their respective Governors to dissolve the Assemblies and hold an election in June, 1977 (while their extended term would have expired in March, 1978). But the Congress Party advised the Chief Ministers not to yield to this appeal or pressure, and contended that the proposition that the English Sovereign can dissolve

[Footnote No. 8 Contd.]

(ii) The term of five years may be extended in case of a Proclamation of Emergency by the President. In such a case, the Union Parliament shall have the power to extend the life of the Legislative Assembly up to a period not exceeding six months after the Proclamation ceases to have effect, subject to the condition that such extension shall not exceed one year at a time [*Article 172(1)*]. A very unique situation arose in 2005 in Bihar where before even the first meeting of the Legislative Assembly, its dissolution had been ordered on the ground that, attempts were being made to cobble a majority by illegal means and lay claim to form the Government in the State, and if these attempts continued, it would amount to tampering with the constitutional provisions. The Supreme Court, while considering the question that whether, the Assembly had been duly constituted or not, so as to enable the Governor to exercise the power of dissolution under Article 174(2)(*b*), observed that the Assembly, for all intends and purposes, is deemed to be duly constituted on issue of notification under section 73 and the duration thereof, is distinct from its due constitution. Five years are to be computed from the date appointed for its first meeting and no longer. There is no restriction under Article 174(2)(*b*) stipulating that the power to dissolve the Legislative Assembly can be exercised only after its first meeting.[9] The constitution of any Assembly can only be under section 73 of the Representation of the People Act, 1951, and the requirement of Article 188 of

[Footnote No. 8 Contd.]

Parliament without the advice of the Prime Minister was wrong and obsolete and that the Crown's prerogative in this behalf had been turned into a privilege of the Prime Minister. In short, under the British Parliamentary system which had been adopted under the Indian Constitution, a Governor could not dissolve the Assembly contrary to the advice of the Chief Minister of the State. It was also urged that Article 356 was not intended to be used for such purposes.

The question was eventually taken to the Supreme Court by some of the affected States by way of a suit (under Article 131) against the Union of India. The suit was dismissed by a Bench of seven Judges, at the hearing on the prayer for temporary injunction, though the Judges gave separate reasons in six concurring judgments [*State of Rajasthan v UOI*, AIR 1977 SC 1361 : (1978) (1) SCR 1]. The Judges agreed on the following points: (i) The reasons behind an Executive decision to dissolve the Legislature are *political* and not justiciable in a court of law. (ii) So also is the question of the President's satisfaction for the purpose of using the power under Article 356, — unless it was shown that there was no satisfaction at all or the satisfaction was based on extraneous grounds [paras 59, 83 (Beg CJ); 124 (Chandrachud, J); 144 (Bhagwati & Gupta, JJ); 170 (Goswami, J); 179 (Untwalia, J); 206 (Fazal Ali, J)]. All the Judges held that on the facts on the record, it was not possible to hold that the order of the President under Article 356, suspending the constitutional system in the relevant States was actuated by *mala fides* or extraneous considerations.

Exercise of power under Article 356 was received again by a nine Judge Bench of the Supreme Court in *S R Bommai v UOI*, 1994 AIR 1918 : (1994) 3 SCC 1. Explaining the *Rajasthan* case it has laid down the following points: (i) Proclamation under Article 356 is subject to judicial review but to a limited extent, eg whether there was any material, whether it was relevant, whether *mala fide* etc. (ii) Till the proclamation is approved by Parliament it is not permissible for the President to take any irreversible action (such as dissolution of the House) under Article 356(1)(a), (b), or (c). (iii) Even if approved by the Parliament the Court may order *status quo ante* to be restored. (iv) If the ruling party in the State suffers a defeat in election to the Lok Sabha it will not be a ground for exercise of power under Article 356.

9. *Rameshwar Prasad v UOI*, AIR 2006 SC 980 : (2006) 2 SCC 1.

the Constitution suggests that the Assembly comes into existence even before its first sitting commences.[10]

7. Qualifications for Membership of the State Legislature. A person shall not be qualified to be chosen to fill a seat in the Legislature of a State unless he —

(a) is a citizen of India;

(b) is, in the case of a seat in the Legislative Assembly, not less than 25 years of age and, in the case of a seat in the Legislative Council, not less than 30 years of age; and

(c) possesses such other qualifications as may be prescribed in that behalf by or under any law made by Parliament [*Article 173*].

Thus, the Representation of the People Act, 1951, has provided that a person shall not be elected either to the Legislative Assembly or the Council, unless he is himself an elector for any Legislative Assembly constituency in that State.

8. Disqualifications for Membership. The disqualifications for membership of a State Legislature as laid down in Article 191 of the Constitution are analogous to the disqualifications laid down in Article 102 relating to membership of either House of Parliament. Thus, a person shall be disqualified for being chosen as, and for being a member of the Legislative Assembly or Legislative Council of a State if he—

(a) holds any office of profit under the Government of India or the Government of any State, other than that of a Minister for the Indian Union or for a State or an office declared by a law of the State not to disqualify its holder (many States have passed such laws declaring certain offices to be offices the holding of which will not disqualify its holder for being a member of the Legislature of that State);

(b) is of unsound mind as declared by a competent court;

(c) is an undischarged insolvent;

(d) is not a citizen of India or has voluntarily acquired the citizenship of a foreign State or is under any acknowledgment of allegiance or adherence to a foreign State;

(e) is so disqualified by or under any law made by Parliament (in other words, the law of Parliament may disqualify a person for membership even of a State Legislature, on such grounds as may be laid down in such law). Thus, the Representation of the People Act, 1951, has laid down some grounds of disqualification, eg, conviction by a court, having been found guilty of a corrupt or illegal practice in relation to election, being a director or managing agent of a corporation in which Government has a financial interest (under conditions laid down in that Act).

Further, he shall be disqualified for being a member of the Legislative Assembly or Legislative Council of a State if he is so disqualified under the Tenth Schedule. If any question arises as to whether a member of a House has become

10. *Special Reference No 1 of 2002 (popularly known as the Gujarat Assembly Election matter),* (2002) 8 SCC 237.

subject to disqualification under the Tenth Schedule, the question shall be referred for the decision of the Chairman or, as the case may be, the Speaker of such House and his decision shall be final. However, where the question which has arisen is as to whether the Chairman or the Speaker of a House has become subject to such disqualification, the question shall be referred for the decision of such member of the House as the House may elect in this behalf and his decision shall be final. [Article 191(2) and Para 6(1) to Schedule Tenth].

The only purpose of entrusting the work of adjudicating the disqualification petitions to the Speaker/Chairman was to avoid dilly-dallying in the courts of law or the Election Commission's office. Also the Parliament decided to entrust the important question of adjudication of disqualification petitions, on account of defection, to the Speaker/Chairman expecting him to decide them fearlessly and expeditiously. Parliament was conscious of the potential long delays that could arise if the petitions were left to be decided through court proceedings. To avoid such potential delays, that would defeat the purpose of the Tenth Schedule, the Parliament therefore intended to have a forum which facilitated the quick disposal of the disqualification proceedings.[11]

8a. Question whether Member is Disqualified or not?

Article 192 lays down that if any question arises as to whether a member of a House of the Legislature of a State has become subject to any of the disqualifications mentioned above, the question shall be referred to the Governor of that state for decision who will act according to the opinion of the Election Commission. His decision shall be final and not liable to be questioned in any court of law.

9. Legislative Procedure for Bills.

The legislative procedure in a State Legislature having two Chambers is broadly similar to that in Parliament, save for differences on certain points to be explained presently.

I. *As regards Money Bills,* the position is the same. The Legislative Council shall have no power save to make recommendations to the Assembly for amendments or to withhold the Bill for a period of 14 days from the date of receipt of the Bill. In any case, the will of the Assembly shall prevail, and the Assembly is not bound to accept any such recommendations. It follows that there cannot be any deadlock between the two Houses at all as regards Money Bills.

II. *As regards Bills other than Money Bills,* too, the only power of the Council is to interpose some *delay* in the passage of the Bill for a period of time (three months) [*Article 197(1)(b)*] which is, of course, larger than in the case of Money Bills. The Legislative Council of a State, thus, shall not be a revising but mere *advisory* or *dilatory* Chamber. If it disagrees to such a Bill, the Bill must have *second journey* from the Assembly to the Council, but ultimately the view of the Assembly shall prevail and in the second journey, the Council shall have no power to withhold the Bill for more than a month [*Article 197(2)(b)*].

Herein the procedure in a State Legislature differs from that in the Parliament, and it renders the position of the Legislative Council even weaker than that of the Council of the States. The difference is as follows:

---

11. *Padi Kaushik Reddy v State of Telangana,* AIR 2025 SC 3618 : AIROnline 2025 SC 687.

While disagreement between the two Houses of Parliament is to be resolved by a *joint sitting*, there is *no such provision* for solving differences between the two Houses of the State Legislature—in this latter case, the will of the lower House, *viz.*, the Assembly, shall ultimately prevail and the Council shall have no more power than to interpose some delay in the passage of the Bill to which it disagrees.

This difference of treatment in the two cases is due to the adoption of two different principles as regards the Union and the State Legislatures. (a) As to Parliament—it has been said that since the Upper House represents the federal character of the Constitution, it should have a status better than that of a mere dilatory body. Hence, the Constitution provides for a joint sitting of both Houses in case of disagreement between the House of the People and the Council of States, though of course, the House will ultimately have an upper hand, owing to its numerical majority at the joint sitting; (b) As regards the two Houses of the State Legislature, however, the Constitution of India adopts the English system founded on the Parliament Act, 1911, *viz.*, that the Upper House must eventually give way to the Lower House which represents the will of the people. Under this system, the Upper House has no power to obstruct the popular House other than to effect some delay. This democratic provision has been adopted in *our* Constitution in the case of the State Legislature inasmuch as in this case, no question of federal importance of the Upper House arises.

9a. Summarised Legislative Procedure for Bills.

The provisions as regards Bills *other than Money Bills* may now be summarised:

(a) *Parliament:* If a Bill (other than a Money Bill) is passed by one House and (i) the other House rejects it or does not return it within six months; or (ii) the two Houses disagree as to amendment, the President may convene a joint sitting of the Houses, for the purpose of finally deliberating and voting on the Bill. At such joint sitting, the vote of the *majority of both Houses present and voting shall prevail* and the Bill shall be deemed to have been passed by both Houses with such amendments as are agreed to by such majority; and the Bill shall then be presented for his assent [*Article 108*].

(b) *State Legislature:* (i) If a Bill (other than a Money Bill) is passed by the Legislative Assembly and the Council: (a) rejects the Bill; or (b) passes it with such amendments as are not agreeable to the Assembly; or (c) does not pass the Bill within *three months* from the time when it is laid before the Council—the Legislative Assembly may again pass the Bill with or without further amendments, and transmit the Bill to the Council again [*Article 197(1)*].

If on this second occasion, the Council—(a) again rejects the Bill; or (b) proposes amendments; or (c) does not pass it *within one month* of the date on which it is laid before the Council, the Bill shall be deemed to have been passed by both Houses, and then presented to the Governor for his assent [*Article 197(2)*].

In short, in the State Legislature, a Bill as regards which the Council does not agree with the Assembly, shall have two journeys from the Assembly to the Council. In the first journey, the Council shall not have the power to withhold the Bill for more than three months and in the second journey, not more than one month, and at the end of this period, the Bill shall be deemed to have been passed by both the Houses, even though the Council remains altogether inert [*Article 197*].

(ii) The foregoing provision of the Constitution is applicable only as regards Bills *originating in the Assembly.* There is no corresponding provision for Bills originating in the Council. If, therefore, a Bill passed by the Council is transmitted to the Assembly and rejected by the latter, there is an end to the Bill.

The relative positions of the two Houses of the Union Parliament and of a State Legislature may be graphically shown as follows:

I. As regards *Money Bills, the position* is similar at the Union and the States:

(a) A Money Bill cannot originate in the Second Chamber or Upper House (ie, the Council of States or the Legislative Council).

(b) The Upper House (*i.e.*, the Council of States or the Legislative Council) has no power to amend or reject such Bills. In either case, the Council can only make recommendations when a Bill passed by the lower House (*i.e.*, the House of the People or the Legislative Assembly, as the case may be) is transmitted to it. It finally rests with the lower House to accept or reject the recommendations made by the Upper House. If the House of the People or the Legislative Assembly (as the case may be) does not accept any of the recommendations, the Bill is deemed to have been passed by the Legislature in the form in which it was passed by the lower House and then presented to the President or the Governor (as the case may be), for his assent. If the lower House, on the other hand, accepts any of the recommendations of the Upper House, then the Bill shall be deemed to have been passed by the Legislature in the form in which it stands after acceptance of such recommendations.

On the other hand, if the Upper House does not return the Money Bill transmitted to it by the Lower House, within a period of 14 days from the date of its receipt in the Upper House, the Bill shall be deemed to have been passed by the Legislature, at the expiry of the period of 14 days, and then presented to the President or the Governor, as the case may be, even though the Upper House has not either given its assent or made any recommendations.

(c) There is no provision for resolving any deadlock as between the two Houses, as regards Money Bills, because no deadlock can possibly arise. Whether in Parliament or in a State Legislature, the will of the lower House (House of the People or the Legislative Assembly) shall prevail, in case the Upper House does not agree to the Bill as passed by the lower House.

II. *As regards Bills other than Money Bills*:

Parliament	*State Legislature*
(a) Such Bills may be introduced in either House of Parliament.	(a) Such Bills may be introduced in either House of a State Legislature.
(b) A Bill is deemed to have been passed by Parliament only if both Houses have agreed to the Bill in its	(b) The Legislative Council has no co-ordinate power, and in a case of disagreement between the two

Parliament	*State Legislature*
original form or with amendments agreed to by both Houses. In case of disagreement between the two Houses in any of the following manner, the deadlock may be solved only by a joint sitting of the two Houses, if summoned by the President.	Houses, the will of the Legislative Assembly shall ultimately prevail. Hence, there is no provision for a joint sitting for resolving a deadlock between the two Houses.
(c) The disagreement may take place if a House, on receipt of a Bill passed by the other House— (i) rejects the Bill; or (ii) proposes amendments as are not agreeable to the other House; or (iii) does not pass the Bill within six months of its receipt of the Bill.	(c) A disagreement between the two Houses may take place if the Legislative Council, *on receipt of a Bill passed by the Assembly*— (i) rejects the Bill; or (ii) makes amendments to the Bill, which are not agreed to by the originating House; or (iii) does not pass the Bill within three months from the date of its receipt from the originating House. While the period for passing a Bill received from the lower House is six months in the case of the Council of States, it is three months only in the case of the Legislative Council.
(d) In a case of disagreement, a passing of the Bill by the House of the People, a second time, cannot over-ride the Council of States. The only means of resolving the deadlock is a Joint sitting of the two Houses. But if the President, in his discretion, does not summon a joint sitting, there is an end of the Bill and, thus, the Council of States has effective power, subject to a joint sitting, of preventing the passing of a Bill.	(d) In case of such disagreement, a passing of the Bill by the Assembly for a second time is sufficient for the passing of the Bill by the Legislature, and if the Bill is so passed and transmitted to the Legislative Council again, the only thing that the Council may do is to withhold it for a period of one month from the date of its receipt of the Bill on its second journey. If the Council either rejects the Bill again, or proposes amendments not agreeable to the Assembly or allows one month to elapse without passing the Bill, the Bill shall be deemed to have been passed by the State Legislature in the form in which it is passed by the Assembly for the second time, with such amendments, if any, as have been made by the Council and as are agreed to by the Assembly.

Parliament	*State Legislature*
	(e) The foregoing procedure applies *only* in the case of disagreement relating to a Bill *originating in the Legislative Assembly.* In the case of a Bill originating in the Legislative Council and transmitted to the Assembly, after its passage in the Council, if the Legislative Assembly either rejects the Bill or makes amendments which are not agreed to by the Council, there is an immediate end of the Bill, and no question of its passage by the Assembly would arise.

10. Utility of the Second Chamber in a State. It has been clear that the position of Legislative Council is inferior to that of the Legislative Assembly so much so that it may well be considered as a surplusage.

(a) The very composition of the Legislative Council, renders its position weak, being partly elected and partly nominated, and representing various interests.

(b) Its very existence depends upon the will of the Legislative Assembly, because the latter has the power to pass a resolution for the abolition of the second Chamber by an Act of Parliament.

(c) The Council of Ministers is responsible only to the Assembly.

(d) The Council cannot reject or amend a Money Bill. It can only withhold the Bill for a period not exceeding 14 days or make recommendations for amendments.

(e) As regards ordinary legislation (ie, with respect to Bills other than Money Bills), too, the position of the Council is nothing but subordinate to the Assembly, for it can at most interpose a delay of four months (in two journeys) in the passage of a Bill originating in the Assembly and, in case of disagreement, the Assembly will have its way without the concurrence of the Council.

In the case of a Bill originating in the Council, on the other hand, the Assembly has the power of rejecting and putting an end to the Bill forthwith.

It will thus be seen that the second Chamber in a State is not even a revising body like the second Chamber in the Union Parliament which can, by its dissent, bring about a deadlock, necessitating a joint sitting of both Houses to effect the passage of the Bill (other than a Money Bill). Nevertheless, by reason of its composition by indirect election and nomination of persons having special knowledge, the Legislative Council commands a better caliber and even by its dilatory power, it serves to check hasty legislation by bringing to light the shortcomings or defects of any ill-considered measure.

11. Governor's Power when a Bill is Presented.

When a Bill is presented before the Governor after its passage by the Houses of the Legislature, it will be open to the Governor to take any of the following steps:

(a) He may declare his *assent* to the Bill, in which case, it would become law at once; or,

(b) He may declare that he withholds his assent to the Bill, in which case the Bill fails to become a law; or,

(c) He may, in the case of a Bill other than a Money Bill, return the Bill with a message.

(d) The Governor may reserve[12] a Bill for the consideration of the President. In one case reservation is compulsory, *viz.,* where the law in question would derogate from the powers of the high court under the Constitution.

In the case of a Money Bill, so reserved, the President may either declare his assent or withhold his assent. But in the case of a Bill other than a Money Bill, the President may, instead of declaring his assent or refusing it, direct the Governor to *return* the Bill to the Legislature for reconsideration. In the latter case, the Legislature must reconsider the Bill within six months and if it is passed again, the Bill shall be presented to the President again. But it shall not be obligatory upon the President to give his assent in this case too [*Article 201*].

It is clear that a Bill which is reserved for the consideration of the President shall have no legal effect until the President declares his assent to it. But no time limit is imposed by the Constitution upon the President either to declare that he assents or that he withholds his assent. As a result, it would be open to the President to keep a Bill of the State Legislature pending at his hands for an indefinite period of time, without expressing his mind.

It should also be noted that there is a third alternative for the President which was demonstrated in the case of the Kerala Education Bill, *viz,* that when a reserved Bill is presented to the President he may, for the purpose of deciding whether he should assent to, or return the Bill, refer to the Supreme Court, under Article 143, for its advisory opinion where any doubts as to the constitutionality of the Bill arise in the President's mind.

12. Veto Powers of President and Governor, Compared.

The veto powers of the President and Governor may be presented graphically, as follows:

President	*Governor*
(A) 1. May assent to the Bill passed by the Houses of Parliament.	1. May assent to the Bill passed by the State Legislature.
2. May declare that he withholds his assent, in which case, the Union Bill fails to become law.	2. May declare that he withholds his assent, in which case, it fails to become law.

12. The entire function of reservation and veto is discretionary and non-justiciable [*Hoechst Pharmaceuticals v State of Bihar*, AIR 1953 SC 1019 : (1983) 3 SCR 130, para 89].

President	*Governor*
3. In case of a Bill other than a Money Bill, may return it for reconsideration by Parliament, with a message to both Houses. If the Bill is again passed by Parliament, with or without amendments, and again presented to the President, the President shall have no other alternative than to declare his assent to it.	3. In case of a Bill other than a Money Bill, may return it for reconsideration by the State Legislature, with a message. If the Legislature again passes the Bill with or without amendments, and it is again presented to the Governor, the Governor shall have no other alternative than to declare his assent to it.
	4. Instead of either assenting to, withholding assent from, or returning the Bill for reconsideration by the State Legislature, Governor may *reserve* a Bill for consideration of the President, in any case he thinks fit. Such reservation is, however, obligatory if the Bill is so much derogatory to the powers of the high court that it would endanger the constitutional position of the high court, if the Bill became law.
(B) In the case of a State Bill reserved by the Governor for the President's consideration (as stated in para 4 of column 2): (a) If it is a Money Bill, the President may either declare that he assents to it or withholds his assent to it. (b) If it is a Bill other than a Money Bill, the President may — (i) declare that he assents to it or that he withholds his assent from it, or (ii) return the Bill to the State Legislature with a message for reconsideration, in which case, the State Legislature must reconsider the Bill within six months, and if it is passed again, with or without amendments, it must be again presented, *direct*, to the President for his assent, but the President is *not* bound to give his assent, even though the Bill has been passed by the State Legislature, for a second time.	Once the Governor reserves a Bill for the President's consideration, the subsequent enactment of the Bill is in the hands of the President and the Governor shall have no further part in its career.

13. Ordinance-making Power of Governor.

The Governor's power to make Ordinances [*Article 213*], having the force of an Act of the State Legislature, is similar to the Ordinance-making power of the President in the following respects:

(a) The Governor shall have this power only when the Legislature, or both Houses thereof, are not in session;

(b) It is not a discretionary power, but must be exercised with the aid and advice of ministers;

(c) The Ordinance must be laid before the State Legislature when it re-assembles, and shall automatically cease to have effect at the expiration of six weeks from the date of re-assembly, unless disapproved earlier by that Legislature.

(d) The Governor himself shall be competent to withdraw the Ordinance at any time.

(e) The scope of the Ordinance-making power of the Governor is co-extensive with the legislative powers of the State Legislature, and shall be confined to the subjects in Lists II and III of Schedule VII.

But as regards repugnancy with a Union law relating to a *concurrent* subject the Governor's Ordinance will prevail notwithstanding repugnancy, if the Ordinance had been made in pursuance of "instructions" of the President.

The peculiarity of the Ordinance-making power of the Governor is that he cannot make Ordinances without "instructions" from the President if—

(a) A Bill containing the same provisions would under the Constitution have required the previous sanction of the President for the introduction thereof into the Legislature;[13] or

(b) the Governor would have deemed it necessary to reserve a Bill containing the same provisions for the consideration of the President;[14] or

(c) an Act of the Legislature of the State containing the same provisions would under this Constitution have been invalid unless, having been reserved for the consideration of the President, it had received the assent of the President[15] [*Article* 213].

14. Ordinance-making Power of President and Governor, Compared.

The Ordinance-making powers of the President and a Governor may be graphically presented as follows:

President	*Governor*
1. Can make Ordinance only when either of the two Houses of Parliament is not in session.	1. Can make Ordinance only when the State Legislature or either of the two Houses (where the State

13. *E.g.*, An Ordinance imposing reasonable restrictions upon inter-State trade or commerce [*Article 304, proviso*].
14. *E.g.*, An Ordinance which might affect the powers of the Union [*Article 220*].
15. *E.g.*, An Ordinance affecting powers of the high court [*second proviso to Article 200*].

<table>
<tr><th>President</th><th>Governor</th></tr>
<tr><td></td><td>Legislature is bi-cameral) is not in session.</td></tr>
<tr><td colspan="2">The President or Governor must be satisfied that circumstances exist which render it necessary for him to take immediate action.</td></tr>
<tr><td></td><td>But Governor cannot make an Ordinance relating to three specified matters, without instructions from President (see above).</td></tr>
<tr><td>2. Ordinance has the same force and is subject to the same limitations as an Act of Parliament.</td><td>2. Ordinance has the same force and is subject to the same limitations as an Act of the State Legislature.</td></tr>
<tr><td></td><td>But as regards repugnancy with a Union law relating to a Concurrent subject, if the Governor's Ordinance has been made in pursuance of "instructions of the President", the Governor's Ordinance shall prevail as if it were an Act of the State Legislature which had been reserved for the consideration of the President and assented to by him.</td></tr>
<tr><td>3. (a) Must be laid before both Houses of Parliament when it re-assembles.</td><td>3. (a) Must be laid before the Legislative Assembly or before both Houses of the State Legislature (where it is bi-cameral), when the Legislature re-assembles.</td></tr>
<tr><td>(b) Shall cease to operate on the expiry of six weeks from the re-assembly of Parliament or, if, before that period, resolutions disapproving the Ordinance are passed by both Houses, from the date of the second of such resolutions.</td><td>(b) Shall cease to operate on the expiry of six weeks from the re-assembly of the State Legislature or, if before the expiry of that period, resolutions disapproving the Ordinance are passed by the Assembly or, where there are two Houses the resolution passed by the Assembly is agreed to by the Council, from the date of the passing of the resolution by the Assembly in the first case, and of the agreement of the Council in the second case.</td></tr>
</table>

15. Privileges of a State Legislature.

The privileges of the Legislature of a State are similar to those of the Union Parliament inasmuch as the constitutional provisions [*Articles 105 and 194*] are identical. The question of the privileges of a State Legislature has been brought to the notice of the public, particularly in relation to the power of the Legislature to punish for contempt and the jurisdiction of the courts in respect thereof. Though all aspects of this question have not yet been settled, the following propositions may be formulated from the decisions of the Supreme Court:

(a) Each House of the State Legislature has the power to punish for breach of its privileges or for contempt.

(b) Each House is the sole judge of the question whether any of its privileges has, in particular case, been infringed, and the courts have no jurisdiction to interfere with the decision of the House on this point.

The court cannot interfere with any action taken for contempt unless the Legislature or its duly authorised officer is seeking to assert a privilege not known to the law of Parliament; or the notice issued or the action taken was without jurisdiction.

(c) No House of the Legislature has, however, the power to create for itself any new privilege not known to the law and the courts possess the power to determine whether the House in fact possesses a particular privilege.

(d) It is also competent for a high court to entertain a petition for *habeas corpus* under Article 226 or for the Supreme Court, under Article 32, challenging the legality of a sentence imposed by a Legislature for contempt on the ground that it has violated a fundamental right of the petitioner and to release the prisoner on bail, pending disposal of that petition.

(e) But once a privilege is held to exist, it is for the House to judge the occasion and its manner of exercise. The court cannot interfere with an *erroneous* decision by the House or its Speaker in respect of a breach of its privilege.

16. New States Added Since 1950.

Apart from those States which have merely changed their names (*e.g.*, Madras has changed its name to *Tamil Nadu;* Mysore to *Karnataka;* United Provinces was renamed Uttar Pradesh immediately after the adoption of the Constitution), there has been an addition of various items in the list of States in the First Schedule to the Constitution, by reason of which a brief note should be given as to the *new* items to make the reader familiar as to their identity.

(1) *Andhra Pradesh:* The State of "Andhra" was created by the Andhra State Act, 1953, comprising certain areas taken out of the State of Madras, and it was renamed "Andhra Pradesh" by the States Reorganisation Act, 1956.

(2) *Gujarat and Maharashtra:* The Bombay Reorganisation Act, 1960 split up the State of Bombay into two States, Gujarat and Maharashtra.

(3) *Kerala:* The State of Kerala was created by the States Reorganisation Act, 1956, in place of the Part B State of Travancore-Cochin of the original Constitution.

(4) *Nagaland:* Nagaland was created a separate State by the State of Nagaland Act, 1962, by taking out the Naga Hills-Tuensang area out of the State of Assam.

(5) *Haryana:* By the Punjab Reorganisation Act, 1966, the 17th State of the Union of India was constituted by the name of Haryana, by carving out a part of the territory of the State of Punjab.

(6) *Karnataka:* The State of Mysore was formed by the States Reorganisation Act, 1956, out of the original Part B State of Mysore. It has been renamed, in 1973, as *Karnataka.*

(7) *Himachal Pradesh:* Some of the Union Territories had, of late, been demanding promotion to the status of a State. Of these, Himachal Pradesh became the fore-runner on the enactment of the State of Himachal Pradesh Act, 1970, by which Himachal Pradesh was added as the 18th State in the list of States, and omitted from the list of Union Territories, in the First Schedule of the Constitution.

(8) *Manipur and Tripura:* Manipur and Tripura were also lifted up from the status of Union Territories (original Part C States), by the North-Eastern Areas (Reorganisation) Act, 1971.

(9) *Meghalaya:* Meghalaya was initially created a "sub-State" or "autonomous State" within the State of Assam, by the Constitution (22nd Amendment) Act, 1969, by the insertion of Articles 241 and 371A. Subsequently, it was given the full status of a state and admitted in the First Schedule as the 21st State, by the North-Eastern Area (Reorganisation) Act, 1971.

(10) *Sikkim:* As has been explained earlier, Sikkim (a Protectorate of India) was given the status of an "associate State" by the Constitution (35th Amendment) Act, 1974, and thereafter added to the First Schedule as the 22nd State, by the Constitution (36th Amendment) Act, 1975.

(11) *Mizoram:* By the State of Mizoram Act, 1986, Mizoram was elevated from the status of a Union Territory to be the 23rd State in the First Schedule of the Constitution.

(12) *Arunachal Pradesh:* Statehood was conferred on the Union Territory of Arunachal Pradesh, by enacting the State of Arunachal Pradesh Act, 1986.

(13) *Goa:* Goa was separated from Daman and Diu and made a State, by the Goa, Daman and Diu Reorganisation Act, 1987.

(14) *Chhattisgarh:* Chhattisgarh was carved out of the territories of the Madhya Pradesh by the Madhya Pradesh Reorganisation Act, 2000.

(15) *Uttaranchal:* Initially, Uttaranchal was created out of the territories of the Uttar Pradesh by the Uttar Pradesh Reorganisation Act, 2000. It was renamed as Uttarakhand by the Uttaranchal (Alteration of Name) Act, 2006.

(16) *Jharkhand:* Jharkhand was created by carving out a part of the territories of the Bihar by the Bihar Reorganisation Act, 2000.

(17) *Telangana:* Telangana was created by carving out a part of the territory of Andhra Pradesh by the Andhra Pradesh Reorganisation Act, 2014.

CHAPTER 15

JAMMU & KASHMIR

1. Peculiar Position and Special Status.

THE erstwhile State of Jammu & Kashmir held a peculiar position under the Constitution of India. It formed a part of the "territory of India" as defined in Article 1 of the Constitution, being the 15th State included in the First Schedule of the Constitution. In the original Constitution, Jammu & Kashmir was specified as a "Part B" State. The States Reorganisation Act, 1956, abolished the category of Part B States, and the Constitution (Seventh Amendment) Act, 1956, which implemented the changes introduced by the former Act, included Jammu & Kashmir in the list of the "States" of the Union of India, all of which were now included in one category.

Nevertheless, the special Constitutional position which Jammu & Kashmir enjoyed under the original Constitution [*Article 370*] was maintained, so that all the provisions of the Constitution of India relating to the States in the First Schedule were *not* applicable to Jammu & Kashmir even though it was one of the States specified in that Schedule.

2. History of the Integration of Jammu and Kashmir with India.

To understand why Jammu & Kashmir, being a State included in the First Schedule of the Constitution of India, was accorded a separate treatment, a retrospect of the development of the constitutional relationship of the State with India becomes necessary. Under the British regime, Jammu & Kashmir was an Indian State ruled by a hereditary Maharaja. On 26 October 1947, when the State was attacked by Azad Kashmir Forces with the support of Pakistan, the Maharaja (Sir Hari Singh) was obliged to seek the help of India, after executing an Instrument of Accession similar to that executed by the Rulers of other Indian States. By the Accession, the Dominion of India acquired jurisdiction over the State with respect to the subjects of Defence, External Affairs, and Communications, and like other Indian States which survived as political units at the time of the making of the Constitution of India, the State of Jammu & Kashmir was included as a Part B State in the First Schedule of the Constitution of India, as it was promulgated in 1950.

2a. Position of the State under the Original Constitution of India.

But though the State was included as a Part B State, all the provisions of the Constitution applicable to Part B States were not extended to Jammu & Kashmir. This peculiar position was due to the fact that having regard to the circumstances in which the State acceded to India, the Government of India had declared that it was the people of the State of Jammu & Kashmir, acting through their Constituent Assembly, who were to finally determine the Constitution of the State and the jurisdiction of the Union of

India. The applicability of the provisions of the Constitution regarding this State were, accordingly, to be in the nature of an interim arrangement. (This was the substance of the provision embodied in Article 370 of the Constitution of India.)

2b. Implications of the Accession.

Since the liberality of the Government of India has been misunderstood and misinterpreted in interested quarters, overlooking the *legal* implications of the Accession of the State to India, we should pause for a moment to explain these legal implications lest they be lost sight of in the turmoil of political events which have clouded the patent fact of the Accession. The first thing to be noted is that the Instrument of Accession signed by Maharaja Hari Singh on 26 October 1947, was in the *same form*[1] as was executed by the Rulers of the numerous other States which had acceded to India following the enactment of the Indian Independence Act, 1947. The legal consequences of the execution of the Instrument of Accession by the Ruler of Jammu & Kashmir cannot, accordingly, be in any way different from those arising from the same fact in the case of the other Indian States. It may be recalled[2] that owing to the lapse of paramountcy under section 7(1)(b) of the Indian Independence Act, 1947, the Indian States regained the position of absolute sovereignty which they had enjoyed prior to the assumption of suzerainty by the British Crown. The Rulers of the Indian States thus became unquestionably competent to accede to either of the newly created Dominions of India and Pakistan, in exercise of their sovereignty. The legal basis[3] as well as the form of Accession were the same in the case of those States which acceded to Pakistan and those which acceded to India. There is, therefore, no doubt that by the act of Accession the State of Jammu & Kashmir became *legally and irrevocably* a part of the territory of India and that the Government of India was entitled to exercise jurisdiction over the State with respect to those matters to which the Instrument of Accession extended. If, in spite of this, the Government of India had given an assurance to the effect that the Accession or the constitutional relationship between India and the State would be subject to confirmation by the people of the State, under no circumstances can any *third party* take advantage of such extra-legal assurances and claim that the legal act had not been completed.

2c. Articles of the Constitution which Apply of their Own Force to the State.

When India made her Constitution in 1949, it is natural that this dual attitude of the Government of India should be reflected in the position offered to the State of Jammu & Kashmir within the framework of that Constitution. The act of Accession was unequivocally given legal effect by declaring Jammu & Kashmir a part of the territory of India [*Article* 1]. But the application of the other provisions of the Constitution of India to Jammu & Kashmir was placed on a tentative basis, subject to the eventual approval of the Constituent Assembly of the State. The Constitution thus provided that the only Articles of the Constitution which would apply of their own force to Jammu & Kashmir were—*Articles* 1 and 370. The application of the other Articles was to be determined by the President in consultation with the Government of the State

1. *Vide White Paper on Indian States*, 1950, Ministry of States, Government of India, Part 11, (MS 6) rule, pp 111, 165.
2. *Vide* Author's *Commentary on the Constitution of India*, 5th Edn, vol 4, p 38.
3. Sections 5–6 of the Government of India Act, 1935, read with section 7(1)(b) of the Indian Independence Act, 1947.

[*Article 370*]. The legislative authority of Parliament over the State was confined to those items of the Union and Concurrent Lists as corresponded to matters specified in the Instrument of Accession. The above interim arrangement was to continue until the Constituent Assembly for Jammu & Kashmir made its decision. It would then communicate its recommendations to the President, who would either abrogate Article 370 or make such modification as might be recommended by that Constituent Assembly.

2d. The Constitution Order of 1950.

In pursuance of the above provisions of the Constitution, the President made the Constitution (Application to Jammu & Kashmir) Order, 1950, in consultation with the Government of the State of Jammu & Kashmir, specifying the matters with respect to which the Union Parliament would be competent to make laws for Jammu & Kashmir, relating to the three subjects of Defence, Foreign Affairs, and Communications, with respect to which Jammu & Kashmir had acceded to India.

2e. Subsequent Constitutional Orders.

Next, there was an Agreement between the Government of India and of the State at Delhi in June 1952, as to the subjects over which the Union should have jurisdiction over the State, pending the decision of the Constituent Assembly of Jammu & Kashmir. The Constituent Assembly of Jammu & Kashmir ratified the Accession to India, and also the decision arrived at by the Delhi Agreement as regards the future relationship of the State with India, early in 1954. In pursuance of this, the President, in consultation with the State Government, made the *Constitution (Application to Jammu & Kashmir), Order, 1954,* which came into force on 14 May 1954. This Order implemented the Delhi Agreement as ratified by the Constituent Assembly and superseded the Order of 1950. According to this Order, in short, the jurisdiction of the Union extended to *all* Union subjects under the Constitution of India (subject to certain slight alterations) instead of only the three subjects of Defence, Foreign Affairs and Communications with respect to which the State had acceded to India in 1947. This Order, as amended from time to time dealt with the entire Constitutional position of the State within the framework of the Constitution of India, excepting only the internal constitution of the State Government, which was to be framed by the Constituent Assembly of the State.[4]

3. Making of the State Constitution.

It has already been explained how from the beginning it was declared by the Government of India that, notwithstanding the Accession of the State of Jammu & Kashmir to India by the then Ruler, the future Constitution of the State as well as its relationship with India were to be finally determined by an elected Constituent Assembly of the State. With these objects in view, the people of the State elected a sovereign Constituent Assembly which met for the first time on 31 October 1951.

The Constitution (Application to Jammu & Kashmir) Order, 1954, which settled the constitutional relationship of the State of Jammu & Kashmir, did not

4. Author's *Commentary on The Constitution of India*, 6th Edn, vol P, p 27. Momentous other changes were proposed to be introduced after the agreement arrived at between the Government of India and Sheikh Abdullah, in February 1975. But this agreement could not be implemented owing to difference in matter of detail.

disturb the previous assurances as regards the framing of the *internal* Constitution of the State by its own people. While the Constitution of the other Part B States was laid down in Part VII of the Constitution of India (as promulgated in 1950), the State Constitution of Jammu & Kashmir was to be framed by the Constituent Assembly of that State. In other words, the provisions governing the Executive, Legislature, and Judiciary of the State of Jammu & Kashmir were to be found in the Constitution drawn up by the people of the State, and the corresponding provisions of the Constitution of India were not applicable to that State.

The first official act of the Constituent Assembly of the State was to put an end to the hereditary princely rule of the Maharaja. It was one of the conditions of the acceptance of the accession by the Government of India that the Maharaja would introduce popular government in the State. In pursuance of this understanding, immediately after the Accession, the Maharaja invited Sheikh Mohammad Abdullah, President of the All Jammu & Kashmir National Conference, to form an interim Government, and to carry on the administration of the State. The interim Government later changed into a full-fledged Cabinet, with Sheikh Abdullah as the first Prime Minister. The Abdullah Cabinet, however, would not rest content with anything short of the abdication of the ruling Maharaja Sir Hari Singh. In June 1949, thus, Maharaja Hari Singh was obliged to abdicate in favour of his son Yuvaraj Karan Singh. The Yuvaraj was later *elected* by the Constituent Assembly of the State (which came into existence on 31 October 1951) as the "*Sadar-i-Riyasat*". Thus, came to an end the princely rule in the State of Jammu & Kashmir and the head of the State was henceforth to be an elected person. The Government of India accepted this position by making a Declaration of the President under Article 370(3) of the Constitution (15 November 1952) to the effect that for the purposes of the Constitution, "Government" of the State of Jammu & Kashmir shall mean the *Sadar-i-Riyasat* of Jammu & Kashmir, acting on the advice of the Council of Ministers of the State. Subsequently, however, the name of *Sadar-i-Riyasat* was changed to that of Governor.

We have already seen that in February 1954, the Constituent Assembly of Jammu & Kashmir ratified the State's Accession to India, thus fulfilling the moral assurance given in this behalf by the Government of India. We have also seen that this act of the Constituent Assembly was followed up by the promulgation by the President of India of the Constitution (Application to Jammu & Kashmir) Order, 1954, placing on a final footing the applicability of the provisions of the Constitution of India governing the relationship between the Union and this State.

The making of the State Constitution for the internal governance of the State was now the only task left to the Constituent Assembly. As early as November 1951, the Constituent Assembly had made the Jammu & Kashmir Constitution (Amendment) Act, which gave legal recognition to the transfer of power from the hereditary Maharaja to the popular Government headed by an elected *Sadar-i-Riyasat*. For the making of the permanent Constitution of the State, the Constituent Assembly set up several Committees and in October 1956, the Drafting Committee presented the Draft Constitution, which after discussion, was finally adopted on 17 November 1957, and given effect to from 26 January 1957. The State of Jammu & Kashmir thus acquired the distinction of having a *separate Constitution for the administration of the State*, in place of the provisions of Part VI of the Constitution of India, which govern all the other States of the Union.[5]

3a. Important Provisions of the State Constitution. The more important provisions of the State Constitution of Jammu & Kashmir were as follows:

(1) The Constitution declared the State of Jammu and Kashmir to be "an integral part of Union of India".

(2) The territory of the State comprised of all the territories, which, on 15 August 1947, were under the sovereignty or suzerainty of the Ruler of the State (*i.e.*, including the Pakistan-occupied area of Jammu & Kashmir). The executive and legislative powers of the State extended to all matters, except those for which Parliament had powers to make laws for the State under the provisions of the Constitution of India.

(3) Under the original Constitution of Jammu & Kashmir, there was a difference between this State and other States of India as regards the Head of the State Government. While in the rest of India, the head of the State Executive is called "Governor" and he is appointed by the President [*Articles* 152, 155], the Executive Head of the State of Jammu & Kashmir was called *Sadar-i-Riyasat* and he was to be elected by the State Legislative Assembly. This anomaly was, however, removed by the Constitution of Jammu & Kashmir (Sixth Amendment) Act, 1965, as a result of which the nomenclature was changed from *Sadar-i-Riyasat* to "Governor" , and the Governor was to be "appointed by the President under his hand and seal" [Sections 26–27] as in other States [*Article 155*]. In the result, there were now *no differences on this point*, between Jammu & Kashmir and other States. As in other States, the executive power of the State vested with the Governor and was exercised by him with the advice of the Council of Ministers (except in the matter of appointment of the Chief Minister [Section 36]. The power of issuing a Proclamation for introducing "Governor's Rule" in case of breakdown of constitutional machinery [section 92]) was also vested with the Governor. The Governor held office for a term of five years. The Council of Ministers, headed by the Chief Minister, were collectively responsible to the Legislative Assembly.

(4) The Legislature of the State consisted of the Governor and two Houses, known respectively as the Legislative Assembly and the Legislative Council. The Legislative Assembly consisted of one hundred members chosen by direct election from territorial constituencies in the State; and two women members nominated by the Governor. Twenty-four seats in the Legislative Assembly remained vacant, to be filled by representatives of people living in Pakistan-occupied areas of the State. The Legislative Council consisted of 36 members. Eleven members were to be elected by the members of the Legislative Assembly from amongst persons who were residents of the Province of Kashmir, provided that of the members so elected at least one was to be a resident of Tehsil Ladakh and at least one a resident of Tehsil Kargil, the two outlying areas of the State. Eleven members were to be elected by the members of the Legislative Assembly from amongst persons who were residents of the Jammu Province. The

5. The very definition of "State" (in Article 152) for the purpose of Part VI excludes the State of Jammu & Kashmir.

remaining 14 members were to be elected by various electorates, such as municipal councils, and such other local bodies.

(5) Every judge of the High Court was to be appointed by the President after consultation with the Chief Justice of India and the Governor, and in the case of appointment of a judge other than the Chief Justice, the Chief Justice of the High Court.

(6) Every member of the civil service or one holding a civil post held office under the pleasure of the Governor.

4. Indira-Abdullah Agreement of 1975.

Notwithstanding the liberal measures introduced in the State by the adoption of a separate State Constitution, the pro-Pakistani elements in Jammu & Kashmir continued their agitation for the holding of a plebiscite to finally determine whether the State should accede to India or Pakistan and there were violent incidents initiated by the "Plebiscite Front",—a pro-Pakistani party which had been formed with the avowed object of secession from India. Sheikh Abdullah got involved in these anti-Indian movements and went on criticising the Indian policy towards the State, as a result of which he had to be placed under preventive detention in 1955. After a short release in 1964 on the profession of a changed attitude, he was again detained in 1965 under the DIR, and eventually externed from the State in 1971. This was followed by a period of blowing hot and cold, leading to a series of negotiations between the representatives of India and the Plebiscite Front, and an agreement was eventually reached and announced, on 24 February 1975.[6]

The net political result of this Agreement was that the demand for plebiscite was abandoned by Abdullah and his followers, and on the other hand, it was agreed that the special status of the State of Jammu & Kashmir would continue to remain under the provisions of Article 370 of the Constitution of India, which was described as a "temporary" measure in the original Constitution. A halt was, thus, cried to the progress of integration of this State with the Union of India, which had started in 1954, by giving larger autonomy to the State Assembly in certain matters.

It should, however, be mentioned that owing to differences over matters arising out of the Agreement, it was not implemented by issuing a fresh Presidential Order under Article 370.

5. Constitution (Application to Jammu and Kashmir) Order, 2019.

On 5 August 2019, in exercise of the powers conferred by clause (1) of Article 370 of the Constitution, the President of India issued the Constitution (Application to Jammu and Kashmir) Order, 2019. The aforesaid Presidential Order came into force at once, and superseded the Constitution (Application to Jammu and Kashmir) Order, 1954, as amended from time to time. All the provisions of the

---

6. *Vide Statesman*, Calcutta, 25 February 1975, pp 1, 7. He was released shortly after this Agreement and made the Chief Minister in February 1975, on the resignation of the Mir Qasim ministry. At the election held in July 1975, Sheikh Abdullah was elected to the Jammu & Kashmir Assembly and his Chief Ministership was thus upheld by election. He was retaining that office till his death in 1982.

Indian Constitution, as amended from time to time, became applicable to the State of Jammu and Kashmir. This would imply that the State's separate Constitution stands inoperative, including the privileges sanctioned by the Article 35A.

Article 370(1) grants the President the authority to apply other provisions of the Constitution of India, subject to such exceptions and modifications as the President may specify by issuing an order. Drawing on the authority available under Article 370(1), the Constitution (Application to Jammu and Kashmir) Order, 2019, added Clause (4) to Article 367 of the Constitution of India. The newly added Clause (4) provides that:

> For the purposes of the Constitution as it applies in relation to the State of Jammu and Kashmir —
>
> (a) references to this Constitution or to the provisions thereof shall be construed as references to the Constitution or the provisions thereof as applied in relation to the said State;
>
> (b) references to the person for the time being recognized by the President on the recommendation of the Legislative Assembly of the State as the Sadar-i-Riyasat of Jammu and Kashmir, acting on the advice of the Council of Ministers of the State for the time being in office, shall be construed as references to the Governor of Jammu and Kashmir;
>
> (c) references to the Government of the said State shall be construed as including references to the Governor of Jammu and Kashmir acting on the advice of his Council of Ministers; and
>
> (d) in proviso to clause (3) of Article 370 of this Constitution, the expression "Constituent Assembly of the State referred to in clause (2)" shall read "Legislative Assembly of the State".

6. Modification of Article 370.

Both Houses of Parliament also passed resolutions recommending the modification of Article 370 of the Constitution of India. Later, on 6 August 2019, in exercise of the powers conferred by Clause (3) of Article 370 read with clause (1) of Article 370 of the Constitution of India, the President made a declaration that, as from the 6 August 2019, all clauses of Article 370 shall cease to be operative except the following which shall read as under, namely:

> 370. All provisions of this Constitution, as amended from time to time, without any modifications or exceptions, shall apply to the State of Jammu and Kashmir notwithstanding anything contrary contained in article 152 or article 308 or any other article of this Constitution or any other provision of the Constitution of Jammu and Kashmir or any law, document, judgement, ordinance, order, by-law, rule, regulation, notification, custom or usage having the force of law in the territory of India, or any other instrument, treaty or agreement as envisaged under article 363 or otherwise.

Article 370 of the Constitution of India stood modified with this declaration made by the President of India. As a result of the said declaration and the 2019 Presidential Order, the special status of the State of Jammu and Kashmir under the Constitution by virtue of Article 370 virtually came to an end.

7. The Jammu and Kashmir Reorganisation Act, 2019.

The Jammu and Kashmir Reorganisation Bill, 2019, was introduced in Rajya Sabha on 5 August 2019. It was passed by the Rajya Sabha on the same day, and by Lok Sabha on 6 August 2019. The Bill received Presidential assent on 9 August 2019, after which it was published in the Gazette of India. A notification published on the same day provided for the formation of Union Territories with effect from 31 October 2019.

The Jammu and Kashmir Reorganisation Act, 2019, provides for the reorganisation of the erstwhile State of Jammu and Kashmir into: (i) the Union Territory of Jammu and Kashmir with a legislature; and (ii) the Union Territory of Ladakh (comprising Kargil and Leh Districts) without a legislature.

Section 5 of the Act provides that on and from the appointed day, *i.e.*, 31 October 2019, the Governor of the existing State of Jammu and Kashmir shall be the Lieutenant Governor for the Union Territory of Jammu and Kashmir, and Union territory of Ladakh for such period as may be determined by the President.

Section 13 of the Act provides that on and from the appointed day, the provisions contained in Article 239A, which are applicable to the "Union territory of Puducherry", shall also apply to the "Union territory of Jammu and Kashmir".[7]

Section 14 of the Act provides for a Legislative Assembly for the Union Territory of Jammu and Kashmir and that the total number of seats to be filled by persons chosen by direct election shall be 107.

Section 57 provides that, on and from the appointed day (*i.e.*, 31 October 2019), the Legislative Council of the existing State of Jammu and Kashmir shall stand abolished, and that all Bills pending in the Legislative Council immediately before the appointed day, shall lapse on the abolition of the Council.

Section 75 of the Act provides that (a) the High Court of Jammu and Kashmir shall be the common High Court for the Union Territory of Jammu and Kashmir and Union Territory of Ladakh; (b) the judges of the High Court of Jammu and Kashmir for the existing State of Jammu and Kashmir, holding office immediately before the appointed day, shall become on that day the judges of the common High Court.

The Fifth Schedule of the Act lists 106 central Acts that are made applicable to Union Territories of Jammu and Kashmir and Ladakh with effect from 31 October 2019. Further, 153 state laws of Jammu and Kashmir have been repealed. In addition, 166 state laws will remain in force, and seven laws will be applicable with amendments.

---

7. As far as the Legislative Assembly of the Union territory of J&K is concerned, Article 170 will have no application as it forms a part of Chapter III of Part VI which deals with only the State Legislature. It has no application to the Legislatures of Union Territories. The reason is that the Legislative Assemblies of the concerned Union Territories will be governed by the law made by the Parliament in accordance with Article 239A and not by the provisions of Chapter III of Part VI [*Haji Abdul Gani Khan v UOI*, 2023 SCC OnLine SC 138].

Section 47 of the Jammu and Kashmir Reorganisation Act, 2019 provides for official language or languages of the Union territory of Jammu and Kashmir and language or languages to be used in Legislative Assembly of the Union territory of Jammu and Kashmir. The said section provides that the Legislative Assembly may by law adopt any one or more of the languages in use in the Union Territory of Jammu and Kashmir or Hindi as the official language or languages to be used for all or any of the official purposes of the Union Territory of Jammu and Kashmir.

In the light of above, and for preserving Urdu and English which are used as official languages of the Union Territory of Jammu and Kashmir, and simultaneously elaborating its ambit by including languages spoken by a majority of the population, Parliament has enacted the Jammu and Kashmir Official Languages Act, 2020. The Act provides that Kashmiri, Dogri, Urdu, Hindi and English shall be the official languages for all official purposes of the Union territory.

8. Apex Court Upholding the Abrogation of Article 370.

By an Order, dated 11-12-2023 in Writ Petition (Civil) No. 1099 of 2019 & Others, the Apex Court[8] has upheld the President's power to abrogate Article 370 without the recommendations of the Jammu & Kashmir Constituent Assembly. The following important conclusions are drawn from the said Apex Court order:

(a) The State of Jammu and Kashmir did not retain any element of sovereignty after the execution of the Instrument of Accession and the issuance of the Proclamation dated 25-11-1949 by which the Constitution of India was adopted.

(b) The State of Jammu and Kashmir does not have 'internal sovereignty' and Article 370 was a feature of asymmetric federalism and not of sovereignty.

(c) It can be garnered from the historical context for the inclusion of Article 370 and the placement of this Article in Part XXI of the Constitution that it is a temporary provision.

(d) The power under Article 370(3) did not cease to exist upon the dissolution of the Constituent Assembly of J&K. When the Constituent Assembly was dissolved, only the transitional power recognised in the proviso to Article 370(3) which empowered the Constituent Assembly to make its recommendations ceased to exist. It did not affect the power held by the President under Article 370(3).

(e) Article 370 cannot be amended by exercise of power under Article 370(1)(*d*). Recourse must have been taken to the procedure contemplated by Article 370(3) if Article 370 is to cease to operate or is to be amended or modified in its application to the State of J&K.

(f) Para. 2 of CO 272 by which Article 370 was amended through through 367 is *ultra vires* Article 370(1)(d) because it modifies, in effect, Article 370 without following the procedure prescribed to modify Article 370. An interpretation clause cannot be used to bypass the procedure laid down for amendment. However, the

8. *Article 370 of the Constitution, In re*, LNIND 2023 SC 726 : 2023 SCC OnLine SC 1647.

exercise of power by the President under Article 370(1)(*d*) to issue CO 272 is not *mala fide.* The President in exercise of power under Article 370(3) can unilaterally issue a notification that Article 370 ceases to exist. The President did not have to secure the concurrence of the Government of the State or Union Government acting on behalf of the State Government under the second proviso to Article 370(1)(d) while applying all the provisions of the Constitution to Jammu and Kashmir because such an exercise of power has the same effect as an exercise of power under Article 370(3) for which the concurrence or collaboration with the State Government was not required.

Para. 2 of CO 272 applying all the provisions of the Constitution of India to the State of J&K is valid. Such an exercise of power is not *mala fide* merely because all the provisions were applied together without following a piece-meal approach.

(g) The President had the power to issue a notification declaring that Article 370(3) ceases to operate without the recommendation of the Constituent Assembly. The continuous exercise of power under Article 370(1) by the President indicates that the gradual process of constitutional integration was ongoing. The declaration issued by the President under Article 370(3) is a culmination of the process of integration and as such is a valid exercise of power. Thus, CO 273 is valid. Following the application of the Constitution of India in its entirety to the State of Jammu and Kashmir by CO 273, the Constitution of the State of J&K is inoperative and is declared to have become redundant.

PART IV

ADMINISTRATION OF UNION TERRITORIES

CHAPTER 16

ADMINISTRATION OF UNION TERRITORIES AND ACQUIRED TERRITORIES

1. Genesis of Union Territories. AS stated earlier, in the original Constitution of 1949, States were divided into three categories and included in Parts A, B, and C of the First Schedule of the Constitution.

Part C States were 10 in number, namely—Ajmer, Bhopal, Bilaspur, Coorg, Delhi, Himachal Pradesh, Kutch, Manipur, Tripura and Vindhya Pradesh. Of these, Himachal Pradesh, Bhopal, Bilaspur, Kutch, Manipur, Tripura and Vindhya Pradesh had been formed by the integration of some of the smaller Indian States. The States of Ajmer, Coorg and Delhi were Chief Commissioner's Provinces under the Government of India Acts, 1919 and 1935, and were thus administered by the Centre even before the Constitution.

The special feature of these Part C States was that they were administered by the President through a Chief Commissioner or a Lieutenant-Governor, acting as his agent. Parliament had legislative power relating to any subject as regards the Part C States, but the Constitution empowered Parliament to create a Legislature as well as a Council of Advisers or Ministers for a Part C State. In exercise of this power, Parliament enacted the Government of Part C States Act, 1951, by which a Council of Advisers or Ministers was set up in each Part C State, to advise the Chief Commissioner, under the overall control of the President, and also a Legislative Assembly to function as the Legislature of the State, without derogation to the plenary powers of Parliament.

In place of these Part C States, the Constitution (Seventh Amendment) Act, 1956 substituted the category of "Union Territories" which are also similarly administered by the Union. As a result of the reorganisation of the States by the States Reorganisation Act, 1956, the Part C States of Ajmer, Bhopal, Coorg, Kutch, and Vindhya Pradesh were merged into other adjoining States.

2. Union Territories. The list of Union Territories, accordingly, included the remaining Part C States of Delhi, Himachal Pradesh[1]

---

1. Himachal Pradesh has since been transferred to the category of States, by the State of Himachal Pradesh Act, 1970, and Manipur and Tripura, by the NE Areas (Reorganisation) Act, 1971. Similarly, by the State of Mizoram Act, 1986, (wef 20-2-1987); the State of Arunachal Pradesh Act, 1986 (wef 20-2-1987) and the Goa, Daman and Diu Reorganisation Act, 1987, (wef 30-5-1987) the Union Territories of Mizoram, Arunachal Pradesh and Goa have been elevated to Statehood. The Principal Seat of the Gauhati High Court is at Guwahati, Assam. Apart from the Principal Seat, the high court has three outlying Benches, *viz.*, Kohima Bench for the State of Nagaland (established on

[Footnote No. 1 Contd.]

(which included Bilaspur), Manipur, and Tripura.[1] To these were added the Andaman and Nicobar Islands, and the Laccadive and Amindivi Islands. Under the original Constitution, the Andaman and Nicobar Islands were included in Part D of the First Schedule. The Laccadive, Minicoy and Amindivi Islands (renamed "Lakshadweep" in 1973), on the other hand, were included in the territory of the State of Madras. The States Reorganisation Act and the Constitution (Seventh Amendment) Act, 1956 abolished Part D of the First Schedule and constituted it a separate Union Territory.

By the Constitution (10th, 12th, 14th and 27th) Amendment Acts, some others were added to the list of Union Territories.

Since some of the erstwhile Union Territories (Himachal Pradesh, Manipur, Tripura, Mizoram, Arunachal Pradesh[1] and Goa) have been lifted up into the category of "States", the number of Union Territories is, at present, *eight* [see Table III, *post*].

Though all these Union Territories belong to one category, there are some differences in the actual system of administration as between the several Union Territories owing to the provisions of the Constitution as well as of Acts of Parliament which have been made in pursuance of the Constitutional provisions.

3. Administrator.

Article 239(1) provides that, save as otherwise provided by Parliament by law, every Union Territory shall be administered by the President acting, to such extent as he thinks fit, through an Administrator to be appointed by him with such designation as he may specify.[2] Instead of appointing an Administrator from outside, the President may appoint the Governor of a State as the Administrator of an adjoining Union Territory; and where a Governor is so appointed, he shall exercise his functions as such Administrator independently of his Council of Ministers [*Article 239(2)*].

All the Union Territories are thus administered by an Administrator as the agent of the President, and not by a Governor acting as the head of a State.

4. Provision for Legislative Assembly and Council of Ministers.

In 1962, however, Article 239A (amended by the 37th Amendment, 1975) was introduced in the Constitution, to empower Parliament to create a Legislature or Council of Ministers or both for some of the Union Territories. By virtue of this power, Parliament enacted the Government of Union Territories Act, 1963, providing for a Legislative Assembly as well as a

---

[Footnote No. 1 Contd.]

1 December 1972), Aizawl Bench for the State of Mizoram (established on 5 July 1990) and Itanagar Bench for the State of Arunachal Pradesh (established on 12 August 2000). The Gauhati High Court occupied a unique position of being a common high court of seven States of North East India, till 23 March 2013, the date of functioning of separate high courts in Meghalaya, Manipur and Tripura.

2. Heterogeneous designations have been specified by the President in the case of the different Union Territories:

   (a) *Administrator*—Chandigarh; Dadra & Nagar Haveli and Daman & Diu; and Lakshadweep.

   (b) *Lieutenant Governor*—Andaman and Nicobar Islands; Jammu & Kashmir; Ladakh; NCT of Delhi; and Puducherry.

   Thus, there does not exist a homogeneous class of Union Territories with similar governance structures.

Council of Ministers to advise the Administrator, in these Union Territories. Puducherry alone is now left in this category; all other Union Territories have become States.

There was no established constitutional convention that the names for nominations to Members of the Legislative Assembly in the UT of Puducherry must emanate from the Chief Minister or that such nominations could be made only after the concurrence of the Chief Minister.[3]

On 1 February 1992, Articles 239AA and 239AB (inserted by Constitution 69th Amendment, 1991) came into force. To supplement these provisions, the Government of National Capital Territory of Delhi Act, 1991 was enacted. Delhi has a Legislative Assembly and a Council of Ministers. NCT of Delhi is accorded a *sui generis* status, setting it apart from other UTs.

The Government of Delhi has all the legislative powers in the State List [excepting entries 1 (Public Order), 2 (Police) and 18 (Land)] and the Concurrent List. In addition to the entries in the Union List, Parliament has legislative competence over all matters in State and Concurrent Lists, including the entries which have been kept out of the legislative domain of Government of Delhi. The Union of India has executive power only over the three entries in List II over which Government of Delhi does not have legislative competence. The executive power of Government of Delhi with respect to State and Concurrent Lists shall be subject to the executive power expressly conferred upon the Union by the Constitution or by a law enacted by Parliament. Further, the phrase "insofar as any such manner is applicable to Union Territories" cannot be read to further exclude the legislative power of Government of Delhi over entries in the State or Concurrent List, over and above those subjects which have been expressly excluded. The Government of India has legislative and executive power over "Services" [List II, Entry 41] because—(i) the definition of "State" under section 3(58) of the General Clauses Act, 1897, applies to the term "State" in Part XIV of the Constitution. Thus, Part XIV is applicable to Union Territories; and (ii) the exercise of rule-making power under proviso to Article 309 does not oust the legislative power of the appropriate authority to make laws over Entry 41 of the State List.[4]

The Lieutenant Governor cannot exercise his discretion in each and every matter and by and large, his discretionary powers are limited to the three matters over which the legislative power of the Delhi Legislature Assembly stands excluded by Article 239AA(3)(*a*). The meaning of "aid and advice" employed in Article 239AA(4) has to be construed to mean that the Lieutenant Governor of the NCT of Delhi is bound by the "aid and advice" of the Council of Ministers and this position holds true so long as the Lieutenant Governor does not exercise his power under the proviso to clause (4) of Article 239AA.[5] The Lieutenant Governor may act in his discretion only in two classes of matters: *firstly*, where the matter deals with issues which are beyond the powers of the Legislative Assembly and where the President has delegated the powers and functions to the LG in relation to such matter; and *secondly*, matters which by

3. *K Lakshminarayanan v UOI*, (2020) 14 SCC 664.
4. *Government of NCT of Delhi v UOI*, (2023) 9 SCC 1.
5. *Government of NCT of Delhi v UOI*, (2018) 8 SCC 501 : (2018) 8 Scale 72 : LNIND 2018 SC 308.

law require him to act in his discretion or where he is exercising judicial or *quasi*-judicial functions.[6]

Under the Transaction of Business of Government of NCT of Delhi Rules, 1993, the Lieutenant Governor shall be kept informed about the decisions taken by the Council of Ministers. This requirement is mandatory.[7]

Parliament had enacted the Government of National Capital Territory of Delhi (Amendment) Act, 2021. It amends certain provisions in the Government of National Capital Territory of Delhi Act, 1991, relating to powers and responsibilities of the Legislative Assembly and the Lieutenant Governor. The Amendment Act clarifies that the expression "Government", which in the context of legislations to be passed by the Legislative Assembly of Delhi, shall mean the Lieutenant Governor of the National Capital Territory of Delhi. [*See* Chapter 6, *ante*].

Similarly, after the pronouncement of the judgment in *Government of NCT of Delhi v UOI*,[8] the President in exercise of powers under Article 123 of the Constitution promulgated the Government of National Capital Territory of Delhi (Amendment) Ordinance, 2023, which amends the Government of NCT of Delhi Act, 1991, to provide for a comprehensive scheme of administration of services deployed in the functioning of NCTD and other allied issues thereby balancing the local and domestic interests of the people staying in the NCTD with the democratic will of the entire nation reflected through the President of India. This matter has been referred to the Constitution Bench to decide the contours of the power of Parliament to enact a law under Article 239AA(7); and whether Parliament can abrogate the constitutional principles of governance for NCT of Delhi.[9]

5. Legislative and Presidential Powers.

Parliament has exclusive legislative power over a Union Territory, including matters which are enumerated in the State List [*Article 246(4)*]. But so far as the two groups of Island Territories, *i.e.*, Dadra and Nagar Haveli and Daman and Diu, and Pondicherry are concerned, the President has a legislative power, namely, to make regulations for the peace, progress and good government of these Territories. This power of the President overrides the legislative power of Parliament inasmuch as a regulation made by the President as regards these Territories may repeal or amend any Act of Parliament which is for the time being applicable to the Union Territory [*Article 240(2)*]. But the President's power to make regulations shall remain suspended *while* the Legislature is functioning in any of these States,—to be revived as soon as such Legislature is dissolved or suspended.

6. High Courts.

Parliament may by law constitute a high court for a Union Territory or declare any court in any such Territory to be a high court for all or any of the purposes of this Constitution [*Article 241*]. Until such legislation is made the existing high courts relating to such territories shall

6. *Government of NCT of Delhi v UOI*, (2023) 9 SCC 1.
7. *State (NCT of Delhi) v UOI*, (2020) 12 SCC 259.
8. *Government of NCT of Delhi v UOI*, (2023) 9 SCC 1.
9. *Government of NCT of Delhi v UOI*, 2023 SCC OnLine SC 856. See also *Government of NCT of Delhi v UOI*, (2024) 2 SCC 300.

continue to exercise their jurisdiction. In the result, the Punjab and Haryana High Court acts as the High Court of Chandigarh; the Lakshadweep is under the jurisdiction of the Kerala High Court; the Calcutta High Court has got jurisdiction over the Andaman and Nicobar Islands [*vide* Table XVI], the Madras High Court has jurisdiction over Pondicherry; the Bombay High Court over Dadra and Nagar Haveli and Daman and Diu; and the Gauhati High Court (Assam) still having jurisdiction over Mizoram and Arunachal Pradesh. However, with the enactment of the State of Mizoram Act, 1986 (Act 34 of 1986) and the State of Arunachal Pradesh Act, 1986 (Act 69 of 1986), the States of Mizoram and Arunachal Pradesh attained statehood on 20 February 1987, and as such, the states of Mizoram and Arunachal Pradesh are full fledged states and have lost the status of Union Territories; but, the Gauhati High Court is still the common high court for the states of Mizoram and Arunachal Pradesh.[1] The Territory of Goa, Daman and Diu had a Judicial Commissioner but the jurisdiction of the Bombay High Court has been extended to this Territory and further with the passing of the Goa, Daman & Diu Re-organization Act, 1987 by the Parliament conferring Statehood to Goa, the High Court of Bombay became the common high court for the states of Maharashtra, Goa, and for the Union Territories of Dadra and Nagar Haveli, and Daman and Diu wef 30-5-1987. Delhi has a separate high court of its own since 1966.

7. Acquired Territories.

There are no separate provisions in the Constitution relating to the administration of acquired territories, but the provisions relating to Union Territories will extend by virtue of their definition of "Union Territory" [*Article 366(30)*], as including "any other territory comprised within the territory of India but not specified in that Schedule". Thus, the Territory of Pondicherry, Karaikal, Yanam and Mahe, was being administered by the President of India through a Chief Commissioner until it was made a Union Territory, in 1962. Parliament has plenary power of legislation regarding such territory as in the case of the Union Territories [*Article 246(4)*].

continue to exercise their jurisdiction. In the case of the Punjab and Haryana High Court, however, the Union Territory of Chandigarh, the Lakshadweep is under the jurisdiction of the Kerala High Court, [illegible] then Goa, Daman and Diu [illegible] over the Andaman and Nicobar Islands [illegible] the Madras High Court has jurisdiction over Pondicherry, the Bombay High Court over Dadra and Nagar Haveli and Daman and Diu, and the Gauhati High Court [illegible] still having jurisdiction over Mizoram and Arunachal Pradesh. However, with the creation of the State of Mizoram by the [illegible] Act of 1986 and [illegible] Arunachal Pradesh Act, 1986 (Act 69 of 1986), the Union of Mizoram and Arunachal Pradesh [illegible] such [illegible] Territories, but [illegible] High Court is still the [illegible] for the States of Mizoram and Arunachal Pradesh. The [illegible] Goa, Daman and Diu [illegible] Delhi is [illegible] the [illegible] the Delhi High Court [illegible] the Territory [illegible] the passing of [illegible] Act [illegible] with [illegible] the Union Territory [illegible] the [illegible] High Court for [illegible] Goa, Daman and Diu [illegible] Delhi has [illegible] since 1966.

There are no separate provisions in the Constitution relating to the administration of [illegible] but the provisions relating to Union Territories will obviously extend to [illegible] Territories [illegible] of [illegible] including [illegible] territory comprised within the territory of India but not specified [illegible] the [illegible] was being [illegible] India through [illegible] in [illegible] of the [illegible]

PART V

LOCAL GOVERNMENT

PART IX

LOCAL GOVERNMENT

CHAPTER 17

THE NEW SYSTEM OF PANCHAYATS, MUNICIPALITIES, AND CO-OPERATIVE SOCIETIES

1. History.

THE village *Panchayat* was a unit of local administration since the early British days, but they had to work under Government control. When Indian leaders pressed for local autonomy at the national level, the British Government sought to meet this demand by offering concession at the lowest level, at the initial stage, by giving powers of self-government to Panchayats in rural areas and municipalities in urban areas, under various local names under different enactments, eg, the Bengal Local Self-Government Act, 1885; the Bengal Village Self-Government Act, 1919; the Bengal Municipal Act, 1884.

In the Government of India Act, 1935, the power to enact legislation was specifically given to the Provincial Legislature by Entry 12 in the Provincial Legislative List. By virtue of this power, new Acts were enacted by many other States vesting powers of administration, including criminal justice, in the hands of the Panchayats.

Notwithstanding such existing legislation, the makers of the Constitution of Independent India were not much satisfied with the working of these local bodies as institutions of popular government and, therefore, a Directive was included in the Constitution of 1949 in Article 40 as follows:

> The State shall take steps to organise village panchayats and endow them with such powers and authority as may be necessary to enable them to function as units of self-government.

But notwithstanding this Directive in Article 40, not much attention was given to hold elections in these local units as units of representative democracy in the country as a whole. During the time of Mr Rajeev Gandhi, it was considered necessary to further the organisation of these local units by inserting specific provisions in the Constitution itself on the basis of which the Legislatures of the various States might enact detailed laws according to the guidelines provided by the Constitutional provisions.

2. The 73rd and 74th Constitution Amendment Acts.

The ideas so evolved, culminated in the passing of Constitution 73rd and 74th Amendment Acts, 1992, which inserted Parts IX and IXA in the Constitution. While Part IX relates to the Panchayats, containing Articles 243 to 243-O, Part IXA relates to the Municipalities, containing Articles 243P to243ZG. The provisions in Parts IX and IXA are more or less parallel or analogous.

2a. Special Features of the New System.

Before entering into details, it may be pointed out that the new system contained certain novel provisions, for example, for direct election by the people in the same manner as at the Union and State levels; reservation of seats for women; an Election Commission to conduct election, a Finance Commission to ensure financial viability of these institutions.

Another striking feature is that the provisions inserted in the Constitution by Articles 243–243ZG are in the nature of basic provisions which are to be supplemented by laws made by the respective State Legislatures, which will define the details as to the powers and functions of the various organs, just mentioned.

It is to be recalled that "local government" including self-government institutions in both urban and rural areas is an exclusive State subject under Entry 5 of List II of the Seventh Schedule, so that the Union cannot enact any law to create rights and liabilities relating to these subjects. What the Union has, therefore, done is to outline the scheme which would be implemented by the several States by making laws, or amending their own existing laws to bring them in conformity with the provisions of the 73rd and 74th Constitution Amendment Acts.

After implementing legislation was enacted by the States, elections have taken place in most of the States, and the Panchayats and Municipalities have started functioning under the new law.

3. The 97th Constitution Amendment Act, 2011.

The Parliament passed the Constitution (97th Amendment) Act, 2011 with an objective to promote voluntary formation, autonomous functioning, democratic control and professional management of Co-operative Societies. The Amendment inserted "co-operative societies" in Part III, in Article 19(1)(c); inserted a new "Article 43B" in Part IV and further inserted Parts IXB in the Constitution containing Articles 243ZH to 243ZT. Soon after passing of the Constitution (97th Amendment) Act, 2011, much controversy has arisen with regard to the constitutional validity of the said Amendment Act and the real intention of Parliament in encroaching upon the subject which belongs to States. Moreover, various restrictions have been imposed upon the State Legislatures while enacting law relating to Co-operative Societies which was earlier unfettered prior to the incorporation of Part IXB. For instance, in Article 243ZI, it is said that the Legislature of a State may, by law, make provisions with respect to the incorporation, regulation and winding-up of co-operative societies based on the principles of voluntary formation, democratic member-control, members' economic participation and autonomous functioning *but such law must be subject to the provisions of Part IXB.* In Article 243ZJ, a definite restriction has been imposed upon the State Legislatures regarding fixation of maximum number of Directors of a Co-operative Society *which shall not exceed 21.* Further, the State Legislatures have been asked to provide for reservation of one seat for the Scheduled Castes or the Scheduled Tribes and two seats for women on board of every co-operative society consisting of individuals as members and having members from such class or category of persons. Similarly, in sub-Article (2) of Article 243ZJ, the duration of the term of office of the elected members of the board and its office bearers has been fixed to be five years and in sub-Article (3) thereof, a further direction has been given upon State Legislatures in the matter of enacting law relating to Co-Operative Societies regarding co-option of the member in the board of director and further provisions regarding the rights of such co-opted members have also been made. Similarly in Article 243ZK, a further condition has been imposed that the election of a board shall be conducted before the expiry of the term of the board so as to ensure that the newly elected members of the board assume office immediately on the expiry of the term of the office of members of the outgoing board. In Article 243ZL, a further condition has been imposed that no board shall be suspended or kept under suspension for a period exceeding six months and has also provided various conditions under which a board may be superseded or kept under suspension. In Article 243ZM, it is mandatorily prescribed that the account of every society should be audited within six months from the close of the financial year to which the accounts relate. Article 243ZP casts a duty upon the society to file returns within the period fixed there in and there is no scope of ignoring the same. Article 243ZQ prescribes the acts which would be the offences relating to the co-operative societies and the State Legislature cannot deviate from those mandates.

Further, the law relating to Co-operative Societies is still in List II of the Seventh Schedule, without bringing the subject of Co-operative Societies either into List I or List III, by way of this amendment, the Parliament has controlled the said power without complying with the provisions of Article 368(2) of the Constitution by taking ratification of the majority of the State Legislatures.

Amid aforesaid controversy, a PIL was filed in the Gujarat High Court in 2012 for declaring the Constitution (97th Amendment) Act 2011 as *ultra vires* the Constitution. The Gujarat High Court, considering the aforesaid aspects of the controversy and in the light of the various judgments of the Supreme Court, *vide* order(2) dated 22 April 2013, held that the amendment is violating the basic structure of the Constitution so long as the subject of "Co-operative Societies" is in the List II of the Seventh Schedule and at the same time, the provisions of Article 368(2) has not been complied with.[1] The Constitution has not permitted curtailment of the power of the State Legislatures over the subject mentioned in List II without taking recourse to Article 368(2), and as such, the curtailment is violative of the principle of federalism[2] which has been declared as basic structure of the Constitution by the Hon'ble Supreme Court.

Against the Order/Judgment dated 22 April 2013 of the Gujarat High Court in WP (PIL) No 166 of 2012, the Union of India preferred an appeal bearing CA No 9108–9109/2014 titled, "*UOI v Rajendra N Shah*" to the

1. *Rajendra N Shah v UOI,* (2013) 2 GLR 1698, Gujarat High Court delivered its Judgment dated 22 April 2013 WP (PIL) No 166 of 2012 and declared the Constitution (97th Amendment) Act 2011 inserting Part IXB containing Articles 243ZH–243ZT as *ultra vires* the Constitution of India for not taking recourse to Article 368(2) of the Constitution providing for ratification by the majority of the State Legislatures.
2. *Automobile Transport v State of Rajasthan,* AIR 1962 SC 1406 : (1963) 1 SCR 491, p *1415–16.* In *Kesavananda Bharati v State of Kerala,* AIR 1973 SC 1461, some of the judges (paras 302, 599, 1681) considered federalism to be one of the "basic features" of *our* Constitution. A nine-judge Supreme Court Bench has in *S R Bommai v UOI,* AIR 1994 SC 1918 : (1994) 3 SCC 1, laid down that the Constitution is federal and some of the judges characterised federalism as its basic feature.

Supreme Court. The Supreme Court by a majority of 2:1 upheld the judgment of the High Court except to the extent that it had struck down Part IX-B of the Constitution in its entirety. The Supreme Court held that since the Constitutional (97th Amendment) Act dealt with an entry which was an exclusive state subject, it required a ratification by at least one-half of the state legislatures as per Article 368(2) of the Constitution. The Supreme Court held that that Part IX-B is operative only insofar as it concerns Multi-State Cooperative Societies both within various States and in Union Territories of India.[3] [See, further, under Chapter 34—How the Constitution has worked, *post*].

3. *UOI v Rajendra N Shah,* CA No 9108–9109/2014, decided on 20 July 2021 (SC).

CHAPTER 18

PANCHAYATS

1. Three-tier system.

PART IX of the Constitution envisages a three-tier system of Panchayats,[1] namely, (a) The village level; (b) The District Panchayat at the district level; (c) The Intermediate Panchayat which stands between the village and district Panchayats in the States where the population is above 20 lakhs.

2. Composition.

All the seats in a Panchayat shall be filled by persons chosen by direct election from territorial constituencies in the Panchayat area. The electorate has been named 'Gram Sabha' consisting of persons registered in the electoral rolls relating to a village comprised within the area of a Panchayat. In this way, representative democracy will be introduced at the grass roots.

The Chairperson of each Panchayat shall be elected according to the law passed by a State and such State Law shall also provide for the representation of Chairpersons of Village and Intermediate Panchayats in the District Panchayat, as well as members of the Union and State Legislature in the Panchayats above the village level.

3. Reservation of Seats.

Article 243D provides that seats are to be reserved for: (a) Scheduled Castes,[2] and (b) Scheduled Tribes. The reservation shall be in proportion to their population. If, for example, the Scheduled Castes constitute 30% of the population and the Scheduled Tribes 21%, then 30% and 21% seats shall be reserved for them respectively.

Out of the seats so reserved not less than one-third of the seats shall be reserved for women belonging to Scheduled Castes and Scheduled Tribes, respectively.

Not less than one-third of the total number of seats to be filled by direct elections in every Panchayat shall be reserved for women.

A State may by law make provision for similar reservation of the offices of Chairpersons in the Panchayats at the village and other levels.

These reservations favouring the Scheduled Castes and Tribes shall cease to be operative as specified in Article 334 (at present 80 years, *i.e.*, upto 24 January 2030).[3]

---

1. For the text of the 73rd Amendment Act relating to Panchayats [*Articles* 243-243-O], see Author's *Constitution Amendment Acts,* 7th Edn, pp 170-77; *Shorter Constitution of India,* 16th Edn, 2021.
2. Excluding in the State of Arunachal Pradesh.
3. In Article 334 of the Constitution, for the words "sixty years", the words "seventy years" was substituted vide The Constitution (Ninety Fifth Amendment) Act, 2009 with effect from 25 January 2010. This period has been further extended to 80 years by the Constitution (104th Amendment) Act, 2019 (wef 25-1-2020).

A State may by law also reserve seats or offices of Chairpersons in the Panchayat at any level in favour of backward classes of citizens.

4. Duration of Panchayat.

Every *Panchayat* shall continue for five years from the date of its first meeting. But it can be dissolved earlier in accordance with the procedure prescribed by State law. Elections must take place before the expiry of the above period. In case it is dissolved earlier, then the elections must take place within six months of its dissolution. A Panchayat reconstituted after premature dissolution (*i.e.*, before the expiry of the full period of five years) shall continue only for the remainder of the period. But if the remainder of the period is less than six months it shall not be necessary to hold elections.

5. Qualification for Membership.

Article 243F provides that all persons who are qualified to be chosen to the State Legislature shall be qualified to be chosen as a member of a Panchayat. The only difference is that a person who has attained the age of 21 years will be eligible to be a member (in case of State Legislature the prescribed age is 25 years—Article 173). If a question arises as to whether a member has become subject to any disqualification, the question shall be referred to such authority as the State Legislature may provide by law.

6. Powers, Authority and Responsibilities of Panchayats.

State Legislatures have the legislative power, to confer on the Panchayats such powers and authority as may be necessary to enable them to function as institutions of self-government [*Articles 243G-243H*]. They may be entrusted with the responsibility of: (a) preparing plans for economic development and social justice; (b) implementation of schemes for economic development and social justice; and (c) in regard to matters listed in the 11th Schedule (inserted by the 73rd Amendment). The list contains 29 items, *e.g.*, land improvement, minor irrigation, animal husbandry, fisheries, education, women and child development etc. The 11th Schedule thus distributes powers between the State Legislature and the Panchayat just as the Seventh Schedule distributes powers between the Union and the State Legislature.

7. Powers to Impose Taxes and Financial Resources.

A State may by law authorise a Panchayat to levy, collect and appropriate taxes, duties, tolls etc. The law may lay down the procedure to be followed as well as the limits of these exactions. It can also assign to a Panchayat various taxes, duties etc. collected by the State Government. Grants-in-aid may be given to the Panchayats from the Consolidated Fund of the State.

8. Panchayat Finance Commissions.

Within one year from 24 April 1993, *i.e.*, the date on which the Constitution 73rd Amendment came into force and afterwards every five years the State Government shall appoint a Finance Commission to review the financial position of the Panchayats and to make recommendations as to—

(a) the distribution between the State and the Panchayats of the net proceeds of taxes, duties, tolls and fees leviable by the State which may be divided between them and how allocation would be made among various levels of Panchayats;

(b) what taxes, duties, tolls and fees may be assigned to the Panchayats;

(c) grant-in-aid to the Panchayats.

The report of the Commission, together with a memorandum of action taken on it, shall be laid before the State Legislature. These provisions are modelled on Article 280 which contains provisions regarding appointment of a Finance Commission for distribution of finances between the Union and the States.

9. State Election Commission. Article 243K is designed to ensure free and fair elections to the Panchayats.

Article 243K provides for the Constitution of a State Election Commission consisting of a State Election Commissioner to be appointed by the Governor. Powers of superintendence, direction and control of elections to the Panchayats, including preparation of electoral rolls for it shall vest in the State Election Commission. To ensure the independence of the Commission it is laid down that State Election Commissioner can be removed only in the same manner and on the same grounds as a Judge of a High Court. The State Legislatures have the power to legislate on all matters relating to elections to Panchayats.

10. Bar to Interference by Courts in Electoral Matters. As under Article 329, courts shall have no jurisdiction to examine the validity of a law, relating to delimitation of constituencies or the allotments of seats, made under Article 243K. An election to a Panchayat can be called in question only by an election petition which should be presented to such authority and in such manner as may be prescribed by or under any law made by the State Legislature.

CHAPTER 16

MUNICIPALITIES AND PANCHAYATS

[illegible] to the Panchayats.

The report of the Commission together with a memorandum of action taken on it shall be laid before the State Legislature. These provisions are modelled on Article 280, which contains provisions regarding appointment of a Finance Commission for distribution of finances between the Union and the States.

State Election Commission. Article 243K [illegible] Elections to the Panchayats.

Article 243K provides for the constitution of a State Election Commission [illegible] superintendence, direction and control of elections to the Panchayats [illegible]

[illegible]

[illegible]

CHAPTER 19

MUNICIPALITIES AND PLANNING COMMITTEES

1. Municipalities and Planning Committees. PART IXA, which came into force on 1 June 1993, gives a constitutional foundation to the local self-government units in urban areas. In fact, such institutions are in existence all over the country.

Some of the provisions are similar to those contained in Part IX, *e.g.*, Reservation of Seats, Finance Commission, Election Commission etc.

This Part gives birth to two types of bodies:

(i) Institutions of self-government [*Article 243Q*], and

(ii) Institutions for planning [*Articles 243ZD and 243ZE*].

2. Three-tier System. Institutions of self-government, called by a general name "municipalities" are of three types:

(a) Nagar Panchayat, for a transitional area, ie an area which is being transformed from a rural area to an urban area.

(b) Municipal Council for a smaller urban area.

(c) Municipal Corporation for a larger urban area.

Article 243Q makes it obligatory for every State to constitute such units. But if there is an urban area or part of it where municipal services are being provided or proposed to be provided by an industrial establishment in that area then considering also the size of the area and other factors, the Governor may specify it to be an industrial township. For such an area it is not mandatory to constitute a municipality.

The members of a municipality would generally be elected by direct election. **3. Composition of Municipalities.** The Legislature of a State may by law provide for representation in a municipality of (i) persons having special knowledge or experience in municipal administration, (ii) Members of Lok Sabha, State Assembly, Rajya Sabha and Legislative Council, and (iii) the Chairpersons of Committees constituted under clause (5) of Article 243S. The Chairperson shall be elected in the manner provided by the Legislature.

For one or more wards comprised within the territorial area of a municipality **4. Wards Committee.** having a population of three lacs or more it would be obligatory to constitute Ward Committees. The State Legislature shall make provision with respect to its composition, territorial area and the manner in which the seats in a ward committee shall be filled.

5. Other Committees. It is open for the State Legislature to constitute Committees in addition to the wards committees.

6. Reservations of Seats. As in Part IX, reservations of seats are to be made in favour of the Scheduled Castes and Scheduled Tribes in every municipality.

Out of the total number of seats to be filled by direct elections, at least one-third would be reserved for women. This includes the quota for women belonging to Scheduled Castes and Tribes.

It has been left to the State Legislature to prescribe by law the manner of reservation of the offices of the Chairpersons of Municipalities.

All reservations in favour of Scheduled Castes and Tribes shall come to an end with the expiry of the period specified in Article 334.

It is permissible for a State Legislature to make provisions for reservation of seats or offices of chairpersons in favour of backward classes.

7. Duration of Municipalities. Every Municipality shall continue for five years from the date of its first meeting. But it may be dissolved earlier according to law. Article 243Q further prescribes that before dissolution a reasonable opportunity of being heard must be given to the municipality. Elections to constitute a municipality shall be completed before the expiry of the period of five years. If the municipality has been superseded before the expiry of its term, the elections must be completed within six months of its dissolution. A Municipality constituted after its dissolution shall continue only for the remainder of the term. But if the remainder of the period is less than six months it shall not be necessary to hold elections.

It has been provided that no amendment of the law in force shall cause dissolution of a municipality before the expiry of the five years term.

8. Qualification for Membership. Article 243V lays down that all persons who are qualified to be chosen to the State legislature shall be qualified for being a member of a municipality. There is an important difference. Persons who have attained the age of 21 years will be eligible to be a member. While the constitutional requirement is that for election to the State legislature of a State a person must have attained the age of 25 years [*Article 173*].

9. Powers, Authority and Responsibilities of Municipalities. Legislatures of States have been conferred the power [*Article 243W*] to confer on the municipalities all such powers and authority as may be necessary to enable them to function as institutions of self-government. It has specifically been mentioned that they may be given the responsibility of (a) preparation of plans for economic development and social justice, (b) implementation of schemes as may be entrusted to them, and (c) in regard to matters listed in the 12th Schedule. This Schedule contains 18 items, *e.g.*, Urban Planning, Regulation of Land Use, Roads and Bridges, Water Supply, Public Health, Fire Services, Urban Forestry, Slums, etc.

10. Power to Impose Taxes and Financial Resources.

A State Legislature may by law authorise a municipality to levy, collect and appropriate taxes, duties, tolls, etc. The law may lay down the limits and prescribe the procedure to be followed. It can also assign to a municipality various taxes, duties etc. collected by the State Government. Grants-in-aid may be given to the municipalities, from the Consolidated Fund of the State.

11. Panchayat Finance Commission.

The Finance Commission appointed under Article 243-I (see Chapter 18 under Panchayat Finance Commission) shall also review the financial position of the municipalities and make recommendations as to —

(a) the distribution between the State and the Municipalities of the net proceeds of taxes, duties, tolls and fees leviable by the State which may be divided between them and allocation of shares amongst different levels of Municipalities.

(b) the taxes, duties, tolls and fees that may be assigned to the Municipalities.

(c) grants-in-aid to the Municipalities.

(d) the measures needed to improve the financial position of the Municipalities.

(e) any other matter that may be referred to it by the Governor.

12. Elections to Municipalities.

The State Election Commission appointed under Article 243K shall have the power of superintendence, direction and control of (i) the preparation of electoral rolls for, and (ii) the conduct of all elections to the Municipalities. State Legislatures have been vested with necessary power to regulate by law all matters relating to elections to municipalities.

13. Bar to Interference by Courts in Electoral Matters.

The courts shall have no jurisdiction to examine the validity of a law, relating to delimitation of constituencies or the allotment of seats made under Article 243ZA. An election to a municipality can be called in question only by an election petition which should be presented to such authority and in such manner as may be prescribed by or under any law made by the State Legislature.

14. Committees for (a) District Planning and (b) Metropolitan Planning.

Apart from giving constitutional recognition to municipalities, the 74th Amendment[1] lays down that in every State two committees shall be constituted:

(1) At the district level, a District Planning Committee [*Article 243ZD*].

(2) In every metropolitan area, a Metropolitan Planning Committee [*Article 243ZE*].

---

1. For the text of the 74th Amendment Act relating to Municipalities [Articles 243P–243ZG], see Author's *Constitution Amendment Acts*, 7th Edn, pp 177–84; *Shorter Constitution of India,* 16th Edn, 2021.

The composition of the committees and the manner in which the seats are to be filled are to be provided by a law to be made by the State Legislature. But it has been laid down that, —

(a) in case of the District Planning Committee at least four-fifth of the members shall be elected by the elected members of the district level *Panchayat* and of the municipalities in the district from amongst themselves. Their proportion would be in accordance with the ratio of urban and rural population of the district.

(b) in case of Metropolitan Planning Committee at least two-third of the members of the committee shall be elected by the members of the municipalities and Chairpersons of the Panchayats in the Metropolitan area from amongst themselves. The proportion of seats to be shared by them would be based on the ratio of the population of the municipalities and of the *Panchayats* in the area.

The State Legislature would by law make provision with respect to (i) the functions relating to district planning that may be assigned to the district committees, and (ii) the manner in which the Chairperson of a district committee may be chosen.

The Committee shall prepare and forward the development plan to the State Government. In regard to the Metropolitan Planning Committee which is to prepare a development plan for the whole Metropolitan area, the State Legislature may by law make provision for:

(1) the representation of the Central and State Governments and of such organisations and institutions as may be deemed necessary,

(2) the functions relating to planning and co-ordination for the Metropolitan area,

(3) the manner in which the Chairpersons of such committees shall be chosen.

The development plan shall be forwarded to the State Government.

15. Addition to the Duties of the Finance Commission under Article 280.

This part adds one more function to the duties cast on the Finance Commission appointed by the President under Article 280. The Commission will make recommendations in regard to the measures needed to augment the Consolidated Fund of a State to supplement the resources of the Municipalities in the State on the basis of the recommendations made by the State Finance Commission.

PART VI

ADMINISTRATION OF SPECIAL AREAS

CHAPTER 20

ADMINISTRATION OF SCHEDULED AND TRIBAL AREAS

1. Scheduled Areas, and Scheduled Tribes of specified States.

THE Constitution makes special provisions for the Administration of certain areas called 'Scheduled Areas' in States other than Assam, Meghalaya, Tripura and Mizoram even though such areas are situated within a State or Union Territory [*Article 244(1)*], presumably because of the backwardness of the people of these Areas. Subject to legislation by Parliament, the power to declare any area as a 'Scheduled Area' is given to the President [Fifth *Schedule, paras 6-7*] and the President has made the Scheduled Areas Order, 1950, in pursuance of this power. These are Areas inhabited by Tribes specified as 'Scheduled Tribes', in States *other than* Assam, Meghalaya Tripura and Mizoram.[1] Special provisions for the administration of such Areas are given in the Fifth Schedule.

Any person eligible to vote who is ordinarily residing in the Scheduled Area has a right to vote, even if he is a non-Tribal.[2]

1a. Administration and Control.

The Fifth Schedule of the Constitution deals with the administration and control of Scheduled Areas as well as of Scheduled Tribes *in States other than Assam, Meghalaya, Tripura and Mizoram.* The main features of the administration provided in this Schedule are as follows:

The executive power of the Union shall extend to giving directions to the respective States regarding the administration of the Scheduled Areas [*Fifth Schedule, para* 3]. The Governors of the States in which there are 'Scheduled Areas'[1] have to submit reports to the President regarding the administration of such Areas, annually or whenever so required by the President [*Fifth Schedule, para 3*]. Tribes Advisory Councils are to be constituted to give advice on such matters as welfare and advancement of the Scheduled Tribes in the States as may be referred to them by the Governor [*Fifth Schedule, para 4*].

The Governor is authorised to direct that any particular Act of Parliament or of the Legislature of the State shall not apply to a Scheduled Area or shall apply, only subject to exceptions or modifications. The Governor is also authorised to

---

1. These States, presently, are—Andhra Pradesh (including Telangana), Chhattisgarh, Gujarat, Himachal Pradesh, Jharkhand, Madhya Pradesh, Maharashtra, Odisha and Rajasthan.
2. *Adivasis for Social and Human Rights Action v UOI*, (2023) SCC OnLine SC 601 : AIR 2023 SC 2658.

make regulations to prohibit or restrict the transfer of land by, or among members of, the Scheduled Tribes, regulate the allotment of land, and regulate the business of money-lending. All such regulations made by the Governor must have the assent of the President [*Fifth Schedule* V, *para 5*].

The foregoing provisions of the Constitution relating to the administration of the Scheduled Areas and Tribes may be altered by Parliament by ordinary legislation, without being required to go through the formalities relating to the amendment of the Constitution [*Fifth Schedule, para 7(2)*].

The Constitution provides for the appointment of a Commission to report on the administration of the Scheduled Areas and the welfare of the Scheduled Tribes in the States. The President may appoint such Commission at any time, but the appointment of such Commission at the end of ten years from the commencement of the Constitution is obligatory [*Article 339(1)*]. A Commission was accordingly appointed (with Sri UN Dhebar as Chairman) in 1960 and it submitted its report to the President towards the end of 1961.

All the Central and the State laws which are applicable to the entire State of Orissa will continue to apply to the Scheduled Area unless, in exercise of powers under sub-clause (1) of clause 5 of the Fifth Schedule, there is a specific notification issued by the Hon'ble Governor making a particular enactment inapplicable, either fully or partially. The power of the Hon'ble Governor is restricted to directing that a particular law will not apply to the Scheduled Area or it will apply with such modifications as may be specified in the notification issued under sub-clause (1) of clause 5 of the Fifth Schedule or while making Regulations in terms of sub-clause (2) of clause 5 of the Fifth Schedule. This power does not supersede the Fundamental Rights under Part III of the Constitution of India.[3]

2. Tribal Areas.

The Tribal Areas in the States of Assam, Meghalaya, Tripura[4] and Mizoram are separately dealt with [*Article 244(2)*], and provisions for their administration are to be found in the Sixth Schedule to the Constitution.

The Tribal Areas in Assam, Meghalaya, Tripura and Mizoram are specified in the Table appended to the Sixth Schedule (para 20) in the Constitution, which has undergone several amendments. Originally, it consisted of two Parts, A and B. But since the creation of the States of Nagaland, the Table (as amended in 1972, 1984, 1988 and 2003)[4] includes 10 areas, in four Parts:

Part I—1. The North Cachar Hills District; 2. The Karbi Anglong District; 3. The Bodoland Territorial Areas District.

Part II—1. The Khasi Hills District; 2. The Jaintia Hills District; 3. The Garo Hills District (in Meghalaya).

Part IIA—Tripura Tribal Areas District.

3. *Adivasis for Social and Human Rights Action v UOI,* (2023) SCC OnLine SC 601 : AIR 2023 SC 2658.
4. Meghalaya was added by the North-Eastern Areas (Reorganisation) Act, 1971. Tripura by the Constitution (49th Amendment) Act, 1984 and Mizoram by State of Mizoram Act, 1986. The Sixth Schedule to the Constitution (Amendment) Act, 2003 (44 of 2003).

Part III—1. The Chakma District; 2. The Mara District; 3. The Lai District.

While the administration of Scheduled Areas in States *other than* Assam, Meghalaya, Tripura and Mizoram[5] is dealt with in the Fifth Schedule, the Sixth Schedule deals with the tribal areas in Assam, Meghalaya, Tripura and Mizoram.[2]

These Tribal Areas are to be administered as autonomous districts. These autonomous districts are not outside the executive authority of the State concerned but provision is made for the creation of District Councils and Regional Councils for the exercise of certain legislative and judicial functions. These Councils are primarily representative bodies and they have got the power of law-making[6] in certain specified fields such as management of a forest other than a reserved forest, inheritance of property, marriage and social customs, and the Governor may also confer upon these Councils the power to try certain suits or offences.[7] These Councils have also the power to assess and collect land revenue and to impose certain specified taxes. The laws made by the Councils shall have, however, no effect unless assented to by the Governor.

With respect to the matters over which the District and Regional Councils are thus empowered to make laws, Acts of the State Legislature shall not extend to such Areas unless the relevant District Council so directs by public notification.[8] As regards other matters, the President with respect to a Central Act and the Governor with respect to a State Act, may direct that an Act of Parliament or of the State Legislature shall *not* apply to an autonomous district or shall apply only subject to exceptions or modifications as he may specify in his notification.

These Councils shall also possess judicial power, civil and criminal, subject to the jurisdiction of the High Court as the Governor may from time to time specify.

5. *Adivasis for Social and Human Rights Action v UOI*, (2023) SCC OnLine SC 601 : AIR 2023 SC 2658.
6. Para 3, Sixth Schedule.
7. Para 4, Sixth Schedule.
8. Paras 12, 12A, 12AA and 12B, Sixth Schedule.

PART VII

THE JUDICATURE

CHAPTER 21

ORGANISATION OF THE JUDICIARY IN GENERAL

No federal distribution of judicial powers.

It has already been pointed out that notwithstanding the adoption of a federal system, the Constitution of India has not provided for a double system of courts as in the United States. Under our Constitution, there is a single integrated system of courts for the Union as well as the States which administer both Union and State laws, and at the head of the entire system stands the Supreme Court of India. Below the Supreme Court stand the High Courts of the different States and under each High Court there is a hierarchy of other courts which are referred to in the Constitution as 'subordinate courts', i.e., courts subordinate to and under the control of the High Court (Arts. 233-237).

The organisation of the subordinate judiciary varies slightly from State to State but the essential features may be explained with reference to a State which has been given [illegible] of the system [illegible] of the State.

The Supreme Court [illegible] constitution [illegible] and [illegible] concrete steps [illegible] taken [illegible].

As regards [illegible] justice [illegible] courts [illegible]

[illegible] courts.

[illegible] Constitution [illegible] regional [illegible] and [illegible] of the lowest [illegible].

The District [illegible] the next higher civil courts [illegible] above the [illegible] unlimited pecuniary jurisdiction over civil suits [illegible].

CHAPTER 21

ORGANISATION OF THE JUDICIARY IN GENERAL

1. No Federal Distribution of Judicial Powers.

IT has already been pointed out that notwithstanding the adoption of a federal system, the Constitution of India has not provided for a double system of courts as in the *United States*. Under *our* Constitution, there is a single integrated system of courts for the Union as well as the States which administer both Union and State laws, and at the head of the entire system stands the Supreme Court of India. Below the Supreme Court stands the High Courts of the different States[1] and under each High Court, there is a hierarchy of other courts which are referred to in the Constitution as "subordinate courts", *i.e.*, courts subordinate to and under the control of the High Court [*Articles 233–237*].

The organisation of the subordinate judiciary varies slightly from State to State, but the essential features may be explained with reference to Table XV, *post,* which has been drawn with reference to the system obtaining in the majority of the States.

The Supreme Court has issued a direction[2] to the Union and the States to constitute an All India Judicial Service and to bring about uniformity in designation of officers both in criminal and civil side. The Central Government is preparing to make a fresh attempt at reaching a consensus with States though concrete steps in this direction are yet to be taken by the Government in this regard.

2. The Hierarchy of Courts.

At the lowest stage, the two branches of justice—civil and criminal—are bifurcated. The Union Courts and the Bench Courts constituted under the Village Self-Government Acts, which constituted the lowest civil and criminal courts respectively, have been substituted by Panchayat Courts set up under post-Constitution State legislation. The Panchayat Courts also function on two sides, civil and criminal, under various regional names, such as the *Nyaya Panchayat, Panchayat Adalat, Gram Kutchery,* and the like. In some states, the Panchayat Courts, are the criminal courts of the lowest jurisdiction, in respect of petty cases.

The Munsiff's Courts are the next higher civil courts, having jurisdiction as determined by high courts. Above the Munsiffs are Subordinate Judges who have got unlimited pecuniary jurisdiction over civil suits and hear first appeals from

1. For a list of high courts, their seat and territorial jurisdiction, see Table XVI.
2. *All India Judges Association v UOI,* AIR 1992 SC 165.

the judgments of Munsiffs. The District Judge hears first appeals from the decisions of Subordinate Judges and also from the Munsiffs (unless they are transferred to a Subordinate Judge) and himself possesses unlimited original jurisdiction, both civil and criminal. Suits of a small value are tried by the Provincial Small Causes Courts.

The District Judge is the highest judicial authority (civil and criminal) in the district. He hears appeals from the decisions of the superior Magistrates and also tries the more serious criminal cases, known as the Sessions cases. A Subordinate Judge is sometimes vested also with the powers of an Assistant Sessions Judge, in which case he combines in his hands both civil and criminal powers like a District Judge.

Since the enactment of the Criminal Procedure Code, 1973, the trial of criminal cases is done exclusively by "Judicial Magistrates". The Chief Judicial Magistrate is the head of the criminal courts within the district. In Calcutta and other "metropolitan areas", there are Metropolitan Magistrates. The Judicial and Metropolitan Magistrates, discharging judicial functions, under the administrative control of the State high court, are to be distinguished from Executive Magistrates who discharge the executive function of maintaining law and order, under the control of the State Government.

There are special arrangements for civil judicial administration in the "Presidency towns", which are now called "metropolitan areas". The original side of the high court at Calcutta tries the bigger *civil* suits arising within the area of the Presidency town. Suits of lower value within the city are tried by the City Civil Court and the Presidency Small Causes Court. But the Original *Criminal* jurisdiction of all high courts, including Calcutta, has been taken away by the Criminal Procedure Code, 1973.

The high court is the supreme judicial tribunal of the State—having both Original and Appellate jurisdiction. It exercises appellate jurisdiction over the District and Sessions Judge, the Presidency Magistrates and the Original Side of the high court itself (where the Original Side still continues). There is a high court for each of the States, except Nagaland, Mizoram, and Arunachal Pradesh, which have the three respective benches of the High Court of Gauhati as their common high court;[3] and Haryana, which has a common High Court (at Chandigarh) with Punjab. The High Court of Judicature at Hyderabad functioned as the common High Court for the State of Telangana and the State of Andhra Pradesh with effect from 2 June 2014 by virtue of section 30(1) of Part IV of the Andhra Pradesh Reorganisation Act, 2014. As per the Order of the Government of India, dated 26 December 2018, the common High Court of Judicature at Hyderabad has been bifurcated and new High Courts namely, High Court for the State of Telangana and High Court of Andhra Pradesh have been established. The seat of High Court of Andhra Pradesh has been established at

3. Three separate high courts have been established in Meghalaya, Manipur and Tripura by the President of India, in exercise of the powers conferred by sub-section (2) of section 28A of the North Eastern Areas (Reorganisation) Act, 1971 and has appointed the Principal Seats of the High Court of Manipur, High Court of Meghalaya, and High Court of Tripura at Imphal, Shillong, and Agartala respectively from the 23 March 2013.

Amravati while the seat of the High Court of Telangana is Hyderabad.[5] The Bombay High Court is common for the States of Maharashtra and Goa (and also for the Union Territories of Dadra and Nagar Haveli and Daman and Diu).

The Jammu and Kashmir Reorganisation Act, 2019 provides that the High Court of Jammu and Kashmir shall be the common High Court for the Union territory of Jammu and Kashmir and Union territory of Ladakh. It provides that the Judges of the High Court of Jammu and Kashmir for the erstwhile State of Jammu and Kashmir holding office immediately before 31 October 2019 shall become on that day the Judges of the common High Court which has now been renamed as High Court of Jammu & Kashmir and Ladakh.

The Supreme Court has appellate jurisdiction over the high courts and is the highest tribunal of the land. The Supreme Court also possesses original and advisory jurisdictions which will be fully explained hereafter (in Chapter 22).

5. The State of Telangana was separated from Andhra Pradesh on 2 June 2014, as a new 29th State of India, with the city of Hyderabad as its capital *vide* the Andhra Pradesh Reorganisation Act, 2014.

CHAPTER 22

THE SUPREME COURT

PARLIAMENT has the power to make laws regulating the constitution, organisation, jurisdiction and powers of the Supreme Court. Subject to such legislation, the Supreme Court consists of the Chief Justice of India and not more than *thirty-three*[1] other Judges [*Article 124*].

1. Constitution of the Supreme Court.

Besides, the Chief Justice of India has the power, with the previous consent of the President, to request a retired Supreme Court Judge to act as a Judge of the Supreme Court for a temporary period. Similarly, a high court Judge may be appointed *ad hoc* Judge of the Supreme Court for a temporary period if there is a lack of quorum of the permanent Judges [*Articles 127–128*].[2]

2. Appointment of Judges.

Every Judge of the Supreme Court shall be appointed by the President of India. The President shall, in this matter, consult other persons besides taking the advice of his Ministers. In the matter of appointment of the Chief Justice of India, he shall consult such Judges of the Supreme Court and of the high courts as he may deem necessary. A nine-Judge Bench of the Supreme Court has laid down that the senior-most Judge of the Supreme Court considered fit to hold the office should be appointed to the office of Chief Justice of India.[3] And in the case of

---

1. The Constitution provided for seven Judges besides the Chief Justice, subject to legislation by Parliament. Parliament has enacted the Supreme Court (Number of Judges) Acts, 1956, 1986 and 2008, raising this number to 30 and further raised to 33 by the Supreme Court (Number of Judges) Amendment Act, 2019 (37 of 2019) as published in the Gazette of India, Extraordinary Part II section 1 dated 09 August 2019.
2. Vide the Constitutional (99th Amendment) Act, 2014 in Article 127 of the Constitution, in clause (1), for the words, *"the Chief Justice of India may, with the previous consent of the President"*, the words, "*the National Judicial Appointments Commission on a reference made to it by the Chief Justice of India, may with the previous consent of the President*" shall be substituted, and further in Article 128 of the Constitution, for the words "*the Chief Justice of India*", the words, "*the National Judicial Appointments Commission*" shall be substituted. This Amendment Act was held invalid by the Supreme Court.
3. *Supreme Court Advocates-on-Record Association v UOI,* AIR 1994 SC 268, pp 685, 688, 692, 693 : (1993) 4 SCC 441 (nine-Judge Bench). Pursuant to public interest petitions filed by the Supreme Court Advocates-On-Recorded Association seeking relief of filling up of vacancies, a bench of nine judges over-ruled the judgment in *SP Gupta v UOI,* AIR 1982 SC 149 (1981) which had upheld the primacy of the executive in the appointment of judges in the superior courts. Later, in *Re Special Reference No 1 of 1998,* AIR 1999 SC 1, the court has, with a view to making consultation more informed, transparent and meaningful, held that the Chief Justice of India must consult four senior most judges in the selection process.

appointment of other Judges of the Supreme Court, consultation with the Chief Justice of India, in addition to the above, is obligatory [*Article 124(2)*]. Consultation would generally mean concurrence.[3] The above provision, thus, modifies the mode of appointment of Judges by the Executive—by providing that the Executive should consult members of the Judiciary itself, who are well-qualified to give their opinion in this matter.[4]

In a reference[5] (not as a review or reconsideration of the *Second Judges case*) made by the President under Article 143 relating to the consultation between the Chief Justice of India and his brother Judges in matters of appointment of the Supreme Court Judges and the relevance of seniority in making such appointments, the nine-Judge Bench opined:

1. The opinion of the CJI, having primacy in the consultative process and reflecting the opinion of the judiciary, has to be formed on the basis of consultation with the *collegium,* comprising of the CJI and the four senior most Judges of the Supreme Court. The Judge, who is to succeed the CJI should also be included, if he is not one of the four senior most Judges. Their views should be obtained in writing.
2. Views of the senior most Judges of the Supreme Court, who hail from the high courts where the persons to be recommended are functioning as Judges, if not the part of the *collegium,* must be obtained in writing.
3. The recommendation of the *collegium* alongwith the views of its members and that of the senior most Judges of the Supreme Court who hail from the high courts where the persons to be recommended are functioning as Judges should be conveyed by the Chief Justice of India to the Government of India.
4. The substance of the views of the others consulted by the Chief Justice of India or on his behalf, particularly those of non-Judges (Members of the Bar) should be stated in the memorandum and be conveyed to the Government of India.
5. Normally, the *collegium* should make its recommendation on the basis of consensus but in case of difference of opinion no one would be appointed, if the CJI dissents.

---

4. *Constituent Assembly Debates,* vol 8, 258. But there is no such safeguard in the case of appointment of a Chief Justice, and when AN Ray J, was appointed Chief Justice, after superseding three senior Judges — Hedge, Grover and Shelat, there was an uproar in which the Supreme Court Bar Association joined, that the Senior Judges had been superseded solely because their judgment in *Kesavananda's* case (AIR 1973 SC 1461 : (1973) 4 SCC 225) had been unfavourable to the Government.

   Again, in January 1977 instead of HR Khanna J the senior most Judge MU Beg J was made the Chief Justice of India. Justice Khanna resigned just as the three Judges had done a few years back. It was said the supersession was because of his dissenting judgment in *ADM Jabalpur v Shivkant Shukla,* AIR 1976 SC 1207 : (1976) 2 SCC 521.

   After the judgment referred to in fn 3 above viz *Supreme Court Advocates-on-Record Association v UOI,* (1993) 4 SCC 441, pp 685, 688, 692, 693, it appears that discretion of the executive has been curtailed.
5. *Re Special Reference No 1 of 1998,* (1998) 7 SCC 739. The Bench expressed its optimistic view that the successive CJIs shall henceforth act in accordance with *the Second Judges case* and the opinion in the instant reference.

6. If two or more members of the *collegium* dissent, CJI should not persist with the recommendation.
7. In case of non-appointment of the person recommended, the materials and information conveyed by the Government of India, must be placed before the original *collegium* or the reconstituted one, if so, to consider whether the recommendation should be withdrawn or reiterated. It is only if it unanimously reiterated that the appointment must be made.
8. The CJI may, in his discretion, bring to the knowledge of the person recommended the reasons disclosed by the Government of India for his non-appointment and ask for his response thereto, which, if made, be considered by the *collegium* before withdrawing or reiterating the recommendation.
9. Merit should be predominant consideration though inter-seniority among the Judges in their high courts and their combined seniority on all India basis should be given weight.
10. Cogent and good reasons should be recorded for recommending a person of outstanding merit regardless of his lower seniority.
11. For recommending one of several persons of more or less equal degree of merit, the factor of the high courts not represented on the Supreme Court, may be considered.
12. The Judge passed over can be reconsidered unless for strong reasons, it is recorded that he be never appointed.
13. The recommendations made by the CJI without complying with the norms and requirements, are not binding on the Government of India.

3. NJAC Judgment.

The 99th Constitutional (Amendment) Act, 2014[6] and the National Judicial Appointment Commission Act, 2014[7] were enacted with a view to bring more transparency in the judicial appointments. (see Chapter 4, *ante*).

In Article 124, for the words "after consultation with such of the Judges of the Supreme Court and of the high courts in the States as the President may deem necessary for the purpose", the words, figures and letter "on the recommendation of the National Judicial Appointments Commission referred to in article 124A" were substituted. Further, three new Articles, *viz.*, Articles 124A, 124B and 124C were also inserted in the Constitution which are as under:

> 124A. (1) There shall be a Commission to be known as the National Judicial Appointments Commission consisting of the following, namely:—
>
> (a) the Chief Justice of India, Chairperson, ex officio;
>
> (b) two other senior Judges of the Supreme Court next to the Chief Justice of India—Members, ex officio;

6. The Constitutional (99th Amendment) Act, 2014 as published in the Gazette of India, Extra Ordinary Part II dated 31 December 2014 which was held invalid by the Supreme Court.
7. National Judicial Appointment Commission Act, 2014 (No 40 of 2014) as published in the Gazette of India, Extra Ordinary Part II dated 31 December 2014 which was held invalid by the Supreme Court.

(c) the Union Minister in charge of Law and Justice—Member, ex officio;

(d) two eminent persons to be nominated by the committee consisting of the Prime Minister, the Chief Justice of India and the Leader of Opposition in the House of the People or where there is no such Leader of Opposition, then, the Leader of single largest Opposition Party in the House of the People— Members:

Provided that one of the eminent person shall be nominated from amongst the persons belonging to the Scheduled Castes, the Scheduled Tribes, Other Backward Classes, Minorities or Women:

Provided further that an eminent person shall be nominated for a period of three years and shall not be eligible for renomination.

(2) No act or proceedings of the National Judicial Appointments Commission shall be questioned or be invalidated merely on the ground of the existence of any vacancy or defect in the constitution of the Commission.

124B. It shall be the duty of the National Judicial Appointments Commission to—

(a) recommend persons for appointment as Chief Justice of India, Judges of the Supreme Court, Chief Justices of High Courts and other Judges of High Courts;

(b) recommend transfer of Chief Justices and other Judges of High Courts from one High Court to any other High Court; and

(c) ensure that the person recommended is of ability and integrity.

124C. Parliament may, by law, regulate the procedure for the appointment of Chief Justice of India and other Judges of the Supreme Court and Chief Justices and other Judges of High Courts and empower the Commission to lay down by regulations the procedure for the discharge of its functions, the manner of selection of persons for appointment and such other matters as may be considered necessary by it.

As per the amended provisions of the Constitution, the Commission was to consist of: a) Chief Justice of India (Chairperson, *ex officio*); b) Two other senior judges of the Supreme Court next to the Chief Justice of India—*ex officio*; c) The Union Minister of Law and Justice, *ex-officio*; d) Two eminent persons (to be nominated by a committee consisting of the Chief Justice of India, Prime Minister of India and the Leader of opposition in the Lok Sabha or where there is no such Leader of Opposition, then, the Leader of single largest Opposition Party in Lok Sabha), provided that of the two eminent persons, one person would be from the Scheduled Castes or Scheduled Tribes or OBC or minority communities or a woman. The eminent persons shall be nominated for a period of three years and shall not be eligible for re-nomination.

As per the amended Constitution, the functions of the Commission were to: (i) recommend persons for appointment as Chief Justice of India, Judges of the Supreme Court, Chief Justices of high courts and other Judges of high courts; (ii) recommend transfer of Chief Justices and other Judges of high courts from one high court to any other high court; and (iii) ensure that the persons recommended are of ability, merit and other criteria mentioned in the regulations related to the Act.

However, it is noteworthy that several writ petitions were filed in the Supreme Court challenging the 99th Constitutional Amendment, 2014 and the National

Judicial Appointment Commission Act, 2014, and disposing of the above appeals, the five Judge Bench of the Supreme Court declared the 99th Amendment to be unconstitutional on the grounds that it violates the basic principles of "Independence of Judiciary" and "Separation of Powers" which in turn violates the basic structure of the Indian Constitution. (Refer Chapter 4, *ante*).

4. Qualifications for appointment as Judge.

A person shall not be qualified for appointment as a Judge of the Supreme Court unless he is: (a) a citizen of India; and (b) either—(i) a distinguished jurist; or (ii) has been a high court Judge for at least five years; or (iii) has been an Advocate of a high court (or two or more such courts in succession) for at least 10 years [*Article 124(3)*].

5. Tenure of Judges.

No minimum age is prescribed for appointment as a Judge of the Supreme Court, nor any fixed period of office. Once appointed, a Judge of the Supreme Court may cease to be so, on the happening of any one of the following contingencies (other than death): (a) On attaining the age of 65 years; (b) On resigning his office by writing addressed to the President; (c) On being removed by the President upon an address to that effect being passed by a special majority of each House of Parliament (*viz.*, a majority of the total membership of that House and by majority of not less than two-thirds of the members of that House present and voting).

The only grounds upon which such removal may take place are: (1) "proved misbehaviour" and (2) "incapacity". In Article 124(4) of the Constitution, "misbehaviour" means wrong conduct or improper conduct. Every act or conduct or error of judgment or negligence by a Constitutional authority *per se* does not amount to misbehaviour. Misconduct implies a creation of some degree of *mens rea* by the doer. Wilful abuse of constitutional office, wilful misconduct in the office, corruption, lack of integrity or any other offence involving moral turpitude would be "misbehaviour".[8]

6. Impeachment of a Judge.

The combined effect of Article 124(4) and the Judges (Inquiry) Act, 1968 is that the following procedure is to be observed for removal of a Judge. This is commonly known as impeachment—

(1) A motion addressed to the President signed by at least 100 members of the Lok Sabha or 50 members of the Rajya Sabha is delivered to the Speaker or the Chairman.

(2) The motion is to be investigated by a Committee of three (two Judges of the Supreme Court and a distinguished jurist).

(3) If the Committee finds the Judge guilty of misbehaviour or that he suffers from incapacity the motion (para 1, above) together with the report of the Committee is taken up for consideration in the House where the motion is pending.

(4) If the motion is passed in each House by majority of the total membership of that House and by a majority of not less than two-thirds of that House present and voting the address is presented to the President.

---

8. *Re Reference under Article 317(1) of the Constitution of India*, (2009) 1 SCC 337, p 345 : [2009] 2 Mad LJ 1055.

(5) The Judge will be removed after the President gives his order for removal on the said address.

The procedure for impeachment is the same for Judges of the Supreme Court and the High Courts. After the Constitution this procedure was started against Shri R Ramaswamy in 1991–93. The Committee found the Judge guilty. In the Lok Sabha the Congress Party abstained from voting and so the motion could not be passed with requisite majority.

7. Salaries, etc. A Judge of the Supreme Court gets a salary of Rs 2,50,000 *per mensem*[9] and the use of an official residence free of rent. The salary of the Chief Justice is Rs 2,80,000.[10]

8. Independence of Supreme Court Judges, how secured. The independence of the Judges of the Supreme Court is sought to be secured by the Constitution in a number of ways:

(a) Though the appointing authority is the President, acting with the advice of his Council of Ministers, the appointment of the Supreme Court Judge has been lifted from the realm of pure politics by requiring the President to consult the Chief Justice of India in the matter.[4]

(b) By laying down that a Judge of the Supreme Court shall not be removed by the President, except on a joint address by both Houses of Parliament (supported by a majority of the total membership and a majority of not less than two-thirds of the members present and voting, in each House), on ground of proved misbehaviour or incapacity of the Judge in question [*Article 124(4)*].

This provision is similar to the rule prevailing in England since the Act of Settlement, 1701, to the effect that though Judges of the Superior Courts are appointed by the Crown, they do not hold office during his pleasure, but hold their office "on good behaviour" and the Crown may remove them only upon a joint address from both Houses of Parliament.

(c) By fixing the salaries of the Judges by the Constitution, and providing that though the allowances, leave and pension may be determined by law made by Parliament, these shall not be varied to the disadvantage of a Judge during his term of office. In other words, he will not be affected adversely by any changes made by law since his appointment [*Article 125(2)*].

But it will be competent for the President to override this guarantee, under a Proclamation of "Financial Emergency" [*Article 360(4)(b)*].

(d) By providing that the administrative expenses of the Supreme Court, the salaries and allowances, etc., of the Judges as well as of the staff of the Supreme Court shall be "charged upon the Consolidated Fund of India", *i.e.*, shall not be subject to vote in Parliament [*Article 146(3)*].

(e) By forbidding the discussion of the conduct of a Judge of the Supreme Court (or of a high court) in Parliament, except upon a motion for an address to the President for the removal of the Judge [*Article 121*].

---

9. The salaries of Judges of the Supreme Court and the High Courts have been enhanced *vide* the High Court and Supreme Court Judges (Salaries and Conditions of Service) Amendment Act, 2018 (10 of 2018) (w.r.e.f. 1-1-2016).

10. *Re Reference under Article 317(1) of the Constitution of India*, (2009) 1 SCC 337, p 345 : [2009] 2 Mad LJ 1055.

(f) By laying down that after retirement, a Judge of the Supreme Court shall not plead or act in any court or before any authority within the territory of India[11] [*Article 124(7)*].

[It is to be noted that there are analogous provisions in the case of High Court Judges; see Chapter 23, *post.*]

9. Position of the Supreme Court under the Constitution.

It has been rightly said that the jurisdiction and powers of our Supreme Court are in their nature and extent wider than those exercised by the highest court of any other country.[12] It is at once a federal court, a court of appeal and a guardian of the Constitution, and the law declared by it, in the exercise of any of its jurisdictions under the Constitution, is binding on all other courts within the territory of India [*Article 141*].

The foreign decisions only have persuasive value in our country and are not binding authorities on our courts.[13]

In case where there is a conflict between two or more judgments of Supreme Court, the judgment of the larger bench would be followed.[14] A decision or judgment can be said to be *per incuriam* if it is not possible to reconcile its ratio with that of a previously pronounced judgment of a co-equal or larger Bench.[15]

10. Compared with the American Supreme Court.

Our Supreme Court possesses larger powers[16] than the American Supreme Court in several respects—

Firstly, the American Supreme Court's appellate jurisdiction is confined to cases arising out of the federal relationship or those relating to the constitutional validity of laws and treaties. But *our* Supreme Court is not only a federal court and a guardian of the Constitution, but also the highest court of appeal in the land, relating to civil and criminal cases [*Articles* 133–134], apart from cases relating to the interpretation of the Constitution.

Secondly, our Supreme Court has an extraordinary power to entertain appeal, without any limitation upon its discretion, from the decision not only of any court but also of any tribunal within the territory of India except from decision of any court or tribunal constituted by or under any law relating to the Armed Forces [*Article* 136]. No such power belongs to the American Supreme Court.

Thirdly, while the American Supreme Court has denied to itself any power to advise the Government and confined itself only to the determination of actual

---

11. But, curiously, there is no bar against a retired Judge from being appointed to any office under the Government [as there is in the case of the Comptroller and Auditor-General: Article 148(4)]; and the expectation of such employment after retirement indirectly detracts from the independence of the Judges from executive influence. In fact, retired Judges have been appointed to hold offices such as that of Governor, Ambassador and the like, apart from membership of numerous Commissions or Boards.
12. *Attorney-General of India,* (1956) SCR 8; AK Aiyar, *The Constitution and Fundamental Rights,* 1955, p 15.
13. *Aruna Ramchandra Shanbang v UOI,* AIR 2011 SC 1290, p 1326 : (2011) 4 SCC 454.
14. *Pyare Mohan Lal v State of Jharkhand,* AIR 2010 SC 3753 : (2010) 10 SCC 693, p 704.
15. *Banwari v Haryana State Industrial and Infrastructure Development Corporation Limited,* AIR 2025 SC 165 : AIROnline 2024 SC 841.
16. *Vide* Author's *Constitutional Law of India,* Prentice-Hall of India, 1991, pp 168 *et seq.*

controversies between parties to a litigation, *our* Supreme Court is vested by the Constitution itself with the power to deliver advisory opinion on any question of fact or law that may be referred to it by the President [*Article* 143].

The power of Supreme Court to make rules to regulate its own procedure is only subject to two limitations:

(i) These rules are subject to the laws made by Parliament.

(ii) These rules being in the nature of subordinate legislation cannot override the constitutional provisions [*Article 145*].[17]

The Supreme Court Rules, 2013 having a statutory force have to be strictly adhered to and followed by all concerned. No practice could be permitted to overrule the Statutory Rules.[18]

10a. As a Federal Court.

Every federal Constitution, whatever the degree of cohesion it aims at, involves a distribution of powers between the Union and the units composing the Union, and both Union and State Governments derive their authority from, and are limited by the same Constitution. In a unitary Constitution, like that of England, the local administrative or legislative bodies are mere subordinate bodies under the central authority. Hence, there is no need of judicially determining disputes between the central and local authorities. But in a federal Constitution, the powers are divided between the national and State Governments, and there must be some authority to determine disputes between the Union and the States or the States *inter se* and to maintain the distribution of powers as made by the Constitution.

Though *our* federation is not in the nature of a treaty or compact between the component units, there is, nevertheless, a division of legislative as well as administrative powers between the Union and the States. Article 131 of *our* Constitution, therefore, vests the Supreme Court with original and exclusive jurisdiction to determine justiciable disputes between the Union and the States or between the States *inter se*.

10b. As a Court of Appeal.

Like the House of Lords in England, the Supreme Court of India is the final appellate tribunal of the land, and in some respects, the jurisdiction of the Supreme Court is even wider than that of the House of Lords. As regards *criminal* appeals, an appeal lies to the House of Lords only if the Attorney-General certifies that the decision of the Court of Criminal Appeal involves a point of law of exceptional public importance and that it is desirable in the public interest that a further appeal should be brought. But in cases specified in clauses (*a*) and (*b*) of Article 134(1) of *our* Constitution (death sentences), an appeal will lie to the Supreme Court as of right.

As to appeals from high courts in *civil* cases, however, the position has been altered by an amendment of Article 133(1) by the Constitution (30th Amendment) Act, 1972, which has likened the law to that in England. Civil appeals from the decisions of the Court of Appeal lie to the House of Lords only if the Court of Appeal or the House of Lords grants leave to appeal. Under

17. *Yomeshbhai P Bhatt v State of Gujarat*, (2011) 6 SCC 312, p *315*.
18. *Supreme Court Bar Association v State of Uttar Pradesh*, AIR 2025 SC 1863 : 2025 INSC 364.

Article 133(1) of *our* Constitution as it originally stood, an appeal to the Supreme Court lay as of right in cases of higher value (as certified by the high court). But this value test and the category of appeal as of right has been abolished by the amendment of 1972, under which appeal from the decision of a high court in a civil matter will lie to the Supreme Court only if the high court certifies that the case involves "a substantial question of law of general importance" and that "the said question needs to be decided by the Supreme Court".[19] The Supreme Court can not interfere, with the finding of fact, arrived at by the final court of fact and affirmed by the high court in second appeal unless there is some infirmity for which the court can hold the findings arbitrary or perverse.[20]

But the right of the Supreme Court to entertain appeal, *by special leave,* in any cause or matter determined by any court or tribunal in India, save military tribunals, is unlimited [*Article 136*].

10c. As a Guardian of the Constitution. As against unconstitutional acts of the Executive the jurisdiction of the courts is nearly the same under all constitutional systems. But not so is the control of the Judiciary over the Legislature.

It is true that there is no express provision in *our* Constitution empowering the *courts* to invalidate laws; but the Constitution has imposed definite limitations upon each of the organs of the state, and any transgression of those limitations would make the law *void*. It is for the courts to decide whether any of the constitutional limitations has been transgressed or not,[21] because the Constitution is the organic law subject to which ordinary laws are made by the Legislature which itself is set up by the Constitution.

Thus, Article 13 declares that any law which contravenes any of the provisions of the Part on Fundamental Rights, shall be *void*. But, as *our* Supreme Court has observed,[22] even without the specific provision in Article 13 (which has been inserted only by way of abundant caution), the court would have the powers to declare any enactment which transgresses a fundamental right as invalid.

Similarly, Article 254 says that in case of inconsistency between Union and State laws in certain cases, the State law shall be *void*.

The limitations imposed by *our* Constitution upon the powers of Legislatures are—(a) Fundamental rights conferred by Part III; (b) Legislative competence; (c) Specific provisions of the Constitution imposing limitations relating to particular matters.[23]

It is clear from the above that (apart from the jurisdiction to issue the writs to enforce the fundamental rights, which has been explained earlier) the jurisdiction of the Supreme Court is three-fold: (a) Original; (b) Appellate; and (c) Advisory.

---

19. *Attorney-General of India,* (1956) SCR 8; AK Aiyar, *The Constitution and Fundamental Rights,* 1955, p 15.
20. *Madan Kishore v Major Sudhir Sewal,* (2008) 8 SCC 744, p *752* : (2008)(12 Scale 20.
21. *AK Gopalan v State of Madras,* AIR 1950 SC 27 : (1950) SCR 88 p *100*; *Reference Under Article 143,* AIR 1965 SC 745, p *762*.
22. *Aruna Ramchandra Shanbang v UOI,* AIR 2011 SC 1290, p 1326 : (2011) 4 SCC 454.
23. *Vide* Author's *Constitutional Law of India,* Prentice-Hall of India, 1991, p 270.

11. Original jurisdiction of Supreme Court.

The Original jurisdiction of the Supreme Court is dealt with in Article 131 of the Constitution. The functions of the Supreme Court under Article 131 are purely of a federal character and are confined to disputes between the Government of India and any of the States of the Union, the Government of India and any State or States on one side and any other State or States on the other side, or between two or more States *inter se*. In short, these are disputes between different units of the federation which will be within the exclusive original jurisdiction of the Supreme Court. The Original jurisdiction of the Supreme Court will be *exclusive*, which means that no other court in India shall have the power to entertain any such suit. On the other hand, the Supreme Court in its original jurisdiction will not be entitled to entertain any suit where *both* the parties are not units of the federation. If any suit is brought either against the State or the Government of India by a private citizen, that will *not lie* within the original jurisdiction of the Supreme Court but will be brought in the ordinary courts under the ordinary law.

Again, one class of disputes, though a federal nature, is excluded from this original jurisdiction of the Supreme Court, namely, a dispute arising out of any treaty, agreement, covenant, engagement; "*sanad*" or other similar instrument which, having been entered into or executed before the commencement of this Constitution continues in operation after such commencement or which provides that the said jurisdiction shall not extend to such a dispute.[24] But these disputes may be referred by the President to the Supreme Court for its *advisory* opinion.

The jurisdiction under Article 131 of the Constitution would only be subject to any other provision in the Constitution which provides for entertaining a dispute between the parties mentioned therein. There is only one such other provision in the Constitution, which is Article 262. Article 262 of the Constitution deals with adjudication of disputes relating to waters of inter-State rivers or river valleys. It provides that the Parliament may by law provide for the adjudication of such disputes or complaints excluding the jurisdiction of all courts including this Court. As such, ordinarily a dispute with respect to the use, distribution or control of the waters of, or in, any inter-State river or river valley between two States could have fallen under Article 131 of the Constitution but because of the words "subject to the provisions of this Constitution" used therein and in view of Article 262, such a dispute would not be entertainable under Article 131 of the Constitution. Merely because, in any of the proceedings initiated under Article 32 or Article 136 or even Article 226 of the Constitution, one of the parties is common, the pendency of such proceedings would not come in the way of a specific party mentioned in Article 131 of the Constitution to take recourse to the remedy available therein. A remedy under Article 131 of the Constitution is a special remedy available only to the parties mentioned therein and for the purposes mentioned therein.[25]

It may be noted that until 1962, no suit in the original jurisdiction had been decided by the Supreme Court. It seems that the disputes, if any, between the Union and the units or between the units *inter se* had so far been settled by

24. Article 131, proviso, as amended by the Constitution (seventh Amendment) Act, 1956.
25. *State of West Bengal v UOI*, AIR 2024 SC 3499 : AIR Online 2024 SC 471.

negotiation or agreement rather than by adjudication. The first suit, brought by the State of West Bengal against the Union of India in 1961, to declare the unconstitutionality of the Coal Bearing Areas (Acquisition and Development) Act, 1957, was dismissed by the Supreme Court.[26]

Besides these, the Supreme Court has original jurisdiction in transfer of cases as provided under Constitution of India and the laws which are as under:

(a) Article 139A(1) of the Constitution of India, 1950 provides that where cases involving the same or substantially the same questions of law are pending before the Supreme Court and one or more high courts or before two or more high courts, and the Supreme Court is satisfied, on its own motion, or on an application made by the Attorney-General for India or by a party to any such case, that such questions are substantial questions of general importance, the Supreme Court may withdraw the case or cases pending before the high court or the high courts and dispose of all the cases itself.

(b) Article 139A(2) of the Constitution of India, 1950 provides that the Supreme Court may, if it deems it expedient so to do for the ends of justice, transfer any case, appeal or other proceedings pending before any high court to any other high court.

(c) Section 25 of the Code of Civil Procedure, 1908 provides that Supreme Court may transfer any suit, appeal or other proceedings from a high court or other civil court in one State to a high court or other civil court in any other State.

(d) Section 406 of the Code of Criminal Procedure, 1973 provides that Supreme Court may transfer any particular case or appeal from one high court to another high court or from a criminal court subordinate to one high court to another criminal court of equal or superior jurisdiction, subordinate to another high court.

In this context, it should be further noted that there are certain provisions in the Constitution which exclude from the original jurisdiction of the Supreme Court certain disputes, the determination of which is vested in other tribunals:

(i) Disputes specified in the proviso to Articles 131 and 363(1).

(ii) Complaints as to interference with inter-State water supplies, referred to the statutory tribunal mentioned in Article 262, if Parliament so legislates.

Since Parliament has enacted the Inter-State Water Disputes Act (33 of 1956), Article 262 has now to be read with section 11 of that Act.

(iii) Matters referred to the Finance Commission [*Article* 280].

(iv) Adjustment of certain expenses as between the Union and the States under Articles 257(4), and 258(3).

(v) Adjustment of certain expenses as between the Union and the States [*Article* 290].

---

26. *State of West Bengal v UOI,* AIR 1963 SC 1241 : (1964) 1 SCR 371.

12. Writ jurisdiction of the Supreme Court. The jurisdiction of the Supreme Court to entertain an application under Article 32 for the issue of a Constitutional writ for the enforcement of Fundamental Rights, is sometimes treated as an "original" jurisdiction of the Supreme Court. It is no doubt original in the sense that the party aggrieved has the right to directly move the Supreme Court by presenting a petition, instead of coming through a high court by way of appeal. Nevertheless, it should be treated as a separate jurisdiction since the dispute in such cases is not between the units of the Union but an aggrieved individual and the Government or any of its agencies. Hence, the jurisdiction under Article 32 has no analogy to the jurisdiction under Article 131.

The contours of the court's writ jurisdiction have been established in several decisions of the Supreme Court. Where the law provides for a hierarchy of appeals, the parties must exhaust the available remedies before resorting to writ jurisdiction of the Supreme Court. At the same time, the Supreme Court in a catena of decisions has held that this doctrine is not a rule of law, but essentially a rule of policy, convenience and discretion. Thus, where there is failure of principles of natural justice or where the orders or proceedings are wholly without jurisdiction warrants, the Supreme Court may exercise its writ jurisdiction even if the parties had other adequate legal remedies.[27]

13. Appellate jurisdiction of Supreme Court. The Supreme Court is the highest court of appeal from all courts in the territory of India, the jurisdiction of the Judicial Committee of the Privy Council to hear appeals from India having been abolished on the eve of the Constitution. The *Appellate* jurisdiction of the Supreme Court may be divided under three heads:

(i) Cases involving interpretation of the Constitution—civil, criminal or otherwise.

(ii) Civil cases, irrespective of any Constitutional question.

(iii) Criminal cases, irrespective of any Constitutional question.

Apart from appeals to the Supreme Court by special leave of that court under Article 136, an appeal lies to the Supreme Court from any judgment, decree or final order in a civil proceeding of a high court in two classes of cases —

(A) Where the case involves a substantial question of law as to the *interpretation of the Constitution,* an appeal shall lie to the Supreme Court on the certificate of the high court that such a question is involved or on the leave of the Supreme Court where the high court has refused to grant such a certificate but the Supreme Court is satisfied that a substantial question of law as to the interpretation of the Constitution is involved in the case [*Article 132*].

(B) In cases where no *Constitutional* question is involved, appeal shall lie to the Supreme Court if the high court certifies that the following conditions are satisfied [*Article 133(1)*]—

27. See *UP State Spinning Co Ltd v RS Pandey,* (2005) 8 SCC 264 : (2005) JT 12 SC 242 : (2006) 1 LLJ 254; *State of Uttar Pradesh v Mohammad Nooh,* AIR 1958 SC 86 : (1958) 1 SCR 595 : (1958) SCJ 242; *Harbanslal Sahnia v Indian Oil Corporation Ltd,* AIR 2003 SC 2120 : (2003) AIR SCW 126 : (2003) 2 SCC 107; *Shrimanth Balasaheb Patil v Hon'ble Speaker, Karnataka Legislative Assembly,* (2020) 2 SCC 595 : (2020) SCC OnLine SC 1454 : (2020) 1 Mad LJ 335.

(i) that the case involves a substantial question of law of general importance;

(ii) that in the opinion of the high court the said question should be decided by the Supreme Court.

13a. Criminal.

Prior to the Constitution, there was no court of criminal appeal over the high courts. It was only in a limited sphere that the Privy Council entertained appeals in criminal cases from the high courts by *special leave* but there was no appeal *as of right*. Article 134 of the Constitution for the first time provides for an appeal to the Supreme Court from any judgment, final order or sentence in a criminal proceeding of a high court, as of right, in two specified classes of cases —

(a) where the high court has on an appeal reversed an order of acquittal of an accused person and sentenced him to death;

(b) where the high court has withdrawn for trial before itself any case from any court subordinate to its authority and has in such trial convicted the accused and sentenced him to death.

In these two classes of cases relating to a sentence of death by the high court, appeal lies to the Supreme Court as a right.

Besides the above two classes of cases, an appeal may lie to the Supreme Court in any criminal case if the high court certifies that the case is a fit one for appeal to the Supreme Court. The certificate of the high court would, of course, be granted only where some substantial question of law or some matter of great public importance or the infringement of some essential principles of justice are involved. Appeal may also lie to the Supreme Court (under *Article* 132) from a criminal proceeding if the high court certifies that the case involves a substantial question of law as to the interpretation of the Constitution.

Except in the above cases, no appeal lies from a criminal proceeding of the high court to the Supreme Court under the Constitution but Parliament has been empowered to make any law conferring on the Supreme Court further powers to hear appeals from criminal matters.

13b. Appeal by Special Leave.

While the Constitution provides for regular appeals to the Supreme Court from decisions of the high courts in Articles 132–134, there may still remain some cases where justice might require the interference of the Supreme Court with decisions not only of the high courts outside the purview of Articles 132–134 but also of any other court or tribunal within the territory of India. Such residuary power outside the ordinary law relating to appeal is conferred upon the Supreme Court by Article 136. This Article is worded in the widest terms possible —

> 136. (1) Notwithstanding anything in this Chapter, the Supreme Court may, in its discretion, grant special leave to appeal from any judgment, decree determination, sentence or order in any cause or matter passed or made by any court or tribunal in the territory of India.
>
> (2) Nothing in clause (1) shall apply to any judgment, determination, sentence or order passed or made by any court or tribunal constituted by or under any law relating to the Armed Forces.

It vests in the Supreme Court a plenary jurisdiction in the matter of entertaining and hearing appeals, by granting special leave, against any kind of judgment or order made by any court or tribunal (except a military tribunal) in any proceeding and the exercise of the power is left entirely to the *discretion* of the Supreme Court unfettered by any restrictions and this power cannot be curtailed by any legislation short of amending the Article itself. It has been observed by the Supreme Court that it would be better to use the said power with circumspection, rather than to limit the power forever.[28]

Article 136 confers plenary powers on this Court to interfere in suitable cases. This Article can be invoked by a party in a petition for special leave to appeal from any judgement, decree, determination, sentence or order in any cause or matter passed or made by a Court or Tribunal within the territory of India. The reach of the extraordinary powers vested in this Court under Article 136 of the Constitution is boundless. Such unbridled powers have been vested in Court, not just to prevent the abuse of the process of any court or to secure the ends of justice as contemplated in Section 482, CrPC, but to ensure dispensation of justice, correct errors of law, safeguard fundamental rights, exercise judicial review, resolve conflicting decisions, inject consistency in the legal system by settling precedents and for myriad other to undo injustice, wherever noticed and promote the cause of justice at every level. The fetters on this power are self imposed and carefully tampered with sound judicial discretion.[29]

When the Supreme Court exercises its discretionary jurisdiction under Article 136 of the Constitution, it is in order to ensure that there is no miscarriage of justice. If finding of acquittal by high court is found to be misconceived and perverse, this court can quash such order of acquittal under Article 136 of the Constitution.[30] This wide power is not, however, to be exercised by the Supreme Court so as to entertain an appeal in *any* case where no appeal is otherwise provided by the law or the Constitution. It is a special power which is to be exercised only under *exceptional circumstances* and the Supreme Court has already laid down the principles according to which this extraordinary power shall be used, *eg*, where there has been a violation of the principles of natural justice. An appeal by special leave is not a regular appeal. Merely because a different view is possible on the evidence adduced at the trial is no ground for the court to upset the opinion of the courts below. The court would reappreciate evidence only to find out whether there has been any illegality, material irregularity or miscarriage of justice.[31] In *civil cases* the special leave to appeal under this Article would not be granted unless there is some substantial question of law or general public interest involved in the case. Similarly, in *criminal* cases the Supreme Court will not interfere under Article 136 unless it is shown that exceptional and special circumstances exist, that

28. *Mathai v George*, (2016) 7 SCC 700 : (2016) 2 Scale 102.
29. *Karnataka Emta Coal Mines Limited v Central Bureau of Investigation*, AIR 2024 SC 5081 : AIROnline 2024 SC 587.
30. *State of Rajasthan v Islam*, AIR 2011 SC 2317, p *2319* : (2011) 6 SCC 343; see also *SB Minerals v MSPL Ltd*, AIR 2010 SC 1137 : 2009 (14) Scale 202.
31. *Amitava Banerjee v State of West Bengal*, AIR 2011 SC 2913, p *2917*: [2011]12 SCR 160; see also *A Subhash Babu v State of Andhra Pradesh*, AIR 2011 SC 3031 : (2011) 7 SCC 616 (court has power to mould relief).

substantial and grave injustice has been done and that the case in question presents features of sufficient gravity to warrant a review of the decision appealed against.[32] The suspension of sentence, pending any appeal by a convicted person and consequential release on bail is not a matter of course and the appellate court is required to record reasons in writing for suspending the sentence and release of convict on a bail pending appeal.[33] Similarly, it will not substitute its own decision for the determination of a *tribunal* but it would interfere to quash the decision of a quasi-judicial tribunal under its extraordinary powers conferred by Article 136 when the tribunal has either exceeded its jurisdiction or has approached the question referred to in a manner which is likely to result in injustice or has adopted a procedure which runs counter to the established rules of natural justice.[34] Where findings of facts recorded by the trial court are affirmed by the high court in appeal, the Supreme Court will be reluctant to interfere with such findings in exercise of jurisdiction under Article 136 of the Constitution unless there are very strong reasons to do so.[35]

Article 136 does not confer a right of appeal on any party, but confers a discretionary power on the Supreme Court to interfere in appropriate cases. This power can be exercised in spite of other provisions for appeal contained in the Constitution, or any other law.[36]

A pure finding of fact based on appreciation of evidence does not call for interference in exercise of power under Article 136 of the Constitution.[37]

There is no tangible justification to allow the appellants to raise a new plea for the first time, the determination of which would require detailed investigation into issue of facts.[38] The point can be raised before the Supreme Court for the first time where it goes to the root of the matter and for consideration of this point no further investigation in the facts of the case is necessary.[39]

Supreme Court while hearing appeal under Article 136 of the Constitution is not inhibited by observations made at the time of admitting SLP limiting the

---

32. *Pritam Singh v State*, AIR 1950 SC 169.
33. *Kanaka Rekha Naik v Manoj Kumar Pradhan*, AIR 2011 SC 799 : (2011) 4 SCC 596, p 600; see also *Bikram Dorjee v State of West Bengal*, AIR 2009 SC 2539 : (2009) 14 SCC 233 (sentence reduced).
34. *DC Mills v CIT*, AIR 1955 SC 65 : [1955] 1 Mad LJ (SC) 60; *Ismail Faruqui v UOI*, (1994) 6 SCC 360; *Special Reference No 1 of 1993*, (1993) 1 SCC 642.
35. *Saradamani Kandappan v S Rajalakhmi*, AIR 2011 SC 3234, p *3242*: (2011) 12 SCC 18.
36. *N Natarajan V BK Subba Rao*, AIR 2003 SC 541 : (2003) 2 SCC 76 : (2002) 9 Scale 16. Under Article 136 of the Constitution of India, the Supreme Court entertains appeals by special leave, where substantial questions of law or questions of public importance are involved. The Supreme Court does not ordinarily interfere with concurrent findings of fact under Article 136. See also *Rajendra Diwan v Pradeep Kumar Raniwala*, AIR Online 2019 SC 1711 : (2019) SCC OnLine SC 1586 : LNIND 2019 SC 991
37. *Pramod Buildings & Developers (P) Ltd v Shanta Chopra*, AIR 2011 SC 1424, p *1428*: (2011) 4 SCC 741, see also *Khilan Singh v State of MP*, AIR 2010 SC 2485 : (2010) 3 SCC 678 (in absence of any infirmity, no exercise of powers under Article 136); *Mahesh Dattatray Tirthakar v State of Maharashtra*, AIR 2009 SC 2238 : (2009) 11 SCC 141 (reversal of finding of fact, not justified).
38. *Abdul Khader v Tarabai*, AIR 2011 SC 2229 : (2011) 6 SCC 199, p *206* .
39. *Sehla Burney v Syed Alimosa Raza*, (2011) 6 SCC 529, p *534*: (2011) 4 Scale 838.

points for consideration. The court can at the time of final hearing consider the entire perspective to do final justice in the matter.[40]

A litigant who is aggrieved by a decision rendered by this Court in a special leave petition or in a civil appeal arising therefrom can seek its review by invoking the review jurisdiction and thereafter through a curative petition. But such a decision cannot be assailed in a writ proceeding under Article 32 of the Constitution.[41]

14. Advisory jurisdiction of the Supreme Court. Besides the above regular jurisdiction of the Supreme Court, it shall have an *advisory* jurisdiction, to give its *opinion,* on any question of law or fact of public importance as may be referred to it for consideration by the President.

Article 143 of the Constitution lays down that the Supreme Court may be required to express its opinion in two classes of matters, in an advisory capacity as distinguished from its judicial capacity:

(a) In the first class, any question of law may be referred to the Supreme Court for its opinion if the President considers that the question is of such a nature and of such public importance that it is expedient to obtain the opinion of the Supreme Court. It has been observed by the Supreme Court that Article 143 does not restrict the President to obtain opinion only on a pure question of law as the bare perusal of the Article shows that the President is authorised to refer to the court any question of law or fact. It is within the discretion of the court, subject to certain parameters to decide whether to refuse or to answer a question on reference.[42]

It differs from a regular adjudication before the Supreme Court in this sense that there is no litigation between two parties in such a case and that the opinion given by the Supreme Court on such a reference is not binding upon the Government itself and further that the opinion is not executable as a judgment of the Supreme Court. The opinion is only advisory and the Government may take it into consideration in taking any action in the matter but it is not bound to act in conformity with the opinion so received. The chief utility of such an advisory judicial opinion is to enable the Government to secure an authoritative opinion either as to the validity of a legislative measure before it is enacted or as to some other matter which may not go to the courts in the ordinary course and yet the Government is anxious to have authoritative legal opinion before taking any action.

Up to 2023, there were *fifteen* cases of reference of this class made by the President.[43] It may be mentioned that though the opinion of the Supreme Court on such a reference may not be binding on the Government, the propositions of law declared by the Supreme Court even on such a reference are binding on the subordinate courts. In fact, the propositions laid down in the *Delhi Laws* case

40. *Yomeshbhai Pranshankar Bhatt v State of Gujarat,* AIR 2011 SC 2328, p *2331.*
41. *Satish Chander Sharma v State of Himachal Pradesh,* AIR 2025 SC 2050 : 2025 INSC 491.
42. *Re Punjab Termination of Agreement Act,* 2004, AIR 2016 SC 5145 : (2017) 1 SCC 121.
43. *Re Delhi Laws Act, 1912,* AIR 1951 SC 332 : (1951) SCR 747 [regarding the validity of the Delhi Laws Act, 1912].

have been frequently referred to and followed since then by the subordinate courts. A decision of the Supreme Court on a question of law is binding on all courts and authorities and the President could refer a question of law only if the Supreme Court had not decided it. A decision of the Supreme Court which is neither without jurisdiction nor *per incuriam* nor in violation of the principle of natural justice or of any provision of the Constitution would be binding and operate as *res judicata* and such a decision would not be open to reconsideration in a reference under Article 143 as that would amount to the court sitting in appeal over its own decision.[44] The Supreme Court is entitled to decline to answer a question posed to it under Article 143 if it is superfluous or unnecessary. The Supreme Court for the first time declined to answer a Reference ie, Special Reference No 1 of 1993. The court can pass interim orders in a pending reference.[45] A Presidential reference was made in the backdrop of the decision rendered by the Supreme Court in *Centre for Public Interest Litigation* case,[46]; wherein eight questions were referred to the Hon'ble Supreme Court for its opinion/ advice, however the Hon'ble Supreme Court only considered five questions and declined to give its opinion on remaining three questions.[47]

(b) The second class of cases belong to the disputes arising out of pre-Constitution treaties and agreements which are excluded by Article 131, proviso, from the Original Jurisdiction of the Supreme Court, as we have already seen. In other words, though such disputes cannot come to the Supreme Court as a litigation under its Original jurisdiction, the subject-matter of such disputes may be referred to by the President for the opinion of the Supreme Court in its advisory capacity.

In *Re the Kerala Education Bill,* 1957 the Supreme Court (seven Judges Bench) observed that the advisory Jurisdiction conferred by Article 143(1) is different from that conferred by Article 143(2) of the Constitution in that the latter made it obligatory on the court to answer the reference.[48] Further in Special Reference No 1 of 1964, the Supreme Court (seven Judges Bench) observed that it is not obligatory on the Supreme Court to answer a Reference under Article 143(1), the word used in that Article being "may" in contrast to the word "shall" used in Article 143(2).[49] Besides this, section 53K of the Competition Commission Act, 2002 confers advisory jurisdiction upon the Supreme Court.

15. Miscellaneous jurisdiction of the Supreme Court. There are provisions for reference to this court under Article 317(1) of the Constitution, section 257 of the Income-tax Act 1961and section 35H of the Central Excise and Salt Act, 1944, section 14(1) and section 17(1) of the Right to Information Act, 2005.

---

44. *Re Cauvery Water Dispute Tribunal,* AIR 1992 SC 522 : (1993) Supp 1 SCC 96.
45. *Babri Masjid Case, Special Reference No 1 of 1993,* (1994) 1 SCC 642.
46. *Centre for Public Interest Litigation v UOI,* AIR 2012 SC 10 : (2012) 3 SCC 1, popularly known as "2G Spectrum case".
47. *Re Special Reference No 1 of 2012,* (2012) 10 SCC 1.
48. *Re Kerala Education Bill,* AIR 1958 SC 956 [regarding the constitutionality of the Kerala Education Bill].
49. *Special Reference I of 1964 (Re UP Legislature),* AIR 1965 SC 745.

Appeals also lie to the Supreme Court under section 116A of the Representation of the People Act, 1951; section 55 of the Monopolies and Restrictive Trade Practices Act, 1969; section 38 of the Advocates Act, 1961; section 19(1)(b) of the Contempt of Courts Act, 1971; section 130E of the Customs Act, 1962; section 35L of the Central Excise and Salt Act, 1944; section 14 of the Terrorist Affected Areas (Special Courts) Act, 1984; section 16 of the Terrorist and Disruptive Activities (Prevention) Act, 1985; section 17 of the Terrorist and Disruptive Activities (Prevention) Act, 1987; section 10 of the Trial of Offences relating to Transactions in Securities Act, 1992 and section 23 of the Consumer Protection Act, 1986, section 379 of the Code of Criminal Procedure, 1973 read with section 2 of the Supreme Court (Enlargement of Criminal Appellate Jurisdiction) Act, 1970, section 18 of the Telecom Regulatory Authority of India Act, 1997, section 15(z) of the Securities and Exchange Board of India Act, 1992, section 261 of the Income-Tax Act, 1961.

16. Power to Punish for Contempt of Court and to do Complete Justice.

Under Articles 129 and 142 of the Constitution, the Supreme Court has been vested with power to punish for contempt of court including the power to punish for contempt of itself. In case of contempt, other than the contempt referred to in rule 2, Part I of the Rules to Regulate Proceedings for Contempt of the Supreme Court, 1975, the court may take action: (a) *suo motu*; or (b) on a petition made by Attorney General, or Solicitor General; or (c) on a petition made by any person, and in the case of a criminal contempt with the consent in writing of the Attorney General or the Solicitor General. For exercising the *suo motu* power for contempt under Article 129 of the Constitution of India, the limitation provided in section 20 of the 1971 Act has no application. Under Article 142, the Supreme Court can grant appropriate relief for doing complete justice: (i) where there is some manifest illegality; or (ii) where there is manifest want of jurisdiction; or (iii) where some pulpable injustice is shown to have resulted. It is advisable to leave this power undefined and uncatalogued, so that it remains elastic enough, to be moulded to suit the given situation. There cannot be any defined parameters, within the framework whereof, the Supreme Court would exercise jurisdiction under Article 142 of the Constitution. The complexity of administration, and of human affairs, would give room for the exercise of the power vested in the Supreme Court under Article 142, in a situation where clear injustice appears to have been caused, to any party to a *lis*. In the absence of any legislation to the contrary, it would be open to this court, to remedy the situation.[50] The power under Article 142 is not limitless. It authorises the court to pass orders to secure complete justice in the case before it. Article 142 embodies both the notion of justice, equity and good conscience as well as a supplementary power to the court to effect complete justice.[51]

The scope of contempt jurisdiction extends to, punishing contemnors for violating the court's orders; punishing contemnors for disobeying the court's orders; punishing contemnors for breach of undertakings given to the courts. It also extends to enforcement of the court's orders. Contempt jurisdiction even extends to punishing those who scandalize (or lower the authority of) any court; punishing those who interfere in due course of judicial proceedings; and

50. *Nidhi Kaim v State of Madhya Pradesh*, (2017) 4 SCC 1 : (2017) 2 Scale 626.
51. *M Siddiq v Mahant Suresh Das*, (2019) 8 Mad LJ 117 : LNIND 2019 SC 891.

punishing those who obstruct the administration of justice. In exercise of contempt jurisdiction, courts have the power to enforce compliance of judicial orders, and also, the power to punish for contempt. In a significant case, a seven-Judge Bench of Supreme Court initiated *suo moto* contempt proceedings against a High Court Judge for the first time and imposed a punishment of six months in exercise of its powers under Article 129 of the Constitution and the Contempt of Courts Act, 1971.[52] Besides this, the Supreme Court is empowered under Article 137 of the Constitution of India, 1950 to review its own judgments/orders. The fundamental right to life under Article 21 of the Constitution, viewed in the light of irreversibility of a death sentence, mandate that oral hearing be given at the review stage in death sentence cases in open court, and not by circulation.

17. Curative Petition.

Further as laid down by the Supreme Court in the case of *Rupa Ashok Hurra v Ashok Hurra,*[53] even after dismissal of a review petition under Article 137 of the Constitution, Supreme Court, may entertain a curative petition and reconsider its judgment/order, in exercise of its inherent powers in order to prevent abuse of its process, to cure gross miscarriage of justice and such a petition can be filed only if a Senior Advocate certifies that it meets the requirements of this case. Such a petition is to be first circulated, in chambers, before a Bench comprising of three senior-most judges and such serving judges who were members of the Bench which passed the judgment/order, subject matter of the petition.

The curative petition is not a second review. The guiding principle for the exercise of curative jurisdiction is the duty of the Supreme Court to avert manifest injustice.[54] The exercise of the curative jurisdiction of this Court should not be adopted as a matter of ordinary course. The curative jurisdiction should not be used to open the floodgates and create a fourth or fifth stage of court intervention in an arbitral award, under this Court's review jurisdiction or curative jurisdiction, respectively.[55]

18. Election Petitions.

Election Petitions under Part III of the Presidential and Vice-Presidential Elections Act, 1952 are also filed directly in the Supreme Court.

19. The 42nd, 43rd and 44th Constitution Amendments.

The jurisdiction of the Supreme Court, as outlined in the foregoing pages, was curtailed by the 42nd Amendment of the Constitution (1976), in several ways. But some of these changes have been recoiled by the Janata Government, by repealing them by the 43rd Amendment Act, 1977, so that the reader need not bother about them. The provisions so repealed are Articles 32A, and 144A.

But there are several other provisions which were introduced by the 42nd Amendment Act, 1976, but the Janata Government failed to dislodge them, owing to the opposition of the Congress Party in the *Rajya Sabha.* These are —

---

52. *Re CS Karnan,* Suo motu CP No. 1 of 2017.
53. *Rupa Ashok Hurra v Ashok Hurra,* AIR 2002 SC 1771 : 2002 (4) SCC 388.
54. *Surendra Koli v State of Uttar Pradesh,* AIR 2025 SC 5591 : AIROnline 2025 SC 1057.
55. *Delhi Metro Rail Corporation Ltd. v Delhi Airport Metro Express Pvt. Ltd.,* AIR 2024 SC 2070 : 2024 INSC 292.

(i) *Articles 323A-323B*: The intent of these two new Articles was to take away the jurisdiction of the Supreme Court under Article 32 over orders and decisions of Administrative Tribunals. These Articles could, however, be implemented only by legislation which Mrs Gandhi's *first* Government had no time to undertake.

Article 323A has been implemented by the Administrative Tribunals Act, 1985 [see, further, under Chapter 30, *post*].

But subsequently, the position turned out to be otherwise as the Supreme Court declared the Articles 323A, clause 2(d) and 323B, clauses 3(d) and also the "exclusion of jurisdiction" clauses in all the legislations enacted in pursuance of these Articles, unconstitutional to the extent they excluded the jurisdiction of the high courts and the Supreme Court under Articles 226/227 and 32.[56]

(ii) *Articles 368(4) and (5):* These two clauses were inserted in Article 368 with a view to preventing the Supreme Court from invalidating any Constitution Amendment Act on the theory of "basic features of Constitution" or anything of that nature.

Curiously, however, these clauses have been emasculated by the Supreme Court itself, striking them down on the ground that they are violative of two "basic features" of the Constitution—(a) the limited nature of the amending power under Article 368, and (b) judicial review—in the *Minerva Mills* case.[57]

20. Office of Chief Justice and the Right to Information Act, 2005. A five-judge bench of the Supreme Court with a 3:2 majority ruled that the office of Chief Justice of India (CJI) comes under the purview of the Right to Information (RTI) Act. The Supreme Court held that the public interest test would be applied to determine whether information should be furnished or would be exempt.

The Supreme Court held that the Chief Justice and the Supreme Court are not two distinct and separate public authorities, *albeit* the latter is a public authority and the Chief Justice and the judges together form and constitute the public authority, that is, the Supreme Court of India.[58]

21. Social Justice Bench of Supreme Court. The Constitution of India in its Preamble has assured the people a three-dimensional justice including social justice. Under the domain of "social justice", several cases highlighting social issues are included, *viz.* the release of surplus food-grains lying in stocks for the use of people living in the drought affected areas, to frame a fresh scheme for public distribution of food-grains, to take steps to prevent untimely death of women and children for want of nutritious food, providing hygienic mid-day meals, besides issues relating to children, to provide night shelter to destitutes and homeless, to provide medical facilities to all the citizens irrespective of their economic conditions, to provide hygienic drinking water, to provide safety and secured living conditions for the fair gender who are forced into prostitution, etc. are pending in the Supreme

56. *L Chandra Kumar v UOI,* AIR 1997 SC 1125 : (1997) 3 SCC 261.
57. *Minerva Mills v UOI,* AIR 1980 SC 1789, paras 22–26, 28, 93–94 : (1980) 3 SCC 625.
58. *Central Public Information Officer, Supreme Court Of India v Subhash Chandra Agarwal,* AIR Online 2019 SC 1449 : (2019) SCC OnLine SC 1459 : LNIND 2019 SC 899.

Court for several years. In order to give a specialised approach for their early disposal so that the masses will realize the fruits of the rights provided to them by the constitutional text, the Hon'ble Chief Justice of India Shri H L Dattu has ordered constitution of a Special Bench titled as the "Social Justice Bench" to deal especially with the matters relating to society and its members, to secure social justice, one of the ideals of the Indian Constitution. This Bench, comprising of Hon'ble Mr Madan B Lokur J and Hon'ble Mr Uday U Lalit J, has started functioning from 12 December 2014 and in order to ensure that these matters are monitored on a regular basis, they will continue to sit on every working Friday at 2 pm. Not only pending cases, but fresh matters will also be dealt with by this Special Bench. The social justice bench of the Supreme Court has directed all the State Governments/Union Territories to make sure that free medical treatment is provided to all the acid attack victims in government as well as private hospitals. Criminal action can be taken against hospital/clinic for refusal to treat any victim of an acid attack.[59]

59. *Laxmi v UOI,* (2014) SCC 4 427, WP (Crl) No 129 of 2006, decided on 10 April 2015 (SC Social Justice Bench) (Bench: Madan B Lokur, Uday Umesh Lalit, JJ).

CHAPTER 23

THE HIGH COURT

1. High Court of a State. THERE shall be a high court in each State [*Article 214*] but Parliament has the power to establish a common high court for two or more States[1] [*Article 231*]. The high court stands at the head of the Judiciary in the State [see Table XVI, *post*].

2. Constitution of High Courts. Every high court shall consist of a Chief Justice and such other judges as the President of India may from time to time appoint.

Besides, the President has the power to appoint: (i) *additional* judges for a temporary period not exceeding two years, for the clearance of arrears of work in a high court; (ii) an acting judge, when a permanent judge of a high court (other than a Chief Justice) is temporarily absent or unable to perform his duties or is appointed to act temporarily as Chief Justice. The acting judge holds office until the permanent Judge resumes his office. But neither an additional nor an acting Judge can hold office beyond the age of 62 years.[2]

3. Appointment and Conditions of the Office of a Judge of a High Court. Every judge of a high court shall be appointed by the President. In making the appointment, the President shall consult the Chief Justice of India (CJI), the Governor of the State (and also the Chief Justice of that high court in the matter of appointment of a judge other than the Chief Justice).

(a) Participatory Consultative Process: A nine-judges Bench of the Supreme Court[3] has held that:

(1) The process of the appointment of the judges of the high courts is an integrated "participatory consultative process" for selecting the best and most suitable persons available for appointment; and all the constitutional functionaries must perform this duty collectively with a view primarily to reach an agreed decision, subserving the Constitutional purpose, so that the occasion of primacy does not arise.

(2) Initiation of the proposal for appointment in the case of high court must invariably be made by the Chief Justice of that high court.

(3) In the event of conflicting opinions by the constitutional functionaries, the opinion of the judiciary "symbolised by the view of the Chief Justice of India"

---

1. For a list of High Courts, their seat and territorial jurisdiction, see Table XVI, *post*.
2. By the Constitution (15th Amendment) Act, 1963, the age of retirement of High Court Judges has been raised from 60 to 62.
3. *Supreme Court Advocates-on-Record Association v UOI,* AIR 1994 SC 268 : (1993) 4 SCC 441.

formed by him in consultation with two senior-most judges of the Supreme Court who come from that State, would have supremacy.

(4) No appointment of any judge of a high court can be made unless it is in conformity with the opinion of the CJI.

(5) In exceptional cases alone, for stated strong cogent reasons, disclosed to the CJI, indicating that the recommendee is not suitable for appointment, that the appointment recommended by the CJI may not be made. However, if the stated reasons are not accepted by the CJI and the other Judges of the Supreme Court, consulted by him in the matter, on reiteration of the recommendation by the CJI, the appointment should be made as a healthy convention.

Subsequently, the President of India in exercise of his powers under Article 143 made a Reference[4] to the Supreme Court (SC) relating to the consultation between the CJI and his brother judges in matters of appointments of the high court judges, but not as a review or reconsideration of the *Supreme Court Advocates case* (*Second Judges case*) above. The SC opined that "consultation with the CJI" implies consultation with a plurality of judges in the formation of opinion. His sole opinion does not constitute consultation. Only a *collegium* comprising the CJI and two senior-most judges of the SC, as was in the *Second Judges case* above, should make the recommendation. The *collegium* in making its decision should take into account the opinion of the CJ of the high court concerned which "would be entitled to the greatest weight," the views of the other judges of the high court who may be consulted and the views of the other judges of the SC "who are conversant with the affairs of the high court concerned." The views of the judges of the SC who were puisne judges of the high court or CJ, thereof, will also be obtained irrespective of the fact that the HC is not their parent HC and they were transferred there. All these views should be expressed in writing and be conveyed to the Government of India alongwith the recommendation of the *collegium*. The recommendations made by the CJI without complying with the norms and requirements of the consultation process, as afore stated, are not binding upon the Government of India.

The Union of India is the ultimate authority to approve the recommendations for appointment as a judge. The view that without consultation with the collegium the opinion of CJI is not legal, cannot be sustained. If the factors which render an additional judge unsuitable for appointment as a permanent judge exist, it would not only be improper but also undesirable to continue him as Additional Judge.[5]

(b) NJAC declared Unconstitutional: After creation of the National Judicial Appointment Commission under Article 124A *vide* the Constitutional (99th Amendment) Act, 2014[6] and the National Judicial Appointment Commission Act, 2014,[7] (wef 13-4-2015), the prevailing practice of "collegium system" with regard to the appointment of the Supreme Court and high court was bought to

4. *Re Special Reference No 1 of 1998*, AIR 1999 SC 1 : (1998) 7 SCC 739 [nine Judge Bench].
5. *Shanti Bhushan v UOI*, (2009) 1 SCC 657, pp 675, 676 : [2009] 3 Mad LJ 144.
6. The Constitutional (99th Amendment) Act, 2014 (wef 13-4-2015).
7. The National Judicial Appointment Commission Act, 2014 (wef 13-4-2015).

an end. (See chapter 22). Accordingly, Articles 217, 222, 224, 224A and 231 were also amended as under:

> In article 217 of the Constitution, in clause (1), for the portion beginning with the words "after consultation", and ending with the words "the High Court", the words, figures and letter "on the recommendation of the National Judicial Appointments Commission referred to in article 124A" shall be substituted.
>
> In article 222 of the Constitution, in clause (1), for the words "after consultation with the Chief Justice of India", the words, figures and letter "on the recommendation of the National Judicial Appointments Commission referred to in article 124A" shall be substituted.
>
> In article 224 of the Constitution,—(*a*) in clause (1), for the words "the President may appoint", the words "the President may, in consultation with the National Judicial Appointments Commission, appoint" shall be substituted; (*b*) in clause (2), for the words "the President may appoint", the words "the President may, in consultation with the National Judicial Appointments Commission, appoint" shall be substituted.
>
> In article 224A of the Constitution, for the words "the Chief Justice of a high court for any State may at any time, with the previous consent of the President", the words "the National Judicial Appointments Commission on a reference made to it by the Chief Justice of a high court for any State, may with the previous consent of the President" shall be substituted.
>
> In article 231 of the Constitution, in clause (2), sub-clause (*a*) shall be omitted.

The constitutionality of the provisions of the Constitutional (99th Amendment) Act, 2014 and the National Judicial Appointment Commission Act, 2014 were challenged in the Supreme Court. In response to the same, five-Judge Bench of the Supreme Court declared the 99th Amendment Act, 2014 as well as the National Judicial Appointments Commission Act, 2014 to be unconstitutional. (Refer Chapter 4, *ante*).

4. Salaries, etc.

A judge of a high court gets a salary of Rs 2,25,000 *per mensem* while the Chief Justice gets Rs 2,50,000 *per mensem*.[8] He is also entitled to such allowances and rights in respect of leave and pension as Parliament may from time to time determine, but such allowances and rights cannot be varied by Parliament to the disadvantage of a Judge after his appointment [*Article 221*].

5. Qualifications for Appointment as High Court Judge.

The qualifications laid down in the Constitution for being eligible for appointment as a Judge of the high court are that —

(a) he must be a citizen of India, not being over 62 years; and

(b) must have—

(i) held for at least 10 years a judicial office in the territory of India; or

(ii) been for at least 10 years an advocate of a high court or of two or more such courts in succession [*Article 217(2)*].

8. The salaries of Chief Justice and other Judges of the High Courts has been enhanced *vide* the High Court and Supreme Court Judges (Conditions of Service) Amendment) Act, 2018 (10 of 2018) (wref 1-1-2016).

6. Independence of the Judges. As in the case of the judges of the Supreme Court, the Constitution seeks to maintain the independence of the judges of the high courts by a number of provisions:

(a) By laying down that a judge of the high court shall not be removed, except in the manner provided for the removal of a judge of the Supreme Court, that is, upon an address of each House of Parliament (passed by a special majority [*Article 218*];

(b) By providing that the expenditure in respect of the salaries and allowances of the judges shall be charged on the Consolidated Fund of the State [*Article 202(3)(d)*];

(c) By specifying in the Constitution the salaries payable to the judges and providing that the allowances of a judge or his rights in respect of absence or pension shall not be varied by Parliament to his disadvantage after his appointment [*Article 221*], except under a Proclamation of Financial Emergency [*Article 360(4)(b)*];

(d) By laying down that after retirement a permanent judge of high court shall not plead or act in a court or before any authority in India, except the Supreme Court and a high court other than the high court in which he had held his office [*Article 220*].

7. Control of the Union over High Courts. As Sir Alladi Krishnaswami explained in the Constituent Assembly,[9] while ensuring the independence of the judiciary, the Constitution placed the high courts under the control of the Union in certain important matters, in order to keep them outside the range of "provincial politics". Thus, even though the high court stands at the head of the State judiciary, it is not so sharply separated from the federal Government as the highest court of an American State (called the State Supreme Court) is. The control of the Union over a high court in India is exercised in the following matters:

(a) Appointment [*Article 217*], transfer[10] from one high court to another [*Article 222*] and removal [*Article 217(1), proviso (b)*], and determination of dispute as to age [*Article 217(3)*], of judges of high courts.

Now the power to transfer of the high court judges remains no more a method of control over the high court by the Union Government as the Supreme Court has prescribed a procedure for the purpose in a Reference[11] made by the President of India in exercise of his powers under Article 143. The Supreme Court opined that the Chief Justice of India should obtain the views of the Chief Justice of the high court from which the proposed transfer is to be effected as also that of the Chief Justice of the high court to which the transfer is to be effected (as was stated in the *Second Judges case* in 1993). The Chief Justice of India should also take into account the views of one or more Supreme Court judges who are in position to provide material which would assist in the process of deciding whether or not a proposed transfer should take place. These views should be expressed in writing and should be considered by CJI and the four

9. *Constituent Assembly Debates,* dated 22 November 1948.
10. *SP Gupta v President of India,* AIR 1982 SC 149 (seven-Judge Bench).
11. *Re Special Reference No 1 of 1998,* (1998) 7 SCC 739.

senior most puisne judges of the Supreme Court. These views and those of each of the four senior most judges should be conveyed to the Government of India with the proposal of transfer.

What applies to the transfer of puisne judges of a high court applies as well to the transfer of the Chief Justice of a high court as a Chief Justice of another high court except that in this case, only the views of one or more knowledgeable Judges need be taken into account.

These factors, including the response of the high court Chief Justice or the puisne judge proposed to be transferred, to the proposal to transfer him, should be placed before the *collegium*—the CJI and his first four puisne judges—to be taken into account by it before reaching a final conclusion on the proposal.

(b) The Constitution and organisation of High Courts and the power to establish a common high court for two or more States and to extend the jurisdiction of a high court to, or to exclude its jurisdiction from, a Union Territory, are all exclusive powers of the Union Parliament.

It should be pointed out in the present context that there are some provisions introduced into the original Constitution by subsequent amendments, which affect the independence of high court judges, as compared with Supreme Court judges:

(a) Article 224 was introduced by substitution, in 1956, to provide for the appointment of additional Judges to meet "any temporary increase in the business of a High Court". An additional judge, so appointed, holds office for two years, but he may be made permanent at the end of that term. There is no such corresponding provision for the Supreme Court. It was introduced in the case of the high courts because of the problem of arrears of work, which was expected to disappear in the near future. Now that the problem of arrears has become a standing problem which is being met by the addition of more Judges, there is no particular reason why the make-shift device of additional appointment should continue. The inherent vice of this latter device is that it keeps an additional judge on probation and under the tutelage of the Chief Justice as well as the Government[10] as to whether he would get a permanent appointment at the end of two years. So far as the judicial power of a high court judge is concerned, he ranks as an equal to every other member of a Bench and is not expected, according to any principle relating to the administration of justice, to "agree" with the Chief Justice or any other senior member of a Bench where his learning, conscience or wisdom dictates otherwise, or to stay his hands where the merits of a case require a judgment against the Government. The fear of losing his job on the expiry of two years obviously acts as an inarticulate obsession upon an additional judge.

(b) Similarly, clause (3) was inserted in Article 217 in 1963, giving the President, in consultation with the Chief Justice of India, the final power to determine the age of high court Judge, if any question is raised by any-body in that behalf. By the same amendment of 1963 (15th Amendment), clause (2A) was inserted in Article 124, laying down that a similar question as to the age of a Supreme Court judge shall be determined in such manner as Parliament may by law provide. A high court judge's position has thus become not only unnecessarily inferior to that of a Supreme Court judge but even to that of a subordinate judicial officer, because any administrative determination of the latter's age is open to challenge in a court of law, but in the case of a high court judge, it is made "final" by the Constitution itself.[12] There is, apparently, no impelling reason why a provision similar to clause (2A) to Article 124 shall not be introduced in Article 217, in place of clause (3), in question.

(c) Another agency of control over high court judges is the provision in Article 222(1) for their transfer from one high court to another, which has been given a momentum in 1994 by transferring as many as 50 judges at a time.[13] In order that the power of the President to order such transfer is not used as a punitive measure, the Supreme Court has laid down[14] that while no consent of the judge concerned would be required, the President would not be competent to exercise the power except on the recommendation of the Chief Justice of India.

8. Territorial Jurisdiction of a High Court. Except where Parliament establishes a common high court for two or more States [*Article 231*] or extends the jurisdiction of a high court to a Union Territory, the jurisdiction of the high court of a State is co-terminous with the territorial limits of that State.[15]

As has already been stated, Parliament has extended the jurisdiction of some of the high courts to their adjoining Union Territories, by enacting the States Reorganisation Act, 1956. Thus, the jurisdiction of the Calcutta high court extends to the Andaman and Nicobar Islands; that of the Kerala high court extends to the Lakshadweep [see Table XVII].

9. Jurisdiction of High Courts. The Constitution does not make any provision relating to the general jurisdiction of the high courts but maintains their jurisdiction as it existed at the commencement of the Constitution, with this improvement that any restrictions upon their jurisdiction as to revenue matters that existed prior to the Constitution shall no longer exist [*Article 225*].

The existing jurisdictions of the high courts are governed by the Letters Patent and Central and State Acts; in particular, their civil and criminal jurisdictions are primarily governed by the two Codes of Civil and Criminal Procedure.

9a. Original. The High Courts at the three Presidency towns of Calcutta, Bombay and Madras had an original jurisdiction, both civil and criminal, over cases arising within the respective Presidency towns. The original *criminal* jurisdiction of the high courts has, however, been completely taken away by the Criminal Procedure Code, 1973.[16]

---

12. In this context, see *UOI v Jyoti Prakash*, AIR 1971 SC 1093, and the comments of the author thereon, Author's *Commentary on the Constitution of India*, 6th edn, vol G, pp 246ff.
13. *Statesman,* Calcutta, 14 April 1994, 16 April 1994, p 5.
14. *SC Advocates v UOI,* AIR 1994 SC 268 : (1993) 4 SCC 441, para 472, — nine-judges Bench.
15. See Table XVI as to the territorial jurisdiction of the several High Courts. Delhi which was under the jurisdiction of the Punjab High Court has now its own High Court since 1996.
16. *Basu's Criminal Procedure Code*, Prentice-Hall of India, 1979, p 29.

Though city civil courts have also been set up to try civil cases within the same area, the original civil jurisdiction of these high courts has not altogether been abolished but retained in respect of actions of higher value.

9b. Appellate. The appellate jurisdiction of the high court, similarly, is both civil and criminal.

(I) On the civil side, an appeal to the high court is either a first appeal or a second appeal:

(i) Appeal from the decisions of District judges and from those of Subordinate judges in cases of a higher value (broadly speaking), lie direct to the high court, on questions of fact as well as of law.

(ii) When any court subordinate to the high court (ie, the District judge or Subordinate judge) decides an appeal from the decision of an inferior court, a second appeal lies to the high court from the decision of the lower appellate court, but only on question of law and procedure, as distinguished from questions of fact [*section 100, CPC*].

(iii) Besides, there is a provision for appeal under the Letters Patent of the Allahabad, Bombay, Calcutta, Madras and Patna High Courts. These appeals lie to the appellate side of the high court from the decision of a single judge of the high court itself, whether made by such judge in the exercise of the original or appellate jurisdiction of the high court.

(II) The criminal appellate jurisdiction of the high court is not less complicated. It consists of appeals from the decisions of—

(a) A Sessions Judge or an Additional Sessions Judge, where the sentence is of imprisonment exceeding seven years;

(b) An Assistant Sessions Judge, Metropolitan Magistrate or other Judicial Magistrates in certain specified cases other than "petty" cases [*sections 374 and 376, CrPC, 1973*]

10. High Court's Power of Superintendence.

Every high court has a power of superintendence over all courts and tribunals throughout the territory in relation to which it exercises jurisdiction, excepting military tribunals [*Article 227*]. This power of superintendence is a very wide power inasmuch as it extends to all courts as well as tribunals within the State, whether such court or tribunal[15] is subject to the *appellate* jurisdiction of the high court or not. Further, this power of superintendence would include a revisional jurisdiction to intervene in cases of gross injustice or non-exercise or abuse of jurisdiction or refusal to exercise jurisdiction, or in case of an error of law apparent on the face of the record, or violation of the principles of natural justice, or arbitrary or capricious exercise of authority, or discretion or arriving at a finding which is perverse or based on no material, or a flagrant or patent error in procedure, even though no appeal or revision against the orders of such tribunal was otherwise available. Judicial orders of a civil court are not amenable to writ of *certiorari* under Article 226 of the Constitution. The high court however can exercise supervisory jurisdiction over civil courts in respect of such judicial orders. The scope of Article 227, however, is different from Article 226.[17] The High Court, in exercise of its power under Article 227 of the Constitution,

17. *Radhey Shyam v Chhabi Nath*, AIR 2015 SC 3269 : (2015) 5 SCC 423.

would not interfere with the orders of the trial court when the orders of trial court were passed on sound consideration of law and facts and not arbitrary.[18]

The power of superintendence conferred by Article 227 is supervisory and not appellate. This power of judicial superintendence must be exercised sparingly, to keep subordinate courts and tribunals within the limits of their authority. Jurisdiction under Article 227 cannot be exercised in the cloak of an appeal in disguise.[19]

11. Control over Subordinate Courts.

As the head of the judiciary in the State, the high court has got an administrative control over the subordinate judiciary in the State in respect of certain matters, besides its appellate and supervisory jurisdiction over them. The Subordinate Courts include District Judges, judges of the City Civil Courts as well as the Metropolitan Magistrates and members of the judicial service of the State.

The control over the Judges of these Subordinate Courts is exercised by the high courts in the following matters —

(a) The high court is to be consulted by the Governor in the matter of appointing, posting and promoting District judges [*Article 233*].

(b) The high court is consulted, along with the State Public Service Commission, by the Governor in appointing persons (other than District Judges) to the judicial service of the State [*Article 234*].

(c) The control over district courts and courts subordinate thereto, including the posting and promotion of, and the grant of leave to, transfers of, disciplinary control over including inquiries, suspension and punishment, and compulsory retirement of, persons belonging to the judicial service and holding any post inferior to the post of a district judge is vested in high court [*Article 235*].

(d) Every high court has power of superintendence over all courts and tribunals throughout the territories in relation to which it exercises jurisdiction except over a court or tribunal constituted by or under any law relating to the Armed Forces. [*Article 227*].

Control over the subordinate courts is the collective and individual responsibility of the high court.[20]

12. The 42nd, 43rd and 44th Constitutional Amendments.

The foregoing survey of the jurisdiction of a high court under the original Constitution was drastically curtailed in various ways, by the Constitution (42nd Amendment) Act, 1976, which has been referred to at the end of chapter 22 *ante,* in the context of the Supreme Court, but the new provisions in Articles 226A and 228A which had been inserted by the Constitution

18. *Puran Ram v Bhaguram,* AIR 2008 SC 1960 : (2008) 4 SCC 102, p 109; see also *TS Ashok v Alex Thompson,* (2011) 2 Ker LT 1037 (includes judicial superintendence).

19. *Rajendra Diwan v Pradeep Kumar Ranibala,* AIR Online 2019 SC 1711 : (2019) SCC OnLine SC 1586 : LNIND 2019 SC 991.

20. *High Court of Judicature at Bombay v Shirish Kumar Rangrao Patil,* AIR 1997 SC 2631 : (1997) 6 SCC 339.

(42nd Amendment) Act, 1976, have all been omitted by the 43rd Amendment Act, 1977, *and the original position has been restored.*

In this context, we must mention Articles 323A–323B, inserted by the 42nd Amendment Act. Parliament has passed the Administrative Tribunals Act, 1985, implementing Article 323A, under which the Central Government has set up Central Administrative Tribunals with respect to services under the Union.

As a result, all courts of law including the high court shall cease to have any jurisdiction to entertain any litigation relating to the recruitment and other service matters relating to persons appointed to the public services of the Union, whether in its original or appellate jurisdiction. The Supreme Court has, however, been spared its special leave jurisdiction of appeals from these Tribunals, under Article 136 of the Constitution. But subsequently, the position turned out to be otherwise as the Supreme Court declared the Article 323A, clause 2(d) and Article 323B, clause 3(d) and also the "exclusion of jurisdiction" clauses in all the legislations enacted in pursuance of these Articles, unconstitutional to the extent they excluded the jurisdiction of the High Courts and the Supreme Court under Articles 226/227 and 32.[21]

The 18th Law Commission in its 215th Report in December, 2008 recommended the Supreme Court to reconsider its decision in *L Chandra Kumar*[22] *especially in the light of the facts that the Supreme Court* in *S P Sampath Kumar,*[23] wherein the Supreme Court directed the carrying out of certain measures with a view to ensuring the functioning of the Administrative Tribunals along constitutionally sound principles. The changes were brought about in the Act by an amending Act (Act 19 of 1986). Jurisdiction of the Supreme Court under Article 32 was restored. Constitutional validity of the Act was finally upheld in *S P Sampath Kumar* subject, of course, to certain amendments relating to the form and content of the Administrative Tribunals. Thus became the Administrative Tribunals an effective and real substitute for the High Courts. However, in 1997, a seven-Judge Bench of the Supreme Court in *L Chandra Kumar* held that clause 2(d) of Article 323A and clause 3(d) of Article 323B, to the extent they empower Parliament to exclude the jurisdiction of the high courts and the Supreme Court under Articles 226/227 and Article 32 of the Constitution, are unconstitutional. Section 28 of the Act and the "exclusion of jurisdiction" clauses in all other legislations enacted under the aegis of Articles 323A and 323B would, to the same extent, be unconstitutional. The court held that the jurisdiction conferred upon the high courts under Articles 226/227 and upon the Supreme Court under Article 32 of the Constitution is part of the inviolable basic structure of our Constitution. All decisions of the Administrative Tribunals are subject to scrutiny before a Division Bench of the high court within whose jurisdiction the Tribunal concerned falls. As a result, orders of the Administrative Tribunals are being routinely appealed against in High Courts, whereas this was not the position prior to the *L Chandra Kumar*'s case. On 18 March 2006, the Administrative Tribunals (Amendment) Bill, 2006 (Bill No XXVIII of 2006) was introduced in Rajya Sabha to amend the Act by incorporating therein, *inter alia*, provisions empowering the Central Government to abolish Administrative Tribunals, and for appeal to high court to bring the Act in line with *L Chandra Kumar*.

21. *L Chandra Kumar v UOI,* AIR 1997 SC 1125 : (1997) JT 3 SC 589 : (1997) 3 SCC 261.
22. *L Chandra Kumar v UOI,* AIR 1997 SC 1125 : (1997) JT 3 SC 589 : (1997) 3 SCC 261.
23. *S P Sampath Kumar v UOI,* AIR 1987 SC 386 : (1987) 1 SCC 124.

Article 323-A does not preclude the Union Government from abolishing SATs because it is an enabling provision which confers the Union Government with the power to establish an administrative tribunal at its discretion (upon receiving a request from the relevant State Government in terms of the Administrative Tribunals Act). The legal and factual context of the power to establish administrative tribunals, the purpose of this power and the intention of the legislature establish that there is no duty to exercise the power conferred by the Administrative Tribunals Act, such that the enabling provision becomes a mandatory provision.[24]

13. Jurisdiction over Administrative Tribunals.

By reason of the extension of Governmental activities and the complicated nature of issues to be dealt with by the administration, many modern statutes have entrusted administrative bodies with the function of deciding disputes and quasi-judicial issues that arise in connection with the administration of such laws, either because the ordinary courts are already overburdened to take up these new matters or the disputes are of such a technical nature that they can be decided only by persons who have an intimate knowledge of the working of the Act under which it arises. Thus, in India, quasi-judicial powers have been vested in administrative authorities such as the Transport Authorities under the Motor Vehicles Act; and the Rent Controller under the State Rent Control Acts. Besides, there are special tribunals which are not a part of the judicial administration but have all the "trappings" of a court. Nevertheless, they are not courts in the proper sense of the term, in view of the special procedure followed by them. All these tribunals have one feature in common, *viz.* that they determine questions affecting the rights of the citizens and their decisions are binding upon them.

Since the decisions of such tribunals have the force or effect of a judicial decision upon the parties, and yet the tribunals do not follow the exact procedure adopted by courts of justice, the need arises to place them under the control of superior courts to keep them within the proper limits of their jurisdiction and also to prevent them from committing any act of gross injustice.

In *England,* judicial review over the decisions of the quasi-judicial tribunals is done by the high court in the exercise of its power to issue the prerogative writs.

In *India,* there are several provisions in the Constitution which place these tribunals under the control and supervision of the superior courts of the land, *viz,* the Supreme Court and the high courts:

(i) If the tribunal makes an order which infringes a fundamental right of a person, he can obtain relief by applying for a writ of *certiorari* to quash that decision, either by applying for it to the Supreme Court under Article 32 or to the high court under Article 226. Even apart from the infringement of the fundamental right, a high court is competent to grant a writ of *certiorari,* if the tribunal either acts without jurisdiction or in excess of its jurisdiction as conferred by the statutes by which it was created, or it makes an order contrary to the rules of natural justice or where there is some error of law apparent on the face of its record.

---

24. *Orissa Administrative Tribunal Bar Association v UOI,* 2023 SCC OnLine SC 309.

(ii) Besides the power of issuing the writs, every high court has a general power of superintendence over all the tribunals functioning within its jurisdiction under Article 227 and this superintendence has been interpreted as both administrative and judicial superintendence. Hence, even where the writ of *certiorari* is not available but a flagrant injustice has been committed or is going to be committed, the high court may interfere and quash the order of a tribunal under Article 227.[25]

(iii) Above all, the Supreme Court may grant special leave to appeal from any determination made by any tribunal in India, under Article 136 wherever there exist extraordinary circumstances calling for interference of the Supreme Court. Broadly speaking, the Supreme Court can exercise this power under Article 136 over a tribunal wherever a writ for *certiorari* would lie against the tribunal; for example, where the tribunal has either exceeded its jurisdiction or has approached the question referred to it in a manner which is likely to result in injustice or has adopted a procedure which runs counter to the established rules of natural justice. The extraordinary power would, however, be exercised by the Supreme Court in rare and exceptional circumstances and not to interfere with the decisions of such tribunals as a court of appeal.

13a. Armed Forces Tribunal.

In 2007, the Armed Forces Tribunal was constituted whose appeal also lies directly to the Supreme Court. The Supreme Court in the matter of *UOI v Brig PS Gill*[26] observed that:

> A conjoint reading of Sections 30 and 31 can lead to only one conclusion viz. there is no vested right of appeal against a final order or decision of the Tribunal to this Court other than those falling under Section 30(2) of the Act. The only mode to bring up the matter to this Court in appeal is either by way of certificate obtained from the Tribunal that decided the matter or by obtaining leave of this Court under Section 31 for filing an appeal depending upon whether this Court considers the point involved in the case to be one that ought to be considered by this Court.

13b. National Green Tribunal.

The Supreme Court in *Vellore Citizens' Welfare Forum v UOI,*[27] requested the Madras high court to constitute "Green Bench" to deal with the case and other environmental matters, since the right to clean environment has been construed as a part of the right to life under Article 21 of the Constitution. In 2010, the Parliament enacted the National Green Tribunal Act, 2010 to constitute the National Green Tribunal. The Tribunal has original jurisdiction on matters of "substantial question relating to environment". The appellate jurisdiction of the National Green Tribunal is under: (i) under section 28 of the Water (Prevention and Control of Pollution) Act, 1974; (ii) under section 29 of the Water (Prevention

25. The 42nd Amendment Act, 1976, also took away this jurisdiction of the High Courts over tribunals, under Article 227(1), by omitting the word "tribunals" therefrom; but the 44th Amendment Act, 1978, has *restored* the word, so that a High Court retains its power of superintendence over any tribunal within its territorial jurisdiction. This jurisdiction of the High Court was taken away in respect of Administrative Tribunals set up under Article 323A, by the Administrative Tribunals Act, 1985 but the provisions in these Articles and in the legislations enacted in pursuance thereof excluding the jurisdiction of SC and HCs under Articles 32 and 226/227 have been declared to be unconstitutional by the Supreme Court in *L Chandra Kumar v UOI,* AIR 1997 SC 1125 : (1997) 3 SCC 261.
26. *UOI v Brig PS Gill,* AIR 2012 SC 1280 : (2012) 4 SCC 463.
27. *Vellore Citizens' Welfare Forum v UOI,* AIR 1996 SC 2826 : (1996) 5 SCC 647.

and Control of Pollution) Act, 1974; (iii) under section 33A of the Water (Prevention and Control of Pollution) Act, 1974; (iv) under section 13 of the Water (Prevention and Control of Pollution) Cess Act, 1977; (v) under section 2 of the Forest (Conservation) Act, 1980; (vi) under section 31 of the Air (Prevention and Control of Pollution) Act, 1981; (vii) under section 5 of the Environment (Protection) Act, 1986; (viii) against an order made granting environmental clearance in the area, in which any industries, operations or processes or class of industries, operations and processes shall not be carried out or shall be carried out subject to certain safeguards under the Environment (Protection) Act, 1986; (ix) against an order refusing to grant environmental clearance for carrying out any activity or operation or process under the Environment (Protection) Act, 1986; (x) against any determination of benefit sharing or order by the National Biodiversity Authority or a State Biodiversity Board under the provisions of the Biological Diversity Act, 2002. Any person aggrieved by an order under the aforesaid provisions can file an appeal before the National Green Tribunal within a period of 30 days from the date on which the order or decision or direction or determination is communicated to him. Against the order of Green Tribunal, an appeal can be filed only in the Supreme Court under section 22 of the National Green Tribunal Act, 2010. The jurisdiction of high courts over the Green Tribunal has been excluded under the 2010 Act.

14. National Tax Tribunal held Unconstitutional.

However, the Supreme Court in "*Madras Bar Association v UOI*"[28] held (per majority) that the jurisdiction to adjudicate upon questions of law/substantial questions of law of the high court under any ordinary law may be transferred to an appropriately constituted tribunal. Therefore, the validity of the Constitution (42nd Amendment) Act, 1976 insofar as it inserts Article 323B is reaffirmed. However, the National Tax Tribunal (NTT) Act, 2005 is unconstitutional, as in transferring the abovesaid power from a traditional court to an alternative court/tribunal, the salient characteristics of the court were sought to be replaced and not incorporated in the court/tribunal created. Especially the provisions in the NTT Act, 2005, *viz.* sections 5, 6, 7, 8 and 13 dealing with the constitution of Benches of NTT, qualifications, appointment, terms of office of Chairperson and Members, are thus unconstitutional. Since the aforesaid provisions, constitute the edifice of the NTT Act, and without these provisions the remaining provisions are rendered ineffective and inconsequential, the entire enactment is declared as unconstitutional.

15. Writ Jurisdiction of Supreme Court and High Court.

Besides the above, the Supreme Court as well as the high courts possess what may be called an extraordinary jurisdiction, under Articles 32 and 226 of the Constitution, respectively, which extends not only to inferior courts and tribunals but also to the State or any authority or person, endowed with State authority. The peculiarity of this jurisdiction is that being conferred by the Constitution, it cannot be taken away or abridged by anything short of an amendment of the Constitution itself. As has already been pointed out, the jurisdiction to issue writs under these Articles is larger in the case of high court inasmuch as while the Supreme Court can issue them only where a fundamental right has been infringed, a high court can issue them not only in such cases but

28. *Madras Bar Association v UOI*, (2014) 10 SCC 1 : 2014 (11) Scale 166.

also where an ordinary legal right has been infringed, provided a writ is a proper remedy in such cases, according to well-established principles.

The writ jurisdiction under Article 32/226 of the Constitution of India being special and extraordinary, it should not be exercised casually or lightly on the mere asking of a litigant based on suspicions and conjectures, unless there is credible/trustworthy material on record to suggest that adverse action affecting a right is reasonably imminent or there is a real threat to the rule of law being abrogated. It must be shown, at least *prima facie*, that there is a real potential threat to a right, which is guaranteed by law to the person concerned.[29]

The petitioner should come to the court at the earliest reasonable possible opportunity. Inordinate delay in making the motion for a writ will indeed be a good ground for refusing to exercise such discretionary jurisdiction.[30] For filing of a writ petition, there is no doubt that no fixed period of limitation is prescribed. However, when the extraordinary jurisdiction of the writ court is invoked, it has to be seen as to whether within a reasonable time same has been invoked and even submitting of memorials would not revive the dead cause of action or resurrect the cause of action which has had a natural death.[31] The extraordinary power must be exercised, sparingly, cautiously and in exceptional situations where it becomes necessary to provide credibility and install confidence in investigations or where such an order may be necessary for doing complete justice and enforcing the fundamental rights.[32] The petitioner approaching the Writ Court must come with clean hands, put forward all the facts before the Court without concealing or suppressing anything and seek appropriate relief. Further, if there is no candid disclosure of relevant and material facts or the petitioner is guilty of misleading the Court, his petition should be dismissed at the threshold without considering the merits of the claim.[33]

In *UOI v Rajasthan High Court*,[34] , the Supreme Court held that a *suo moto* exercise of the nature embarked upon the high court encroaches upon the domain of the Executive. The Supreme Court further held that the powers under Article 226 are wide enough to reach out to injustice wherever it may originate. But judges are expected to apply standards which are objective and well-defined by law founded on constitutional principles.

In *Municipal Committee Katra v Ashwani Kumar*, [35] the Court has stated that though, the jurisdiction of the High Court is wide, the High Court in exercise of the extra ordinary writ jurisdiction cannot entertain disputes arising out of purely contractual obligations. [36]

---

29. *Association for Democratic Reforms v Election Commission of India*, AIR 2024 SC 2203 : AIROnline 2024 SC 276 : 2024 INSC 341.
30. *Tridip Kumar Dingal v State of West Bengal*, (2009) 1 SCC 768 (784) : (2009) 3 Serv LR 1.
31. *Mrinmoy Maity v Chhanda Koley*, AIR 2024 SC 2717 : AIROnline 2024 SC 279.
32. *TC Thangraj v V Engammal*, AIR 2011 SC 3010 : (2011) 12 SCC 328, p 332.
33. *HMT Ltd. v Rukmini*, AIR 2024 SC 4677 : AIROnline 2024 SC 628.
34. *UOI v Rajasthan High Court*, AIR 2017 SC 101 : (2017) 2 SCC 599.
35. *Municipal Committee Katra v Ashwani Kumar*, AIR 2024 SC 2855 : AIROnline 2024 SC 323; also see *UOI v Puna Hinda*, (2021) 10 SCC 690.
36. *Municipal Committee Katra v Ashwani Kumar*, AIR 2024 SC 2855 : AIROnline 2024 SC 323; also see *UOI v Puna Hinda*, (2021) 10 SCC 690.

15a. Public Interest Litigation (PIL).

Following English and American decisions, our Supreme Court has admitted exceptions from the strict rules relating to affidavit *locus standi* and the like in the case of a class of litigations, classified as "public interest litigation" (PIL) ie, where the public in general are interested in the vindication of some right or the enforcement of some public duty.[37] The high courts also have started following this practice in their jurisdiction under Article 226,[38] and the Supreme Court has approved this practice, observing that where public interest is undermined by an arbitrary and perverse executive action, it would be the duty of the high court to issue a writ.[39] Public interest litigation serves as an effective tool for addressing the grievances of the public. It must be carefully scrutinised to prevent misuse or abuse by those with ulterior motives. Vexatious petitions disguised as PILs, aiming to address personal grievances, deserve rejection at the threshold.[40] The court must satisfy itself that the party bringing the PIL is litigating *bona fide* for public good. It should not be merely a cloak for attaining private ends of a third party or of the party bringing the petition. The court can examine the previous records of public service rendered by the litigant.[41] An advocate filed a writ petition against the State or its instrumentalities seeking not only compensation to a victim of rape committed by its employees (the railway employees) but also so many other reliefs including eradication of anti-social and criminal activities at the railway stations. The Supreme Court held that the petition was in the nature of a PIL and the advocate could bring in the same for which no personal injury or loss is an essential element.[42]

Writ proceedings under Articles 32 or 226 are not guided by the provisions of the Limitation Act, 1963, but instead, by the Doctrine of Delay and Laches. Without adverting much into its pith and substance, it is ubiquitous that the doctrine of delay and laches cannot be applied *stricto senso* to writ petitions invoking public interest jurisdiction, unless the court is satisfied that the party has not approached it with clean hands.[43]

37. *People's Union v UOI,* AIR 1982 SC 1473, para 1 : [1983] 1 SCR 456.
38. *State of West Bengal v Sampat Lal,* AIR 1985 SC 195, para 10 : [1985] 2 SCR 256.
39. *Chaitanya v State of Karnataka,* AIR 1986 SC 825, para 10 : (1986) 2 SCC 594.
40. *NOIDA Toll Bridge Company Ltd. v Federation of NOIDA Residents Welfare Association,* AIR 2025 SC 393 : 2024 INSC 1027.
41. *Raunaq International Ltd v IVR Construction Ltd,* AIR 1999 SC 393 : (1999) 1 SCC 492, para 12.
42. *Chairman, Railway Board v Chandrima Das,* (2000) 2 SCC 465.
43. *NOIDA Toll Bridge Company Ltd. v Federation of NOIDA Residents Welfare Association,* AIR 2025 SC 393 : 2024 INSC 1027.

PART VIII

THE FEDERAL SYSTEM

CHAPTER 24

DISTRIBUTION OF LEGISLATIVE AND EXECUTIVE POWERS

1. Nature of the Union. THE nature of the federal system introduced by *our* Constitution has been fully explained in Chapter 5, *ante*.

To recapitulate its essential features: Though there is a strong admixture of unitary bias and the exceptions from the traditional federal scheme are many, the Constitution introduces a federal system as the basic structure of Government of the country. The Union is composed of 28 States[1] and both the Union and the States derive their authority from the Constitution which divides all powers—legislative, executive and financial, as between them. [The judicial powers, as already pointed out (Chapter 22), are, not divided and there is a common Judiciary for the Union and the States.] The result is that the States are not delegates of the Union and that, though there are agencies and devices for Union control over the States in many matters—subject to such exceptions, the States are autonomous within their own spheres as allotted by the Constitution, and both the Union and the States are equally subject to the limitations imposed by the Constitution, say, for instance, the exercise of legislative powers being limited by Fundamental Rights.

Thus, neither the Union Legislature (Parliament) nor a State Legislature can be said to be "sovereign" in the legalistic sense,—each being limited by the provisions of the Constitution effecting the distribution of legislative powers as between them, apart from the Fundamental Rights and other specific provisions restraining their powers in certain matters, *e.g.*, Article 276(2) [limiting the power of a State Legislature to impose a tax on professions]; Article 303 [limiting the powers of both Parliament and a State Legislature with regard to legislation relating to trade and commerce]. If any of these constitutional limitations is violated, the law of the Legislature concerned is liable to be declared invalid by the courts.

2. Scheme of Distribution of Legislative Powers. As has been pointed out at the outset, a federal system postulates a distribution of powers between the federation and the units. Though the nature of distribution varies

1. The creation of Chhattisgarh, Uttaranchal (now Uttarakhand) and Jharkhand States by carving out their territories from the territories of Madhya Pradesh, Uttar Pradesh and Bihar States respectively in 2000 has raised the number of States from 25 to 28. Telangana become the 29th State in 2014. The number has now come down to 28 as the erstwhile State of Jammu and Kashmir has been reorganised into Union Territories of Jammu and Kashmir and Ladakh.

according to the local and political background in each country, the division, obviously, proceeds on two lines—

(a) The *territory* over which the Federation and the Units shall, respectively, have their jurisdiction.

(b) The *subjects* to which their respective jurisdiction shall extend.

The distribution of legislative powers in *our* Constitution under both heads is as follows:

2a. Territorial Extent of Union and State Legislations.

As regards the territory with respect to which the Legislature may legislate, the State Legislature naturally suffers from a limitation to which Parliament is not subject, namely, that the territory of the Union being divided amongst the States, the jurisdiction of each State must be confined to its own territory. When, therefore, a State Legislature makes a law relating to a subject within its competence, it must be read as referring to persons or objects situated within the territory of the State concerned. A State Legislature can make laws for the whole or any part of the State to which it belongs [*Article 245(1)*]. It is not possible for a State Legislature to enlarge its territorial jurisdiction under any circumstances except when the boundaries of the State itself are widened by an Act of Parliament.

Parliament has, on the other hand, the power to legislate for "the whole or any part of the territory of India", which includes not only the States but also the Union Territories or any other area, for the time being, included in the territory of India [*Article 246(4)*]. It also possesses the power of "extra-territorial legislation" [*Article 245(2)*], which no State Legislature possesses. This means that laws made by Parliament will govern not only persons and property within the territory of India but also Indian subjects resident and their property situated *anywhere* in the world. No such power to affect persons or property outside the borders of its own State can be claimed by a State Legislature in India.

While Parliament has exclusive power under Article 246(1) of the Constitution to make laws with respect to the matters enumerated in the Union List, the State Legislature has exclusive power to make laws with respect to matters enumerated in the State List, subject to clauses (1) and (2) of Article 246. Along with the Union Legislature, the State Legislature is also competent to enact laws in respect of the matters enumerated in the Concurrent List, subject to the provisions of Article 246(1).

The Constitution (101st Amendment) Act, 2015 was passed by the Lok Sabha on 6 May 2015 which provides that the Parliament has exclusive power to make laws with respect to goods and services tax (GST) where the supply of goods, or of services, or both takes place in the course of inter-State trade or commerce [*Article 246A(2)*].

The plenary territorial jurisdiction of Parliament is, however, subject to some special provisions of the Constitution—

(i) As regards to some of the Union Territories, such as the Andaman and *Lakshadweep* group of Islands, Regulations may be made by the President to have the same force as Acts of Parliament and such

Regulations may repeal or amend a law made by Parliament in relation to such Territory [*Article 240(2)*].[2]

(ii) The application of Acts of Parliament to any Scheduled Area may be barred or modified by notifications made by the Governor [*Para 5 of the Fifth Schedule*].[2]

(iii) Besides, the Governor of Assam may, by public notification, direct that any other Act of Parliament shall not apply to an autonomous district or an autonomous region in the State of Assam or shall apply to such district or region or part thereof subject to such exceptions or modifications as he may specify in the notification [*Para 12(1)(b) of the Sixth Schedule*].[3] Similar power has been vested in the President as regards the autonomous district or region in Meghalaya, Tripura and Mizoram by paras 12A, 12AA and 12B of the Sixth Schedule.

It is obvious that the foregoing special provisions have been inserted in view of the backwardness of the specified areas to which the indiscriminate application of the general laws might cause hardship or other injurious consequences.

2b. Distribution of Legislative Subjects.

As regards the *subjects* of legislation, the Constitution adopts from the Government of India Act, 1935, a *threefold* distribution of *legislative* powers between the Union and the States [*Article 246*]. While in the *United States* and *Australia,* there is only a single enumeration of powers,—only the powers of the Federal Legislature being enumerated—in *Canada* there is a double enumeration, and the Government of India Act, 1935, introduced a scheme of threefold enumeration, namely, Federal, Provincial and Concurrent. The Constitution adopts this scheme from the Act of 1935 by enumerating possible subjects of legislation under three Legislative Lists in Seventh Schedule of the Constitution (see Table XVIII, *post*).[4]

List I or the *Union* List includes 98 subjects over which the Union shall have exclusive power of legislation. These include defence, foreign affairs, banking, insurance, currency and coinage, Union duties and taxes.

List II or the *State* List comprises 59 items or entries over which the State Legislature shall have exclusive power of legislation, such as public order and police, local government, public health and sanitation, agriculture, forests, fisheries, State taxes and duties.

List III gives *concurrent* powers to the Union and the State Legislatures over 52 items, such as Criminal law and procedure, Civil procedure, marriage, contracts, torts, trusts, welfare of labour, economic and social planning and education.

In case of *overlapping* of a matter as between the three Lists, predominance has been given to the Union Legislature, as under the Government of India Act,

---

2. See Author's *Constitutional Law of India,* Prentice-Hall of India, 6th Edn, 1991, pp 265, and 458.
3. See Author's *Constitutional Law of India,* Prentice-Hall of India, 6th Edn, 1991, p 467.
4. As stated earlier, the distribution does not apply to the Union Territories, in regard to which Parliament is competent to legislate with respect to any subject, including those which are enumerated in the "State List".

1935. Thus, the power of the State Legislature to legislate with respect to matters enumerated in the State List has been made subject to the power of Parliament to legislate in respect of matters enumerated in the Union and Concurrent Lists, and the entries in the State List have to be interpreted accordingly.

In the *concurrent* sphere, in case of repugnancy between a Union and a State law relating to the *same* subject, the former prevails. If, however, the State law was reserved for the assent of the President and has received such assent, the State law may prevail notwithstanding such repugnancy, but it would still be competent for Parliament to override such State law by subsequent legislation [*Article 254(2)*].[5] Repugnancy between two statutes would arise if there is a direct conflict between the two provisions of law made by the Parliament and the law made by the State Legislative occupies the same filed and the provisions of both laws are firstly inconsistent. However, incidental touching by one in the field of other is immaterial.[6]

In *M Karunanidhi v UOI,*[7] the principles to be applied for determining repugnancy between a law made by Parliament and law made by State legislature were considered by a Constitution Bench. In this case, the Supreme Court laid down the following tests:

> 35. 1. That in order to decide the question of repugnancy it must be shown that the two enactments contain inconsistent and irreconcilable provisions, so that they cannot stand together or operate in the same field.
>
> 2 That there can be no repeal by implication unless the inconsistency appears on the face of the two statutes.
>
> 3 That where the two statutes occupy a particular field, but there is room or possibility of both the statutes operating in the same field without coming into collision with each other, no repugnancy results.
>
> 4 That where there is no inconsistency but a statute occupying the same field seeks to create distinct and separate offences, no question of repugnancy arises and both the statutes continue to operate in the same field.[8]

3. Residuary Powers.

The vesting of residual power under the Constitution follows the precedent of *Canada,* for, it is given to the Union instead of the States (as in the *USA* and *Australia*). In this respect, the Constitution differs from the Government of India Act, 1935, for, under that Act, the residual powers were vested neither in the Federal nor in the State Legislature, but were placed in the hands of the Governor-General; the Constitution vests the residuary power, *i.e.,* the power to legislate with respect to any matter *not* enumerated in any one of the three Lists—in the Union legislature [*Article 248*],[9] and the final determination as to whether a particular matter falls under the residuary power or not is that of the courts.

5. See Author's *Constitutional Law of India,* Prentice-Hall of India, 1991, pp 281–84.
6. *K T Plantation Pvt Ltd v State of Karnataka,* AIR 2011 SC 3430, p 3451 : (2011) 9 SCC 1; see also *A Subhash Babu v State of A P,* AIR 2011 SC 3031: (2011) 7 SCC 616.
7. *M Karunanidhi v UOI,* AIR 1979 SC 898 : (1979) 3 SCR 254.
8. *M Karunanidhi v UOI,* AIR 1979 SC 898 : (1979) 3 SCC 431 : [1979] 3 SCR 254; *West UP Sugar Mills Association v State of Uttar Pradesh,* (2020) 4 Mad LJ 384 : LNIND 2020 SC 250.
9. *M Karunanidhi v UOI,* AIR 1979 SC 898 : (1979) 3 SCC 431 : [1979] 3 SCR 254, p 279.

It should be noted, however, that since the three Lists attempt at an exhaustive enumeration of all possible subjects of legislation, and the courts interpret the ambit of the enumerated powers liberally, the scope for the application of the residuary power will be very narrow.[10]

4. Exceptional Circumstances under Scheme of Distribution of Legislative Powers.

While the foregoing may be said to be an account of the normal distribution of the legislative powers, there are certain exceptional circumstances under which the above system of distribution is either suspended or the powers of the Union Parliament are extended over State subjects. These exceptional or extraordinary circumstances are —

(a) *National interest:* Parliament shall have the power to make laws with respect to any matter included in the State List, for a temporary period, if the Council of States declares by a resolution of two-third of its members present and voting, that it is necessary in the national interest that Parliament shall have power to legislate over such matters. Each such resolution will give a lease of one year to the law in question.

A law made by Parliament, which Parliament would not but for the passing of such resolution have been competent to make, shall, to the extent of the incompetency, cease to have effect on the expiration of a period of six months after the resolution has ceased to be in force, except as respects things done or omitted to be done before the expiration of the said period [*Article 249*]. The resolution of the Council of States may be renewed for a period of one year at a time.

(b) *Proclamation of Emergency:* While a Proclamation of "Emergency" made by the President is in operation, Parliament shall have similar power to legislate with respect to State subjects.

A law made by Parliament, which Parliament would not but for the issue of such Proclamation have been competent to make, shall, to the extent of incompetency, cease to have effect on the expiration of a period of six months after the Proclamation has ceased to operate, except as respects things done or omitted to be done before the expiration of the said period [*Article 250*].

(c) *By agreement between States:* If the Legislatures of two or more States resolve that it shall be lawful for Parliament to make laws with respect to any matters included in the State List relating to those States, Parliament shall have such power as regards such States. It shall also be open to any other State to adopt such Union legislation in relation to itself by a resolution passed in that behalf in the Legislature of the State. In short, this is an extension of the jurisdiction of Parliament by consent of the State Legislatures [*Article 252*].[8]

Thus, though Parliament has no competence to impose an estate duty with respect to *agricultural* lands, Parliament, in the Estate Duty Act, 1953, included the agricultural lands situated in certain States, by virtue of resolutions passed by

---

10. See *Second Gift Tax Officer v Hazareth*, AIR 1970 SC 999 : (1970) 1 SCC 749; *UOI v H S Dhillon*, (1971) 2 SCC 779 : (1971) 1 SCR 195; *Azam Jha Bahadur (Dead) By His Legal Representatives v Expenditure*, (1971) 3 SCC 621; *Shorter Constitution of India*, 14th Edn, 2008, Schedule VII, under "General Rules for interpretation of the Entries" *etc.*

the Legislatures of such States, under Article 252, to confer such power upon Parliament. That Act has since been repealed.

Other examples of such legislation are: Prize Competition Act, 1955; Urban Land (Ceiling and Regulation) Act, 1976; Water (Prevention and Control of Pollution) Act, 1974.

(d) *To implement treaties:* Parliament shall have the power to legislate with respect to any subject for the purpose of implementing treaties or international agreements and conventions. In other words, the normal distribution of powers will not stand in the way of Parliament to enact legislation for carrying out its international obligations, even though such legislation may be necessary in relation to a State subject [*Article 253*].

Examples of such legislation are the Geneva Convention Act, 1960; the Anti-Hijacking Act, 1982; the United Nations (Privileges and Immunities) Act, 1947.

(e) *Under a Proclamation of Failure of Constitutional Machinery in the States:* When such a Proclamation is made by the President, the President may declare that the powers of the Legislature of the State shall be exercisable by or under the authority of Parliament [*Article 356(1)(b)*].

5. Interpretation of Legislative Lists.

The interpretation of over 200 Entries in the three Legislative Lists is no easy task for the courts and the courts have to apply various judicial principles to reconcile the different Entries, a discussion of which would be beyond the scope of the present work.[11] Suffice it to say that —

(a) Each Entry is given the widest import that its words are capable of, without rendering another Entry nugatory.[12]

(b) In order to determine whether a particular enactment falls under one Entry or the other, it is the "pith and substance" of such enactment and not its legislative label that is taken account of.[13] If the enactment substantially falls under an Entry over which the Legislature has jurisdiction, an incidental encroachment upon another Entry over which it had no competence will not invalidate the law.[10]

(c) On the other hand, where a Legislature has no power to legislate with respect to a matter, the courts will not permit such Legislature to transgress its own powers or to encroach upon those of another Legislature by resorting to any device or "colourable legislation".[14]

(d) The motives of the Legislature are, otherwise, irrelevant for determining whether it has transgressed the constitutional limits of its legislative power.[15]

11. *Vide* Author's *Commentary on the Constitution of India,* 5th Edn, vol 4, pp 95 *et seq.* and *Shorter Constitution of India,* 14th Edn, 2008, Schedule VII, under "General Rules for interpretation of the Entries" *etc*; *Constitutional Law of India,* 6th Edn, pp 475–500.
12. *State of Bombay v Balsara,* AIR 1951 SC 318 : (1951) 2 SCR 682; *Ramakrishna v Municipal Committee,* (1950) SCR 15, p *25.*
13. *Amar Singh v State of Rajasthan,* AIR 1955 SC 504 : (1955) 2 SCR 303, p *325.*
14. *KCG Narayana Deo v State of Orissa,* (1954) SCR 1.
15. *P H Paul Manoj Pandian v P Veldurai,* (2011) 5 SCC 214.

6. Distribution of Executive Powers.

The distribution of *executive* powers between the Union and the States is somewhat more complicated than that of the legislative powers.

I. In general, it follows the scheme of distribution of the legislative powers. In the result, the executive power of a State is, in the main, co-extensive with its legislative powers—which means that the executive power of State shall extend only to its own territory and with respect to those subjects over which it has legislative competence. The limitations on the exercise of executive power by the Government are twofold, first, if any Act or law has been made by the State legislature conferring any function or any other authority, in that case the Governor is not empowered to make any order in regard to that matter in exercise of his executive power nor can the Governor exercise such power in regard to that matter through officers subordinate to him. Secondly, the vesting in the Governor with the executive power of the State Government does not create any embargo for the legislature of the State from making and/or enacting any law conferring functions on any authority subordinate to the Governor [*Article 162*].[16] Conversely, the *Union* shall have exclusive executive power over: (a) the matters with respect to which Parliament has exclusive power to make laws (*i.e.*, matters in List I of Seventh Schedule), and (b) the exercise of its powers conferred by any treaty or agreement [*Article 73*]. On the other hand, a State shall have exclusive executive power over matters included in List II [*Article 162*].

II. It is in the *concurrent* sphere that some novelty has been introduced. As regards matters included in the Concurrent Legislative List (*i.e.*, List III), the executive function shall *ordinarily* remain with the States, but subject to the provisions of the Constitution or of any law of Parliament conferring such function expressly upon the Union. Under the Government of India Act, 1935, the Centre had only a power to give directions to Provincial Executive to execute a Central law relating to a Concurrent subject. But this power of giving directions proved ineffective; so, the Constitution provides that the Union may, whenever it thinks fit, itself take up the administration of Union laws relating to any Concurrent subject.

In the result, the executive power relating to concurrent subjects remains with the States, except in two cases—

(a) Where a law of Parliament relating to such subjects vests some executive function specifically in the Union, *e.g.*, the Land Acquisition Act, 1894; the Industrial Disputes Act, 1947 [*proviso to Article 73(1)*]. So far as these functions specified in such Union law are concerned, it is the Union and not the States which shall have the executive power while the rest of the executive power relating to the subjects shall remain with the States.

(b) Where the provisions of the Constitution itself vest some executive functions upon the Union. Thus,

(i) The executive power to implement any treaty or international agreement belongs exclusively to the Union, whether the subject appertains to the Union, State or Concurrent List [*Article 73(1)(b)*].

16. *P H Paul Manoj Pandian v P Veldurai,* (2011) 5 SCC 214, p 230.

(ii) The Union has the power to give directions to the State Governments as regards the exercise of their executive power, in certain matters—

(I) *In Normal times:*

(a) To ensure due compliance with Union laws and existing laws which apply in that State [*Article 256*].

(b) To ensure that the exercise of the executive power of the State does not interfere with the exercise of the executive power of the Union [*Article 257(1)*].

(c) To ensure the construction and maintenance of the means of communication of national or military importance by the State [*Article 257(2)*].

(d) To ensure protection of railways within the State [*Article 257(3)*].

(e) To ensure drawing and execution of schemes specified in the directions to be essential for the welfare of the Scheduled Tribes in the States [*Article 339(2)*].

(f) To secure the provision of adequate facilities for instruction in the mother-tongue at the primary stage of education to children belonging to linguistic minority groups [*Article 350A*].

(g) To ensure the development of the Hindi language [*Article 351*].

(h) To ensure that the government of a State is carried on in accordance with the provisions of the Constitution [*Article 355*].

(II) *In Emergencies:*

(a) During a Proclamation of Emergency, the power of the Union to give directions extends to the giving of directions as to the *manner* in which the executive power of the State is to be exercised, relating to any matter [*Article 353(a)*]. (So as to bring the State Government under the complete control of the Union, without suspending it).

(b) Upon a Proclamation of failure of constitutional machinery in a State, the President shall be entitled to assume to himself all or any of the executive powers of the State [*Article 356(1)*].

(III) *During a Proclamation of Financial Emergency:*

(a) To observe canons of financial propriety, as may be specified in the directions [*Article 360(3)*].

(b) To reduce the salaries and allowances of all or any class of persons serving in connection with the affairs of the Union including the Judges of the Supreme Court and high courts [*Article 360(4)(b)*].

(c) To require all Money Bills or other Financial Bills to be reserved for the consideration of the President after they are passed by the Legislature of the State [*Article 360(4)*].

III. While as regards the legislative powers, it is not competent for the Union [apart from Article 252, see *ante*] and a State to encroach upon each other's exclusive jurisdiction by mutual consent, this is possible as regards executive powers. Thus, with the consent of the Government of a State, the Union may entrust its own executive functions relating to any matter to such State Government or its officers [*Article 258(1)*]. Conversely, with the consent of the Union Government, it is competent for a State Government to entrust any of its executive functions to the former [*Article 258A*].

IV. On the other hand, under Article 258(2), a law made by Parliament relating to a Union subject may *authorise* the Central Government to delegate its functions or duties to the State Government or its officers (irrespective of the consent of such State Government).

[illegible]

[illegible] the consent of the Government of a State, [illegible] relating to [illegible] [illegible] of Commission [illegible] the consent of the [illegible] Government to entrust any of its executive functions [illegible]

(iv) [illegible] other [illegible] [illegible] a law made by Parliament [illegible] [illegible] the Central Government [illegible] [illegible]

Need for Dispute Settlement of Inter-State and Resources [illegible]

[illegible]

[illegible] Bodies [illegible] [illegible] the lines of the [illegible] [illegible] India Act, 1935 [illegible]

[illegible]

CHAPTER 25

DISTRIBUTION OF FINANCIAL POWERS

1. Need for Distribution of Financial Resources. NO system of federation can be successful unless both the Union and the States have at their disposal adequate financial resources to enable them to discharge their respective responsibilities under the Constitution.

To achieve this object, *our* Constitution has made elaborate provisions, mainly following the lines of the Government of India Act, 1935, relating to the distribution of the taxes as well as non-tax revenues and the power of borrowing, supplemented by provisions for grants-in-aid by the Union to the States.

Before entering into these elaborate provisions which set up a complicated arrangement for the distribution of the financial resources of the country, it has to be noted that the object of this complicated machinery is an equitable distribution of the financial resources between the two units of the federation, instead of dividing the resources into two watertight compartments, as under the usual federal system. A fitting introduction to this arrangement has been given by our Supreme Court,[1] in these words:

> Sources of revenue which have been allocated to the Union are not meant entirely for the purposes of the Union but have to be distributed according to the principles laid down by Parliamentary legislation as contemplated by the Articles aforesaid. Thus, all the taxes and duties levied by the Union ... do not form part of the Consolidated Fund of India but many of these taxes and duties are distributed amongst the States and form part of the Consolidated Fund of the States. Even those taxes and duties which constitute the Consolidated Fund of India may be used for the purposes of supplementing the revenues of the States in accordance with their needs. The question of distribution of the aforesaid taxes and duties amongst the States and the principles governing them, as also the principles governing grants-in-aid ... are matters which have to be decided by a high-powered Finance Commission, which is a responsible body designated to determine those matters in an objective way... The Constitution-makers realised the fact that those sources of revenue allocated to the States may not be sufficient for their purposes and that the Government of India would have to subsidise their welfare activities... Realising the limitations on the financial resources of the States and the growing needs of the community in a welfare State, the Constitution has made... specific provisions empowering Parliament to set aside a portion of its revenues... for the benefit of the States, not in stated proportions but according to their needs ... The resources of the Union Government are not meant exclusively for the benefit of the Union activities ... In other words, the Union and the States together form one organic whole for the purposes of utilisation of the resources of territories of India as a whole.

---

1. *Coffee Board v CTO,* AIR 1971 SC 870 : (1971) 1 SCJ 14.

2. Principles Underlying Levy and Distribution of Tax Revenues.

The Constitution makes a distinction between the legislative power to levy a tax and the power to *appropriate* the proceeds of a tax so levied. In *India,* the powers of a Legislature in these two respects are not identical.

(A) The legislative power to make a law for imposing a tax is divided as between the Union and the States by means of specific Entries in the Union and State Legislative Lists in Schedule VII (see Table XVIII, *post*). Thus, while the State Legislature has the power to levy an estate duty in respect of agricultural lands [Entry 48 of List II], the power to levy an estate duty in respect of non-agricultural land belongs to Parliament [Entry 87 of List I]. Similarly, it is the State Legislature which is competent to levy a tax on agricultural income [Entry 46 of List II], while Parliament has the power to levy income-tax on all incomes other than agricultural [Entry 82 of List I].

The residuary power as regards taxation (as in general legislation) belongs to Parliament [Entry 97 of List I] and the gift tax and expenditure tax have been held to derive their authority from this residuary power. There is no concurrent sphere in the matter of tax legislation.

Before leaving this topic, it should be pointed out that though a State Legislature has the power to levy any of the taxes enumerated in the State Legislative List, in case of certain taxes, this power is subject to certain limitations imposed by the substantive provisions of the Constitution. Thus—

(a) *Professions tax:* While Entry 60 of List II of Seventh Schedule authorises a State Legislature to levy a tax on profession, trade, calling or employment, the total amount payable in respect of any one person to the State or any other authority in the State by way of such tax shall not exceed Rs 2,500[2] *per annum* [*Article 276(2)*].

(b) *Sales tax:* The power to impose taxes on "sale or purchase of goods other than newspapers" belongs to the State. But "taxes on imports and exports" [Entry 83, List I] and "taxes on sales in the course of inter-State trade and commerce" [Entry 92A, List I] are exclusive Union subjects. Article 286 is intended to ensure that sales taxes imposed by States do not interfere with imports and exports or inter-State trade and commerce, which are matters of national concern, and should, therefore, be beyond the competence of the States. Hence, certain limitations have been laid down by Article 286 upon the power of the States to enact sales tax legislation:

1. (a) No tax shall be imposed on sale or purchase which takes place *outside the State.*

(b) No tax shall be imposed on sale or purchase which takes place *in the course of import* into or *export* out of India.[3]

2. In connection with inter-state trade and commerce there are two limitations—

(i) The power to tax sales taking place "in the course of inter-State trade and commerce"[4] is within the exclusive competence of Parliament [Entry 92A, List I].

2. The maximum limit of the professions tax has been raised from Rs 250 to Rs 2500, by the Constitution (60th Amendment) Act, 1988.

3. *State of J&K v Caltex,* AIR 1966 SC 1350 : (1966) 3 SCR 149.

(ii) Even though a sale does not take place "in the course of" inter-State trade or commerce, State taxation would be subject to restrictions and conditions imposed by Parliament if the sale relates to "goods declared by Parliament to be of *special importance* in inter-State trade and commerce". In pursuance of this power, Parliament has declared sugar, tobacco, cotton, silk and woollen fabrics to be goods of special importance in inter-State trade and commerce, by enacting the Additional Duties of Excise (Goods of Special Importance) Act, 1957[5] [*Section* 7], and imposed special restrictions upon the States to levy tax on the sales of these goods.

(c) *Tax on consumption or sale of electricity:* Save insofar as Parliament may by law otherwise provide, no law of a State shall impose, or authorise the imposition of, a tax on the consumption or sale of electricity (whether produced by a Government or other persons) which is —

(i) consumed by the Government of India, or sold to the Government of India for consumption by that Government; or

(ii) consumed in the construction, maintenance or operation of any railway by the Government of India, or a railway company operating that railway, or sold to that Government or any such railway company for consumption in the construction, maintenance or operation of any railway [*Article* 287].

(d) *Exemption of Union and State properties from mutual taxation:* The property of the Union shall, save insofar as Parliament may by law otherwise provide, be exempt from all taxes imposed by a State or by any authority within a State [*Article* 285(1)].

Conversely, the property and income of a State shall be exempt from Union taxation [*Article* 289(1)]. There is, however, one exception in this case. If a State enters into a trade or business, other than a trade or business which is declared by Parliament to be incidental to the ordinary business of government, it shall not be exempt from Union taxation [*Article* 289(2)]. The immunity, again, relates to a tax on property. Hence, the property of a State is not immune from customs duty.[1]

(B) Even though a Legislature may have been given the power to levy a tax because of its affinity to the subject-matter of taxation, the yield of different taxes coming within the State legislative sphere may not be large enough to serve the purposes of a State. To meet this situation, the Constitution makes special provisions:

(i) Some duties are leviable by the Union; but they are to be collected and entirely appropriated by the States after collection.

(ii) There are some taxes which are both levied and collected by the Union, but the proceeds are then assigned by the Union to those States within which they have been levied.

(iii) Again, there are taxes which are levied and collected by the Union but the proceeds are distributed between the Union and the State.

4. *Re Sea Customs Act,* AIR 1963 SC 1760, p *1771* : (1964) 3 SCR 787.
5. Repealed by Act 12 of 2017 (w.e.f. 1-7-2017).

The distribution of the tax-revenue between the Union and the States, according to the foregoing principles, stands as follows:

(A) Taxes belonging to the Union exclusively:

1. Customs. 2. Corporation tax. 3. Taxes on capital value of assets of individuals and Companies. 4. Surcharge on income tax, etc. 5. Fees in respect of matters in the Union List (List I).

(B) Taxes belonging to the States exclusively:

1. Land Revenue. 2. Stamp duty except in documents included in the Union List. 3. Succession duty, Estate duty, and Income tax on *agricultural land.* 4. Taxes on passengers and goods carried on inland waterways. 5. Taxes on lands and buildings, mineral rights. 6. Taxes on animals and boats, on road vehicles, on advertisements, on consumption of electricity, on luxuries and amusements, etc. 7. Taxes on entry of goods into local areas. 8. Sales Tax. 9. Tolls. 10. Fees in respect of matters in the State List. 11. Taxes on professions, trades, etc., not exceeding Rs 2,500 per annum (List II).

(C) Duties Levied by the Union but Collected and Appropriated by the States:

Stamp duties on bills of Exchange, etc., and Excise duties on medicinal and toilet preparations containing alcohol, though they are included in the Union List and *levied* by the Union, shall be collected by the States insofar as leviable within their respective territories, and shall form part of the States by whom they are collected [*Article 268*].

(D) Taxes Levied as well as Collected by the Union, but Assigned to the States within which they are Leviable:

(a) Duties on succession to property other than agricultural land. (b) Estate duty in respect of property other than agricultural land. (c) Terminal taxes on goods or passengers carried by railway, air or sea. (d) Taxes on railway fares and freights. (e) Taxes on stock exchange other than stamp duties. (f) Taxes on sales of and advertisements in newspapers. (g) Taxes on the sale or purchase of goods other than newspapers, where such sale or purchase takes place in the course of inter-State trade or commerce. (h) Taxes on inter-State consignment of goods [*Article 269*].

(E) Taxes Levied and Distributed between Union and the States:

The Constitution (80th Amendment) Act, 2000 amended Article 270 as well as omitted Article 272 to implement the Tenth Finance Commission's recommendation to simplify the tax structure. The amended Article 272 as it stands after the Constitution (Eightieth Amendment) Act, 2000 and the Constitution (Eighty-eighth Amendment) Act, 2003 provides that all taxes and duties referred to in the Union List [except the duties and taxes referred to in Articles 268, 269 and 269A respectively], surcharge on taxes and duties referred to in Article 271 and any cess levied for specific purposes under any law made by Parliament shall be levied and collected by the Government of India and shall be distributed between the Union and the States in the manner provided in clause (2) [*Article 270*].

(F) The principal sources of non-tax revenues of the Union are the receipts from:

Railways; Posts and Telegraphs; Broadcasting; Opium; Currency and Mint; Industrial and Commercial Undertakings of the Central Government relating to the subjects over which the Union has jurisdiction.

Of the Industrial and Commercial Undertakings relating to Central subjects may be mentioned—The Industrial Finance Corporation; Air India; Indian Airlines; Industries in which the Government of India have made investments, such as the Steel Authority of India; the Hindustan Shipyard Ltd; the Indian Telephone Industries Ltd.

(G) The States, similarly, have their receipts from:

Forests, Irrigation and Commercial Enterprises (like Electricity, Road Transport) and Industrial Undertakings (such as Soap, Sandalwood, Iron and Steel in Karnataka, Paper in Madhya Pradesh, Milk Supply in Mumbai, Deep-sea Fishing and Silk in West Bengal).

(*H*) *Grants-in-aid*:

Even after the assignment to the States of a share of the Central taxes, the resources of all the States may not be adequate enough. The Constitution, therefore, provides that grants-in-aid shall be made in each year by the Union to such States as Parliament may determine to be in need of assistance; particularly, for the promotion of welfare of tribal areas, including special grants to Assam in this respect [*Article 275*].

3. Constitution and Functions of the Finance Commission.

Articles 270, 273, 275 and 280 provide for the constitution of a Finance Commission (at five-year intervals) to recommend to the President certain measures relating to the distribution of financial resources between the Union and the States—for instance, the percentage of the net proceeds of income-tax which should be assigned by the Union to the States and the manner in which the share to be assigned shall be distributed among the States [*Article 280*].

The constitution of the Finance Commission is laid down in Article 280, which has to be read with the Finance Commission (Miscellaneous Provisions) Act of 1951, which has supplemented the provisions of the Constitution. Briefly speaking, the Commission has to be constituted by the President, every five years. The Chairman must be a person having "experience in public affairs"; and the other four members must be appointed from amongst the following—

(a) A high court judge or one qualified to be appointed as such; (b) a person having special knowledge of the finances and accounts of the Government; (c) a person having wide experience in financial matters and administration; (d) a person having special knowledge of economics.

It shall be the duty of the Commission to make recommendations to the President as to—

(a) the distribution between the Union and the States of the net proceeds of taxes which are to be, or may be, divided between them under this chapter and the allocation between the States of the respective shares of such proceeds;

(b) the principles which should govern the grants-in-aid of the revenues of the States out of the Consolidated Fund of India;

(c) the measures needed to augment the Consolidated Fund of a State to supplement the resources of the Panchayats in the State;[6]

(d) the measures needed to augment the Consolidated Fund of a State to supplement the resources of the Municipalities in the State;[7]

(e) any other matter referred to the Commission by the President in the interests of sound finance.

3a. The First Finance Commission. The First Finance Commission was constituted in 1951, with Sri Neogy as the Chairman, and it submitted its report in 1953. Government accepted its recommendations which, *inter alia,* were that—

(a) 55 per cent of the net proceeds of income-tax shall be assigned by the Union to the States and that it shall be distributed among the States in the shares prescribed by the Commission.

(b) The Commission laid down the principles for guidance of the Government of India in the matter of making general grants-in-aid to States which require financial assistance and also recommended specific sums to be given to certain States such as West Bengal, Punjab, Assam, during the five years from 1952 to 1957.

3b. The Second Finance Commission. A Second Finance Commission, with Sri Santhanam as the Chairman, was constituted in 1956. Its report was submitted to Government in September, 1957 and its recommendations were given effect to for the quinquennium commencing from April, 1957.

3c. The Third Finance Commission. A Third Finance Commission, with Sri A K Chanda as its Chairman, was appointed in December, 1960. It submitted its report in 1962.

3d. The Fourth Finance Commission. The Fourth Finance Commission with Dr Rajamannar retired Chief Justice of the Madras High Court, as its Chairman, was constituted in May, 1964.

3e. The Fifth Finance Commission. A Fifth Finance Commission, headed by Sri Mahavir Tyagi, was constituted in March, 1968, with respect to the quinquennium commencing from 1 April 1969. It submitted its final report in July 1969, and recommended that the States' share of income-tax should be raised to 75% and of Union Excise duties should be raised to 20%.

3f. The Sixth Finance Commission. The Sixth Finance Commission, headed by Sri Brahmananda Reddy, submitted its Report in October, 1973. This Commission was, for the first time, required to go into the question of the debt position of the States and their non-plan capital gap.

3g. The Seventh Finance Commission. A Seventh Finance Commission was appointed in June, 1977 in relation to the next quinquennium from 1979, with Sri Shelat, a retired Judge of the Supreme Court as its Chairman. It submitted its report in October, 1978.

6. Inserted by the Constitution (73rd Amendment) Act, 1992, wef 24-4-1993.
7. Inserted by the Constitution (74th Amendment) Act, 1992, wef 1-7-1993.

3h. The Eighth Finance Commission. The Eighth Finance Commission was set up in 1982, with ex-Minister, Shri Y B Chavan as its head.

The Eighth Finance Commission submitted its report in 1984, but its recommendations, granting moneys to the States, were not implemented by the Government of India, on the ground of financial difficulties and late receipt of the Commission's Report. Obviously, this placed some of the States in financial difficulty and the State of West Bengal raised vehement protest against this unforeseen situation. Responsible authorities in West Bengal threatened litigation but eventually nothing was done presumably because the matter was non-justiciable. Article 280(3) enjoins the Finance Commission to make "recommendations" to the President and the only duty imposed on the President, by Article 281, is to lay the recommendations of the Commission before each House of Parliament. It is nowhere laid down in the Constitution that the recommendations of the Commission shall be binding upon the Government of India or that it would give rise to a legal right in favour of the beneficiary States to receive the moneys recommended to be offered to them by the Commission. Of course, non-implementation would cause grave dislocation in States which might have acted upon their anticipation founded on the Commission's Report. The remedy for such dislocation or injustice lies only in the ballot box.

3i. The Ninth Finance Commission. The Ninth Finance Commission, headed by Shri NKP Salve, submitted its Reports in 1988 and 1989; all its recommendations have been accepted by the Government.

3j. The Tenth Finance Commission. The 10th Finance Commission was constituted on 16 June 1992, with Shri K C Pant as its Chairman. It submitted its report on 26 November 1994.

3k. The Eleventh Finance Commission. The 11th Finance Commission was constituted on 3 July 1998. It submitted its report on 7 July 2000.

3l. The Twelfth Finance Commission. The 12th Finance Commission was constituted on 1 November 2002 with Dr. C Rangarajan as its Chairman. It submitted its report on 17 December 2004.

3m. The Thirteenth Finance Commission. The 13th Finance Commission was constituted on 1 November 2007 with Shri Vijay Kelkar as its Chairman and has submitted its report in December, 2009.

3n. The Fourteenth Finance Commission. The President of India constituted 14th Finance Commission *vide* notification as published in the Gazette of India dated 2 January 2013 consisting of Dr. Y V Reddy, former Governor, Reserve bank of India as Chairman and four other members — former Finance Secretary Sushma Nath, NIPFP Director M Govinda Rao, Planning Commission Member Abhijit Sen and Former Acting Chairman of National Statistical Commission Sudipto Mundle. The five-member panel is to submit its report by 31 October 2014. Apart from its recommendations on the sharing of tax proceeds between the Centre and the States which will apply for a five-year period beginning 1 April 2015, the Commission has been asked to suggest steps for pricing of public utilities such as electricity and water in an independent manner and also look into issues like disinvestment, GST compensation, sale of non-priority PSUs and subsidies.

Among other things, the Commission would look into the "need for insulating the pricing of public utility services like drinking water, irrigation, power and public transport from policy fluctuations through statutory provisions".

The 14th Finance Commission has submitted its recommendations for the period 2015-16 to 2020-21. They are likely to have major implications for the Center-State relations.

3o. The Fifteenth Finance Commission.

The 15th Finance Commission was constituted in November 2017 to give recommendations on the transfer of resources from the Centre to States for the five-year period from 2020 to 2025. The 15th Finance Commission has been constituted with the objective of strengthening the co-operative federalism and improving the quality of public spending and help protect fiscal stability. It is required to: (i) review the impact of the 14th Finance Commission's recommendations on the fiscal position of the centre; (ii) review the debt level of the centre and states, and recommend a roadmap; (iii) study the impact of GST on the economy; and (iv) recommend performance-based incentives for states based on their efforts to control population, promote ease of doing business, and control expenditure on populist measures, among others.

3p. The Sixteenth Finance Commission.

The 16th Finance Commission was constituted on 31 December 2023 with Shri Arvind Panagariya [Former Vice-Chairman, Niti Aayog] as its Chairman. This Commission was made to make recommendations as to the following matters: (i) the distribution between the Union and the States of the net proceeds of taxes which are to be, or may be, divided between them under Chapter I, Part XII of the Constitution and the allocation between the States of the respective shares of such proceeds; (ii) the principles which should govern the grants-in-aid of the revenues of the States out of the Consolidated Fund of India and the sums to be paid to the States by way of grants-in-aid of their revenues under article 275 of the Constitution for the purposes other than those specified in the provisos to clause (1) of that article; and (iii) the measures needed to augment the Consolidated Fund of a State to supplement the resources of the Panchayats and Municipalities in the State on the basis of the recommendations made by the Finance Commission of the State. The Commission may review the present arrangements on financing Disaster Management initiatives, with reference to the funds constituted under the Disaster Management Act, 2005 (53 of 2005), and make appropriate recommendations thereon. This Commission has been requested to make its recommendations available by 31 October 2025 covering an award period of 5 years commencing 1 April 2026.

4. Safeguarding the Interests of the States in the Shared Taxes.

By way of safeguarding the interests of the States in the Union taxes which are divisible according to the foregoing provisions, it is provided by the Constitution [*Article 274*] that no Bill or amendment which—

(a) varies the rate of any tax or duty in which the States are interested; or

(b) affects the principles on which moneys are distributable according to the foregoing provisions of the Constitution; or

(c) imposes any surcharge on any such tax or duty for the purposes of the Union,

shall be introduced or moved in Parliament except on the recommendation of the President.

Subject to the above condition, however, it is competent for Parliament to increase the rate of any such tax or duty (by imposing a surcharge) for purposes of the Union [*Article 271*]. The power to levy surcharge on income tax is traceable to Article 271 read with Entry 82, and not to section 4 of the Act.[8]

5. Financial Control by the Union in Emergencies. As in the legislative and administrative spheres, so in financial matters, the normal relation between the Union and the States (under Articles 268–279) is liable to be modified in different kinds of emergencies. Thus,

(a) While a Proclamation of Emergency [*Article 352(1)*] is in operation, the President may by order direct that, for a period not extending beyond the expiration of the financial year in which the Proclamation ceases to operate, all or any of the provisions relating to the division of the taxes between the Union and the States and grants-in-aid shall be suspended [*Article* 354]. In the result, if any such order is made by the President, the States will be left to their narrow resources from the revenues under the State List, without any augmentation by contributions from the Union.

(b) While a Proclamation of Financial Emergency [*Article 360(1)*] is made by the President, it shall be competent for the Union to give directions to the States—

(i) to observe such canons of financial propriety and other safeguards as may be specified in the directions;

(ii) to reduce the salaries and allowances of all persons serving in connection with the affairs of the State, including high court Judges;

(iii) to reserve for the consideration of the President all money and financial Bills, after they are passed by the Legislature of the State [*Article 360*].

6. Borrowing Powers of the Union and the States. The Union shall have unlimited power of borrowing, upon the security of the revenues of India either within India or outside. The Union Executive shall exercise the power subject only to such limits as may be fixed by Parliament from time to time [*Article 292*].

The borrowing power of a State is, however, subject to a number of constitutional limitations:

(i) It cannot borrow outside India. Under the *Government of India Act, 1935,* the States had the power to borrow outside India with the consent of the Centre. But this power is totally denied to the States by the Constitution; the Union shall have the sole right to enter into the international money market in the matter of borrowing.

---

8. *CIT (Central)-I, New Delhi v Vatika Township Pvt Ltd,* (2015) 1 SCC 1 : (2014) 10 Scale 510. (Bench: RM Lodha, Jagdish Singh Kehar, J Chelameswar, AK Sikri, and Rohinton Fali Nariman).

(ii) The State Executive shall have the power to borrow, within the territory of India upon the security of the revenues of the State; subject to the following conditions:

(a) Limitations as may be imposed by the State Legislature.

(b) If the Union has guaranteed an outstanding loan of the State, no fresh loan can be raised by the State without consent of the Union Government.

(c) The Government of India may itself offer a loan to a State, under a law made by Parliament. So long as such a loan or any part thereof remains outstanding, no fresh loan can be raised by the State without the consent of the Government of India. The Government of India may impose terms in giving its consent as above [*Article* 293].

7. Demand for more Financial Power by States.

Before closing this chapter, it should be pointed out that there is a growing demand from some of the States for greater financial powers, by amending the Constitution, if necessary, which was stoutly resisted by Prime Minister Desai.[9] There are two relevant considerations on this issue:

(i) The steps taken by Pakistan to make nuclear bombs together with the equivocal conduct of China leave no room for complacence in the matter of defence. Hence, the Union cannot yield to any weakening of its resources that would prejudice the defence potential of the country.

(ii) On the other hand, the welfare activities of the States involving huge expenditure, natural calamities, etc., which could not be fully envisaged in 1950, call for a revision of the financial provisions of the Constitution.

The entire subject of "Centre-State Relations" has been reviewed by the Sarkaria Commission.

8. GST Council.

The Constitution (101st Amendment) Act, 2016, has been enacted which has introduced National Goods and Services Tax in India from 1 July 2017. The GST is a comprehensive indirect tax levy on manufacture, sale and consumption of goods as well as services at the national level. It has replaced all indirect taxes levied on goods and services by the Indian Central and State Governments.

9. Mrs Gandhi's second Government has also adhered to the recommendations of the Administrative Reforms Commission that no amendment of the Constitution is necessary to alter the relation between the Centre and the States, on the ground, *inter alia,* that the financial deficiencies of particular States are being periodically examined and provided for by the Finance Commission, by making larger grants to those States from the Union revenues, according to the provisions of the Constitution.

CHAPTER 26

ADMINISTRATIVE RELATIONS BETWEEN THE UNION AND THE STATES

1. Need for co-ordination between the Units of the Federation.

ANY federal scheme involves the setting up of dual governments and division of powers. But the success and strength of the federal polity depends upon the maximum of co-operation and co-ordination between the governments. The topic may be discussed under two heads:

(a) Relation between the Union and States;

(b) Relation between the States *inter se.*

In the present chapter, the former aspect will be discussed, and the inter-State relations will be dealt with in the next chapter.

2. Techniques of Union control over States.

It would be convenient to discuss this matter under two heads—(i) in emergencies; (ii) in normal times.

I. *In Emergencies:* It has already been pointed out that in "emergencies", the government under the Indian Constitution will work as if it were a unitary government. This aspect will be more fully discussed in Chapter 28, *post.*

II. *In Normal times:* Even in normal times, the Constitution has devised techniques of control over the States by the Union to ensure that the State Governments do not interfere with the legislative and executive policies of the Union and also to ensure the efficiency and strength of each individual unit which is essential for the strength of the Union.

Some of these avenues of control arise out of the executive and legislative powers vested in the President, in relation to the States, *e.g.*:

(i) The power to appoint and dismiss the Governor [*Articles 155 and 156*]; the power to appoint other dignitaries in the State, *e.g.*, judges of the high court; Members of the State Public Service Commission [*Articles 217 and 317*].

(ii) Legislative powers, *e.g.*, previous sanction to introduce legislation in the State Legislature [*Article 304, proviso*]; assent to specified legislation which must be reserved for his consideration [*Article 31A(1), 1st proviso; and Article 31C, proviso*]; instruction of President required for the Governor to make Ordinance relating to specified matters [*Article 213(1), proviso*]; veto power in respect of other State Bills reserved by the Governor [*Article 200, 1st proviso*].

These having been explained in the preceding chapters, in the present chapter we shall discuss other specific agencies for Union control, namely:

(i) Directions to the State Government;

(ii) Delegation of Union functions;

(iii) All-India Services;

(iv) Grant-in-aid;

(v) Inter-State Councils;

(vi) Inter-State Commerce Commission [*Article 307*].

3. Directions by the Union to State Governments.

The idea of the Union giving directions to the States is foreign and repugnant to a truly federal system. But this idea was taken by the framers of *our* Constitution from the Government of India Act, 1935, in view of the peculiar conditions of this country and, particularly, the circumstances out of which the federation emerged.

The circumstances under which and the matters relating to which it shall be competent for the Union to give directions to a State have already been stated. The sanction prescribed by the Constitution to secure compliance with such directions remains to be discussed.

It is to be noted that the Constitution prescribes a coercive sanction for the enforcement of the directions issued under any of the foregoing powers, namely, the power of the President to make a Proclamation under Article 356. This is provided in Article 365 as follows:

> Where any State has failed to comply with, or to give effect to, any directions given in the exercise of the executive power of the Union under any of the provisions of this Constitution, it shall be lawful for the President to hold that a situation has arisen in which the Government of the State cannot be carried on in accordance with the provisions of this Constitution.

And as soon as a Proclamation under Article 356 is made by the President he will be entitled to assume to himself any of the functions of the State Government as are specified in that Article.

4. Delegation of Union functions.

It has already been stated that with the consent of the Government of a State, President may entrust to that Government executive functions of the Union relating to any matter [*Article 258(1)*]. While legislating on a Union subject, Parliament may delegate powers to the State Governments and their officers insofar as the statute is applicable in the respective states [*Article 258(2)*].

Conversely, a State Government may, with the consent of the Government of India, confer administrative functions upon the latter, relating to state subjects [*Article 258A*].

Thus, where it is inconvenient for either Government to directly carry out its administrative functions, it may have those functions executed through the other Government.

5. All-India Services.

It has been pointed out earlier that besides persons serving under the Union and the states, there will be certain services "common to the Union and the States". These are called "All-India Services", of which the Indian Administrative Service and the Indian Police Service are the existing examples [*Article 312(2)*]. But the Constitution gives the power to create additional All-India Services.[1] If the Council of States declares by a resolution supported by not less than two-thirds of the members present and voting that it is necessary or expedient in the national interests so to do, Parliament may by law provide for the creation of one or more all-India services common to the Union and the states and regulate the recruitment, and the conditions of service of persons appointed, to any such service [*Article 312(1)*].

As explained by Dr Ambedkar in the Constituent Assembly, the object behind this provision for All-India Services is to impart a greater cohesion to the federal system and greater efficiency to the administration in both the Union and the States:

> The dual policy which is inherent in a federal system is followed in all federations by a dual service. In all Federations, there is a Federal Civil Service and a State Civil Service. The Indian Federation, though a dual polity, will have a dual service, but with one exception. It is recognised that in every country there are certain parts in its administrative set-up which might be called strategic from the point of view of maintaining the standard of administration... There can be no doubt that the standard of administration depends upon the calibre of the civil servants who are appointed to these strategic posts... The Constitution provides that without depriving the States of their right to form their own civil services there shall be an all-India Service, recruited on an all-India basis with common qualifications, with uniform scale of pay and members of which alone could be appointed to these strategic posts throughout the Union.

6. Grant-in-aid.

As stated earlier, Parliament is given power to make such grants as it may deem necessary to give financial assistance to any State which is in need of such assistance [*Article 275*].

By means of the grants, the Union would be in a position to correct inter-state disparities in financial resources which are not conducive to an all-round development of the country and also to exercise control and co-ordination over the welfare schemes of the states on a national scale.

Besides this general power to make grants to the states for financial assistance, the Constitution provides for specific grants on two matters: (a) For schemes of development, for welfare of Scheduled Tribes and for raising the level of administration of Scheduled Areas, as may have been undertaken by a State with the approval of the Government of India; (b) To the state of Assam, for the development of the tribal areas in that state [*provisos 1 to 2, Article 275(1)*].

7. Inter-State Council.

The President is empowered to establish an inter-state Council [*Article 263*] if at any time it appears to him that the public interests would be served thereby. Though the President is given the power to define the nature of the duties to be performed by the Council, the Constitution outlines the three-fold duties that may be assigned to this body. One of these is—

> The duty of *inquiring* into and *advising* upon disputes which may have arisen between States.

---

1. Until 1961, no additional All-India Services were created, but later on several new All-India Services were created [See Chapter 30, *post*].

The other functions of such Council would be to investigate and discuss subjects of common interest between the Union and the states or between two or more states *inter se, e.g.*, research in such matters as agriculture, forestry, public health and to make recommendation for co-ordination of policy and action relating to such subject.

In exercise of this power, the President has so far established a Central Council of Health,[2] a Central Council of Local Self-Government,[3] and a Transport Development Council,[4] for the purpose of coordinating the policy of the states relating to these matters. In fact, the primary object of an Inter-State Council being co-ordination and federal cohesion, this object has been lost sight of, while creating fragmentary bodies to deal with specified matters relying on the statutory interpretation that the singular "a" before the word "Council" includes the plural.

The Sarkaria Commission has recommended the Constitution of a permanent inter-state Council, which should be charged with the duties set out in (b) and (c) of Article 263. Such a Council, consisting of Prime Minister being Chairman of Council, six Union Cabinet Ministers nominated by Prime Minister, the Chief Ministers of all the states, Chief Ministers of Union Territories having a Legislative Assembly and Administrators of Union Territories not having Legislative Assembly has been created *vide* Inter–State Council Order, 1990, notified through a Presidential Notification No IV/11017/3/90 CSR dated 28 May 1990.[5]

Further, with a view to ensure more harmonious and healthier relationship between the Centre and the states in future as well as for further strengthening of the third-tier of governance, the Government had set up the second Commission on Centre State Relations on 27 April 2007 under the Chairmanship of Justice M M Punchhi, a retired Chief Justice of India. The second Commission on Centre-State Relations has submitted its report on 31 March 2010 and has made 273 recommendations which are still under consideration by the Inter-State Council.[6]

8. Inter-State Commerce Commission.

For the purpose of enforcing the provisions of the Constitution relating to the freedom of trade, commerce and intercourse throughout the territory of India [*Articles 301–305*], Parliament is empowered to constitute an authority similar to the Inter-State Commerce Commission in the *USA* and to confer on such authority such powers and duties as it may deem fit [*Article 307*]. No such Commission has, however, been set up.

---

2. SRO 1418, dated 9 August 1952; *India, 1959*, p 146.
3. *India, 1957*, p 398.
4. *India, 1979*, p 352. Also, Central Council of Indian Medicine, Central Family Welfare Council [*India, 1982*, pp 101, and 108].
5. *Rep of the Administrative Reforms Commission,* 1969, vol 1, pp 32–34; *the Report of the Sarkaria Commission on Inter-State Relations*, Part I, paras 9.3.05–06. State Council Order, 1990 notified through a Presidential Notification No IV/11017/3/90 CSR dated 28 May 1990.
6. Report of Punchhi Commission, March 2010 on Centre-State Relation.

9. Extra-constitutional Agencies for Setting All-India Problems.

Apart from the above constitutional agencies for Union control over the States, to ensure a coordinated development of India notwithstanding a federal system of government, there are some advisory bodies and conferences held at the Union level, which further the co-ordination of state policy and eliminate differences as between the states. The foremost of such bodies is the Planning Commission.

10. Planning Commission or NITI Aayog.

Though the Constitution specifically mentions several Commissions to achieve various purposes, the Planning Commission, as such, is not to be found in the Constitution. "Economic and social planning" is a concurrent legislative power [*Entry* 20, *List* III]. Taking advantage of this Union power, the Union set up a Planning Commission in 1950, but without resorting to legislation. This extra-Constitutional and non-statutory body was set up by a resolution (1950) of the Union Cabinet by Prime Minister Nehru with himself as its first Chairman, to formulate an integrated Five Year Plan for economic and social development and to act as an advisory body to the Union Government, in this behalf.

Set up with this definite object, the Commission's activities have gradually been extended over the entire sphere of the administration excluding only defence and foreign affairs, so much so, that a critic has described it as "the economic Cabinet of the country as a whole", consisting of the Prime Minister and encroaching upon the functions of constitutional bodies, such as the Finance Commission[7] and, yet, not being accountable to Parliament. It has built up a heavy bureaucratic organisation[8] which led Pandit Nehru himself to observe[7]—

> The Commission which was a small body of serious thinkers had turned into a government department complete with a crowd of secretaries, directors and of course a big building.

According to these critics, the Planning Commission is one of the agencies of encroachment upon the autonomy of the states under the federal system. The extent of the influence of this Commission should, however, be precisely examined before arriving at any conclusion. The function of the Commission is to prepare a plan for the "most effective and balanced utilisation of the country's resources", which would initiate "a process of development which will raise living standards and open out to the people new opportunities for a richer and more varied life". It is obvious that the business of the Commission is only to prepare the plans; the implementation of the plans rests with the states because the development relates to mostly state subjects. There is no doubt that in the Union, the Planning Commission has great weight, having the Prime Minister himself as its Chairman. But so far as the states are concerned, the role of the Commission is only advisory. Whatever influence it exerts is only *indirect,* insofar as the states vie with each other in having their requirements included in the national plan. After that is done, the Planning Commission can have no *direct* means of securing the implementation of the plan. If, at that stage, the states are obliged to follow the uniform policy laid down by the Planning Commission, that is because the States cannot do without obtaining financial assistance from the

---

7. Chandra, *Federation in India,* pp 213, *et seq.*
8. Appleby, *Public Administration in India,* p 22.

Union.[9] But, strictly speaking, taking advantage of financial assistance involves voluntary element, not coercion, and even in the *United States* the receipt of federal grants-in-aid is not considered to be a subversion of the federal system, even though it operates as an encroachment upon State autonomy, according to many critics.[10]

But there is justification behind the criticism that there is overlapping of work and responsibility owing to the setting up of two high-powered bodies, *viz.*, the Finance Commission and the Planning Commission and the Administrative Reforms Commission has commented upon it.[11] There is, in fact, no natural division between "plan expenditure" and "non-plan expenditure". The anomaly has been due to the fact that the makers of the Constitution could not, at that time, envisage the creation of a body like the Planning Commission which has subsequently been set up by executive order. Be that as it may be, the need for co-ordination between the two Commissions is patent, and, ultimately, this must be taken over by the Cabinet or a body such as the National Development Council of which we shall speak just now, unless the two Commissions are unified — which would require an amendment of the Constitution because the Finance Commission is mentioned in the Constitution. On 13 August 2014, the Narendra Modi Government scrapped the Planning Commission and replaced it with NITI Aayog (National Institution for Transforming India).

On 1 January 2015, the cabinet of Narendra Modi Government passed a resolution to replace Planning Commission by NITI Aayog[12] (National Institution for Transforming India) which works as a policy think-tank of Government of India and aims to involve the states in economic policy-making in India. It will be providing strategic and technical advice to the Central and the State Governments, ie, by adopting bottom-up approach rather than traditional top-down approach as in planning commission.

The NITI Aayog comprise of the following:

(a) Prime Minister of India as the Chairperson;

(b) Governing Council comprising the Chief Ministers of all the States and Lt. Governors of Union Territories;

(c) Regional Councils will be formed to address specific issues and contingencies impacting more than one state or a region. These will be formed for a specified tenure. The Regional Councils will be convened by the Prime Minister and will comprise of the Chief Ministers of States and Lt Governors of Union Territories in the region. These will be chaired by the Chairperson of the NITI Aayog or his nominee;

(d) Experts, specialists and practitioners with relevant domain knowledge as special invitees nominated by the Prime Minister;

9. Under the Second Five Year Plan, 70% of the "revenue expenditure" and nearly the whole of the "capital expenditure" on the State Plans were financed by grants from the Union (under Article 275 of the Constitution), known as "matching grants".

10. *Vide Basu's Commentary on the Constitution of India,* 5th Edn, vol 4, p 304; *Steward Machine Co v Davis,* (1937) 301 US 548.

11. *Rep of the Administrative Reforms Commission,* vol I, pp 16–19, 26–39.

12. NITI Aayog (National Institution for Transforming India) — Cabinet Resolution dated 1 January 2015 as published in the Gazette of India, Extraordinary Part-I, section 1, dated 7 January 2015.

(e) The full-time organisational framework will comprise of, in addition to the Prime Minister as the Chairperson:

  (i) Vice-Chairperson: To be appointed by the Prime Minister;

  (ii) Members: Full-time;

  (iii) Part-time members: Maximum of two from leading universities, research organisations and other relevant institutions in an ex-officio capacity. Part-time members will be on a rotational basis;

  (iv) Ex-officio members: Maximum of four members of the Union Council of Ministers to be nominated by the Prime Minister;

  (v) Chief Executive Officer: To be appointed by the Prime Minister for a fixed tenure, in the rank of Secretary to the Government of India;

  (vi) Secretariat as deemed necessary.

Aims and Object of NITI Aayog:

- NITI Aayog seeks to provide a critical directional and strategic input into the development process.
- The centre-to-state one-way flow of policy, that was the hallmark of the Planning Commission era, is now sought to be replaced by a genuine and continuing partnership of states.
- NITI Aayog have emerged as a "think-tank" that provide Governments at the Central and State levels with relevant strategic and technical advice across the spectrum of key elements of policy.
- The NITI Aayog also seek to put an end to slow and tardy implementation of policy, by fostering better Inter-Ministry coordination and better Centre-State coordination. It will help evolve a shared vision of national development priorities, and foster cooperative federalism, recognising that strong states make a strong nation.
- The NITI Aayog will develop mechanisms to formulate credible plans to the village level and aggregate these progressively at higher levels of government. It will ensure special attention to the sections of society that may be at risk of not benefitting adequately from economic progress.
- The NITI Aayog will create a knowledge, innovation and entrepreneurial support system through a collaborative community of national and international experts, practitioners and partners. It will offer a platform for resolution of inter-sectoral and inter-departmental issues in order to accelerate the implementation of the development agenda.
- In addition, the NITI Aayog will monitor and evaluate the implementation of programmes and focus on technology upgradation and capacity building.

Through the above, the NITI Aayog will aim to accomplish the following objectives and opportunities:

- An administration paradigm in which the Government is an "enabler" rather than a "provider of first and last resort."

- Progress from "food security" to focus on a mix of agricultural production, as well as actual returns that farmers get from their produce.
- Ensure that India is an active player in the debates and deliberations on the global commons.
- Ensure that the economically vibrant middle-class remains engaged, and its potential is fully realized.
- Leverage India's pool of entrepreneurial, scientific and intellectual human capital.
- Incorporate the significant geo-economic and geo-political strength of the Non-Resident Indian Community.
- Use urbanisation as an opportunity to create a wholesome and secure habitat through the use of modern technology.
- Use technology to reduce opacity and potential for misadventures in governance.

The NITI Aayog aims to enable India to better face complex challenges, through the following:

- Leveraging of India's demographic dividend, and realisation of the potential of youth, men and women, through education, skill development, elimination of gender bias, and employment.
- Elimination of poverty, and the chance for every Indian to live a life of dignity and self-respect.
- Redressal of inequalities based on gender bias, caste and economic disparities.
- Integrate villages institutionally into the development process.
- Policy support to more than 50 million small businesses, which are a major source of employment creation safeguarding of our environmental and ecological assets.

It is expected that through its commitment to a co-operative federalism, promotion of citizen engagement, egalitarian access to opportunity, participative and adaptive governance and increasing use of technology, the NITI Aayog will seek to provide a critical directional and strategic input into the development process.

Criticism: The government's move to replace the Planning Commission with a new institution called "NITI Aayog" was criticised by opposition parties of India. The Congress sought to know whether the reform introduced by the BJP-led government was premised on any meaningful programme or if the move was simply born out of political opposition to the party that ran the Planning Commission for over 60 years.

11. National Development Council. The working of the Planning Commission led to the setting up of another extra-constitutional and extra-legal body, namely, the National Development Council.

This Council was formed in 1952, as an adjunct to the Planning Commission, to associate the states in the formulation of the plans. The functions of the

Council are "to strengthen and mobilise the efforts and resources of the nation in support of the plans; to promote common economic policies in all vital spheres and to ensure the balanced and rapid development of all parts of the country", and in particular, are —

(a) to review the working of the National Plan from time to time;

(b) to recommend measures for the achievement of the aims and targets set out in the National Plan.

Since the middle of 1967, all members of the Union Cabinet, Chief Ministers of states, the Administrators of the Union Territories and members of the Planning Commission have been members of this Council.[13]

Besides the Planning Commission, the annual conferences, whose number is legion, held under the auspices of the Union, serve to evolve co-ordination and integration even in the state sphere. Apart from conferences held on specific problems, there are annual conferences at the highest level, such as the Governors' Conference, the Chief Ministers' Conference, the Law Ministers' Conference, the Chief Justices' Conference, which are of no mean importance from the standpoint of the Union-State as well as inter-state relations. As Appleby[8] has observed, it is by means of such contacts rather than by the use of constitutional coercion, that the Union is maintaining a hold over this sub-continent, having 25 autonomous States (now 28):

> No other large and important national government... is so dependent as India on theoretically subordinate but actually rather *distinct units responsible to a different* political control, for so much of the administration of what are r ecognized as national programmes of great importance to the nation.
>
> The power that is exercised organically in New Delhi is the uncertain and discontinuous power of prestige. It is influence rather than power. Its method is making plans, issuing pronouncements, holding conferences... Any real power in most of the development field is the personal power of particular leaders and the informal, extra-constitutional, extra-administrative power of a dominant party, coherent and strongly led by the same leaders. Dependence of achievement, therefore, is in some crucial ways, apart from the formal organs of governance, in forces which in the future may take quite different forms.[8]

The National Development Council held its 57th meeting in New Delhi on 27 December 2012 and approved the strategy to achieve average growth rate of 8% during the 12th Five Year Plan (2012–2017), to generate 50 million new jobs and to increase investment in infrastructure sector.

The National Development Council is likely to be scrapped and its powers are likely to be transferred to the Governing Council of NITI Aayog. However, no resolution has been passed till date to abolish it.

12. National Integration Council. Another non-constitutional body ie, National Integration Council, originally was a group of senior politicians and public figures in India that looked for ways to address the problems of communalism, casteism and regionalism. The then Prime Minister,

13. *Statesman,* 18 July 1976, p 1.

Shri Jawaharlal Nehru, convened National Integration Conference in September-October 1961 to find ways and means to combat the evils of communalism, casteism, regionalism, linguism and narrow-mindedness, and to formulate definite conclusions in order to give a lead to the country. This Conference decided to set up a National Integration Council (NIC) to review all matters pertaining to national integration and to make recommendations thereon. The NIC was constituted accordingly and held its first meeting in 1962. The National Integration Council has held 16 meetings so far in the year 1962, 1968, 1980, 1984, April 1986, September 1986, April 1990, September 1990, November 1991, December 1991, July 1992, November 1992, August 2005, October 2008, 10 September 2011 and the last 16th meeting was held in September 2013.[14]

A resolution on maintaining communal harmony and ending discrimination by condemning atrocities on Scheduled Castes and Scheduled Tribes was passed in the 16th meeting. The National Integration Council was reconstituted on 28 October 2013 under the Chairmanship of the Prime Minister.

13. Co-operation between Union and States. Apart from the agencies of federal control, there are certain provisions which tend towards a smooth working of both the Union and State Governments, without any unnecessary conflict jurisdiction. These are —

(i) Mutual delegation of functions;

(ii) Immunity from mutual taxation.

(a) As explained already *our* Constitution distributes between the Union and the states not only the legislative power but also the executive power, more or less on the same lines [*Articles 73 and 162*].

The result is that it is not competent for a state to exercise administrative power with respect to Union subjects, or for the Union to take up the administration of any State function, unless authorised in that behalf by any provision in the Constitution. In administrative matters, a rigid division like this may lead to occasional deadlocks. To avoid such a situation, the Constitution has engrafted provisions enabling the Union as well as a state to make a mutual delegation of their respective administrative functions:

(b) As to the delegation of Union functions, there are two methods:

(i) With the *consent* of the State Government, the *President* may, without any legislative sanction, entrust any executive function to that State [*Article 258(1)*].

(ii) Irrespective of any consent of the state concerned, *Parliament* may, while legislating with respect to Union subject, confer powers upon a State or its officers, relating to such subject [*Article 258(2)*]. Such delegation has, in short, a statutory basis.

14. In 2008 the NIC meeting was chaired by Prime Minister Manmohan Singh who had earlier publicly admitted that the ongoing violence against the Christian communities was a matter of great "national shame". On 19 October 2010, the government established a standing committee of the National Integration Council. Home Minister P Chidambaram was appointed as the chairman and four Union Ministers and nine Chief Ministers were appointed members who would decide on agenda items for future council meetings.

(c) Conversely, with the *consent* of the Government of India, the *Governor* of a State may entrust on the Union Government or its officers, functions relating to a state subject, so far as that state is concerned [*Article 258A*].

14. Immunity from Mutual Taxation.

The system of double government set up by a federal Constitution requires, for its smooth working, the immunity of the property of one Government from taxation by another. Though there is some difference between federal Constitutions as to the extent to which this immunity should go, there is an agreement on the principle that mutual immunity from taxation would save a good deal of fruitless labour in assessment and calculation and cross-accounting of taxes between the two governments (Union and State).

This matter is dealt with in Articles 285 and 289 of *our* Constitution, relating to the immunity of the Union and a State, respectively.

The property of the Union shall, save insofar as Parliament may by law otherwise provide, be exempt from all taxes imposed by a State or by any authority within a state [*Article* 285(1)].

Similarly, the property of a State is immune from Union taxation [*Article* 289(1)]. The immunity, however, does not extend to all Union taxes, as held by *our* Supreme Court,[15] but is confined only to such taxes as are levied *on* property. A State is, therefore, not immune from customs duty, which is imposed, not on property, but on the act of import or export of goods.

Not only the "property" but also the "income" of a State is exempted from Union taxation. The exemption is, however, confined to the State Government and does not extend to any local authority situated within a State. The above immunity of the income of a State is, again, subject to an overriding power of Parliament as regards any income derived from a commercial activity. Thus —

(a) Ordinarily, the income derived by a State from commercial activities shall be immune from income-tax levied by the Union.

(b) Parliament is, however, competent to tax the income of a State derived from a commercial activity.

(c) If, however, Parliament declares any apparently trading functions as functions "incidental to the ordinary functions of Government", the income from such functions shall be no longer taxable, so long as such declaration stands.[16]

15. *Re Sea Customs Act*, AIR 1963 SC 1760.
16. *APSRTC v ITO*, AIR 1964 SC 1486, p *1491, 1493* : (1964) 2 Mad LJ 33.

[illegible]

[illegible] the [illegible] of the [illegible] by another. [illegible] the difference between federal [illegible] [illegible]

This matter [illegible] in [illegible] 1938 [illegible] to the [illegible]

The [illegible]

[illegible]

[illegible]

[illegible]

CHAPTER 27

INTER-STATE RELATIONS

1. Inter-State Comity.

THOUGH a federal Constitution involves the sovereignty of the Units within their respective territorial limits, it is not possible for them to remain in complete isolation from each other and the very exercise of internal sovereignty by a Unit would require its recognition by, and co-operation of, the other Units of the federation. All federal Constitutions, therefore, lay down certain rules of comity which the Units are required to observe, in their treatment of each other. These rules and agencies relate to such matters as —

(a) Recognition of the public acts, records and judicial proceedings of each other.

(b) Extra-judicial settlement of disputes.

(c) Co-ordination between States.

(d) Freedom of inter-state trade, commerce and intercourse.

2. Recognition of Public Acts, Records, etc.

Since the jurisdiction of each state is confined to its own territory [*Articles 162 and 245(1)*], the acts and records of one state might have been refused to be recognised in another state, without a provision to compel such recognition. The Constitution, therefore, provides that—

> Full faith and credit shall be given throughout the territory of India to public acts, records and judicial proceedings of the Union and every State [*Article 261(1)*].

This means that duly authenticated copies of statutes or statutory instruments, judgments or orders of one state shall be given recognition in another State in the same manner as the statutes, etc., of the latter state itself. Parliament has the power to legislate as to the mode of proof of such acts and records or the effects thereof [*Article 261(2)*].

3. Extra-judicial Settlement of Disputes.

Since the States, in every federation, normally act as independent units in the exercise of their internal sovereignty, conflicts of interest between the units are sure to arise. Hence, in order to maintain the strength of the Union, it is essential that there should be adequate provision for judicial determination of disputes between the units and for settlement of disputes by extra-judicial bodies as well as their prevention by consultation and joint action. While Article 131 provides for the judicial determination of disputes between states by vesting the Supreme Court with exclusive jurisdiction in the matter, Article 262 provides for the adjudication of *one class* of such disputes by an extra-judicial tribunal, while Article 263 provides for the prevention of inter-state disputes by investigation and recommendation by an administrative body. Thus—

(i) Parliament may by law provide for the adjudication of any dispute or complaint with respect to the use, distribution or control of the waters of, or in, any inter-state river or river valley and also provide for the exclusion of the jurisdiction of all courts, including the Supreme Court, to entertain such disputes [*Article 262*].

In exercise of this power, Parliament has enacted the Inter-State River Water Disputes Act, 1956, providing for the constitution of an *ad hoc* tribunal for the adjudication of any dispute arising between two or more States with regard to the waters of any inter-state river or river valley.

(ii) The President can establish an Inter-State Council for enquiring into and advising upon Inter-State disputes, if at any time it appears to him that the public interests would be served by the establishment of such Council [*Article* 263(a)].

4. Co-ordination between States.

The power of the President to set up Inter-State Councils may be exercised not only for advising upon disputes, but also for the purpose of investigating and discussing subjects in which some or all of the states or the Union and one or more of the states have a common interest. In exercise of this power, the President has already constituted the Central Council of Health, the Central Council of Local Self-Government, the Central Council of Indian Medicine,[1] Central Council of Homeopathy.

In this connection, it should be mentioned that advisory bodies to advise on inter-state matters have also been established under statutory authority:

4a. Zonal Councils.

Zonal Councils have been established by the States Reorganisation Act, 1956 to *advise* on matters of common interest to each of the five zones into which the territory of India has been divided — Northern, Southern, Eastern, Western and Central.

It should be remembered that these Zonal Councils do not owe their origin to the Constitution but to an Act of Parliament, having been introduced by the States Reorganisation Act, as a part of the scheme of reorganisation of the states with a view to securing co-operation and co-ordination as between the states, the Union Territories and the Union, particularly in respect of economic and social development. The creation of the Zonal Councils was a logical outcome of the reorganisation of the states on a linguistic basis. For, if the cultural and economic affinity of linguistic states with their contiguous States was to be maintained and their common interests were to be served by co-operative action, a common meeting ground of some sort was indispensable. The object of these Councils, as Pandit Nehru envisaged it, is to "develop the habit of co-operative working". The presence of a Union Minister, nominated by the Union Government, in each of these Councils (and the Chief Ministers of the states concerned) also furthers co-ordination and national integration through an extra-constitutional advisory organisation, without undermining the autonomy of the states. If properly

1. *India,* 1982, p 101.

worked, these Councils would thus foster the "federal sentiment" by resisting the separatist tendencies of linguism and provincialism.

(i) The *Central* Zone, comprising the states of Uttar Pradesh, Madhya Pradesh, Chhattisgarh and Uttarakhand.

(ii) The *Northern* Zone, comprising the states of Haryana, Himachal Pradesh, Punjab, Rajasthan, Jammu & Kashmir (now reorganised in two Union Territories), and the Union Territories of Delhi & Chandigarh.

(iii) The *Eastern* Zone, comprising the states of Bihar, West Bengal, Orissa, Sikkim and Jharkhand.

(iv) The *Western* Zone, comprising the states of Gujarat, Maharashtra and Goa and the Union Territory of Dadra & Nagar Haveli and Daman & Diu.

(v) The *Southern* Zone, comprising the states of Andhra Pradesh, Karnataka, Tamil Nadu, Kerala, Telangana and the Union Territory of Puducherry. Andaman and Nicobar Islands and Lakshadweep are presently not members but special invitees to the Southern Zonal Council.

(vi) The *North Eastern* Zone, comprising the states of Assam, Meghalaya, Nagaland, Manipur, Tripura, Mizoram, and Arunachal Pradesh.

Each Zonal Council consists of the Chief Minister and two other Ministers of each of the Sates in the Zone and the Administrator in the case of a Union Territory. There is also provision for holding joint meetings of two or more Zonal Councils. The Union Home Minister has been nominated to be the common chairman of all the Zonal Councils.

The Zonal Councils, as already stated, discuss matters of common concern to the States and Territories comprised in each Zone, such as, economic and social planning, border disputes, inter-state transport, matters arising out of the reorganisation of states and the like, and give advice to the Governments of the states concerned as well as the Government of India.[2]

Besides the Zonal Councils, there is a North-Eastern Council, set up under the North-Eastern Council Act, 1971, to deal with the common problems of Assam, Meghalaya, Manipur, Nagaland, Tripura, Arunachal Pradesh and Mizoram.

4b. River Boards.

The River Boards Act, 1956, provides for the establishment of a River Board for the purpose of advising the Governments interested in relation to the regulation or development of an inter-state river or river valley.

4c. Water Disputes Tribunal.

The Inter-State River Water Disputes Act, 1956, provides for the reference of an *inter-State* river dispute for arbitration by a Water Disputes Tribunal, (excluding jurisdiction of the Supreme Court under section 11) whose award would be final according to Article 262(2).

---

2. After a lapse of some three years, sittings of Zonal Councils have been revived from 1978 [*Statesman*, 8 September 1978, p 9]. Yet, it must be said that this scheme has not been fully utilised [see Author's *Comparative Federalism*, 1987, pp 574ff].

5. Freedom of Inter-State Trade, Commerce and Intercourse. The great problem of any federal structure is to minimise Inter-State barriers as much as possible, so that the people may feel that they are members of one nation, though they may, individually, be residents of any of the Units of the Union. One of the means to achieve this object is to guarantee to every citizen the freedom of movement and residence throughout the country. Our Constitution guarantees this right by Article 19(1)(*d*) and (*e*).

No less important is the freedom of movement or passage of commodities and of commercial transactions between one part of the country and another. The progress of the country as a whole also requires free flow of commerce and intercourse as between different parts, without any barrier. This is particularly essential in a federal system. This freedom is sought to be secured by the provisions [*Articles 301 to 307*] contained in Part XIII of *our* Constitution. These provisions, however, are not confined to *inter-State* freedom but include *intra-State* freedom as well. In other words, subject to the exceptions laid down in this Part, no restrictions can be imposed upon the flow of trade, commerce and intercourse, not only as between one state and another but as between any two points within the territory of India whether any state border has to be crossed or not.

Article 301 thus declares—

> Subject to the other provisions of this Part, trade, commerce and intercourse throughout the territory of India shall be free.

Article 303(1) declares that neither Parliament nor the State Legislature shall have power to make any law giving, or authorising the giving of, any preference to one State over another; or making or authorising the making of, any discrimination between one state and another, in the field of trade, commerce or intercourse. Hence, if a state prohibits the sale of lottery tickets of others and promotes that of its own, it would be discriminatory and violative of Article 303.[3]

5a. Limitations Imposed. The limitations imposed upon the above freedom by the other provisions of Part XIII are—

(a) Non-discriminatory restrictions may be imposed by Parliament, in the public interest [*Article* 302].

By virtue of this power, Parliament has enacted the Essential Commodities Act, 1955, which empowers, "in the interest of the general public", the Central Government to control the production, supply and distribution of certain "essential commodities", such as coal, cotton, iron and steel, petroleum.

(b) Even discriminatory or preferential provisions may be made by Parliament, for the purpose of dealing with a scarcity of goods arising in any part of India [*Article* 303(2)].

(c) Reasonable restrictions may be imposed by a state "in the public interest" [*Article* 304(b)].

3. *B R Enterprises v State of Uttar Pradesh*, AIR 1999 SC 1867 : (1999) 9 SCC 700.

(d) Non-discriminatory taxes may be imposed by a state on goods imported from other states or Union Territories, similarly as on *intra-State* goods [*Article* 304(a)].

(e) The appropriate Legislature may make a law [under *Article* 19(6)(ii)] for the carrying on by the state, or by a corporation owned or controlled by the state, of any trade, business, industry or service, whether to the exclusion, complete or partial, of citizens or otherwise.

5b. Freedoms under Articles 19(1)(g) and 301. Before leaving this topic, we should notice the difference in the scope of the provisions of Articles 19(1)(g) and 301 both of which guarantee the freedom of trade and commerce.

Though this question has not been finally settled, it may be stated broadly that Article 19(1)(g) looks at the freedom from the standpoint of the *individual* who seeks to carry on a trade or profession and guarantees such freedom throughout the territory of India subject to reasonable restrictions, as indicated in Article 19(5). Article 301, on the other hand, looks at the freedom from the standpoint of the movement or passage of commodities or the carrying on of commercial transactions between *one place and another,* irrespective of the individuals who may be engaged in such trade or commerce. The only restrictions that can be imposed on the freedom declared by Article 301 are to be found in Articles 302-305. But if either of these freedoms be restricted, the aggrieved individual[4] or even a state[5] may challenge the constitutionality of the restriction, whether imposed by an executive order or by legislation.[4] When there is a violation of Article 301 or 304, there would ordinarily be an infringement of an individual's fundamental right guaranteed by Article 19(1)(g), in which case, he can bring an application under Article 32, even though Article 301 or 304 is not included in Part III as a fundamental right.[6]

4. *Atiabari Tea Co v State of Assam,* AIR 1961 SC 232 : (1961)1 SCR 809; *Automobile Transport v State of Rajasthan,* AIR 1962 SC 1406 : (1962) 1 SCR 491.
5. *State of Rajasthan v Ghasiram Mangilal,* (1969) 2 SCC 710, p 713; *State of Assam v Labanya Prabha,* AIR 1967 SC 1574, p 1578.
6. *Syed Ahmed v State of Mysore,* AIR 1975 SC 1443 : (1975) 2 SCC 131.

CHAPTER 28

EMERGENCY PROVISIONS

1. Emergencies and its Different Kind.

FEDERAL government, according to *Bryce,* means weak government because it involves a division of power. Every modern federation, however, has sought to avoid this weakness by providing for the assumption of larger powers by the federal government whenever unified action is necessary by reason of emergent circumstances, internal or external. But while in countries like the *United States*, this expansion of federal power takes place through the wisdom of judicial interpretation, in *India,* the Constitution itself provides for conferring extraordinary powers upon the Union in case of different kinds of emergencies. As has been stated earlier, the Emergency provisions of *our* Constitution enable the federal government to acquire the strength of a unitary system whenever the exigencies of the situation so demand.

The Constitution provides for *three different kinds* of abnormal situations which call for a departure from the normal governmental machinery set up by the Constitution:— *viz.*, (i) An emergency due to war, external aggression or *armed rebellion*[1] [*Article 352*]; This may be referred to as 'national emergency', to distinguish it from the next category; (ii) Failure of constitutional machinery in the States [*Article 356*]; (iii) Financial emergency [*Article 360*].

An 'armed rebellion' poses a threat to the security of the state as distinguished from 'internal disturbance' contemplated under Article 355.[2]

Where the Constitution simply uses the expression 'Proclamation of Emergency', the reference is [*Article 366(18)*] to a Proclamation of the first category, *i.e.*, under Article 352.

2. 42nd and 44th Constitutional Amendments.

The Emergency provisions in Part XVIII of the Constitution [*Articles* 352-360] have been extensively amended by the 42nd Amendment (1976) and the 44th Amendment (1978) Acts, so that the *resultant* position may be stated for the convenience of the reader, as follows:

3. Proclamation of Emergency.

I. A 'Proclamation of Emergency' may be made by the President at any time he is satisfied that the security of India or any part thereof has been threatened by war, external aggression or *armed rebellion*[1] [*Article 352*]. It may be made even before the *actual occurrence* of any such disturbance, *e.g.*, when external aggression is apprehended.

---

1. Since the amendment of Article 352 in 1978, it is no longer possible to make a Proclamation of Emergency, on the ground of mere 'internal disturbance' which does not constitute an 'armed rebellion'.
2. *Naga People's Movement of Human Rights v UOI,* (1998) 2 SCC 109 (paras 31 and 32) : AIR 1998 SC 431.

An 'Emergency' means the existence of a condition whereby the security of India or any part thereof is threatened by war or external aggression or *armed rebellion.*[1] A state of emergency exists under the Constitution when the President makes a 'Proclamation of Emergency'. The actual occurrence of war or any armed rebellion, is not necessary to justify a Proclamation of Emergency of the President. The President may make such a Proclamation if he is satisfied that there is an imminent danger of such external aggression or *armed rebellion.* But no such Proclamation can be made by the President unless the Union Ministers of Cabinet rank, headed by the Prime Minister, recommend to him, *in writing,* that such a Proclamation should be issued [*Article 352(3)*].

3a. Proclamation of Emergency.

While the 42nd Amendment made the declaration immune from judicial review, that fetter has been removed by the 44th Amendment, so that the constitutionality of the Proclamation can be questioned in a Court on the ground of *mala fides.*[3]

Every such Proclamation must be laid before both Houses of Parliament and shall cease to be in operation unless it is approved by resolutions of both Houses of Parliament within *one month* from the date of its issue.

Until the 44th Amendment of 1978, there was no Parliamentary control over the revocation of a Proclamation, once the issue of the Proclamation had been approved by resolutions of the Houses of Parliament.

4. Termination of Proclamation.

After the 44th Amendment, a Proclamation under Article 352 may come to an end in the following ways:

(a) On the expiry of *one* month from its issue, unless it is approved by resolutions of both Houses of Parliament before the expiry of that period. If the House of the People is dissolved at the date of issue of the Proclamation or within one month thereof, the Proclamation may survive until 30 days from the date of the first sitting of the House after its reconstitution, provided the Council of States has in the meantime approved of it by a resolution [*Clause (4)*].

(b) It will get a fresh lease of six months from the date it is approved by resolutions of both Houses of Parliament [*Clause (5)*], so that it will terminate at the end of six months from the date of last such resolution.

(c) Every such resolution under clauses (4)-(5), must be passed by either House by a majority of the total membership of that House and by a majority of not less than two-thirds of the members of that House present and voting [*Clause (6)*].

(d) The President must issue a Proclamation of revocation any time that the House of the People passes a resolution *disapproving* of the issue or continuance of the Proclamation [*Clause (7)*]. For the purpose of convening a special sitting of the House of the People for passing such a resolution of disapproval, not less than one-tenth of the Members of the House may give a notice in writing to the Speaker or to the President (when the House is not in session) to convene a special sitting of the House for this purpose. A special sitting of the House shall

3. Cf, *State of Rajasthan v UOI,* AIR 1977 SC 1361 (paras 124, and 144): (1977)3 SCC 592; *Minerva Mills v UOI,* AIR 1980 SC 1789 (paras 103-04); *SR Bommai v UOI,* (1994) 3 SCC 1.

be held within 14 days from the date on which the notice is received by the Speaker or as the case may be by the President [*Clause (8)*].

It may be that an armed rebellion or external aggression has affected only a *part* of the territory of India which is needed to be brought under greater control. Hence, it has been provided, by the 44th Amendment, that a Proclamation under Article 352 may be made in respect of the whole of India or only a part thereof.

The Executive and the Legislature of the Union shall have extraordinary powers during an emergency.

5. Effects of Proclamation of Emergency. The effects of a Proclamation of Emergency may be discussed under four heads—(i) Executive; (ii) Legislative; (iii) Financial; and (iv) As to Fundamental Rights.

5a. Executive. When a Proclamation of Emergency has been made, the executive power of the Union shall, during the operation of the Proclamation, extend to the giving of directions to any State as to the manner in which the executive power thereof is to be exercised [*Article 353(a)*].

In normal times, the Union Executive has the power to give directions to a State, which includes only the matters specified in Articles 256-257.

But under a Proclamation of Emergency, the Government of India shall acquire the power to give directions to a State on '*any*' matter, so that though the State Government will not be suspended, it will be under the complete *control* of the Union Executive, and the administration of the country insofar as the Proclamation goes, will function as under a unitary system with local sub-divisions.

5b. Legislative. (a) While a Proclamation of Emergency is in operation, Parliament may, by law, extend the normal life of the House of the People (five years) for a period not exceeding one year at a time and not extending in any case beyond a period of six months after the Proclamation has ceased to operate [*proviso to Article 83(2), ante*]. (This power also was used by Mrs Gandhi in 1976—Act 109 of 1976).

(b) As soon as a Proclamation of Emergency is made, the legislative competence of the Union Parliament shall be automatically widened, and the limitation imposed as regards List II, by Article 246(3), shall be removed. In other words, during the operation of the Proclamation of Emergency, Parliament shall have the power to legislate as regards List II (State List) as well [*Article 250(1)*]. Though the Proclamation *will not suspend the State* Legislature, it will suspend the distribution of legislative powers between the Union and the State, so far as the Union is concerned—so that the Union Parliament may meet the emergency by legislation over any subject as may be necessary as if the Constitution were unitary.

(c) In order to carry out the laws made by the Union Parliament under its extended jurisdiction as outlined above, Parliament shall also have the power to make laws conferring powers, or imposing duties (as may be necessary for the purpose), upon the Executive of the Union in respect of any matter, even though such matter normally belonged to State jurisdiction [*Article 353(b)*].

5c. Financial. During the operation of the Proclamation of Emergency the President shall have the constitutional power to modify the provisions of the Constitution relating to the allocation of financial resources [*Articles 268-279*] between the Union and the States, by his own Order. But no such Order shall have effect beyond the financial year in which the Proclamation itself ceases to operate, and, further, such Order of the President shall be subject to approval by Parliament [*Article 354*].

5d. Fundamental Rights. Articles 358-359 lay down the effects of a Proclamation of Emergency upon fundamental rights. As amended up to 1978, by the 44th Amendment Act, the following results emerge—

I. While Article 358 provides that the state would be free from the limitations imposed by Article 19, so that these rights would be non-existent against the state during the operation of a Proclamation of Emergency, under Article 359, the right to *move the Courts* for the enforcement of the rights or any of them, may be suspended, by Order of the President.

II. While Article 359 would apply to an Emergency declared on any of the grounds specified in Article 352, ie, war, external aggression or armed rebellion, the application of Article 358 is confined to the case of Emergency on grounds of war or external aggression only.

III. While Article 358 comes into operation automatically to suspend Article 19 as soon as a Proclamation of Emergency on the ground of war or external aggression is issued, to apply Article 359, a further Order is to be made by the President, specifying those Fundamental Rights against which the suspension of enforcement shall be operative.

IV. Article 358 suspends Article 19; the suspension of enforcement under Article 359 shall relate only to those Fundamental Rights which are specified in the President's Order, *excepting Articles 20 and 21.* In the result, notwithstanding an Emergency, access to the Courts cannot be barred to enforce a prisoner's or detenu's right under Article 20 or 21.[4]

V. Neither Article 358 nor 359 shall have the effect of suspending the operation of the relevant fundamental right unless the law which affects the aggrieved individual contains a recital to the effect that "such law is in relation to the Proclamation of Emergency". In the absence of such recital in the law itself, neither such law nor any executive action taken under it shall have any immunity from challenge for violation of a fundamental right during operation of the Emergency [*Articles 358(2) and 359(1B)*].

6. Usage of Emergency Powers. A. The *first* Proclamation of Emergency under Article 352 was made by the President on 26 October 1962, in view of the Chinese aggression in the NEFA. It was also provided by a Presidential Order, issued under Article 359, that a person arrested or imprisoned under the Defence of India Act would not be entitled to move any Court for the enforcement of any of his Fundamental Rights under

4. This amendment, saving Articles 20 and 21 from the mischief of Article 359, has been made by the 44th Amendment Act, 1978 in order to *supersede* the view taken in the case of *ADM Jabalpur v Shivkant Shukla*, AIR 1976 SC 1207, that when Article 21 is suspended by an Order under Article 359, the person imprisoned or detained "loses his *locus standi* to regain his liberty on *any* ground".

Articles 14, 19 or 21. This Proclamation of Emergency was revoked by an order made by the President on 10 January 1968.

B. The *second* Proclamation of Emergency under Article 352 was made by the President on 3 December 1971 when Pakistan launched an undeclared war against India.

A Presidential Order under Article 359 was promulgated on 25 December 1974, in view of certain high court decisions releasing some detenus under the Maintenance of Internal Security Act, 1971 for smuggling operations. This Presidential Order suspended the right of any such detenu to move *any* Court for the enforcement of his fundamental rights under Articles 14, 21 and 22, for a period of six months or during the continuance of the Proclamation of Emergency of 1971, whichever expired earlier.

Though there was a ceasefire on the capitulation of Pakistan in Bangladesh in December, 1971, followed by the Shimla Agreement between India and Pakistan, the Proclamation of 1971 was continued, owing to the persistence of hostile attitude of Pakistan. It was thus in operation when the third Proclamation of 25 June 1975 was made.

C. While the two preceding Proclamations under Article 352 were made on the ground of *external* aggression, the *third* Proclamation of Emergency under Article 352 was made on 25 June 1975, on the ground of "*internal* disturbance".[5]

The "internal disturbance", which was cited in the Press Note relating to the Proclamation, was that 'certain persons have been inciting the Police and the Armed Forces against the discharge of their duties and their normal functioning'.[5] Both the second and third proclamations were revoked on 21 March 1977.

It should be noted that after 1978, it is not possible to issue a Proclamation of Emergency on the ground of 'internal disturbance', short of an armed rebellion, for, the words 'internal disturbance' have been substituted by the words 'armed rebellion', by the Constitution (44th Amendment) Act, 1978.[1]

7. Administration of a State in case of Failure of Constitutional Machinery.

II. The Constitution provides for carrying on the administration of a State in case of a failure of the constitutional machinery.

(a) It is a duty of the Union to ensure that the Government of every State is carried on in accordance with the provisions of the Constitution [*Article 355*]. So, the President is empowered to make a Proclamation, when he is satisfied that the Government of a State cannot be carried on in accordance with the provisions of the Constitution, either on the report of the Governor of the State or otherwise [*Article 356(1)*]. (For usage of this power, see *below.*)

(b) Such Proclamation may also be made by the President where any state has failed to comply with, or to give effect to, any directions given by the Union, in the exercise of its executive power to the State [*Article 365*].[6]

5. An official version of the reasons which impelled Mrs Gandhi to assume that 'the security of India was threatened by internal disturbances' may be had from *India, 1976,* pp i-ii. This Proclamation was revoked on 21 March 1977.

By such Proclamation, the President may—

(a) assume to himself all or any of the functions of the Executive of the State or of any other authority save the High Court; and

(b) declare that the powers of the Legislature of the State shall be exercisable by or under the authority of Parliament. In short, by such Proclamation, the Union would assume control over all functions in the State administration, except judicial.

When the State Legislature is thus suspended by the Proclamation, it shall by competent—

(a) for Parliament to delegate the power to make laws for the State to the President or any other authority specified by him; (b) for the President to authorise, when the House of the People is not in session, expenditure from the Consolidated Fund of the State pending the sanction of such expenditure from Parliament; and (c) for the President to promulgate Ordinances for the administration of the State when Parliament is not in session [*Article 357*].

The duration of such Proclamation shall ordinarily be for *two* months. If, however, the Proclamation was issued when the House of the People was dissolved or dissolution took place during the period of the two months above-mentioned, the Proclamation would cease to operate on the expiry of 30 days from the date on which the reconstituted House of the People first met, unless the Proclamation is approved by Parliament. The two months' duration of such Proclamation can be extended by resolutions passed by both Houses of Parliament for a period of six months at a time, subject to a maximum duration of three years [*Article 356(3)-(4)*]; but if the duration is sought to be extended beyond *one* year, two other conditions, as inserted by the 44th Amendment Act, 1978, have to be satisfied, namely, that—

(a) a Proclamation of Emergency is in operation, in the whole of India or as the case may be, in the whole or any part of the State, at the time of the passing of such resolution, and

(b) the Election Commission certifies that the continuance in force of the Proclamation approved under clause (3) during the period specified in such resolution is necessary on account of difficulties in holding general elections to the Legislative Assembly of the state concerned.

By the 42nd Amendment, 1976, the President's satisfaction for the making of a Proclamation under Article 356 had been made immune from judicial review; but the 44th Amendment of 1978 has removed that fetter, so that the courts may now interfere if the Proclamation is *mala fide* or the reasons disclosed for making the Proclamation have no reasonable nexus with the satisfaction of the President.

The Author's views expressed above have been upheld by the Supreme Court in *SR Bommai's* case[7] where a nine-judge Bench held that the validity of a Proclamation under Article 356 can be judicially reviewed to examine: (i) whether it was issued on the basis of any material; (ii) whether the material was relevant; (iii) whether it was issued *mala fide*.

6. *State of Rajasthan v UOI,* AIR 1977 SC 1361 : (1977) 3 SCC 592 (paras 58-59).
7. *SR Bommai v UOI,* (1994) 3 SCC 1.

8. Articles 352 and 356, Compared. The Proclamation in case of failure of the constitutional machinery differs from a Proclamation of 'Emergency' on the following points:

(i) A Proclamation of Emergency may be made by the President only when the *security* of India or any part thereof is threatened by war, external aggression or armed rebellion. A Proclamation in respect of failure of the constitutional machinery may be made by the President when the constitutional government of State cannot be carried on for any reasons, not necessarily connected with *war* or *armed rebellion.*

(ii) When a Proclamation of Emergency is made, the Centre shall get no power to *suspend* the State Government or any part thereof. The State Executive and Legislature would continue in operation and retain their powers. All that the Centre would get are *concurrent* powers of legislation and administration of the state.

But under a Proclamation in case of failure of the constitutional machinery, the State Legislature would be suspended and the executive authority of the state would be assumed by the President in whole or in part. [This is why it is popularly referred to as the imposition of the '*President's rule*'.]

(iii) Under a Proclamation of Emergency, Parliament can legislate in respect of State subjects only by itself; by under a Proclamation of the other kind, it can delegate its powers to legislate for the State—to the President or any other authority specified by him.

(iv) In the case of a Proclamation of failure of constitutional machinery, there is a maximum limitation to the power of Parliament to extend the operation of the Proclamation, namely, three years [*Article* 356(4), *Proviso* 1], but in the case of a Proclamation of Emergency, it may be continued for a period of six months by each resolution of the Houses of Parliament approving its continuance, so that if Parliament so approves, the Proclamation may be continued indefinitely as long as the Proclamation is not revoked or the Parliament does not cease to make resolutions approving its continuance [*new clause* (5) to *Article* 352, inserted by the 44th Amendment Act, 1978].

9. Usage of Power under Article 356(1). It is clear that the power to declare a Proclamation of failure of constitutional machinery in a State has nothing to do with any external aggression or armed rebellion; it is an extraordinary power of the Union to meet a *political* breakdown in any of the units of the federation [or the failure by such Unit to comply with the federal directives [*Article 365*], which might affect the national strength. It is one of the coercive powers at the hands of the Union to maintain the democratic form of government, and to prevent factional strifes from paralysing the governmental machinery, in the states. The importance of this power in the political system of India can hardly be overlooked in view of the fact that it has been used 133 times during the first 78 years of the working of the Constitution (till February 2026). For details, see Table XX, *post*.

9a. Frequent and Improper use of the Power under Article 356, Deprecated. From the foregoing history of the use of the power conferred upon the Union under Article 356, it is evident that it is a drastic coercive power which takes nearly the substance away from the normal federal polity prescribed by the Constitution. It is, therefore, to be always remembered that the provision for such drastic power was defended by Dr Ambedkar in the Constituent Assembly[8] on the plea that the use of this drastic power would be a *matter of the last resort:*

> ....the proper thing we ought to expect is that such articles will never be called into operation and *that they would remain a dead-letter.* If at all they are brought into operation, I hope the President who is endowed with this power *will take proper precautions* before actually suspending the administration of the Province.

It is natural, therefore, that the propriety of the use of this provision (which was envisaged by Dr BR Ambedkar to 'remain a dead-letter'), on numerous occasions (more than any other provision of the Constitution), has evoked criticism from different quarters. The judgment of the Supreme Court in the *Rajasthan* case also did not lay down the law correctly. The views of the Author were expressed in detail in the 16th Edition of this book (at pp 336-37). In view of *SR Bommai's* case (nine-judge Bench) the comments have been replaced by the law as declared by the Supreme Court, which affirm the Author's view.

In 2005, a unique situation had arisen in Bihar where before even the first meeting of the Legislative Assembly, its dissolution had been ordered on the ground that attempts were being made to cobble a majority by illegal means and lay claim to form the Government in the State and if these attempts continued, it would amount to tampering with constitutional provisions. It was alleged that the Governor made no genuine attempt to explore the possibility of forming a government before recommending the dissolution of the House. Further the "indecent haste" with which the Governor acted, showed that his only intention was to prevent Janata Dal (U) leader Nitish Kumar from staking his claim to form the government, as it did not suit the political ambitions of Rashtriya Janata Dal chief Lalu Prasad. There was no explanation by the Government for the hurry shown in getting the Proclamation signed by the President (who was then in Moscow) at midnight. The main question before the court at the outset was whether the dissolution of the Assembly under Article 356(1) of the Constitution could be ordered on the said ground along with another aspect of the matter raising important question of law that: Is it permissible to dissolve the Legislative Assembly under Article 174(2)(b) of the Constitution without its first meeting taking place? It was held that neither Article 172 nor Article 174 prescribe that dissolution of a State Legislature can only be after commencement of its term or after the date fixed for its first meeting. Once the Assembly is constituted, it becomes capable of dissolution.[9] The Supreme Court declared the proclamation dated 23 May 2005 as unconstitutional and observed that if a political party with the support of other political party or other MLA's stakes claim to form a Government and satisfies the Governor about its majority to form a stable Government, the Governor cannot

8. *Constituent Assembly Debates,* IX, p 177.
9. *Rameshwar Prasad v UOI,* (2006) 2 SCC 1; *KK Abu v UOI,* AIR 1965 Ker 229; *Special Reference No 1 of 2002* (popularly known as Gujarat Assembly Election matter) [(2002) 8 SCC 237]

refuse formation of Government and override the majority claim because of his subjective assessment that the majority was cobbled by illegal and unethical means. No such power has been vested with the Governor. Such a power would be against the democratic principles of majority rule. Governor is not an autocratic political Ombudsman. If such a power is vested in the Governor and/or the President, the consequences can be horrendous. The ground of mal-administration by a State Government enjoying majority is not available for invoking power under Article 356. The remedy for corruption or similar ills and evils lies elsewhere and not in Article 356(1). In the same vein, it has to be held that the power under Tenth Schedule for defection lies with the Speaker of the House and not with the Governor. The power conferred by Article 356 upon the President is a conditioned power. It is not an absolute power.

In *SR Bommai's* case, the Court has clearly subscribed to the view that the power under Article 356 is an exceptional power and has to be resorted to only occasionally to meet the exigencies of special situations. The Court quoted the Sarkaria Commission Report to give examples of situations when such power should *not* be used. It made it clear that Article 356 cannot be invoked for superseding a duly constituted ministry and dissolving the Assembly on the sole ground that in the elections to the Lok Sabha, the ruling party in the State suffered a massive defeat.

After *Bommai's* case, it is settled that the courts possess the power to review the Proclamation on the grounds mentioned above [see under "JUDICIAL REVIEW", *ante*]. This will surely have a restraining effect on the tendency to use the power on flimsy grounds.

In *SR Bommai's* case, it has been pronounced that till the Proclamation is approved by both Houses of Parliament, it is not permissible for the President to take any irreversible action under clauses (a), (b) and (c) of Article 356(1). Hence, the Legislative Assembly of a State cannot be dissolved before the Proclamation is approved by both Houses of Parliament.

If the court holds the Proclamation to be invalid then in spite of the fact that it has been approved by the Parliament, the court has the power to restore, in its discretion, *status quo ante,* ie, the court may order that the dissolved Ministry and Assembly will be revived.[7]

9b. Illustrative Cases where Resort to Article 356 would not be Proper. Some of the situations which do *not* amount to failure of Constitutional machinery are given below. They are based on the report of the Sarkaria Commission and have the approval of the Court in *SR Bommai's* case.[10]

(1) a situation of maladministration in a state, where a duly constituted ministry enjoys support of the Assembly.

(2) where a Ministry resigns or is dismissed on losing majority support and the Governor recommends imposition of President's Rule without exploring the possibility of installing an alternative government.

(3) where a Ministry has not been defeated on the floor of the House, the Governor on his subjective assessment recommends supersession and imposition of President's Rule.

10. *SR Bommai v UOI,* (1994) 3 SCC 1, para 82.

(4) where in general elections to the Lok Sabha the ruling party in the state has suffered a massive defeat.

(5) where there is situation of internal disturbance but all possible measures to contain the situation by the Union in discharge of its duty, under Article 355, have not been exhausted.

(6) where no prior warning or opportunity is given to the state Government to correct itself in cases where directives were issued under Articles 256, 257 etc.

(7) where the power is used to sort out intra-party problems of the ruling party.

(8) the power cannot be legitimately exercised on the sole ground of stringent financial exigencies of the state.

(9) the power cannot be invoked merely on the ground that there are serious allegations of corruption against the Ministry.

(10) exercise of the power for a purpose extraneous or irrelevant to those which are permitted by the Constitution would be vitiated by legal *mala fides.*

9c. Proper Occasions for use Suggested.

A proper occasion for use of this power would, of course, be when a Ministry *resigns* after defeat in the Legislature and no other Ministry commanding a majority in the Assembly can at once be formed. Dissolution of the Assembly may be a radical solution, but, that being expensive, a resort to Article 356 may be made to allow the state of flux in the Assembly to subside so as to obviate the need for a dissolution, if possible. A similar situation would arise where the party having a majority *declines* to form a Ministry and the Governor fails in his attempt to find a coalition Ministry. Another obviously proper use is mentioned in Article 365 of the Constitution itself; but curiously, none of the numerous past occasions *specifically* refers to this contingency. The provision in Article 365 relates to the failure of a State Government to carry out the directives of the Union Government which the latter has the authority under the Constitution to issue (*e.g.*, under *Articles* 256, and 257). The Union may also issue such a directive under the implied power conferred by the latter part of Article 355, "to ensure that the government of every state is carried on in accordance with the provisions of this Constitution".[6]

9d. Effect of 44th Amendment.

The only change that the 44th Amendment Act, 1978 (sponsored by the Janata Government), has made in this Article, is to substitute clause (5) to limit the duration of a Proclamation made under Article 356 to a period of *one year* unless a Proclamation of Emergency under Article 352 is in operation and the Election Commission certifies that it is not possible to hold elections to the Legislative Assembly of the state concerned immediately, in which case, it may be extended up to three years, by successive resolutions for continuance being passed by both Houses of Parliament.

It is to be noted that the foregoing amendment has not specified any conditions or circumstances under which the power under Article 356 can be used. Hence, in the light of the *Rajasthan decision,*[6] no legal challenge could be offered when Mrs Gandhi repeated the Janata experiment in February, 1980, in the same nine states, on the same ground, *viz., that* the Janata Party, which was in power in *those* states, was routed in the *Lok Sabha* election.

10. Proclamation of Financial Emergency.

III. If the President is satisfied that a situation has arisen whereby the financial stability or credit of India or of any part of the territory thereof is threatened, he may by a Proclamation make a declaration to that effect [*Article 360(1)*].

The consequences of such a declaration are:

(a) During the period any such Proclamation is in operation, the executive authority of the Union shall extend to the giving of directions to any state to observe such canons of financial propriety as may be specified in the directions.

(b) Any such direction may also include—

  (i) a provision requiring the reduction of salaries and allowances of all or any class of persons serving in connection with the affairs of a state;

  (ii) a provision requiring all Money Bills or other financial Bills to be reserved for the consideration of the President after they are passed by the Legislature of the state.

(c) It shall be competent for the President during the period that any such Proclamation is in operation to issue directions for the reduction of salaries and allowances of all or any class of persons serving in connection with the affairs of the Union including the judges of the Supreme Court and the High Courts [*Article 360(3)-(4)*].

The duration of such Proclamation will be similar to that of a Proclamation of Emergency, that is to say, it shall ordinarily remain in force for a period of *two* months, unless before the expiry of that period, it is approved by resolutions of both Houses of Parliament. If the House of the People is dissolved within the aforesaid period of two months, the Proclamation shall cease to operate on the expiry of thirty days from the date on which the House of the People first sits after its reconstitution, unless before the expiry of that period of thirty days it has been approved by both Houses of Parliament. It may be revoked by the President at any time, by making another Proclamation.

No use of Article 360 has ever been made.

the [illegible] ground [illegible] that the [illegible] in [illegible] was [illegible] by the 44th Amendment.

[illegible] Proclamation [illegible] two months [illegible] unless before the expiry of that period it is approved by [illegible] both Houses of Parliament [illegible] the Constitution, unless [illegible] has been approved by both Houses [illegible] President at any time by making another Proclamation.

PART IX

MISCELLANEOUS

CHAPTER 29

RIGHTS AND LIABILITIES OF THE GOVERNMENT AND PUBLIC SERVANTS

1. Property of the Union and the States.

OUR Constitution views the Union and the States as juristic persons, capable of owning and acquiring property, making contracts, carrying on trade or business, bringing and defending legal actions, just as private persons, subject to modifications specified in the Constitution itself.

The Union and a state can acquire property in several ways—

(a) *Succession:* Broadly speaking, the property, assets, rights and liabilities that belonged to the Dominion of India or a Governor's Province or an Indian State at the commencement of the Constitution devolved by virtue of the Constitution, on the Union or the corresponding State under the Constitution [*Articles 294-295*].

(b) *Bona vacantia:* Any property in the territory of India which, if this Constitution had not come into operation, would have accrued to His Majesty or as the case may be, to the Ruler of an Indian State by escheat or lapse, or as *bona vacantia* for want of a rightful owner, shall, if it is property situate in a state, vest in such state, and shall in any other case, vest in the Union [*Article 296*]. Thus, the disputed property of a person dying a civil death (not heard of for more than seven years) without leaving any heir, would vest in the Gaon Sabha and should be recorded in its name even if no objection has been filed by it.[1]

(c) *Things underlying the ocean:* All lands, minerals and other things of value underlying the ocean within the territorial waters of India shall vest only in the Union [*Article* 297].

(d) *Compulsory acquisition or requisition by law:* Both the Union and State Legislatures shall be competent to compulsorily acquire or requisition property by making law, under Entry 42, List III, Seventh Schedule.

The constitutional obligation to pay compensation has been abolished, by the omission of Article 31(2) by the 44th Amendment Act, 1978.

(e) *Acquisition under executive power:* The Government of India or a State may make contracts and acquire property, say by purchase or exchange, just as a private individual, in exercise of their respective powers, and for the purposes of their respective Governments [*Article 298*] and the decision of the government in granting contracts/licences to private bodies/companies can be questioned only the grounds of bad faith, based on irrational or irrelevant considerations,

1. *Sheo Nand v Deputy Director of Consolidation,* (2000) 3 SCC 103 : AIR 2000 SC 1141.

non-compliance with the prescribed procedure or violation of any constitutional or statutory provision.[2] But for compulsorily taking a person's property, a *law* will be required to authorise it [*Article 300A*].

2. Power to Carry on Trade or Business.

The Union or a State Government is competent to carry on *any* trade or business and make contracts for that purpose, in exercise of its executive power. Such business shall, however, be subject to regulation by the competent Legislature. That is to say, if the Union Government takes up a business relating to a subject (say, agriculture) which is included in the State List, the business will be subject to the legislative jurisdiction of the State Legislature [*Article 298, proviso (a)*].

The Union or a State, while legislating with respect to a trade or business carried on by itself, is immune from a constitutional limitation to which it would have been otherwise subject. If an ordinary law excludes a citizen from carrying on a particular business, wholly or partially, the *reasonableness* of such law has to be tested under Article 19(6). Thus, if the state creates a monopoly in favour of a private trade without any reasonable justification, such law is liable to be held unconstitutional by the courts. But if a law creates a monopoly in favour of the State itself as a trader, whether to the partial or complete exclusion of citizens,[3] the reasonableness of such law cannot be questioned by the Courts [*Exception (ii) to Article 19(6)*].

In short, it is competent for the Union or a State not only to enter into a trade but also to create a monopoly in its own favour in respect of such trade. This is what is popularly known as the 'nationalisation' of a trade.[4]

3. Government Contracts.

As stated already, both the Union and State Governments have the power to enter into contracts like private individuals, in relation to the respective spheres of their executive power. But this contractual power of the Government is subject to some special formalities required by the Constitution, in addition to those laid down by the Law of Contract which governs any contract made in India.

The reason for imposing these special conditions is that contracts by Government raise some problems which do not or cannot possibly arise in the case of contracts entered into by private persons. Thus, there should be a definite procedure according to which contracts must be made by its agents, in order to bind the Government; otherwise public funds may be depleted by clandestine contracts made by any and every public servant. The formalities for contracts made in the exercise of the executive power of the Union or of a State, as laid down in Article 299, are that the contract—

(a) must be executed by a person duly authorised by the President or Governor, as the case may be;

(b) must be executed by such person 'on behalf of' the President or Governor, as the case may be;

(c) must be 'expressed to be made by' the President or Governor, as the case may be.

---

2. *Delhi Science Forum v UOI,* (1996) 2 SCC 405 : AIR 1996 SC 1356.
3. *H C Narayanappa v State of Mysore,* AIR 1960 SC 1073 (*1078*) : [1960] 3 SCR 742; *Parbhani Transport Society v RTA,* AIR 1960 SC 801 : [1960] 3 SCR 177.
4. *Daruka and Co v UOI,* AIR 1973 SC 2711; *Excel Wear v UOI,* AIR 1979 SC 25 (para 24).

If *any* of these conditions are not complied with, the contract is not binding on or enforceable *against* the Government,[5] though a suit may lie against the officer who made the contract, in his personal capacity.

4. Right of Government to Sue and to be Sued.

The right of the Government to sue and its liability to be sued, like a private individual in the ordinary courts, is also subject to certain special considerations.

Article 300(1) of the Constitution says—

> The Government of India may sue or be sued by the name of the Union of India and the Government of a State may sue or be sued by the name of the State and may, subject to any provisions which may be made by Act of Parliament or of the Legislature of such State enacted by virtue of powers conferred by this Constitution, sue or be sued in relation to their respective affairs in the like cases as the Dominion of India and the corresponding Provinces or the corresponding Indian States might have sued or been sued if this Constitution had not been enacted.

This Article, however, does not give rise to any cause of action, but merely says that the State can sue or be sued, as a juristic personality, in matters where a suit would lie against the Government had not the Constitution been enacted, subject to legislation by the appropriate Legislature. No such legislation has, however, been undertaken so far. For the substantive law as to the liability of the State, therefore, we have to refer to the law as it stood before the commencement of the Constitution.

4a. Right to Sue.

So far as the right to sue is concerned, the Government of India may sue by the name of the 'Union of India', while a state may sue by the name of that state, *eg.*, 'State of Bihar'. Either Government may sue not only a private person but also another Government. Thus, the Union may bring a suit against one or more states; while a state may sue another state or the Union [*Article* 131]. It is to be noted that when the suit is against a private individual, the suit will have to be instituted in the court of the lowest jurisdiction, according to the law of procedure; but in the case of a suit between two Governments, it must be instituted in the highest tribunal, namely, the Supreme Court, which has exclusive original jurisdiction over such federal litigation.

4b. Liability to be Sued.

In this matter, a distinction is to be made between contractual liability and the liability for torts or civil wrongs, because such distinction has been observed in India since the days of the East India Company, up to the commencement of the Constitution, and that position is maintained by Article 300 of the Constitution, subject to legislation by Parliament.

(a) *Contract:* In India, direct suit had been allowed against the East India Company, the Secretary of State or the existing Governments in matters of contract, instead of a petition of right by which a British subject sought relief from the Crown, as a matter of grace. The Government of India Acts expressly empowered the Government to enter into contracts with private individuals and the corresponding provision in the Constitution in Article 299(1) maintains that position.

---

5. *Bhikraj v UOI,* AIR 1962 SC 118; *K P Chaudhury v State of MP,* AIR 1967 SC 203 [1969] 2 SCJ 119; *State of UP v Murari Lal,* (1971) 2 SCC 449 : AIR 1971 SC 22210.

Subject to the formalities prescribed by Article 299 and to statutory conditions or limits, the contractual liability of the State, under *our* Constitution, is the same as that of an individual under the ordinary law of contract.

(b) *Torts:* The liability of the State under the existing law, for actionable wrongs committed by its servants, cannot be so simply stated as in the case of contracts. The state of the law is unnecessarily complicated by reason of its being founded on the position of the British Crown under the Common Law and of the East India Company upon its supposed representation of the sovereignty of the Crown, both of which have become archaic, owing to the changes in history and law.

Even in *England*, the Common Law maxim that the 'King can do no wrong' has been superseded by the Crown Proceedings Act, 1947. Nevertheless, in the absence of any such corresponding legislation, Courts in India have no alternative than to follow the existing case-law which is founded on the old English theory of immunity of the State, founded on the maxim 'King can do no wrong'.

The existing law in India, thus, draws a distinction between the sovereign and non-sovereign functions of the Government and holds that Government cannot be sued for torts committed by the Government or its officers in the exercise of its 'sovereign' functions.

Thus, it has been held—

(A) No action lies against the Government for injury done to an individual *in the course of exercise* of the *sovereign functions* to the Government, such as the following:

(i) Commandeering goods during war; (ii) making or repairing a military road; (iii) administration of justice; (iv) improper arrest, negligence or trespass by Police officers; (v) wrongs committed by officers in the performance of duties imposed upon them by the Legislature, unless, of course, the statute itself prescribes the limits or conditions under which the executive acts are to be performed; or the wrongful act was expressly authorised or ratified by the State; (vi) loss of movables from Government custody owing to negligence of officers; (vii) payment of money in custody of Government to a person other than the rightful owner, owing to negligence of an officer in the exercise of statutory duty, where the Government does not derive any benefit from such transaction, *eg*, by a Treasury Officer paying money to a wrong person on a forged cheque owing to negligence in performing his statutory duty to compare the signature.

But gradually the ratio of *Kasturi Lal's* case,[6] and the list of sovereign functions is being limited. The Supreme Court has adopted a pro-people approach. In *Rudul Shah,*[7] in a writ petition, the court ordered compensation to be paid for deprivation of liberty. In *Nagendra Rao,*[8] the Supreme Court

6. *State of Rajasthan v Vidyawati,* AIR 1962 SC 933 (*935*); *Kasturi Lal v State of U.P.,* AIR 1965 SC 1039.

7. *Rudul Sah v State of Bihar,* (1983) 4 SCC 141 : AIR 1983 SC 1086; *Saheli v Commissioner of Police,* (1990) 1 SCC 422 : AIR 1990 SC 513 was also a case in which the State was ordered to pay compensation.

8. *Nagendra Rao v State of AP,* (1994) 6 SCC 205. In this case the State confiscated certain goods. When the Court annulled the confiscation, the State could not return the goods because they had deteriorated. The Court held that the owner was entitled to compensation.

observed that no civilised system can permit an executive to play with the people of a country and claim to be sovereign. To place the state above the law is unjust and unfair to the citizen. In the modern sense the distinction between sovereign and non-sovereign functions does not exist. The ratio of *Kasturi Lal*[6] is available to those rare and limited cases where the statutory authority acts as a delegate of such functions for which it cannot be sued in a Court of law.

The theory of sovereign power, propounded in *Kasturi Lal* case has yielded to new theories and is no longer available in a welfare state in which functions of the government are manifold, all of which cannot be said to be the activities relating to exercise of sovereign powers. Running of a railway is a commercial activity. Establishing the Yatri Niwas at various railway stations to provide lodging and boarding facilities to the passengers on payment of charges is a part of commercial activity of the Union of India which cannot be equated with the exercise of sovereign power. The employees deputed to run the Railways and to manage the establishment, including the railway stations and the Yatri Niwas, are essential components of the government machinery carrying on commercial activity. If any of such employees commits an act of tort, the Union Government can be held liable in damages to the person wronged by those employees. As observed in *Common Cause, A Registered Society v UOI,* (1999) 6 SCC 667, the efficacy of *Kasturi Lal* case as a binding precedent has been eroded. Hence, the Supreme Court upheld the award against the Railways of a compensation of Rs. Ten lakhs by the High Court to a foreign passenger, victim of gang-rape committed by the railway employees in a room of a Railway Yatri Niwas booked in their name.[9]

Likewise, the persons employed in government hospitals cannot claim sovereign immunity and the government will be liable for their tortious acts.[10]

(B) On the other hand, a suit lies against the Government for wrongs done by public servants in the course of transactions which a trading company or a private person could engage in such as the following:

(i) Injury due to the negligence of servants of the Government employed in a dockyard or a railway; (ii) trespass upon or damage done to private property in the course of a dispute as to right to land between Government and the private owner, even though committed in the course of a colourable exercise of statutory powers; (iii) the State is liable to be sued for *restitution of* the profits unlawfully made, just as a private owner, *e.g.*, where Government retains property or moneys unlawfully seized by its officers, a suit lies against the Government for its recovery, with interest; (iv) defamation contained in a resolution issued by Government; (v) injury caused by a Government vehicle while such vehicle was not being engaged in carrying out any sovereign function,[6] or engaged in famine relief work.[11]

5. Suability of Heads of State. Though the state itself is immune from liability in certain cases already noted owing to historical reasons, *our* Constitution does not grant any immunity to a public servant for his official acts which are unlawful under the ordinary law of the land.

9. *Chairman, Railway Board v Chandrima Das,* (2000) 2 SCC 465 : AIR 2000 SC 989.
10. *Achutrao Haribhan Khodwa v State of Maharashtra,* (1996) 2 SCC 634 : AIR 1996 SC 2377.
11. *Shyam Sunder v State of Rajasthan,* AIR 1974 SC 890 (para 21) : (1974) 1 SCC 690.

The only exception to this rule is a limited immunity granted to the heads of State, namely, the President and a Governor,[12] both for their political and personal acts, while in office [*Article 361*].

6. Immunity of President or Governor.

I. *Official Acts:* The immunity given for official acts of the President or the Governor is absolute, but it is limited only to the President and the Governor personally, and no other person can shield himself from legal liability on the plea that it was done under orders or the President or a Governor.

The President or a Governor is immune from legal action and cannot be sued in a court, whether during office or thereafter, for any act done or purported to be done by them or for any contract made [*Article 299(2)*] in exercise of their powers and duties as laid down by the Constitution or by any law made thereunder [*Article 361(1)*]. Though the President is liable to be impeached under Article 61 and the Governors may be dismissed by the President—for any unconstitutional act done in exercise of their official powers, no action lies in the courts.

It follows from the rule of personal immunity that no court can compel the President or the Governor to exercise any power or to perform any duty nor can a court compel him to forbear exercising his power or performing his duties. He is not amenable to the writs or directions issued by any Court.

The remedy to an individual for wrongful official acts of the President or a Governor is twofold—

(i) To bring appropriate proceedings against the respective Government itself, where such proceedings lie [*Article 361(1), proviso 2*].

(ii) To bring an action against the public servant, individually, who has executed the wrongful order of the President or Governor, and must, therefore, answer to the aggrieved individual, under the ordinary law of crimes or civil wrongs, subject to limitations, to be explained shortly.

In this connection, it should be noted that while the Constitution grants personal immunity to the President or a Governor for official acts, no such immunity is granted to their Ministers.[12] But by virtue of the peculiar position of the Ministers as regards official acts of the President or the Governor, as the case may be, it is not possible to make a Minister liable in a court of law, for any official act done in the name of the President or Governor. As pointed out earlier, the position in this respect in India differs from that in the United Kingdom. In *England,* every official act of the Crown must be countersigned by a Minister who is responsible to the law and the courts for that act. But though the principle of ministerial responsibility has been adopted in *our* Constitution, both at the Centre and in the states, the principle of legal responsibility has not been introduced in the English sense. There is no requirement that the acts of the President or of the Governor must be countersigned by a Minister. Further, the

12. The Constitution (41st Amendment) Bill, 1975 sought to amend Article 361, to bar criminal proceedings against the President, Governor *or Prime Minister* even after termination of their office. But this Bill could *not* be passed in the *Lok Sabha* before Mrs Gandhi lost office in 1977. In the result, the Prime Minister has *no* immunity at all, for his or her personal acts.

courts are precluded from enquiring as to what advice was tendered by the Ministers to the President or the Governor. It is clear, therefore, that the Ministers shall not be liable for official acts done on their advice. But there is no immunity for offences committed in their personal capacity.

II. *Personal Acts:* The immunity of the President or a Governor for unlawful personal acts committed by him during the term of his office is limited to the duration of such term.

(a) As regards crimes, no proceedings can be brought against them or continued while they are in office: but there is nothing to prevent such proceedings after their office is terminated[13] by expiry of term, dismissal or otherwise.

(b) As regards civil proceedings, there is no such immunity, but the Constitution imposes a procedural condition:

Civil proceedings may be brought against the President or a Governor, in respect of their *personal* acts, but only if two months' notice in writing has been delivered to the President or Governor.

7. Suability of Public Officials.

As stated before, the Constitution makes no distinction in favour of Government servants as to their personal liability for any unlawful act done by them whether in their official or personal capacity. There is only one provision in the Constitution relating to the liability of public servants; but the general law imposes certain conditions as regards their liability for official acts, in view of their peculiar position. These may be analysed as follows:

(i) *Contract:* If a contract made by a Government servant in his official capacity complies with the formalities laid down in Article 299, it is the Government concerned which will be liable in respect of the contract and not the officer who executed the contract [*Article 299(2)*].

If, however, the contract is not made in term of Article 299(2), the officer who executed it would be *personally* liable under it, even though he may not have derived any personal benefit.

(ii) *Torts:* As stated earlier, in India, the Government is not liable to answer in damages for its 'sovereign' acts. In such cases, the officer through whom such act is done is also immune.

In other cases, action will lie against the Government as well as the officer personally, unless—

(a) the act has been done, *bona fide,* in the performance of duties imposed by a statute;

(b) he is a judicial officer, within the meaning of the Judicial Officers' Protection Act, 1850. This Act gives absolute immunity from a civil proceeding to a judicial officer for acts done in the discharge of his official duty.[13]

But any civil action, whether in contract or in torts, against a public officer "in respect of any act *purported* to be done by such public officer in his official

13. Author's *Commentary on the Constitution of India,* 5th Edn, vol V, p 453.

capacity", is subject to the procedural limitations in sections 80-82 of the Code of Civil Procedure which include a two months' notice as a condition precedent to a suit.

(iii) *Crimes:* The criminal liability of a public servant is the same as that of an ordinary citizen except that—

(a) There is no liability for judicial acts or for acts done in pursuance of judicial orders [*Sections 77-78, Indian Penal Code, 1860*].

(b) Officers, other than judicial, are also immune for any act which they, by reason of some mistake of law or fact, in good faith, believed themselves to be bound by law to do [*Section 76, Indian Penal Code, 1860*].

(c) Where a public servant who is not removable from his office save by or with the sanction of the Central or State Government is accused of an offence, committed by him while acting or purporting to act in the discharge of his official duty, no Court can take cognizance of such offence without the previous sanction of the Central Government or the State Government, as the case may be [*Section 197, Criminal Procedure Code, 1973*].[14]

(iv) For acts done for the maintenance or restoration of order in an area where martial law was in force, Parliament may exempt the officers concerned from liability by validating such acts by making an Act of Indemnity [*Article 34*].

14. Author's *Criminal Procedure Code, 1973*, Prentice-Hall of India, p 520.

CHAPTER 30

THE SERVICES AND PUBLIC SERVICE COMMISSIONS

1. Public Services. ONE of the matters which do not usually find place in a Constitutional document but have been included in *our* Constitution is the Public Services.

2. Position of Civil Servants in a Parliamentary System of Government. The wisdom of the makers of *our* Constitution in giving a Constitutional basis to such matters as are left to ordinary legislation and administrative regulations under other Constitutions may be appreciated if we properly assess the importance of public servants in a modern democratic government.

A notable feature of the Parliamentary system of government is that while the policy of the administration is determined and laid down by ministers responsible to the Legislature, the policy is carried out and the administration of the country is actually run by a large body of officials who have no concern with politics. In the language of Political Science, the officials form the "permanent" Executives as distinguished from the Ministers who constitute the "political" Executive. While the political Executive is chosen from the party in majority in the Legislature and loses office as soon as that party loses its majority, the permanent Executive is appointed by a different procedure and does not necessarily belong to the party in power. It maintains the continuity of the administration and of the neutrality in politics that characterises the civil servants who constitute the permanent Executive and accounts for their efficiency. While the Ministers, generally, cannot claim any expert knowledge about the technique of administration and the details of the administrative departments, the civil servants, as a body, are supposed to be experts in the detailed working of government. One inherent vice in this system of carrying on the administration with the help of these "permanent" civil servants is that they tend to be more and more tied to red-tape and routine and lack that responsiveness to fresh ideas which the political Executive is sure to maintain owing to their responsibility to the Legislature. But with all this inherent vice, the civil servants are *indispensable* to the Parliamentary form of Government.

As the Joint Select Committee on Indian Constitutional Reforms[1] observed—

> The system of responsible Government, to be successful in practical working, requires the existence of a competent and independent Civil Service staffed by persons capable of giving to successive Ministers advice based on long

1. (1933–34) JPC Report, vol 1, para 274.

> administrative experience, secure in their positions, during good behaviour, but required to carry out the policy upon which the Government and Legislature eventually decide.

The reason is that in the modern age, government is not only an art but also a science and, to that extent a business for experts. It has, therefore, naturally fallen into the hands of a very large army of people who have taken up the business of government, being in service of the Government, itself,—as their professional career. Since they cannot be dispensed with, the problem of a modern democracy is how to prevent them from converting the democratic system into a "bureaucracy" or officialdom. The remedy lies not in the assumption of the work of government by the Legislature, for a direct democracy as prevailed in the ancient State is an impossibility under modern conditions. Nor does remedy lie in the assumption of the actual work of administration, as distinguished from the laying down of policies, by the Ministers or the political heads of the Departments, for, as has been already stated, the task is not only technical but enormous, and the Ministers might lose sight of the broader and serious questions of national urgency if they were to enter into the details of the day-to-day administration.

The proper solution of the problem, therefore, is — firstly, to select the right type of men who shall be not only efficient but also honest and who can be trusted with confidence that they would not abuse their position and would be strictly impartial, having no personal or political bias of their own and would be ready to faithfully carry out the policy once it is formulated by the government for the time being in power; secondly, to keep them under proper discipline so that they maintain the proper relationship with their employer, *viz.*, the State; and thirdly, to ensure that for breaches of the rules of discipline, they can be brought under proper departmental action and, for breach of law, made answerable before the courts of law. Once the interests of the State are thus secured, it is equally essential that the security of tenure of public servants who do not contravene the foregoing principles should be ensured. For, the best available talents would never be attracted unless there is a reasonable security against arbitrary action by superior officials who exercise the governmental power as to removal and discipline.

3. Conditions of Service for Public Servants. All the aforesaid objects can be achieved only if there are definite rules and proper safeguards in respect of what is broadly known as the "conditions of service" of public servants and *our* Constitution seeks to lay down some basic principles in this behalf.

It is not that *our* Constitution seeks to make detailed provisions relating to every matter concerning the Public Service. The makers of the Constitution realised that, that was not practicable and therefore, left the recruitment and conditions of service of the public servants of the Union and of the state to be regulated by Acts of the appropriate Legislatures. Pending such legislation, however, these matters were to be regulated by Rules made by the President or by the Governor in connection with the services under the Union and the States respectively [*Article 309*]. Once the Legislature intervenes to enact a law, the power of the executive (the President/the Governor) is totally displaced and the Act of the legislature would have precedence over any rule made by the executive under Article 309[2] but no rule can be framed which affects or impairs the vested rights.[3] However, these rules have equal force of law.[4] Though already some Acts have been passed, for instance, the All-India Services Act, 1951, the larger part of the field is still covered by rules made by the Government, not only under the Constitution, but also those existing from before (that is, made under the Government of India Acts), which are to continue to be in force until superseded by the appropriate authority. It is to be noted, however, that neither a rule nor any Act of the Legislature made in this behalf can have any validity if its provisions are contrary to those of the Constitution. As a matter of fact, our courts have already annulled a number of Service Rules on the ground of contravention of some of the constitutional provisions. For instance, if any rule or order enables the Government to dismiss a Government servant without giving him an opportunity to be heard, such rule would be struck down as unconstitutional owing to contravention of the requirement in Article 311(2).[5]

The two matters which are substantively dealt with by our Constitution are —

(a) Tenure of office of the public servants and disciplinary action against them;

(b) The Constitution and functions of the Public Service Commissions, which are independent bodies to advise the Government on some of the vital matters relating to services.

3a. Tenure of Office.

We have inherited from the British system the maxim that all service is at the pleasure of the Crown, and *our* Constitution, therefore, primarily declares that anybody who holds a post (civil or military) under the Union or a State holds his office during the pleasure of the President or the Governor, as the case may be [*Article 310(1)*]. The power to compulsory retire a government servant is one of the facets of the doctrine of pleasure incorporated in this Article.[6] This means that any Government employee may be dismissed at *any* time and on *any* ground, without giving rise to any cause of action for wrongful dismissal, except where the dismissal is in contravention of the Constitutional safeguards to be mentioned just now.

This right of the Government to dismiss a Government servant at its pleasure cannot be fettered by any contract and any contract made to this effect would be void, for contravention of Article 310(1) of the Constitution which embodies the principle of service at pleasure. This rule is, however, subject to one exception specified in Article 310(2) namely, that where Government is obliged to secure the services of technical personnel or specialists, not belonging to the regular services, by entering into a special contract, without which such persons would not be available for employment

---

2. *A K Krishna v State of Karnataka,* AIR 1998 SC 1050 : (1998) 3 SCC 495.
3. *R S Ajara v State of Gujarat,* (1997) 3 SCC 641 : (1997) 2 SCR 597.
4. *Secretary to Government of Tamil Nadu v D Subramanyan Rajadevan,* AIR 1996 SC 2634 : (1996) 5 SCC 334.
5. *Moti Ram v NEF Ry,* AIR 1964 SC 600, p *610*; *P C Wadhwa v UOI,* AIR 1964 SC 423 : (1964) 4 SCR 598.
6. *Allahabad Bank Officers' Association v Allahabad Bank,* AIR 1996 SC 2030 : (1996) 4 SCC 504.

under the Government. In such cases, compensation would be payable for premature termination of the service if the contract provides for such payment. But even in such cases, no compensation would be payable under the clause if the service is terminated within the contractual period, on the ground of his *misconduct.* It will be payable only —

(a) if the post is abolished before the expiration of the contractual period; or,

(b) if the person is required to vacate his post before the expiry of the contractual period, for reasons *unconnected with misconduct.*

3b. Limitations on Doctrine of Pleasure. While, however, the pleasure of the Crown in England is absolutely unfettered, the Constitution of India subjects the above pleasure to certain exceptions and limitations:

A. In the case of certain high officials, the Constitution lays down specific procedures as to how their service may be terminated. Thus, as has been noted in their proper places earlier, the Supreme Court judges, the Auditor-General, the high court judges and the Chief Election Commissioner shall not be removed from their offices except in the manner laid down in Articles 124, 148, 218, and 324, respectively. These offices thus, constitute exceptions to the general rule of tenure "during pleasure" of Government servants.

B. Though all other Government servants hold office during the pleasure of the President or the Governor (as the case may be), two procedural safeguards are provided for the security of tenure of "*civil*" servants as *distinguished from military personnel,* namely, that—

(a) A civil servant shall not be dismissed or removed by any authority subordinate to that by which he was appointed. In other words, if he is to be removed from service, he is entitled to the consideration of his appointing authority or any other officer of corresponding rank before he is so removed. The object of this provision [*Article 311(1)*] is to save a public servant from the caprices of officers of inferior rank.

(b) The other security which is guaranteed by the Constitution is that no dismissal, removal or reduction in rank shall be ordered against a civil servant unless he has been given a reasonable opportunity of being heard in respect of the charges brought against him.

A. Prior to 1976, this opportunity had to be given at two stages — (a) at the stage of inquiry into the charges; and (b) to make representation against the penalty (such as dismissal, removal, reduction in rank, censure) proposed to be imposed, after the inquiry had been concluded, holding the employee guilty of the charges.

B. But the Constitution (42nd Amendment) Act, 1976, has omitted the right of the employee to make a representation against the penalty proposed, retaining, however, the safeguard that the penalty can be proposed only on the basis of the evidence adduced at the inquiry stage. The result is that the judicial decisions[7] prior to 1976, which required that the "opportunity" under Article 311(2) must be offered at two stages, have been superseded by the 42nd Amendment.

---

7. Eg, *Khem Chand v UOI,* AIR 1958 SC 300 : [1969] 1 Mad LJ 169; *UOI v T R Verma,* AIR 1957 SC 882 : [1958] 1 Mad LJ 67.

Hence, after this amendment of 1976, the expression "reasonable opportunity" must be interpreted to imply that the Government or other authority proceeding against a civil servant must give him—

(i) an opportunity to deny his guilt and establish his innocence, which he can only do if he is told what the charges levelled against him are and the allegations on which such charges are based;

(ii) an opportunity to defend himself by cross-examining the witnesses produced against him and by examining himself or any other witnesses in support of his defence.

Hence, the authority must: (i) frame specific charges with full particularity; (ii) intimate those charges to the Government servant concerned; (iii) give him an opportunity to answer those charges; (iv) after considering his answers, take its decision; and (v) the rules of natural justice should be observed in coming to the finding against the accused.

But no "inquiry" need be held where the employee is given sufficient opportunity to explain his conduct but he does not wilfully avail himself of that opportunity[8] as was done in the case of dismissal of an absconder who failed to respond to show cause why his services be not terminated by way of dismissal as his further retention in service was not desirable.[9] This would not, however, apply where he fails to attend the inquiry owing to default of the Government in allowing him subsistence allowance.[10]

(iii) when the inquiry officer is not the disciplinary authority the delinquent employee has a right to receive a copy of the inquiry officers report before the disciplinary authority arrives at its conclusions. It is a part of the right to defence.[11]

The inquiry must be held and the opportunity to be heard must be given if two conditions are satisfied:

(i) The employee is a member of a civil service of the Union or an all-India service or a civil service of a State or holds a civil post under the Union or a State.

(ii) Such employee is sought to be dismissed, removed or "reduced in rank".

While a person "dismissed" is ineligible for re-employment under the Government, no such disqualification attaches to a person "removed".[12] But two elements are common to "dismissal" and "removal":

(a) Both the *penalties* are awarded on the ground that the conduct of the Government servant is blameworthy or deficient in some respect.

(b) Both entail penal consequences, such as the forfeiture of the right to salary, allowances or pension already acquired, for past services.

---

8. *Shahoodul v Registrar*, AIR 1974 SC 1896.
9. *UOI v Ram Phal,* AIR 1996 SC 1500 : (1996) 7 SCC 546.
10. *Ghanshyam v State of Madhya Pradesh,* AIR 1973 SC 1183 : (1973) 1 SCC 656.
11. *UOI v Ramzan Khan,* AIR 1991 SC 471 : (1991) 1 SCC 588; *Managing Director ECIL Hyderabad v Karunakar,* AIR 1994 SC 1074 : (1993) 4 SCC 727.
12. *Abdul Salam v Sarfaraz,* AIR 1975 SC 1064 : (1975) 1 SCC 669.

4. What Constitutes Dismissal, Removal and Reduction in Rank?

Where no such penal consequence is involved, it would not constitute "dismissal" or "removal", *e.g.*, where a Government servant is "compulsorily retired",[13, 14] without any further penal consequence attached to such order.[15]

As would appear from the decisions of the Supreme Court,[16] the term actually used in the order terminating the officer's services is not conclusive. Words such as "discharged" or "retrenched" may constitute "dismissal" or "removal", if the order entails *penal consequences,* as referred to above. Termination of the services of a temporary employee during the pendency of his criminal trial, for the same assault, was held to be punitive amounting to dismissal.[17]

It is also clear that in order to attract Article 311(2), the termination of services must be *against the will* of the civil servant. Hence, the following orders of termination of service have been held *not* to constitute "dismissal" or "removal":

(a) Termination in accordance with the terms of the contract of employment.[18]

(b) Termination in terms of the conditions of service as embodied in[19] the relevant Department Rules applicable to the Government servant, provided such conditions are not inconsistent with the provisions of the Constitution.

(c) Fixing an age for superannuation or compulsory retirement, and enforcement thereof.[20]

4a. Reduction in Rank.

Reduction in rank means the degradation in rank or status of the officer, directed by way of penalty. It thus involves two elements — (a) reduction in the physical sense, meaning degradation; (b) such degradation or demotion must be by way of penalty.

(a) Reduction in rank in the *physical sense* takes place where the Government servant is reduced to a lower post or to a lower pay-scale. Even reduction to a lower stage in the pay-scale (ordered by way of penalty) would involve a reduction in rank, for the officer loses his rank or seniority in the gradation list of his substantive rank.

(b) As regards the *penal nature* of the reduction, the Supreme Court has applied the test of "right to the rank" in question, in the same manner as the "right to the post" test has been applied in the case of dismissal or removal. Reduction in rank takes place only when a person is reduced from his substantive rank. Hence, (i) Where a Government servant has a *right* to a

13. *Moti Ram v NEF Ry,* AIR 1964 SC 600, p 610; *P C Wadhwa v UOI,* AIR 1964 SC 423 : (1964) 4 SCR 598.
14. *State of Bombay v Doshi,* AIR 1957 SC 892 : 1958 SCR 571.
15. *I N Saxena v State of Madhya Pradesh,* AIR 1967 SC 1264, p *1266* : (1967) 2 SCR 496; *State of Bombay v Nurul Latif,* AIR 1966 SC 269 : (1996) 2 LLJ 595.
16. *Parshottam v UOI,* AIR 1958 SC 36 : (1958) 1 SCR 828.
17. *Nar Singh Pal v UOI,* AIR 2000 SC 1401 : (2000) 3 SCC 588.
18. *Satish Chandra Anand v UOI,* AIR 1953 SC 250.
19. *Hartwell v Uttar Pradesh Government,* AIR 1957 SC 886.
20. *Lakshmana v State of Karnataka,* AIR 1975 SC 1646; *Tara Singh v State of Rajasthan,* AIR 1975 SC 1487.

particular rank, the very reduction from that rank will be deemed to be by way of penalty and Article 311(2) will be attracted, without more. Thus, an officer who holds a permanent post in a substantive capacity, cannot be transferred to a lower post, without complying with Article 311(2). (ii) On the other hand, where a Government servant has no title to a particular rank, under the contract of his employment or conditions of service — there will ordinarily be no reduction in rank within the meaning of Article 311(2),[21] *e.g.*, where a person, who had been promoted to a higher post on an officiating basis[22] or contrary to the statutory recruitment rules[23], is reverted to his substantive post as it is neither punitive nor illegal. But even in this case, the order of reversion will amount to "reduction in rank" so as to attract Article 311(2), if the reversion entails penal consequences, such as postponement of future chances of promotion or the order contains a stigma which indicates that it was penal in nature;[24] though, in the absence of such penal features, the motive of the authority would be irrelevant.[25] Reversion of the employees from their confirmed posts by imposing additional qualifications and functions to their confirmed post would offend Article 311.[26]

4b. No Inquiry to be held and no Opportunity of being Heard in Certain Cases.

It is to be noted that even where a person holding a civil post is dismissed, removed or reduced in rank, no inquiry need be held and no opportunity need be given in three classes of cases, which themselves explain the reasons for the exceptions —

(a) Where a person is dismissed or removed or reduced in rank on the ground of conduct which has led to his conviction on a criminal charge; but such a charge must relate to a misconduct of such magnitude as would have deserved the penalty of dismissal, removal or reduction in rank.[27]

(b) Where an authority empowered to dismiss or remove a person or to reduce him in rank is satisfied that for some reason, to be recorded by that authority in writing, it is not reasonably practicable to hold such inquiry the Supreme Court upheld the concurrent view taken by the disciplinary authority and the appellate authority that holding inquiry into the case of a Head Constable who was working for terrorists and preparing to murder some senior police officers, was not practicable[28]; or

(c) Where the President or Governor, as the case may be, is satisfied that, in the interest of the *security of the State* it is not expedient to hold such inquiry [Second proviso to *Article* 311(2)].[29] In cases where the mere disclosure of the charge might affect the security of the State, the President or the Governor

21. *Shitla v NEF Ry*, AIR 1966 SC 1197; *State of Mysore v Gadgoli*, AIR 1977 SC 1617.
22. *State of Uttar Pradesh v Sughar*, AIR 1974 SC 423; *UOI v Gajendra*, AIR 1972 SC 1329; *Debesh Chandra v UOI*, AIR 1970 SC 77.
23. *Kishore Chandra Panigrahi v State of Orissa*, (1996) 11 SCC 234.
24. *Shitla v NEF Ry*, AIR 1966 SC 1197; *State of Mysore v Gadgoli*, AIR 1977 SC 1617.
25. *State of Bihar v Shiva*, AIR 1971 SC 1011.
26. *Chandraprakash Madhavrao Dadwa v UOI*, (1998) 8 SCC 154.
27. *UOI v Tulsiram*, AIR 1985 SC 1416 : (1985) 3 SCC 398.
28. *Kuldeep Singh v State of Punjab*, AIR 1997 SC 79 : (1996) 10 SCC 659.
29. *UOI v Tulsiram*, AIR 1985 SC 1416, para 70 : (1985) 3 SCC 398.

might exempt the holding of an inquiry[30] but such satisfaction should not be *mala fide*.[31] However, the satisfaction need not be personal as such power is exercised in compliance with Article 166[32] but the Government is required to disclose the nature of activities of the employee which formed the basis of such satisfaction so that the court/tribunal may be able to determine whether there was any reasonable nexus between such activities and the security of the State or not[33] without which the dismissal might be held to be *ultra vires*.[34]

5. Adjudication of Disputes Relating to Recruitment and Conditions of Service of Public Servants.

A radical change has taken place in the Constitutional law relating to services by the 42nd Constitution Amendment Act, 1976, which inserted into the Constitution, Article 323A, to take out the adjudication of disputes relating to the recruitment and conditions of service of the public services of the Union and of the States from the hands of the civil courts and the high courts and to place it before an Administrative Tribunal for the Union or of a State (as the case may be). The 42nd Constitution Amendment Act, 1976 paved way for tribunalisation of the justice dispensation system by introduction of Articles 323A and 323B in the Constitution.

This provision of the Constitution was to come into effect only if it was implemented by a law made by Parliament. That law has been enacted by Parliament in 1985 and brought into force on 2 October 1985, by setting up a Central Administrative Tribunal (with branches in the specified cities).

According to this Administrative Tribunal Act, 1985 (as amended in 1986), the Central Administrative Tribunal will adjudicate disputes and complaints with respect to the "recruitment and conditions of service of persons appointed to public services and posts in connection with the affairs of the Union", excepting—

(a) Members of the Defence Forces.

(b) Officers and Servants of the Supreme Court or of any high court.

(c) Members of the secretarial staff of Parliament, or of any Legislature of any State or Union Territory.

Excluding the above categories, any public servant of the Union who is aggrieved, in the matter of his appointment, removal or reduction in rank or the like, shall have to be contented with administrative justice by a Tribunal instead of by a court of law. The only court to which the aggrieved person might run, as a last resort, is the Supreme Court, under Articles 32 and 136.

The decisions of the Administrative Tribunal can, therefore, be challenged only before the Supreme Court and the high court shall not be competent to interfere under Article 226 or 227. But subsequently, the position turned out to be otherwise as the Supreme Court declared the Articles 323-A, clause 2(d) and 323-B, clause 3(d) and also the "exclusion of jurisdiction" clauses in all the

30. *B C Dass v State of Assam,* (1971) 2 SCC 168.
31. *UOI v Tulsiram,* AIR 1985 SC 1416 : (1985) 3 SCC 398.
32. *Shamsher Singh v State of Punjab,* AIR 1974 SC 2192.
33. *A K Kaul v UOI,* AIR 1995 SC 1403 : (1995) 4 SCC 73.
34. *State of Orissa v Dinabandhu Beheta,* (1997) 10 SCC 383.

legislations enacted in pursuance of these Articles, unconstitutional to the extent they excluded the jurisdiction of the high courts and the Supreme Court under Articles 226/227 and 32.[35]

6. Public Service Commissions.

There shall be a Public Service Commission for the Union; and a Public Service Commission for each State or a Joint Public Service Commission for a group of States if the Parliament provides for the establishment of such a Joint Public Service Commission in pursuance of a resolution to that effect being passed by the State Legislatures concerned. The Union Public Service Commission also may, with the approval of the President, agree to serve the needs of a State, if so requested by the Governor of that State [*Article 315*].

The number[36] of members of the Commission and their conditions of service shall be determined: (a) by the President in the case of the Union or a Joint Commission; and (b) by the Governor of the State in the case of a State Commission; provided that the conditions of service of a member of a Commission shall not be altered to his disadvantage after his appointment.

7. Appointment and Term of Office of Members of Public Service Commissions.

The *appointment* of the Chairman and members of the Commission shall be made — (a) in the case of the Union or a Joint Commission, by the President; and (b) in the case of a State Commission, by the Governor of the State. Half of the members of a Commission shall be persons who have held office under the Government of India or of a State for at least 10 years [*Article 316*].

The *term of service* of a member of a Commission shall be six years from the date of his entering upon office, or until he attains the age of 65 years in the case of the Union Commission or of 62 years[37] in the case of a State or a Joint Commission. But a member's office may be terminated earlier, in any of the following ways:

(i) By *resignation* in writing addressed to — the President in the case of the Union or a Joint Commission, or the Governor in the case of a State Commission.

(ii) By *removal* by the President — (a) if the member is adjudged insolvent; or engages himself during his term in paid employment outside the duties of his office; or is in the opinion of the President infirm in mind or body; (b) on the ground of misbehaviour according to the report of the Supreme Court which shall hold an enquiry on this matter on a reference being made by the President.

Thus, even in the case of a State Commission, it is only the President who can make a reference to the Supreme Court and make an order of removal in pursuance of the report of the Supreme Court. The Governor has only the power to pass an interim order of suspension pending the final order of the President on receipt of the report of the Supreme Court [*Article 317(1)-(2)*].

---

35. *L Chandra Kumar v UOI*, AIR 1997 SC 1125 : (1997) 3 SCC 261.
36. As on 2-2-2024, the number of members of the Union Public Service Commission is 7, excluding the Chairman.
37. Raised from 60 to 62 years by the Constitution (41st Amendment) Act, 1976.

If a member's term comes to an end while a reference under Article 317(1) is pending in the Supreme Court the reference[38] does not become infructuous and the court must answer it.

A member shall be deemed to be guilty of misbehaviour — (i) if he is in any way concerned or interested in any contract made on behalf of the Government of India or of a State; or (ii) if he participates in any way in the profit of such contract or agreement or in any benefit therefrom otherwise than as a member and in common with other members of an incorporated company [*Article 317(4)*].

8. Independence of Public Service Commission. The Constitution seeks to maintain the independence of the Public Service Commission from the Executive in several ways —

(a) The Chairman or a member of a Commission can be removed from office only in the manner and on the grounds specified in the Constitution (see *above*).

(b) The conditions of service of a member of the Public Service Commission shall not be varied to his disadvantage after his appointment [*proviso to Article 318*].

(c) The expenses of the Commission are charged on the Consolidated Fund of India or of the State (as the case may be) [*Article 322*].

(d) Certain disabilities are imposed upon the Chairman and members of the Commission with respect to future employment under the Government [*Article 319*]. Thus, on ceasing to hold office —

(i) The Chairman of the Union Public Service Commission shall be ineligible for further employment either under the Government of India or under the Government of a State;

(ii) the Chairman of a State Public Service Commission shall be eligible for appointment as the Chairman or any other member of the Union Public Service Commission or as the Chairman of any other State Public Service Commission, but not for any other employment either under the Government of India or under the Government of a State;

(iii) a member other than the Chairman of the Union Public Service Commission shall be eligible for appointment as the Chairman of the Union Public Service Commission or as the Chairman of a State Public Service Commission, but not for any other employment either under the Government of India or under the Government of a state;

(iv) a member other than the Chairman of a State Public Service Commission shall be eligible for appointment as the Chairman or any other member of the Union Public Service Commission or as the Chairman of that or any other State Public Service Commission, but not for any other employment either under the Government of India or under the Government of a State.

In short, the bar against employment under the Government is *absolute* in the case of the Chairman of the Union Public Service Commission; while in the case

38. *Re Ref under Article 317(1), Smt. Santosh Chowdhary, Chairman, Punjab Public Service Commission v Krishna Saini, Member of the Commission,* (1990) 4 SCC 262 : [1990] 2 LLJ 368.

of the Chairman of a State Public Service Commission or of the other members of the Union or State Commissions, there is scope of employment in a higher post within the Public Service Commission but not outside.

The Public Service Commissions are *advisory bodies.*[39] It is open to the government to accept the recommendation or depart from it:[40]

9. Duties and Functions of Public Service Commissions. The following are the duties of the Union and the State Public Service Commissions —

(a) To conduct examination for appointments to the services of the Union and the services of the state respectively.

(b) To advise on any matter so referred to them and on any other matter which the President, or, as the case may be, the Governor of a state may refer to the appropriate Commission [*Article 320*].

(c) To exercise such additional functions as may be provided for by an act of Parliament or of the Legislature of a state — as respects the services of the Union or the state and also as respects the services of any local authority or other body corporate constituted by law or of any public institution [*Article 321*].

(d) To present annually to the President or the Governor a report as to the work done by the Union or the State Commission, as the case may be [*Article 323*].

(e) It shall be the duty of the Union Public Service Commission, if requested by any two or more states so to do, to assist those states in framing and operating schemes of joint recruitment for any services for which candidates possessing special qualifications are required [*Article 320(2)*].

(f) The Public Service Commission for the Union, if requested so to do by the Governor of a state, *may*, with the approval of the President, *agree* to serve all or any of the needs of the state.

The Union Public Service Commission or the State Public Service Commission, as the case may be, shall be consulted—

> (a) on all matters relating to methods of recruitment to civil services and for civil posts;
>
> (b) on the principles to be followed in making appointments to civil services and posts and in making promotions and transfers from one service to another and on the suitability of candidates for such appointments, promotions or transfers;
>
> (c) on all disciplinary matters affecting a person serving under the Government of India or the Government of a State in a civil capacity, including memorials or petitions relating to such matters;
>
> (d) on any claim by or in respect of a person who is serving or has served under the Government of India or the Government of a State or under the Crown in India or under the Government of an Indian State, in a civil capacity, that any costs incurred by him in defending legal proceedings instituted against him in respect of acts done or purporting to be done in the execution of his duty should be paid out of the Consolidated Fund of India, or, as the case may be, out of the Consolidated Fund of the State;

---

39. *D'Silva v UOI*, AIR 1962 SC 1130.
40. *H Mukherjee v UOI*, (1994) 1 Supp SCC 250.

(e) on any *claim* for the award of a pension in respect of injuries sustained by a person while serving under the Government of India or the Government of a State or under the Crown in India or under the Government of an Indian State, in a civil capacity, and any question as to the amount of any such award [*Article* 320(3)].

But—

(i) The President or the Governor, as the case may be, as respects the services and posts in connection with the affairs of the Union or of a State, may specify the matters in which either generally, or in any particular class of cases, or in any particular circumstances, it shall *not be necessary for* a Public Service Commission to be consulted. But all such regulations must be laid before the appropriate Legislature and be subject to such modifications as may be made by the Legislature.

(ii) It has been held by the Supreme Court[41] that the obligation of the Government to consult the Public Service Commission in any of the matters specified above does *not* confer any *right* upon any individual who may be affected by any act of the Government done without consulting the appropriate Commission as required by the Constitution. The reason assigned by the court is that the consultation prescribed by the Constitution is to afford proper assistance to the Government, in the matter of assessing the guilt of a delinquent officer, the merits of a claim for reimbursement of legal expenses and the like; and that the function of the Commission being purely advisory,[42] if the Government fails to consult the Commission with respect to any of the specified matters, the resulting act of the Government is not invalidated by reason of such omission and no individual who is affected by such act can seek redress in a court of law against the Government for such irregularity or omission.[43]

10. Report of Public Service Commissions.

As stated already, it shall be the duty of the Union Commission to present annually to the President a report as to the work done by the Commission and on receipt of such report the President shall cause a copy thereof together with a memorandum explaining, as respect the cases, if any, where the advice of the Commission was not accepted, the reason for such non-acceptance, to be laid before each House of Parliament [*Article 323(1)*]. A State Public Service Commission has a similar duty to submit an annual report to the Governor and the latter has a duty to lay a copy of such report before the State Legislature with a memorandum explaining the cases, if any, where the advice of the Commission was not accepted by the Government [*Article 323(2)*].

11. Binding nature of Commission's Advice on Government.

As stated earlier, the function of the Public Service Commission is only advisory, and the Constitution has no provision to make it obligatory upon the Government to act upon the advice of the Commission in any case.[44] The reason is that, under the Parliamentary system of government, it is the Cabinet which is responsible for the proper administration of the country and its responsibility is to Parliament. They cannot, therefore, abjure this ultimate responsibility by

41. *State of Uttar Pradesh v Manbodhan Lal Srivastava*, AIR 1957 SC 912; *Ram Gopal v State of Madhya Pradesh*, AIR 1970 SC 158.
42. *D'Silva v UOI*, AIR 1962 SC 1130.
43. *State of Uttar Pradesh* v *Srivastava*, AIR 1957 SC 912; *Ram Gopal v State of Madhya Pradesh*, AIR 1970 SC 158.
44. *D'Silva v UOI*, AIR 1962 SC 1130.

binding themselves by the opinion of any other body of persons. On the other hand, in matters relating to the recruitment to the Services and the like, it would be profitable for the Ministers to take the advice of a body of experts. It is in this light that Sir Samuel Hoare[45] justified the parallel provisions as to the Public Service Commissions in the Government of India Act, 1935—

> Experience goes to show that they are likely to have more influence if they are advisory than if they have mandatory powers. The danger is that if you give them mandatory powers you then set up two governments.

But, though the Simon Commission[46] was conscious of the fact that left alone, the Ministers might use their position "to promote family or communal interests at the expense of the efficiency or just administration of the services", no safeguard was prescribed in the Government of India Act, 1935 against a flagrant disregard of the recommendations of the Commissions by the Government. In view of the possibility of such abuse, the Constitution has provided the safeguard (referred to above) of the Commission's report being laid before Parliament (or State Legislature), through the President (or the Governor) as the case may be. The Government is under an obligation, while presenting such report, to explain the reasons why in any particular case the recommendation of the Commission has been overridden by the Government. In view of this obligation to submit to Parliament an explanation for non-acceptance of the advice of the Commission, the number of such cases may be said to have been kept at a minimum.

Notwithstanding the above safeguard, there is criticism from certain quarters that patronage is still exercised by the Government by resorting to some devices—

(a) One of these is the system of making *ad hoc* appointments for a temporary period without consulting the Public Service Commission, and then approaching the Commission to approve of the appointment at a time when the person appointed has already been in service for some time and the recommendations of his superiors are available to him, in addition to the experience already gained by him in the work, which puts him at an advantage over the new candidates. The Supreme Court has been deprecating this practice of making *ad hoc* appointments. The Supreme Court did not allow the services of the employees appointed *de hors* the rules, although officiating for a long period of 14 years;[47] that of the *ad hoc* appointees by bypassing the process of recruitment through open competition[48] and a temporary appointee on monthly basis during the period of strike,[49] to be regularised.

(b) Sometimes the rules laying down the qualifications for the office to which such appointment has been made is changed retrospectively to fit in the appointee.

(c) Another complaint is that sometimes the reports are presented before Parliament (or State Legislature as the case may be) long after the year under review. This, however, does not appear to be permissible under the Constitution.

45. 300 Parl Deb, c 858.
46. Simon Commission Rep, vol 1.
47. *E Ramakrishnanv State of Kerala,* (1996) 10 SCC 565 : (1996) 7 Scale 76.
48. *P Ravindran v Union Territory of Pondicherry,* (1997) 1 SCC 350.
49. *UOI v Harish Balkrishna Mahajan,* (1997) 3 SCC 194 : (1997) 10 JT SC 375.

So far as the duty of the Commission to report to the President or the Governor is concerned, the Constitution says that it must be done "annually". Hence, his obligation cannot be postponed for more than a few months from the end of the period under report. The duty of the President or the Governor is to present the report to Parliament or the State Legislature "on receipt of such Report". Though no specific time-limit is imposed, it is clear that it must be done as soon as possible after the receipt of the annual Report and it cannot be construed that the obligation is discharged by presenting the report two or three years after the receipt or by presenting the reports for two or three years in a lump. The presentation before the Legislature must also be an annual affair, and, if the President or the Governor makes delay, it should be the concern of the appropriate Legislature to demand an explanation for such delayed presentation, apart from anything else. If the Legislature slumbers, the entire machinery of Parliamentary government will succumb, not to speak of any particular object of scrutiny by the Legislature.

12. All-India Services.

Another matter relating to the Services which is dealt with by the Constitution is the creation of All-India Services. The All-India Services should be distinguished from Central Services. The "Central Services" is an expression which refers to certain services under the Union, maintained on an all-India basis, for service throughout the country — for instance, the Indian Foreign Service, the Indian Audit and Accounts Service, the Indian Customs and Excise Service and the like. The expression "All-India Service", on the other hand, is a technical one, used by the Constitution to indicate only the Indian Administrative Service and the Indian Police Service and such other services[50] which may be included in this category in the manner provided by Article 312 of the Constitution. That Article provides that if the Council of states declares by a resolution, supported by not less than two-third of the members present and voting, that it is necessary and expedient in the national interest to create an All-India Service, common to the Union and the states, Parliament may provide for its creation by making a law. The practical incident of an All-India Service thus, is that the recruitment to it and the conditions of service under it can be regulated only by an Act of the Parliament. It must be noted that it is by virtue of this power that Parliament has made the All-India Services Act, 1951 and that the conditions of service, recruitment, conduct, discipline and appeal of the members of the All-India Services are now regulated by Rules made under this Act. Since these rules provide that the officers of the All-India Services shall be appointed and controlled by the Union Government, these services constitute an additional agency of control of the Union over the state, insofar as members of these services are posted in key posts in the states.

I. Subject to the power of Parliament, under Article 33, to modify the fundamental rights in their application to members of the Armed Forces and the

---

50. Several new Services have been added to the list of All-India Services, namely, the Indian Engineering Service, the Indian Forest Service and the Indian Medical Service [the All-India Service (Amendment) Act, 1963]; the Indian Statistical Service; Indian Economic Service.

The Supreme Court has directed the Government of India to take steps for setting up an *All-India Judicial Service* [*All India Judges' Association v UOI,* AIR 1992 SC 165, para 10A]. No such Service appears to have been created by now.

Police Forces, the fundamental rights guaranteed by the Constitution are in favour of all "citizens", which obviously include public servants.[51]

II. It follows, therefore, that a civil employee of the Government is entitled to the protection of a fundamental right such as Articles 14,[52] 15,[53] 16,[54] 19,[51] and 20 in the same manner as a private citizen. Thus —

If two sets of rules relating to disciplinary proceedings were in operation at the time when the inquiry was directed against a Government servant, and the inquiry was directed under the set of rules which was more drastic and prejudicial to the interests of such Government servant, the proceedings against him are liable to be struck off as infringing Article 14. In other words, if against two public servants similarly circumstanced enquiries may be directed according to procedure *substantially different*,[52] at the discretion of the Executive authority, exercise whereof is not governed by any principles having any rational relation to the purpose to be achieved by the inquiry, the order selecting a prejudicial procedure, out of the two open for selection, is hit by Article 14.[52]

III. Restrictions upon the rights of the public servants under Article 19 can, therefore, be imposed only on the grounds specified in clauses (2)–(6), and to the extent that the restriction is reasonable.[55]

But while a public servant possesses the fundamental rights as a citizen, the state also possesses, under the proviso to Article 309, the power to regulate their "conditions of service". Now, the interests of service under the state require efficiency, honesty, impartiality and discipline and like qualities on the part of the public servant. The state has thus the Constitutional power to ensure that every public servant possesses these qualities and to prevent any person who lacks these qualities from being in the public service. It seems, therefore, that state regulation of the conditions of service of public servants so as to restrict their fundamental rights will be valid only to the extent that such restriction is reasonably necessary in the interests of efficiency, integrity impartiality, discipline, responsibility and the like which have a "direct, proximate and rational" relation to the conditions of public service as well as the general grounds (eg, public order, under Article 19) upon which the fundamental rights of all citizens may be restricted.[55]

---

51. *Kameshwar v State of Bihar*, AIR 1962 SC 1166; *O K Ghosh v Joseph*, AIR 1963 SC 812.
52. *State of Orissa v Dhirendranath*, AIR 1961 SC 1715; *Jagannath v State of Uttar Pradesh*, AIR 1961 SC 1245.
53. *State of Punjab v Joginder*, AIR 1963 SC 913.
54. *Devadasan v UOI*, AIR 1964 SC 179.
55. *Kameshwar v State of Bihar*, AIR 1962 SC 1166; *O K Ghosh v Joseph*, AIR 1963 SC 812.

CHAPTER 31

ELECTIONS

WHILE the Constitution lays down the procedure for the election of the President[1] [*Article 54*] and the Vice-President[1] [*Article 66*], the procedure for election to the Legislatures of the Union and the States is left to legislation, the Constitution itself providing certain principles. These principles are—

1. Election Provisions.

(a) There is no provision for communal, separate or special representation. There shall be one electoral roll for every territorial constituency for election to either House of Parliament or to the State Legislature and no person shall be excluded from such roll on grounds only of religion, race, caste, sex or any of them [*Article 325*].

(b) The election shall be on the basis of adult suffrage, *ie*, every person who is a citizen of India and who is not less than 18[2] years of age shall be entitled to vote at the election provided he is not disqualified by any provision of the Constitution or of any law made by the appropriate Legislature on the ground of non-residence, unsoundness of mind, crime, or corrupt or illegal practice [*Article 326*].

1a. Power to make Laws.

Subject to the above principles and the other provisions of the Constitution, the power to make laws relating to all matters in connection with the election not only to the Houses of Parliament, but also to the Houses of the Legislature of a State belongs to the Union Parliament [*Article 327; Entry 72, List I, Seventh Schedule*]. The State Legislature has, however, a subsidiary power in this respect. It can legislate on all electoral matters relating to the State Legislature insofar as such matters are not covered by legislation by Parliament. The laws of the State Legislature shall, in other words, be valid only if they are not repugnant to laws made by Parliament and, of course, to the provisions of the Constitution [*Article 328*]. Parliament has enacted the Representation of the People Acts, 1950, 1951, as well as the Delimitation Commission Acts of 1952, 1962, 1972 and 2002 to prescribe the mode of election, and the formation and delimitation of the constituencies relating to election.

The Election Laws (Amendment) Act, 2021 envisages the following: (a) linking of electoral roll with Aadhaar system to curb the menace of multiple enrolment

---

1. See Chapter 11, *ante*.
2. The voting age has been lowered from 21 to 18, by the Constitution (61st Amendment) Act, 1988. Corresponding change had been effected by amending the Constitution of Jammu & Kashmir, by the 21st Amendment, 1989 to that State's Constitution.

of the same person in different places; (b) multiple qualifying dates for enrolment in the electoral roll to expand the voter base; (c) making the statutes gender neutral in line with the avowed policy of gender equality and inclusiveness *vis-à-vis* conduct of the elections; and (d) streamlining the process of conduct of elections with reference to requisitioning of premises for certain purposes, etc.

The Central Government amended the Conduct of Elections Rules, 1961, by bringing the Conduct of Elections (Amendment) Rules, 2022 which increased the maximum limit of expenditure by a candidate for parliamentary and assembly constituencies. In respect of larger States/Union Territories, it has been increased from Rs. 77 lakhs to Rs. 95 lakhs for parliamentary constituencies, and Rs 30.8 lakhs to Rs. 40 lakhs for assembly constituencies. In respect of smaller States/Union Territories, it has been increased from Rs. 59.4 lakhs to Rs. 75 lakhs for parliamentary constituencies, and Rs 22 lakhs to Rs. 28 lakhs for assembly constituencies.

1b. Basis of Voting.

The procedure prescribed by these Acts is voting based on single-member territorial constituencies. While proportional representation has been prescribed for election to the office of the President and the Vice-President, that system has *not* been adopted for election to the Legislature of the Union and the States.

2. Decision of Disputes Relating to Election of Members.

Disputes are bound to arise in the matter of such a big-scale election on various points, such as, whether the procedure for election was properly followed or whether any candidate returned as member suffered from any disqualification under the law or the Constitution, or whether a candidate who ought to have been returned has been, in fact, declared not elected. For the decision of such disputes, the Constitution provides [*Article 329*] that the ordinary courts of the land will have no jurisdiction and that any question relating to an election can be agitated only by an election petition, as provided for by law.

Article 329 provides—

> Notwithstanding anything in this Constitution—
>
> (b) No election to either House of Parliament or to the House or either House of the Legislature of a State shall be called in question except by an election petition presented to such authority and in such manner as may be provided for by or under any law made by the appropriate Legislature.

Under the Representation of the People Act, 1951, the power to decide an election petition is vested in the High Court within the local limits of whose jurisdiction the election to which the election petition relates has been held, with appeal to the Supreme Court.

3. Election Tribunals.

By Article 323B of the Constitution, as inserted by the Constitution (42nd Amendment) Act, 1976, power has been conferred on the appropriate Legislature to set up a Tribunal for the adjudication of disputes relating to elections of the Legislature concerned, by making law, and to provide in such law for the exclusion of all Courts (save that of the Supreme Court under Article 136), to entertain any such matter. In short, when any such law is made in exercise of this power, the High Court will cease to have any jurisdiction over election disputes; they will be determined only by the Administrative Tribunal set up by law, with appeal from the decision of such Tribunal to the Supreme Court by special leave under Article 136.

4. Special Jurisdiction for Adjudicating Election Disputes to Election of President and Vice-President.

In Article 71 of the Constitution, the exclusive forum for adjudicating disputes relating to the election of the President and Vice-President is the Supreme Court. There is no special provision for the Prime Minister or the Speaker of the House of the People, so that any dispute relating to election to these offices is to be determined only by an election petition before the high court, according to Article 329(*b*).

5. Election Commission.

In order to supervise the entire procedure and machinery for election and for some other ancillary matters, the Constitution provides for an independent body, namely, the Election Commission [*Article 324*]. The provisions for the removal of the Election Commissioners make them independent of executive control and ensure an election free from the control of the party in power for the time being.

The Election Commission shall consist of a Chief Election Commissioner and such other Commissioners as the President may, from time to time, fix [*Article 324(2)*].

From the beginning, the Election Commission consisted of the Chief Election Commissioner only. The Congress(I) Government, just a week before the commencement of the Ninth General Election, appointed two more Commissioners on 16 October 1989 making it a multi-member Commission.[3] The National Front Government, on assuming charge, amended the rules to make it again a single-member body wef 2 January 1990. The conditions of service and tenure of office of the Election Commissioner shall be such as Parliament may by law prescribe. Provided that the Chief Election Commissioner cannot be removed from his office except in like manner and on like grounds as a Judge of the Supreme Court. In other words, the Chief Election Commissioner can only be removed by each House of Parliament, by a special majority and on the ground of proved misbehaviour or incapacity (and the other Election Commissioners shall not be removed by the President except on the recommendation of the Chief Election Commissioner).

The Election Commission shall have the power of superintendence, direction and conduct of all elections to Parliament and the State Legislatures and of elections to the offices of the President and Vice-President [*Article 324(1)*].

Regional Commissioners may also be appointed by the President, in consultation with the Election Commission, on the eve of a general election to the House of the People or to the State Legislature, for assisting the Election Commission [*Article 324(4)*].

---

3. According to critics, the haste with which new Members were appointed created a suspicion that it was an attempt to compromise the independence of the Commission.

On 1 October 1993, the Government promulgated an Ordinance[4] (which was subsequently converted into an Act) to provide for the appointment of two Election Commissioners. Soon thereafter two Commissioners were appointed. The distribution of work and the rules for transaction of business made in the Ordinance were challenged in the Supreme Court. The court issued directions and the matter has been finally settled by upholding the validity of the Act.[5]

The Election Commission (Conditions of Service of Election Commissioners and Transaction of Business) Act, 1991 did not provide the procedure for appointment of Election Commissioners, which continued to be decided by the President. Thus, in March 2023, while examining the appointment of the CEC and ECs, the Supreme Court[6] declared that their appointment should not be done solely by the Executive. The Court noted that the ECI should be independent of Executive control. It mandated a selection process, which would hold until Parliament makes a law. The Court directed that the appointment should be done by the President on the recommendation of a Selection Committee, which will consist of: (i) the Prime Minister, (ii) the Leader of Opposition in Lok Sabha, and (iii) the Chief Justice of India.

With effect from 2-2-2024, the Election Commission (Conditions of Service of Election Commissioners and Transaction of Business) Act, 1991 has been repealed and replaced by the Chief Election Commissioner and Other Election Commissioners (Appointment, Conditions of Service and Term of Office) Act, 2023 (49 of 2023). This 2023 Act provides that the appointment of Election Commissioners should be done by the President on the recommendation of a Selection Committee consisting of: (i) the Prime Minister [Chairperson], (ii) the Leader of Opposition in Lok Sabha (or the leader of the single largest party in opposition), and (iii) a Union Cabinet Minister to be nominated by the Prime Minister.

6. Reforms in Electoral Processes.

The Election Commission of India has brought several reforms in the electoral processes, and the Supreme Court of India has also played a pro-active role while passing several leading judgments with regard to electoral reforms, which resulted in a historical voting in the recent parliamentary and legislative elections.

The Election Commission of India told the Supreme Court in 2009 that it wished to offer the voter a '*None of the above*' button on voting machines; the Government, however, has generally opposed this option. On 27 September 2013, the Supreme Court of India pronounced a landmark judgement that the citizens of India have the *Right to Negative Vote* by exercising the *'None of the above' (NOTA)* option in EVMs and ballot papers. The judgment was passed based on a PIL filed by the *People's Union for Civil Liberties,*[7] an NGO in 2009. The Election Commission has

4. The Ordinance has been replaced by Chief Election Commissioner and other Election Commissioners (Condition of Service) Amendment Act, 1993. The name of the original Act has been changed to the Election Commission (Conditions of Service of Election Commissioners and Transaction of Business) Act, 1991.
5. *TN Seshan v UOI,* (1995) 4 SCC 611 : JT 1995 (5) 337.
6. *Anoop Baranwal v UOI (Election Commission Appointments),* (2023) 6 SCC 161.
7. *People's Union for Civil Liberties v UOI,* (2013) 10 SCC 1.

implemented this "none of the above" voting option in EVM machines wef, the five states polls that started from November 2013. However, it does not mean that if 'NOTA' gets the highest votes then the election will be conducted again, rather, even in that case, the candidate with the highest votes will be treated as the elected candidate.[8] The option of NOTA may serve as an elixir in direct elections but in respect of the election to the Council of States (which is a different one), it would not only undermine the purity of democracy but also serve the Satan of defection and corruption.[9] In 2013, the Supreme Court mandated the use of VVPAT (Voter Verified Paper Audit Trail).[10]

8. Election Commission of India, Press Note, 28 October 2013, wrt, NOTA.
9. *Shailesh Manubhai Parmar v Election Commission of India*, AIR 2018 SC 3918: (2018) 9 SCC 100: (2018) 10 SCALE 51.
10. *Dr Subramanian Swamy v Election Commission of India*, AIR 2014 SC 18.

implemented the option of 'None of the Above' voting option in EVM machines in the [illegible] Assembly polls that started from November 2013. However, it does not mean that if NOTA gets the highest votes then the election will be conducted again; rather, even in that case, the candidate with the highest votes will be declared as the elected candidate. The option of NOTA may serve as an [illegible] elections. But, in respect of the election to the Council of States, which is [illegible] different case, it would not only undermine the purity of democracy but also [illegible] the menace of defection and corruption. In 2013, the Supreme Court mandated the use of VVPAT (Voter Verified Paper Audit Trail).

[illegible] Election Commission of India, Press Note, 25 October 2013 [illegible] NOTA.
[illegible] Shailesh Manubhai Parmar v. Election Commission of India, [illegible] (2018)
[illegible]
[illegible] Dr. Subramanian Swamy v. Election Commission of India, (2013) [illegible]

CHAPTER 32

MINORITIES, SCHEDULED CASTES, SCHEDULED TRIBES AND OTHER BACKWARD CLASSES

1. General Introduction.

IT was pointed out at the outset that *our* Constitution, being consecrated by the ideals of equality and justice both in the social and political fields, abolishes any discrimination either against or in favour of any class of persons on the grounds of religion, race or place of birth. It is in pursuance of this ideal that the Constitution did away with *communal* representation or reservation of seats in the Legislature or in the offices on the basis of religion.

It would have been a blunder on the part of the makers of *our* Constitution if, on a logical application of the above principle, they had omitted to make any special provisions for the advancement of those sections of the community who are socially and economically *backward*, for, the democratic march of a nation would be impossible if those who are handicapped are not aided at the start. The principle of democratic equality (as envisaged in the Preamble to the Constitution), indeed, can work only if the nation as a whole is brought on the same level, as far as that is practicable. *Our* Constitution, therefore, prescribes certain temporary measures to help the backward sections to come up to the same level with the rest of the nation, as well as certain permanent safeguards for the protection of the cultural, linguistic and similar rights of any section of the community who might be said to constitute a 'minority' from the numerical, *not communal*, point of view, in order to prevent the democratic machine from being used as an engine of oppression by the numerical majority.

2. Protection of Interests of Minorities.

Any discussion of the provisions of our Constitution for the protection of the interests of the minorities can hardly fail to take notice of the palpably unfair comments of Sir Ivor Jennings[1] on this point:

> Indeed, the most complete disregard of minority claims is one of the most remarkable features of Indian federalism. The existence of competing claims on religious and ethnic grounds was one of the reasons given for the refusal of Indian independence before 1940. By reaction the Congress politicians, who were above all nationalists, tended to minimize the importance of minority interests and emotions.

---

1. Some Characteristics of the Indian Constitution, 1953, p 64.

It is obvious that Sir Ivor would have been satisfied if the framers of *our* Constitution had perpetuated communal representation even after the country had been partitioned on the basis of a two-Nation slogan carried to the point of fanaticism, leading to a well-planned mass massacre. It is somewhat painful to point out to an Englishman that communal representation was not a natural limb of the Indian political system which was 'blindly' amputated by the nationalist Congress leaders but was an artificial growth which had been grafted upon our body politic by the Morley-Minto plan in the name of 'reform'.[2] An impartial student of Indian history may be expected to testify how, once the malignant growth had been implanted into our political life, every opportunity was seized by the imperialistic power to develop it as a wedge to separate the Indian people into two hostile camps so much so that it could eventually be advanced "as one of the reasons for the refusal of Indian independence". After those who were allured by the separatist vision had succeeded in dividing the motherland to create an exclusive home of their own, it must be presumed that those belonging to that very community who elected to remain in their birth-place should prefer to live with the other children of the soil as one family, after giving up all claims to separate treatment in the political *sphere*. It is only there that the objective of 'fraternity' assured by the Preamble would be fulfilled and the "integrity of the Nation" (*ibid*) could be achieved.

That the majority community has not abolished the communal representation with any selfish motives will be apparent from the very fact that notwithstanding the abolition of reservation, members of the minority community have been appointed to the highest offices of President, Vice-President, ministers, ambassadors, governors and judges of the superior courts in such numbers as can hardly be overlooked by an impartial observer. There is no reasonable ground for apprehending that the interests or development of the minority community have suffered because of the abolition of separate electorates on a communal basis.

The real injustice done by Sir Ivor, above all, is the omission to mention the religious, cultural and educational safeguards incorporated in the Constitution to protect the interests of *all minority groups*, whether they are religious, linguistic or cultural minorities. While some of these shall be a permanent feature of the Constitution, there are others of a temporary nature which will continue to operate only so long as the backward communities are lagging behind in the march of the nation. The safeguards for minorities and backward classes may, accordingly, be discussed under two heads—(I) Permanent provisions; and (II) Temporary provisions, which have been discussed below.

2a. Religious Freedom.

Though the provisions guaranteeing religious freedom to every individual cannot, strictly speaking, be said to be specific safeguards in favour of the minorities, they do protect the *religious* minorities if we contrast the provisions of the successive Islamic Constitutions of Pakistan. *Our* Constitution does not contain any provision for the furtherance of any particular religion as may raise legitimate apprehensions in the minds of those who do not belong to that religion.

2. Thanks are due to Prof. Gledhill that he does not fail to notice this [(1959) *Journal of Indian Law Institute*, p 406].

2b. Linguistic and Cultural Rights. Any section of the citizens of India having a distinct language, script or culture of its own shall have the fundamental right to conserve the same [*Article 29(1)*]. This means that if there is a cultural minority which wants to preserve its own language and culture, the state would not by law impose upon it any other culture belonging to the majority of the locality. This provision, thus, gives protection not only to religious minorities but also to linguistic minorities. The promotion of Hindi as the national language or the introduction of compulsory primary education cannot be used as a device to take away the linguistic safeguard of a minority community as guaranteed by Arts. 29-30.[3-4] In fact, both the Union and State Governments have been taking active steps, at Government expense, for the promotion of Urdu in order to appease Muslim sentiments (see next Chapter).

2c. Facilities for Instruction in Mother-tongue. The Constitution directs every State to provide adequate facilities for instruction in the mother-tongue at the primary stage of education to children belonging to linguistic minority groups and empowers the President to issue proper direction to any state in this behalf [*Article 350A*].

Further, a Special Officer for linguistic minorities shall be appointed by the President to investigate all matters relating to the safeguards provided for linguistic minorities under the Constitution and report to the President [*Article* 350B].

2d. National Commission for Minorities. Parliament has enacted the National Commission for Minorities Act, 1992 for monitoring the working of the safeguards provided in the Constitution and in Union and State laws.

2e. No Discrimination in State Educational Institutions. No citizen shall be denied admission into any educational institution maintained by the State or receiving state aid, on grounds only of religion, race, caste, language or any of them [*Article 29(2)*]. This means that there shall be no discrimination against any citizen on the ground of religion, race, caste or language, in the matter of admission into educational institutions maintained or aided by the state. It is a very wide provision intended for the protection not only of the religious minorities but also of 'local' or linguistic minorities, and the provision is attracted as soon as the discrimination is immediately based only on the ground of religion, race, caste, language or any of them.

The Government of Bombay issued an Order which directed that, subject to certain exceptions, no primary or secondary school receiving aid from Government should admit to a class where English was the medium of instruction, any pupil other than a pupil belonging to a section of the citizens the language of which was English, namely Anglo-Indians and citizens of non-Asiatic descent. An Indian citizen, other than an Anglo-Indian citizen, was denied admission to a State-aided school, in pursuance of the above Order. The Supreme Court *held* that the immediate ground for denial of admission of a pupil to such a School where English was the medium of instruction was that

---

3. *Re Kerala Education Bill,* AIR 1958 SC 956.
4. *State of Bombay v Bombay Education Society,* (1955) 1 SCR 568.

the mother-tongue of the pupil was *not* English. It was, thus, a denial of the right conferred by Article 29(2), only on the ground of the language of the pupil. The argument that the object of the denial was to promote the introduction of Hindi or any other Indian language as the medium of instruction in the schools was immaterial in determining whether Article 29(2) had been contravened.[4]

2f. Right to Establish Educational Institutions of their Choice.

All minorities, whether based on religion or language, shall have the fundamental right to establish and administer educational institutions of their choice [*Article 30(1)*]. While Article 29(1) enables the minority to maintain its language or script, the present clause enables them to run their own educational institution, so that the state cannot compel them to attend any other institutions, not to their liking.

By the 1978 amendment, favourable treatment has been accorded to such minority educational institutions in the matter of compensation for compulsory acquisition of property by the state. While, by reason of the repeal of Article 31, all persons have lost their constitutional right to compensation for acquisition of their property by the state, including educational institutions belonging to the majority community, educational institutions established by a minority community lie entrenched in this behalf. Their property cannot be acquired by the state without payment of such compensation as would safeguard their right to exist, as is guaranteed by Article 30(1A).

2g. No Discrimination in State Aid to Educational Institutions.

The State shall not, in granting aid to educational institutions, discriminate against any educational institution on the ground that it is under the management of a minority, whether based on religion or language [*Article 30(2)*].

The ambit of the above educational safeguards of all minority communities, whether religious, linguistic, or otherwise, can be understood only if we notice the propositions evolved by the Supreme Court out of the above guarantees:

(a) Every minority community has the right not only to establish its own educational institutions, but also to impart instruction to the children of its own community in its own language.[4]

(b) Even though Hindi is the national language of India, and Article 351 provides a special directive upon the state to promote the spread of Hindi, nevertheless, the object cannot be achieved by any means which contravenes the rights guaranteed by Articles 29 or 30.[4]

(c) In making primary education compulsory [*Article 45*], the state cannot compel that such education must take place only in the schools owned, aided or recognised by the State so as to defeat the guarantee that a person belonging to a linguistic minority has the right to attend institutions run by the community, to the exclusion of any other school.[3]

(d) Even though there is no constitutional right to receive state aid, if the state does in fact grant aid to educational institutions, it cannot impose such conditions upon the right to receive such aid as would, virtually, drive the members of a religious or linguistic community of their right under Article 30(1). While the state has the right to impose reasonable conditions, it cannot impose such conditions as will substantially deprive the minority community of its rights guaranteed by Article 30(1). Surrender of fundamental rights cannot be exacted as the price of aid doled out by the State. Thus, the state cannot prescribe that if an institution, including one entitled to the protection of Article 30(1), seeks to receive State aid, it must subject itself to the condition that the State may take over the management of the institution or to acquire it on its subjective satisfaction as of certain matters,—for such condition would completely destroy the right of the community to administer the institution.[3]

(e) Similarly, in the matter of the right to establish an institution in relation to recognition by the state, though there is no Constitutional or other right for an institution to receive state recognition and though the state is entitled to impose reasonable conditions for receiving state recognition, *eg,* as to qualifications, it cannot impose conditions the acceptance of which would virtually deprive a minority community of their right guaranteed by Article 30(1).[3]

Where, therefore, the state regulations debar scholars of unrecognised educational institutions from receiving higher education or from entering into the public services, the right to establish an institution under Article 30(1) cannot be effectively exercised without obtaining state recognition. In such circumstances, the state cannot impose it as a condition precedent to state recognition that the institution must not receive any fees for tuition in the primary classes. For, if there is no provision in the state law or regulation as to how this financial loss is to be recouped, institutions, solely or primarily dependent upon the fees charged in the primary classes, cannot exist at all.[3]

(f) Minority institutions protected under Article 30(1) are, however, subject to regulation by the educational authorities of the state to prevent maladministration and to ensure a proper standard of education.[5] But such regulation cannot go to the extent of virtually annihilating the right guaranteed by Article 30(1).[6]

2h. No Discrimination in Public Employment.

No person can be discriminated against in the matter of public employment, on the ground of race, religion or caste [*Article 16(2)*].

3. Safeguards for Advancement of Backward Classes.

While the Constitution has abolished representation on *communal* lines, it has included safeguards for the advancement of the *backward* classes amongst the residents of India (irrespective of their *religious* affiliations), so that the country may be ensured of an all-round development. These provisions fulfil the assurance of "justice, social, economic and political" which has been held out by the very Preamble of the Constitution. A major section of such backward classes has been specified in the Constitution as Scheduled Castes and Scheduled Tribes because their backwardness is patent.

4. Scheduled Castes and Tribes.

There is no definition of Scheduled Castes and Scheduled Tribes in the Constitution itself. But the President is empowered to draw up a list in consultation with the Governor of each state, subject to revision by Parliament [*Articles 341-342*]. The President has made Orders, specifying the Scheduled

5. *State of Kerala v Mother Provincial,* AIR 1970 SC 2079; *St Xavier's College v State of Gujarat,* AIR 1974 SC 1389; *Sidhrajbhai v State of Gujarat,* AIR 1963 SC 540.

Castes and Scheduled Tribes in the different States in India, which have since been amended by Acts of Parliament.[6]

The Resolution passed by the State deleting the caste and merging the said caste in the Scheduled Castes list with another caste was patently illegal, erroneous as the State Government had no competence/ authority/power to tinker with the lists of Scheduled Castes published under Article 341 of the Constitution.[7]

5. Special Provisions for Protection of Interests of Scheduled Castes and Tribes. The Constitution makes various special provisions for the protection of the interests of the Scheduled Castes and Scheduled Tribes. Thus,

(i) Measures for the advancement of the Scheduled Castes and Scheduled Tribes are exempted [*Article 15(4)*] from the general ban against discrimination on the grounds of race, caste, and the like, contained in Article 15. It means that if special provisions are made by the state in favour of the members of these Castes and Tribes, other citizens shall not be entitled to impeach the validity of such provisions on the ground that such provisions are discriminatory against them.

(ii) On the other hand, while the rights of free movement and residence throughout the territory of India and of acquisition and disposition of property are guaranteed to every citizen, in the case of members of the Scheduled Castes and Scheduled Tribes, special restrictions may be imposed by the state as may be required for the protection of their interests. For instance, to prevent the alienation or fragmentation of their property, the state may provide that they shall not be entitled to alienate their property except with the concurrence of a specified administrative authority or except under specified conditions [*Article 19(5)*].

(iii) The claims of the members of the Scheduled Castes and the Scheduled Tribes shall be taken into consideration, consistently with the maintenance of the efficiency of the administration, in the making of appointments[8] to services and posts in connection with the affairs of the Union or of a state [*Article 335*].

(iv) There shall be a National Commission for the Scheduled Castes to be appointed by the President [*Article 338*]. It shall be the duty of this Commission to investigate all matters relating to the safeguards provided for the Scheduled Castes under this Constitution and to report to the President upon the working of those safeguards annually or at such intervals as it may deem fit, and the President shall cause all such reports to be laid before each House of Parliament. A similar provision for similar purposes has been made for the appointment of a National Commission for the Scheduled Tribes by inserting Article 338A.[9]

(v) The President may, at any time, and shall, at the expiration of ten years from the commencement of this Constitution, by Order appoint a Commission to report on the administration of the Scheduled Areas and the welfare of the Scheduled Tribes in the states. The Order may define the composition, powers

6. Scheduled Castes and Scheduled Tribes form 24.56 per cent of the total population of the country (*India 2001*, p 14).
7. *Bhim Rao Ambedkar Vichar Manch Bihar, Patna v State of Bihar*, AIR 2024 SC 3531 : AIROnline 2024 SC 481.
8. *Balaji v State of Mysore*, AIR 1963 SC 649 (*656, 658*).
9. *Vide* The Constitution (89th Amendment) Act, 2003, Section 3 (w.e.f. 19.2.2004).

and procedure of the Commission and may contain such incidental or ancillary provisions as the President may consider necessary or desirable [*Article 339(1)*].

(vi) The executive power of the Union shall extend to the giving of directions to any such state as to the drawing up and execution of schemes specified in the direction to be essential for the welfare of the Scheduled Tribes in the state [*Article 339(2)*].

With a view to associate members of Parliament and other members of the public in the due discharge of the above functions by the Government of India, three Parliamentary Committees have been set up. Their function is to formulate and review the working of schemes for the welfare of the Scheduled Castes and Scheduled Tribes and to advise the Government of India on matters relating to these castes and tribes.

(vii) Financial aid for the implementation of these welfare schemes is provided for in Article 275(1) which requires the Union to give grants-in-aid to the states for meeting the costs of schemes of welfare of the Scheduled Tribes and for raising the level of administration of the Scheduled Areas in a state to that of the administration of the areas of that state.

(viii) Proviso to Article 164 lays down that in the States of Bihar, Madhya Pradesh and Orissa, there shall be a Minister in charge of tribal welfare, who may also be in charge of the welfare of the Scheduled Castes and other backward classes.

In practice, such Welfare Departments have been set up not only in these three states as required by the Constitution, but also in other states.

(ix) Special provisions are laid down in the Fifth and Sixth Schedules of the Constitution, read with Article 244, for the administration of areas inhabited by Scheduled tribes.

Over and above all these, there is a general Directive in Article 46 that the state shall promote with special care the educational and economic interests of the weaker sections of the people, and, in particular, of the Scheduled Castes and the Scheduled Tribes, and shall protect them from social injustice and all forms of exploitation.

Besides, there are temporary provisions for special representation of and reservation of seats for Scheduled Castes and Scheduled Tribes in the Legislatures [*Articles 330, 332, and 334*][10-11] which will be treated separately, hereafter.

---

10. In 2008, out of 543 seats in the House of the People, 84 are reserved for representatives of the Scheduled Castes and 47 for representatives of the Scheduled Tribes. Two President's nominees from Anglo-Indians. In the Legislative Assemblies, on the other hand, out of an aggregate of 4,116 seats, 613 are reserved for the Scheduled Castes and 554 for the Scheduled Tribes [*vide* the Representation of the People (Amendment) Act, 2008, Sec. 8].
11. The period of ten years prescribed in the original Constitution was extended to twenty years by the Constitution (Eigth Amendment) Act, 1959, and, then, to thirty years, by the Constitution (23rd Amendment) Act, 1969, on the ground that the object of the safeguard had not yet been fulfilled. This has been further extended to *40* years, by the Constitution (45th Amendment) Act, 1980, to *fifty* years by the Constitution (62nd Amendment) Act, 1989, w.e.f. 20-12-1989 and to *sixty* years by the Constitution (79th Amendment) Act, 1999, w.e.f. 25-1-2000 [Article 334] and to *seventy* years by the Constitution (95th Amendment) Act, 2010 (w.e.f. 25-1-2010). This period as it relates to the reservation of Scheduled Castes and Scheduled Tribes has been further extended to *80* years by the Constitution (104th Amendment) Act, 2019 (wef 25-1-2020).

By amending Article 338, the Constitution (65th Amendment) Act, 1990, a National Commission has been set up for investigating and reporting on the working of the foregoing safeguards regarding the Scheduled Castes and Scheduled Tribes.[9]

6. Special Provisions for Advancement of Backward Classes.

Not contented with making special provisions for the Scheduled Castes, who form a specific category of socially depressed people (generally identifiable with the Gandhian term '*harijan*'), the Constitution has made separate provisions for the amelioration and advancement of all 'backward classes', in general.

Of course, the Constitution does not define 'backward classes'. The Scheduled Castes and Scheduled Tribes are no doubt backward classes, but the fact that the Scheduled Castes and Scheduled Tribes are mentioned together with the expression 'backward classes' in the foregoing provisions shows that there may be other backward classes of people besides the Scheduled Castes and Scheduled Tribes. The Constitution provides for the appointment of a 'Commission to investigate the conditions of backward classes' [*Article* 340]. Such a Commission was appointed in 1953 (with Kaka Saheb Kalelkar as Chairman), with the following terms of appointment—

(a) To determine the tests by which any particular class or group of people can be called 'backward'.

(b) To prepare a list of such backward communities for the whole of India.

(c) To examine the difficulties of backward classes and to recommend steps to be taken for their amelioration.

This Commission submitted its report to the Government in 1955, but the tests recommended by the Commission appeared to the Government to be too vague and wide to be of much practical value; hence, the State Governments have been authorised to give assistance to the backward classes according to the lists prepared by the State Governments themselves.

The second Backward Classes Commissioner, Mr. B.P. Mandal, submitted his report in 1980. In August 1990, the Government declared reservation of 27% seats in government service on the basis of this report. This was challenged as unconstitutional. A nine-Judge Bench has decided this case in November, 1992, rejecting that challenge.[12]

The court has not itself enumerated the 'backward classes' but has directed the Government to set up a Commission[14] to specify the backward classes, in the light of the principles laid down by the court.[13]

Following the recommendations of the Commission the Central Government has reserved 27% seats in all recruitments to be made from 9 September, 1993.

12. *Indra Sawhney v UOI*, (1992) Supp. (3) SCC 217.
13. Parliament has already enacted the National Commission for Backward Classes Act, 1993, for this purpose. This came into force on 1 February 1993.

It has already been pointed out that the Proviso to Article 164(1) provides for a Minister in charge of the welfare of backward classes and that departments for such welfare have, in fact, been opened in all the states.

7. Special Provisions for Socially and Educationally Backward Classes.

The Constitution (102nd Amendment) Act, 2018 has inserted a new Article 338-B to provide for a Commission for socially and educationally backward classes to be known as the National Commission for Backward Classes. The Chairperson, Vice-Chairperson and other Members of the Commission shall be appointed by the President by warrant under his hand and seal. The Union and every State Government shall consult the Commission on all major policy matters affecting the socially and educationally backward classes.

It is the duty of the Commission—

(a) to investigate and monitor all matters relating to the safeguards provided for the socially and educationally backward classes under the Constitution or under any other law for the time being in force or under any order of the Government;

(b) to inquire into specific complaints with respect to the deprivation of rights and safeguards of the socially and educationally backward classes;

(c) to participate and advise on the socio-economic development of the socially and educationally backward classes and to evaluate the progress of their development under the Union and any state;

(d) to present to the President, annually and at such other times as the Commission may deem fit, reports upon the working of those safeguards;

(e) to make in such reports the recommendations as to the measures that should be taken by the Union or any state for the effective implementation of those safeguards and other measures for the protection, welfare and socio-economic development of the socially and educationally backward classes; and

(f) to discharge such other functions in relation to the protection, welfare and development and advancement of the socially and educationally backward classes as the President may, subject to the provisions of any law made by Parliament, by rule specify.

The President shall cause all such reports to be laid before each House of Parliament along with a memorandum explaining the action taken or proposed to be taken on the recommendations relating to the Union and the reasons for the non-acceptance, if any, of any of such recommendations.

The Constitution (102nd Amendment) Act, 2018 has also inserted another Article 342A to the Constitution of India. The newly added Article 342A provides that the President may with respect to any state or Union territory specify by public notification the socially and educationally backward classes which shall for the purposes of this Constitution be deemed to be socially and educationally backward classes in relation to that state or Union territory.

The Constitution (102nd Amendment) Act, 2018 inserted three new Articles, *i.e.*, Articles 338B, 342A and 366(26C). Article 338B provided Constitutional status to the National Commission for Backward Classes (NCBC). Whereas Article 342A dealt with the Central List of the Socially and Educationally

Backward Classes (commonly known as the Other Backward Classes) and Article 366(26C) defined the Socially and Educationally Backward Classes.

The legislative intent behind the enactment of the Constitution (102nd Amendment) Act, 2018 was to deal with the Central List of the Socially and Educationally Backward Classes (SEBCs). After the enactment of the Constitution (102nd Amendment) Act, 2018, the Maharashtra passed a law that recognised Marathas as SEBCs and provided them the benefit of reservation. This was subsequently challenged before the Supreme Court. In *Jaishri Laxmanrao Patil v UOI*, a Constitutional Bench of the Supreme Court by a 3:2 majority held that the states lack the power to identify SEBCs after the enactment of the Constitution (102nd Amendment) Act, 2018. The decision of the majority stated that after the introduction of Articles 338B and 342A in the Constitution "the final word concerning the exclusion or inclusion (or modification) of SEBCs first rests with the President, and thereafter, in case of exclusion or modification from the previously published list, with the Parliament".

In order to adequately clarify that the State Government and Union territories are empowered to prepare and maintain their own State List/Union territory List of SEBCs and with a view to maintain the federal structure of this country, Parliament enacted the Constitution (105th Amendment) Act, 2021.

8. Special Provisions for Anglo-Indian Community. Even apart from the foregoing safeguards, provisions were made in the Constitution in the interests of the Anglo-Indian community, in view of their peculiar position in Indian society.

An Anglo-Indian is defined in Article 366(2) as—

> A person whose father or any of whose other male progenitors in the male line is or was of European descent but who is domiciled within the territory of India and is or was born within such territory of parents habitually resident therein and not established there for temporary purposes only.

The Special Officer for Scheduled Castes and Scheduled Tribes was to investigate into and report on the working of the foregoing safeguards relating to the Anglo-Indian community [*Article 338(3)*]. This provision has been repealed by the 65th Amendment Act, 1990.

9. Temporary Provisions for Advancement of Backward Classes. Let us now advert to other provisions for the advancement of the Scheduled Castes and Scheduled Tribes as well as the Anglo-Indian community, which were intended to be of a temporary duration,—just sufficient to enable them to come up to the level of the general body of citizens:

(a) Seats shall be reserved in the House of the People[11] for—(a) The Scheduled Castes; (b) The Scheduled Tribes except the Scheduled Tribes in the tribal areas of Assam; and (c) The Scheduled Tribes in the autonomous districts of Assam [*Article 330*].

Seats shall also be reserved for the Scheduled Castes and the Scheduled Tribes, except the Scheduled Tribes in the tribal areas of Assam, in the Legislative Assembly[11] of every State [*Article 332*]. Such reservation will cease on the expiration of *80* years[12] from the commencement of the Constitution [*Article 334*].

Article 334 of the Constitution lays down that the provisions of the Constitution relating to the reservation of seats for the Scheduled Castes and the Scheduled Tribes and the representation of the Anglo-Indian community by nomination in the House of the People and Legislative Assemblies of the states.

(b) The President may, if he is of opinion that the Anglo-Indian community is not adequately represented in the House of the People, nominate not more than two members of that community to the House of the People [*Article 331*]. The Governor has a similar power in respect of the Legislative Assembly of the State, but in the case of a Governor, the maximum quota, fixed by the Constitution (23rd Amendment) Act, 1969 is—*one* member of the community for the Legislative Assembly [*Article 333*]. Such power shall cease after 70 years[12] from the commencement of the Constitution.

(c) The provisions for reservation for Anglo-Indians in certain services of the Union [*Article 336*] or for special educational grants [*Article 337*] have already expired.

CHAPTER 18

LANGUAGES

CHAPTER 33

LANGUAGES

1. Languages.

LANGUAGES offered a special problem to the makers of the Constitution simply because of the plurality of languages used by the vast population of 1,210,854,977 according to 2011 census. It is somewhat bewildering to think that no less than 1,369 spoken languages are current in this sub-continent. This astonishing number reflects the immense linguistic diversity of India.

2. Need of a National Language.

The Constitution of India does not declare Hindi to be a national language. The Supreme Court in *UP Hindi Sahitya Sammelan*,[1] while referring the author's commentary on the Constitution of India observed that:

> Acharya Dr. Durga Das Basu, in his commentary on the Constitution of India, Volume 9, 2011 while dealing with Part XVII under the sub-title "Need for a National Language" observes that the Constitution makers failed to declare one language as the national language of India and what has been provided in the Constitution is mainly a compromise between the diverse claims¥. Dr. Basu then observes that what has been provided in the Constitution is not a national language but – (a) an "official language" for the Union (Articles 343-344); (b) regional official languages for the States (Articles 345-347); and (c) official language (a) for purposes of proceedings in the Supreme Court and High Courts and (b) for Bills, Acts, Ordinances, Regulations, bye-laws at the Union and State level. Dr. Basu in his treatise quotes the Constitutional Law of India by T.K. Tope*, wherein the author has stated that Hindi has not been accepted as the national language by the Constitution; the Constitution has not laid down any language as the national language.

3. Need for an Official Language.

The makers of the Constitution had, therefore, to select some of these languages as the recognised medium of official communication in order to save the country from a hopeless confusion. Fortunately for them, the number of people speaking each of these 1,369 languages was not anything like proportionate and some 22[1] languages (included in the Eighth Schedule of the Constitution, see Table XIX, *post*) could easily be picked up as the major languages of India, used by more than 90% of the total population of the country, and out of them, Hindi, including its kindred variants Urdu and Hindustani, could claim 46%. Hindi Devanagari script was accordingly prescribed as the official language of the Union (subject to the continuance of English for the same purpose for the limited period of 15 years), and, for the

---

1. *UP Hindi Sahitya Sammelan v State of UP*, AIR 2015 SC 1154 : (2014) 9 SCC 716 : (2014) 6 Mad LJ 624 (SC).

development of the Hindi language as a medium of expression for all the elements of the composite culture of India, the assimilation of the expressions used in the other languages specified in the Eighth Schedule was recommended [*Article 351*].

But though one language was thus prescribed for the official purposes of the Union, and the makers of the Constitution sought to afford relief to regional linguistic groups by allowing the respective State Legislatures [*Article 345*] and the President [*Article 347*] to recognise some language or languages other than Hindi as the languages for intra-State official transactions or any of them. These provisions thus recognise the right of the majority of the State Legislature or a substantial section of the population of a state to have the language spoken by them to be recognised for official purposes within the state.

In the result, the provisions of the Constitution relating to Official Language have come to be somewhat complicated [*Articles 343–351*].

4. Official Language of the Union.

The Official language of the *Union* shall be Hindi in Devanagri script [*Article 343*]. But, for a period of 15 years from the commencement of this Constitution, the English language shall continue to be used for *all* the official purposes of the Union for which it was being used immediately before such commencement. Even after the expiry of the above period of 15 years, Parliament *may* by law provide for the use of—

(a) The English language, or

(b) The Devanagri form of numerals, for such purposes as may be specified in the law [*Article 343*].

In short, English would continue to be the official language of the Union side by side with Hindi, until 1965, and thereafter the use of English for any purpose will depend on Parliamentary legislation. Parliament has made this law by enacting the Official Languages Act, 1963, which will be presently noted.

5. Official Language Commission.

The Constitution provides for the appointment of a Commission as well as a Committee of Parliament to advise the President as to certain matters relating to the official language [*Article 344*]. The Official Language Commission is to be appointed at the expiration of five years, and again at the expiration of 10 years, from the commencement of the Constitution. The President shall constitute the Commission with the representatives of the recognised languages specified in the Eighth Schedule.[2] It shall be the duty of the Commission to make recommendations to the President as to—

(a) the progressive use of the Hindi language for the official purposes of the Union;

2. The original Constitution enumerated 14 languages. This number became 15, by the addition of "Sindhi", by the Constitution (21st Amendment) Act, 1967. The 71st Amendment Act, 1992 added Konkani, Nepali and Manipuri to make it 18. The 92nd Amendment Act, 2003 added Bodo, Dogri, Mathilli and Santhali to make it 22. In the Eighth Schedule to the Constitution in entry 15 for the word "Oriya", the word "Odia" substituted by The Constitution (96th Amendment) Act, 2011 as published in The Gazette of India, Extraordinary Part II, section 1, dated 23 September 2011.

(b) restrictions on the use of the English language for any of the official purposes of the Union;

(c) the language to be used for proceedings in the Supreme Court and the High Courts and the texts of legislative enactments of the Union and the States as well as subordinate legislation made thereunder;

(d) the form of numerals to be used for any of the official purposes of the Union;

(e) any other matters referred to the Commission by the President as regards—

(1) the official language of the Union, and

(2) the language for communication between the Union and the States or between one State and another.

In making its recommendations, the Commission shall have due regard to the industrial, cultural and scientific advancement of India and the just claims and interests of persons belonging to the non-Hindi speaking areas in regard to Public Services.

The recommendations of the Commission will be examined by a Joint Parliamentary Committee consisting of 30 members of whom 20 shall be elected from the Lok Sabha and 10 from the Rajya Sabha in accordance with the system of proportional representation by single transferable vote. The Committee will examine the recommendations of the Commission and report their opinion to the President.

5a. Implementation of the Recommendations of First Official Language Commission.

The Official Language Commission was, accordingly, appointed in 1955 with Sri B G Kher as Chairman, and it submitted its report in 1956, which was presented to Parliament in 1957 and examined by a joint Parliamentary Committee. The recommendations of the Parliamentary Committee upon a consideration of the Report of the Official Language Commission were as follows—

(a) The Constitution contains an integrated scheme of official language and its approach to the question is flexible and admits of appropriate adjustment being made within the framework of the scheme.

(b) Different regional languages are rapidly replacing English as a medium of instruction and of official work in the States. The use of an Indian language for the purposes of the Union has thus become a matter of practical necessity, but there *need be no rigid date-line for the change-over.* It should be a natural transition over a period of time effected smoothly and with the minimum of inconvenience.

(c) English should be the principal official language and Hindi, the subsidiary official language till 1965. After 1965, when Hindi becomes the principal official language of Union, *English should continue as the subsidiary official language.*

(d) No restriction should be imposed for the present on the use of English for any of the purposes of the Union and provision should be made in terms of clause (3) of Article 343 for the continued use of English even after 1965 for purposes to be specified by Parliament by law as long as may be necessary.

(e) Considerable importance attaches to the provision in Article 351 that Hindi should be so developed that it may serve as a medium of expression for all elements of the composite culture of India, and every encouragement should be given to the use of *easy* and *simple* diction.

In pursuance of the above recommendations of the Parliamentary Committee, the President issued an Order[3] on 27 April 1960, containing directions by way of implementing the above recommendations. The main direction was as regards the evolution of Hindi terminology for scientific, administrative and legal literature and the translation of English literature on administrative and procedural matters into Hindi. For the evolution of such terminology, the Official Language Commission recommended the Constitution of two *Standing Commissions*: (A) For the development of legal terminology and preparation of authoritative texts of Central Acts in Hindi and other languages a Commission [known as the Official Language (Legislative) Commission] was constituted in 1961. It was abolished in 1976 and its functions have been assigned to the Legislative Department of the Government of India; (B) The other Commission [known as the Commission for Scientific and Technical Terminology] is working under the Ministry of Human Resources.

Of the other recommendations of the Official Language Commission, the following, *inter alia,* were adopted in the President's Order:[2]

(i) English shall continue to be the medium of examination for the recruitment through the Union Public Service Commission but, after some time, Hindi may be admitted as an alternative medium, both Hindi and English being available as the media at the option of the candidate.

(ii) Parliamentary legislation may continue to be in English but an authorised translation should be provided in Hindi. For this purpose, the Ministry of Law has been directed to provide for such translation and also to initiate legislation to provide for an authorised Hindi translation of the text of Acts passed by Parliament.

(iii) Where the original text of Bills introduced or Acts passed by a State Legislature is in a language other than Hindi, a Hindi translation may be published with it besides an English translation as provided in clause (3) of Article 348.

(iv) When the time comes for the change-over, Hindi shall be the language of the Supreme Court.

(v) Similarly, when the time for change-over comes, Hindi shall ordinarily be the language of judgments, decrees or orders of courts, *in all regions;* but, by undertaking necessary legislation, the use of a regional official language may be made optional instead of Hindi, with the previous consent of the President.

6. Official Language of Inter-State Communications

The Constitution further provides that the language for the time being authorised for use in the Union for official purposes (*i.e.,* English) shall be the official language of communication between one state and another state and between a state and the Union. If, however, two or more states agree that the Hindi language should be the official language for communication

3. *India*, 1961, p 547.

between such states, that language may be used for such communication instead of English [*Article 346*].

7. Official Language of a State.

The Legislature of a State may by law[4] adopt any one or more of the languages in use in the state or Hindi as the language to be used for all or any of the official purposes of that state: Provided that, until the Legislature of the State otherwise provides by law, the English language shall continue to be used for those official purposes within the state for which it was being used immediately before the commencement of this Constitution [*Article 345*]. Nothing in Article 345, bars declaring one or more of the languages in use in the state, in addition to Hindi, as the second official language.[1]

7a. Declaration Procedure for non-Hindi Languages.

Hindi has been given a special constitutional status but that does not mean that Article 345 cannot be used for declaring a non-Hindi language as the official language, if the power under Article 345 has been exhausted or exercised once to declare Hindi as the official language of that state. The use of the word "or" before "Hindi" in the Article 345 is for the purpose of dispensing with the requirement of Hindi being "in use" in that particular state. However, for a non-Hindi language to be declared as the official language, the requirement of being "in use" has to be satisfied for exercise of power by the State Legislature under Article 345. Dispensing the requirement of "in use" for Hindi is to facilitate, spread and to absorb the adoption of Hindi across states in terms of Article 351, though it may not be spoken or used by the people in the State. There are many State Legislatures which have adopted other officially recognised language(s) in addition to Hindi such as Bihar, Haryana, Jharkhand, Madhya Pradesh and Uttarakhand. Delhi has also adopted Punjabi and Urdu as other officially recognised languages in addition to Hindi. It is noteworthy that Article 350 confers a constitutional right on every person to submit a representation for redress of any grievance to any office of the Union or the state, in any of the language used in the Union or the state.[1]

The Supreme Court in *UP Hindi Sahitya Sammelan*,[1] upheld the constitutional validity of the Uttar Pradesh Official Language (Amendment) Act, 1989 and the Uttar Pradesh Government notification dated 7 October 1989, notifying the use of Urdu language as the second official language for the seven purposes specified therein.[1]

8. Difference between Articles 345 and 347.

Articles 345 and 347 prescribe two different procedures for making law or issuing directions for recognising a language as the official language. Article 345 deals with the power of the State Legislature, while Article 347 refers to the power of the President of India. The requirements of both these Articles are different. Under Article 347, the requirement of "a substantial portion of the population of a State desire the use of any language spoken by them to be recognised by that State", is not a requirement under Article 345.

---

4. In January 1987, the Goa Legislative Assembly has passed the Goa Language Act, making Konkani as an official language of the Union Territory, in addition to Marathi/Gujarati.

If Hindi is in use in a particular state, then it does not foreclose the state's power or discretion to adopt any language other than Hindi as the official language, provided such language is "in use" in that state. The use of the word "may" in Article 345 indicates that state has discretion in adopting the language or languages in use in the state and so also Hindi. Such discretion can be exercised any number of times by the State Legislature as it deems proper. However, under Article 347, the President of India may respond to a demand for an additional official language where the requirements of Article 347 are fulfilled ie, the President of India must be satisfied that "a substantial portion of the population of a State desire the use of any language spoken by them to be recognised by that State". Article 350B provides a machinery by which the President may make an assessment with respect to the demands of linguistic minorities. The criterion for adoption of one or more of the languages, other than Hindi, in the state is that those languages must be "in the use in State". This criterion must be satisfied at the time the State Legislature exercises its power under Article 345. The State Legislature cannot adopt any language as an official language if such language is not used in the state. However, there is no impediment for the State Legislature to declare Hindi to be an official language even if Hindi is not "in use" in Karnataka. The law-making power of the State Legislature under Article 345 is restricted by virtue of the expression "subject to......" against the direction issued by the President of India under Article 347, meaning thereby, that once directions under Article 347 are issued by the President, the State Legislature cannot tinker with the said direction in any manner. However, in the absence of such direction issued by the President under Article 347 of the Constitution, there is no restriction, restraint or impediment for the State Legislature in adopting one of the languages in use in the state as an official language under Article 345 of the Constitution of India. These are the distinguishing features between Articles 345 and 347.[1]

There is also a provision for the recognition of any other language for the official purposes of a state or any part thereof, upon a substantial popular demand for it being made to the President [*Article 347*].

9. Language to be used in Supreme Court and in High Courts and for Acts, Bills, etc.

Until Parliament by law otherwise provides —

(a) all proceedings in the Supreme Court and in every high court,

(b) the authoritative texts —

(i) of all Bills to be introduced or amendments thereto to be moved in either House of Parliament or in the House or either House of the Legislature of a State,

(ii) of all Acts passed by Parliament or the Legislature of a state and of all Ordinances promulgated by the President or the Governor of a State, and

(iii) of all orders, rules, regulations and bye-laws issued under this Constitution or under any law made by Parliament or the Legislature of a State,

shall be in the English language.

A State Legislature may, however, prescribe the use of any language other than English for Bills and Acts passed by itself, or subordinate legislation made thereunder. Similarly, the Governor of a State may, with the previous consent of the President, authorise the use of Hindi or any other language used for official purposes of the state, in proceedings in the high court of the state, but not in judgments, decrees or orders (which must continue to be in English until Parliament by law otherwise provides) [*Article 348*].

The foregoing provisions of the Constitution *are now to be read subject to* the modifications made by the Official Languages Act, 1963 and the Authorised Translations (Central Laws) Act, 1973 and the new Article 394A, inserted in the Constitution in 1987.

In 1973, Parliament enacted the Authorised Translations (Central Laws) Act, 1973, to provide that when a Central Law is translated into a regional language (other than Hindi), and published in the Official Gazette, under the authority of the President, such translation shall be deemed to be the authorised translation thereof in such language.

10. Article 394A.

The Draft Constitution as well as the Constitution adopted by the Constituent Assembly on the 26 November 1949, was in the English language. After it was officially translated into Hindi, Article 394A was inserted into the Constitution, by the 58th Amendment Act, 1987, in order to give it effective authority. In pursuance of this Article, the President published in the Gazette of India, the Hindi text which, according to clause (2) of Article 394A, shall be construed to have the same meaning as the original text in the English language, and in case of any difficulty arising in this matter, the President shall direct the Hindi text to be suitably revised.

11. The Official Languages Act, 1963.

The provisions of the Official Languages Act (as amended) are—

I. *Continuance of English language for official purposes of the Union and for use in Parliament:* Notwithstanding the expiration of the period of 15 years from the commencement of the Constitution, the English language may, as from the appointed day, continue to be used, *in addition to Hindi,* —

(a) for all the official purposes of the Union for which it was being used immediately before that day; and

(b) for the transaction of business in Parliament.

II. *Authorised Hindi translation of Central Acts, etc.:* (1) A translation in Hindi published under the authority of the President in the Official Gazette on and after the appointed day, —

(a) of any Central Act or of any Ordinance promulgated by the President; or

(b) of any order, regulation or bye-law issued under the Constitution or under any Central Act,

shall be deemed to be authoritative text thereof in Hindi.

(2) As from the appointed day the authoritative text in the English language of all Bills to be introduced or amendments thereto to be moved in either House

of Parliament shall be accompanied by a translation of the same in Hindi authorised in such manner as may be prescribed by rules made under this Act.

III. *Authorised Hindi translation of State Acts in certain cases:* Where the Legislature of a state has prescribed any language other than Hindi for use in Acts passed by the Legislature of the state or in Ordinances promulgated by the Governor of the state, a translation of the same in Hindi, in addition to a translation thereof in the English language as required by clause (3) of Article 348 of the Constitution, may be published on or after the appointed day under the authority of the Governor of the state in the Official Gazette of that state and in such a case, the translation in Hindi of any such Act or Ordinance shall be deemed to be the authoritative text thereof in the Hindi language.

IV. *Optional use of Hindi or other official language in judgments, etc., of High Courts:* As from the appointed day or any day thereafter, the Governor of a state may, with the previous consent of the President, authorise the use of Hindi or the official language of the state, in addition to the English language, for the purposes of any judgment, decree or order passed or made by the high court for that state and where any judgment, decree or order is passed or made in any such language (other than the English language), it shall be accompanied by a translation of the same in the English language issued under the authority of the high court.

V. *Inter-State communications:* (a) English shall be used for purposes of communication between the Union and a state which has *not* adopted Hindi as its official language; (b) Where Hindi is used for purposes of communication between one state and another which has *not* adopted Hindi as its official language, such communication in Hindi shall be accompanied by an English translation thereof.

12. Special Directives Relating to Languages.

The Constitution lays down certain special directives in respect of not only the official language but also the other languages in use in the different parts of the country, in order to protect the interests of the linguistic minorities.

A. As regards the *official* language — the directive is, of course, for the promotion and development of the Hindi language so that it may serve as a medium of expression for all the elements of the composite culture of India and this is laid down as a duty of the Union; and the Union is further directed to secure the enrichment of Hindi, by assimilating without interfering with its genius, the forms, style and expressions, used in the Hindustani and other languages (specified in the Eighth Schedule) and by giving primary importance to *Sanskrit* in this respect [*Article 351*]. The Government of India has already implemented this directive by taking a number of steps for the popularisation of Hindi amongst the non-Hindi speaking people, particularly its own employees.[5] But not enough has been done for the promotion of Sanskrit so as "to secure the enrichment of Hindi *by drawing on Sanskrit*", which the state is enjoined to do, by Article 351. The views of the Author regarding importance of Sanskrit have been supported by the Supreme Court.[6] The court has clearly spelt out that in view of the importance of Sanskrit for

5. *India,* 1984, pp 69ff.
6. *Santosh Kumar v Secretary,* AIR 1995 SC 293 : (1994) 6 SCC 579.

nurturing our cultural heritage it is necessary to include it as an elective subject at the secondary school level. The Education Minister of the Charan Singh Government promised to set up a Sanskrit Academy, but that Government did not survive to implement it.[7]

On the other hand, an Urdu Academy has been set up in West Bengal, at Government expense, on 27 October 1979. There cannot be any objection from any enlightened man to any effort for the promotion of any Indian language, at least any of those specified in the Eighth Schedule. But there is a Constitutional aspect which does not appear to have been duly considered by the authorities. If the newspaper reports be correct, one of the objectives of this Academy is to translate religious scriptures like the Quoran, at the expense of the Academy.[8] If the resources of the Academy be the public revenues, raised by taxation, any appropriation of such resources for the promotion or maintenance of any "particular religion" shall be hit by Article 27. The reason behind Article 27 is that India is a "Secular State" where all religions are on a status of equality so far as the State is concerned. If the contrary be permissible some other State Government may set up a language Academy for the translation and dissemination of the scriptures of the Hindus like the Vedas, Bhagavad-Gita, while another Government may take up the translation and propagation of the Bible and so on, resulting in conflicts between the different religions under the auspices of the state.

If the State really wants to promote the languages at Government expenses, the only constitutional way would be to set up an Academy of languages, embracing *all* the languages in the Eighth Schedule, so that Sanskrit, Urdu, Bengali, etc., would have an equal treatment, and all religious activities should be excluded from the programme of such an Academy, because there being numerous religions in India, there is a likelihood of some religion being excluded in the venture, leading to a violation of Article 27.[9]

As regards research into the Sanskrit language for enriching the vocabulary of Hindi [*Article 351*], a branch should be opened specifically for this purpose and, if any activities are already being undertaken, they should be speeded up and the glossaries produced should be available to the people at a low cost. The extension of such an organisation itself will provide employment to Sanskrit scholars and thus provide incentive to the otherwise unprofitable study of Sanskrit.

---

7. An organisation called *Rashtriya Sanskrit Sansthan* has been set up at New Delhi, but its efforts are primarily directed towards the promotion of the study of Sanskrit at the higher level [*India*, 1987, p 91]. Unless Sanskrit is made a compulsory subject at the root, none would be available in the next generation to carry on post-Graduate study in Sanskrit. The Sansthan should also be transformed into a Sanskrit Academy, with power to translate Sanskrit scriptures and literary works, just as the Urdu Academy established by the LF Government in West Bengal, has.

   In should never be forgotten that Sanskrit is the base of Indian "heritage and culture" which the Constitution seeks to ensure [*Articles* 51A(f); and 351]. Anything added to it has taken place after the Sanskritic culture had prevailed over this land for some 3000 or 4000 years.
8. Such objective will not be covered by Article 350A, noted under head B.
9. See, further, Author's *Commentary on the Constitution of India*, 6th Edn, vol D, pp 220–21.

B. For the protection of the *other* languages in use, the following directives are provided —

(i) For the submission of representation for the redress of any grievance to any officer or authority of the Union or a state, the petitioner is authorised to use any of the languages used in the Union or in the state, as the case may be [*Article 350*]. In other words, a representation *cannot* be rejected on the ground that it is not in Hindi.

(ii) Every state and other local authority within a state is directed to provide adequate facilities for instruction in the *mother-tongue* at the preliminary stage of education to children belonging to linguistic minority groups and the President is authorised to issue such directions to any state as he may consider necessary for the securing of such facilities [*Article 350A*].

(iii) A Special Officer for linguistic minorities shall be appointed by the President to investigate all matters relating to the safeguards provided by the Constitution for linguistic minorities and to report to the President upon those matters. It shall be the duty of the President to cause all such reports to be laid before each House of Parliament and also to be sent to the Government of the State concerned [*Article 350B*].

The Constitution Bench of the Supreme Court has held that "State has no power under Article 350A of the Constitution to compel the linguistic minorities to choose their mother tongue only as a medium of instruction in primary schools."[10] It was held that the imposition of mother tongue affects the fundamental rights under Articles 19, 29 and 30 of the Constitution.

10. *State of Karnataka v Associated Management of (Govt Recognised-Unaided-English Medium) Primary and Secondary Schools,* AIR 2014 SC 2094 : (2014) 9 SCC 485.

CHAPTER 34

HOW THE CONSTITUTION HAS WORKED[1]

1. Constitutional Amendments and Interpretation of Constitutional Provisions.

ONE who has to study the Indian Constitution today may come to grief if he has in his hand only a text of the Constitution as it was promulgated in November 1949, for, momentous changes have since been introduced not only by numerous Amendment Acts but by scores of judicial decisions emanating from the highest tribunal of the land. Nearly every provision of the original Constitution has acquired a gloss either from formal amendment or from judicial interpretation, and an account of the working of the Constitution, over and above this, would in itself be a formidable one.

1a. Constitution—a Living Instrument.

The Constitution of India is a living instrument, with capabilities of enormous dynamism made for a progressive society. Working of such a Constitution depends upon the prevalent atmosphere and conditions. It is wise to remember the words of Dr B R Ambedkar in the Constituent Assembly on 25 November 1949 about working of the Constitution:

> I shall not therefore enter into the merits of the Constitution. Because I feel, however good a Constitution may be, it is sure to turn out bad because those who are called to work it, happen to be a bad lot. However bad a Constitution may be, it may turn out to be good if those who are called to work it, happen to be a good lot. The working of a Constitution does not depend wholly upon the nature of the Constitution. The Constitution can provide only the organs of State such as the Legislature, the Executive and the Judiciary. The factors on which the working of those organs of the State depend on the people and the political parties they will set up as their instruments to carry out their wishes and their politics. Who can say how the people of India and their parties will behave ? Will they uphold constitutional methods of achieving their purposes or will they prefer revolutionary methods of achieving them ? If they adopt the revolutionary methods; however good the Constitution may be, it requires no prophet to say that it will fail. It is, therefore, futile to pass any judgement upon the Constitution without reference to the part which the people and their parties are likely to play.

This sentiment was echoed in the equally memorable words of Dr Rajendra Prasad on 26 November 1949:

> Whatever the Constitution may or may not provide, the welfare of the country will depend upon the way in which the country is administered. That will depend

1. The views expressed herein are of the Author(s) and the Publisher does not necessarily subscribe to these view.

> upon the men who administer it. It is a trite saying that a country can have only the Government it deserves. Our Constitution has provisions in it which appear to some to be objectionable from one point or another. We must admit that the defects are inherent in the situation in the country and the people at large. If the people who are elected are capable and men of character and integrity, they would be able to make the best even of a defective Constitution. If they are lacking in these, the Constitution cannot help the country. After all a Constitution like a machine is a lifeless thing. It acquires life because of the men who control it and operate it, and India needs today nothing more than a set of honest men who will have the interest of the country before them.

The democratic values survive and become successful where the people at large and the persons-in-charge of the institution are strictly guided by the constitutional parameters without paving the path of deviancy and reflecting in action the primary concern to maintain institutional integrity and the requisite constitutional restraints.[2]

1b. Constitutional Amendments.

At the first instance, the passing of 106 Amendment Acts (see Table IV, *post*) in a period of 78 years can hardly be passed over unnoticed. In the *American* Constitution, the process of formal amendment prescribed by the Constitution to changes in social conditions has fallen into the hands of the judiciary even though it ostensibly exercises the function only of interpreting the Constitution. Instead of leaving the matter to the slow machinery of judicial interpretation, *our* Constitution has vested the power in the people's representatives and, though the final power of *interpretation* of the Constitution as it stands at any moment belongs to the *courts,* the power of changing the instrument itself has been given to Parliament (with or without ratification by the State Legislatures) and, if Parliament, acting as the constituent body, considers that the interests of the country so require, it can amend the Constitution as often as it likes. The ease with which these amendments have been enacted demonstrates that our Constitution contains the potentiality of peacefully adopting changes some of which would be considered as revolutionary in other countries.

The real question involved in this context is whether it is the judiciary or a constituent body which should be entrusted with this task of introducing changes in order to keep pace with the exigencies of national and social progress. For reasons good or bad, the framers of our Constitution preferred the legislature as the machinery for introducing changes into the Constitution, but the need for change is acknowledged even in countries like the *USA* where the task has been assumed by the Judiciary, taking advantage of the fact that the amending machinery provided in the Constitution was too heavy and unwieldy for practical purposes.

A little reflection will show that some of these changes, the need for which must be admitted even by critics, could not have been introduced by the courts, by the application of the canons of statutory interpretation which are firmly embedded in our courts. An instance to the point is the insertion of the word "reasonable" to qualify the word "restrictions" in clause (2) of Article 19 (by the First Amendment). Without such a qualification, the engine of judicial review

---

2. See *Manoj Narula v UOI,* (2014) 9 SCC 1 : (2014) 9 Scale 600 : 2015 (2) ALD 84 (SC).

would have been altogether excluded from the field of legislative encroachment upon the freedom of expression, for, it was not open to any court, unless it was determined to do violence to the canons of interpretation, to supply the word "reasonable" which had been inserted by the makers of the Constitution in all other clauses of the Article but omitted from clause (2). The Seventh Amendment, again, was necessary to provide for the territorial reorganisation of the country which could not be made by the makers of the Constitution, before promulgating it in 1949. Similarly, the 10th, 12th, 13th, 14th, 35th, and 36th, and many other Amendments have been necessitated by the acquisition of new territories or the upliftment of the political status of existing territories, which are obviously for the benefit of the nation.

At the same time, one cannot help observing that so frequent and multifarious amendments of the Constitution, some of which might have been avoided or consolidated, have undermined the sanctity of the Constitution as an organic instrument.

Special mention should, however, be made of the 42nd Amendment Act, 1976, by which Congress Government, taking advantage of its monolithic control over the Union as well as the State Legislatures, effected comprehensive changes in the Constitution, overturning some of its bedrocks.[3] So widespread and drastic was the impact of this Amendment Act that it would be proper to call it an Act for "revision", rather than "amendment" of the Constitution.

As a result of popular resentment against such drastic changes, the Janata Party was voted to power at the general election which was held as a result of dissolution of the Lok Sabha at the instance of Mrs Gandhi early in 1977. After several reverses, owing to their lacking a two-third majority in the Rajya Sabha, the Janata Government succeeded in enacting the 43rd and 44th Amendment Acts (1977, 1978), which wiped out many of the new provisions introduced by the 42nd Amendment Act, restoring the pre-1976 text of the Constitution, on many points. But the total elimination of the right to *property* from the part on Fundamental Rights is an additional contribution of the Janata Government.

1c. A Case for Revision of the Constitution, Instead of Piecemeal Amendments.

But in view of the mutilation of the Constitution, so far made by endless piecemeal amendments, inevitably resulting in confusion and inflicting injury upon the dignity and solemnity of the Constitution, an impartial observer may suggest that a Commission for the revision of the Constitution should be set up to examine, objectively, each of the existing provisions in the light of suggestions for amendment from the Government as well as the citizens and to recommend the enactment of one comprehensive Amendment Act or a revision of the Constitution itself. In a country like the United States, where the written Constitution is sanctified as the Bible of the Nation, nobody could imagine that a Government, because it commands unquestionable majority in the Legislature, should amend the Constitution as often demanded by its Departments or in the manner

3. A critical survey of the 42nd and 44th Amendments are to be found in Author's *Constitutional Law of India*, Prentice-Hall of India, 4th Edn, 1985, pp xxxix to lvi; and *Constitution Amendment Acts*.

recommended by the political committees of the party in power, as has happened in the case of the 42nd, 43rd and 44th Amendments in India.

In case the Government ever accepts the author's suggestion to revise the Constitution,[4] the further suggestion is that the Constitution should be amplified, by inserting in it provisions relating to matters on which it is silent, or it is left to conventions or the goodwill of those who are to administer those matters respectively—because in the absence of such codified provisions, much confusion has arisen not only amongst the masses who have little knowledge about the British conventions of Cabinet Government or the common law privileges of the British Parliament, but amongst the administrators themselves. Though many such instances may be found upon a thorough examination, I shall illustrate my point with reference to these two instances.

A. *Conventions:* Though the Cabinet system of government was adopted by the framers of the Indian Constitution both at the Union and state (subject to the discretionary sphere left to the state Governor) levels, the British Cabinet system is a complicated outcome of history and the sagacity of trained politicians and even then, as veteran scholars have pointed out, it is a difficult task to formulate clear-cut propositions, relating to the conventions upon which the system is founded. Naturally, in India, there has been much controversy both at the Centre and the states to what course should be taken by the President or the Governor in the matter of selecting a person to form a government in a situation where no party commands a clear majority; conversely, what action should be taken by the Constitutional Head of the state where it is alleged against a party in power that it has lost majority in the popular House of the Legislature by reason of defection or the like; whether the Constitutional Head has the power to dismiss the Prime Minister or Chief Minister, ie, the Council of Ministers collectively, and, if so, when. Though there is scope for controversy on such questions, it is not wholesome for the country if the Governors of two States or the President of the Union take divergent steps in the same or similar situation. Questions relating to the exercise of the pardoning or Ordinance-making powers have also created confusion. Even though it may not be possible to make comprehensive provisions relating to such matters or to apprehend all possible situations of doubt or controversy, it would be possible and profitable to formulate those propositions which have already been laid down by the Supreme Court or on which there has been a fair amount of consensus amongst the political parties as a result of the working of the Constitution for about 70 years.

B. *Privileges of Legislatures:* When the Constitution was drafted in 1948–49, the uncodified privileges of the British House of Commons were sanctified by the Indian Constitution, but *only as a temporary measure,* because it was not practicable, at once, to grapple with the difficult problem of codifying the mass of British precedents which constitute the foundation of privileges of Parliament in England. But almost more than six decades have passed since then, and today, even if the task of a fairly exhaustive codification may not be completed all at

4. Subsequent to the publication of this suggestion at p 361 of the 11th edition, Government of India had appointed the Sarkaria Commission, under pressure of political circumstances. The scope of this Commission, however, was a review of the Centre-State relations, ie, the *federal* provisions and not a comprehensive revision of the Constitution as suggested by the Author. Ere long, this shall have to be undertaken.

once, many of the principles have been settled by judicial decisions of the highest court and the consensus of precedents laid down by the Presiding Officers of the Houses of the Union and State Legislatures. It is not conducive to a smooth working of the Parliamentary system in this poor and developing country to have a war between the courts and the legislatures as has happened on occasions[5]—a repetition of which can be averted only by a proper solution embodied in the Constitution itself. Those who still argue in favour of a "high court of Parliament", exercising powers and privileges, such as the British House of Commons, are blinded by the initial fallacy that we have a written Constitution which *limits* the powers of all the organs of the state, including the legislatures and that the latter cannot claim any overriding power (in the name of privileges) to interfere with the jurisdictions vested in the superior courts by Articles 32 and 226 of the Constitution itself. The Constitution-amending body can no longer fight shy of facing this unfortunate and uncanny problem of which there cannot be any authoritative solution so long as the Constitution itself is not amended, to incorporate that solution which is acceptable to the special majority of the constituent body. Even if the code of privileges be not exhaustive, it is better to start with a nucleus rather than a vacuum.

2. Implementation of Directive Principles.

Of the achievements of the executive and the legislature in the working of the Constitution, one cannot fail to refer to the progress made in implementation of the Directive Principles of State Policy, which shows that the Government in power has not taken them as "pious homilies", as was apprehended by critics when they were engrafted into the Constitution. Though the implementation of these Directives falls mostly within the province of the states, the Union has offered its guidance and assistance through the Planning Commission. The Constitution of India, it should be remembered, was not intended to serve merely as a charter of government but as a means to achieve the social and economic transformation of the country peacefully and this goal has been achieved to the extent that the Government has succeeded in implementing the Directive Principles.

By the insertion of Article 31C by the Constitution (25th Amendment) Act, 1971, the Congress Government demonstrated that it was determined to implement the directives and that if the Fundamental Rights came in the way, it would not hesitate to amend even the Fundamental Rights. The Supreme Court has also adhered to this view,[6] though in its earlier decisions, it had imputed pre-eminence to the Fundamental Rights.

---

5. See Author's *Commentary on the Constitution of India,* 6th Edn, vol F, pp 248–50.
6. *Kesavananda Bharati v State of Kerala,* AIR 1973 SC 1461. The process of supplanting the Fundamental Rights by the Directive Principles, however, received a set-back at the hands of a 4:1 decision of a Constitution Bench of the Supreme Court in the much-debated case of the *Minerva Mills v UOI,* AIR 1980 SC 1789 (paras 60, 70, and 80) : (1981) SCR 1 206, as a result of which the extension of the protection of Article 31C to legislation to implement "all or any" of the Directives in Part IV, made by the 42nd Amendment of 1976, was held to be void on the ground that it disturbed the basic structure of the Constitution which rested on a balance between the Fundamental Rights and the Directives, by excluding judicial review altogether in respect of such laws. The result of this decision was that a legislation to implement only the Directive under Article 39(b)–(c) would receive the protection of Article 31C, as prior to 1976.

[Footnote No. 6 Contd.]

The greatest failure of the Government in implementing the Directives has been with respect to the enactment of a uniform civil code [*Article 44*], which we shall presently see.

In enforcing the Directive for Prohibition of consumption of intoxicants, too, some Governments are giving more importance to revenue than the "fundamental principle of governance" embodied in Article 47. That is why it has not been substantially implemented in the course of almost more than six decades. Some State Governments have gone to the extent of withdrawing it after having once imposed Prohibition.

3. Trend towards the Unitary System.

In the federal sphere, it may be stated that most of the formal and informal changes which have taken place since the commencement of the Constitution have been to strengthen Central control over the states more and more. While the federal system, by its nature, has generated state consciousness more than under the British regime, the Centre has been endeavouring more and more to assume control over the states not only by Constitutional amendment (chapter 5, *ante*) and legislation but also by setting up extra-Constitutional bodies like the Planning Commission,[7] the National Development Council,[8] and numerous Conferences. As regards the predominant position of the Planning Commission, a learned author[9] observed—

> The emergence of the Planning Commission as a super-government has disturbed the concept of the autonomy of the States. It has also impinged on the authority of the States in matters vital to its administration such as education, health and other welfare services.

The Planning Commission has now been replaced by a new institution called NITI Aayog. A Cabinet resolution was passed and the Union Government of India announced the formation of NITI Aayog on 1 January 2015.

No less momentous is the increasing dependence of the States upon the Union in the matter of finance. Not only is the financial strength of a state dependent upon the share of the taxes and grants-in-aid as may be allotted to it by the union upon the recommendations of the Finance Commission, there is a general sense of irresponsibility in financial matters in the states founded upon the assumption that the Union will ultimately come to its aid or, else, the National Plan will fail.

But, notwithstanding this unitary trend, federation has not yet proved to be a failure in India, particularly because the Supreme Court has steadfastly enforced

---

[Footnote No. 6 Contd.]

While the Indira Government had been seeking to get the decision in the *Minerva Mills* case overruled, another Division Bench [in *Sanjeev Coke Co v Bharat Coking Coal Ltd*, AIR 1983 SC 239, *para* 13 : (1983) 1 SCR 1000] came to the rescue of the Government in an indirect way, by indicting the view taken by four of the judges of the Supreme Court [Chinnappa Reddy, Venkataramaiah, Baharul Islam and Bhagwati, JJ (who had dissented in the *Minerva Mills* case)]. In the opinion of these four judges, the decision in the *Minerva Mills* case as regards Article 31C was *obiter*, ie, uncalled for by the pleadings in the case.

7. *India*, 1984, pp 231ff.
8. Chanda, *Federal Finance*, pp 279, *et seq.*
9. Chanda, *Federal Finance*, p 186.

the distribution of powers laid down in the Constitution,[10] without acknowledging any pre-eminence of the Union so as to obliterate that federal distribution, except in solitary instances so far.[11]

The trend towards greater cohesion is, in fact, an index not of the failure but of the success of the federal system of India. One of the defects of a federation, according to classical writers, is its weakness. Credit must go to India if she succeeds in attaining unitary strength upon the foundation of a federal governmental system over an unwieldy territory inhabited by heterogeneous elements with radically conflicting ideologies. The founders of *our* Constitution had realised that a federal system was the only system suitable to a country like ours, consisting of so many heterogeneous elements. But, in view of our external dangers, existing and potential, they sought to impart into the federal system the elements of adjustment by resorting to which the system might acquire the strength of a unitary system in case of external aggression or other extraordinary circumstances. That it has succeeded in attaining this objective[12] has been demonstrated by the working of our governmental system since the ominous aggression which had been set in motion by China in October 1962.

4. Separatist Forces at Work.

Unfortunate happenings in some of the States have demonstrated that strong Central control is needed in India if not only federalism but the very existence of the Union of India is to be saved from separatist forces fighting for fragmentation and aggressive provincialism, which, if undeterred, would undermine that national unity and integrity which forms the foundation-stone of the Constitution.

4a. The Sikhs.

So far as the Sikh demand[13] was concerned, it would have, if acceded to, put an end to the federal Constitution and was bound to raise similar demands from other states and minority communities,[14] leading to the break-up of India as a nation. Though Anandpur Saheb resolution,[15] which the Akalis intended to impose upon the Union by

10. See, for instance, *Atiabari Tea Co v State of Assam,* 1961 AIR SC 232 : (1961) 1 SCR 809, p *860*; *Automobile Transport v State of Rajasthan,* AIR 1962 SC 1406, p *1416* : (1963) 1 SCR 491; *S Kodar v State of Kerala,* AIR 1974 SC 2272 : (1974) 4 SCC 422.

11. Cf, *State of West Bengal v UOI,* AIR 1963 SC 1241 : (1964) 1 SCR 371: (*vide* Author's *Comparative Federalism,* Prentice-Hall of India, 1987, pp 167ff).

12. It would have been impossible to achieve this strength over-night if the unitary elements in the Constitution had not been utilised by the Union in times of peace to make the country understand that strength lay in greater cohesion and unity. The Author is therefore unable to agree that "the most surprising thing about Indian politics during the last ten years is that, while keeping intact the formal legal relations, the distribution of functions, powers and finances between the Union and the States has been altered to an extent that was *not at all contemplated by the Constituent Assembly*" (Santhanam, Union-State Relations, 1960, vii).

13. An elaborate treatment of this topic is to be found in Author's *Constitutional Aspects of Sikh Separatism,* Prentice-Hall of India, 1985. [Reference in the following footnotes is to pages of this booklet].

14. Many Opposition Parties joined with the Akalis to form the "*Opposition Conclave*", DD Basu, *Constitutional Aspects of Sikh Separatism,* Prentice-Hall of India, 1985, p 6.

15. A resolution adopted by the Akalis at the Anandpur Gurudwara on 16 October 1973 and ratified by the All India Akali Sammelan in October 1978, at Ludhiana [*Vide* D D Basu, *Constitutional Aspects of Sikh Separatism,* Prentice-Hall of India, 1985, pp 2ff].

force[16] did not itself speak of secession from the Union or to start an independent State of Khalisthan that was at the back of the movement, as evidenced by extraneous evidence.[17] Apart from that, the demand that, after the formation of a compact state with adjoining Sikh majority territories, the Union would have jurisdiction over that state only with respect to five subjects, *viz.,* Defence, External Affairs, Posts and Telegraphs, Currency and Railway, put their case even higher than that of the erstwhile State of Jammu & Kashmir. The Anandpur Saheb resolution would have ousted the jurisdiction of the Union over the entire Concurrent List, and a substantial portion of the Union List, eg, those relating to communications other than Railways, Posts and Telegraphs, Banking, Insurance, Public Debt of the Union, Reserve Bank of India, Trade and Commerce with foreign countries, regulation of national industries, inter-State waterways, institutions of higher education, Elections to Parliament, Supreme Court and High Courts, Union taxation, and the like. The Akalis could not claim inspiration from the instance of Jammu & Kashmir, because while the latter had a history of its own, with international implications, Punjab had all along been an integral Province of India and, further, the Akalis did not constitute the entire Sikh population of Punjab,—the other Sikhs did not support the Akali demand; nay, they failed to win over the Sikh President of India or even the Sikh Chief Minister of the State of Punjab. On the other hand, within the Akali party, sprang up several leaders and in May 1985, the leaders gave way to terrorists, led by the father of the Khalistan demand, Sant Bhindranwale.[18]

Subsequent to the preceding events in July 1985 (after the accession of Sri Rajiv Gandhi as Prime Minister), a momentous event took place, namely, that an agreement (called the "Punjab Accord")[19] was entered into between the Prime Minister of India and Sant Longowal—the head of the predominant group amongst the Akalis. According to this Accord, *inter alia,* the Anandpur Resolution was to be referred to the Sarkaria Commission and some Hindi-speaking areas of Punjab were to be transferred to Haryana in lieu of Chandigarh which would come over to Punjab from Haryana.

---

16. Raising a volunteer force of One lakh at the first instance [*Statesman,* 14 March 1983] and a "*suicide squad*", D D Basu, *Constitutional Aspects of Sikh Separatism,* Prentice-Hall of India, 1985, pp 15–16.
17. It is not correct to say that the agitation for "Khalistan" is the work of a group of terrorists. The steps in which it has advanced from Akali organisations cannot be overlooked; 54th All-India Educational Conference of the Chief Khalsa Dewan—asserting that the Sikhs were a *separate* Nation and should also be admitted to the UN as a member—"Khalistan" [18 March 1981]; Reiterated by the Shiromani Gurudwara Prabandhak Committee [*Times of India,* 30 August 1981]; Anandpur Sahib Resolution; as presented by the Akali Dal (Talwandi) at the World Sikh Convention [April 1981],—asserting that the Sikhs are a separate Nation and that this status of the Sikh Nation has been recognised by the major Powers of the World; letter written by the Akali Leader Bhindrawale to Jagjit Singh, the "Khalistan" leader in London [*Statesman,* 6 January 1983]; Sant Longowal's thesis that Sikhs are a "separate race" [*Statesman,* 16 June 1983]; harbouring extremist leaders and criminals [*Statesman,* 20 June 1983, p 7; D D Basu, *Constitutional Aspects of Sikh Separatism,* Prentice-Hall of India, 1985,, pp 1, 15–18].
18. *Ananda Bazar Patrika,* 18 May 1985.
19. *Statesman,* 25 July 1985.

The Punjab Accord, however, failed to make any settlement of the Punjab problem (upto July 1992) for the following reasons—

(a) The Chief Minister (Surjeet Singh Barnala) failed to submit the State Government's case to the Sarkaria Commission.

(b) The Commission appointed to find out the Hindi-speaking areas of Punjab which were to be given over to Haryana in lieu of Chandigarh failed to complete its work owing to repeated objections of various sorts being raised by the Punjab Government.

(c) The Mann Group, elected to Parliament in November, 1989, raised new demands every day thus deferring any amicable settlement with the National Front Government which was ready for a talk.

(d) Terrorism was continuing unabated and each morning's newspaper reports some dozen murders, bank loot, and the like.[20]

In deference to the opposition to any further extension of President's Rule (which had been imposed in 1987), election was held in Punjab in February, 1992, at which Congress (I) formed Government with Mr Beant Singh as the Chief Minister.

4b. The Assamese.

The case of the agitators in Assam is peculiar. They did not demand secession, but they wanted "Assam for Assamese".[21] Though at the beginning, their demand was mystified by the intervention of political parties, the massacre of hundreds of Bengalis—Hindus and Muslims—developments since January, 1983 leave no doubt that the agitators were determined to purge Assam of all people who were not of Assamese origin. These non-Assamese, however, consist of different categories:

In so far as the *citizens* of other States, such as West Bengal or Bihar, are concerned, who have settled in Assam for purposes of profession or business, the agitators must remember that these citizens of India have a fundamental right to reside and settle in "any part of the territory of India", under Article 19(1)(e). To oust them from the State of Assam by violence would be to give a decent burial to the Constitution, and if Assam is allowed to succeed, other States would most likely follow, breaking federal India into pieces.

---

20. Cf, *Statesman,* 15 April 1987. [The Chief Minister thinks that it may be abated by the Government of India releasing the army deserters and mutineers who are detained in the Jodhpur Jail, as demanded by the AISSF (*Statesman,* 14 March 1987). It is impossible for any Government to give a blanket amnesty to mutineers if mutiny in place of discipline is to be prevented from being the order of the day, in the ranks of those who are entrusted with the defence of the State. To meet the demand halfway, Government of India has announced its decision to review the cases of these detainees *individually.* It does not appear, however, that anybody has given the assurance that the released mutineers or deserters will not swell the ranks of terrorists.]

21. The present agitation, in fact, is not a new movement, but is a logical sequel of the "*Bangal Khedao*" movement which started as a language drive, some three decades ago. It would be an eye-opener to many people in other parts of India, that one group of the agitators calls its movement as "the 18th war of *independence*", to carve out a separate homeland for the Assamese who belong to the Mongolian stock, with a separate flag [*Time,* 7 March 1983].

The first task of the Government and the agitators should, therefore, be to identify these "citizens of India", *i.e.,* those who have acquired citizenship of India under Article 5 or 6 of the Constitution or under the provisions of the Citizenship Act, 1955. These people are not "foreign nationals". They can be found out only through some peaceful machinery and not force.[22–23]

4c. The Bangladeshi Infiltration. Not only the security of India but the entire social and political structure of India has been threatened by the mass infiltration of Bangladeshis into the border States of Assam and West Bengal.

The question involved is not communal but legal, namely that of sovereignty. No independent state, other than India, would welcome infiltrators from another state. As early as 1964–65, cases brought before the Calcutta high court clearly demonstrated that large number of immigrants had overstayed after expiry of their visas, with the support of their kinsmen or friends in the bordering districts of West Bengal. In pursuance of the judgments passed in these cases, the police pushed back many of these immigrants into Bangladesh, but the operation was stalled by the utterance of a Chief Minister of Bengal that he himself was neither a Hindu nor a Muslim, and that he would view the problem of illegal immigration or infiltration as a *humanitarian* problem caused by a shortage of food or employment in Bangladesh.[24]

The Government of India also shut their eyes to the problem even when some leaders in Bangladesh threatened to conduct a "long march" of Pakistani nationals through India or even when the infiltrants demanded Indian citizenship at a mammoth gathering at the Calcutta Press Club under the nose of the police.[25] They were roused to their senses only when the infiltrators reached the capital city of Delhi (as did Bahadur Shah Zafar), and when they are demanding Indian citizenship on the strength of their ration cards and entries in

22. Good sense has prevailed with the agitators to realise this [*Statesman,* 23 March 1983, p 1]. But though the Tribunals set up for this purpose [*Statesman,* 7 June 1983] has done substantial work by May 1987, there has been a stalemate in finalising the decisions of the Tribunal owing to a controversy on principles.

23. On 16 August 1985, the Government signed an agreement with Assam leaders as a result of which elections were conducted, leading to the Assam Gana Parishad taking up administration of the State. Subsequently the ULFA (United Liberation Front of Assam) started a reign of terror by murdering non-Assamese and extorting money from them. It reached a point where people left as if there was no government in Assam. Consequently, President's Rule was declared on 28 November 1990, after dismissing the Assam Gana Parishad Government headed by Mahanta owing to its failure to combat terrorism.

    An election was held in 1992 leading to a Congress (I) Government under Hiteswar Saikia as the Chief Minister. He is still struggling against the ULFA and Bodo militants.

24. Critics say that the illegal immigrants have been entertained by the parties in power by granting them ration cards and eventually entering their names in the electoral roll [*Cf, Ali Ahmad v Electoral Registration Officer*, AIR 1965 Cal 1, paras 1, 6], in order to gain their votes.

25. *Statesman,* 13 February 1991; *Anandabazar,* 15 February 1991.

the electoral roll,[26] and forming Muslim pockets[27] which would lead to a demand for their autonomy.

It is a pity that the same Central Government who had earlier overlooked the illegal immigration as a human problem later held it to be a serious threat to the integrity of India[27] at a conference of Chief Ministers called by the Centre, and the same party in West Bengal which had so long prized the votes of the infiltrators,[27] made a clean breast of the *modus operandi* adopted and the seriousness of the problems created by them.[27]

Apart from anything else, infiltration has thus come to operate as a divisive force threatening the integrity of India, which can be rooted only by firmly carrying out a plan of action after realising the gravity of the situation, instead of using the illegal infiltrants as pawns in the game of vote-hunting.

4d. Language as a Separatist Force. Another such division factor is that the people having a separate language must have a separate political status and autonomy. The initial blunder of the Government in this behalf was committed when the states were reorganised on a primarily linguistic basis and that current is still unimpeded, thus raising the original number of states in Parts A–B (18) to 28 and the scramble for *Gorkhaland, Bodoland, Jharkhand, Uttarakhand* and the like is continuing at different levels[28]

26. If they succeed in this plan, they will simply fulfil their pledge to "recover Hindusthan by a joke" (*larke lia Pakistan, larke lenge Hindusthan*), which was their slogan at the time of the Referendum held in 1947 in Sylhet.

27. *Anandabazar,* 8 August 1992; *Statesman,* 15 February 1991; 2 August 1991.

28. The secessionist nature of the *Gorkhaland* agitation is veiled and equivocal and not so patent as in the case of that for *Khalistan,* and that is why the Government of India was initially misled to assume that the *Gorkhaland* agitation was not anti-national, until the Government of West Bengal came out with a well-documented White Paper (in two Parts) which gives written evidence of what the GNLF (Gorkha National Liberation Front) means, according to its "President" Ghising.

The *Gorkhaland* agitation relates to the West Bengal District of Darjeeling where a large number of Nepalis reside as immigrants (for work), under a reciprocal treaty of friendship between India and Nepal of 1950. The GNLF claim that Darjeeling was a part of Nepal and came to the British Government by way of cession from Nepal is, however, not correct because the territory of Darjeeling belonged to Sikkim and Bhutan and the British acquired the territory by grant, agreement or annexation of which the other party was not Nepal but Sikkim or Bhutan, during the 19th century. Nepal entered into the 1950 Agreement with India, because the immigrants to Darjeeling were people of Nepali origin (*Gorkhas*) whereas many Indians were similarly residing in Nepal, so that "reciprocal rights and privileges" were to interest to both Nepal and India.

The agitation for Gorkhaland took a concrete shape by the submission of a Memorandum by the GNLF leader to the King of Nepal on 23 December 1983 (Appendix A to the WP, Part I). This contained clearly a demand for creating a separate State for the Gorkhas in the territory of Darjeeling, which the Memorandum claimed to be a ceded territory of Nepal. The appeal was to the King of Nepal to revoke all treaties and agreements which might stand in the way of severing Gorkhaland from India. It also spoke of the "right of *self-determination*" of the Gorkhas and copies of this Memorandum were simultaneously sent to the heads of foreign States, such as the USA, France, Pakistan, Britain, the United Nations besides India. There was *not a word* in this Memorandum as to Gorkhaland being created as a separate State *within* the Union of India. The birth of the Gorkhaland movement was thus clearly for *secession* from India.

[Footnote No. 28 Contd.]

[Jharkhand and Uttaranchal (Uttarakhand) have been created as new states by carving their territories out of the territories of the Bihar and the Uttar Pradesh in 2000. Besides Chhattisgarh, as a new state, has been created by carving it out of the territory of Madhya Pradesh in 2000. (see Table III)]. To concede any form of separate status, such as the formation of a Union Territory, ultimately leads to the demand for full-fledged Statehood.

A formidable corollary from the linguistic demand is the struggle for getting one's language included in the Eighth Schedule of the Constitution. Obviously, there is little material gain from such inclusion. The only two relevant provisions of the Constitution are Articles 344(1) and 351. The former gives the people representing a language specified in the Eighth Schedule to have a member in the Official Language Commission and the latter gives that language to be considered for contribution towards the development of the Hindi language. The real motive behind the struggle for inclusion of a particular language, therefore, is *political,* namely, to lay the corner-stone for demanding a separate political entity for the people speaking that language, as in the case of Gorkhaland.[30] Be that as it may, the demand for every language to be included in the Eighth Schedule is wild because there are as many as 1652 languages in India. Hence, there must be standard according to which the status of the Eighth Schedule may be conferred on a language. Unfortunately, there is no such standard laid down in the Constitution itself and that is opening an avenue for diverse factions to raise demands which, if conceded, would lead to a suicidal fragmentation of the Union. Outside the Constitution, of course, there is an understanding that only languages which are spoken by over one lakh of people are entitled to enter into the Eighth Schedule. But this understanding is too feeble to resist indiscriminate claims from any faction which may gather force enough to intimidate the Government.

[Footnote No. 28 Contd.]

As Appendix B to the WP (Part I) shows, on 2 June 1985, the GNLF leader made a speech wherein he admitted that the Government of Nepal or the UN had not responded to his claim for a separate sovereign State. This speech was, in fact, made after the Government of India, realising its initial blunder, told the GNLF leader that there would be no talk with him until he gave up his claim for a sovereign State outside India. In para 2 of this speech, therefore, the leader says that "we do not want to get separated from India.....but have demanded.....separate State within Indian Union". Curiously, however, in the succeeding paragraphs, he reiterated his story that Darjeeling came to the British by way of cession from Nepal, and in the concluding paragraph he clearly urged for a "separate sovereign" State, just as other small countries had been recognised as separate States by the UN.

The Author had, in a previous edition suggested that if the Government of India does not create a separate State it would have to offer regional autonomy after its terms were settled by a tripartite talk between India, West Bengal and Gorkha leaders. This has come to be true. In July 1988, an agreement was signed creating a Darjeeling Gorkha Hill Council, followed by election in pursuance thereof, and Subhas Ghising was elected Chairman of the Council.

Later, the Gorkhaland Territorial Administration ('GTA') was formed in 2012 to replace the Darjeeling Gorkha Hill Council. GTA presently consists of three hill subdivisions Darjeeling, Kurseong, Mirik, some areas of Siliguri subdivision of Darjeeling district and the whole of Kalimpong district under its authority.

It is lamentable that notwithstanding the foregoing warning offered by the Author in the 13th Edition of his *Introduction to the Constitution of India,* Government of India failed to amend the Constitution to lay down any definite standard for inclusion in the Eighth Schedule and, instead, they have been obliged to amend the Eighth Schedule itself[29] to include three new languages, *viz., Konkani, Manipuri* and *Nepali and further by 92nd Amendment Act, 2003 new languages like Bodo, Dogri, Maithili and Santhali were included* because for the time being, their demand became irresistible.

5. Judicial Review. The most remarkable achievement in post-Constitution India is the exercise of the power of judicial review by the superior courts. So long as this power is wielded by the courts effectively and fearlessly, democracy will remain ensured in India and, with all its shortcomings, the Constitution will survive. The numerous applications for the Constitutional writs before the high courts and the Supreme Court and their results testify to the establishment in India of "limited Government", or, "the Government of laws, not of men", as they call it in the United States of America. The Supreme Court has well performed its task of protecting the rights of the individual against the Executive, against oppressive legislation and even against the legislature itself, when it becomes over-zealous in asserting its privileges not only against the individual but even against the judges.[30]

At the same time, it should be observed that neither the guarantee of Fundamental Rights nor its adjunct—Judicial Review—could have full play during the first quarter of a century of the working of *our* Constitution owing to their erosion by Proclamations of Emergency over a substantial period of time.

The period of 15 years, when Articles 14, 19, 21 and 22 remained suspended owing to the operation of Article 358 and of orders under Article 359, can hardly be overlooked. It is true that the emergency provisions are as much a part of the Constitution of India as any other, and that history has proved the need for such powers to meet extraordinary situations, but, broadly speaking, if the application of the emergency provisions overshadows the other features of the Constitution, the balance between the "normal" and the "emergency" provisions is palpably destroyed. Of course, the Janata Government has hemmed in the emergency provisions in Articles 352 and 356, by giving a larger control to Parliament over the exercise of such power, under the 44th Amendment Act, 1978. Nevertheless, even apart from emergency, there has been an astounding erosion of Fundamental Rights owing to multiple amendments of the Constitution.

As I pointed out in the previous editions, the means to prevent any such conflict between competing interests is to process all proposals for constitutional amendment through an expert and objective machinery, which would ensure the progressive adaptation of the Constitution to the copernican changes in the social, economic and political background, apart from the views of the political

---

29. By the Constitution (71st Amendment) Act, 1992 [see Table XIX, *post*].
30. *Cf, Reference under Article 143,* AIR 1965 SC 745.

supporters of the party in power and the bureaucrats.[31] This purpose would not be served by Sarkaria Commission, which was confined to "Centre-State Relations".

It can be served only by setting up a Commission for the comprehensive revision of the Constitution which has also been mutilated by multiple amendments during more than half century of its working, as mentioned at the outset of this chapter. Any piecemeal reference to the existing Law Commission, with respect to particular provisions of the Constitution will only aggravate the anomaly.

5a. Role of Judiciary.

Even though the power of formal amendment has been conferred upon Parliament by Article 368 of the Constitution and the scope of resorting to the Judiciary to introduce changes has been reduced by making the process of amendment easier than in the USA, the working of *our* Constitution has opened the avenue for judicial review in India in nearly the same way as in the USA.

Paradoxically, the urge for judicial intervention has arisen from the very tendency of the legislature to make frequent amendments to the Constitution, which were eating into the vitals of the Constitution (which the Supreme Court called its "basic features"). Hence, asserted the court, it could set aside even an Act to amend the Constitution, not only on (i) a *procedural* ground, *viz.*, that the procedure laid down in Article 368 has not been complied by the relevant Bill, but on, (ii) the *substantive* ground, *viz.*, that the amending Act has violated one or other of the basic features of the Constitution.[32]

Conversely, it has come to be held that if the legislature is not prompt enough to implement the provisions of the Constitution, the court has the duty to make the changes necessary to adopt the demands of a progressive society.[33] In this mission, the court has propounded two doctrines—

(a) The court is the exclusive and final interpreter of all provisions of the Constitution.[32]

(b) The court has the duty to make the ideals enshrined in the Constitution a reality,[34] and to meet the needs of social change in a welfare society.[33]

---

31. The Author is tempted to reproduce what he said in this context more than two decades ago: "Fragmental changes ... cannot achieve the purpose where the change in the public opinion is so rapid as in India today. In fact, each step ahead in material or social advancement is enlarging the mental horizon as well as the demands of the masses. If this is to be met halfway, by way of averting anything like a revolution, an overall rethinking is necessary. . ." [Author's Tagore Law Lectures on *Limited Government and Judicial Review,* pp. 13–14].
32. *State of Rajasthan v UOI,* AIR 1977 SC 1361, p *1413* : (1978) 1 SCR 1, CB; *Minerva Mills v UOI,* AIR 1980 SC 1789 : (1981) 1 SCR 206, paras 21, 26, 93–94, 104, CB; *Kihoto Hollohan v Zachillhu,*: AIR 1993 SC 412 : (1992) 1 SCR 686, paras 18, 46, 104, CB; *SR Bommai v UOI,* AIR 1994 SC 1918 : (1994) 3 SCC 1, para 30,—nine judges; *AK Kaul v UOI,* 1995 AIR SC 1403 : (1995) 4 SCC 73, para 12.
33. *State of Karnataka v Appa Balu Ingale,* AIR 1993 SC 1126 : (1995) Supp 4 SCC 469.
34. *Ravichandran v Bhattacharjee,* (1995) 5 SCC 457 : (1995) JT 6 SC 339.

(c) This duty would extend even to the implementation of the "Directive Principles" in Part IV, which were "not enforceable by any court" according to the Constitution itself [*Article 37*].[35]

5b. Judicial Activism.

If a rose has its thorns, so must Judicial Review—the flower of Indian constitutionalism—has its thorns, as has been demonstrated by the fact that, during the last decade *our* Supreme Court has been evolving novel doctrines, such as that of "basic structure" or "basic features" or "prospective overruling" or "unenumerated" fundamental rights—the foundation for which is not apparent on the face of the Constitution. In the present context, suffice it to point out that if this trend is not curbed, it would lead to unwholesome consequences, however well-intentioned the authors of such judicial innovations might be; for instance—

(a) It would add to the confusion and uncertainty, which has been introduced by the multiple amendments made by the legislature, to the dismay not only of the general public but also of the administrators and the courts themselves, in applying the written Constitution—the very object of which is to infuse certainty and order into the political system.

(b) It would engender bitterness between the legislature and the judiciary, if either of them seeks to checkmate the other[36]—by means of amendment or judicial activism.

(c) There is no knowing how far such novel doctrines may be extended, for, the final say, in the matter, rests with the Supreme Court itself. The result would be an amendment of the Constitution by the Judiciary, while Article 368 of the Constitution specifically places the power of amendment in the legislative machinery.[37]

6. Dangerous Anti-national Trends in Minority Demands.

The present chapter would be incomplete without recounting the ominous trends which have been revealed since the General Election of 1980 as regards the ever-aggressive demands of the religious minorities—which run counter to the very foundations of the existing Constitution and which seek to ride roughshod over the pronouncements of the highest tribunal of the land—not only on the ground that they are inconsistent with the provisions of the Constitution but because they are not consonant with the separatist

---

35. *Bandhua Mukti Morcha v UOI,* AIR 1984 SC 802 (para 10) : 1984 SCR (2) 67; *State of HP v HPSRC,* (1995) 4 SCC 507 (para 17); *State of Maharashtra v Manubhai,* 1996 AIR, 1 : (1995) 5 SCC 730; *Vishal v UOI,* 1990 SCR (2) 861 : AIR 1990 SC 1412 (paras 8, 14); *Indra Sawhney v UOI,* (1990 to 1992) Supp (3) SCC 217 (paras 22-28)—Nine Judges.

36. This hoax has already raised its head under the Deve Gowda Coalition Ministry, in 1996.

37. An example of this is a direction by the Supreme Court for creation of an All-India Judicial Service. The Constitution (*Article* 312) lays down that for creation of an All-India Service, Rajya Sabha must pass a resolution with the support of two-thirds of the members present and then Parliament may provide for it by enacting a law. A directive by the Court cannot supplant a clear constitutional provision. Similarly to state that "consultation" means "concurrence" is also stretching the language to a breaking point and is nothing but amending the Constitution under the colour of interpretation [*Supreme Court Advocates v UOI,* (1993) 4 SCC 441 and *Re Special Reference No. 1 of 1998,* (1998) 7 SCC 739 (nine-Judge Bench)].

ambitions of the religious minorities. The most grievous feature of this post-Independence development is that the minorities have held up their vote as a bait and political leaders of the majority community *belonging to different parties* have indiscriminately swallowed that bait in their election manifestos and alliances, irrespective of the *ideologies* which ushered in the independence of India and which form the bed-rock of the existing Constitution. In this background, it is the duty of an impartial academician to point out to a nationalist Indian (every Indian citizen cannot be assumed to have narrow political ambitions) that to accept such anti-nationalist demands of the minorities.

Space would not permit a full treatment of all the demands hoisted by the religious minorities and for a fuller treatment, the reader should read the Author's *Commentary on the Constitution of India,* 6th Edn, volume D, pp 217–28; and 232–37, where, though published early in 1978, these dangerous minority ideologies had been anticipated. The broader propositions involved may, however, be mentioned for the consideration of the average reader:

A. The major demand of the Muslim minority community now is for a proportional representation in the legislatures and in the services, according to their number.[38]

This is, in fact, a resurrection of that baneful plant of the "communal award" which had been inserted into the Indian body politic by the British Prime Minister Ramsay MacDonald and which had its inevitable culmination in the bloody partition of India.

It is to prevent any repetition of such anti-national cleavages that the framers of the Constitution of free India proclaimed the unity of the Nation to be the objective, in its Preamble, abolishing any reservation or representation on the basis of the religious colour of any individual or community; and such reservation, if made now, would violate the guarantee of equality in Articles 15(1) and 16(1)–(2), as explained by the Supreme Court.[39–40] Of course, all these guarantees acknowledge the constitutionality of reservation or other special provisions in the interests of the "backward classes", so that any community

38. All-Indian Muslim Conference at Lucknow [*Statesman,* 29 December 1978; 11 December 1979]; See also Muslim League's demand in Kerala [*Statesman,* 27 February 1983].
39. *Nain Sukh v State of UP,* AIR 1953 SC 384, p *385* : 1953 SCR 1184; *State of Madras v Champakam Dorairajan,* 1951 AIR 226 : (1951) SCR 525, pp *530, 533*; *Triloki Nath Tiku v State of Jammu & Kashmir,* AIR 1969 SC 1 : (1969) 1 SCR 103.
40. On this point, it is worthwhile to reproduce the illuminating words of Ahmadi, J, as he then was, in the nine-Judge case of *SR Bommai v UOI,* AIR 1994 SC 1918 : (1994) 3 SCC 1—

"*The experience of partition of the country and its aftermath had taught lessons which were too fresh to be forgotten by our Constitution-makers.* It was perhaps for that reason that our founding fathers thought a strong centre was essential to ward off separatist tendencies and consolidate the *unity and integrity* of the country" (para 21).

"The British policy of divide and rule, aggravated by *separate electorates based on religion,* had added a new dimension of mixing religion with politics which had to be countered....." (para 24).

"Since it was felt that *separate electorates for minorities were responsible for communal* and separatist tendencies, the Advisory Committee resolved that the system of reservation for minorities, excluding SC/ST, *should be done away with .....*" (para 26).

See also *R C Poudyal v UOI,* AIR 1993 SC 1804 : (1993) 1 SCR 891, paras 30–33.

which is *socially or educationally* backward may be entitled to special consideration under the existing Constitution [*Article* 15(4)], irrespective of its religious complexion.

To accede to these patently anti-national demands would need multiple amendments of the Constitution involving a decent burial of the doctrines of equality which the Supreme Court has built up[39] during nearly more than half a century, and to re-instal the monster of communal representation[40] which was banished from this land by the fathers of the Constitution.

B. Another demand of a minority community is that the Minority Commission, set up administratively, during the Desai regime, should be given a constitutional footing and a *binding force* to its recommendations.[38]

Apart from the fact that none of the various investigatory Commissions set up by the existing Constitution has got more than recommendatory status, the broad consideration against any such drastic proposal is that, if conceded, it would mean a government by the Minority Commission, resulting in the abdication of the government by the peoples' representatives voted to power. To quote the words of Sir Samuel Hoare, who rejected the suggestion that the recommendation of the Public Service Commission should be binding on the Government (see chapter 30, *ante*)—

> The danger is that if you give them mandatory powers you then set up two governments.

Besides, what would happen if the members of the Minority Commission (which must necessarily be a collegiate body representing the various minority communities) fail to agree (as has already happened since one of the Members of an erstwhile Commission, Professor John, in a reasoned discourse, exposed the blatantly unreasonable, anti-national and anti-majority views and outlook of some of his colleagues)?[41] When the Commission is divided, it is obvious that Government must have the discretion to find out which of its views is consonant with reason and national interests. Even when the Minority Commission speaks in one voice, it cannot claim an imperative command simply because it is *not a body responsible to the people.*

Besides, what should be the proper jurisdiction of the Minority Commission, what would happen to any recommendation of the Commission which is *ultra vires* or outside that jurisdiction and who will decide whether any of its recommendations is beyond its jurisdiction? Insurmountable confusion and chaos would result if, in spite of these considerations, binding force is given to the recommendations of the Minority Commission.

The only proper jurisdiction of any such Commission, under the existing Constitution, would be the matters included in Articles 25–30.[42]

It is to be noted that Parliament has enacted the National Commission for Minorities Act on 17 May 1992, but that its recommendations [*section* 9(1)(c),

---

41. *Statesman,* 30 November 1979 (Zakir Hussain Memorial Lecture).
42. It should be noted that so far as the linguistic interests of Minorities are concerned there is already a provision for the appointment of a Special Officer for linguistic minorities, in Article 350B.

and (2)–(3)], have *not* been given any obligatory force. The Act defines "minority" as a community notified as such by the Central Government.[43]

C. Another demand advanced on behalf of the Muslims is that the Directive in Article 44 for establishing "a uniform civil code throughout the territory of India" should not be applicable to the Muslims who should be allowed to be governed by the *Shariat* as their personal law.[44]

This demand, again, seeks to put the clock back. At the time when the Constitution was framed, all such claims were considered and rejected on the grounds that: (a) matters like marriage, inheritance and the like falling under the category of "personal law" are secular matters having no essential relation to religion;[45] and that (b) without a common civil code, *inter alia,* the people of India, belonging to heterogeneous elements, could never be united into a nation. The provision in Article 44 is nothing but an implementation of the objective of "fraternity, unity and integrity of the Nation" which is not only enshrined in the Preamble to the Constitution, but is since buttressed by the Fundamental Duties in Article 51A(c), and (e) [*see* chapter 8].

It may be mentioned that when the Law Commission of India took up the question of framing a common code of marriage and divorce, not only the

---

43. Parliament has enacted on 17 May 1992, the National Commission for Minorities Act, 1992 for constituting a statutory Commission. The Act defines "minority" as a community notified as such by the Central Government.

    The functions assigned to the National Commission for Minorities are to (see section 9)—

    (a) evaluate the progress of the development of minorities under the Union and States;

    (b) monitor the working of the safeguards provided in the Constitution and in laws enacted by Parliament and the State Legislatures;

    (c) make recommendations for the effective implementation of the safeguards for the protection of the interests of minorities by the Central Government or the State Governments;

    (d) look into specific complaints regarding deprivation of rights and safeguards of the minorities and take up such matters with the appropriate authorities;

    (e) cause studies to be undertaken into problems arising out of any discrimination against minorities and recommend measures for their removal;

    (f) conduct studies, research and analysis on the issues relating to socio-economic and educational development of minorities;

    (g) suggest appropriate measures in respect of any minority to be undertaken by the Central Government or the State Governments;

    (h) make periodical or special reports to the Central Government on any matter pertaining to minorities and in particular difficulties confronted by them; and

    (i) any other matter which may be referred to it by the Central Government.

    For the full text of this Act, see Author's *Human Rights in Constitutional Law, App I.*

44. The *Jamiat-ulama-i-Hind* goes to the extent of urging for the deletion of Article 44 [*Statesman,* dated 2 October 1979, p 3] or to exempt Muslims from its operation [*Statesman,* 8 April 1985].

45. This view has been supported by many Muslim Judges and scholars who possess special knowledge about the Shariat [see Author's *Commentary on the Constitution of India,* 6th (Silver Jubilee) Edn, vol D, pp 222–23].

Muslims but the Christians too opposed the move and that the very government which had induced the Hindus to give up their scriptural laws relating to these matters, gave way to the minority resistance, for "political" reasons. Now that Article 51A has been embodied in the Constitution, a constitutional lawyer might urge that any opposition to Article 44 by any member of any minority community would be a violation of Article 51A, and any Government which yields thereto would be a party to such violation of the Constitution.[46]

It is curious that while polygamy has been either abolished or controlled by Islamic States like Turkey and Bangladesh and is discouraged even in Pakistan, Indian Muslims are pressing to uphold it as their religious right, founded on the *Shariat*[47] and eventually protected as a fundamental right, by the Constitution of India.[48]

---

46. If Government yields to this demand of the Muslim now, could it resist a similar demand of the Christians and the nascent demand of the Akali leader that there should be a separate code of personal laws for the Sikhs [*Statesman,* 16 June 1983]. For similar demand for Christian converts; which has been turned down by the Supreme Court, see *Soosai v UOI,* AIR 1986 SC 733 : (1985) 3 SCR Supl 242, para 8.

47. *Ananda Bazar Patrika,* dated 5 February 1982.

48. A Muslim divorced wife brought an application for maintenance under section 125 of the Criminal Procedure Code, which was decreed. The husband appealed to the Supreme Court on the ground that section 125 should not apply to Muslims as it is contrary to Muslim personal law. The Supreme Court rejected this contention upon the interpretation of section 125, namely, that it applied to all "persons", irrespective of their religion or personal law, and dismissed the husband's appeal.

In the judgment [*Mohd Ahmed Khan v Shah Bano,* AIR 1985 SC 945 : 1985 SCR (3) 844,para 32], the Supreme Court observed that it was a pity that the State had not made any attempt to make a common Civil Code even though Article 44 issued a clear mandate on the State in this behalf,—whether the lead came from the Muslim community or not:

"*A belief seems to have gained ground* that it is for the Muslim community to take a lead in the matter of reforms of their personal law. A common Civil Code will help the cause of national integration by removing disparate loyalties to laws which have conflicting ideologies . . . *It is the State which is charged with the duty of securing* a uniform Civil Code for the citizens of the country. . ."

The Supreme Court repeated its views on Article 44 in *Jorden v Chopra,* AIR 1985 SC 935 : (1985) 1 SCR Supl 704, para 1.

As a learned Professor of the Bombay University, Professor Siddiqui, observed, if the State took the lead, ultimately the Muslim community would accept it because it was in accord with the notions of modern civilised society.

"The issue should not be decided in terms of textual conformity with the Koran but in the context of *modern civilised society.* And then even if the law goes against the Koran, the Government must enact it. Ultimately, the community will accept it" [*Sunday Observer,* 6 May 1984].

Overriding the clear observations of the Supreme Court and rejecting the protests of a large section of the Muslim community, including learned scholars, however, the Congress(I) Government enacted the Muslim Women (Protection of Rights on Divorce) Act, 1966, providing that the statutory provisions contained in this Act should govern, unless the divorced woman and her former husband apply to the court that they would prefer to be governed by the provisions of section 125, the Code of Criminal Procedure, 1973, as to the right of maintenance of the divorced wife.

[Footnote No. 48 Contd.]

As against this, the Government of India, in 1986, undertook legislation[48] to supersede the law declared by the Supreme Court in *Shah Bano's* case[49] and deprived the Muslim women of the rights that they enjoyed in common with all other women. Such legislation retards the unity of the Nation as envisaged in the Preamble to the Constitution and at the same time, relegated India to a backward status even in the progressive Muslim world.

D. Once one particular community is permitted to urge anti-national demands, it is natural that *other* minority communities will start clamouring for other privileges which might serve their own sectional interests.

The advocates of guaranteeing further minority rights in India, supplanting the existing Constitution, if necessary, pretend to overlook the following broad considerations which distinguish the status of minorities in India from the international problem of minorities in post-War Europe which have inspired the International movement for minority safeguards:

(a) In the international sphere, the demand for special safeguards to protect the cultural or linguistic identity of minority communities has emerged from the principle that owing to war or like circumstances causing territorial changes *without the consent* of the people residing in those territories, the identity of such communities who have been torn asunder by circumstances beyond their control should be preserved from ethnic extinction, by affording proper safeguards through international charters and national Constitutions.

The partition of India which left a portion of the Muslim community in India took place in the *opposite* way. The pre-independence demand of the Muslim community led by their acknowledged leader, Mr. Jinnah, was to have a separate homeland for the Muslims who, it was asserted, constituted a nation separate from the Hindus. The British Rulers conceded to this demand overruling the contention of the nationalist Indians that the Muslims and Hindus as well as the other people residing in India constituted one Nation and not two or more. The result of the acceptance of the two-nation theory was the lamentable partition of India and the creation of a separate Dominion, named Pakistan. As a sequel of such division, the Hindu leaders in India could have insisted upon an exchange of population between Pakistan and India, so that all the Muslims in undivided India could be transferred to Pakistan. But they did not prevent any Muslim from staying behind in India, *as an Indian.* Those who remained in India, did so *of their free will and option.* The partition was the seeking of their own community and *not the result of any circumstances beyond their control,* such as the First or Second World War which created the international minority problem in the world.

Of course, in consonance with the liberal attitude of the Hindu leaders, the framers of the Constitution of independent India embodied certain safeguards for minorities in like manner as the International Charters. But these safeguards

[Footnote No. 48 Contd.]

The Congress (I) Government thus, gave way to the Muslim fundamentalists to violate the Supreme Court decisions as well as the Constitution, which enjoined the State to make a common Civil Code, overriding any personal law to the contrary. It was more surprising that the National Front Government's Law Minister had dittoed, declaring that there would be no common Civil Code unless the Muslim community wanted it.

49. *Mohd Ahmed Khan v Shah Bano,* AIR 1985 SC 945 : (1985) 3 SCR 844 :.

were extended to all numerical minorities of all religions, languages and cultures and not to the Muslims in particular. The Muslims who opted not to go to Pakistan did so with their *eyes open* as to the safeguards they might get under the draft Constitution and not because of any covenant that they would be allowed *to demand more and more to serve their sectional interests.*

It is to be noted that the Universal Declaration did not contain any provision in respect of minorities so that the makers of the Indian Constitution had no international obligation to include in the Constitution of 1949 any special provisions to protect the minorities. Subsequent thereto, in 1966, the International Covenant on Civil and Political Rights was adopted, including Article 27[39] as follows:

> **Article 27**. In those States in which ethnic, religious or linguistic minorities exist, persons belonging to such minorities shall not be denied the right, in community with the other members of their group, to enjoy their own culture, to profess and practise their own religion, or to use their own language.

Few people appreciate that these rights were anticipated by the makers of the Indian Constitution of 1949 and guaranteed them as the fundamental rights of the minorities in Articles 25, 29, and 30.

But to urge for *political* or other rights not provided for by the Constitution, would be not only unconstitutional but anti-national, because the makers of the Constitution wanted to build up *one* Nation, namely, India, in which persons belonging to the majority and the minority would embrace themselves into a fraternity [Preamble]. To refuse to enter into the mainstream of Indian Fraternity on the plea of Muslim identity is nothing but a vestige of the two-nation theory which the fathers of the Indian Constitution sought to banish once for all as a result of their bitter experience culminating in the lamentable Partition.[40]

(b) In the International sphere, it has been emphatically made clear[50] that the only object of offering the minority safeguards was to protect the minority from discrimination by the majority who administer a country under a representative system of democracy. But this is on the condition that the minority "must be loyal to the State of which they are nationals",[50] and must not set up an "*imperium in imperio*" founded on their minority status.

The framers of the Indian Constitution, too, fondly believed that, having established a secular State (ie, a State which has no established religion of its own, and treats all religions equally) and offered safeguards for the preservation of the religious, cultural and linguistic identity of the minorities —not only Muslims, but all the minorities who remained in India as Indian citizens, would be united as one nation by the bond of "fraternity" (Preamble).

(c) I must, with profound regret, point out that there are Muslims, who are not even willing to call India their "motherland", on the ground that Bankim Chandra's *Vande Mataram,* which was adopted by the 1896-session of the Indian National Congress, seeks to deify the motherland, while any kind of imputation of personality to God smacks of idolatry, as condemned by Islam. On this point, the reader may at once refer to page 18 of *India, 1987,* where the translation of the first stanza of this song (by Sri Aurobindo) has been reproduced. To express

50. Resolution of the UN Sub-Commission on the Prevention of Discrimination and Protection of Minorities (1950).

gratitude to the soil from which you sprang and which sustains you with milk and honey every moment of your life is not idolatry, simply because it is called "mother".[51] In fact, the country of one's origin can only be described either as "fatherland" or as "motherland". Since some political leaders who are not themselves Muslims, sometimes fan communal sentiments only to gain political favours from the minority community, it would be worthwhile to reproduce relevant provisions from the Constitutions of Russia and China, both of which have a considerable Muslim population who are obliged to swear by these provisions, without demur.

Article 62 of the 1977 Constitution of the USSR says—

> Defence of the Socialist Motherland is the sacred duty of every citizen of the USSR. Betrayal of the Motherland is the gravest of crimes against the people.

The 1993-Constitution of the Russian Federation says—

> Article 59.1.—The protection of the *fatherland* is the duty and obligation of the Russian Federation.

Article 55 of the 1982-Constitution of the Chinese Republic repeats, in no less emphatic terms:

> It is the sacred duty of every citizen to defend the *motherland* and resist aggression.

It would be pertinent, in this context, to mention that the erstwhile ruling party in Turkey was named the "Motherland Party".

Any sane man must concede that what is not anti-Islamic elsewhere cannot be anti-Islamic in India simply because the Muslim vote is covetable to every party which seeks to come to power.

The reason why the song *Vande Mataram* was adopted as complementary to the National Anthem *Jana-Gana Mana* may be explained in the words of the President of the Constituent Assembly, on the 24 January 1950, which were adopted with applause:

> The composition consisting of the words and music known as Jana Gana Mana is the National Anthem of India, subject to such alterations in the words as the Government may authorise as occasion arises; and the song Vande Matram, which has played a historic part in the struggle for Indian freedom, shall be honoured equally with Jana Gana Mana and shall have equal status with it.

To resist the play of the *tune* of this song on the ground that it would impair communal harmony because it is an emblem of idolatry which is repugnant to Islam, is to forget the following facts:

(a) That it was sung in the 1896-session of the Indian National Congress, after omitting the larger part of the song which depicted the hands and limbs of the motherland (in order to obviate any objection from the Muslims) and retaining only some 20 words at the beginning of the song, for official use.

(b) That it is that trimmed composition which is printed at page 18 of India, 1988–89, as the counterpart of the National Anthem.

---

51. Of course, in some later stanzas, the motherland is described as having hands and voices, but that is nothing but a poetic way of portraying the hands and voices of all children of the soil, to whom the poet appealed for fighting for their independence, as one man. The object is not in any way different from the patriotic songs of other lands.

(c) That the tune of that clipped composition that is played in the All India Radio and the TV at the beginning of each day's programme.

(d) That whatever might be the objection to particular words used in the latter portion of the song, the same cannot be raised as an objection to the *music* representing the earlier part of the composition, except by a handful of men who have forgotten that what they could do during the days of the Muslim League cannot be done today *because of the partition of India intervening.*

(e) That this music is an emblem not of communalism but of India's freedom.

(f) To protest against it today is to turn the table up-side down, taking recourse to religious fanaticism.[52]

The Ministry of Home Affairs has issued guidelines in February 2026, wherein the Union government has directed States and other government bodies that, at events where both are performed, the national song Vande Mataram should precede the national anthem Jana Gana Mana.[53]

There is little doubt that this country, inhabited by heterogeneous elements belonging to different races and religions, can maintain her independence, only if she stands as one man, inspired by a national sentiment. Every American, whether of English, Hebrew, Italian or Negro origin, regards the United States as his motherland for which he must fight against dangers at home or abroad, and that is why she has maintained her independence as a mighty Nation, notwithstanding so much of difference in race, religion and culture amongst her variegated population. The situation in India is just to the contrary. As in other matters, in India, even constitutional and legal questions are muddled up with politics, which, of course, means *power politics.* Few leaders today think of the Nation (as did the members of the First National Congress of 1885), apart from the interests of the political parties to which they belong and through which machine they scramble their way to the seat of power. It is even risky for an impartial academician to express his conclusions derived from a non-political interpretation of the Constitution to which everybody in India must profess to swear allegiance. It is difficult to convince people engrossed in power politics that to love his motherland is the birthright of *everyone* born in this country and that it does not need to don any particular cap or to hoist the banner of any particular hue.

Those who believe that communal harmony and the unity of India can be achieved only by granting more and more *extra*-Constitutional privileges forget the adage—"once an infant always an infant"; and also the fact that communalism is a vicious circle : the cry of "Muslim in danger" gave birth to Hindu fundamentalism and, similarly, the slogan of "Muslim sentiments" has given rise to the plea of "Hindu sentiments".[54] There will be no end to these

52. It sounds ironical to hear that the objection to *Vande Mataram,* which figured in the 11-point demands of Mr Zinnah 1938, could be resounded through the mouth of the Muslims in the 1992-Parliament, ie, 45 years after the partition of India. Eventually, the Parliament (of partitioned India) had to adopt a resolution (23 December 1992) that every session of Parliament shall close with the *music* of *Vande Mataram.*

53. *https://www.mha.gov.in/sites/default/files/NationalSongEng_06022026.pdf* (last accessed in February 2026).

54. The demand for *namaz* on the highway has been reciprocated by that of *moha-arati* on the highway [*Statesman,* 10 February 1993], forgetting that both are equally untenable under the law [*vide* p 24, C7, vol C/1].

pernicious currents or cross-currents so long as everybody is not told firmly that all of us, including the administrators, are bound by the Constitution which we adopted as the "People of India"—under which there is no room for Hindu Indians or Muslim Indians, but there is only one Nation, namely, India, which is solidly bound by a tie of fraternity. If we have any respect for the Constitution of India, we must tear off from the political history of India those baneful pages which have become anachronistic and stand in the way of our national unity even after the adoption of the Preamble to the Constitution of *divided* India.

Let me, in the present context, stray into a personal (but relevant) digression. As a schoolboy (not knowing anything about politics or communalism), I was attracted by the national songs which inspired the "non-Co-operation" meetings and processions. One of the few that I still remember was—

Ekbar tora ma baliye dak jagata-janara sravana jurak
Tris koti kanthe mayere dakile thas dik sukhe hasibe . . .

It depicted India as our motherland and exhorted all the people, without any exception, to call her "mother". The Muslim leaders who participated in these meetings and processions never objected to this representation of one's birth-place as "mother" nor did the Muslim masses ever imagine that "Muslim sentiments" would be prejudiced thereby, just as a staunch Hindu did not object to the singing of another piece—

Ram Rahim no juda karo bhai, dilki sachha rakho ji . . .

which exhorted the Hindus not to treat Ram and Rahim as different entities.

If today, more than half a century after independence, we are on the reverse gear, it is for the political parties to search their heart to find if they are in any way responsible for this great "Fall" for which divided India shall have to lament through all futurity. It is no good throwing mud on each other. All of us have forgotten the history of our independence, the ideals of those who brought about that independence, and the Constitution which enshrines those ideals.

In fact, decline of national sentiments has generated obnoxious selfishness and greed, forgetting all the while that members of Parliament own the vote of the people on the shameless profession that they would *serve* the country. The result has been a fall of the ideal of Parliamentary democracy for which the Nationalists fought the crusade for independence. Few Parliamentarians today are duly cognizant of the basic provisions of the Constitution, the fundamental law of the land—and the respect which it demands.

7. Failure of Parliamentary Democracy.

The narrow-mindedness and selfishness of the "representatives" of the people was shamefacedly illustrated when on the last day of sitting of the Ninth Lok Sabha, the MPs unanimously voted for ensuring their pension, and at an enhanced rate, even though the Lok Sabha was dissolved after a short duration—without caring to see that a bill or motion having financial liability could not be introduced without the President's recommendation [*Article 117(1)*].

A more fundamental cause of the trend towards the failure of Parliamentary democracy is that since the beginning of the present decade, violence and extermination of opponents is being resorted to as an easier mode of winning an election. The foundation of Parliamentary democracy is an "appeal from the bullet to the ballot".

Amidst this abysmal gloom, a ray of hope has been flashed by the fact that by the 61st Amendment Act 1988—amending Article 326—the voting age has been lowered from 21 to 18 years, as a result of which younger blood has been infused into the electorate of India, since the 1989—General Election. The result has been that it would no longer lie in the mouth of the elders to keep students away from politics. What the students have so long been doing surreptitiously in the educational institutions, they will now do it as a matter of right. Now, therefore, it will be a concern of every young man to be apprised of the objectives of each of the political parties and to decide which way he himself would be inclined. All this means degeneration of academic education, no doubt, but it will bring forth a new generation of students who would realise that they are not tools in the political machinery, to be wielded by political leaders to serve their selfish ends —but the very foundation of parliamentary democracy in India.

7a. Lowering of Voting Age.

Of course, mere lowering of the voting age will not give a young man an opportunity to enter into the administration at once, so long as the qualifying age of membership of the Legislature is not lowered down from 25 years for the House of the People or the Legislative Assembly of a State. The period between 18 and 25 is the brewing time given to the younger generation to equip themselves for taking up the reins of government from professional politicians who have repeatedly proved their failure. Time has come for them to realise that they cannot reach their objective by political slogans or breaking their heads on the streets, but by acquiring political education and encyclopaedic knowledge ranging from nuclear science to agriculture and the mass of laws by which this vast country is governed—so that they can usher in an age of efficient administration, if and when they come to power.

At an election held in the UK or the USA, hardly a life is lost in the election campaign, during which opposing contestants address newsmen and the voters from the same platform—presenting alternative programme to solve the same national problems, from which the electorate can make their choice for a new Government.

In India, on the other hand, it has become commonplace that when a political leader is determined to win an election at any cost he has to use younger people as tools in his election campaign of bloodshed. It is young people who either kill or are killed. At the General Election of Parliament held in November 1989, over 100 lives were lost in the election clashes and a similar figure is to be attributed to the State Assembly election in several States which took place in February, 1990. At the election for the 10th Lok Sabha held in 1991 the death toll has exceeded 289 (present position is not available). Side by side was the open declaration of a Chief Minister that, whatever might be the result of a poll, the issue of a certificate of the Returning Officer was under his control. This cannot be brushed aside as a hyperbole because it was attended with unlawful practices which led to unprecedented intervention by the Election Commission in some such States.

This is not Parliamentary democracy, but its death-knell. It will be a glorious failure of democracy in India if the younger generation does not cry a halt to this scheme of massacre. It is for them to rise as a man to protest against the nefarious mandates of the heads of various political parties.

Every Indian must look forward, to build up an India which will stand as a man against whatever calamity befalls our lot. The responsibility therefore lies on the younger generation to build up a united and stronger India, where each man will play the role of a poet, philosopher, warrior, and administrator, rolled in one, in the cause of the Motherland—which stands paramount to the narrower interests of his family, community or political affiliation.

8. Glaring Events Changing the Constitutional History.

Before concluding, I should mention certain glaring events which have changed the background in the history of Constitutional development in India. So long there was one major political party, namely the Congress, while there were a number of groups or factions, composed of dissidents, apart from the Leftists parties who held views radically different from the rest. The decline of Communism in Europe, including the USSR itself, has made it impossible for the Leftist to present an alternative government at the Union level. Instead has emerged the Bharatiya Janata Party (known as the BJP), as an effective Opposition party, with evident potentiality.

8a. Controversy as to the True meaning of "Secularism".

It seems that at future elections, the issue will be as to the meaning of "Secularism" in the Indian Constitution. The case of the BJP is that secularism means *equal* treatment of all the religions and not a favourable treatment (extra-constitutional) of the minority, or rather, the Muslims (who constitute the major group amongst the minorities), in order to secure their votes, which is decisive because the majority, that is the Hindus, are divided into numerous political parties. According to the BJP, what the ruling parties have been doing so long is to pamper "Muslim sentiments", for which there is no provision in the Constitution over and above the safeguards embodied in Articles 29, and 30, and the like. The Constitution, on the other hand, promises equality to every individual, irrespective of religion [*Articles 15 and 16*].[55]

8b. Unstable Governments in 90s.

In the 1996 Lok Sabha Election, although BJP got the highest number of seats, it could not attain absolute majority. It seemed that at the next general elections the political parties would be compelled to fight the elections being divided mainly into two camps—(a) BJP; and (b) non-BJP. This did actually happen in 1996, but in a different manner—the anti-BJP parties united against the BJP, but without surrendering their separate entities. The result was formation of Coalition Governments formed by 13 minority parties, headed by Mr HD Deve Gowda and later on by Mr IK Gujral, which tottered ever since their formation and collapsed within a year of their formation. In 1998 Parliamentary elections, the BJP emerged as a single largest party and again a coalition Government was formed headed by Mr Atal Bihari Bajpayee with a political uncertainty to complete its full term.

---

55. Whatever be the merits of the arguments of the BJP, the Supreme Court has thrown cold water upon it by laying down in the nine-Judge *Bommai's* Case, *SR Bommai v UOI,* AIR 1994 SC 1918 : (1994) 3 SCC 1, that "Secularism" under the Constitution requires that.

Both at the elections held in 1989 and 1991 (for the 9th and 10th Lok Sabhas, respectively), the largest single party has failed to secure an absolute majority; yet, in order to avoid another election, it was allowed to form a government with the tacit support of some other parties who, however, refused to enter into a coalition government and share the responsibilities of the party in power. The result has been the successive fall of a minority government as soon as the supporting party withdraws its support on some issue on which it has taken a contrary stand. This has happened to the governments headed by Mr VP Singh and Chandra Shekhar.

8c. 16th, 17th and 18th Lok Sabha Elections.

The Indian General Election of 2014 was held to constitute the 16th Lok Sabha, for electing the members of Parliament for all the 543 parliamentary constituencies in India. It ran in nine phases from 7 April 2014 to 12 May 2014, and was the longest election in the country's history. According to the Election Commission of India, approximately 814.5 million people were eligible to vote, with an increase of 100 million voters since the last general election in 2009, thence, making it the largest-ever election in the world. Over 23 million or 2.88% of the total eligible voters were aged 18–19 years. A total of 8,251 candidates contested for the 543 Lok Sabha seats. The average election turnout over all nine phases was around 66.38% , the highest ever in the history of the Indian General Elections. It was for the first time since the 1984 Indian General Elections that a party won enough seats to govern, without any support from the other parties. The United Progressive Alliance (UPA), led by the Indian National Congress, won 58 seats, 44 (8.1%) of which were won by the Congress, that won 19.3% of all votes.

The Indian General Election of 2019 was held to constitute the 17th Lok Sabha. The 2019 General Election ran in seven phases from 11 April 2014 to 19 May 2019. *Bharatiya Janata Party* won 303 seats and emerged as the largest party in the elections and formed the government. Narendra Modi was sworn in as the Prime Minister on 30 May 2019.

In 2024, the General Election was held to constitute the 18th Lok Sabha in India from 19 April to 1 June 2024 in seven phases. BJP won 240 seats and Narendra Modi was sworn in as the Prime Minister on 9 June 2024.

8d. Civil Society Movement Transformed into AAP Political Party.

The fledgling Aam Aadmi Party, born from the crucible of the anti-corruption movement that began in 2011, generated a new and a never before witnessed kind of energy and hope in the country. For the first time, a civil society movement transformed itself into a political o rganization and challenged the established political parties. Similar attempts were made in the 1960s and 70s which however, did not succeed.

8e. Regain Credibility of Parliamentary Process.

If the parliamentary process is to regain credibility, it is necessary for both the government as well as the opposition members to make an effort. In this regard, the former President Mukherjee made a balanced intervention. "Indians don't send their representatives to Parliament to watch them disrupt it. Unfortunately, this problem has intensified over the years. For instance, the last Lok Sabha functioned for just over half the sittings of the first one".

8f. Resort to Presidential System, no Solution.

Some people think that since we have failed in the game of parliamentary democracy, we should now try our hand at the Presidential form of Government. Without going into the merits and demerits of the two systems, a jurist should point out that this will *not be possible* because an amendment of the Constitution, which will be necessary for the purpose, will not be tolerated by the Supreme Court so long as the 13-Judge dogma that the Parliamentary system of Government is a "basic feature" of our Constitution[56] is not turned down by a larger Bench—which would be another Herculean task.

We have, therefore, to remain contended with the Parliamentary system.

Apart from this, unless corruption is rooted out from the grass roots, a change over to the Presidential system will merely result in the installation of irresponsibility and autocracy; wherefrom shall we get a "clean" President and a nationally inspired electorate to keep him under control?

A cool thinking of all the foregoing considerations will enable us to realise that in order to save our democracy, each one of us should make a *sincere* and concerted effort to root out dishonesty and corruption, withdraw all support from "political murders" and communal riots and should love our country as we love our mother. This can be achieved if only we realise the *true* tenets of our respective religions, for no religion teaches otherwise. Definitely, India is evolving as a responsible and a responsive democracy.

56. *Kesavananda Bharati v State of Kerala,* AIR 1973 SC 1461 (13-Judges).

TABLES

TABLE I

FACTS TO START WITH

1. The Constituent Assembly had its first sitting on 9 December 1946.

2. The Draft Constitution of India, which was prepared by the Drafting Committee of the Constituent Assembly and presented by it to the President of the Constituent Assembly on 21 February 1948, contained 315 Articles and Eight Schedules. The Constitution of India, as adopted on 26 November 1949, contained 395 Articles and Eight Schedules. After subsequent amendments, the Constitution as it stood on 01-05-2024, contained 469 Articles and 12 Schedules.

3. General elections have been held in 1951, 1957, 1962, 1967, 1971, 1977, 1980, 1984, 1989, 1991, 1996, 1998, 1999, 2004, 2009, 2014, 2019 and 2024 (ongoing). Every man and woman of 18 and over is an elector for the House of the People and respective Legislative Assembly. At the fifth general election held in 1971, the number of persons on the electoral roll was 290 million, which is more than the population of the USA or the USSR. On the revision of the electoral roll, in 1986, this number rose up to 361 million; and as a result of the lowering of the voting age to 18, in the 1989-election, the number exceeded 490 million. In the 1996 polls, the number of voters was more than 590 million. In 14th Lok Sabha general election in 2004, the number of voters was 67,14,87,930. In 15th General Election in 2009, it was 714 million. In 16th Lok Sabha General Election in 2014, the number of voters was 834082814 and in 17th General Election, it was 910512091. In the ongoing 18th General Election, the total count of voters is 96.8 crores.

4. India (*i.e.*, *Bharat*) has—

(a) *Area-related:*

(i) an area of over 32,87,263 sq kms (or 12,69,000 sq miles), of which 1,12,348 sq kms are included in the 8 Union Territories and the rest in the 28 States. Its forest cover comprises 21.7% of its area. India is the 7th largest country in the world.

(ii) 6,40,932 villages as against 7,933 towns, 5,924 sub-districts and 640 districts; and 68.85% of the population (*i.e.*, 83.38 crores) live in villages, and the rest 37.71 crores in urban areas as per 2011 census.

(b) *Population-related:*

(i) a population of 1,210,854,977 [comprising 62.33 crore males and 58.76 crore females] as per 2011 census[1] (about 17.3% of the world population and ranks 2nd in the world)—of whom Hindus constitute 79.8%, Muslims 14.23%, Christians 2.3%, Sikhs 1.72%,

---

1. Due to the outbreak of the COVID-19 Pandemic, the Census 2021 and related field activities have been postponed until further orders. The population is estimated to have reached 1,363 million in 2021 and is projected to reach 1,522.3 million by 2036 [*Source:* India 2024, A Reference Material, 68th Edition, 2024, published by the Director General, Publications Division, Ministry of I&B, Government of India].

Buddhists 0.7%, Jains 0.37%, and other religions constitute 0.9%; who speak as many as 1,369 languages, of which 22 languages have already been included in the Eighth Schedule of the Constitution. The Indian population increased with a decadal growth of 17.7% (*i.e.*, addition of 181.5 million population). Transgender population was counted officially for the first time in 2011 census which stood at 4,90,000.

(ii) population density of 382 per sq. km. in 2011. Bihar being the most thickly populated State with a population density of 1,106 persons per sq. km. followed by West Bengal at 1,028 and Kerala at 860. NCT of Delhi's population density was the highest at 11,320 persons per sq. km.

(iii) overall sex ratio of 1020 females for every 1,000 males for the period 2019-2021. However, the child sex ratio born in the last five years (females per 1,000 males) is 929.[2]

(iv) a total fertility rate (TFR) of 2.5 in 2010 to 2.0[3] in 2020; crude birth rate (CBR) of 19.5 per 1000 population, and crude death rate (CDR) of 6 per 1000 population, in 2020; and drastically able to reduce the infant mortality rate (IMR) from 47 in 2010 to 28 in 2020.

(v) total number of households at 248.8 million—of which 202.4 million are Hindu, 31.2 million are Muslim, 6.3 million are Christian, 4.1 million are Sikh, and 1.9 million are Jain. There are more than 3 million places of worship in India.

(vi) about 455.8 million people which were treated as migrants by place of last residence, and 141.9 million were considered to be migrants between 2001 and 2011.

(c) *Literacy rate:* the literacy rate (*i.e.*, taking population from age 7 or more into account) of 73% [64.6% among females and 80.9% among males] as per 2011 census (with a decadal growth of 8.2%). Kerala being the most literate state with 94% literacy followed by Lakshadweep 91.8%, and Bihar the least with 61.8%.

(d) *Income:* a per capita net national income of Rs 1,219,680 in 2025-26.[4]

5. National Symbols:

(a) *National Flag:* It is a tricolour panel made up of three rectangular panels or sub-panels of equal width, which was adopted by the Constituent Assmbly of India on 22-7-1947. Top panel being saffrom (*kesari*), middle panel being white bearing at its centre the

2. *https://www.mohfw.gov.in/sites/default/files/NFHS-5_Phase-II_0.pdf* (last accessed in January 2026).
3. India has achieved the replacement level of fertility (*i.e.*, a TFR of about 2.1 children per woman) according to the National Family Health Survey-5 report released in 2022.
4. *https://www.indiabudget.gov.in/economicsurvey/doc/stat/tab1.1.pdf* (last accessed in January 2026).

design of Ashoka Chakra in navy blue colour with 24 equally spaced spokes, and bottom panel being green. The ratio of the length to the height (width) shall be 3:2.

(b) *State Emblem:* The State Emblem of India is an adaptation of the Lion Capital of Asoka at Sarnath. The motto "Satyamev Jayate"—Truth alone triumps—written inDevanagri script below the profile of the Lion Capital is part of the State Emblem. The official seal of the Government of India also lies in the State Emblem.

(c) *National Anthem:* The song "Jana Gana Mana", composed originally in Bangla by Rabindranath Tagore, was adopted in its Hindi version by the Constituent Assembly as the National Anthem of India on 24-1-1950. It was first sung on 27-12-1911 at the Calcutta Session of the INC. The playing time of the full version, which consists of 5 stanzas, is approximately 52 seconds.

(d) *National Song:* The song "Vande Mataram", composed in Sanskrit by Bankimchandra Chatterji, was a source of inspiration to the people in their struggle for freedom. It has an equal status with the National Anthem. The first political occasion when it was sung was the 1896 session of the INC.

(e) *National Animal and Bird:* Tiger and Peacock have been renotified as national animal and national bird, respectively, by the Wildlife Division of the then Ministry of Environment and Forests in 2011.

(f) *National Calendar:* Based on the *Saka* era with Chaitra as its first month and a normal year of 365 days, the National Calendar[5] was adopted from 22-3-1957 along with the Gregorian calendar for the following official purposes, namely, (i) Gazette of India, (ii) news broadcast by All India Radio, (iii) calendars issued by the Government of India, and (iv) Government communications addressed to the public.

5. Dates of the National Calendar have a permanent correspondence with the dates of ther Gregorian Calendar. Normally, 1 Chaitra falling on March 22, and on March 21, in case of a leap year.

TABLE II

STATEWISE MEMBERSHIP OF THE CONSTITUENT ASSEMBLY OF INDIA AS ON 31 DECEMBER 1947

PROVINCES — 229

	No. of members		*No. of members*
1. Madras	49	7. C.P. and Berar	17
2. Bombay	21	8. Assam	8
3. West Bengal	19	9. Orissa	9
4. United Provinces	55	10. Delhi	1
5. East Punjab	12	11. Ajmer-Merwara	1
6. Bihar	36	12. Coorg	1

INDIAN STATES — 70

1. Alwar	1	19. Tripura, Manipur and Khasi States Group	1
2. Baroda	3		
3. Bhopal	1	20. U.P. States Group	1
4. Bikaner	1	21. Eastern Rajputana States Group	3
5. Cochin	1		
6. Gwalior	4	22. Central India States Group (including Bunldelkhand and Malwa)	3
7. Indore	1		

	No. of members		No. of members
8. Jaipur	3		
9. Jodhpur	2	23. Western India States Group	4
10. Kolhapur	1		
11. Kotah	1	24. Gujarat States Group	2
12. Mayurbhanj	1	25. Deccan and Madras States Group	2
13. Mysore	7		
14. Patiala	2	26. Punjab States Group	3
15. Rewa	2	27. Eastern States Group I	4
16. Travancore	6	28. Eastern States Group II	3
17. Udaipur	2	29. Residuary States Group	4
18. Sikkim and Cooch Behar Group	1		

Thus, total number of Provinces (229) and Indian States (70) = 299

TABLE III

TERRITORY OF INDIA

(A) *As in the Original Constitution (1949)* UNION				(B) *After Seventh Amendment, 1956 till date* UNION		
States in Part A	*States in Part B*	*States in Part C*	*Territories in Part D*	*States (and their Capitals)*	*Union Territories (and their Capitals)*	*Other acquired territories*
1. Assam	1. Hyderabad	1. Ajmer	1. The Andaman and Nicobar Islands	1. Andhra Pradesh[1] (Amaravati)	1. Andaman & Nicobar Islands (Port Blair)	
2. Bihar	2. Jammu and Kashmir	2. Bhopal	2. Acquired Territories (if any)	2. Arunachal Pradesh[2] (Itanagar)	2. Chandigarh[6] (Chandigarh)	
3. Bombay	3. Madhya Bharat	3. Bilaspur		3. Assam[3] (Dispur)	3. Dadra and Nagar Haveli[7] & Daman and Diu[8] (Daman)	
4. Madhya Pradesh	4. Mysore	4. Cooch-Behar		4. Bihar[4] (Patna)	4. Government of NCT of Delhi[9] (Delhi)	
5. Madras	5. Patiala and East Punjab States Union	5. Coorg		5. Chhattisgarh[5] (Raipur)		
6. Orissa	6. Rajasthan	6. Delhi				
7. Punjab	7. Saurashtra	7. Himachal Pradesh				

1. State reorganised to form a new State "Telangana" by the Andhra Pradesh Reorganisation Act, 2014 (6 of 2014), section 10 (w.e.f. 2-6-2014).
2. Arunachal Pradesh was elevated from the status of Union Territory to Statehood by the State of Arunachal Pradesh Act, 1986 (69 of 1986), section 4 (w.e.f. 20-2-1987).
3. State reorganised to form a new State "Meghalaya" by the N.E. Areas (Reorganisation) Act, 1971 (81 of 1971), section 9 (w.e.f. 21-1-1972).
4. State reorganised to form a new State "Jharkhand" by the Bihar Reorganisation Act, 2000 (30 of 2000), section 5 (w.e.f. 15-11-2000).
5. Added by the Madhya Pradesh Reorganisation Act, 2000 (28 of 2000), section 5 (w.e.f. 1-11-2000).
6. Inserted by the Punjab Reorganisation Act, 1966 (31 of 1966), section 7 (w.e.f. 1-11-1966).
7. Inserted by the Constitution (10th Amendment) Act, 1961 (w.e.f. 11-8-1961).
8. Daman and Diu, as a Union Territory, was inserted by the Constitution (12th Amendment) Act, 1962 (w.e.f. 20-12-1961).
   Two Union Territories "Dadra and Nagar Haveli" and "Daman and Diu" merged into a single Union territory *vide* Act 44 of 2019, section 3 (w.e.f. 26-1-2020).
9. Delhi was renamed as the "National Capital Territory of Delhi" by the Constitution (69th Amendment) Act, 1991, by inserting Articles 239AA and 239AB in the Constitution, w.e.f. 1-2-1992.

(A) *As in the Original Constitution (1949)* UNION				(B) *After Seventh Amendment, 1956 till date* UNION		
States in Part A	*States in Part B*	*States in Part C*	*Territories in Part D*	*States (and their Capitals)*	*Union Territories (and their Capitals)*	*Other acquired territories*
8. The United Provinces 9. West Bengal	8. Travancore-Cochin 9. Vindhya Pradesh	8. Kutch 9. Manipur 10. Tripura		6. Goa[10] (Panaji) 7. Gujarat[11] (Gandhinagar) 8. Haryana[12] (Chandigarh) 9. Himachal Pradesh[13] (Shimla) 10. Jharkhand[14] (Ranchi) 11. Karnataka[15] (Bengaluru) 12. Kerala (Thiruvananthapuram) 13. Madhya Pradesh[16] (Bhopal)	5. Jammu & Kashmir[17] [Srinagar (in summer) and Jammu (in winter)] 6. Ladakh[18] (Leh) 7. Lakshadweep[19] (Kavaratti) 8. Puducherry[20] (Puducherry)	

10. Inserted by the Constitution (12th Amendment) Act, 1962 as a Union Territory. Elevated to the status of a State by the Goa, Daman and Diu Reorganisation Act, 1987 (18 of 1987), section 5 (w.e.f. 30-5-1987).
11. Substituted for "Bombay" by the Bombay Reorganisation Act (11 of 1960), section 4 (w.e.f. 1-5-1960).
12. Inserted by the Punjab Reorganisation Act, 1966 (31 of 1966), section 7 (w.e.f. 1-11-1966).
13. Inserted by the State of Himachal Pradesh Act, 1970 (53 of 1970), section 4 (w.e.f. 25-1-1971).
14. Added by the Bihar Reorganisation Act, 2000 (30 of 2000), section 5 (w.e.f. 15-11-2000).
15. The name of "Mysore" changed to "Karnataka" by the Mysore State (Alteration of Name) Act, 1973 (31 of 1973), section 5 (w.e.f. 1-11-1973).
16. State reorganised to form a new State "Chhattisgarh" by the Madhya Pradesh Reorganisation Act, 2000 (28 of 2000), section 5 (w.e.f. 1-11-2000).
17. Jammu & Kashmir was a State up to 30-10-2019. Downgraded to Union Territory with Legislature by the Jammu and Kashmir Reorganisation Act, 2019 (34 of 2019), section 6 (w.e.f. 31-10-2019).
18. Ladakh was part of State of Jammu & Kashmir up to 30-10-2019. Reconstituted as a Union Territory by the Jammu and Kashmir Reorganisation Act, 2019 (34 of 2019), section 6 (w.e.f. 31-10-2019).
19. The Laccadive, Minicoy and Amindivi Islands were renamed as "Lakshadweep" by the Laccadive, Minicoy and Amindivi Islands (Alteration of Name) Act, 1973.
20. Inserted by the Constitution (14th Amendment) Act, 1962 (w.e.f. 16-8-1962). Further, the name of "Pondicherry" substituted as "Puducherry" by the Pondicherry (Alteration of Name) Act, 2006, section 4 (w.e.f. 1-10-2006).

(A) *As in the Original Constitution (1949)* UNION				(B) *After Seventh Amendment, 1956 till date* UNION		
States in Part A	*States in Part B*	*States in Part C*	*Territories in Part D*	*States (and their Capitals)*	*Union Territories (and their Capitals)*	*Other acquired territories*
				14. Maharashtra[21] (Mumbai)		
				15. Manipur[22] (Imphal)		
				16. Meghalaya[23] (Shillong)		
				17. Mizoram[24] (Aizawl)		
				18. Nagaland[25] (Kohima)		
				19. Odisha[26] (Bhubaneshwar)		
				20. Punjab[27] (Chandigarh)		
				21. Rajasthan (Jaipur)		
				22. Sikkim[28] (Gangtok)		
				23. Tamil Nadu[29] (Chennai)		
				24. Telangana[30] (Hyderabad)		

21. Substituted for "Bombay" by the Bombay Reorganisation Act (11 of 1960), section 4 (w.e.f. 1-5-1960).
22. Elevated to the status of a State by the N.E. Areas (Reorganisation) Act, 1971 (81 of 1971), section 9 (w.e.f. 21-1-1972).
23. Added by the N.E. Areas (Reorganisation) Act, 1971 (81 of 1971), section 9 (w.e.f. 21-1-1972).
24. Elevated to the status of a State by the State of Mizoram Act, 1986 (34 of 1986), section 4 (w.e.f. 20-2-1987).
25. Elevated to the status of a State by the State of Nagaland Act, 1962 (27 of 1962), section 4 (w.e.f. 1-12-1963).
26. The name of "Orissa" changed to "Odisha" by the Orissa (Alteration of Name) Act, 2011 (15 of 2011), section, 6 (w.e.f. 1-11-2011).
27. State reorganised to form a new State "Haryana" by the Punjab Reorganisation Act, 1966 (31 of 1966), section 7 (w.e.f. 1-11-1966).
28. Added by the Constitution (36th Amendment) Act, 1975, section 2 (w.r.e.f. 26-4-1975).
29. The name of "Madras" changed to "Tamil Nadu" by the Madras State (Alteration of Name) Act, 1968 (53 of 1968), 3 (w.e.f. 14-1-1969).
30. Added by the Andhra Pradesh Reorganisation Act, 2014 (6 of 2014), section 10 (w.e.f. 2-6-2014).

(A) *As in the Original Constitution (1949)* UNION				(B) *After Seventh Amendment, 1956 till date* UNION		
States in Part A	*States in Part B*	*States in Part C*	*Territories in Part D*	*States (and their Capitals)*	*Union Territories (and their Capitals)*	*Other acquired territories*
				25. Tripura[31] (Agartala) 26. Uttar Pradesh[32] (Lucknow) 27. Uttarakhand[33] (Dehradun) 28. West Bengal (Kolkata)		

31. Elevated to the status of a State by the N.E. Areas (Reorganisation) Act, 1971 (81 of 1971), section 9 (w.e.f. 21-1-1972).
32. State reorganised to form a new State "Uttarakhand" by the Uttar Pradesh Reorganisation Act, 2000 (29 of 2000), section 5 (w.e.f. 9-11-2000).
33. Added by the Uttar Pradesh Reorganisation Act, 2000 (29 of 2000), section 5 (w.e.f. 9-11-2000). Name substituted by the Uttaranchal (Alteration of Name) Act, 2006 (52 of 2006), section 4 for "Uttaranchal" (w.e.f. 1-1-2007).

TABLE IV

OVERVIEW OF ALL 106 CONSTITUTIONAL AMENDMENTS

Sl. No.	*The Constitution (...... Amendment) Act*	*Date of assent by President*	*Date of commen-cement*	*Whether ratified by more than half of State Legislatures, as required by the proviso to Article 368?*	*Amendments made*
1.	2.	3.	4.	5.	6.
1.	The Constitution (First Amendment) Act, 1951	18-6-1951	18-6-1951 (retrospect-tive in part)	... ...	Articles amended — 15, 19, 85, 87, 174, 176, 341, 342, 372, 376. Articles inserted — 31A, 31B. Schedule added — Ninth.
2.	The Constitution (Second Amendment) Act, 1952	1-5-1953	1-5-1953	Since the Amendment Bill sought to make a change in the representation of States in Parliament, it had to be referred to the Legislatures of the States in Parts A and B for their ratification. The Bill was accordingly passed in Parliament on 19 December 1952, and then referred to the States. On receiving the ratification of not less than one-half of the State Legislatures, the President gave his assent on 1 May 1953.	Article amended — 81.
3.	The Constitution (Third Amendment) Act, 1954	22-2-1955	22-2-1955	The Bill was passed by Parliament on 28 September 1954. Since the Bill sought to amend a List of the Seventh Schedule, it required ratification by the Legislatures	Schedule amended — Seventh [List III, Entry 33].

1.	2.	3.	4.	5.	6.
				of not less than one-half of the States specified in Parts A and B of the First Schedule. After having received such ratification, the President gave his assent on 22 February 1955.	
4.	The Constitution (Fourth Amendment) Act, 1955	27-4-1955	27-4-1955	. . . . . .	Articles amended — 31, 31A, 305. Schedule amended — Ninth.
5.	The Constitution (Fifth Amendment) Act, 1955	24-12-1955	24-12-1955	. . . . . .	Article amended — 3.
6.	The Constitution (Sixth Amendment) Act, 1956	11-9-1956	11-9-1956	The Bill was passed by Parliament on 31 May 1956. It required ratification by not less than half of the State Legislatures because it sought to amend the Legislative Lists. Having received such ratification, the Bill was assented to by the President on 11 September 1956.	Articles amended — 269, 286. Schedule amended — Seventh [List II, Entry 54; and List I, Entry 92A (inserted)].
7.	The Constitution (Seventh Amendment) Act, 1956	19-10-1956	1-11-1956	For obvious reasons, this Bill required ratification. Hence, it was referred to the State Legislatures, having been passed by Parliament on 11 September 1956. After obtaining the required ratification, the President gave his assent.	Articles amended — 1, 49, 80, 81, 82, 131, 153, 158, 168, 170, 171, 216, 217, 220, 222, 224, 230, 231, 232, 239, 240, 298, 371. Articles inserted — 258A, 290A, 350A, 350B, 372A, 378A. Schedules amended—First, Second, Fourth, and Seventh [List I, Entries 32, 67 and 79; List II, Entries 12 and 24; and List III, Entry 40].

1.	2.	3.	4.	5.	6.
					Articles omitted — 238, 242, 243, 259, 278, 306, 379 to 391. Schedule omitted — Part B of Second Schedule.
8.	The Constitution (Eighth Amendment) Act, 1959	5-1-1960	5-1-1960	. . . . . .	Article amended — 334.
9.	The Constitution (Ninth Amendment) Act, 1960	28-12-1960	17-1-1961	Views of the Legislature of the State of West Bengal ascertained, under Article 3, but ratification was not required as mere territorial change was not a matter specified in the proviso to Article 368.	Schedule amended — First [to transfer certain territories from the States of Assam, Punjab, West Bengal and the Union Territory of Tripura to Pakistan, implementing the Indo-Pakistan agreements of different dates].
10.	The Constitution (Tenth Amendment) Act, 1961	16-8-1961	11-8-1961 (retrospectively)	. . . .	Article 240 and First Schedule amended — to incorporate Dadra and Nagar Haveli as a Union Territory.
11.	The Constitution (Eleventh Amendment) Act, 1961	19-12-1961	19-12-1961		Article amended – 66(1) Article inserted – 71(4) to narrow down grounds for challenging validity of election of President or Vice-President.
12.	The Constitution (Twelfth Amendment) Act, 1962	27-3-1962	20-12-1961 (retrospectively)	. . . . . .	Article 240 and First Schedule amended — to incorporate Goa, Daman and Diu as a Union Territory.
13.	The Constitution (Thirteenth Amendment) Act, 1962	28-12-1962	1-12-1963	Yes.	Article 371A inserted — to make special provisions for the administration of the State of Nagaland.

1.	2.	3.	4.	5.	6.
14.	The Constitution (Fourteenth Amendment) Act, 1962	28-12-1962	28-12-1962 [But Article 240 and First Sch. came into force on 16-8-1962 (retrospectively)	Yes.	Articles amended – 81 and 240. Article inserted – 239A. Schedules amended – First and Fourth.
15.	The Constitution (Fifteenth Amendment) Act, 1963	5-10-1963	5-10-1963	Yes	Articles amended – 124, 128, 217, 222, 224, 226, 297, 311, 316. Article inserted – 224A. Schedule amended – Seventh [List I, Entry 78]. The more important of these changes are — the raising of the age of retirement of a High Court Judge from 60 to 62; the extension of the jurisdiction of a High Court to issue writs under Article 226 to a Government or authority situated outside its territorial jurisdiction where the cause of action arises within such jurisdiction; modifying the procedure imposed by Article 311 upon the pleasure of the President or Governor to dismiss a civil servant.
16.	The Constitution (Sixteenth Amendment) Act, 1963	5-10-1963	5-10-1963	Yes.	Amends Article 19 to enable Parliament to make laws providing restrictions upon the freedom of expression questioning the sovereignty or integrity of the Union of India, with

1.	2.	3.	4.	5.	6.
					consequential changes in Articles 84, 173 and Third Schedule.
17.	The Constitution (Seventeenth Amendment) Act, 1964	20-6-1964	20-6-1964	. . . . . .	Amends Article 31A (definition of "estate" amended with retrospective effect); Entries 21–64 added to the Ninth Schedule.
18.	The Constitution (Eighteenth Amendment) Act, 1966	27-8-1966	27-8-1966	. . . . . .	Adding Explanations to Article 3 to clarify that the Parliament has the power to create a new State or Union Territory. Provision was made for the formation of two States, Punjab and Haryana, by reorganising Punjab on linguistic basis.
19.	The Constitution (Nineteenth Amendment) Act, 1966	11-12-1966	11-12-1966	. . . . . .	Amending Article 324 to clarify the duties of the Election Commission.
20.	The Constitution (Twentieth Amendment) Act, 1966	22-12-1966	22-12-1966	. . . . . .	Article 233A inserted to validate the appointment of District Judges.
21.	The Constitution (Twenty-first Amendment) Act, 1967	10-4-1967	10-4-1967	. . . . . .	Includes "Sindhi" in the list of languages in the Eighth Schedule.
22.	The Constitution (Twenty-second Amendment) Act, 1969	25-9-1969	25-9-1969	Yes.	Inserted Articles 244A, 371B and clause (1A) in Article 275 – to constitute an autonomous State within the State of Assam (Meghalaya) comprising certain areas specified in Part A of the Sixth Schedule.

1.	2.	3.	4.	5.	6.
23.	The Constitution (Twenty-third Amendment) Act, 1970	23-1-1970	23-1-1970	Yes.	Amending Articles 330, 332, 333, 334 (to extend the period of reservation for Scheduled Castes and Tribes).
24.	The Constitution (Twenty-fourth Amendment) Act, 1971	5-11-1971	5-11-1971	Yes.	Inserting clause (4) in Article 13; amending Article 368. The object of the amendment was to clarify that the Parliament has the power to amend every part of the Constitution. The intention was to wipe out the effect of *Golak Nath*. After this amendment the President is bound to assent to a Constitution Amendment Bill.
25.	The Constitution (Twenty-fifth Amendment) Act, 1971	20-4-1972	20-4-1972	Yes.	Clause (2) of Article 31 amended and clause (2B) inserted; and Article 31C inserted. The jurisdiction of the courts to determine the adequacy of compensation on acquisition of property was taken away. A new clause was added to lay down that no law which declared that it was for giving effect to the principles specified in clauses (b) and (c) of Article 39 would be called in question on the ground that it is inconsistent with the fundamental rights.
26.	The Constitution (Twenty-sixth Amendment) Act, 1971	28-12-1971	28-12-1971	. . . . . .	Omitting Articles 291 and 362; inserting Article 363A; amending Article 366(22). The recognition to the Rulers of Princely States was withdrawn and their privy purses were abolished.

1.	2.	3.	4.	5.		6.
27.	The Constitution (Twenty-seventh Amendment) Act, 1971	30-12-1971	section 3 from 30-12-1971, and rest from 15-2-1972	. . .	. . .	Amending Articles 239A and 240; inserting Articles 239B and 371C. Two new Union Territories, *viz.*, Mizoram and Arunachal Pradesh, were formed.
28.	The Constitution (Twenty-eighth Amendment) Act, 1972	27-8-1972	29-8-1972	. . .	. . .	Inserting Article 312A; omitting Article 314. The conditions of service and privileges of former Indian Civil Service officers were abolished.
29.	The Constitution (Twenty-ninth Amendment) Act, 1972	9-6-1972	9-6-1972	. . .	. . .	Adding items 65–66 to the Ninth Schedule.
30.	The Constitution (Thirtieth Amendment) Act, 1972	22-2-1973	27-2-1973	Yes.		Amending Article 133(1). Appeals to the Supreme Court were curtailed. Only such appeals can be brought which involve a substantial question of law.
31.	The Constitution (Thirty-first Amendment) Act, 1973	17-10-1973	17-10-1973	. . .	. . .	Amending Articles 81, 33 and 332. Elected seats in Lok Sabha increased from 525 to 545.
32.	The Constitution (Thirty-second Amendment) Act, 1973	3-5-1974	1-7-1974	. . .	. . .	Amending Article 371(1) and inserting Articles 371D and 371E; amending Entry 63 of List I, Seventh Schedule. The object was to include six provisions in regard to Andhra Pradesh.

1.	2.	3.	4.	5.	6.
33.	The Constitution (Thirty-third Amendment) Act, 1974	19-5-1974	19-5-1974	. . . . . .	Amending Articles 101 and 190. It was provided that if a member of a State Legislature or Parliament sends his resignation, the Chairman or Speaker would satisfy himself that it is voluntary and genuine.
34.	The Constitution (Thirty-fourth Amendment) Act, 1974	7-9-1974	7-9-1974	Yes.	Adding items 67–86 to the Ninth Schedule.
35.	The Constitution (Thirty-fifth Amendment) Act, 1974	22-2-1975	1-3-1975	Yes.	Inserting Article 2A and amending Articles 80–81; adding Tenth Schedule. Sikkim was made an associate State.
36.	The Constitution (Thirty-sixth Amendment) Act, 1975	16-5-1975	26-4-1975	Yes.	Omitting Article 2A and Schedule X; adding item 22 to Schedule I; inserting Article 371F; adding Entry 22 to Schedule IV. Sikkim was made a full fledged State
37.	The Constitution (Thirty-seventh Amendment) Act, 1975	3-5-1975	3-5-1975	. . . . . .	Amending Articles 239A and 240. Provision was made for a legislative Assembly and Council of Ministers for the Union Territory of Arunachal Pradesh.
38.	The Constitution (Thirty-eighth Amendment) Act, 1975	1-8-1975	1-8-1975	Yes.	Amending Articles 123, 213, 239B, 352, 356, 359, 360. Declaration of Emergency by the President and promulgation of Ordinances by the President or Governor made issues over which the judiciary would not be able to exercise its power of review.

1.	2.	3.	4.	5.	6.
39.	The Constitution (Thirty-ninth Amendment) Act, 1975	10-8-1975	10-8-1975	Yes.	Amending Articles 71 and 329; inserting Article 329A; adding Entries 87–124 to Schedule IX. Questions regarding elections of President, Vice-President, Prime Minister and Speaker of Lok Sabha taken out of the purview of the Judiciary.
40.	The Constitution (Fortieth Amendment) Act, 1976	27-5-1976	27-5-1976	... ...	Substituting Article 297; adding Entries 125–188 to Schedule IX. It was provided that all lands, minerals etc. underlying the ocean within the territorial waters or the continental shelf or the exclusive economic zone of India shall vest in the Union. Power to determine the limits of territorial waters, continental shelf etc. was vested in Parliament.
41.	The Constitution (Forty-first Amendment) Act, 1976	7-9-1976	7-9-1976	... ...	Amending Article 316. Upper age for members of State Public Service Commission raised from 60 to 62.
42.	The Constitution (Forty-second Amendment) Act, 1976	18-12-1976	Different dates, commencing from 3-1-1977, 1-2-1977 and 1-4-1977	Yes.	Amending Preamble, Articles 31C, 39, 55, 74, 77, 81, 82, 83, 100, 102, 105, 118, 145, 166, 170, 172, 189, 191, 194, 208, 217, 225, 227, 228, 311, 312, 330, 352, 353, 356, 357, 358, 359, 366, 368, 371F, Seventh Schedule. Substituting Articles 103, 150, 192, 226. inserting Articles 31D, 32A, 39A, 43A, 48A, 51A, 131A, 139A, 144A, 226A, 228A, 257A, 323A, 323B.

1.	2.	3.	4.	5.	6.
					This amendment was almost a complete revision of the Constitution and many material changes were incorporated. It was enacted during an emergency. The next Government that came into power in 1977 repealed most of the amendments.
43.	The Constitution (Forty-third Amendment) Act, 1977	13-4-1978	13-4-1978	Yes.	Omitting Articles 31D, 32A, 131A, 144A, 226A and 228A; amending Articles 145, 226, 228 and 366. This amendment omitted many articles inserted by the 42nd Amendment Act. Some articles were changed.
44.	The Constitution (Forty-fourth Amendment) Act, 1978	30-4-1979	Different dates as notified by Central Government, for different provisions: 20-6-1979, 1-8-1979 and 6-9-1979	Yes.	Omitting Articles 19(1)(f), 31, 77(4), 123(4), 166(4), 213(4), 239B(4), 257A and 329A. Inserting Articles 30(1A), 134A, 300A and 361A. Amending and substituting Articles 19(1), 22, 30, 31A, 31C, 38, 71, 74, 77, 83, 103, 105, 123, 132-134, 139A, 150, 166, 172, 192, 194, 213, 217, 225, 226, 227, 239B, 329, 352, 356, 358, 359, 360, 361 and 371F. Entry 130 of Schedule IX omitted. Cancelling the amendments made by the 42nd Amendment Act to Articles 100, 102, 105, 118, 191, 194 and 208. (6 clauses of the Bill were rejected by the Rajya Sabha). The changes made by the 42nd Amendment Act were

1.	2.	3.	4.	5.	6.
					repealed or altered and the Constitution was brought back in its original form. But the Right to Property was taken away from the Chapter of Fundamental Rights and put as a new Article 300A.
45.	The Constitution (Forty-fifth Amendment) Act, 1980	14-4-1980	25-1-1980	Yes.	Extending reservation under Article 334 from 30 to 40 years.
46.	The Constitution (Forty-sixth Amendment) Act, 1982	2-2-1983	2-2-1983	. . . . . .	Amending Articles 269, 286, 366 and Seventh Schedule, List I [relating to Sales Tax].
47.	The Constitution (Forty-seventh Amendment) Act, 1984	26-8-1984	26-8-1984	. . . . . .	Adding Entries 189–202 to the Ninth Schedule.
48.	The Constitution (Forty-eighth Amendment) Act, 1984	26-8-1984	26-8-1984	. . . . . .	Inserting proviso to clause (5) of Article 356 to extend President's rule in Punjab.
49.	The Constitution (Forty-ninth Amendment) Act, 1984	11-9-1984	1-4-1985	. . . . . .	Amending Article 244, Fifth & Sixth Schedules. Sixth Schedule was made applicable to Tripura.
50.	The Constitution (Fiftieth Amendment) Act, 1984	11-9-1984	11-9-1984	. . . . . .	Substituting Article 33. Its scope was enlarged and many other Forces were included in its ambit.
51.	The Constitution (Fifty-first Amendment) Act, 1984	29-4-1985	16-6-1986	Yes.	Amending Articles 330 and 332.
52.	The Constitution (Fifty-second Amendment) Act, 1985	15-2-1985	1-3-1985	. . . . . .	Amending Articles 101, 102, 190 and 191; adding Tenth Schedule (anti-defection). It was declared that a

1.	2.	3.	4.	5.	6.
					member who defects from his party would become subject to disqualification.
53.	The Constitution (Fifty-third Amendment) Act, 1986	14-8-1986	20-2-1987	. . . . . .	Adding Article 371G [Mizoram was made a State].
54.	The Constitution (Fifty-fourth Amendment) Act, 1986	14-3-1987	1-4-1986	. . . . . .	Amending Articles 125, 221 and Second Schedule. Appropriate provisions were made to increase the salary of the Judges of the Supreme Court and High Courts.
55.	The Constitution (Fifty-fifth Amendment) Act, 1986	23-12-1986	20-2-1987	. . . . . .	Inserting Article 371-H [State of Arunachal Pradesh was formed].
56.	The Constitution (Fifty-sixth Amendment) Act, 1987	23-5-1987	30-5-1987	. . . . . .	Inserting Article 371-I [The Union Territory of Goa, Daman, Diu was divided. Goa was made a State and provision for a State assembly were inserted. Daman and Diu to be a Union Territory].
57.	The Constitution (Fifty-seventh Amendment) Act, 1987	15-9-1987	21-9-1987	. . . . . .	Clause (3A) inserted in Article 332. Articles 330 and 332 were amended to make provision for reservation of seats for Scheduled Tribes of Nagaland, Meghalaya, Mizoram and Arunachal Pradesh, in the Lok Sabha and in the legislative assemblies of Nagaland and Meghalaya.
58.	The Constitution (Fifty-eighth Amendment) Act, 1987	9-12-1987	9-12-1987	. . . . . .	Inserting Article 394A. The people had been demanding that the authoritative text of the Constitution should be published in Hindi. This

1.	2.	3.	4.	5.	6.
					amendment authorised the President to publish the authoritative text of the Constitution in Hindi.
59.	The Constitution (Fifty-ninth Amendment) Act, 1988	30-3-1988	30-3-1988	. . . . . .	Inserting Article 359A; Amending Article 356 to provide that the declaration of emergency may remain in operation up to three years.
60.	The Constitution (Sixtieth Amendment) Act, 1988	20-12-1988	20-12-1988	. . . . . .	Amending Article 276 to increase the limit of profession-tax from Rs 250 to Rs 2,500.
61.	The Constitution (Sixty-first Amendment) Act, 1989	28-3-1989	28-3-1989	Yes.	Amending Article 326 to reduce the voting age from 21 to 18 years.
62.	The Constitution (Sixty-second Amendment) Act, 1989	25-1-1990	20-12-1989	Yes.	Amending Article 334 to increase the period of reservation of seats for Scheduled Castes and Tribes for 10 years.
63.	The Constitution (Sixty-third Amendment) Act, 1989	6-1-1990	6-1-1990	. . . . . .	Omitting proviso to Article 356(5), and Article 359A.
64.	The Constitution (Sixty-fourth Amendment) Act, 1990	16-4-1990	16-4-1990	. . . . . .	Amending Article 356 [as normalcy could not be restored in Punjab, emergency was to be continued].
65.	The Constitution (Sixty-fifth Amendment) Act, 1990	7-6-1990	12-3-1992	. . . . . .	Amending Article 338 to provide for a National Commission for Scheduled Castes and Scheduled Tribes.

1.	2.	3.	4.	5.		6.
66.	The Constitution (Sixty-sixth Amendment) Act, 1990	7-6-1990	7-6-1990	. . .	. . .	Inserting Entries 203-257 in the Ninth Schedule.
67.	The Constitution (Sixty-seventh Amendment) Act, 1990	4-10-1990	4-10-1990	. . .	. . .	Amending Article 356(4), third proviso, extending President's Rule in Punjab to four years.
68.	The Constitution (Sixty-eighth Amendment) Act, 1991	12-3-1991	12-3-1991	. . .	. . .	Amending Article 356(4), third proviso, extending the period to five years.
69.	The Constitution (Sixty-ninth Amendment) Act, 1991	12-12-1991	1-2-1992	. . .	. . .	Inserting Articles 239AA and 239AB to provide for a Legislative Assembly and Council of Ministers for the Union Territory of Delhi.
70.	The Constitution (Seventieth Amendment) Act, 1992	12-8-1992	21-12-1991 [for Article 239AA]; and 1-6-1995 [for Article 54]	Yes.		Amending Articles 54 and 239AA to include Members of Legislative Assemblies of Union Territories of Delhi and Pondicherry in the electoral college.
71.	The Constitution (Seventy-first Amendment) Act, 1992	31-8-1992	31-8-1992	. . .	. . .	Inserting entries 7, 9, 11 and reinserting some entries in Eighth Schedule
72.	The Constitution (Seventy-second Amendment) Act, 1992	5-12-1992	5-12-1992	. . .	. . .	Inserting clause (3B) in Article 332.
73.	The Constitution (Seventy-third Amendment) Act, 1992	20-4-1993	24-4-1993	Yes.		Inserting Part IX, containing Articles 243, 243A–243-O; Eleventh Schedule [pertaining to Panchayats].
74.	The Constitution (Seventy-fourth Amendment) Act, 1992	20-4-1993	1-6-1993	Yes.		Inserting Part IXA, containing Articles 243P–243ZG; Twelfth Schedule [pertaining to Nagarpalika

1.	2.	3.	4.	5.	6.
					(Municipalities)]. Amended Article 280(3).
75.	The Constitution (Seventy-fifth Amendment) Act, 1993	5-2-1994	15-5-1994	Yes.	Inserting sub-clause (h) in Article 323B(2).
76.	The Constitution (Seventy-sixth Amendment) Act, 1994	31-8-1994	31-8-1994	Yes.	Inserting entry 257A in the Ninth Schedule
77.	The Constitution (Seventy-seventh Amendment) Act, 1995	17-6-1995	17-6-1995	. . . . . .	Inserting clause (4A) in Article 16.
78.	The Constitution (Seventy-eighth Amendment) Act, 1995	30-8-1995	30-8-1995	. . . . . .	Further addition of 27 entries to the Ninth Schedule to the Constitution.
79.	The Constitution (Seventy-Ninth Amendment) Act, 1999	21-1-2000	25-1-2000	Yes.	Substituting "sixty years" for the words "fifty years" in Article 334.
80.	The Constitution (Eightieth Amendment) Act, 2000	9-6-2000	1-4-1996 [for Article 270]; and 9-6-2000 [for others]	. . . . . .	Substituting new clauses for clauses (1) and (2) of Article 269; new Article for Article 270 and omitting Article 272.
81.	The Constitution (Eighty-First Amendment) Act, 2000	9-6-2000	9-6-2000	. . . . . .	Inserting clause (4B) in Article 16.
82.	The Constitution (Eighty-Second Amendment) Act, 2000	8-9-2000	8-9-2000	. . . . . .	Inserting a proviso to Article 335.

1.	2.	3.	4.	5.	6.
83.	The Constitution (Eighty-Third Amendment) Act, 2000	8-9-2000	8-9-2000	. . . . . .	Inserting clause (3A) in Article 243M.
84.	The Constitution (Eighty-fourth Amendment) Act, 2001	21.2.2002	21.2.2002	Yes	Substitution of the figure "2026" relating to census in Articles 55, 81, 82, 170, 330 and 332 for the figure "2000".
85.	The Constitution (Eighty-fifth Amendment) Act, 2001	4.1.2002	17.6.1995	. . . . . .	Substitution of certain words in Article 16(4A) to protect consequential seniority of reserved category retrospectively.
86.	The Constitution (Eighty-sixth Amendment) Act, 2002	12.12.2002	1-4-2010	. . . . . .	Insertion of Article 21A, substitution of Article 45 and insertion of Article 51A(k).
87.	The Constitution (Eighty-seventh Amendment) Act, 2003	22.6.2003	22.6.2003	. . . . . .	Substitution of the figure "2001" relating to census in Articles 81, 82, 170 and 330 for the figure "1991".
88.	The Constitution (Eighty-eighth Amendment) Act, 2003	8.5.2003	(yet to be notified)	. . . . . .	Insertion of Article 268A, substitution of the words, figures and letter "Articles 268, 268A and 269" for the words and figures "Articles 268 and 269" in Article 270 and insertion of Entry 92C in Union List.
89.	The Constitution (Eighty-ninth Amendment) Act, 2003	28.9.2003	19.2.2004	. . . . . .	Amendment of Article 338 and insertion of Article 338A.
90.	The Constitution (Ninetieth Amendment) Act, 2003	28.9.2003	28.9.2003	. . . . . .	Insertion of a proviso to Article 332(6).

1.	2.	3.	4.	5.	6.
91.	The Constitution (Ninety-first Amendment) Act, 2003	1.1.2004	1.1.2004	. . . . . .	Amendment of Articles 75, 164 and Schedule X, insertion of Article 361B.
92.	The Constitution (Ninety-second Amendment) Act, 2003	7.1.2004	7-1-2004	. . . . . .	Addition of "Bodo", "Dogri", "Maithilli" and "Santhali" languages in Schedule VIII.
93.	The Constitution (Ninety-third Amendment) Act, 2005	20.1.2006	20.1.2006	. . . . . .	Insertion of clause (5) in Article 15.
94.	The Constitution (Ninety-fourth Amendment) Act, 2006	12.6.2006	12-6-2006	Yes	Amendment of Article 164.
95.	The Constitution (Ninety-fifth Amendment) Act, 2009	18.1.2010	25.1.2010	. . . . . .	Amendment of Article 334.
96.	The Constitution (Ninety-sixth Amendment) Act, 2011	23.9.2011	23-9-2011	. . . . . .	Amendment of Eighth Schedule.
97.	The Constitution (Ninety-seventh Amendment) Act, 2011	12.1.2012	15-2-2012	. . . . . .	Amendment of Article 19, insertion of Article 43B, insertion of Part IX-B consisting of Articles 243ZH–243ZT.
98.	The Constitution (Ninety-Eighth Amendment) Act, 2012	1.1.2013	1.10.2013	. . . . . .	Insertion of New Article 371J
99.	The Constitution (Ninety-Ninth Amendment) Act, 2014	31.12.2014	13.04.2015	. . . . . .	Insertion of Articles 124A, 124B, 124C Amendment of Articles 124, 127, 128, 217, 222, 224, 224A, 231

1.	2.	3.	4.	5.		6.
100.	The Constitution (One Hundredth Amendment) Act, 2015	28-5-2015	31-7-2015	. . .	. . .	Amendment to First Schedule with regard to States of Assam, West Bengal, Meghalaya and Tripura.
101.	The Constitution (One Hundred and First Amendment) Act, 2016	8-9-2016	12-9-2016 (for Article 279); and 16-9-2016 (for other Articles)	. . .	. . .	Amendment of Articles 248,249, 250, 268, 269, 270, 271, 286, 366, 368, Sixth Schedule, Seventh Schedule. New Articles 246A, 269A, 279A inserted and Article 268A omitted.
102.	The Constitution (One Hund-red and Second) Amendment Act, 2018	11-8-2018	15-8-2018	. . .	. . .	Amendment of Article 338(10) & Article 366 and New Articles 338B and 342A inserted.
103.	The Constitution (One Hundred and Third) Amendment Act, 2019.	12-1-2019	14-1-2019	. . .	. . .	Inserting of clause (6) in Articles 15 & 16.
104	The Constitution (One Hundred and Fourth) Amendment Act, 2019	21-1-2020	25-1-2020	. . .	. . .	Amendment of Article 334.
105	The Constitution (One Hundred and Fifth) Amendment Act, 2021	18-8-2021	15-9-2021	. . .	. . .	Amendment of Articles 338B, 342A and 366.
106	The Constitution (One Hundred and Sixth) Amendment Act, 2023	28-9-2023	(yet to be notified)	. . .	. . .	Article 239AA(2) amended; and Articles 330A, 332A and 334A inserted – to allocate 33% of seats for women in Lok Sabha, State Legislative Assemblies and Delhi Legislative Assembly.

TABLE V

FUNDAMENTAL RIGHTS [PART III OF THE CONSTITUTION]

Right to Equality	*Right to Freedom*	*Right against Exploitation*	*Right to Freedom of Religion*	*Cultural and Educational Rights*	*Right to Property*[1]	*Right to Constitutional Remedies*
1. Equality before law and equal protection of laws within territory of India [Article 14]. 2. Prohibition of discrimination on grounds of religion, race, caste, sex or place of birth [Article 15]. 3. Equality of opportunity in matters of public employment [Article 16]. 4. Abolition of untouchability [Article 17]. 5. Abolition of titles [Article 18].	1. Freedom of speech and expression; assembly; association; movement; residence and settlement; ....[1] profession, occupation, trade or business [Article 19]. 2. Protection in respect of conviction for offences [Article 20]. 3. Protection of life and personal liberty [Article 21]. 4. Right to education [Article 21A].[2] 5. Protection against arrest and detention in certain cases [Article 22].	1. Prohibition of traffic in human beings and forced labour [Article 23]. 2. Prohibition of employment of children in any factory or mine or in any other hazardous employment [Article 24].	1. Freedom of conscience and free profession, practice and propagation of religion [Article 25]. 2. Freedom to manage religious affairs [Article 26]. 3. Freedom as to payment of taxes for promotion of any particular religion [Article 27]. 4. Freedom as to attendance at religious instruction or religious worship in certain educational institutions [Article 28].	1. Protection of interests of minorities [Article 29]. 2. Right of minorities to establish and administer educational institutions [Article 30].		Remedies for enforcement of guaranteed fundamental rights conferred by Part III by moving the Supreme Court for issuing directions, orders, or writs of *habeas corpus, mandamus,* prohibition, *certiorari* and *quo warranto* [Article 32].

1. The fundamental right of 'right to property' omitted from Part III of the Constitution, by the Constitution (44th Amendment) Act, 1978, section 5 (w.e.f. 20-6-1979), though it is still a constitutional right in view of insertion of Article 300A from the same date.
2. Inserted by the Constitution (Eighty-sixth Amendment) Act, 2002, section 2 (w.e.f. 1-4-2010).

TABLE VI

DIRECTIVE PRINCIPLES OF STATE POLICY [PART IV OF THE CONSTITUTION]

Directives in the Nature of Ideals of the State:	*Directives Shaping the Policy of the States:*	*Non-justiciable Rights of Citizens:*
1. The State shall strive to promote the welfare of the people by securing and effectively protecting a social order permeated by social, economic and political justice [Article 38(1)]; *to minimise inequality in income, and endeavour to eliminate inequality in status, facilities and opportunities, amongst individuals and groups of people* [Article 38(2)].[1]	1. To establish economic democracy and justice by securing certain economic rights (to be enumerated in the next column).	1. Right to adequate means of livelihood [Article 39(a)].
2. The State shall direct its policy towards securing equitable distribution of the material resources of the community to subserve the common good, and prevention of concentration of wealth and means of production to the common detriment [Articles 39(b) and (c)].	2. To organise village panchayats as units of self-government [Article 40].	2. Right of equal pay for equal work [Article 39(d)].
3. The State shall endeavour to secure just and human conditions of work and for maternity relief [Article 42].	3. To promote cottage industries in rural areas [Article 43].	3. Right against exploitation (whether economic or health) [Article 39(e)].
4. The State shall endeavour to secure work, a living wage, a decent standard of living and social and cultural opportunities for all workers [Article 43].	4. To promote voluntary formation, autonomous functioning, democratic control and professional management of co-operative societies [Article 43B].[2]	4. *Right of children and the young to be protected against exploitation and to opportunities for healthy development, consonant with freedom and dignity* [Article 39(f)].[4]
5. The State shall endeavour to raise the level of nutrition and standard of living and to improve public health [Article 47].	5. To secure a uniform civil code for the citizens [Article 44].	5. *Right to equal opportunity for justice and free legal aid* [Article 39A].[4]
	6. *To provide early childhood care and education for all children until they are more than 6 years old* [Article 45].[3]	6. Right to work, to education and to public assistance in case of unemployment, old age, sickness and disablement, and in other cases of undeserved want [Article 41].
	7. To promote educational and economic interests of weaker sections (particularly SCs and STs) and to protect them from social injustice and all forms of injustice [Article 46].	7. Right for just and humane conditions of work and maternity relief [Article 42].

1. Added by the Constitution (44th Amendment) Act, 1978, section 9 (w.e.f. 20-6-1979).
2. Added by the Constitution (97th Amendment) Act, 2011, section 3 (w.e.f. 15-2-2012).
3. Subs. by the Constitution (86th Amendment) Act, 2002, section 3 (w.e.f. 1-4-2010).
4. Added by the Constitution (42nd Amendment) Act, 1976, section 7 (w.e.f. 3-1-1977).

Directives in the Nature of Ideals of the State:	*Directives Shaping the Policy of the States:*	*Non-justiciable Rights of Citizens:*
		8. Right to a living wage and conditions of work ensuring decent standard of life for workers [Article 43].
6. The State shall endeavour to promote international peace and security, maintain just and honourable relations between nations, foster respect for international law and treaty obligations, and encourage settlement of international disputed by arbitration [Article 51].	8. To prohibit consumption of liquor and intoxicating drugs (except for medicinal purposes) [Article 47].	9. *Right of workers to participate in management of industries* [Article 43A].[5]
	9. To organise agriculture and animal husbandry on modern and scientific lines; to preserve and improve the breeds; and to prohibit slaughter of cows, calves, and other milch and draught cattle [Article 48].	10. Right of children (up to 6 years of age) of early childhood care and free and compulsory education [Article 45].[6]
	10. *To protect and improve the environment and to safeguard forests and wild life* [Article 48A].[7]	
	11. To protect and maintain monuments or places of artistic or historic interest declared to be of national importance by or under law made by Parliament [Article 49].	
	12. To separate the Judiciary from the Executive [Article 50].	

5. Added by the Constitution (42nd Amendment) Act, 1976, section 7 (w.e.f. 3-1-1977).
6. Subs. by the Constitution (86th Amendment) Act, 2002, section 3 (w.e.f. 1-4-2010).
7. Added by the Constitution (42nd Amendment) Act, 1976, section 7 (w.e.f. 3-1-1977).

TABLE VII

FUNDAMENTAL DUTIES OF CITIZENS[1] [PART IVA OF THE CONSTITUTION]

(a) To abide by the Constitution and respect its ideals and institutions, the National Flag and the National Anthem.

(b) To cherish and follow the noble ideals which inspired our national struggle for freedom.

(c) To uphold and protect the sovereignty, unity and integrity of India.

(d) To defend the country and render national service when called upon to do so.

(e) To promote harmony and the spirit of common brotherhood amongst all the people of India transcending religious, linguistic and regional or sectional diversities; to renounce practices derogatory to the dignity of women.

(f) To value and preserve the rich heritage of our composite culture.

(g) To protect and improve the natural environment including forests, lakes, rivers and wild life, and to have compassion for living creatures.

(h) To develop the scientific temper, humanism and the spirit of inquiry and reform;

(i) To safeguard public property and to abjure violence.

(j) To strive towards excellence in all spheres of individual and collective activity so that the nation constantly rises to higher levels of endeavour and achievement.

[2](k) A parent or guardian to provide opportunities for education to his child or, as the case may be, ward between the age of six and fourteen years.

1. Added by the Constitution (42nd Amendment) Act, 1976, section 11 (w.e.f. 3-1-1077).
2. Inserted by the Constitution (86th Amendment) Act, 2002, section 4 (w.e.f. 1-4-2010).

TABLE VIII

GOVERNMENT OF THE UNION

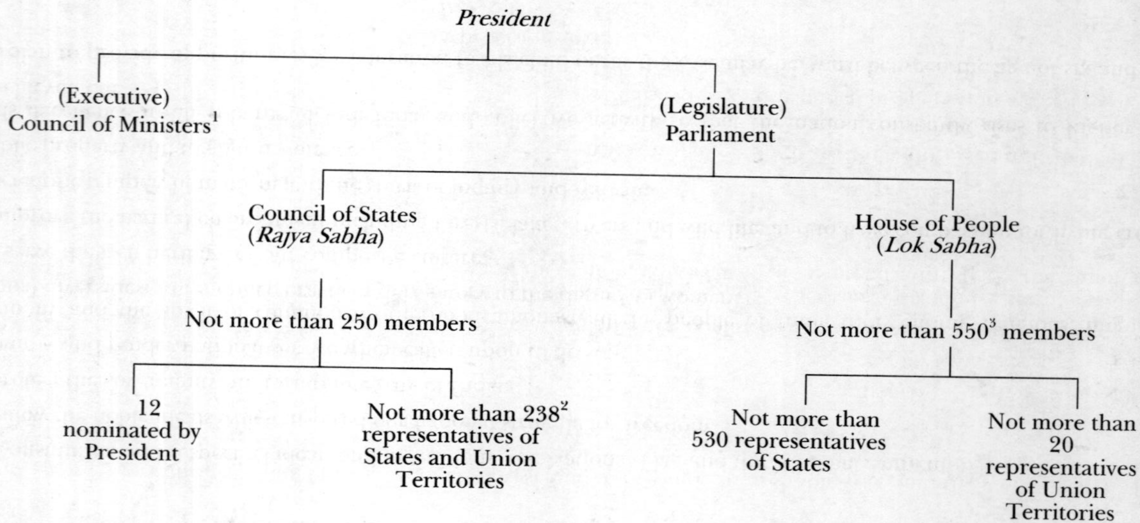

1. As on 02-02-2026, the Council of Ministers with Portfolios consisted of—
   (a) 31 Ministers in the Cabinet, including the Prime Minister; and
   (b) 41 Ministers of State [including 5 Ministers of State (Independent Charge)].
2. See Table XI, *post.*
3. See Table XII, *post.*

TABLE IX

OFFICES OF PRESIDENT AND VICE-PRESIDENT COMPARED

President	*Vice-President*
(i) Election :	
Elected by members of an electoral college consisting of the elected members of (a) both Houses of Parliament; and (b) Legislative Assemblies of States (including the NCT of Delhi and Puducherry).	Elected by members of an electoral college consisting of members of both Houses of Parliament.
Both elections to be in accordance with the system of proportional representation by single transferable vote, and the voting shall be by secret ballot.	
(ii) Qualifications for Election :	
(a) Must be a citizen of India;	
(b) Must have completed the age of 35 years; and	
(c) Must be qualified for election of House of the People.	(c) Must be qualified for election to Council of States.
(d) Must not hold any office of profit under the Government of India or of a State or any other authority under the control of either Government, excepting the offices of President or Vice-President of the Union, Governor of any State, or Minister of the Union or of any State.	
(iii) Term of Office :	
Five years from the date of entering office :	
(a) May resign earlier by writing addressed to Vice-President.	(a) May resign earlier by writing addressed to President.
(b) May be removed by the process of impeachment provided in Article 61.	(b) May be removed by a resolution passed by a majority of all the then members of Council of States and agreed to by House of the People.
Both eligible for re-election any number of times, subject to other provisions of the Constitution.	
(iv) Powers and Functions :	
(a) The executive power in the Union is vested in him, and he exercises it on the aid and advice of the Council of Ministers of the Union.	(a) When a vacancy arises in the office of President, he has to act as President until a new President is elected and enters upon office.
(b) Various appointments are to be made by him such as the Prime Minister, other Council of Ministers on the advice of the Prime Minister, Attorney-General for India.	(b) Except when a vacancy arises in office of President, he acts as an *ex-officio* Chairman of the Rajya Sabha.

TABLE X

IMPORTANT CONSTITUTIONAL POSTS

A. TABLE OF RANK AND PRECEDENCE OF REPUBLIC OF INDIA

1. President

2. Vice-President

3. Prime Minister

4. Governors of States within their respective States

5. Former Presidents

5A. Deputy Prime Minister

6. Chief Justice of India
Speaker of Lok Sabha

7. Cabinet Ministers of the Union
Chief Ministers of States within their respective States
Deputy Chairman, NITI Aayog
Former Prime Ministers
Leaders of Opposition in Rajya Sabha and Lok Sabha

7A. Holders of Bharat Ratna decoration

8. Ambassadors Extraordinary and Plenipotentiary and High Commissioners of Commonwealth countries accredited to India
Chief Ministers of States outside their respective States
Governors of States outside their respective States

9. Judges of Supreme Court

9A. Chairperson, Union Public Service Commission
Chief Election Commissioner
Comptroller & Auditor General of India

10. Deputy Chairman, Rajya Sabha
    Deputy Chief Ministers of States
    Deputy Speaker, Lok Sabha
    Members of the NITI Aayog
    Ministers of State of the Union {and any other Minister in the Ministry of Defence for defence matters}

11. Attorney General of India.
    Cabinet Secretary.
    Lieutenant Governors within their respective Union Territories

12. Chiefs of Staff holding the rank of full General or equivalent rank.

13. Envoys Extraordinary and Ministers Plenipotentiary accredited to India.

14. Chairmen and Speakers of State Legislatures within their respective States.
    Chief Justices of High Courts within their respective jurisdictions

15. Cabinet Ministers in States within their respective States
    Chief Ministers of Union Territories and Chief Executive Councillor, Delhi within their respective Union Territories
    Deputy Ministers of the Union

16. Officiating Chiefs of Staff holding the rank of Lieutenant General or equivalent rank.

17. Chairman, Central Administrative Tribunal.
    Chairman, Minorities Commission
    Chairperson, National Commission for Scheduled Castes
    Chairperson, National Commission for Scheduled Tribes
    Chief Justices of High Courts outside their respective jurisdictions
    Puisne Judges of High Courts within their respective jurisdictions

18. Cabinet Ministers in States outside their respective States
    Chairmen and Speakers of State Legislatures outside their respective States
    Chairman, Monopolies and Restrictive Trade Practices Commission
    Deputy Chairmen and Deputy Speakers of State Legislatures within their respective States
    Ministers of State in States within their respective States
    Ministers of Union Territories and Executive Councilors, Delhi, within their respective Union Territories.
    Speakers of Legislative Assemblies in Union Territories and Chairman of Delhi Metropolitan Council within their respective Union Territories.

19. Chief Commissioners of Union Territories not having Councils of Ministers, within their respective Union Territories.
    Deputy Ministers in States within their respective States.
    Deputy Speakers of Legislative Assemblies in Union Territories and Deputy Chairman of Metropolitan Council Delhi, within their respective Union Territories.

20. Deputy Chairman and Deputy Speakers of State Legislatures, outside their respective states.
    Ministers of State in States outside their respective States
    Puisne Judges of High Courts outside their respective jurisdictions.

21. Members of Parliament.

22. Deputy Ministers in State outside their respective States

23. Army Commanders/ Vice-Chief of the Army Staff or equivalent in other services
    Chief Secretaries to State Governments within their respective States
    Commissioner for Linguistic Minorities
    Commissioner for Scheduled Castes and Scheduled Tribes
    Members, Minorities Commission
    Members, National Commission for Scheduled Castes
    Members, National Commission for Scheduled Tribes
    Officers of the rank of full General or equivalent rank
    Secretaries to the Government of India (including officers holding this office ex-officio).
    Secretary, Minorities Commission.
    Secretary, Scheduled Castes and Scheduled Tribes Commission.
    Secretary to the President.
    Secretary to the Prime Minister.
    Secretary, Rajya Sabha/Lok Sabha
    Solicitor General
    Vice-Chairman, Central Administrative Tribunal

24. Officers of the rank of Lieutenant General or equivalent rank.

25. Additional Secretaries to the Government of India.
    Additional Solicitor General
    Advocate Generals of States.
    Chairman, Tariff Commission

Charge d' Affairs and Acting High Commissioners a pied and ad interim
Chief Ministers of Union Territories and Chief Executive Councillor, Delhi outside their respective Union Territories
Chief Secretaries of State Governments outside their respective States.
Deputy Comptroller and Auditor General
Deputy Speakers of Legislative Assemblies in Union Territories and Deputy Chairman, Delhi Metropolitan Council, outside their respective Union Territories.
Director, Central Bureau of Investigation
Director General, Border Security Force.
Director General, Central Reserve Police.
Director, Intelligence Bureau
Lieutenant Governors outside their respective Union Territories.
Members, Central Administrative Tribunal
Members, Monopolies and Restrictive Trade Practices Commission
Members, Union Public Service Commission
Ministers of Union Territories and Executive Councillors, Delhi, outside their respective Union Territories.
Principal Staff Officers of the Armed Forces of the rank of major General or equivalent rank
Speakers of Legislative Assemblies in Union Territories and Chairman of Delhi, Metropolitan Council, outside their respective Union Territories

26. Joint Secretaries to the Government of India and officers of equivalent rank.
Officers of the rank of Major-General or equivalent rank.

NOTES

Note 1.—The order in this Table of Precedence is meant for State and Ceremonial occasions and has no application in the day-to-day business of Government.

Note 2.—Persons in the Table of Precedence will take rank in order of the number of the articles. The entries in the same article are arranged alphabetically. Those included in the same article will take precedence inter se according to date of entry into that article. However, where the dignitaries of different States and Union Territories included in the same article are present at a function outside their States or Union Territories and there is difficulty in ascertaining their dates of entry, they may be assigned precedence inter se in the alphabetical order of the name of States and Union Territories concerned after those whose precedence is determined according to date of entry into that article.

Note 3.—In Article 7, former Prime Ministers will take precedence over the Cabinet Ministers of the Union and the Leaders of Opposition in the Rajya Sabha and the Lok Sabha. The Chief Ministers of States within their respective States will take precedence over the Cabinet Ministers of the Union in official functions held in the respective States.

Note 4.—In Article 8:

(a) Ambassadors Extraordinary and Plenipotentiary and High Commissioners of Commonwealth countries accredited to India will en bloc rank above Governors of States outside their respective States;

(b) Governors of States outside their respective States will en bloc rank above Chief Ministers of States outside their respective States.

Note 5.—The Ministry of External Affairs may assign appropriate ranks to foreign dignitaries and Indian Ambassadors, High Commissioners and Ministers Plenipotentiary during their visit to India.

Note 6.—Notwithstanding the procedure laid down in Note 2, the rank inter se and precedence of the persons in Article 10 shall be assigned in the following order:

(1) Deputy Chairman, Rajya Sabha.

(2) Deputy Speaker, Lok Sabha.

(3) Ministers of State of the Union and any other Minister in the Ministry of Defence for defence matters.

(4) Deputy Chief Ministers of States.

(5) Members of NITI Aayog.

However, the Deputy Chief Ministers of States outside their respective States will always rank below all other dignitaries figuring in this article.

Note 7.—The Chairmen of State Legislative Councils will rank above the Speakers of Legislative Assemblies in cases where they were elected on the same date.

Note 8.—When Members of Parliament are invited *en bloc* to major State functions, the enclosures reserved for them should be next to the Chief Justice, Speaker of the Lok Sabha, Ambassadors etc.

Note 9.—Speakers of Legislative Assemblies in Union Territories and Chairman of the Delhi Metropolitan Council, Delhi, will take precedence over Ministers and Executive Councillors, included in the same article.

Note 10.—In Article 23:

(a) Secretaries in the Ministry of External Affairs other than the Foreign Secretary, between themselves, will take precedence in the order of their seniority in Grade-I of the Indian Foreign Service and both of them will take precedence after the Foreign Secretary.

(b) Members of the Minorities Commission and the Scheduled Castes and Schedule Tribes Commission will always take precedence over the Secretaries of these Commissions;

(c) In official functions held at Delhi/New Delhi, Army Commanders/Vice Chief of the Army Staff or equivalent in other Services will always rank after Secretaries to the Government of India.

Note 11.—In Article 25:

(a) Additional Secretaries in the Ministry of External Affairs, among themselves, will take precedence in the order of their seniority in Grade-II of the Indian Foreign Service;

(b) Additional Solicitor General will take precedence above the Advocate General of States;

(c) Lieutenant Governors will take precedence over the Chief Ministers and Chief Executive Councillor, Delhi, and the latter will take precedence over Speakers of Legislative Assemblies and Chairman, Metropolitan Council, Delhi;

(d) Deputy Speakers of Legislative Assemblies of Union Territories and Deputy Chairman of Delhi Metropolitan Council will take precedence after Ministers of Union Territories and Executive Councillors, Delhi.

Note 12.—For the purpose of Article 26, the posts equivalent to the posts of Joint Secretaries to the Government of India will be determined by the Ministry of Home Affairs.

B. PRESIDENTS OF INDIA

	Name	Tenure
1.	Dr. Rajendra Prasad (1884–1963)	26 January 1950 — 13 May 1962 [1st President]
2.	Dr. Sarvepalli Radhakrishnan (1888–1975)	13 May 1962 — 13 May 1967 [2nd President]
3.	Dr. Zakir Hussain (1897–1969)	13 May 1967 — 3 May 1969 (Died) [3rd President]
4.	Varahagiri Venkata Giri (1894–1980)	3 May 1969 — 20 July 1969 (Acting)
5.	Justice Muhammad Hidayatullah (1905–1992)	20 July 1969 — 24 August 1969 (Acting)
6.	Varahagiri Venkata Giri (1894–1980)	24 August 1969 — 24 August 1974 [4th President]
7.	Dr. Fakhruddin Ali Ahmed (1905–1977)	24 August 1974 — 11 February 1977 (Died) [5th President]
8.	Basappa Danappa Jatti (1912–2002)	11 February 1977 — 25 July 1977 (Acting)

Name	Tenure
9. Neelam Sanjiva Reddy (1913–1996)	25 July 1977 — 25 July 1982 [6th President]
10. Giani Zail Singh (1916–1994)	25 July 1982 — 25 July 1987 [7th President]
11. Justice Muhammad Hidayatullah (1905–1992)	6 October 1982 — 31 October 1982 (discharged the functions of the President)
12. Ramaswamy Venkataraman (1910–2009)	25 July 1987 — 25 July 1992 [8th President]
13. Dr. Shankar Dayal Sharma (1918–1999)	25 July 1992 — 25 July 1997 [9th President]
14. Dr. K.R. Narayanan (1920–2005)	25 July 1997 — 25 July 2002 [10th President]
15. Dr. A.P.J. Abdul Kalam (1931–2015)	25 July 2002 — 25 July 2007 [11th President]
16. Pratibha Devisingh Patil (1934-present)	25 July 2007 — 25 July 2012 [12th President]
17. Pranab Mukherjee (1935–2020)	25 July 2012 — 25 July 2017 [13th President]
18. Ram Nath Kovind (1945-present)	25 July 2017 — 25 July 2022 [14th President]
19. Droupadi Murmu (1958-present)	25 July 2022 onwards [15th President]

C. VICE-PRESIDENTS OF INDIA

Name	Tenure
1. Dr. Sarvepalli Radhakrishnan (1888-1975)	13 May 1952 — 13 May 1962 [1st Vice-President]
2. Dr. Zakir Hussain (1897-1969)	13 May 1962 — 13 May 1967 [2nd Vice-President]
3. Varahagiri Venkatagiri (1894–1980)	13 May 1967 — 3 May 1969 (Resigned) [3rd Vice-President]

Name	Tenure
4. Gopal Swarup Pathak (1896–1982)	31 August 1969 — 31 August 1974 [4th Vice-President]
5. Basappa Danappa Jatti (1912–2002)	31 August 1974 — 31 August 1979 [5th Vice-President]
6. Justice Mohammad Hidayatullah (1905-1992)	31 August 1979 — 31 August 1984 [6th Vice-President]
7. Ramaswamy Venkataraman (1910-2009)	31 August 1984 — 24 July 1987 (Resigned) [7th Vice-President]
8. Dr. Shanker Dayal Sharma (1918-1999)	3 September 1987 — 24 July 1992 (Resigned) [8th Vice-President]
9. Dr. K R Narayanan (1920-2005)	21 August 1992 — 24 July 1997 (Resigned) [9th Vice-President]
10. Krishan Kant (1927-2002)	21 August 1997 — 27 July 2002 (Died) [10th Vice-President]
11. Bhairon Singh Shekhawat (1925-2010)	19 August 2002 — 21 July 2007 (Resigned) [11th Vice-President]
12. Mohammad Hamid Ansari (1937-present)	11 August 2007 — 11 August 2017 [12th Vice-President]
13. Muppavarapu Venkaiah Naidu (1948-present)	11 August 2017 — 11 August 2022 [13th Vice-President]
14. Jagdeep Dhankar (1951-present)	11 August 2022 - 21 July 2025 (resigned) [14th Vice-President]
15. C. P. Radhakrishnan (1957-present)	12 September 2025 onwards [15th Vice-President]

D. PRIME MINISTERS OF INDIA

Name	Tenure
1. Jawaharlal Nehru (1889–1964)	15 August 1947 — 27 May 1964 (Died) [1st Prime Minister]
2. Gulzari Lal Nanda (1898–1997)	27 May 1964 — 9 June 1964 (Acting)
3. Lal Bahadur Shastri (1904–1966)	9 June 1964 — 11 January 1966 (Died) [2nd Prime Minister]

Name	Tenure
4. Gulzari Lal Nanda (1898–1997)	11 January 1966 — 24 January 1966 (Acting)
5. Indira Gandhi (1917–1984)	24 January 1966 — 24 March 1977 [3rd Prime Minister]
6. Morarji Desai (1896–1995)	24 March 1977 — 28 July 1979 (Resigned) [4th Prime Minister]
7. Charan Singh (1902–1987)	28 July 1979 — 14 January 1980 (Resigned) [5th Prime Minister]
8. Indira Gandhi (1917–1984)	14 January 1980 — 31 October 1984 (Died)
9. Rajiv Gandhi (1944–1991)	31 October 1984 — 1 December 1989 [6th Prime Minister]
10. Vishwanath Pratap Singh (1931-2008)	2 December 1989 — 10 November 1990 (Resigned) [7th Prime Minister]
11. Chandra Shekhar (1927–2007)	10 November 1990 — 21 June 1991 (Resigned) [8th Prime Minister]
12. P V Narasimha Rao (1921-2004)	21 June 1991 — 16 May 1996 [9th Prime Minister]
13. Atal Bihari Bajpayee (1924–2018)	16 May 1996 — 1 June 1996 (Resigned) [10th Prime Minister]
14. H D Deve Gowda (1933-present)	1 June 1996 — 20 April 1997 (Resigned) [11th Prime Minister]
15. I K Gujral (1919–2012)	21 April 1997 — 18 March 1998 (Resigned) [12th Prime Minister]
16. Atal Bihari Bajpayee (1924–2018)	19 March 1998 — 22 May 2004
17. Dr. Manmohan Singh (1932-2024)	22 May 2004 — 26 May 2014 [13th Prime Minister]
18. Narendra Modi (1950-present)	26 May 2014 onwards [14th Prime Minister]

E. CHIEF JUSTICES OF INDIA

Name	Tenure
Harilal J. Kania	26-01-1950 — 06-11-1951
M. Patanjali Sastri	07-11-1951 — 03-01-1954
M.C. Mahajan	04-01-1954 — 22-12-1954
B.K. Mukherjea	23-12-1954 — 31-01-1956
S.R. Das	01-02-1956 — 30-09-1959
B.P. Sinha	01-10-1959 — 31-01-1964
P.B. Gajendragadkar	01-02-1964 — 15-03-1966
A.K. Sarkar	16-03-1966 — 29-06-1966
K. Subba Rao	30-06-1966 — 11-04-1967
K.N. Wanchoo	12-04-1967 — 24-02-1968
M. Hidayatullah	25-02-1968 — 16-12-1970
J.C. Shah	17-12-1970 — 21-01-1971
S.M. Sikri	22-01-1971 — 25-04-1973
A.N. Ray	26-04-1973 — 28-01-1977
M.H. Beg	29-01-1977 — 21-02-1978
Y.V. Chandrachud	22-02-1978 — 11-07-1985
P.N. Bhagwati	12-07-1985 — 20-12-1986
R.S. Pathak	21-12-1986 — 18-06-1989
E.S. Venkataramiah	19-06-1989 — 17-12-1989
S. Mukherjee	18-12-1989 — 25-09-1990
Ranganath Misra	25-09-1990 — 24-11-1991
K.N. Singh	25-11-1991 — 12-12-1991
M.H. Kania	13-12-1991 — 17-11-1992
L.M. Sharma	18-11-1992 — 11-02-1993

Name	Tenure
M.N. Venkatachaliah	12-02-1993 — 24-10-1994
A.M. Ahmadi	25-10-1994 — 24-03-1997
J.S. Verma	25-03-1997 — 17-01-1998
M.M. Punchhi	18-01-1998 — 09-10-1998
A.S. Anand	10-10-1998 — 31-10-2001
S.P. Bharucha	01-11-2001 — 05-05-2002
B.N. Kirpal	06-05-2002 — 07-11-2002
G.B. Patnaik	08-11-2002 — 18-12-2002
V.N. Khare	19-12-2002 — 01-05-2004
S. Rajendra Babu	02-05-2004 — 31-05-2004
R.C. Lahoti	01-06-2004 — 31-10-2005
Y.K. Sabharwal	01-11-2005 — 13-01-2007
K.G. Balakrishnan	14-01-2007 — 12-05-2010
S.H. Kapadia	12-05-2010 — 28-09-2012
Altamas Kabir	29-09-2012 — 18-07-2013
P. Sathasivam	19-07-2013 — 26-04-2014
R.M. Lodha	27-04-2014 — 27-09-2014
H.L. Dattu	28-09-2014 — 2-12-2015
T.S. Thakur	03-12-2015 — 03-01-2017
J.S. Khehar	04-01-2017 — 27-08-2017
Dipak Misra	28-08-2017 — 02-10-2018
Ranjan Gogoi	03-10-2018 — 17-11-2019
S.A. Bobde	18-11-2019 — 23-04-2021
NV Ramana	24-04-2021 — 26-08-2022
U.U. Lalit	27-08-2022 — 08-11-2022
D.Y. Chandrachud	09-11-2022 — 10-11-2024
Sanjiv Khanna	11-11-2024 — 13-05-2025
B R Gavai	14-05-2025 — 23-11-2025
Surya Kant	24-11-2025 — 09-02-2027

F. LOK SABHA & ITS SPEAKERS

Lok Sabha			Speaker(s)		
	Date of first meeting after its constitution	*Date of dissolution*	*Name*	*From*	*To*
First Lok Sabha	13 May 1952	4 April 1957	Ganesh Vasudev Mavalankar M Ananthasayanam Ayyanger	15 May 1952 8 March 1956	27 February 1956 10 May 1957
Second Lok Sabha	10 May 1957	31 March 1962	M Ananthasayanam Ayyanger	11 May 1957	16 April 1962
Third Lok Sabha	16 April 1962	3 March 1967	Hukam Singh	17 April 1962	16 March 1967
Fourth Lok Sabha	16 March 1967	27 December 1970	Neelam Sanjiva Reddy Dr. Gurdial Singh Dhillon	17 March 1967 8 August 1969	19 July 1969 19 March 1971
Fifth Lok Sabha	19 March 1971	18 January 1977	Dr. Gurdial Singh Dhillon Bali Ram Bhagat	22 March 1971 5 January 1976	1 December 1975 25 March 1977
Sixth Lok Sabha	25 March 1977	22 August 1979	Neelam Sanjiva Reddy K.D. Hegde	26 March 1977 21 July 1977	13 July 1977 21 January 1980
Seventh Lok Sabha	21 January 1980	31 December 1984	Dr. Balram Jakhar	22 January 1980	15 January 1985
Eighth Lok Sabha	15 January 1985	27 November 1989	Dr. Balram Jakhar	16 January 1985	18 December 1989
Ninth Lok Sabha	18 December 1989	13 March 1991	Rabi Ray	19 December 1989	9 July 1991
Tenth Lok Sabha	9 July 1991	10 May 1996	Shivraj V. Patil	10 July 1991	22 May 1996
Eleventh Lok Sabha	22 May 1996	4 December 1997	P.A. Sangma	23 May 1996	23 March 1998
Twelfth Lok Sabha	23 March 1998	26 April 1999	G.M.C. Balayogi	24 March 1998	20 October 1999
Thirteenth Lok Sabha	20 October 1999	6 February 2004	G.M.C. Balayogi Manohar Ganjan Joshi	22 October 1999 10 May 2002	3 March 2002 2 June 2004

Lok Sabha			Speaker(s)		
	Date of first meeting after its constitution	*Date of dissolution*	*Name*	*From*	*To*
Fourteenth Lok Sabha	2 June 2004	18 May 2009	Somnath Chatterjee	4 June 2004	31 May 2009
Fifteenth Lok Sabha	1 June 2009	18 May 2014	Meira Kumar	1 June 2009	18 May 2014
Sixteenth Lok Sabha	4 June 2014	24 May 2019	Sumitra Mahajan	6 June 2014	17 June 2019
Seventeenth Lok Sabha	17 June 2019	Till date	Om Birla	19 June 2019	Till date

G. CHIEF ELECTION COMMISSIONERS OF INDIA

Name	Tenure
1. Sukumar Sen	21 March 1950 to 19 December 1958
2. KVK Sundaram	20 December 1958 to 30 September 1967
3. SP Sen Verma	1 October 1967 to 30 September 1972
4. Dr Nagendra Singh	1 October 1972 to 6 February 1973
5. T Swaminathan	7 February 1973 to 17 June 1977
6. SL Shakdhar	18 June 1977 to 17 June 1982
7. RK Trivedi	18 June 1982 to 31 December 1985
8. RVS Peri Sastri	1 January 1986 to 25 November 1990
9. VS Ramadevi	26 November 1990 to 11 December 1990
10. TN Seshan	12 December 1990 to 11 December 1996
11. MS Gill	12 December 1996 to 13 June 2001
12. J.M. Lyngdoh	14 June 2001 to 7 Feb 2004
13. T.S. Krishna Murthy	8 Feb 2004 to 15 May 2005
14. B.B. Tandon	16 May 2005 to 29 June 2006
15. N. Gopalaswami	30 June 2006 to 20 April 2009
16. Navin B. Chawla	21 April 2009 to 29 July 2010

Name	Tenure
17. S.Y. Quraishi	30 July 2010 to 10 June 2012
18. V.S. Sampath	11 June 2012 to 15 Jan 2015
19. H.S. Brahma	16 Jan 2015 to 18 April 2015
20. Nasim Zaidi	19 April 2015 to 05 July 2017
21. A K Joti	06 July 2017 to 22 January 2018
22. O. P. Rawat	23 January 2018 to 01 December 2018
23. Sunil Arora	02 December 2018 to 12 April 2021
24. Sushil Chandra	13 April 2021 to 14 May 2022
25. Rajiv Kumar	15 May 2022 to 18 February 2025
26. Gyanesh Kumar	19 February 2025 – till date

H. CABINET SECRETARIES

Name	Tenure
1. N.R. Pillai	06 February 1950 to 13 May 1953
2. Y.N. Sukthankar	14 May 1953 to 31 July 1957
3. M.K. Vellodi	01 August 1957 to 04 June 1958
4. Vishnu Sahay	01 July 1958 to 10 November 1960
5. B.N. Jha	10 November 1960 to 08 March 1961
6. Vishnu Sahay	09 March 1961 to 15 April 1962
7. S.S. Khera	15 April 1962 to 18 November 1964
8. Dharam Vira	18 November 1964 to 27 June 1966
9. D.S. Joshi	27 June 1966 to 31 December 1968
10. B. Sivaraman	01 January 1969 to 30 November 1970
11. T. Swaminathan	01 December 1970 to 02 November 1972
12. B.D. Pande	02 November 1972 to 31 March 1977
13. N.K. Mukarji	31 March 1977 to 31 March 1980

Name	Tenure
14. S.S. Grewal	02 April 1980 to 30 April 1981
15. C.R. Krishnaswamy Rao	30 April 1981 to 08 February 1985
16. P.K. Kaul	08 February 1985 to 22 August 1986
17. B.G. Deshmukh	23 August 1986 to 27 March 1989
18. T.N. Seshan	27 March 1989 to 23 December 1989
19. V.C. Pande	23 December 1989 to 11 December 1990
20. Naresh Chandra	11 December 1990 to 31 July 1992
21. S. Rajgopal	01 August 1992 to 31 July 1993
22. Zafar Saifullah	31 July 1993 to 31 July 1994
23. Surendra Singh	01 August 1994 to 31 July 1996
24. T.S.R. Subramanian	01 August 1996 to 31 March 998
25. Prabhat Kumar	01 April 1998 to 31 October 2000
26. T.R. Prasad	01 November 2000 to 31 October 2002
27. Kamal Pande	01 November 2002 to 14 June 2004
28. B. K. Chaturvedi	14 June 2004 to 13 June 2007
29. K. M. Chandrasekhar	14 June 2007 to 13 June 2011
30. Ajit Kumar Seth	14 June 2011 to 13 June 2015
31. Pradeep Kumar Sinha	13 June 2015 to 30 August 2019
32. Rajiv Gauba	30 August 2019 to 30 August 2024
33. Dr. T.V. Somanathan	30 August 2024 till date

I. CHIEFS OF DEFENCE STAFF (CDS)

Name	Tenure
1. Bipin Rawat	January 1 2020 - December 8 2021
2. Anil Chauhan	September 30 2022 till date

J. CHIEFS OF ARMY STAFF

Name	Tenure
1. Sir Francis Robert Roy Bucher	01 January 1948 to 15 January 1949
2. KM Cariappa	16 January 1949 to 14 January 1953
3. KS Rajendra Sinhji	15 January 1953 to 14 May 1955
4. SM Shrinagesh	15 May 1955 to 07 May 1957
5. KS Thimayya	08 May 1957 to 07 May 1961
6. PN Thapar	08 May 1961 to 19 November 1962
7. JN Chaudhuri	20 November 1962 to 07 June 1966
8. PP Kumaramangalam	08 June 1966 to 07 June 1969
9. SHFJ Manekshaw	08 June 1969 to 15 January 1973
10. GG Bewoor	16 January 1973 to 31 May 1975
11. TN Raina	01 June 1975 to 31 May 1978
12. OP Malhotra	01 June 1978 to 31 May 1981
13. KV Krishna Rao	01 June 1981 to 31 July 1983
14. AS Vaidya	01 August 1983 31 January 1986
15. K Sundarji	01 February 1986 to 31 May 1988
16. VN Sharma	30 June 1988 to 30 June 1990
17. SF Rodrigues	01 July 1990 to 30 June 1993
18. BC Joshi	01 July 1993 to 19 November 1994
19. S Roy Chowdhury	22 November 1994 to 30 September 1997
20. VP Malik	01 October 1997 to 30 September 2000
21. S Padmanabhan	01 October 2000 to 30 December 2002
22. NC Vij	31 December 2002 to 31 January 2005
23. JJ Singh	01 February 2005 to 30 September 2007
24. Deepak Kapoor	30 September 2007 to 30 March 2010
25. VK Singh	31 March 2010 to 31 May 2012
26. Bikram Singh	01 June 2012 to 31 July 2014
27. Dalbir Singh	01 August 2014 to 31 December 2016

Name	Tenure
28. Bipin Rawat	31 December 2016 to 31 December 2019
29. MM Naravane	31 December 2019 to 30 April 2022
30. Manoj Pande	30 April 2022 to 30 June 2024
31. Upendra Dwivedi	30 Jun 2024 to Till Date

K. CHIEFS OF NAVAL STAFF

Name	Tenure
1. J.T.S. Hall	August 15, 1947, to August 14 1948
2. Sir Edward Parry	August 15, 1948, to October 13 1951
3. Sir Mark Pizey	October 14, 1951, to 21 July 1955
4. Sir Stephen Carlill	July 22, 1955 to April 21, 1958
5. R.D. Katari	April 22, 1958, to June 4 1962
6. B.S. Soman	June 05, 1962, to March 3 1966
7. A.K. Chatterjee	March 04, 1966, to February 27 1970
8. S.M. Nanda	February 28, 1970, to February 28 1973
9. S.N. Kohli	March 01, 1973, to February 28 1976
10. J.L. Cursetji	March 01, 1976, to February 28 1979
11. R.L. Pereira	March 01, 1979, to February 28 1982
12. O.S. Dawson	March 01, 1982, to November 30 1984
13. R.H. Tahiliani	December 01, 1984, to November 30 1987
14. J.G. Nadkarni	December 01, 1987, to November 30 1990
15. Ramdas	December 01, 1990, to September 30 1993
16. V.S. Shekhawat	October 01, 1993, to September 30 1996
17. Vishnu Bhagwat	October 01, 1996, to December 30 1998

Name	Tenure
18. Sushil Kumar	December 31, 1998, to December 29 2001
19. Madhvendra Singh	December 29, 2001, to July 31 2004
20. Arun Prakash	August 01, 2004, to October 30 2006
21. Suresh Mehta	October 30, 2006, to August 31 2009
22. Nirmal Verma	August 31, 2009, to August 31 August 2012
23. Devender Kumar Joshi	August 31, 2012, to February 26 2014
24. RK Dhowan	February 26, 2014, to May 31 2016
25. Sunil Lanba	May 31, 2016, to May 31 2019
26. Karambir Singh	May 31, 2019, to November 30, 2021
27. R Hari Kumar	November 30, 2021 to April 30, 2024
28. Dinesh Kumar Tripathi	April 30th, 2024 – Present

L. CHIEFS OF AIR STAFF

Name	Tenure
1. Sir Thomas Walker Elmhirst	15 August 1947 - 22 February 1950
2. Ronald Ivelaw-Chapman	22 February 1950 - 09 December 1951
3. Sir Gerald Ernest Gibbs	10 December 1951 - 31 March 1954
4. Subroto Mukerjee	01 April 1954 - 08 November 1960
5. Aspy Merwan Engineer	01 December 1960 - 31 July 1964
6. Arjan Singh	01 August 1964 - 15 July 1969
7. Pratap Chandra Lal	16 July 1969 - 15 January 1973
8. Om Prakash Mehra	16 January 1973 - 31 January 1976
9. Hrushikesh Moolgavkar	01 February 1976 - 31 August 1978

Name	Tenure
10. Idris Hassan Latif	01 September 1978 - 31 August1981
11. Dilbagh Singh	01 September 1981 - 03 September 1984
12. Lakshman Madhav Katre	04 September 1984 - 01 July 1985
13. Denis Anthony La Fontaine	03 July 1985 - 31 July 1988
14. Surinder Kumar Mehra	01 August 1988 - 31 July 1991
15. Nirmal Chandra Suri	31 July 1991 - 31 July 1993
16. Swaroop Krishna Kaul	01 August 1993 - 31 December 1995
17. Satish Kumar Sareen	31 December 1995 - 31 December 1998
18. Anil Yashwant Tipnis	31 December 1998 - 31 December 2001
19. S Krishnaswamy	31 December 2001 - 31 December 2004
20. SP Tyagi	31 December 2004 - 31 March 2007
21. FH Major	31 March 2007 - 31 May 2009
22. Pradeep Vasant Naik	31 May 2009 - 31 July 2011
23. NAK Browne	02 August 2011 - 31 December 2013
24. Arup Raha	01 January 2014 - 31 December 2016
25. BS Dhanoa	01 January 2017 - 30 September 2019
26. Rakesh Kumar Singh Bhadauria	30 September 2019 - 30 September 2021
27. VR Chaudhari	30 September 2021 - 30 September 2024
28. AP Singh	30 September 2024 - Till date

TABLE XI

REPRESENTATION OF STATES AND UNION TERRITORIES IN THE COUNCIL OF STATES (RAJYA SABHA)[1]

For each State or Union territory specified in the first column of the following table, there shall be allotted the number of seats specified in the second column thereof opposite to that State or that Union territory, as the case may be.

TABLE

1. Andhra Pradesh	[2][11]
[3][2. Telangana	7]
3. Assam	7
[*]4. Bihar	[4][16]

1. Subs. by the Constitution (Seventh Amendment) Act, 1956, sec. 3(2), for the Fourth Schedule (w.e.f. 1-11-1956).
2. Subs. by the Andhra Pradesh Reorganisation Act, 2014 (6 of 2014), sec. 12(a), for "18" (w.e.f. 2-6-2014).
3. Ins. by the Andhra Pradesh Reorganisation Act, 2014 (6 of 2014), sec. 12(c).

* Entry numbers have been re-numbered by (i) the Jammu and Kashmir Reorganisation Act, 2019 (34 of 2019), sec. 8(b) (w.e.f. 31-10-2019); (ii) the Bombay Reorganisation Act, 1960 (11 of 1960), sec. 6(c) (w.e.f. 1-5-1960); (iii) the State of Nagaland Act, 1962 (27 of 1962), sec. 6(b)(i) (w.e.f. 1-12-1963); (iv) the Punjab Reorganisation Act, 1966 (31 of 1966), sec. 9(a) (w.e.f. 1-11-1966); (v) the State of Himachal Pradesh Act, 1970 (53 of 1970), sec. 5(a) (w.e.f. 25-1-1971); (vi) the North Eastern Areas (Reorganisation) Act, 1971 (81 of 1971), sec. 10(a) (w.e.f. 21-1-1972); (vii) the Constitution (Thirty-sixth Amendment) Act, 1975, sec. 4(b) (w.e.f. 26-4-1975); (viii) the State of Mizoram Act, 1986 (34 of 1986), sec. 5(a) (w.e.f. 20-2-1987); (ix) the Goa, Daman and Diu Reorganisation Act, 1987 (18 of 1987), sec. 6(a) (w.e.f. 30-5-1987); (x) the Madhya Pradesh Reorganisation Act, 2000 (28 of 2000), sec. 7(a) (w.e.f. 1-11-2000); (xi) the Uttar Pradesh Reorganisation Act, 2000 (29 of 2000), sec. 7(a) (w.e.f. 9-11-2000); (xii) the Bihar Reorganisation Act, 2000 (30 of 2000), sec. 7(a) (w.e.f. 15-11-2000) and (xiii) the Andhra Pradesh Reorganisation Act, 2014 (6 of 2014), sec. 12(b) (w.e.f. 2-6-2014 vide S.O. 655(E), dated 4th March 2014).

4. Subs. by the Bihar Reorganisation Act, 2000 (30 of 2000), sec. 7(b), for "22" (w.e.f. 15-11-2000).

[5][*5. Jharkhand	6]
[6][*6. Goa	1]
[7][*7. Gujarat	11]
[8][*8. Haryana	5]
*9. Kerala	9
*10. Madhya Pradesh	[9][11]
[10][*11. Chattisgarh	5]
[11][*12. Tamil Nadu]	[12][18]
[13][*13. Maharashtra	19]
[14][*14. Karnataka]	12
*15. [15][Odisha]	10

5. Ins. by the Bihar Reorganisation Act, 2000 (30 of 2000), sec. 7(c) (w.e.f. 15-11-2000).

* Entry numbers have been re-numbered by (i) the Jammu and Kashmir Reorganisation Act, 2019 (34 of 2019), sec. 8(b) (w.e.f. 31-10-2019); (ii) the Bombay Reorganisation Act, 1960 (11 of 1960), sec. 6(c) (w.e.f. 1-5-1960); (iii) the State of Nagaland Act, 1962 (27 of 1962), sec. 6(b)(i) (w.e.f. 1-12-1963); (iv) the Punjab Reorganisation Act, 1966 (31 of 1966), sec. 9(a) (w.e.f. 1-11-1966); (v) the State of Himachal Pradesh Act, 1970 (53 of 1970), sec. 5(a) (w.e.f. 25-1-1971); (vi) the North Eastern Areas (Reorganisation) Act, 1971 (81 of 1971), sec. 10(a) (w.e.f. 21-1-1972); (vii) the Constitution (Thirty-sixth Amendment) Act, 1975, sec. 4(b) (w.e.f. 26-4-1975); (viii) the State of Mizoram Act, 1986 (34 of 1986), sec. 5(a) (w.e.f. 20-2-1987); (ix) the Goa, Daman and Diu Reorganisation Act, 1987 (18 of 1987), sec. 6(a) (w.e.f. 30-5-1987); (x) the Madhya Pradesh Reorganisation Act, 2000 (28 of 2000), sec. 7(a) (w.e.f. 1-11-2000); (xi) the Uttar Pradesh Reorganisation Act, 2000 (29 of 2000), sec. 7(a) (w.e.f. 9-11-2000); (xii) the Bihar Reorganisation Act, 2000 (30 of 2000), sec. 7(a) (w.e.f. 15-11-2000) and (xiii) the Andhra Pradesh Reorganisation Act, 2014 (6 of 2014), sec. 12(b) (w.e.f. 2-6-2014 vide S.O. 655(E), dated 4th March 2014).

6. Ins. by Goa, Daman and Diu Reorganisation Act, 1987 (18 of 1987), sec. 6(b) (w.e.f. 30-5-1987).
7. Subs. by the Bombay Reorganisation Act, 1960 (11 of 1960), sec. 6(a), for entry 4 (w.e.f. 1-5-1960).
8. Ins. by the Punjab Reorganisation Act, 1966 (31 of 1966), sec. 9(b) (w.e.f. 1-11-1966).
9. Subs. by the Madhya Pradesh Reorganisation Act, 2000 (28 of 2000), sec. 7(b), for "16" (w.e.f. 1-11-2000).
10. Ins. by Madhya Pradesh Reorganisation Act, 2000 (28 of 2000), sec. 7(c) (w.e.f. 1-11-2000).
11. Subs. by the Madras State (Alteration of Name) Act, 1968 (53 of 1968), sec. 5(2), for "8. Madras" (w.e.f. 14-1-1969).
12. Subs. by the Andhra Pradesh and Madras (Alteration of Boundaries) Act, 1959 (56 of 1959), sec. 8(a), for "17" (w.e.f. 1-4-1960).
13. Ins. by the Bombay Reorganisation Act, 1960 (11 of 1960), sec. 6(b) (w.e.f. 1-5-1960).
14. Subs. by the Mysore State (Alternation of Name) Act, 1973 (31 of 1973), sec. 5(2), for "10. Mysore" (w.e.f. 1-11-1973).
15. Subs. by the Orissa (Alteration of Name) Act, 2011 (15 of 2011), sec. 7, for "Orissa" (w.e.f. 1-11-2011, *vide* G.S.R. 791(E), dated 1st November, 2011).

*16. Punjab	[16][7]
*17. Rajasthan	10
*18. Uttar Pradesh	[17][31]
[18][19. [19][Uttarakhand]	3]
*20. West Bengal	16
[20]*[***]	
[21][*21. Nagaland	1]
[22][*22. Himachal Pradesh	3]
[23][*23. Manipur	1]
*24. Tripura	1
*25. Meghalaya	1

16. Subs. by the Punjab Reorganisation Act, 1966 (31 of 1966), sec. 9(c), for "11" (w.e.f. 1-11-1966).
17. Subs. by the Uttar Pradesh Reorganisation Act, 2000 (29 of 2000), sec. 7(b), for "34" (w.e.f. 9-11-2000).
18. Ins. by the Uttar Pradesh Reorganisation Act, 2000 (29 of 2000), sec. 7(c) (w.e.f. 9-11-2000).
19. Subs. by the Uttaranchal (Alteration of Name) Act, 2006 (52 of 2006), sec. 5, for "Uttaranchal" (w.e.f. 1-1-2007).

* Entry numbers have been re-numbered by (i) the Jammu and Kashmir Reorganisation Act, 2019 (34 of 2019), sec. 8(b) (w.e.f. 31-10-2019); (ii) the Bombay Reorganisation Act, 1960 (11 of 1960), sec. 6(c) (w.e.f. 1-5-1960); (iii) the State of Nagaland Act, 1962 (27 of 1962), sec. 6(b)(i) (w.e.f. 1-12-1963); (iv) the Punjab Reorganisation Act, 1966 (31 of 1966), sec. 9(a) (w.e.f. 1-11-1966); (v) the State of Himachal Pradesh Act, 1970 (53 of 1970), sec. 5(a) (w.e.f. 25-1-1971); (vi) the North Eastern Areas (Reorganisation) Act, 1971 (81 of 1971), sec. 10(a) (w.e.f. 21-1-1972); (vii) the Constitution (Thirty-sixth Amendment) Act, 1975, sec. 4(b) (w.e.f. 26-4-1975); (viii) the State of Mizoram Act, 1986 (34 of 1986), sec. 5(a) (w.e.f. 20-2-1987); (ix) the Goa, Daman and Diu Reorganisation Act, 1987 (18 of 1987), sec. 6(a) (w.e.f. 30-5-1987); (x) the Madhya Pradesh Reorganisation Act, 2000 (28 of 2000), sec. 7(a) (w.e.f. 1-11-2000); (xi) the Uttar Pradesh Reorganisation Act, 2000 (29 of 2000), sec. 7(a) (w.e.f. 9-11-2000); (xii) the Bihar Reorganisation Act, 2000 (30 of 2000), sec. 7(a) (w.e.f. 15-11-2000) and (xiii) the Andhra Pradesh Reorganisation Act, 2014 (6 of 2014), sec. 12(b) (w.e.f. 2-6-2014 vide S.O. 655(E), dated 4th March 2014).

20. Entry 21 relating to Jammu and Kashmir deleted by the Jammu and Kashmir Reorganisation Act, 2019 (34 of 2019), sec. 8(a) (w.e.f. 31-10-2019).
21. Ins. by the State of Nagaland Act, 1962 (27 of 1962), sec. 6(b)(ii) (w.e.f. 1-12-1963).
22. Ins. by the State of Himachal Pradesh Act, 1970 (53 of 1970), sec. 5(a) (w.e.f. 25-1-1971).
23. Subs. by the North Eastern Areas (Reorganisation) Act, 1971 (81 of 1971), sec. 10(a) for entries 19 to 22 (w.e.f. 21-1-1972).

[24][*26. Sikkim	1]
*27. Mizoram	1
*28. Arunachal Pradesh	1
*29. Delhi	3
[25][*30. [26][Puducherry].	1]
[27][31. Jammu and Kashmir	4]
Total	[28][233]]

24. Ins. by the Constitution (Thirty-sixth Amendment) Act, 1975, sec. 4(a) (w.e.f. 26-4-1975).
25. Ins. by the Constitution (Fourteenth Amendment) Act, 1962, sec. 6(a) (w.e.f. 28-12-1962).
26. Subs. by the Pondicherry (Alteration of Name) Act, 2006 (44 of 2006), sec. 6, for "Pondicherry" (w.e.f. 1-10-2006).
27. Ins. by the Jammu and Kashmir Reorganisation Act, 2019 (34 of 2019), sec. 8(c) (w.e.f. 31-10-2019).
28. Subs. by the Goa, Daman and Diu Reorganisation Act, 1987 (18 of 1987), sec. 6(c), for "232" (w.e.f. 30-5-1987). Earlier the figures were changed by (i) the Bombay Reorganisation Act, 1960 (11 of 1960), sec. 6(d) (w.e.f. 1-5-1960); (ii) the State of Nagaland Act, 1962 (27 of 1962), sec. 6(b)(iii); (iii) the Punjab Reorganisation Act, 1966 (31 of 1966), sec. 9(c) (w.e.f. 1-11-1966); (iv) the North-Eastern Areas (Reorganisation) Act, 1971 (81 of 1971), sec. 10(b) (w.e.f. 21-1-1972); (v) the Constitution (Thirty-sixth Amendment) Act, 1975, sec. 4(c) (w.e.f. 26-4-1975).

TABLE XII

ALLOCATION OF SEATS IN THE HOUSE OF THE PEOPLE[1]

Name of the State/Union territory	Number of seats in the House as constituted in 2004 on the basis of the Delimination of Parliamentary and Assembly Constituencies Order, 1976 as amended from time to time			Number of seats in the House as subsequently constituted as per the Delimitation of Parliamentary and Assembly Constituencies Order, 2008		
	Total	Reserved for the Scheduled Castes	Reserved for the Scheduled Tribes	Total	Reserved for the Scheduled Castes	Reserved for the Scheduled Tribes
1	**2**	**3**	**4**	**5**	**6**	**7**
I. STATES:						
1. Andhra Pradesh[2]	42	6	2	42	7	3
2. Arunachal Pradesh	2	—	—	2	—	—
3. Assam	14	1	2	14	1	2
4. Bihar	40	7	—	40	6	—
5. Chhattisgarh	11	2	4	11	14	

1. Subs. by Act 10 of 2008, sec. 8, for *THE FIRST SCHEDULE* (w.e.f. 16-4-2008). Earlier *THE FIRST SCHEDULE* was amended by Act 67 of 1951, sec. 5 (w.e.f. 31-10-1951); by Act 32 of 1954, sec. 9 (w.e.f. 28-5-1954); by Act 58 of 1958, sec. 12 (w.e.f. 30-12-1958); by Act 35 of 1961, sec. 3(2)(b) (w.r.e.f. 11-8-1961); by Act 1 of 1962, sec. 3(2)(b) (w.r.e.f. 5-3-1962); by Act 27 of 1962, sec. 9 (w.e.f. 4-9-1962); by Act 20 of 1963, sec. 57(1)(b) and Sch. II (w.e.f. 13-5-1963) and was substituted by Act 47 of 1966, sec. 13 (w.e.f. 14-12-1966); and was amended by Act 10 of 1976, sec. 2 and Sch. (w.r.e.f. 9-9-1975); and was again substituted by Act 88 of 1976, Sec. 7 (w.e.f. 2-9-1976); and amended by Act 69 of 1986, sec. 8(1) (w.e.f 20-2-1987); by Act 18 of 1987, sec. 8 (w.e.f. 30-5-1987); by Act 23 of 2001 sec. 9 (w.e.f. 1-11-2000); by Act 29 of 2009 sec. 9 (w.e.f. 9-11-2000) and by Act 30 of 2000, sec. 9 (w.e.f. 15-11-2000).
2. See also The Andhra Pradesh Reorganisation Act, 2014 (6 of 2014), sec. 14, 15 and Second Sch.

1	2	3	4	5	6	7
6. Goa	2	—	—	2	—	—
7. Gujarat	26	2	4	26	2	4
8. Haryana	10	2	—	10	2	—
9. Himachal Pradesh	4	1	—	4	1	—
[3]10. [4][***]						
11. Jharkhand	14	1	5	14	1	5
12. Karnataka	28	4	—	28	5	2
13. Kerala	20	2	—	20	2	—
14. Madhya Pradesh	29	4	5	29	4	6
15. Maharashtra	48	3	4	48	5	4
16. Manipur	2	—	1	2	—	1
17. Meghalaya	2	—	—	2	—	2
18. Mizoram	1	—	1	1	—	1
19. Nagaland	1	—	—	1	—	—
20. Orissa	21	3	5	21	3	5
21. Punjab	13	3	—	13	4	—
22. Rajasthan	25	4	3	25	4	3
23. Sikkim	1	—	—	1	—	—
24. Tamil Nadu	39	7	—	39	7	—

3. Refer the Jammu and Kashmir Reorganisation Act, 2019 (34 of 2019) (w.e.f. 31-10-2019), section 10, which stood as under:
"*10. Representation in House of the People.*–On and from the appointed day, there shall be allocated five seats to the successor Union territory of Jammu and Kashmir and one seat to Union territory of Ladakh, in the House of the People, and the First Schedule to the Representation of the People Act, 1950 (43 of 1950) shall be deemed to be amended accordingly."

4. Entry 10 related to Jammu and Kashmir deleted by the Jammu and Kashmir Reorganisation Act, 2019 (34 of 2019), sec. 10 (w.e.f. 31-10-2019). Entry 10, before deletion stood as under:
"10. Jammu and Kashmir 6 — — 6 — —"

1	2	3	4	5	6	7
25. Tripura	2	—	1	2	—	1
26. Uttarakhand	5	—	—	5	1	—
27. Uttar Pradesh	80	18	—	80	17	—
28. West Bengal	42	8	2	42	10	2
II. UNION TERRITORIES:						
1. Andaman and Nicobar Islands	1	—	—	1	—	—
2. Chandigarh	1	—	—	1	—	—
3. [5]Dadra and Nagar Haveli	1	—	1	1	—	1
[5]Daman and Diu	1	—	—	1	—	—
4. Delhi	7	1	—	7	1	—
5. Lakshadweep	1	—	1	1	—	1
6. Puducherry	1	—	—	1	—	—
[6,7][7. Jammu and Kashmir	5	—	—	5	—	—
8. Ladakh	1	—	—	1	—	—]
Total:	**543**	**79**	**41**	**543**	**84**	**47]**

5. Refer the Dadra and Nagar Haveli and Daman and Diu (Merger of Union Territories) Act, 2019 (44 of 2019) [w.e.f. 26-1-2020, vide S.O. 4542(E), dated 19th December, 2019]. Section 6, which stood as under:

   "*6. Allocation of seats in House of People.*–On and from the appointed day, there shall be allocated two seats to the Union territory of Dadra and Nagar Haveli and Daman and Diu in the House of the People and the First Schedule to the Representation of the People Act, 1950 (43 of 1950) shall be deemed to be amended accordingly.".

6. Refer the Jammu and Kashmir Reorganisation Act, 2019 (34 of 2019) (w.e.f. 31-10-2019), section 10 which stood as under:

   "*10. Representation in House of the People.*–On and from the appointed day, there shall be allocated five seats to the successor Union territory of Jammu and Kashmir and one seat to Union territory of Ladakh, in the House of the People, and the First Schedule to the Representation of the People Act, 1950 (43 of 1950) shall be deemed to be amended accordingly."

7. Ins. by the Jammu and Kashmir Reorganisation Act, 2019 (34 of 2019), sec. 10 (w.e.f. 31-10-2019).

TABLE XIII

GOVERNMENT OF STATES

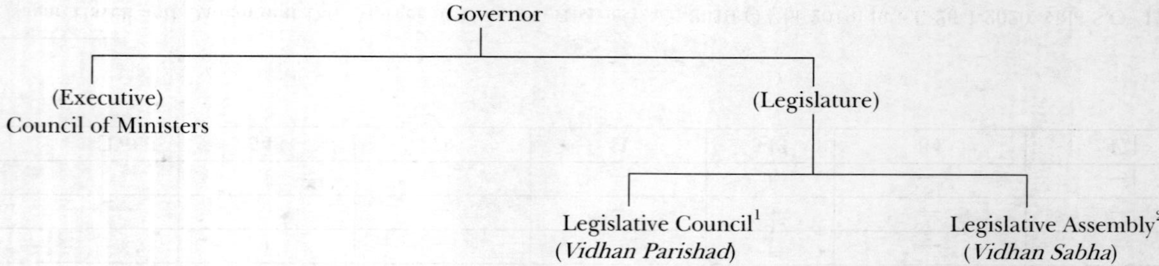

1. The total number of seats in the States which have a Legislative Council is 594. [see Table XIV].
2. The total number of seats in the Legislative Assemblies of the States and Union Territories is 4116. [see Table XIV].

TABLE XIV

MEMBERSHIP OF LEGISLATIVE ASSEMBLIES AND LEGISLATIVE COUNCILS

[*Vide* sections 7 and 7A read with Second Schedule[1] and section 10 read with Third Schedule to the Representation of the People Act, 1950]

Name of the State/Union territory	Number of seats in the House as constituted on the basis of the Delimitation of Parliamentary and Assembly Constituencies Order, 1976 as amended from time to time			Number of seats in the House as subsequently constituted as per the Delimitation of Parliamentary and Assembly Constituencies Order, 2008		
	Total	Reserved for the Scheduled Castes	Reserved for the Scheduled Tribes	Total	Reserved for the Scheduled Castes	Reserved for the Scheduled Tribes
1	**2**	**3**	**4**	**5**	**6**	**7**
I. STATES:						
[2][1. Andhra Pradesh	294	39	15	175	29	7]

1. Subs. by Act 10 of 2008, sec. 8, for THE SECOND SCHEDULE (w.e.f. 16-4-2008). Earlier THE SECOND SCHEDULE was amended by Act 58 of 1958, sec. 13 (w.e.f. 30-12-1958); by Act 11 of 1960, sec. 13 (w.e.f. 25-4-1960); by Act 27 of 1962, sec. 11(2)(h) (w.e.f. 4-9-1962); by Act 20 of 1963, sec. 57(1)(b) (w.e.f. 13-5-1963) and was substituted by Act 47 of 1966, sec. 14 (w.e.f. 14-12-1966) and amended by Act 61 of 1968, sec. 4(b) (w.e.f. 31-12-1968) and was again substituted by Act 88 of 1976, sec. 7 (w.e.f. 2-9-1976) and amended by Act 28 of 2000, sec. 12(2) (w.e.f. 1-11-2000); by Act 29 of 2000, sec. 12(2) (w.e.f. 9-11-2000) and by Act 30 of 2000, sec. 12(2) (w.e.f 15-11-2000).
2. Subs. by Act 6 of 2014, sec. 17(2)(a), for

1	2	3	4	5	6	7
"Andhra Pradesh	294	39	15	294	48	19".

(w.e.f. 2-6-2014, vide S.O. 655(E), dated 4th March, 2014).

1	2	3	4	5	6	7
2. Arunachal Pradesh	60	—	59	60	—	59
3. Assam	126	8	16	126	8	16
4. Bihar	243	39	—	243	38	2
5. Chhattisgarh	90	10	34	90	10	29
6. Goa	40	1	—	40	1	—
7. Gujarat	182	13	26	182	13	27
8. Haryana	90	17	—	90	17	—
9. Himachal Pradesh	68	16	3	68	17	3
[3][***]						
[4][10]. Jharkhand	81	9	28	81	9	28
[4][11]. Karnataka	224	33	2	224	36	15
[4][12]. Kerala	140	13	1	140	14	2
[4][13]. Madhya Pradesh	230	34	41	230	35	47
[4][14]. Maharashtra	288	18	22	288	29	25
[4][15]. Manipur	60	1	19	60	1	19
[4][16]. Meghalaya	60	—	55	60	—	55

3. Entry 10 relating to Jammu and Kashmir deleted by Act 34 of 2019, sec. 14(9)(a) (w.e.f. 31-10-2019). Under the Constitution of Jammu and Kashmir, the number of seats in the Legislative Assembly of that State excluding the 24 seats earmarked for Pakistan occupied territory was 87 out of which 7 seats had been reserved for the Scheduled Castes in pursuance of the Jammu and Kashmir Representation of the People Act, 1957. Entry 10, before deletion, stood as under:

"Jammu and Kashmir	76	6	—	".

4. Entries 11 to 29 renumbered as 10 to 28 thereof by Act 34 of 2019, sec. 14(9)(b) (w.e.f. 31-10-2019).

1	2	3	4	5	6	7
[5][17]. Mizoram	40	—	39	40	—	[6][39]
[5][18]. Nagaland	60	—	59	60	—	59
[5][19]. Orissa	147	22	34	147	24	33
[5][20]. Punjab	117	29	—	117	34	—
[5][21]. Rajasthan	200	33	24	200	34	25
[5][22]. Sikkim	32	2	12**	32	2	12**
[5][23]. Tamil Nadu	234	42	3	234	44	2
[7][[5][24]]. Telangana	—	—	—	119	19	12]
[8][[5][25]]. Tripura	60	7	20	60	10	20
[8][[5][26]]. Uttarakhand	70	12	3	70	13	2
[8][[5][27]]. Uttar Pradesh	403	89	—	403	85	—
[8][[5][28]]. West Bengal	294	59	17	294	68	16
II. UNION TERRITORIES:						
1. Delhi	70	13	—	70	12	—
2. Puducherry	30	5	—	30	5	—
[9][3. Jammu and Kashmir	90	7	9	90	7	9

**Reserved 1 seat for Sanghas and 12 seats for the Sikkimese of Bhutia Lepcha origin.]

5. Entries 11 to 29 renumbered as 10 to 28 thereof by Act 34 of 2019, sec. 14(9)(b) (w.e.f. 31-10-2019).
6. Subs. by Act 41 of 2009, sec. 3, for "38" (w.e.f. 1-2-2010).
7. Ins. by Act 6 of 2014, sec. 17(2)(c).
8. Entries 25 to 28 renumbered as entries 26 to 29 by Act 6 of 2014, sec. 17(2)(b).
9. Subs. by the Jammu and Kashmir Reorganisation (Amendment) Act, 2023 (35 of 2023), sec. 2(ii), for Serial number 3 relating to "Jammu and Kashmir" and their entries under column (2) to (7) [*Date of enforcement yet to be notified. For present status, see Notification issued by the concerned Ministry or the Gazette of India*]. Earlier serial no. 3 was inserted by Act 34 of 2019, sec. 14(10)(a) (w.e.f. 31-10-2019). and corrected by corrigenda, published in the Gazette of India, Extra., Pt. II, sec. 1, No. 58, dated 12th September, 2019, for "5. Jammu". Serial no. 3 before substitution by Act 35 of 2023 stood as under:

"3. Jammu and Kashmir 83 6 - 83 6 -".

ALLOCATION OF SEATS IN THE LEGISLATIVE COUNCILS[10]

	Number to be elected or nominated under article 171(3)					
	Total number of seats	Sub-clause (a)	Sub-clause (b)	Sub-clause (c)	Sub-clause (d)	Sub-clause (e)
1	**2**	**3**	**4**	**5**	**6**	**7**
[11][1. Andhra Pradesh	58	20	5	5	20	8]
[12][2. Bihar	75	24	6	6	27	12]
[13][***]						
3. Madhya Pradesh	90	31	8	8	31	12
[14][***]						
[15][5. Maharashtra	78	22	7	7	30	12]
[16][6. Karnataka	75	25	7	7	25	11]
[17][7. Tamil Nadu	78	26	7	7	26	12]

10. Subs. by Act 37 of 1957, sec. 12(b), for THE THIRD SCHEDULE (w.e.f. 18-9-1957).
11. Subs. by Act 12 of 2015, sec. 3(ii), for entry 1 relating to Andhra Pradesh (w.e.f. 30-3-2015, vide G.S.R. 334(E), dated 29th April, 2015). Earlier entry 1 was substituted by Act 6 of 2014, sec. 23(2)(i)(a) (w.e.f. 2-6-2014, vide S.O. 655(E), dated 4th March, 2014). Earlier entry 1 was inserted by Act 1 of 2006, sec. 4(a) (w.e.f. 11-1-2006). Earlier to that entry 1 was omitted by Act 34 of 1985, sec. 5(a) (w.e.f. 1-6-1985).
12. Subs. by Act 30 of 2000, sec. 17, for entry 2 relating to Bihar (w.e.f. 15-11-2000).
13. Entry relating to Bombay omitted by Act 11 of 1960, sec. 21(a) (w.e.f. 1-5-1960).
14. Entry relating to Tamil Nadu omitted by Act 40 of 1986, sec. 5(a) (w.e.f. 1-11-1986).
15. Ins. by Act 11 of 1960, sec. 21(b) (w.e.f. 1-5-1960)
16. Subs. by Act 31 of 1987, sec. 2, for entry 6 relating to Karnataka (w.e.f. 8-9-1987). Earlier the word Karnataka was substituted by the Mysore State (Alteration of Name) (Adaptation of Laws on Union Subject Order, 1974, sec. 3 and Sch., for the word "Mysore" (w.e.f. 1-11-1973).
17. Ins. by Act 16 of 2010, sec. 4(a) (w.e.f. 18-5-2010).

1	2	3	4	5	6	7
[18][7A. Telangana	40	14	3	3	14	6]
[19][***]						
[20][8. Uttar Pradesh	100	36	8	8	38	10]
[21][***]						

18. Ins. by Act 6 of 2014, sec. 23(2)(i)(b) (w.e.f. 2-6-2014, vide S.O. 655(E), dated 4th March, 2014).
19. Entry relating to Punjab omitted by Act 46 of 1969, sec. 5(a) (w.e.f. 7-1-1970).
20. Subs. by Act 7 of 2004, sec. 2, for entry 8 (w.r.e.f. 9-11-2000). Earlier entry 8 was substituted by Act 29 of 2000, sec. 18 (w.e.f. 9-11-2000).
21. Entry relating to West Bengal omitted by Act 20 of 1969, sec. 5(a) (w.e.f. 1-8-1969).

TABLE XV
THE JUDICIARY

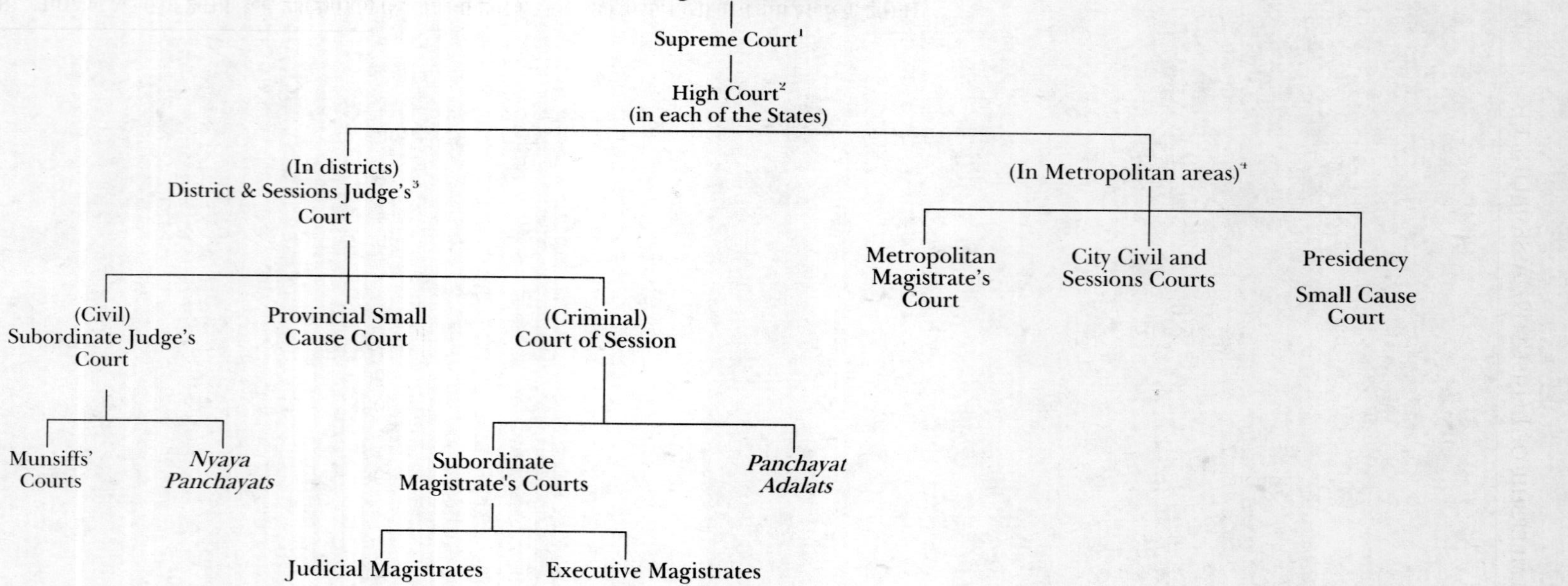

1. Chief Justice and 33 other Judges, *i.e.*, total 34 Judges. As of 3-8-2023, there were 2 vacancies in the Supreme Court.
2. The total sanctioned strength of permanent Judges and additional Judges in different High Courts is 1114 of which 778 Judges were in position while vacancies were 336 as on 3-8-2023.
3. As per reply of the then Minister of Law and Justice Shri Kiren Rijiju in the Rajya Sabha to the Unstarred Question No. 1869, answered on 22-12-2022, the total sanctioned strength at District and subordinate Courts was 25,042; working strength was 19192; and total vacancies were 5,850. Note that the sanctioned strength is 25,423 in the year 2023 as per reply of Shri Arjun Ram Meghwal [Minister of State (Independent Charge) of the Ministry of Law and Justice] in the Lok Sabha to the Unstarred Question No. 946, answered on 8-12-2023 on the question raised by Shri Dushyant Singh.
4. The Bharatiya Nagarik Suraksha Sanhita, 2023 [which replaced the CrPC, 1973, with effect from 1-7-2024] removed/abolished the classification of Metropolitan Areas and Metropolitan Magistrates to bring uniformity in classes of Courts and Judges across India.

TABLE XVI

JURISDICTION AND SEATS OF HIGH COURTS

Name	Year of Establishment	Territorial Jurisdiction	Principal Seat (and Bench, if any)
Allahabad	1866	Uttar Pradesh	Prayagraj (Bench at Lucknow)
Andhra Pradesh[1]	1954	Andhra Pradesh	Amaravati
Bombay	1862	Maharashtra, Goa, UT of Dadra and Nagar Haveli & Daman and Diu	Mumbai (Bench at Nagpur, Panaji, Kolhapur and Aurangabad)
Calcutta	1862	West Bengal and UT of Andaman and Nicobar Islands	Kolkata (Circuit Benches at Port Blair and Jalpaiguri)
Chhattisgarh	2000	Chhattisgarh	Bilaspur
Delhi	1966	NCT of Delhi	New Delhi
Gauhati	1948	Assam, Nagaland, Mizoram and Arunachal Pradesh	Guwahati (Benches at Kohima, Aizawl and Itanagar)
Gujarat	1960	Gujarat	Ahmedabad (Sola)
Himachal Pradesh	1971	Himachal Pradesh	Shimla
Jammu & Kashmir and Ladakh	1957	UTs of Jammu & Kashmir and Ladakh	Jammu and Srinagar
Jharkhand	2000	Jharkhand	Ranchi
Karnataka	1884	Karnataka	Bengaluru (Benches at Dharwad and Gulbarga)

1. On 26-12-2018, the President of India issued orders bifurcating the High Court of Judicature at Hyderabad for the State of Telangana and the State of Andhra Pradesh into the High Court for the State of Telangana with the principal seat at Hyderabad and the High Court of Andhra Pradesh with the principal seat at Amaravati, which came into effect from 1-1-2019.

Name	Year of Establishment	Territorial Jurisdiction	Principal Seat (and Bench, if any)
Kerala	1956	Kerala and UT of Lakshadweep	Kochi
Madhya Pradesh	1956	Madhya Pradesh	Jabalpur (Benches at Gwalior and Indore)
Madras	1862	Tamil Nadu and UT of Puducherry	Chennai (Bench at Madurai)
Manipur	2013	Manipur	Imphal
Meghalaya	2013	Meghalaya	Shillong
Orissa	1948	Odisha[2]	Cuttack
Patna	1916	Bihar	Patna
Punjab and Haryana	1966	Punjab, Haryana and UT of Chandigarh	Chandigarh
Rajasthan	1950	Rajasthan	Jodhpur (Bench at Jaipur)
Sikkim	1975	Sikkim	Gangtok
Telangana[3]	2019	Telangana	Hyderabad
Tripura[4]	2013	Tripura	Agartala
Uttarakhand[5]	2000	Uttarakhand	Nainital

2. Substituted by the Orissa (Alteration of Name) Act, 2011, section 3, for "Orissa
3. On 26-12-2018, the President of India issued orders bifurcating the High Court of Judicature at Hyderabad for the State of Telangana and the State of Andhra Pradesh into the High Court for the State of Telangana with the principal seat at Hyderabad and the High Court of Andhra Pradesh with the principal seat at Amaravati, which came into effect from 1-1-201
4. Added by the North Eastern Areas (Reorganisation) and Other Related Laws (Amendment) Act, 2012.
5. Substituted by the Uttaranchal (Alteration of Name) Act, 2006, section 4, for "Uttaranchal".

TABLE XVII

TERRITORIAL JURISDICTION OF BENCHES OF CENTRAL ADMINISTRATIVE TRIBUNAL

Sl No.	Bench	Jurisdiction of the Bench
1	2	3
1.	Principal Bench (New Delhi)	National Capital Territory (NCT) of Delhi
2.	Ahmedabad Bench	State of Gujarat
3.	Allahabad Bench	(a) State of Uttar Pradesh excluding the Districts mentioned against Serial Number 4 under the jurisdiction of Lucknow Bench; and (b) State of Uttaranchal (Uttarakhand)
4.	Lucknow Bench	Districts of Lucknow, Hardoi, Kheri, Rai Barelli, Sitapur, Unnao, Faizabad, Ambedkar Nagar, Bahraich, Shravasti, Barabanki, Gonda, Balrampur, Pratapgarh and Sultanpur in the State of Uttar Pradesh
5.	Bangalore Bench	State of Karnataka
6.	Calcutta Bench	States of Sikkim and West Bengal and Union Territory of Andaman and Nicobar Islands
7.	Chandigarh Bench	States of Jammu & Kashmir, Haryana, Himachal Pradesh and Punjab and the Union Territory of Chandigarh
8.	Cuttack Bench	State of Odisha[1]
9.	Ernakulam Bench	State of Kerala and Union Territory of Lakshadweep
10.	Guwahati Bench	States of Assam, Manipur, Meghalaya, Nagaland, Tripura, Arunachal Pradesh and Mizoram
11.	Hyderabad Bench	State of Andhra Pradesh
12.	Jabalpur Bench	States of Madhya Pradesh and Chattisgarh
13.	Jodhpur Bench	State of Rajasthan excluding the Districts mentioned against Serial Number 14 under the jurisdiction of Jaipur Bench

1. Substituted by the Orissa (Alteration of Name) Act, 2011, section 3, for "Orissa".

Sl No.	Bench	Jurisdiction of the Bench
1	2	3
14.	Jaipur Bench	Districts of Ajmer, Alwar, Baran, Bharatpur, Bundi, Dausa, Dholpur, Jaipur, Jhalawar, Jhunjhunu, Kota, Sawai Madhopur, Sikar, Tonk and Karauli in the State of Rajasthan
15.	Chennai Bench	States of Tamil Nadu and Union Territory of Pondicherry[2]
16.	Mumbai Bench	States of Maharashtra and Goa, and Union Territories of Dadra and Nagar Haveli and Daman and Diu.
17.	Patna Bench	States of Bihar and Jharkhand
18.	Jammu Bench	(a) Districts of Doda, Jammu, Kathua, Kishtwar, Poonch, Rajouri, Ramban, Reasi, Samba, Udhampur in the Union Territory of Jammu and Kashmir; and (b) Leh district in the Union Territory of Ladakh
19.	Srinagar Bench	(a) Districts of Anantnag, Bandipora, Baramulla, Budgam, Ganderbal, Kulgam, Kupwara, Pulwama, Shopiam, Srinagar in the Union Territory of Jammu and Kashmir; and (b) Kargil district in the Union Territory of Ladakh

2. Substituted by the Pondicherry (Alteration of Name) Act, 2006, section 4, for "Pondicherry".

Note.–Parliament had enacted the Administrative Tribunals Act, 1985 which came into force in July, 1985 and the Administrative Tribunals were established in November, 1985 at Delhi, Mumbai, Calcutta and Allahabad. As of 15-4-2024, there are 19 Benches and 19 Circuit Benches in the Central Administrative Tribunal all over India.

TABLE XVIII

DISTRIBUTION OF LEGISLATIVE POWER

List I—Union List	List II—State List	List III—Concurrent List
1. Defence of India and every part thereof including preparation for defence and all such acts as may be conducive in times of war to its prosecution and after its termination of effective demobilisation. 2. Naval, military and air forces; any other armed forces of the Union. [1][2A. Deployment of any armed force of the Union or any other force subject to the control of the Union or any contingent or unit thereof in any State in aid of the civil power; powers, jurisdiction, privileges and liabilities of the members of such forces while on such deployment.] 3. Delimitation of cantonment areas, local self-government in such areas, the constitution and powers within such areas of cantonment authorities and the regulation of house accommodation (including the control of rents) in such areas.	1. Public order (but not including [2][the use of any naval, military or air force or any other armed force of the Union or of any other force subject to the control of the Union or of any contingent or unit thereof] in aid of the civil power). [3][2. Police (including railway and village police) subject to the provisions of entry 2A of List I.] 3. [4][***] Officers and servants of the High Court; procedure in rent and revenue courts; fees taken in all courts except the Supreme Court. 4. Prisons, reformatories, Borstal institutions and other institutions of a like nature, and persons detained therein; arrangements with other States for the use of prisons and other institutions.	1. Criminal law, including all matters included in the Indian Penal Code at the commencement of this Constitution but excluding offences against laws with respect to any of the matters specified in List I or List II and excluding the use of naval, military or air forces or any other armed forces of the Union in aid of the civil power. 2. Criminal procedure, including all matters included in the Code of Criminal Procedure at the commencement of this Constitution. 3. Preventive detention for reasons connected with the security of a State, the maintenance of public order, or the maintenance of supplies and services essential to the community; persons subjected to such detention.

1. Ins. by the Constitution (Forty-second Amendment) Act, 1976, sec. 57(a) (w.e.f. 3-1-1977).
2. Subs. by the Constitution (Forty-second Amendment) Act, 1976, sec. 57(b)(i), for certain words (w.e.f. 3-1-1977).
3. Subs. by the Constitution (Forty-second Amendment) Act, 1976, sec. 57(b)(ii), for entry 2 (w.e.f. 3-1-1977).
4. Certain words omitted and transferred to entry 11A in List III by the Constitution (Forty-second (Amendment) Act, 1976, sec. 57(b)(iii) (w.e.f. 3-1-1977).

List I—Union List	List II—State List	List III—Concurrent List
4. Naval, military and air force works. 5. Arms, firearms, ammunition and explosives. 6. Atomic energy and mineral resources necessary for its production. 7. Industries declared by Parliament by law to be necessary for the purpose of defence or for the prosecution of war. 8. Central Bureau of Intelligence and Investigation. 9. Preventive detention for reasons connected with Defence, Foreign Affairs, or the security of India; persons subjected to such detention. 10. Foreign affairs; all matters which bring the Union into relation with any foreign country. 11. Diplomatic, consular and trade representation. 12. United Nations Organisation. 13. Participation in international conferences, associations and other bodies and implementing of decisions made thereat.	5. Local government, that is to say, the constitution and powers of municipal corporations, improvement trusts, district boards, mining settlement authorities and other local authorities for the purpose of local self-government or village administration. 6. Public health and sanitation; hospitals and dispensaries. 7. Pilgrimages, other than pilgrimages to places outside India. 8. Intoxicating liquors, that is to say, the production, manufacture, possession, transport, purchase and sale of intoxicating liquors. 9. Relief of the disabled and unemployable. 10. Burials and burial grounds; cremations and cremation grounds. [5][***] 12. Libraries, museums and other similar institutions controlled or financed by the State; ancient and historical monuments and records other than those [6][declared by or under law made by Parliament] to be of national importance.	4. Removal from one State to another State of prisoners, accused persons and persons subjected to preventive detention for reasons specified in entry 3 of this List. 5. Marriage and divorce; infants and minors; adoption; wills, intestacy and succession; joint family and partition; all matters in respect of which parties in judicial proceedings were immediately before the commencement of this Constitution subject to their personal law. 6. Transfer of property other than agricultural land; registration of deeds and documents. 7. Contracts, including partnership, agency, contracts of carriage, and other special forms of contracts, but not including contracts relating to agricultural land. 8. Actionable wrongs. 9. Bankruptcy and insolvency. 10. Trust and Trustees. 11. Administrators-general and official trustees.

5. Entry 11 omitted by the Constitution (Forty-second Amendment) Act, 1976, sec. 57(b)(iv) (w.e.f. 3-1-1977).
6. Subs. by the Constitution (Seventh Amendment) Act, 1956, sec. 27, for "declared by Parliament by law" (w.e.f. 1-11-1956).

List I—Union List	List II—State List	List III—Concurrent List
14. Entering into treaties and agreements with foreign countries and implementing of treaties, agreements and conventions with foreign countries. 15. War and peace. 16. Foreign jurisdiction. 17. Citizenship, naturalisation and aliens. 18. Extradition. 19. Admission into, and emigration and expulsion from, India; passports and visas. 20. Pilgrimages to places outside India. 21. Piracies and crimes committed on the high seas or in the air; offences against the law of nations committed on land or the high seas or in the air. 22. Railways. 23. Highways declared by or under law made by Parliament to be national highways. 24. Shipping and navigation on inland waterways, declared by Parliament by law to be national waterways, as regards mechanically propelled vessels; the rule of the road on such waterways. 25. Maritime shipping and navigation, including shipping and navigation on tidal waters; provision of education and training for the mercantile marine and regulation of such education and training provided by States and other agencies.	13. Communications, that is to say, roads, bridges, ferries, and other means of communication not specified in List I; municipal tramways; ropeways; inland waterways and traffic thereon subject to the provisions of List I and List III with regard to such waterways; vehicles other than mechanically propelled vehicles. 14. Agriculture, including agricultural education and research, protection against pests and prevention of plant diseases. 15. Preservation, protection and improvement of stock and prevention of animal diseases; veterinary training and practice. 16. Pounds and the prevention of cattle trespass. 17. Water, that is to say, water supplies, irrigation and canals, drainage and embankments, water storage and water power subject to the provisions of entry 56 of List I. 18. Land, that is to say, right in or over land, land tenures including the relation of landlord and tenant, and the collection of rents; transfer and alienation of agricultural land; land improvement and agricultural loans; colonization.	[7][11A. Administration of justice; constitution and organisation of all courts, except the Supreme Court and the High Courts.] 12. Evidence and oaths; recognition of laws, public acts and records, and judicial proceedings. 13. Civil procedure, including all matters included in the Code of Civil Procedure at the commencement of this Constitution, limitation and arbitration. 14. Contempt of court, but not including contempt of the Supreme Court. 15. Vagrancy; nomadic and migratory tribes. 16. Lunacy and mental deficiency, including places for the reception or treatment of lunatics and mental deficients. 17. Prevention of cruelty to animals. [8][17A. Forests.] [8][17B. Protection of wild animals and birds.] 18. Adulteration of foodstuffs and other goods.

7. Ins. by the Constitution (Forty-second Amendment) Act, 1976, sec. 57(c)(i) (w.e.f. 3-1-1977).
8. Ins. by the Constitution (Forty-second Amendment) Act, 1976, sec. 57(c)(ii) (w.e.f. 3-1-1977).

List I—Union List	List II—State List	List III—Concurrent List
26. Lighthouses, including lightships, beacons and other provisions for the safety of shipping and aircraft.	[9][***]	19. Drugs and poisons, subject to the provisions of entry 59 of List I with respect to opium.
27. Ports declared by or under law made by Parliament or existing law to be major ports, including their delimitation and the constitution and powers of port authorities therein.	21. Fisheries.	20. Economic and social planning.
28. Port quarantine, including hospitals connected therewith; seamen's and marine hospitals.	22. Courts of wards subject to the provisions of entry 34 of List I; encumbered and attached estates.	[12][20A. Population control and family planning.]
29. Airways; aircraft and air navigation; provision of aerodromes; regulation and organisation of air traffic and of aerodromes; provision for aeronautical education and training and regulation of such education and training provided by States and other agencies.	23. Regulation of mines and mineral development subject to the provisions of List I with respect to regulation and development under the control of the Union.	21. Commercial and industrial monopolies, combines and trusts.
30. Carriage of passengers and goods by railway, sea or air, or by national waterways in mechanically propelled vessels.	24. Industries subject to the provisions of [10][entries 7 and 52] of List I.	22. Trade unions; industrial and labour disputes.
31. Posts and telegraphs; telephones, wireless, broadcasting and other like forms of communication.	25. Gas and gas-works.	23. Social security and social insurance; employment and unemployment.
	26. Trade and commerce within the State subject to the provisions of entry 33 of List III.	24. Welfare of labour including conditions of work, provident funds, employers' liability, workmen's compensation, invalidity and old age pensions and maternity benefits.
	27. Production, supply and distribution of goods subject to the provisions of entry 33 of List III.	[13][25. Education, including technical education, medical education and universities, subject to the provisions of entries 63, 64, 65 and 66 of List I; vocational and technical training of labour.]
	28. Markets and fairs.	26. Legal, medical and other professions.
	[11][***]	
	30. Money-lending and money-lenders; relief of agricultural indebtedness.	

9 Entries 19 and 20 omitted by the Constitution (Forty-second Amendment) Act, 1976, sec. 57(b)(iv) (w.e.f. 3-1-1977) [*Entry 19 Transferred to List III, as Entry 17A and Entry 20 Transferred to List III, as Entry 17B*].

10. Subs. by the Constitution (Seventh Amendment) Act, 1956, sec. 28, for "entry 52" (w.e.f. 1-11-1956).

11. Entry 29 omitted by the Constitution (Forty-second Amendment) Act, 1976, sec. 57(b)(iv) (w.e.f. 3-1-1977) [*Transferred to List III, as Entry 33A*].

12. Ins. by the Constitution (Forty-second Amendment) Act, 1976, sec. 57(c)(iii) (w.e.f. 3-1-1977).

13. Subs. by the Constitution (Forty-second Amendment) Act, 1976, sec. 57(c)(iv), for entry 25 (w.e.f. 3-1-1977).

List I—Union List	List II—State List	List III—Concurrent List
32. Property of the Union and the revenue therefrom, but as regards property situated in a State [14][***] subject to legislation by the State, save in so far as Parliament by law otherwise provides. [15][***] 34. Courts of wards for the estates of Rulers of Indian States. 35. Public debt of the Union. 36. Currency, coinage and legal tender; foreign exchange. 37. Foreign loans. 38. Reserve Bank of India. 39. Post Office Savings Bank. 40. Lotteries organised by the Government of India or the Government of a State. 41. Trade and commerce with foreign countries; import and export across customs frontiers; definition of customs frontiers. 42. Inter-State trade and commerce. 43. Incorporation, regulation and winding up of trading corporations, including banking, insurance and financial corporations but not including co-operative societies.	31. Inns and inn-keepers. 32. Incorporation, regulation and winding up of corporation, other than those specified in List I, and universities; unincorporated trading, literary, scientific, religious and other societies and associations; co-operative societies. 33. Theaters and dramatic performances; cinemas subject to the provisions of entry 60 of List I; sports, entertainments and amusements. 34. Betting and gambling. 35. Works, lands and buildings vested in or in the possession of the State. [16][***] 37. Elections to the Legislature of the State subject to the provisions of any law made by Parliament. 38. Salaries and allowances of members of the Legislature of the State, of the Speaker and Deputy Speaker of the Legislative Assembly and, if there is a Legislative Council, of the Chairman and Deputy Chairman thereof.	27. Relief and rehabilitation of persons displaced from their original place of residence by reason of the setting up of the Dominions of India and Pakistan. 28. Charities and charitable institutions, charitable and religious endowments and religious institutions. 29. Prevention of the extension from one State to another of infectious or contagious diseases or pests affecting men, animals or plants. 30. Vital statistics including registration of births and deaths. 31. Ports other than those declared by or under law made by Parliament or existing law to be major ports. 32. Shipping and navigation on inland waterways as regards mechanically propelled vessels, and the rule of the road on such waterways, and the carriage of passengers and goods on inland waterways subject to the provisions of List I with respect to national waterways.

14. The words and letters "specified in Part A or Part B of the First Schedule" omitted by the Constitution (Seventh Amendment) Act, 1956, sec. 29 and Sch. (w.e.f. 1-11-1956).
15. Entry 33 omitted by the Constitution (Seventh Amendment) Act, 1956, sec. 26 (w.e.f. 1-11-1956).
16. Entry 36 omitted by the Constitution (Seventh Amendment) Act, 1956, sec. 26 (w.e.f. 1-11-1956).

List I—Union List	List II—State List	List III—Concurrent List
44. Incorporation, regulation and winding up of corporations, whether trading or not, with objects not confined to one State, but not including universities. 45. Banking. 46. Bills of exchange, cheques, promissory notes and other like instruments. 47. Insurance. 48. Stock exchanges and futures markets. 49. Patents, inventions and designs; copyright; trade-marks and merchandise marks. 50. Establishment of standards of weight and measure. 51. Establishment of standards of quality for goods to be exported out of India or transported from one State to another. 52. Industries, the control of which by the Union is declared by Parliament by law to be expedient in the public interest. 53. Regulation and development of oil fields and mineral oil resources; petroleum and petroleum products; other liquids and substances declared by Parliament by law to be dangerously inflammable. 54. Regulation of mines and mineral development to the extent to which such regulation and development under the control of the Union is	39. Powers, privileges and immunities of the Legislative Assembly and of the members and the committees thereof, and, if there is a Legislative Council, of that Council and of the members and the committees thereof; enforcement of attendance of persons for giving evidence or producing documents before committees of the Legislature of the State. 40. Salaries and allowances of Ministers for the State. 41. State public services; State Public Service Commission. 42. State pensions, that is to say, pensions payable by the State or out of the Consolidated Fund of the State. 43. Public debt of the State. 44. Treasure trove. 45. Land revenue, including the assessment and collection of revenue, the maintenance of land records, survey for revenue purposes and records of rights, and alienation of revenues. 46. Taxes on agricultural income. 47. Duties in respect of succession to agricultural land.	[17][33. Trade and commerce in, and the production, supply and distribution of,— (a) the products of any industry where the control of such industry by the Union is declared by Parliament by law to be expedient in the public interest, and imported goods of the same kind as such products; (b) foodstuffs, including edible oilseeds and oils; (c) cattle fodder, including oilcakes and other concentrates; (d) raw cotton, whether ginned or unginned, and cotton seed; and (e) raw jute.] [18][33A. Weights and measures except establishment of standards.] 34. Price control. 35. Mechanically propelled vehicles including the principles on which taxes on such vehicles are to be levied. 36. Factories. 37. Boilers. 38. Electricity.

17. Subs. by the Constitution (Third Amendment) Act, 1954, sec. 2, for entry 33 (w.e.f. 22-2-1955).
18. Ins. by the Constitution (Forty-second Amendment) Act, 1976, sec. 57(c)(v) (w.e.f. 3-1-1977).

List I—Union List	List II—State List	List III—Concurrent List
declared by Parliament by law to be expedient in the public interest. 55. Regulation of labour and safety in mines and oilfields. 56. Regulation and development of inter-State rivers and river valleys to the extent to which such regulation and development under the control of the Union is declared by Parliament by law to be expedient in the public interest. 57. Fishing and fisheries beyond territorial waters. 58. Manufacture, supply and distribution of salt by Union agencies, regulation and control of manufacture, supply and distribution of salt by other agencies. 59. Cultivation, manufacture, and sale for export, of opium. 60. Sanctioning of cinematograph films for exhibition. 61. Industrial disputes concerning Union employees. 62. The institutions known at the commencement of this Constitution as the National Library, the Indian Museum, the	48. Estate duty in respect of agricultural land. 49. Taxes on lands and buildings. 50. Taxes on mineral rights subject to any limitations imposed by Parliament by law relating to mineral development. 51. Duties of excise on the following goods manufactured or produced in the State and countervailing duties at the same or lower rates on similar goods manufactured or produced elsewhere in India:— (a) alcoholic liquors for human consumption; (b) opium, Indian hemp and other narcotic drugs and narcotics, but not including medicinal and toilet preparations containing alcohol or any substance included in sub-paragraph (b) of this entry. [19][***] 53. Taxes on the consumption or sale of electricity.	39. Newspapers, books and printing presses. 40. Archaeological sites and remains other than those [20][declared by or under law made by Parliament] to be of national importance. 41. Custody, management and disposal of property (including agricultural land) declared by law to be evacuee property. [21][42. Acquisition and requisitioning of property.] 43. Recovery in a State of claims in respect of taxes and other public demands, including arrears of land-revenue and sums recoverable as such arrears, arising outside that State. 44. Stamp duties other than duties or fees collected by means of judicial stamps, but not including rates of stamp duty. 45. Inquiries and statistics for the purposes of any of the matters specified in List II or List III.

19. Entry 52 omitted by the Constitution (One Hundred and First Amendment) Act, 2016, sec. 17(b)(i) (w.e.f. 16-9-2016, *vide* S.O. 2986(E), dated 16th September, 2016). Entry 52, before omission, stood as under:
"52. Taxes on the entry of goods into a local area for consumption, use or sale therein.".
20. Subs. by the Constitution (Seventh Amendment) Act, 1956, sec. 27, for "declared by the Parliament by law" (w.e.f. 1-11-1956).
21. Subs. by the Constitution (Seventh Amendment) Act, 1956, sec. 26, for entry 42 (w.e.f. 1-11-1956).

List I—Union List	List II—State List	List III—Concurrent List
Imperial War Museum, the Victoria Memorial and the Indian War Memorial, and any other like institution financed by the Government of India wholly or in part and declared by Parliament by law to be an institution of national importance. 63. The institutions known at the commencement of this Constitution as the Banaras Hindu University, the Aligarh Muslim University and the [22][Delhi University; the University established in pursuance of article 371E;] any other institution declared by Parliament by law to be an institution of national importance. 64. Institutions for scientific or technical education financed by the Government of India wholly or in part and declared by Parliament by law to be institutions of national importance. 65. Union agencies and institutions for—	[23][54. Taxes on the sale of petroleum crude, high speed diesel, motor spirit (commonly known as petrol), natural gas, aviation turbine fuel and alcoholic liquor for human consumption, but not including sale in the course of inter-State trade or commerce or sale in the course of international trade or commerce of such goods.] [24][***] 56. Taxes on goods and passengers carried by road or on inland waterways. 57. Taxes on vehicles, whether mechanically propelled or not, suitable for use on roads, including tramcars subject to the provisions of entry 35 of List III. 58. Taxes on animals and boats. 59. Tolls. 60. Taxes on professions, trades, callings and employments. 61. Capitation taxes.	46. Jurisdiction and powers of all courts, except the Supreme Court, with respect to any of the matters in this List. 47. Fees in respect of any of the matters in this List, but not including fees taken in any court. *See* also Notes on Articles 245, 246, 248 and 254.

22. Subs. by the Constitution (Thirty-second Amendment) Act, 1973, sec. 4, for "Delhi University and" (w.e.f. 1-7-1974).
23. Subs. by the Constitution (One Hundred and First Amendment) Act, 2016, sec. 17(b)(ii), for Entry 54 (w.e.f. 16-9-2016, *vide* S.O. 2986(E), dated 16th September, 2016). Earlier Entry 54 was substituted by the Constitution (Sixth Amendment) Act, 1956, sec. 2(b) (w.e.f. 11-9-1956). Entry 54, before substitution by the Constitution (One Hundred and First Amendment) Act, 2016, stood as under:
   "54. Taxes on the sale or purchase of goods other than newspapers, subject to the provisions of entry 92A of List I.".
24. Entry 55 omitted by the Constitution (One Hundred and First Amendment) Act, 2016, sec. 17(b)(iii) (w.e.f. 16-9-2016, *vide* S.O. 2986(E), dated 16th September, 2016). Earlier Entry 55 was amended by the Constitution (Forty-second Amendment) Act, 1976, sec. 57(b)(v) (w.e.f. 3-1-1977). Entry 55, before omission, stood as under:
   "55. Taxes on advertisements other than advertisements published in the newspapers and advertisements broadcast by radio or television.".

List I—Union List	List II—State List	List III—Concurrent List
(a) professional, vocational or technical training, including the training of police officers; or (b) the promotion of special studies or research; or (c) scientific or technical assistance in the investigation or detection of crime. 66. Co-ordination and determination of standards in institutions for higher education or research and scientific and technical institutions. 67. Ancient and historical monuments and records, and archaeological sites and remains, [25][declared by or under law made by Parliament] to be of national importance. 68. The Survey of India, the Geological, Botanical, Zoological and Anthropological Surveys of India; Meteorological organisations. 69. Census. 70. Union Public Services; All-India Services; Union Public Service Commission. 71. Union pensions, that is to say, pensions payable by the Government of India or out of the Consolidated Fund of India.	[26][62. Taxes on entertainments and amusements to the extent levied and collected by a Panchayat or a Municipality or a Regional Council or a District Council.] 63. Rates of stamp duty in respect of documents other than those specified in the provisions of List I with regard to rates of stamp duty. 64. Offences against laws with respect to any of the matters in this List. 65. Jurisdiction and powers of all courts, except the Supreme Court, with respect to any of the matters in this List. 66. Fees in respect of any of the matters in this List, but not including fees taken in any court.	

25. Subs. by the Constitution (Seventh Amendment) Act, 1956, sec. 27, for "declared by Parliament by law" (w.e.f. 1-11-1956).
26. Subs. by the Constitution (One Hundred and First Amendment) Act, 2016, sec. 17(b)(iv), for Entry 62 (w.e.f. 16-9-2016, *vide* S.O. 2986(E), dated 16th September, 2016). Entry 62, before substitution, stood as under:
"62. Taxes on luxuries, including taxes on entertainments, amusements, betting and gambling. ".

List I—Union List	List II—State List	List III—Concurrent List
72. Elections to Parliament, to the Legislatures of States and to the offices of President and Vice-President; the Election Commission. 73. Salaries and allowances of members of Parliament, the Chairman and Deputy Chairman of the Council of States and the Speaker and Deputy Speaker of the House of the People. 74. Powers, privileges and immunities of each House of Parliament and of the members and the Committees of each House; enforcement of attendance of persons for giving evidence or producing documents before committees of Parliament or commissions appointed by Parliament. 75. Emoluments, allowances, privileges, and rights in respect of leave of absence, of the President and Governors; salaries and allowances of the Ministers for the Union; the salaries, allowances, and rights in respect of leave of absence and other conditions of service of the Comptroller and Auditor-General. 76. Audit of the accounts of the Union and of the States. 77. Constitution, organisation, jurisdiction and powers of the Supreme Court (including contempt of such Court), and the fees taken therein; persons entitled to practise before the Supreme Court.		

List I—Union List	List II—State List	List III—Concurrent List
78. Constitution and organisation [27][(including vacations)] of the High Courts except provisions as to officers and servants of High Courts; persons entitled to practise before the High Courts.		
[28][79. Extension of the jurisdiction of a High Court to, and exclusion of the jurisdiction of a High Court from, any Union territory.]		
80. Extension of the powers and jurisdiction of members of a police force belonging to any State to any area outside that State, but not so as to enable the police of one State to exercise powers and jurisdiction in any area outside that State without the consent of the Government of the State in which such area is situated; extension of the powers and jurisdiction of members of a police force belonging to any State to railway areas outside that State.		
81. Inter-State migration; inter-State quarantine.		
82. Taxes on income other than agricultural income.		
83. Duties of customs including export duties.		

27. Ins. by the Constitution (Fifteenth Amendment) Act, 1963, sec. 12 (with retrospective effect).
28. Subs. by the Constitution (Seventh Amendment) Act, 1956, sec. 29 and Sch., for entry 79 (w.e.f. 1-11-1956).

List I—Union List	List II—State List	List III—Concurrent List
[29][84. Duties of excise on the following goods manufactured or produced in India, namely:— (a) petroleum crude; (b) high speed diesel; (c) motor spirit (commonly known as petrol); (d) natural gas; (e) aviation turbine fuel; and (f) tobacco and tobacco products.] 85. Corporation tax. 86. Taxes on the capital value of the assets, exclusive of agricultural land, of individuals and companies; taxes on the capital of companies. 87. Estate duty in respect of property other than agricultural land. 88. Duties in respect of succession to property other than agricultural land. 89. Terminal taxes on goods or passengers, carried by railway, sea or air; taxes on railway fares and freights. 90. Taxes other than stamp duties on transactions in stock exchanges and futures markets.		

29. Subs. by the Constitution (One Hundred and First Amendment) Act, 2016, sec. 17(a)(i), for entry 84 (w.e.f. 16-9-2016, *vide* S.O. 2986(E), dated 16th September, 2016). Entry 84, before substitution, stood as under:

"84. Duties of excise on tobacco and other goods manufactured or produced in India except—

(a) alcoholic liquors for human consumption;

(b) opium, Indian hemp and other narcotic drugs and narcotics,

but including medicinal and toilet preparations containing alcohol or any substance included in sub-paragraph (b) of this entry.".

List I—Union List	List II—State List	List III—Concurrent List
91. Rates of stamp duty in respect of bills of exchange, cheques, promissory notes, bills of lading, letters of credit, policies of insurance, transfer of shares, debentures, proxies and receipts. [30][***] [31][92A. Taxes on the sale or purchase of goods other than newspapers, where such sale or purchase takes place in the course of inter-State trade or commerce.] [32][92B. Taxes on the consignment of goods (whether the consignment is to the person making it or to any other person), where such consignment takes place in the course of inter-State trade or commerce.] [33][***] 93. Offences against laws with respect to any of the matters in this List. 94. Inquiries, surveys and statistics for the purpose of any of the matters in this List.		

30. Entry 92 omitted by the Constitution (One Hundred and First Amendment) Act, 2016, sec. 17(a)(ii) (w.e.f. 16-9-2016, *vide* S.O. 2986(E), dated 16th September, 2016). Entry 92, before omission, stood as under:
    "92. Taxes on the sale or purchase of newspapers and on advertisements published therein.".
31. Ins. by the Constitution (Sixth Amendment) Act, 1956, sec. 2(a) (w.e.f. 11-9-1956).
32. Ins. by the Constitution (Forty-sixth Amendment) Act, 1982, sec. 5 (w.e.f. 2-2-1983).
33. Entry 92C omitted by the Constitution (One Hundred and First Amendment) Act, 2016, sec. 17(a)(ii) (w.e.f. 16-9-2016, *vide* S.O. 2986(E), dated 16th September, 2016). Earlier Entry 92C was inserted by the Constitution (Eighty-eighth Amendment) Act, 2003, sec. 4 (enforcement date was not notified). Entry 92C, before omission, stood as under:
    "92C. Taxes on services.".

List I—Union List	List II—State List	List III—Concurrent List
95. Jurisdiction and powers of all courts, except the Supreme Court, with respect to any of the matters in this List; admiralty jurisdiction. 96. Fees in respect of any of the matters in this List, but not including fees taken in any court. 97. Any other matter not enumerated in List II or List III including any tax not mentioned in either of those Lists.		

TABLE XIX

LANGUAGES

[Articles 344(1), 351 read with Eighth Schedule]

1. Assamese.
2. Bengali.
[1][3. Bodo.]
[2][4. Dogri.]
*5. Gujarati.
*6. Hindi.
*7. Kannada.
*8. Kashmiri.
[2][*9. Konkani.]
[3][*10. Mathilli.]
*11. Malayalam.
[4][*12. Manipuri.]
*13. Marathi.
[5][*14. Nepali.]

1. Ins. by the Constitution (Ninety-second Amendment) Act, 2003, sec. 2(a) (w.e.f. 7-1-2004).
2. Ins. by the Constitution (Seventy-first Amendment) Act, 1992, sec. 2(a) (w.e.f. 31-8-1992).
* Entry numbers have been re-numbered by (i) the Constitution (Twenty-first Amendment) Act, 1967, sec. 2(a) (w.e.f. 10-4-1967); (ii) by the Constitution (Seventy-first Amendment) Act, 1992, sec. 2 (w.e.f. 31-8-1992) and (iii) by the Constitution (Ninety-second Amendment) Act, 2003, sec. 2 (w.e.f. 7-1-2004).
3. Ins. by the Constitution (Ninety-second Amendment) Act, 2003, sec. 2(c) (w.e.f. 7-1-2004).
4. Ins. by the Constitution (Seventy-first Amendment) Act, 1992, sec. 2(b) (w.e.f. 31-8-1992).

*15. [6][Odia].
*16. Punjabi.
*17. Sanskrit.
[7][*18. Santhali.]
[8][*19. Sindhi.]
*20. Tamil.
*21. Telugu.
*22. Urdu.

5. Ins. by the Constitution (Seventy-first Amendment) Act, 1992, sec. 2(c) (w.e.f. 31-8-1992).
6. Subs. by the Constitution (Ninety-sixth Amendment) Act, 2011, sec. 2, for "Oriya" (w.e.f. 23-9-2011).
7. Ins. by the Constitution (Ninety-second Amendment) Act, 2003, sec. 2(e) (w.e.f. 7-1-2004).
8. Ins. by the Constitution (Twenty-first Amendment) Act, 1967, sec. 2(b) (w.e.f. 10-4-1967).

TABLE XX

PRESIDENT'S RULE IN STATES AND UNION TERRITORIES

Sl. No.	State/U.T.	No. of times President's rule imposed	Duration of President's rule	
			From	To
1	2	3	4	5
1.	Andhra Pradesh	3	[1]15-11-1954 18-1-1973 28-2-2014	29-3-1955 10-12-1973 8-6-2014
2.	Arunachal Pradesh	2	3-11-1979 25-1-2016	18-1-1980 19-2-2016
3.	Assam	4	12-12-1979 30-6-1981 19-3-1982 28-11-1990	5-12-1980 13-1-1982 27-2-1983 30-6-1991
4.	Bihar	8	29-6-1968 4-7-1969 9-1-1972 30-4-1977 17-2-1980 28-3-1995 12-2-1999 7-3-2005	26-2-1969 16-2-1970 19-3-1972 24-6-1977 8-6-1980 5-4-1995 9-3-1999 24-11-2005

1. In the erstwhile Andhra State.

1	2	3	4	5
5.	Delhi	1	14-2-2014	11-2-2015
6.	Goa	5	2-12-1966 27-4-1979 14-12-1990 9-2-1999 4-3-2005	5-4-1967 16-1-1980 25-1-1991 9-6-1999 7-6-2005
7.	Gujarat	5	12-5-1971 9-2-1974 12-3-1976 17-2-1980 19-9-1996	17-3-1972 18-6-1975 24-12-1976 8-6-1980 23-10-1996
8.	Haryana	3	21-11-1967 30-4-1977 6-4-1991	22-5-1968 21-6-1977 23-7-1991
9.	Himachal Pradesh	2	30-4-1977 15-12-1992[2]	22-6-1977 3-12-1993
10.	Jammu and Kashmir	9	26-3-1977 6-3-1986 19-1-1990 18-10-2002 11-7-2008 9-1-2015 8-1-2016 19-6-2018 [3]31-10-2019	9-7-1977 7-11-1986 9-10-1996 2-11-2002 5-1-2009 1-3-2015 4-4-2016 30-10-2019 Present
11.	Jharkhand	3	19-1-2009 1-6-2010 18-1-2013	29-12-2009 11-9-2010 12-7-2013

2. Writ Petition challenging Proclamation brought before the Supreme Court has been dismissed and the validity of these Proclamations have been upheld by a 9-Judge Bench [*Bommai v UOI,* AIR 1994 SC 1918, paras 91(x), p 366].
3. Imposed under section 73 of the J&K Reorganisation Act, 2019 as Article 356 does not apply to Union Territories.

1	2	3	4	5
12.	Karnataka	6	19-3-1971 31-12-1977 21-4-1989 10-10-1990 9-10-2007 20-11-2007	20-3-1972 28-2-1978 30-11-1989 17-10-1990 11-11-2007 27-5-2008
13.	Kerala	5	[4]23-3-1956 31-7-1959 10-9-1964 1-8-1970 1-12-1979	5-4-1957 22-2-1960 6-3-1967 4-10-1970 25-1-1980
14.	Madhya Pradesh	4	[5]8-4-1949 29-4-1977 18-2-1980 15-12-1992[2]	13-3-1952 25-6-1977 8-6-1980 7-12-1993
15.	Maharashtra	3	17-2-1980 28-9-2014 12-11-2019	8-6-1980 31-10-2014 23-11-2019
16.	Manipur	11	12-1-1967 25-10-1967 17-10-1969 28-3-1973 16-5-1977 14-11-1979 28-2-1981 7-1-1992 31-12-1993 2-6-2001 13-02-2025	19-3-1967 18-2-1968 22-3-1972 3-3-1974 28-6-1977 13-1-1980 18-6-1981 7-4-1992 13-12-1994 6-3-2002 4-2-2026
17.	Meghalaya	2	11-10-1991 18-3-2009	5-2-1992 12-5-2009

4. In the erstwhile Travancore-Cochin.
5. In the erstwhile Vindhya Pradesh.

1	2	3	4	5
18.	Mizoram	3	11-5-1977 10-11-1978 7-9-1988	1-6-1978 8-5-1979 24-1-1989
19.	Nagaland	4	20-3-1975 7-8-1988 2-4-1992 3-1-2008	25-11-1977 25-1-1989 22-2-1993 12-3-2008
20.	Odisha	6	25-2-1961 11-1-1971 3-3-1973 16-12-1976 30-4-1977 17-2-1980	23-6-1961 3-4-1971 6-3-1974 29-12-1976 26-6-1977 9-6-1980
21.	Patiala and East Punjab States Union (PEPSU)	1	5-3-1953	8-3-1954
22.	Puducherry	7	18-9-1968 3-1-1974 28-3-1974 12-11-1978 24-6-1983 4-3-1991 25-2-2021	17-3-1969 6-3-1974 2-7-1977 16-1-1980 16-3-1985 3-7-1991 7-5-2021
23.	Punjab	8	20-6-1951 5-7-1966 23-8-1968 14-6-1971 30-4-1977 17-2-1980 10-10-1983 11-5-1987	17-4-1952 1-11-1966 17-2-1969 17-3-1972 20-6-1977 6-6-1980 29-9-1985 25-2-1992
24.	Rajasthan	4	13-3-1967 29-4-1977 16-2-1980 15-12-1992[2]	26-4-1967 22-6-1977 6-6-1980 4-12-1993

1	2	3	4	5
25.	Sikkim	2	18-8-1978 25-5-1984	18-10-1979 8-3-1985
26.	Tamil Nadu	4	31-1-1976 17-2-1980 30-1-1988 30-1-1991	29-6-1977 8-6-1980 26-1-1989 23-6-1991
27.	Tripura	3	1-11-1971 5-11-1977 11-3-1993	20-3-1972 5-1-1978 10-4-1993
28.	Uttar Pradesh	9	25-2-1968 1-10-1970 13-6-1973 30-11-1975 30-4-1977 17-2-1980 6-12-1992 18-10-1995 8-3-2002	26-2-1969 18-10-1970 8-11-1973 21-1-1976 23-6-1977 9-6-1980 4-12-1993 21-3-1997 3-5-2002
29.	Uttarakhand	1	27-3-2016	11-5-2016
30.	West Bengal	5	1-7-1962 20-2-1968 19-3-1970 28-6-1971 30-4-1977	8-7-1962 25-2-1969 2-4-1971 19-3-1972 21-6-1977
		133		

SUBJECT INDEX